Linux Administration:
A Beginner's Guide,
Fourth Edition

STEVE **SHAH** AND WALE **SOYINKA**

McGraw-Hill/Osborne

New York   Chicago   San Francisco
Lisbon   London   Madrid   Mexico City   Milan
New Delhi   San Juan   Seoul   Singapore   Sydney   Toronto

The McGraw·Hill Companies

McGraw-Hill/Osborne
2100 Powell Street, 10th Floor
Emeryville, California 94608
U.S.A.

To arrange bulk purchase discounts for sales promotions, premiums, or fund-raisers, please contact **McGraw-Hill**/Osborne at the above address.

Linux Administration: A Beginner's Guide, Fourth Edition

1234567890 CUS CUS 0198765

ISBN 0-07-226259-1

Acquisitions Editor
Jane Brownlow
Project Editor
Emily Rader
Acquisitions Coordinator
Jennifer Housh
Copy Editor
Robert Campbell
Proofreaders
Andrea Fox
Paul Medoff

Indexer
Valerie Robbins
Composition
International Typesetting
and Composition
Illustration
International Typesetting
and Composition
Series Design
Peter F. Hancik

This book was composed with Adobe® InDesign®.

Dedicated to my family, for their infinite support, patience, and love.

—Steve Shah

I would like to dedicate the portions of this book for which I am responsible to everybody who likes open-source software and everybody who has contributed to open-source software in one form or another.

—Wale Soyinka

ABOUT THE AUTHORS

Steve Shah is the Director of Product Management at the NetScaler division of Citrix Systems, where he is responsible for the Security and Layer 4–7 switching capabilities of the company's award-winning application delivery systems. Prior to NetScaler, Steve played a similar role at Array Networks, where he did everything from kernel-level TCP/IP hacking to product management. Before Array Networks, he was a member of Alteon Web Systems, where he lead the development effort of their SSL accelerator product.

In addition to the *Linux Administration: A Beginners Guide*, Steve is a contributor to several editions of *UNIX Unleashed*, *RedHat Linux Unleashed*, *Using Linux*, and *Content Delivery Networks*. He holds a B.S. in Computer Science with a minor in Creative Writing and an M.S. in Computer Science from UC Riverside. Steve has been programming since 1986, performing system administration since 1992, and doing product management since 2001.

When Steve isn't either working or hacking on some part of Linux that fascinates him (which his better half, Heidi, will argue does not exist), he tries his hand at being a better DJ and photographer. You can read Steve's blog at http://www.planetoid.org/blog.

Wale Soyinka is a Systems & Network Engineering consultant with several years experience in the field. He holds a BSc in Mathematics/Statistics. He has written several Linux administration training materials used as part of the curriculum in some Community Colleges in the Bay Area. He is also the author of a projects lab manual, *Microsoft Windows 2000 Managing Network Environments*, which is part of the Microsoft certification series published by Prentice Hall. He currently participates in several open source discussions and projects. His interests are very wide and varied.

CONTENTS

Part II

Single-Host Administration

Part III

Security and Networking

ACKNOWLEDGMENTS

'm insane. This book is proof of that.

Between work and other responsibilities, I figured I'd pile on a book project thinking it wouldn't be too bad . . . Well, I thank God for my wonderful wife Heidi for putting up with it even after she told me I was being insane. She is better than I deserve.

Before Heidi came to my rescue, my parents Manjari and Jagdish Shah were directly responsible for giving me the tools, love, and encouragement to pursue my interests.

My coauthor, Adewale Soyinka, has been absolutely fantastic to work with. His thoughts, feedback, and insistence that we always do it the right way have helped make this book something we are both proud of. The people behind the scenes at Osborne have also been instrumental in making this book happen. Jane Brownlow (the person responsible for the first edition of this book!), Jennifer Housh, Emily Rader, and the entire editing team helped us get everything together to make the best book possible. I'm extremely grateful that they have had the patience to work through all the details with us on making this book happen.

Last, but certainly not least, are my friends at NetScaler. Their relentless energy and teamwork kept my spirits flying even when I was physically exhausted. They are an incredible group to work with.

—Steve

The list of people that I would like to acknowledge is rather long—and as such I will try to create a "catch all" that will reflect the individuals and groups that deserve it. This simply includes everybody that has ever believed in me and provided me with one opportunity or the other to experience various aspects of my life until now. You know who you are, and I thank you and remain forever indebted to you.

—Wale

INTRODUCTION

On October 5, 1991, Linus Torvalds posted this message to the newsgroup comp.os.minix. (There was, after all, a time when newsgroups were not polluted with spam.)

```
Do you pine for the nice days of minix-1.1, when men were men and wrote
their own device drivers? Are you without a nice project and just dying
to cut your teeth on a OS you can try to modify for your needs? Are you
finding it frustrating when everything works on minix? No more all-nighters
to get a nifty program working? Then this post might be just for you :-)
```

Linus went on to introduce the first cut of Linux to the world. Unbeknownst to him, he had unleashed what was to become one of the world's most popular operating systems, second only to Microsoft Windows. Fourteen years later, an entire industry has grown up around Linux. Chances are, you've probably already used it in one form or another. (Got a TiVo? You've used Linux.)

TIP For the full wit of Linus Torvalds' first post, search for "Linus' first post about Linux" in Google. The first link will lead you to the entry on Google Groups. You can also learn more about Linux's history at http://en.wikipedia.org/wiki/Linux_kernel.

The Linux of yesteryear is not at all like the Linux of today. When the authors first installed Slackware in 1994, getting the basic peripherals to work was a challenge. Linux's GUI environment, for instance, required hours of tweaking. The process could cause your monitor to make the dreaded "click" sound, which would mean that you overclocked a setting and would have to buy a new monitor. Similarly, making software downloaded from the Internet work typically required the administrator to debug source code problems. Linux may have been a solid operating system, but it was not for the faint of heart.

Most every Linux distribution today, by contrast, practically installs and configures itself. Almost every conceivable peripheral works out of the box. Ironically, getting software to work on *other* UNIX platforms is now somewhat of a challenge because most new software is written on Linux systems and requires porting. (Godspeed if you still administer Irix or HPUX.)

This change brings with it an entire industry of support, infrastructure options, and even enterprise class software. After all, when the likes of Oracle make their first release of new software available for Linux *before* any other operating system, you know you've got some serious momentum going.

This book, originally written in 1999/2000, has changed significantly with the times as well. The fourth edition represents significant updates to reflect the current state of Linux, the choices available for administrators, and the market realities of running an enterprise class server in an Internet-centric world where everything from security to performance to basic access needs to be readily available.

This book is *not* a blow-by-blow account of why other operating systems and their users are fools for their decisions. Linux, like any technology, is a tool. Our goal is to arm you with the best information possible about running a Linux server so that you can make the best decision for your solution. Operating system religion has no place here.

WHO SHOULD READ THIS BOOK

The title of this book includes "Beginners Guide," and that's mostly true. What the title should say is "Beginners to Linux Guide" because we do make a few assumptions about you, the reader.

First, we assume that you are already familiar with the care and feeding of Windows at "power user" level or better. We assume that you are familiar with the terms necessary to run a small- to medium-sized Windows network. Any experience with bigger networks or advanced Windows technologies such as Active Directory will allow you to get more from the book but is not required.

We make this assumption because we did not want to write a guide for dummies. There are already enough books on the market that tell you what to click without telling you why; this book is not meant to be among those ranks. Furthermore, we did not want to waste time writing about information that we believe is common knowledge for power users of Windows. Other people have already done an excellent job at conveying that information, and there is no reason to repeat that work here.

In addition to your Windows background, we assume that you're interested in having more information about the topics here than the material we have written alone. After all, we've only spent 30–40 pages on topics that have entire books devoted to them! For this reason, we have scattered references to other books throughout the chapters. We urge you to take advantage of these recommendations. No matter how advanced you are, there is always something new to learn.

WHAT'S IN THIS BOOK?

Linux Administration: A Beginner's Guide, is broken into five parts.

Part I: Installing Linux as a Server

Part I includes three chapters (Chapter 1, "Technical Summary of Linux Distributions and Windows 2003"; Chapter 2, "Installing Linux in a Server Configuration"; and Chapter 3, "Installing Software") that give you a firm handle on what Linux is, how it compares to Windows in several key areas, how to install Fedora Core, and, finally, how to install source code and prepackaged software. Ideally, this should be enough information to get you started and help you draw parallels to how Linux works based on your existing knowledge of Windows.

Part II: Single-Host Administration

Part II covers the necessary material to manage a single system that is disconnected from a network. While this may seem useless at first, it is the foundation on which many other concepts are built, and these concepts are essential to understand even after a system is connected to a network.

There are seven chapters in this part. Chapter 4, "Managing Users," covers the necessary information on how to add, remove, and otherwise manage users. The chapter also introduces the basic concepts of multiuser operation and how a user applies to application security. In Chapter 5, "The Command Line," we begin covering the basics of working with the Linux command line so that you can become comfortable dropping out of the graphical environment provided by default. While it is possible to administer a system from within the graphical desktop, the greatest power comes from being comfortable with both the CLI and the GUI. (This is true for Windows, too. Don't believe that? Open a command prompt, run **netsh**, and try to do what **netsh** does in the GUI.)

Once you are comfortable with the CLI, you begin Chapter 6, "Booting and Shutting Down," which documents the entire booting and shutting down process. This includes the necessary detail on how to start up services and properly shut them down during these cycles so that you can reliably add new services later on in the book without any difficulty.

Chapter 7, "File Systems," continues with the basics of file systems—their organization, creation, and, most importantly, their management. The basics of operation continue in Chapter 8, "Core System Services," with coverage of basic tools, such as **xinetd** for scheduling applications to run at specified times. **Xinetd** is the Linux equivalent of

Windows' **svchost** and **syslog**, which manage logging for all applications in a unified framework. One may think of **syslog** as a more flexible version of the Event Viewer.

We finish this section with Chapter 9, "Compiling the Linux Kernel," and Chapter 10, "Knobs and Dials: The proc File System," which cover the kernel and kernel-level tweaking through **/proc**. Kernel coverage documents the process of compiling and installing your own custom kernel in Linux. This capability is one of the points that gives Linux administrators an extraordinary amount of fine-grained control over how their systems operate. The viewing of kernel-level configuration and variables through the **/proc** file system shown in Chapter 10 allows administrators to fine-tune their kernel operation in what amounts to an arguably better and easier way than Windows' **regedit**.

Part III: Security and Networking

Previous editions of this book had security and networking at the back of the book. This was done because at the time the only real extensions to the book that were covered were advanced networking concepts that don't apply to most administrators. The last few years have significantly changed.

With the ongoing importance of security on the Internet as well as compliancy issues with Sarbanes Oxley and HIPAA, the use of Linux in security situations has risen dramatically. Thus, we decided to move coverage up before introducing network-based services, which could be subject to network attacks.

We kick off this section with Chapter 11, "TCP/IP for System Administrators," which provides a detailed overview of TCP/IP in the context of what system administrators need to know. The chapter provides a lot of detail on how to use troubleshooting tools like **tcpdump** to capture packets and read them back, as well as a step-by-step analysis of how TCP connections work. These tools should enable you to effectively troubleshoot network peculiarities.

Chapter 12, "Network Configuration," returns to administration issues by focusing on basic network configuration. This includes setting up IP addresses, routing entries, and even setting up multiple IP addresses. We extend past the basics in Chapter 13, "Configuring the Linux Firewall," by going into advanced networking concepts and showing you how to build a Linux-based firewall.

Chapter 14, "Local Security," and Chapter 15, "Network Security," discuss aspects of system and network security in detail. They include Linux-specific issues as well as general security tips and tricks so that you can better configure your system and protect it against attack.

Part IV: Internet Services

The remainder of the book is broken into two distinct parts: Internet and intranet services. We define Internet services as those that you may consider running on a Linux system exposed directly to the Internet. Examples of this include Web and DNS services.

We start this section off with Chapter 16, "DNS." In this section, we cover the information you need to know to install, configure, and manage a DNS server. In addition to the actual details of running a DNS server, we provide a detailed background on how DNS works and several troubleshooting tips, tricks, and tools. From DNS we move on to Chapter 17, "FTP," and cover the installation and care of FTP servers. Like the DNS chapter, we also include a background on the FTP protocol itself and some notes on its evolution.

Chapter 18, "Setting Up Your Web Server Using Apache," moves onto what may be considered one of the most popular uses of Linux today: running a Web server with the Apache Web server. In this chapter, we cover the information necessary to install, configure, and manage the Apache Web server, with additional detail given to setting up and configuring virtual hosting.

Chapter 19, "SMTP," and Chapter 20, "POP and IMAP," dive into e-mail through the setup and configuration of SMTP, POP, and IMAP servers. We cover the information needed to configure all three, as well as show how they interact with one another, are testable via the CLI and Telnet, and can be used in heterogeneous environments. What you may find a little different about this book from other books on Linux is that we have chosen to cover the Postfix SMTP server instead of the classic Sendmail server because it provides a more flexible server with a better security record.

We end the part with Chapter 21, "The Secure Shell (SSH)." Setting up and managing the SSH service is a requirement for any server you set up, regardless of the server's mail function.

Part V: Intranet Services

We define intranet services as those that are typically run behind a firewall for internal users only. Even in this environment, Linux has a lot to offer. We start off by looking at NFS in Chapter 22, "Network File System (NFS)." NFS has been around for close to 20 years now and has evolved and grown to fit the needs of its users very well. In this chapter, we cover Linux's NFS server capabilities, including how to set up both clients and servers as well as troubleshooting. From NFS we move on to NIS in Chapter 23, "Network Information Service (NIS)." NIS is typically deployed alongside NFS servers to provide a central naming service for all users within a network. We pay special attention to scaling issues and how you can make NIS work in a large user-base environment.

Chapter 24, "Samba," continues the idea of sharing disks and resources with coverage of the Samba service. Using Samba, administrators can share disks and printing facilities with Windows users without having to install any special client software. Thus, Linux can become an effective server able to support UNIX systems running NFS as well as Windows systems running Samba.

We revisit directory services in Chapter 25, "LDAP," with coverage of LDAP and how administrators can use this standard service for providing user directories for multiple operating systems as well as mail directories for both Windows and UNIX systems.

In Chapter 26, "Printing," we take a tour of the Linux printing subsystem. The printing subsystem combined with Samba allows administrators to support seamless printing from Windows desktops. The result is a powerful way of centralizing printing options for Linux, Windows, and even Mac OS X users on a single server.

Chapter 27, "DHCP," covers another common use of Linux systems: DHCP servers. In this chapter, we cover how to deploy the ISC DHCP server, which offers a powerful array of features and access controls that are not traditionally exposed in graphical-based DHCP administration tools.

We end with Chapter 28, "Backups." Backups are arguably one of the most critical pieces of administration. Linux comes with two common means of providing backups that are easy to use and readily usable by tape drives. We cover both and explain how they can be used as part of a backup schedule. In addition to the mechanics of backups, we discuss general backup design and how you can optimize your backup system.

Updates and Feedback

While we hope that we publish a book with no errors, this isn't always possible. You can find an errata list for this book posted at http://www.planetoid.org/linux. If you find any errors, we welcome your submissions for errata updates.

We also welcome your feedback and comments. Unfortunately, our day jobs prevent us from answering detailed questions, so if you're looking for help on a specific issue, you may find one of the many online communities a better choice. (A great place to start is http://www.linux.org/.) However, if you have two cents to share about the book, we welcome your thoughts. You can send us e-mail at linuxadmin@planetoid.org.

PART I

Installing Linux as a Server

CHAPTER 1

Technical Summary of Linux Distributions and Windows 2003

Linux has hit the mainstream. A quick walk through any local major computer and electronics retail store will show this—the software offerings include boxed versions of various Linux distributions! What was only a hacker's toy a couple of years ago has grown up tremendously and is known for its stable and fast server performance. If more proof be needed, just note a common question that is now asked of CTOs of Fortune 500 companies. The question is "What is your Linux strategy"?

With the KDE and GNOME environments, Linux is also making inroads into the Windows desktop market. In this chapter, we will take a look at the technical differences between Linux and Windows .NET Server (likely the platform you are considering replacing with Linux). This chapter also explains the GNU (GNU's Not UNIX) license, which may help you understand why much of Linux is the way it is.

LEARNING ABOUT THE LINUX OPERATING SYSTEM

Usually people understand Linux to be an entire package of developer tools, editors, GUIs, networking tools, and so forth. More formally, such packages are called *distributions*. You've most likely heard of the Linux distributions named Red Hat, Fedora Core, Mandrake, and SuSE, which have received a great deal of press and have been purchased for thousands of installations. Noncommercial distributions of Linux such as Debian are less well known and haven't reached the same scale of popularity, but they are out there and in active use by their respective (and very dedicated) communities.

What's interesting about all Linux distributions is that almost all of the tools with which they ship were not written by the companies themselves. Rather, other people have released their programs with licenses, allowing their redistribution with source code. By and large, these tools are also available on other variants of UNIX, and some of them are becoming available under Windows as well. The makers of the distribution simply bundle them up into one convenient package that's easy to install. (Some distribution makers also develop value-added tools that make their distribution easier to administer or compatible with more hardware, but the software that they ship is generally written by others.)

So if we consider a distribution everything you need for Linux, what then *is* Linux exactly? Linux itself is the core of the operating system: the *kernel*. The kernel is the program acting as Chief of Operations. It is responsible for starting and stopping other programs (such as editors), handling requests for memory, accessing disks, and managing network connections. The complete list of kernel activities could easily be a chapter in itself, and in fact, several books documenting the kernel's internal functions have been written.

The kernel is known as a nontrivial program. It is also what puts the Linux into all those Linux distributions. All distributions use essentially the same kernel, and thus the fundamental behavior of all Linux distributions is the same.

Kernel Differences

Each company that sells a Linux distribution of its own will be quick to tell you that its kernel is better than others. How can a company make this claim? The answer comes from the fact that each company now maintains its own patch set. In order to make sure that the kernels largely stay in sync, most do adopt patches that are put into Linus' tree (as published on http://www.kernel.org). The only difference is that vendors typically do not make a release of every kernel version that is released onto kernel.org. Instead, they take a foundation, apply their custom patches to it, run the kernel through a simple QA process, and then take it out to production. This helps organizations have confidence that their kernels have been sufficiently baked, thus mitigating any perceived risk of running open-source operating systems.

The only exception to this rule revolves around security issues. If a security issue is found with a Linux kernel, vendors are quick to adopt the necessary patches to fix the problem immediately. A new release of the kernel is made within a short time period (commonly less than 24 hours) so that administrators can be sure that their installations are secure. Thankfully, exploits against the kernel itself are rare.

So if each vendor maintains their own patch set, what exactly is it patching? This answer varies from vendor to vendor, depending on each vendor's focus market. Red Hat, for instance, is largely focused on providing enterprise-grade reliability and solid efficiency for application servers. This may be different than the mission of the Fedora Core team, which is more interested in trying new technologies quickly, and even more different than the approach of a vendor that is trying to put together a desktop-oriented Linux system.

What separates one distribution from the next is the value-added tools that come with each one. For example, Red Hat includes a very useful tool that makes configuring the graphical interface a very straightforward task. Asking "Which distribution is better?" is much like asking "Which is better, Coke or Pepsi?" Almost all colas have the same basic ingredients—carbonated water, caffeine, and high-fructose corn syrup—thereby giving the similar effect of quenching thirst and bringing on a small caffeine-and-sugar buzz. In the end, it's a question of requirements: Do you need commercial support? Did your application vendor recommend one distribution over another? Does the package updating infrastructure suit your site's administrative style better than another distribution? When you review your requirements, you'll find that there is likely a distribution that is geared toward your exact needs.

WHAT ARE FREE SOFTWARE AND GNU ALL ABOUT?

In the early 1980s, Richard Stallman began a movement within the software industry. He preached (and still does) that software should be free. Note that by free, he doesn't mean in terms of price, but rather free in the same sense as freedom. This meant shipping not just a product, but the entire source code as well.

Stallman's policy was, somewhat ironically, a return to classic computing, when software was freely shared among hobbyists on small computers and given as part of the hardware by mainframe and minicomputer vendors. (It was not until the late 1960s that IBM considered selling application software. Through the 1950s and most of the 1960s, they considered software merely a tool for enabling the sales of hardware.)

This return to openness was a wild departure from the early 1980s conventions of selling prepackaged software, but Stallman's concept of free software was in line with the initial distributions of UNIX from Bell Labs. Early UNIX systems did contain full source code. Yet by the late 1970s, source code was typically removed from UNIX distributions and could be acquired only by paying large sums of money to AT&T (now SBC). The Berkeley Software Distribution (BSD) maintained a free version, but its commercial counterpart, BSDi, had to deal with many lawsuits from AT&T until it could be proved that nothing in the BSD kernel was from AT&T.

The idea of giving away source code is a simple one: Users of the software should never be forced to deal with a developer who might or might not support that user's intentions for the software. The user should never have to wait for bug fixes to be published. More important, code developed under the scrutiny of other programmers is typically of higher quality than code written behind locked doors. The greatest benefit of free software, however, comes from the users themselves: Should they need a new feature, they can add it to the program and then contribute it back to the source, so that everyone else can benefit from it.

From this line of thinking has sprung a desire to release a complete UNIX-like system to the public, free of license restrictions. Of course, before you can build any operating system, you need to build tools. And this is how the GNU project was born.

NOTE GNU stands for GNU's Not UNIX—recursive acronyms are part of hacker humor. If you don't understand why it's funny, don't worry. You're still in the majority.

What Is the GNU Public License?

A very important thing to emerge from the GNU project has been the *GNU Public License (GPL)*. This license explicitly states that the software being released is free, and no one can ever take away these freedoms. It is acceptable to take the software and resell it, even for a profit; however, in this resale, the seller must release the full source code, including any changes. Because the resold package remains under the GPL, the package can be distributed for free and resold yet again by anyone else for a profit. Of primary importance is the liability clause: the programmers are not liable for any damages caused by their software.

It should be noted that the GPL is not the only license used by free software developers (although it is arguably the most popular). Other licenses, such as BSD and Apache, have similar liability clauses but differ in terms of their redistribution. For instance, the BSD license allows people to make changes to the code and ship those changes without having to disclose the added code. (The GPL would require that the added code be shipped.) For more information about other open-source licenses, check out http://www.opensource.org.

Historical Footnote

A couple of years ago, Red Hat started a commercial offering of their erstwhile free product (Red Hat Linux). The commercial release was the Red Hat Enterprise Linux (RHEL) series. Because the foundation for RHEL is GPL, individuals interested in maintaining a free version of Red Hat's distribution have been able to do so. Furthermore, as an outreach to the community Red Hat created the Fedora Core Project, which is considered the testing grounds for new software before it is adopted by the RHEL team. The Fedora Core Project is freely distributed and can be downloaded from http://fedora.redhat.com.

The Advantages of Free Software

If the GPL seems a bad idea from the standpoint of commercialism, consider the recent surge of successful freeware packages—they are indicative of a system that does indeed work. This success has evolved for two reasons. First, as mentioned earlier, errors in the code itself are far more likely to be caught and quickly fixed under the watchful eyes of peers. Second, under the GPL system, programmers can release code without the fear of being sued. Without that protection, no one would ever release his or her code.

This concept of course begs the question of why anyone would release his or her work for free. Most projects don't start out as full-featured, polished pieces of work. They may begin life as a quick hack to solve a specific problem bothering the programmer. As a quick-and-dirty hack, the code has no sales value. But when this code is shared and consequently improved upon with others who have similar problems and needs, it becomes a useful tool. Other program users begin to enhance it with features they need, and these additions travel back to the original program. The project thus evolves as the result of a group effort and eventually reaches full refinement. This polished program may contain contributions from possibly hundreds, if not thousands, of programmers who have added little pieces here and there. In fact, the original author's code is likely to be little in evidence.

There's another reason for the success of generally licensed software. Any project manager who has worked on commercial software knows that the *real* cost of development software isn't in the development phase. It's really in the cost of selling, marketing, supporting, documenting, packaging, and shipping that software. A programmer carrying out a weekend hack to fix a problem with a tiny, kludged program may lack the interest, time, and money to turn that hack into a profitable product.

When Linus Torvalds released Linux in 1991, he released it under the GPL. As a result of its open charter, Linux has had a notable number of contributors and analyzers. This participation has made Linux very strong and rich in features. Torvalds himself estimates that since the v.2.2.0 kernel, his contributions represent only 5% of the total code base.

Since anyone can take the Linux kernel (and other supporting programs), repackage them, and resell them, some people have made money with Linux. As long as these individuals release the kernel's full source code along with their individual packages, and as long as the packages are protected under the GPL, everything is legal. Of course, this means that packages released under the GPL can be resold by other people under other names for a profit.

In the end, what makes a package from one person more valuable than a package from another person consists of the value-added features, support channels, and documentation. Even IBM can agree to this; it's how they made most of their money from 1930 to 1970 and now in the late 1990s and early 2000s with IBM Global Services. The money isn't in the product; it's in the services that go with it.

UNDERSTANDING THE DIFFERENCES BETWEEN WINDOWS AND LINUX

As you might imagine, the differences between Microsoft Windows and the Linux operating system cannot be completely discussed in the confines of this section. Throughout these chapters, topic by topic, we'll examine the specific contrasts between the two systems. In some chapters, you'll find that we don't derive any comparisons because a major difference doesn't really exist.

But before we attack the details, let's take a moment to discuss the primary architectural differences between the two operating systems.

Single Users vs. Multiple Users vs. Network Users

Windows was designed according to the "one computer, one desk, one user" vision of Microsoft's cofounder Bill Gates. For the sake of discussion, we'll call this philosophy *single-user.* In this arrangement, two people cannot work in parallel running (for example) Microsoft Word on the same machine at the same time. (On the other hand, one might question the wisdom of doing this with an overwhelmingly weighty program like Word!) You can buy Windows and run what is known as Terminal Server, but this requires huge computing power and lots of money in licensing. Of course, with Linux you don't run into the cost problem, and Linux will run fairly well on just about any hardware.

Linux borrows its philosophy from UNIX. When UNIX was originally developed at Bell Labs in the early 1970s, it existed on a PDP-7 computer that needed to be shared by an entire department. It required a design that allowed for *multiple users* to log in to the central machine at the same time. Various people could be editing documents, compiling programs, and doing other work at the exact same time. The operating system on the central machine took care of the "sharing" details, so that each user seemed to have an individual system. This multiuser tradition continued through today, on other versions of UNIX as well. And since Linux's birth in the early 1990s, it has supported the multiuser arrangement.

NOTE   Most people believe that with the advent of Windows 95, the term "multitasking" was invented. UNIX has had this capability since 1969! You can be rest assured that the concepts put into Linux have had many years to develop and prove themselves.

Today, the most common implementation of a multiuser setup is to support *servers*— systems dedicated to running large programs for use by many clients. Each member of a department can have a smaller workstation on the desktop, with enough power for day-to-day work. When they need to do something requiring significantly more CPU power or memory, they can run the operation on the server.

"But hey! Windows can allow people to offload computationally intensive work to a single machine!" you may argue. "Just look at SQL Server!" Well, that position is only half correct. Both Linux and Windows are indeed capable of providing services such as databases over the network. We can call users of this arrangement *network users,* since they are never actually logged into the server but rather send requests to the server. The server does the work and then sends the results back to the user via the network. The catch in this case is that an application must be specifically written to perform such server/client duties. Under Linux, a user can run any program allowed by the system administrator on the server without having to redesign that program. Most users find the ability to run arbitrary programs on other machines to be of significant benefit.

The Monolithic Kernel and the Micro-Kernel

In operating systems, there are two forms of kernels. You have a monolithic kernel that provides all the services the user applications need. And then you have the micro-kernel, a small core set of services and other modules that perform other functions.

Linux for the most part adopts the monolithic kernel architecture; it handles everything dealing with the hardware and system calls. Windows works off a micro-kernel design. The kernel provides a small set of services and then interfaces with other executive services that provide process management, I/O management, and other services. It has yet to be proved which methodology is truly the best way.

Separation of the GUI and the Kernel

Taking a cue from the Macintosh design concept, Windows developers integrated the graphical user interface (GUI) with the core operating system. One simply does not exist without the other. The benefit to this tight coupling of the operating system and user interface is consistency in the appearance of the system.

Although Microsoft does not impose rules as strict as Apple's with respect to the appearance of applications, most developers tend to stick with a basic look and feel among applications. One reason this is dangerous is that the video card driver is now allowed to run at what is known as "Ring 0" on a typical *x*86 architecture. Ring 0 is a protection mechanism—only privileged processes can run at this level, and typically user processes run at Ring 3. Since the video card is allowed to run at Ring 0, the video card could misbehave (and it does!), which can bring down the whole system.

On the other hand, Linux (like UNIX in general) has kept the two elements—user interface and operating system—separate. The X Window System interface is run as a user-level application, which makes it more stable. If the GUI (which is very complex for both Windows and Linux) fails, Linux's core does not go down with it. The process simply crashes and you get a terminal window. The X Window System also differs from the Windows GUI in that it isn't a complete user interface. It only defines how basic objects should be drawn and manipulated on the screen.

The most significant feature of the X Window System is its ability to display windows across a network and onto another workstation's screen. This allows a user sitting on host A to log in to host B, run an application on host B, and have all of the output routed back to host A. It is possible for two people to be logged in to the same machine, running a Linux equivalent of Microsoft Word (such as OpenOffice) at the same time.

In addition to the X Window System core, a window manager is needed to create a useful environment. Linux distributions come with several window managers and include support for GNOME and KDE, both of which are available on other variants of UNIX as well. If you're concerned with speed, you can look into the WindowMaker and FVWM window managers. They might not have all the glitz of KDE or GNOME, but they are really fast. When set as default, both GNOME and KDE offer an environment that is friendly even to the casual Windows user.

So which is better—Windows or Linux—and why? That depends on what you are trying to do. The integrated environment provided by Windows is convenient and less complex than Linux, but it lacks the X Window System feature that allows applications to display their windows across the network on another workstation. Windows' GUI is consistent but cannot be turned off, whereas the X Window System doesn't have to be running (and consuming valuable memory) on a server.

The Network Neighborhood

The native mechanism for Windows folk to share disks on servers or with each other is through the Network Neighborhood. In a typical scenario, users *attach* to a share and have the system assign it a drive letter. As a result, the separation between client and server is clear. The only problem with this method of sharing data is more people-oriented than technology-oriented: people have to know which servers contain which data.

With Windows, a new feature borrowed from UNIX has also appeared: *mounting*. In Windows terminology, it is called *reparse points*. This is the ability to mount a CD-ROM drive into a directory on your C drive. This may seem a little strange, but as you get used to Linux you'll understand this is the *only* way mounting works. The amazing thing is that on Windows you cannot mount network shares this way. You have to map a network share to a drive letter.

Linux, using the Network File System (NFS), has supported the concept of mounting since its inception. In fact, the Linux Automounter can dynamically mount and unmount partitions on an as-needed basis.

A common example of mounting partitions under Linux involves mounted home directories. The user's home directories reside on a server, and the client mounts the directories at boot time (automatically). So **/home** exists on the client, but **/home/ username** exists on the server.

Under Linux NFS, users never have to know server names or directory paths, and their ignorance is your bliss. No more questions about which server to connect to. Even better, users need not know when the need arises to change the server configuration. Under Linux, you can change the names of servers and adjust this information on client-side systems without making any announcements or having to reeducate users. Anyone who has ever had to reorient users to new server arrangements is aware of the repercussions that can occur.

Printing works much in the same way. Under Linux, printers receive names that are independent of the printer's actual host name. (This is especially important if the printer doesn't speak TCP/IP.) Clients point to a print server whose name cannot be changed without administrative authorization. Settings don't get changed without your knowing it. The print server can then redirect all print requests as needed. The Linux uniform interface will go a long way toward improving what may be a chaotic printer arrangement in your installation. This also means you don't have to install print drivers in several locations.

NOTE   If you intend to use Linux to serve Windows/NT/98 clients via the Samba package, you'll still have to deal with notifying users about server shares and printer assignments. You can read more about Samba in Chapter 24.

The Registry vs. Text Files

Think of the Windows Registry as the ultimate configuration database—thousands upon thousands of entries, very few of which are completely documented, some located on servers and some located on clients.

"What? Did you say your Registry *got corrupted*?" <maniacal laughter> "Well, yes, we can try to restore it from last night's backups, but then Excel starts acting funny and the technician (who charges $50 just to answer the phone) said to reinstall...."

In other words, the Windows Registry system is, at best, very difficult to manage. Although it's a good idea in theory, most people that have serious dealings with it don't emerge from battle without a scar or two.

Linux does not have a registry. This is both a blessing and a curse. The blessing is that configuration files are most often kept as a series of text files (think of the Windows .INI files before the days of the Registry). This setup means you're able to edit configuration files using the text editor of your choice rather than tools like **regedit**. In many cases, it also means you can liberally comment those configuration files so that six months from now you won't forget why you set something up in a particular way. With most tools that come with Linux, configuration files exist in the **/etc** directory or one of its subdirectories.

More on Configuration Files

An interesting side effect of having configuration files exist as a series of text files is that configuration of these files can be automated. This is very useful in situations where a large number of workstations needs to be deployed or new workstations are added frequently. You can easily set up Linux on a CD-ROM disc that simply mounts an NFS share and begins a customized installation. While you can do this on Windows, the supported way involves using binary differences called sys-diffs and automated install scripts (.ini files). The other way is to use clone tools like Norton Ghost and duplicate the install.

The problem with this is that each Windows box has a Security Identifier (SID) associated with it and this is stored all throughout the Registry. Automated installs of Windows can be done; it just takes a lot more effort.

The curse of a no-registry arrangement is that there is no standard way of writing configuration files. Each application or server can have its own format. Many applications are now coming bundled with GUI-based configuration tools to alleviate some of these problems. So you can do a basic setup easily, and then manually edit the configuration file when you need to do more complex adjustments.

In reality, having text files hold configuration information usually turns out to be an efficient method. Once set, they rarely need to be changed; even so, they are straight text files and thus easy to view when needed. Even more helpful is that it's easy to write scripts to read the same configuration files and modify their behavior accordingly. This is especially helpful when automating server maintenance operations, which is crucial in a large site with many servers.

Domains and Active Directory

If you've been using Windows long enough, you may remember the Windows NT domain controller model. If twinges of fear ran through you when reading the last sentence, you may still be suffering from the shell shock of having to maintain Primary Domain Controllers (PDCs), Backup Domain Controllers (BDCs), and their synchronization.

Microsoft, fearing revolt from administrators all around the world, gave up on the Windows NT model and created Active Directory (AD). The idea behind AD was simple: provide a repository for any kind of administrative data, whether it is user logins, group information, or even just telephone numbers, and manage authentication and authorization for a domain. The domain synchronization model was also changed to follow a DNS-style hierarchy that has proved to be far more reliable. NTLM was also dropped in favor of Kerberos. (Note that AD is still compatible with NTLM.)

While running **dcpromo** may not be anyone's idea of a fun afternoon, it is easy to see that AD works pretty well.

Linux does not have a tightly coupled authentication/authorization and data store model the way that Windows does with Active Directory. Instead, Linux uses an abstraction model that allows for multiple types of stores and authentication schemes to work without any modification to the applications. This is accomplished through the Password Authentication Models (PAM) infrastructure and the name resolution libraries that provide a standard means of looking up group information for applications and a flexible way of storing that group information using a variety of schemes.

For administrators looking to Linux, this abstraction layer can seem peculiar at first. However, consider that you can use anything from flat files, to NIS, to LDAP or Kerberos for authentication. This means you can pick the system that works best for you. For example, if you have an existing UNIX infrastructure that uses NIS, you can simply make your Linux systems plug into that. On the other hand, if you have an existing AD infrastructure, you can use PAM with Samba or LDAP to authenticate against the domain. Use Kerberos? No problem. And of course, you can choose to make your Linux system not interact with any external authentication system. In addition to being able to tie into multiple authentication systems, Linux can easily use a variety of tools, such as OpenLDAP, to keep directory information available as well.

OTHER REFERENCES

If you are interested in getting under the hood of the technology revolution (and it's always helpful to know how things work), the following texts are recommended:

▼ *Computer: A History of the Information Machine,* by Martin Campbell-Kelly and William Aspray (HarperCollins, 1997)

▲ *A Quarter Century of Unix,* by Peter Salus (Addison-Wesley, 1994)

Neither of these texts discusses Linux specifically. *A Quarter Century of Unix* does tell the Linux history up to the point where the system was just becoming a serious player. Peter Salus writes an interesting discussion of why Linus Torvalds saw a need to create Linux in the first place.

To get the scoop on Linux itself, start with the Linux home page at http://www.linux.org.

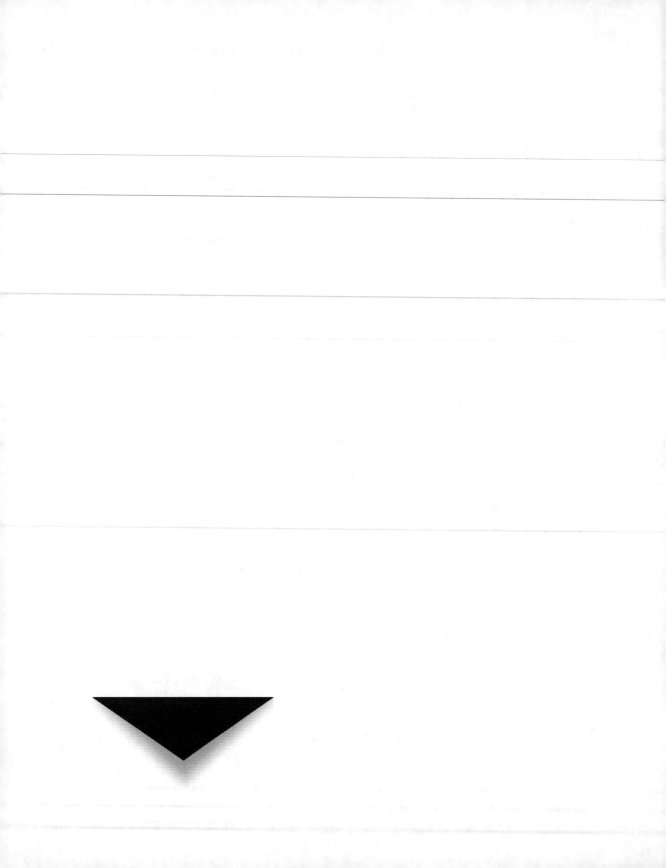

CHAPTER 2

Installing Linux in a Server Configuration

A key attribute in Linux's recent success is the remarkable improvement in installation tools. What once was a mildly frightening process many years back has now become almost trivial. Even better, there are many ways to install the software; optical media (CD/DVD-ROMs) are no longer the only choice (although they are still the most common). Network installations are part of the default list of options as well, and they can be a wonderful help when installing a large number of hosts.

Most default configurations where Linux is installed are already capable of becoming servers. This is due to an unfortunate, slightly naive design decision: being designated a server means that the machine serves everything! From disk services to printers to mail to news to . . . it's all turned on from the start. Proper practice dictates that a so-called server should be dedicated to performing only one or two specific tasks. Any other installed and irrelevant services simply take up memory and exert a drag on performance. In this chapter, we discuss the installation process as it pertains to servers and their dedicated functions.

HARDWARE AND ENVIRONMENTAL CONSIDERATIONS

As with any operating system, before getting started with the installation process, you should determine what hardware configurations would work. Each commercial vendor publishes a hardware compatibility list (HCL) and makes it available on its Web site. For example, Red Hat's HCL is at http://hardware.redhat.com/hcl (Fedora Core's HCL can be safely assumed to be similar to Red Hat's), SuSE's HCL database can be found at http://hardwaredb.suse.de, and a more generic HCL for most Linux flavors can be found at http://www.tldp.org/HOWTO/Hardware-HOWTO.

These sites provide a good starting reference point when you are in doubt concerning a particular piece of hardware. However, keep in mind that new Linux device drivers are being churned out on a daily basis around the world and no one single site can keep up with the pace of development in the open-source community. In general, most popular Intel-based and AMD-based configurations work without difficulty.

A general suggestion that applies to all operating systems (OSes) is to avoid cutting-edge hardware and software configurations. While they appear to be really impressive, they haven't had the maturing process some of the slightly older hardware has gone through. For servers, this usually isn't an issue, since there is no need for a server to have the latest and greatest toys, such as fancy video cards and sound cards. After all, your main goal is to provide a stable and available server for your users.

SERVER DESIGN

When a system becomes a server, its stability, availability, and performance become a significant issue. These three factors are usually improved through the purchase of more hardware, which is unfortunate. It's a shame to pay thousands of dollars extra to get a system capable of achieving in all three areas when you could have extracted the desired level of performance out of existing hardware with a little tuning. With Linux, this is not hard. Even better, the gains are outstanding.

The most significant design decision you must make when managing a server configuration is not technical but administrative. You must design a server to be *unfriendly* to casual users. This means no cute multimedia tools, no sound card support, and no fancy Web browsers (when at all possible). In fact, it should be a rule that casual use of a server is strictly prohibited.

Another important aspect of designing a server is making sure that it has a good environment. As a system administrator, you must ensure the physical safety of your servers by keeping them in a separate room under lock and key (or the equivalent). The only access to the servers for nonadministrative personnel should be through the network. The server room itself should be well ventilated and kept cool. The wrong environment is an accident waiting to happen. Systems that overheat and nosy users who think they know how to fix problems can be as great a danger to server stability as bad software (arguably even more so).

Once the system is in a safe place, installing battery backup is also crucial. Backup power serves two key purposes:

▼ To keep the system running during a power failure so that it may gracefully shut down, thereby avoiding data damage or loss

▲ To ensure that voltage spikes, drops, and other noises don't interfere with the health of your system

Here are some specific things you can do to improve your server performance:

▼ Take advantage of the fact that the graphical user interface is uncoupled from the core operating system, and avoid starting the X Window System (Linux's GUI) unless someone needs to sit on a console and run an application. After all, like any other application, the X Window System requires memory and CPU time to work, both of which are better off going to the more essential server processes instead.

■ Determine what functions the server is to perform, and disable all other functions. Not only are unused functions a waste of memory and CPU time, but they are just another issue you need to deal with on the security front.

▲ Unlike some other operating systems, Linux allows you to pick and choose the features you want in the kernel. (You'll learn about this process in Chapter 9.) The default kernel will already be reasonably well tuned, so you won't have to worry about it. But if you do need to change a feature or upgrade the kernel, be picky about what you add. Make sure you really need a feature before adding it.

> **NOTE** You may hear an old recommendation that you recompile your kernel to make the most effective use of your system resources. This is no longer entirely true—the other reasons to recompile your kernel might be to upgrade or add support for a new device.

Uptime

All of this chatter about taking care of servers and making sure silly things don't cause them to crash stems from a long-time UNIX philosophy: *Uptime is good. More uptime is better.*

The UNIX (Linux) **uptime** command tells the user how long the system has been running since its last boot, how many users are currently logged in, and how much load the system is experiencing. The last two are useful measures that are necessary for day-to-day system health and long-term planning. (For example, the server load has been staying high lately, so maybe it's time to buy a faster/bigger/better server.)

But the all-important number is how long the server has been running since its last reboot. Long uptimes are a sign of proper care, maintenance, and, from a practical standpoint, system stability. You'll often find UNIX administrators boasting about their server's uptimes the way you hear car buffs boast about horsepower. This is also why you'll hear UNIX administrators cursing at system changes (regardless of operating system) that require a reboot to take effect. You may deny caring about it now, but in six months you'll probably scream at anyone who reboots the system unnecessarily. Don't bother trying to explain this phenomenon to a nonadmin, because they'll just look at you oddly. You'll just know in your heart that your uptime is better than theirs.

DUAL-BOOTING ISSUES

If you are new to Linux, you may not be ready to commit to a complete system when you just want a test drive. All distributions of Linux can be installed on only certain partitions of your hard disk while leaving others alone. Typically, this means allowing Microsoft Windows to coexist with Linux.

Because we are focusing on server installations, we will not cover the details of building a dual-booting system; however, anyone with a little experience in creating partitions on a disk should be able to figure this out. If you are having difficulty, you may want to refer to the installation guide that comes with your distribution.

Some quick hints: if a Windows 95/98 partition currently consumes an entire hard disk as drive C, you can use the **fips** tool to repartition the disk. Simply defragment and then run **fips.exe**. If you are using Windows NT/2000/XP with NTFS and have already allocated all the disk with data on each partition, you may have to move data around a bit by hand to free up a partition. Because of its complexity, it is slightly more tricky to resize an NTFS-formatted partition. Nonetheless, it is still very possible. Some of the newer Linux distributions will even offer to automatically resize your NTFS partition for you during the OS install.

> **NOTE**   From the perspective of flexibility, NTFS doesn't sound like a good thing, but in reality it is. If you have to run Windows NT or 2000, use NTFS.

You may find using a commercial tool such as PartitionMagic to be especially helpful, because it offers support for NTFS, FAT32, and regular FAT, as well as a large number of other file system types. Its user interface is also significantly nicer than **fips**.

METHODS OF INSTALLATION

With the improved connectivity and speed of both local area networks and Internet connections, it is becoming an increasingly popular option to perform installations over the network rather than using a local CD-ROM.

Network-based installations are especially very useful when there is a need to roll out Linux on a large number of systems. This method provides a fast installation procedure in which many systems can be installed at the same time.

Depending on the particular Linux distribution and the network infrastructure already in place, one can design network-based installations around several protocols. Some of the more popular protocols over which network-based installations are done are listed here:

▼   **FTP**   This is one of the earliest methods for performing network installations.

■   **HTTP**   The installation tree is served from a Web server.

■   **NFS**   The distribution tree is shared/exported on an NFS server.

▲   **SMB**   This method is relatively new and not all distributions support it. The install tree can be shared on a Samba server or shared from a Windows box.

The other, more typical, method of installation is through the use of optical media provided by the vendor. All the commercial distributions of Linux have boxed sets of their brand of Linux that contain the install media. They usually also make CD/DVD-ROM images (ISOs) of the OS available on their FTP and/or HTTP sites. The distros (distributions) that don't make their ISOs available will usually have a stripped version of the OS available in a repository tree on their site.

We will be performing a server class install in this chapter using a DVD image that was burnt to a DVD. Of course, once you have gone through the process of installing from an optical medium (CD/DVD-ROM), you will find performing the network-based installations to be very straightforward. A side note regarding automated installations is that server-type installs aren't well suited to automation, because each server usually has a unique task; thus, each server will have a slightly different configuration. For example, a server dedicated to handling logging information sent to it over the network is going to have especially large partitions set up for the appropriate logging directories, compared to a file server that performs no logging of its own. (The obvious exception is for server farms where you have large numbers of replicated servers. But even those installations have their nuances that require attention to detail specific to the installation.)

INSTALLING FEDORA CORE LINUX

In this section, you will install the Fedora Core 4 version of Linux on a stand-alone system. We will take a liberal approach to the process, installing all of the tools possibly relevant to server operations. Later chapters explain each subsystem's purpose and help you determine which ones you really need to keep.

NOTE   Don't worry if you chose to install a distribution other than Fedora; luckily, most of the concepts carry over among the various distributions. Some installers are just prettier than others.

Project Prerequisites

First you need to download the ISOs for Fedora Core 4 that you will be installing. Fedora's project Web page has a listing of several mirrors located all over the world. You should of course choose the mirror geographically closest to you. The list of mirrors can be found at http://fedora.redhat.com/download/mirrors.html.

The DVD image used for this installation was downloaded from ftp://download .fedora.redhat.com/pub/fedora/linux/core/4/i386/iso/FC4-i386-DVD.iso.

The next step is to burn the ISO to a suitable medium. In this case we need to burn the ISO to a blank DVD. Use your favorite CD/DVD burning program to burn the image. Remember that the file you downloaded is already an exact image of a DVD medium and so should be burnt as such. Most CD/DVD burning programs have an option to create a CD or DVD from an image.

If you burn the file you downloaded as you would a regular data file, you will end up with a single file on the root of your DVD-ROM. This is not what you want.

The system you are installing on should have a DVD-ROM drive.

NOTE   Fedora install images are also available as a set of four CD-ROM images. You can perform the installation using the four CD-ROMS, but we have decided to perform the install using a DVD-ROM, mostly for sake of convenience. Using a single DVD helps you avoid having to swap out CDs in the middle of the install, because all the required files are already on a single DVD as opposed to multiple CDs, and also because the chances of having a bad installation medium are reduced (i.e., there is a higher probability of having one bad CD out of four than of having one bad DVD out of one.)

Let's begin the installation process.

Carrying Out the Installation

1. To start the installation process, boot off the DVD-ROM. This will present you with a splash screen (see illustration) introducing you to Fedora Core. At the bottom of the screen will be a prompt that reads

    `boot:`

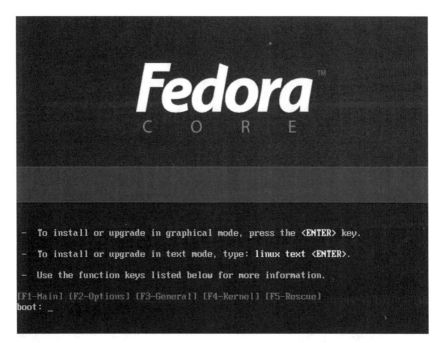

2. If you do not press any key, the prompt will automatically time out and begin the installation process. You can press ENTER to start the process immediately.

3. At the CD Found screen, press ENTER to test/verify your install media. Note that the test performed here is not always perfect. But for the majority of times when it does work, it can save you the trouble of starting the installation only to find out halfway through that the installer will abort because of a bad disc.

    Press ENTER again at the Media Check screen to begin testing.

4. After the media check runs to completion, you should get a Media Check Result screen that reports PASS. At this point it is safe to select OK to continue with the installation.

    If you don't have any other install media to test, select Continue at the next screen.

5. Select Next at the Welcome To Fedora Core screen.

6. Select the language you want use to perform the installation in this screen (see illustration). The interface works much like any other Windows-style interface. Simply point to your selection and click. When you are ready, click the Next button in the lower-right portion of the screen. English (English) is selected on our sample system.

Fedora
C O R E

Language Selection

Choose the language you would like to use during this installation.

What language would you like to use during the installation process?

Catalan (Català)
Chinese(Simplified) (简体中文)
Chinese(Traditional) (繁體中文)
Croatian (Hrvatski)
Czech (Čeština)
Danish (Dansk)
Dutch (Nederlands)
English (English)
Estonian (eesti keel)
Finnish (suomi)
French (Français)
German (Deutsch)
Gujarati (ગુજરાતી)
Hindi (हिन्दी)
Hungarian (magyar)

Hide Help   Release Notes   Back   Next

7. Select your keyboard type. This next screen allows you to select the layout type for the keyboard. The right pane of the dialog box lists the various possible layouts that are supported.

   The most common option will be the U.S. English layout. Select U.S. English and click Next to continue.

NOTE After you click Next at this point, the installer will quickly search your hard drive for any existing Linux installations. If any is found, you might be prompted with a different screen to perform an upgrade or a reinstallation of the OS found. If you are instead installing on a brand new hard disk, you will not get any such screen.

Installation Type

The installation type screen presents you with a set of preconfigured installation classes (types). The options are Personal Desktop, Workstation, Server, and Custom. The different classes comprise packages and options that the team of Fedora developers think should make up a certain installation type. Even though we had earlier claimed that we are going to install Linux in a server-type configuration, we will not select the preconfigured Server option for two reasons: one, we want to have as much control as possible over how the system is built, and two, we presume that you are a free thinker and you will not let a bunch of developers and/or authors tell you what to do.

1. Select the Custom radio button.

2. Click Next, as shown here:

Disk Partitioning Setup

This portion of the installation is probably the part that most new Linux users find the most awkward. This is because of the different naming conventions that Linux uses. This needn't be so—all it takes is a slight mind shift. You should also keep in mind that *"a partition is a partition is a partition"* in Linux or Windows.

What follows is a quick overview of the partitioning scheme you will be employing for this installation. The equivalent partitions in the Windows world are also given in the overview:

▼ **/** The root partition/volume is identified by a forward slash (/). All other directories are attached (mounted) to this parent directory. It is equivalent to the system drive (**C:**) in Windows.

■ **/boot** This partition/volume contains almost everything required for the boot process. It stores data that is used before the kernel begins executing user programs. The equivalent of this in Windows is what known as the system partition (*not* the boot partition).

■ **/usr** This is where all of the program files will reside (similar to **C:\Program Files** in Windows).

■ **/home** This is where everyone's home directory will be (assuming this server will house them). This is useful for keeping users from consuming an entire disk and leaving other critical components without space (such as log files). This directory is synonymous with **C:\Documents and Settings** in Windows XP/200*x*.

■ **/var** This is where system/event logs are generally stored. Because log files tend to grow in size quickly and can also be affected by outside users (for instance, individuals visiting a Web site), it is important to store the logs on a separate partition so that no one can perform a denial-of-service attack by generating enough log entries to fill up the entire disk. Logs are generally stored in the **C:\WINDOWS\system32\config** directory in Windows.

■ **/tmp** This is where temporary files are placed. Because this directory is designed so that it is writable by any user (similar to the **C:\Temp** directory under Windows), you need to make sure arbitrary users don't abuse it and fill up the entire disk. You ensure this by keeping it on a separate partition.

▲ **Swap** This is where the virtual memory file is stored. This isn't a user-accessible file system. Although Linux (and other flavors of UNIX, as well) can use a normal disk file to hold virtual memory the way Windows does, you'll find that having it on its own partition improves performance. You will typically want to configure your swap file to be double the physical memory that is in your system. This is referred to as the paging file in Windows.

Each of these partitions is mounted at boot time. The mount process makes the contents of that partition available as if it were just another directory on the system. For example, the root directory (/) will be on the first (root) partition. A subdirectory called **/usr** will exist on the root directory, but it will have nothing in it. A separate partition can then be mounted such that going into the **/usr** directory will allow you to see the contents of the newly mounted partition. All the partitions, when mounted, appear as a unified directory tree rather than as separate drives; the installation software does not differentiate one partition from another. All it cares about is which directory each file goes into. As a result, the installation process automatically distributes its files across all the mounted partitions, as long as the mounted partitions represent different parts of the directory tree where files are usually placed.

The Disk Druid partitioning tool (see Step 3 in the upcoming list) was developed by Red Hat as an easy way to create partitions and associate them to the directories they will be mounted as. When starting Disk Druid, you will see all of the existing partitions on your disk, if any. Each partition entry will show the following information:

▼ **Device**   Linux associates each partition with a separate device. For the purpose of this installation, you need to know only that under IDE disks, each device begins with /dev/hd*XY*, where *X* is *a* for an IDE master on the first chain, *b* for an IDE slave on the first chain, *c* for an IDE master on the second chain, or *d* for an IDE slave on the second chain, and where *Y* is the partition number of the disk. For example, /dev/hda1 is the first partition on the primary chain, primary disk. SCSI follows the same basic idea, except instead of starting with /dev/hd, each partition starts with /dev/sd and follows the format /dev/sd*XY*, where *X* is a letter representing a unique physical drive (*a* is for SCSI ID 1, *b* is for SCSI ID 2, and so on). The *Y* represents the partition number. Thus, /dev/sdb4 is the fourth partition on the SCSI disk with ID 2. The system is a little more complex than Windows, but each partition's location is explicit—no more guessing, "What physical device does drive E: correspond to?"

■ **Mount point**   The location where the partition is mounted.

■ **Type**   This field shows the partition's type (for example, ext2, ext3, swap, or vfat).

■ **Format**   This field indicates whether or not the partition will be formatted.

■ **Size (MB)**   This field shows the partition's size (in MB).

■ **Start**   This field shows the cylinder on your hard drive where the partition begins.

▲ **End**   This field shows the cylinder on your hard drive where the partition ends.

For the sake of simplicity, you will use only some of the disk boundaries described earlier for your installation. In addition, you will also leave some free space (unpartitioned space) that we can play with in a later chapter (Chapter 7). You will carve up your hard disk into

/boot partition

/ partition

SWAP partition

/home partition

/tmp partition

FREE SPACE / UN-PARTITIONED AREA

The sample system that this installation is being performed on has a 10GB hard disk. You will use the sizes below as a guideline on how to allocate the various sizes for each partition/volume. You should, of course, adjust the suggested sizes to suit the overall size of the disk you are using.

Mount Point	Size
/boot	200MB
/	5GB
SWAP	512MB
/home	3GB
/tmp	512MB
FREE SPACE	~ 512MB

NOTE The /boot partition can not be created on a Logical Volume Management (LVM) partition type. The Fedora boot loader cannot read LVM type partitions. This is true at the time of this writing but may change in the future.

Now that you have some background on partitioning under Linux, let's go back to the installation process itself:

1. Select the Manually Partition With Disk Druid option and click Next.

2. If you are performing the installation on a brand new hard disk, you might get a Warning dialog box that will pop up prompting you to initialize the drive. Select Yes when prompted.

3.   Next you will be presented with the Disk Setup screen, as shown here:

4.   Click New. The Add Partition dialog box appears; complete it with the information that follows for the corresponding fields:

Mount Point	/boot
File System Type	ext3
Allowable Drives	hda
Size (MB)	200
Additional Size Options	Fixed Size
Force to be a primary partition	Leave unchecked

The completed dialog box should resemble the one shown here. Click the OK button when done.

Add Partition	
Mount Point:	/boot ▾
File System Type:	ext3 ⬍
	☑ hda 10237 MB VMware Virtual IDE Hard Drive
Allowable Drives:	
Size (MB):	200 ⬍
Additional Size Options	
⦿ Fixed size	
○ Fill all space up to (MB):	200
○ Fill to maximum allowable size	
☐ Force to be a primary partition	
	✗ Cancel ⏎ OK

5. You will create the / (root), /home, /tmp, and swap containers on an LVM-type partition. Therefore, you will first need to create the parent physical volume. Click New. The Add Partition dialog box appears. The physical volume will be created with the information that follows:

Mount Point	Leave this field blank
File System Type	physical volume (LVM)
Allowable Drives	hda
Size (MB)	9216 (Approximately 9.0GB)
Additional Size Options	Fixed Size
Force to be a primary partition	Leave unchecked

The completed dialog box should resemble the one shown here. Click the OK button when done.

6. Click the LVM button. The Make LVM Volume Group dialog box will appear. Accept the default values already provided for the various fields (Volume Group Name, Physical Extent, etc.). Click Add. The Make Logical Volume dialog box will appear. Complete the fields in the dialog box with the information that follows:

Mount Point	/
File System Type	ext3
Logical Volume Name	LogVol00
Size (MB)	5120 (approximately 5GB)

The completed dialog box should resemble the one shown here. Click OK when done.

7. Click Add again in the Make LVM Volume Group dialog box. The Make Logical Volume dialog box will appear. Complete the fields in the dialog box with the information that follows:

Mount Point	Leave blank
File System Type	swap
Logical Volume Name	LogVol01
Size (MB)	512 (approximately double the total amount of RAM available)

The completed dialog box should resemble the one shown here. Click the OK button when done.

Make Logical Volume	
Mount Point:	<Not Applicable>
File System Type:	swap
Logical Volume Name:	LogVol01
Size (MB):	512
	(Max size is 4064 MB)
	Cancel OK

8. Click Add again in the Make LVM Volume Group dialog box. The Make Logical Volume dialog box will appear. Complete the fields in the dialog box with the information that follows:

Mount Point	/home
File System Type	ext3
Logical Volume Name	LogVol02
Size (MB)	3072 (Approximately 3GB)

Click the OK button when done.

9. Click Add again in the Make LVM Volume Group dialog box. The Make Logical Volume dialog box will appear. Complete the fields in the dialog box with the information that follows:

Mount point	/tmp
File System Type	ext3
Logical Volume Name	LogVol03
Size (MB)	480 (or "Use up all the remaining free space on the Volume group")

Click OK when done.

10.   The completed Make LVM Volume Group dialog box should resemble the one shown here:

Click the OK button to close the dialog box.

11.   You will be returned to the main Disk Setup screen. The final screen should be similar to the one shown here:

You will notice that we have some free unpartitioned space left under the device column. This was done deliberately so that you can play with that space in later chapters without necessarily having to reinstall the entire operating system to create free space.

12. Click Next to complete the disk partitioning portion of the installation.

Boot Loader Configuration

GRUB is one of the popular *boot managers* for Linux. A boot manager handles the process of actually starting the load process of an operating system. If you're familiar with Windows NT, you have already dealt with the NT Loader (NTLDR), which presents the menu at boot time.

The boot loader configuration screen has multiple sections (see Figure 2-1). The top of the screen tells you where the boot loader is being installed. On our sample system, it is being installed on the Master Boot Record (MBR) of /dev/hda. The MBR is the very

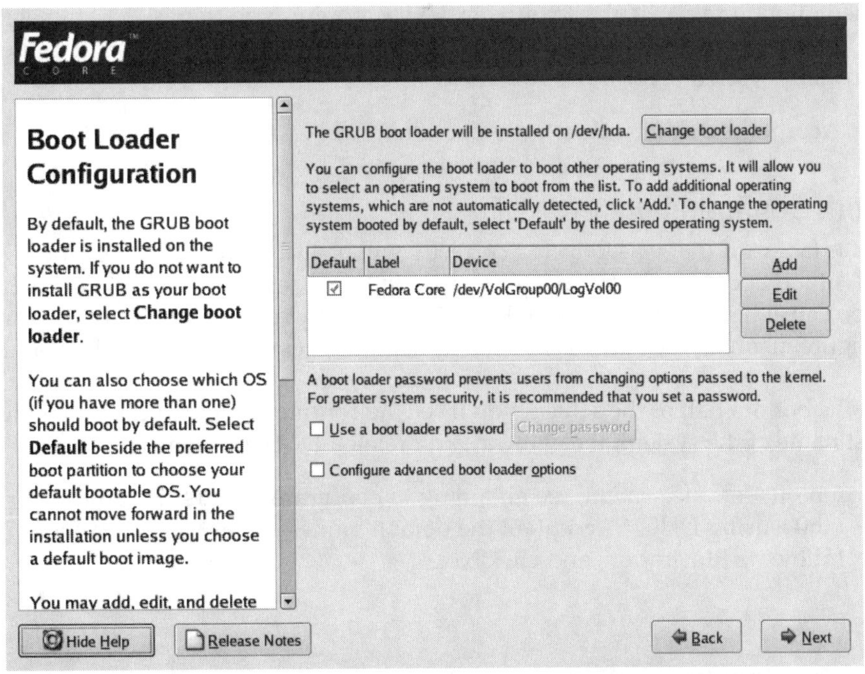

Figure 2-1. Boot loader configuration screen

first thing the system will read when booting a system. It is essentially the point where the built-in hardware tests finish and pass off control to the software.

There is also a button at the top of the screen that lets you change the boot loader. Typically, unless you really know what you are doing, you want to accept the defaults provided here.

The next section of the screen lets you configure the boot loader to boot other operating systems.

If you are installing Linux on a hard disk that already has some other operating system (e.g., Windows or some other flavor of Linux), this is where the dual-booting functionality will be configured. On a system that is configured to support both Windows and Linux, you will see your choices here. If your system is set up only for Linux (as we assume here), you will see one entry.

NOTE The exception is for SMP-based systems that will see two entries. The first entry is usually to set up to support for a multiple processor system, usually followed by a backup entry for a uniprocessor-enabled kernel.

The last option, labeled Configure Advanced Boot Loader Options, allows you to enter kernel parameters to be used at boot time. Most people can ignore this box. If the documentation for a particular feature or device requires you to pass a parameter here, add it; otherwise, leave the option alone. To reiterate, most of the default values provided usually work fine for most purposes.

1. Accept the default values provided and click Next.

Network Configuration

Each interface card that was detected correctly will be listed under the Network Devices section. Ethernet devices in Linux are named eth0, eth1, eth2, and so on. For each interface, you can either configure it using DHCP or manually set the IP address. If you choose to configure manually, be sure to have the IP, netmask, network, and broadcast addresses ready.

On the bottom half of the screen, you'll see the configuration choices for configuring the host name of the system, the gateway, and related DNS information.

1. On our sample system, we are going to configure the first Ethernet interface—eth0—using DHCP. Accept all the default values in this screen, as shown in the following illustration, and click Next.

Fedora
CORE

Network Configuration

Any network devices you have on the system are automatically detected by the installation program and shown in the **Network Devices** list.

To configure the network device, first select the device and then click **Edit**. In the **Edit Interface** screen, you can choose to have the IP and Netmask information configured by DHCP or you can enter it manually. You can also choose to make the device active at boot time.

If you do not have DHCP client

Network Devices

Active on Boot	Device	IP/Netmask	
☑	eth0	DHCP	Edit

Hostname

Set the hostname:
- ⦿ automatically via DHCP
- ○ manually [localhost.localdomain] (ex. "host.domain.com")

Miscellaneous Settings

Gateway: [ ][ ][ ][ ]
Primary DNS: [ ][ ][ ][ ]
Secondary DNS: [ ][ ][ ][ ]
Tertiary DNS: [ ][ ][ ][ ]

[🛈 Hide Help] [📄 Release Notes]   [⬅ Back] [➡ Next]

NOTE   Don't worry if you know that you don't have a DHCP server available on your network that will provide your new system with IP configuration information. The Ethernet interface will simply remain unconfigured. The host name of the system will also be automatically set to localhost.localdomain in the absence of a capable DHCP server that can automatically allocate host names.

Firewall Configuration

The next leg of the installation deals with the security-related options available.

The first option lets you decide if you want to enable the firewall or not enable the firewall. Under this section you also have the option of configuring the firewall to allow access to specific services hosted on your computer.

NOTE   This section of the install is a common source of confusion for people who are new to Linux. The sample services listed (Remote Login, Web Server, File Transfer, Mail Server) refer to services that you want to run on your local system and that you want to make accessible externally (ingress traffic). For example, if you want to run a Web server on your server to host a Web site, then you can punch a hole in the firewall to allow access to Web server (HTTP, HTTPS) traffic. Leaving the HTTP, HTTPS unchecked in this screen will *not* prevent your Web browser from displaying Web pages hosted on other systems (egress traffic).

The other section of the screen deals with security-enhanced Linux (SELinux) configuration.

SELinux provides finer-grained security controls than those traditionally available in Linux systems. During the installation, it can be set up in a Disabled state, an Active state, or a Warn-Only state.

1. Accept the defaults in this screen, but in addition select the check box to allow Remote Login (SSH) through the firewall, as shown here:

2. Click Next when done.

Time Zone Selection

The time zone configuration screen, shown next, allows you to select the time zone in which the machine is located:

If your system's hardware clock keeps time in UTC, be sure to click the System Clock Uses UTC check box so that Linux can determine the difference between the two and display the correct local time.

1. Scroll through the list of locations and select the nearest city to your time zone. You can also use the interactive map to select a specific city (marked by a yellow dot) to set your time zone.

2. Click Next when done.

Set the Root Password

The next part of the installation allows you to set a password for the root user, also called the superuser. It is the most privileged account on the system and typically has full control of the system. It is equivalent to the Administrator account in the Windows operating system. Thus, it is crucial that you protect this account with a good password. Be sure not to pick dictionary words or names as passwords, as they are easy to guess and crack.

1. Pick a very good password and enter it in the Root Password text box.

2. Enter the same password again in the Confirm text box.

3. Click Next.

Package Group Selection

This is the part of the installation where you can select what packages (applications) get installed onto the system. Fedora categorizes these packages into several high-level categories. The available categories are Desktops, Applications, Servers, Development, System, and Miscellaneous. Under each category are the available package groups (X Window System, Editors, Development Tools, etc.). This organization allows you to make a quick selection of what type of packages you want installed and safely ignore the details.

Looking at the choices shown here, you see the menu of top-level package groups that Fedora gives you. You can simply pick the groups that interest you or scroll to the bottom of the list and pick Everything to have all of the packages installed (be warned: a full/everything install can require upward of 7GB of disk space!), or select the option to install only the minimum required.

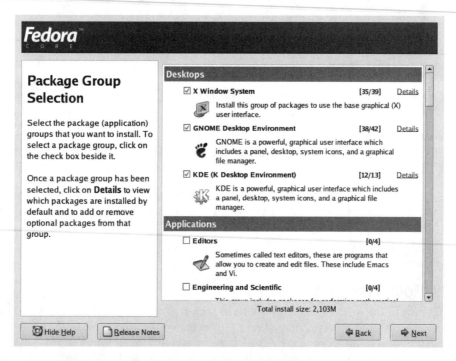

The GNOME Desktop Environment might already be selected for you—GNOME is a very popular desktop environment. In addition to the package groups that are selected by default, select the KDE (K Desktop Environment) package group. This additional selection will allow you to sample some of the available desktop environments (graphical user interfaces, or GUIs) that are available to Linux. There is an age-old holy war regarding which of the desktop environments is the best, but you will have to play around with them to decide for yourself.

1. Accept the defaults and also select the KDE (K Desktop Environment) package group.

2. Click Next.

About to Install

The installer will begin the actual installation (laying out the partitions, formatting the partitions with a file system, writing the operating system to the disk, etc.) after you click Next in this screen. If you develop cold feet at this point, you can still safely back out of the installation without any loss of data (or self esteem). To quit the installer, simply reset your system by pressing CTRL-ALT-DELETE on the keyboard or by pushing the reset or power switch for the system.

1. Click Next to begin.

NOTE   If you are installing from a set of CDs, the installer will inform you of the particular discs you need to have handy to complete the installation. You will not get this warning if you are performing a network-based installation or using a DVD. (The steps here are being performed using a DVD.)

2. The installation will begin, and the installer will show the progress of the installation, as shown here:

Fedora™
CORE

Installing Packages

We have gathered all the information needed to install Fedora Core on the system. It may take a while to install everything, depending on how many packages need to be installed.

Fedora™
C O R E

Installing e2fsprogs-1.37-4.i386 (3 MB)
Utilities for managing the second extended (ext2) filesystem.

🔅 Hide Help   📄 Release Notes   ⬅ Back   ➡ Next

This is also a good time to study the Release Notes. Click the Release Notes button at the left-hand side of the screen to launch another window to view the notes.

3. Remove the installation medium from the drive and click the Reboot button in the final screen shown here:

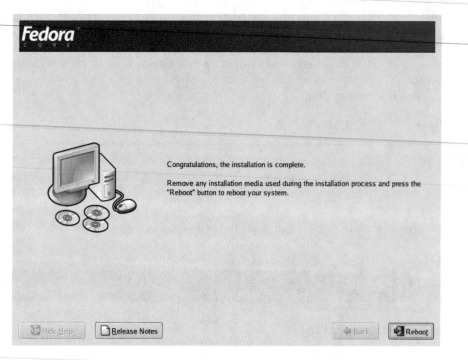

Initial System Configuration

The system will reboot itself. After the boot process completes, you will have to click through a quick customization process (Fedora and RHEL call this process "The Setup Agent"). This is a one-time process, and you will not have to go through it again for future reboots. It is here that you can set the system time and date, add users to the system, install additional software, and so on.

1. Click Next when you are presented with the Welcome screen, shown next:

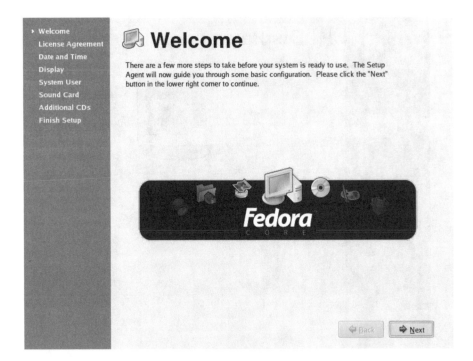

2. You will next be prompted to read and agree to the license agreement before proceeding. Select the Yes, I Agree To The License Agreement radio button and click Next.

3. In the Date and Time screen, make sure that the current date and time shown reflect the actual current date and time. Click Next when done.

4. At the Display section, shown next, the Setup Agent will try to probe for the type of video card and monitor that you have attached to the system. If the values detected are incorrect, you can use the buttons to select the correct values for your hardware. If you are unsure about any particular setting, you may safely accept the automatically probed defaults. Click Next when done.

Welcome
License Agreement
Date and Time
▸ Display
System User
Sound Card
Additional CDs
Finish Setup

Display

Please select the resolution and color depth that you wish to use:

Unknown monitor with VMWare   [Configure...]

Resolution: [800x600   ▲▼]

Color Depth: [Millions of Colors   ▲▼]

[⇐ Back]   [⇒ Next]

5. Next you will be presented with a dialog box with which you can create a user account, but you will skip the creation of any additional user at this time. Click Next.

A warning dialog box will appear, as shown here, urging you to create a nonprivileged user account; select Continue.

Warning

It is highly recommended that a personal user account be created. If you continue without an account, you can only log in with the root account, which is reserved for administrative use only.

[Continue]   [Create account]

6. If a sound card is detected on your system, you will get the Sound Card screen. Click the Play Test Sound button if indeed you have a sound card on your system. Follow the subsequent prompts and click Next when done.

7. The Additional CDs section allows you to install additional packages that you did not install during the installation, and some other third-party software may be installed here.

You have no additional software you want to install, so click Next.

8. The system is now set up and ready for use. Click Next to exit the Setup Agent, shown here, and continue:

9. You will be presented with the Fedora login screen, shown here:

SUMMARY

You have successfully completed the installation process. If you are still having problems with the installation, be sure to visit Fedora's Web site at http://fedora.redhat.com and take a look at the various manuals available.

The version release notes are also a very good resource for specific installation issues. Even though the install process discussed in this chapter used Fedora Core as the operating system of choice, you can rest assured that the installation steps for RHEL version 4 are virtually identical. The install steps also introduced you to some Linux/UNIX-specific concepts that will be covered in better detail in later chapters (e.g., hard disk naming conventions and partitioning under Linux).

CHAPTER 3

Installing Software

System administrators deal with software or application management on systems in various ways. You have the class of system administrators that like to play it safe and generally abide by the principle "if it's not broken, don't fix it." This approach has its benefits as well as its drawbacks. One of the benefits is that the system tends to be more stable and behave in a predictable manner. Nothing has changed drastically on the system, and so it should pretty much be the same way it was yesterday, last week, last month, etc. The drawback to this approach is that the system might lose the benefits of bug fixes and security fixes that are available for the various installed applications.

Another class of system administrators take the exact opposite approach: they like to install the latest and greatest piece of software available out there. This approach also has its benefits and drawbacks. One of its benefits is that the system tends to stay current as security flaws in applications are discovered and fixed. The obvious drawback is that some of the newer software might not have had time to benefit from the maturing process that comes with age and hence may behave in slightly unpredictable ways.

Regardless of your system administration style, you will find that a great deal of your time will be spent interacting with the various software components of the system, keeping them up to date, maintaining what you already have installed, or installing new software.

There are a couple of basic approaches to installing software on a Linux system. One approach is to use the package manager for the distribution. A common method for Fedora Core and Red Hat Enterprise Linux is to use the Red Hat Package Manager (RPM). Another approach is to compile and install the software by hand using the standard GNU compilation method or the specific software directives. We will cover these methods in this chapter.

THE RED HAT PACKAGE MANAGER

The Red Hat Package Manager (RPM) allows the easy installation and removal of software packages (typically, precompiled software). A package consists of an archive of files and other metadata.

It is wonderfully easy to use, and several graphical interfaces have been built around it to make it even easier. Several Linux distributions (distros) and various third parties use this tool to distribute and package their software. In fact, almost all of the software mentioned in this book is available in RPM form. The reason you'll go through the process of compiling software yourself in other chapters is so that you can customize the software to your system, as such customizations might not be readily achievable in an RPM.

An RPM file is a package that contains files needed for the software to function correctly. These files can be configuration files, binaries, and even pre- and post-scripts to run while installing the software.

NOTE In the present context, we are assuming that the RPM files contain precompiled binaries, but adhering to the open-source principle, the various commercial Linux distros are obliged to make the source code for most GNU binaries available. (Some Linux vendors stick to this principle more than others.) Several Linux vendors therefore make the source code for their binaries available in RPM form. For instance, Fedora and SuSE make source code available as an RPM, and it is becoming increasingly common to download and compile source code in this fashion.

The RPM tool performs the installation and uninstallation of RPMs. The tool also maintains a central database of what RPMs you have installed, where they are installed, when they were installed, and other information about the package.

In general, software that comes in the form of an RPM is less work to install and maintain than software that needs to be compiled. The trade-off is that by using an RPM, you accept the default parameters supplied in the RPM. In most cases, these defaults are acceptable. However, if you need to be more intimately aware of what is going with a piece of software, you may find that by compiling the source yourself, you will learn more about what package components and options exist and how they work together.

Assuming that all you want to do is install a simple package, RPM is perfect. There are several great resources for RPM packages, including the following:

▼ http://www.rpmfind.net

■ http://rpm.pbone.net

■ ftp://ftp.redhat.com

■ http://mirrors.kernel.org

▲ http://freshrpms.net

Of course, if you are interested in more details about RPM itself, you can visit the RPM Web site at http://www.rpm.org. RPM comes with Fedora Core, SuSE, Mandrake, countless other Red Hat derivatives, and most surprising of all, the Red Hat version of Linux! If you aren't sure if RPM comes with your distribution, check with your vendor.

NOTE Although the name of the package says "Red Hat," the software can be used with other distributions as well. In fact, RPM has even been ported to other operating systems, such as Solaris and IRIX. The source code to RPM is open source software, so anyone can take the initiative to make the system work for them.

The primary functions of the Red Hat Package Manager are

▼ Querying, installing, and uninstalling software

■ Maintaining a database that stores various items of information about the packages

▲ Packaging other software into an RPM form

The following sections examine some of these functions by using actual examples.

Table 3-1, which includes frequently used RPM options, is provided for reference purposes only.

Command-Line Option	Description
`--install`	This installs a new package.
`--upgrade`	This upgrades or installs the package currently installed to a newer version.
`--erase`	Removes or erases an installed package.
`--query`	This is the option used for querying.
`--force`	This is the sledgehammer of installation. Typically, you use it when you're knowingly installing an odd or unusual configuration, and RPM's safeguards are trying to keep you from doing so. The `--force` option tells RPM to forego any sanity checks and just do it, even if it thinks you're trying to fit a square peg into a round hole. Be careful with this option.
`-h`	Prints hash marks to indicate progress during an installation. Use with the `-v` option for a pretty display.
`--percent`	Prints the percentage completed to indicate progress. It is handy if you're running RPM from another program, such as a Perl script, and you want to know the status of the install.
`-nodeps`	If RPM is complaining about missing dependency files but you want the installation to happen anyway, passing this option at the command line will cause RPM to not perform any dependency checks.
`-q`	Queries the RPM system for information.
`--test`	This option does not perform a real installation; it just checks to see whether an installation would succeed. If it anticipates problems, it displays what they'll be.
`-V`	Verifies RPMs or files on the system.
`-v`	Tells RPM to be verbose about its actions.

Table 3-1.   Common RPM Options

Querying with RPM (Getting to Know One Another)

One of the best ways to begin any relationship is by getting to know the other party. Some of the relevant information might be the person's name, what that person does for a living, date of birth, likes or dislikes, etc. The same rules apply to RPM-type packages. After you obtain a piece of software (from the Internet, from the distribution's CD/DVD, from a third party, etc.), you should get to know the software before making it a part of your life . . . sorry, your system. This functionality was built into RPM from the beginning, and it is very easy to use.

When you get used to Linux/UNIX, you may find that software names are somewhat intuitive and you can usually tell what a package is just by looking at it's name. For example, to the uninitiated it may not be immediately obvious that a file named **gcc-3.8.2-6.rpm** is a package for the "GNU compiler collection." But once you get used to the system and you know what to look for, it becomes more intuitive. You can also use RPM to query for other types of information, such as the package's build date, its weight . . . sorry, its size, its likes and dislikes . . . sorry, its dependencies, etc.

Let's start by trying a few things using RPM. Begin by logging in to the system and starting a terminal (as described in the following sidebar, "Getting Down to Business").

Getting Down to Business

The previous chapter walked you through the installation process. Now that you have a working system, you will need to log in to the system to carry out the exercises in this and other chapters of the book. Most of the exercises will implicitly ask you to type a command. Although it may seem like stating the obvious, whenever you are asked to type in a command, you will have to type it into a console at the shell prompt. This is akin to the DOS prompt in Microsoft Windows but stupendously more powerful.

There are a couple of ways to do this. One way is to use a nice windowed (GUI) terminal or the system console. The windowed consoles are known as terminal emulators (or pseudo-terminals), and there are tons of them.

After logging in to your chosen desktop (GNOME, KDE, XFCE, etc.), you can usually launch a pseudo-terminal by right-clicking the desktop and selecting Launch Terminal from the context-sensitive menu. If you don't have that particular option, look for an option in the menu that says Run Command. After the Run dialog box appears, you can then type the name of a terminal emulator into the Run text box. A popular terminal emulator program that is almost guaranteed (or your money back!) to exist on all Linux systems is the venerable **xterm**. If you are in a GNOME desktop, the **gnome-terminal** is the default. If you are using KDE, the default is **konsole**.

Querying for All Packages

Use the **rpm** command to list all the packages that are currently installed on your system. At the shell prompt type

```
[root@serverA ~]# rpm  --query -all
```

This will give you a long listing of software installed.

NOTE Like most Linux commands, the **rpm** command also has its own long or short (abbreviated) forms of options or arguments. For example, the short form of the **--query** option is **-q**, and the short form of **--all** is **-a**. We will mostly use short forms in this book but will occasionally use the long forms just so that you can see their relationship.

Querying Details for a Specific Package

Let's zero in on one of the packages listed in the output of the preceding command, the bash application. Use **rpm** to see if you indeed have the bash application installed on your system.

```
[root@serverA ~]# rpm --query  bash
bash-3.0-17
```

The output should be something similar to this. It shows that you do indeed have the package called bash installed. It also shows the version number appended to the package name. Note that the version number of the output on your system might be different. But the main package name will almost always be the same, i.e., bash is bash is bash is bash in SuSE, Fedora, Mandrake, RHEL, etc.

Which brings us to the next question: what is bash and what does it do? To find out, type

```
[root@serverA ~]# rpm -qi  bash
Name        : bash              Relocations: /usr
Version     : 3.0               Vendor: Red Hat, Inc.
Release     : 17                Build Date: Tue 19 Oct 2004 12:40:09 PM PDT
Install Date: Sat 22 Jan 2007 08:15:12 PM PST
Build Host  : bugs.build.redhat.com
Group       : System Environment/Shells    Source RPM: bash-3.0-17.src.rpm
Size        : 5112768                       License: GPL
Signature   : DSA/SHA1, Wed 20 Oct 2005 09:07:11 AM PDT, Key ID b44269d04f2a6fd2
Packager    : Red Hat, Inc. <http://bugzilla.redhat.com/bugzilla>
Summary     : The GNU Bourne Again shell (bash).
Description :
The GNU project Bourne Again shell (bash) is a shell or command
language interpreter that is compatible with the Bourne shell
(sh). Bash incorporates useful features from the Korn shell (ksh) and
the C shell (csh) and most sh scripts can be run by bash without
modification. Bash is the default shell for Red Hat Linux.
```

This output gives us a lot of information. It shows the version number, the release, the description, the packager, and more.

The bash package looks rather impressive. Lets see what else comes with it.

```
[root@serverA ~]# rpm -ql bash
```

This lists all the files that come with the bash package.

To list the configuration files (if any) that come with the bash package, type

```
[root@serverA ~]# rpm -qc bash
/etc/skel/.bash_logout
/etc/skel/.bash_profile
/etc/skel/.bashrc
```

The querying capabilities of **rpm** are very extensive. RPM packages have a lot of information stored in so-called TAGs. These tags make up the metadata of the package. You can query the RPM database for specific information using these tags. For example, to find out the date that the bash package was installed on your system, you can type

```
[root@serverA ~]# rpm -q --qf "[ %{INSTALLTIME:date} \n]"  bash

Sat 22 Jan 2007 08:15:12 PM PST
```

NOTE   Because bash is a standard part of most Linux distros and would have been installed when you initially installed the OS, you will find that its install date will be very close to the day you installed the OS.

To find out what package group the bash application comes under, type

```
[root@serverA ~]# rpm -q --qf "[ %{GROUP} \n]"  bash

System Environment/Shells
```

You can, of course, always query for more than one package at the same time and also query for multiple tag information. For example, to display the names and package groups for the bash and xterm packages, type

```
[root@serverA ~]# rpm -q --qf "[%{NAME} - %{GROUP} - %{SUMMARY} \n]" bash xterm
 bash -  System Environment/Shells -  The GNU Bourne Again shell (bash).
 xterm -  User Interface/X -  xterm terminal emulator for the X Window System
```

To determine what other packages on the system depend on the bash package, type

```
[root@serverA ~]# rpm -q --whatrequires bash
```

TIP   The RPM queries just made were done on software that is currently installed on the system. You can perform similar queries on other software that you get from other sources as well, for instance, software that you are planning to install that you have obtained from the Internet or from the distribution CD/DVD. Similar queries can also be performed on packages that have not yet been installed. To do this, you simply add the **-p** option to the end of the query command. For example, to query an uninstalled package named "joe-3.1-8.i386.rpm," you would type **rpm -qip joe-3.1-8.i386.rpm**.

Installing with RPM (Moving in Together)

Okay, you are now both ready to take the relationship to the next stage. You have both decided to move in together. This can be a good thing because it allows both of you to see and test how truly compatible you are.

This stage of relationships is akin to installing the software package on your system, i.e., moving the software into your system.

In the following project steps, you will install the application called "joe" onto your system. First you will need to get a copy of the RPM package for joe. You can get this program from several places (the install CDs/DVD, the Internet, etc.). The example that follows uses a copy of the program that came with the DVD used during the installation.

The CD/DVD needs to be mounted in order to access its content. To mount it, insert the DVD into the drive and launch a console. If you don't see an icon for the DVD appear on the desktop after a brief delay, then you will have to manually mount the device. At the shell prompt, type

```
[root@serverA RPMS]# mount /media/dvd
```

or

```
[root@serverA RPMS]# mount /media/cdrom
```

The RPM files are stored under the **Fedora/RPMS** directory under the mount point of your DVD/CD device, e.g., the **/media/dvd/Fedora/RPMS** directory.

NOTE   If you don't have a Fedora Core CD or DVD, you can download the RPM we will be using in the next section from http://mirrors.kernel.org/fedora/core/4/i386/os/Fedora/RPMS/joe-3.1-8.i386.rpm.

Let's step through the process of installing an RPM.

1. Launch a virtual terminal.
2. Assuming your distribution install disc is mounted at the **/media/dvd** mount point, change to the directory that usually contains the RPM packages on the DVD. Type

    ```
    [root@serverA ~]# cd /media/dvd/Fedora/RPMS/
    ```

    You can first make sure that the file you want is indeed in that directory. Use the **ls** command to list all the files that start with the letters "joe" in the directory. Type

```
[root@serverA RPMS]# ls  joe*
joe-3.1-8.i386.rpm
```

NOTE If you are using the installation CDs instead of the DVD, the file might be located on the second CD of the four-CD set.

3. Now that you have confirmed that the file is there, perform a test install of the package (this will run through all the motions of installing the package without actually installing anything on the system). This is useful in making sure that all the needs (dependencies) of a package are met. Type

```
[root@serverA RPMS]# rpm --install --verbose --hash --test joe-3.1-8.i386.rpm

warning: joe-3.1-8.i386.rpm: V3 DSA signature: NOKEY, key ID 4f2a6fd2
Preparing...               ######################################### [100%]
```

Everything looks okay (except the warning message about the signature, which we can safely ignore for now).

4. Go ahead and perform the actual installation. Type

```
[root@serverA RPMS]# rpm -ivh   joe-3.1-8.i386.rpm

warning: joe-3.1-8.i386.rpm: V3 DSA signature: NOKEY, key ID 4f2a6fd2
Preparing...             ######################################### [100%]
1:joe                    ######################################### [100%]
```

5. Run a simple query to confirm that the application is now installed on your system. Type

```
[root@serverA RPMS]# rpm -q joe
joe-3.1-8
```

The output shows that joe is now available on the system. Joe is a simple text editor. You can launch it by simply typing **joe** at the shell prompt. To quit joe, press CTRL-SHIFT-C.

As you can see, installing packages via RPM can be very easy. But there are times when installing packages is a little more tricky. This is usually due to the issues of failed dependencies. For example, the package joe might require the bash package to be already installed on the system before it can be successfully installed itself.

Let's step through installing a more complex package to see how dependencies are handled with RPM. Assuming you are still in the Fedora RPMS directory, do the following:

1. Install the package by typing

```
[root@serverA RPMS]# rpm -ivh gcc-4*.rpm
warning: gcc-4*.rpm: V3 DSA signature: NOKEY, key ID 4f2a6fd2
error: Failed dependencies:
        glibc-devel >= 2.2.90-12 is needed by gcc-4*
```

The preceding output does not look very good. The last line tells us that gcc* depends on another package, called glibc-devel*.

2. Fortunately, because we have access to the DVD that contains all the packages for this distro in a single directory, we can easily add the additional package to our install list. Type

```
[root@serverA RPMS]# rpm -ivh gcc-4*.rpm \
glibc-devel-*.rpm
warning: gcc-4*.rpm: V3 DSA signature: NOKEY, key ID 4f2a6fd2
error: Failed dependencies:
 glibc-headers is needed by glibc-devel-*
 glibc-headers = 2.3.3 is needed by glibc-devel-*
```

Uh-oh . . . it looks like this particular partner is not going to be easy to move in. The output again tells us that the glibc-devel* package depends on another package, called glibc-headers*.

3. Add the newest dependency to the install list. Type

```
[root@serverA RPMS]# rpm -ivh gcc-4*.rpm \
glibc-devel-*.rpm  glibc-headers-*.rpm
warning: gcc-4*.rpm: V3 DSA signature: NOKEY, key ID 4f2a6fd2
error: Failed dependencies:
    kernel-headers is needed by glibc-headers-*
        kernel-headers >= 2.2.1 is needed by glibc-headers-*
```

After all we have given to this relationship, all we get is more complaining. The last requirement is one of those nonintuitive package names that you will rarely come across, because that dependency is actually satisfied by a package called "glibc-kernheaders*" and *not* "kernel-headers*" as we might have thought.

4. Looks like we are getting close to the end. We add the final required package to the list. Type

```
[root@serverA RPMS]# rpm -ivh  gcc-4*.rpm  \
glibc-devel-*.rpm glibc-headers-*.rpm \
glibc-kernheaders-*.rpm

warning: gcc-4*.rpm: V3 DSA signature: NOKEY, key ID 4f2a6fd2
Preparing...                ####################################### [100%]
   1:glibc-kernheaders      ####################################### [ 25%]
   2:glibc-headers          ####################################### [ 50%]
   3:glibc-devel            ####################################### [ 75%]
   4:gcc                    ####################################### [100%]
```

It was tough, but you managed to get the software installed.

TIP When you perform multiple RPM installations in one shot as you did in the previous step, this is called an RPM *transaction*.

A very popular option used in installing packages via RPM is the **-U** (for Upgrade) option. It is especially useful when you want to install a newer version of a package that already exists. It will simply upgrade the already-installed package to the newer version. This option also does a good job of keeping your custom configuration for an application intact. For example, if you had joe-7-8.rpm installed and you wanted to upgrade to joe-8.0.rpm, you would type **rpm -Uvh joe-8.0.rpm**.

It should also be noted that you can also use the **-U** option to perform a regular installation of a package even when you are not upgrading.

Uninstalling with RPM (Ending the Relationship)

Things didn't quite work out the way you both had anticipated. Now it is time to end the relationship. The other partner was never any good anyhow . . . so we'll simply clean them out of our system (literally).

Cleaning up after itself is one of the areas in which RPM truly excels, and this is one of its key selling points as a software manager in Linux systems. Because a database of various pieces of information is stored and maintained along with each installed package, it is easy for RPM to refer to its database to collect information about what was installed and where.

NOTE A slight caveat applies here. Much as with Windows install/uninstall tools, all the wonderful things that RPM can do are also dependent on the packager of the software. For example, if an application were badly packaged and its removal scripts were not properly formatted, then you might still end up with bits of the package on your system even after uninstalling. This is one of the reasons you should always get software only from trusted sources.

Removing software with RPM is quite easy and can be done in a single step. For example, to remove the joe package that we installed earlier, we simply need to use the **-e** option like so:

```
[root@serverA RPMS]#  rpm -e joe
```

This command will usually not give you any feedback if everything went well. To get more verbose output for the uninstallation process, add the **-vvv** option to the command.

A handy feature of RPM is that it will protect you from removing packages that are needed by other packages. For example, if we try to remove the glibc-headers package (something that we saw gcc depended on), we'd see the following:

```
[root@serverA RPMS]# rpm -e glibc-headers
error: Failed dependencies:
        glibc-headers is needed by (installed) glibc-devel-*
        glibc-headers = 2.3.3 is needed by (installed) glibc-devel-*
```

NOTE Remember that the glibc-headers* package required this package. And so RPM will do its best in helping you maintain a stable software environment. But if you are adamant and desperate to shoot yourself in the foot, RPM will also allow you to do that (perhaps because you know what you are doing). If, for example, you wanted to forcefully uninstall the glibc-devel package, you would add the `--nodeps` option to the uninstallation command.

Other Things You Can Do with RPM

In addition to basic installation and uninstallation of packages with RPM, there are numerous other things you can do with it as well. In this section, we walk through what some of these functions are.

Verifying Packages

A very useful option to the RPM tool is the ability to verify a package. What happens is that RPM looks at the package information in its database, which is assumed to be good. It then compares that information with the binaries and files that are on your system.

In today's Internet world, where being hacked is a real possibility, this kind of test should tell you instantly if anyone has done something to your system.

For example, to verify that the bash package is as it should be, type

```
[root@serverA ~]# rpm -V bash
```

The absence of any output is a good sign.

You can also verify specific files on the file system that a particular package installed. For example, to verify the **/bin/ls** command is valid, you would type

```
[root@serverA ~]# rpm -Vf /bin/ls
```

Again, the lack of output is a good thing.

If something was amiss, for example if the **/bin/ls** command has been replaced by a dud version, the verify output might be similar to the one here:

```
[root@serverA ~]# rpm -Vf   /bin/ls
SM5....TC    /bin/ls
```

If something is wrong, as in the preceding example, RPM will inform you of what test failed. Some example tests are the MD5 checksum test, file size, and modification times. The moral of the story is: RPM is an ally in finding out what is wrong with your system.

Table 3-2 provides a summary of the various error codes and their meanings.

If you want to verify all the packages installed on your system, type

```
[root@serverA ~]# rpm -Va
```

This command verifies *all* of the packages installed on your system. That's a lot of files, so you might have to give it some time to complete.

Code	Meaning
S	File size differs
M	Mode differs (includes permissions and file type)
5	MD5 sum differs
D	Device major/minor number mismatch
L	readLink-path mismatch
U	User ownership differs
G	Group ownership differs
T	mTime differs

Table 3-2. RPM Verification Error Attributes

Package Validation

Another feature of RPM is that the packages can be digitally signed. This provides a form of built-in authentication mechanism that allows a user to ascertain that the package in his or her possession was truly packaged by the party the user thinks provided the package and also that the package has not been tampered with along the line somewhere.

You sometimes need to manually tell your system whose digital signature to trust. This explains the warnings in the earlier projects when you were trying to install a package (such as this message: "warning: joe-3.1-8.i386.rpm: V3 DSA signature: NOKEY, key ID 4f2a6fd2"). To prevent this warning message, you should import Fedora's digital key into your system's key ring. Type

```
[root@serverA ~]# rpm --import   /usr/share/rhn/RPM-GPG-KEY-fedora
```

You might also have to import some other vendors' keys into the key ring. To be extra certain that even the local key you have is not a dud, you can import the key directly from the vendor's Web site. For instance, to import a key from Fedora's project site, you would type

```
[root@serverA ~]# rpm --import \
http://download.fedora.redhat.com/pub/fedora/linux/core/3/i386/os/RPM-GPG-KEY-fedora
```

GUI RPM Package Managers

For those who like a good GUI tool to help simplify their lives, several package managers with GUI front ends are available. Doing all the dirty work behind these pretty GUI front ends is RPM. The GUI tools allow you to do quite a few things without forcing you to remember command-line parameters. Some of the more popular ones with each distribution or desktop environment are listed in the sections that follow.

Fedora

You can launch the GUI package management tool (Figure 3-1) in Fedora by clicking Main menu | System Settings | Add/Remove Applications. You can also launch the Fedora package manager from the command line simply by typing

```
[root@serverA ~]# system-config-packages
```

SuSE

In SuSE, most of the system administration is done via a tool called YaST. YaST (see Figure 3-2) is made up of different modules. For adding and removing packages graphically on the system, the relevant module is called **sw_single**. So to launch this

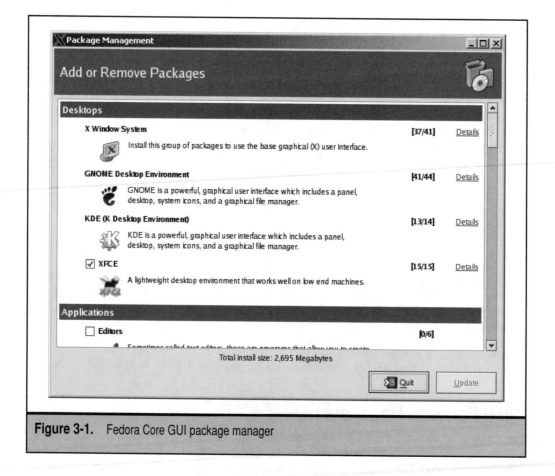

Figure 3-1.   Fedora Core GUI package manager

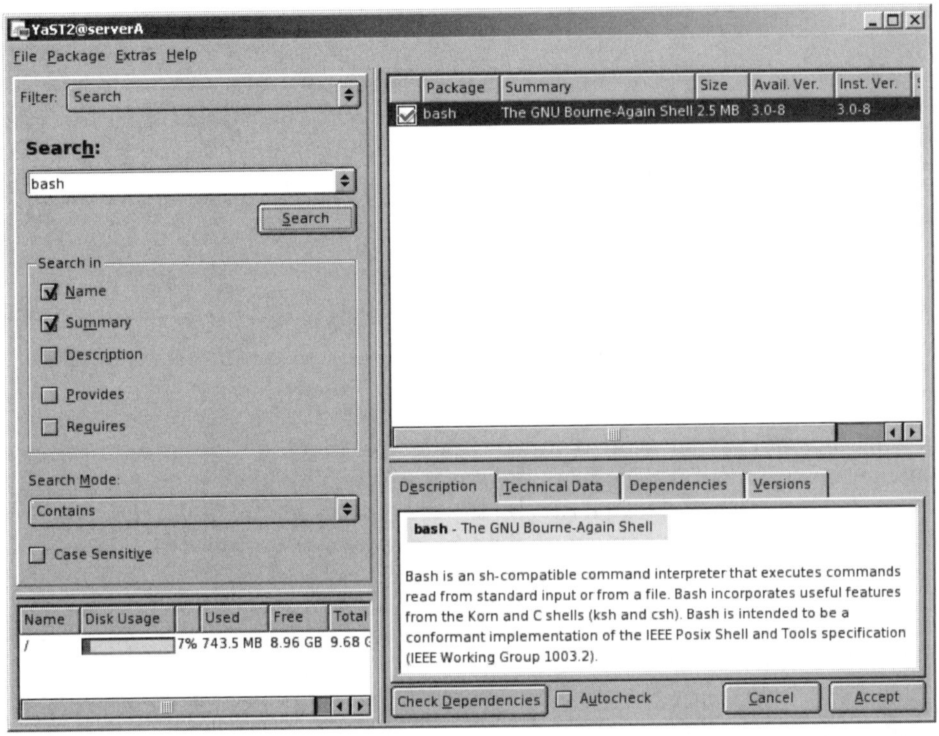

Figure 3-2. SuSE GUI package management tool

module from the command line of a system running the SuSE version of Linux, you would type

```
serverA:~ # yast2   sw_single
```

Yum

Yum is one of the newer methods of software management on Linux systems. It is basically a wrapper program for RPM with great enhancements. It has been around for a while but has become more widely used and adopted as major Linux vendors decided to concentrate more on their (more profitable) commercial product offerings. Yum appears to be one of those disruptive technologies because it has radically changed the traditional approach to package management. Popular large sites that serve as repositories for open-source software have had to slightly retool to now also maintain and accommodate "Yumified" repositories.

According to the Yum project's Web page, "Yum is an automatic updater and package installer/remover for rpm systems. It automatically computes dependencies and figures out what things should occur to install packages. It makes it easier to maintain groups of machines without having to manually update each one using rpm."

This summary is an understatement. Yum can do a lot beyond that. There are certain new Linux distributions that rely heavily on the capabilities provided by Yum.

Using Yum is very simple on supported systems. You mostly need a single configuration file (**/etc/yum.conf**) that points to a Yum-enabled (Yumified) software repository. Fortunately several Linux distributions now ship with Yum already installed and preconfigured. Fedora Core is one such distro.

To use Yum on a Fedora Core system—to install a package called "gcc," for example—from the command line, you would type

```
[root@serverA ~]# yum install gcc
```

Yum will automatically take care of any dependencies that the package might need and install the package for you. (The first time it is run, it will build up its local cache.)

Yum also has extensive search capabilities that will help you find a package even if you don't know the correct name for the package. All you need to know is a part of the name. For example, if you want to search for all packages that have the word "header" in the name, you can try a Yum option like this:

```
[root@serverA ~]# yum search headers
```

This will return a long list of matches to you. You can then look through the list and pick the package that you want.

NOTE By default Yum tries to access repositories that are located somewhere out on the Internet. Therefore, your system needs to be able to access the Internet to use it in its default state. You can also always create your own local software repository on the local file system or on your LAN and Yumify it. Simply copy the entire contents of the distribution media (DVD/CD) somewhere and run the **yum-arch** command against the directory location.

COMPILE AND INSTALL GNU SOFTWARE

One of the key benefits of open-source software is that you have access to the source code. If the developer chooses to stop working on it, you can continue (if you know how to). If you find a problem, you can fix it. In other words, you are in control of the situation and not at the mercy of a commercial developer you can't control. But having the source code means you need to be able to compile it, too. Otherwise, all you have is a bunch of text files that can't do much.

Although almost every piece of software in this book is available as an RPM, we will step through the process of compiling and building software from source. This has the added benefit of allowing you to pick and choose compile-time options, which is something you can't do with prebuilt RPMs. Also, an RPM might be compiled for a specific architecture such as the Intel 486, but that same code might run better if you compile it natively on your, say, Intel Pentium 4–class CPU.

In this section, we will step through the process of compiling the Hello package, a GNU software package that might seem useless at first but exists for good reasons. Most GNU software conforms to a standard method of compiling and installing, and the "hello" software tries to conform to this standard and so makes an excellent example.

Getting and Unpacking the Package

The other relationship left a bad taste in your mouth, but you are ready to try again. Perhaps things didn't quite work out because there were so many other factors to deal with . . . RPM with its endless options and seemingly convoluted syntax. And so out with the old, in with the new. Maybe you'll be luckier this time around if you have more control over the flow of things.

Although a little more involved, working directly with source code will give you more control over the software and how things shape out.

Software that comes in source form is generally made available as a *tarball*—that is, it is archived into a single large file and then compressed. The tools commonly used to do this are **tar** and **gzip**: **tar** handles the process of combining many files into a single large file, and **gzip** is responsible for the compression.

NOTE   Do not confuse the Linux **gzip** program with the MS Windows WinZip program. They are two different programs that use two different (but comparable) methods of compression. The Linux **gzip** program can handle files that are compressed by WinZip, and the WinZip program knows how to deal with tarballs.

Let's try installing hello, one step at a time:

1. We'll begin by first obtaining a copy of the hello source code.

NOTE   Typically, a single directory is selected in which to build and store tarballs. This allows the system administrator to keep the tarball of each package in a safe place in the event he or she needs to pull something out of it later. It also lets all the administrators know which packages are installed on the system in addition to the base system. A good directory for this is **/usr/local/src**, since software local to a site is generally installed in **/usr/local**.

Pull down a copy of the hello program used in this example from http://www.gnu.org/software/hello or directly from http://ftp.gnu.org/gnu/hello/hello-2.1.1.tar.gz.

The latest version of the program available at the time of this writing was **hello-2.1.1.tar.gz**. Save the file to the **/usr/local/src/** directory.

TIP A quick way to download a file from the Internet (via FTP or HTTP) is using the command-line utility called **wget**. For example, to pull down the hello program while at a shell prompt, you'd simply type:

```
# wget http://ftp.gnu.org/gnu/hello/hello-2.1.1.tar.gz
```

And the file will be automatically saved into your present working directory (PWD).

2. After downloading the file, you will need to unpack (or **untar**) it. When unpacked, a tarball will generally create a new directory for all of its files. The hello tarball (**hello-2.1.1.tar.gz**), for example, creates the subdirectory **hello-2.1.1**. Most packages follow this standard. If you find a package that does not follow it, it is a good idea to create a subdirectory with a reasonable name and place all the unpacked source files there. This allows multiple builds to occur at the same time without the risk of the two builds conflicting. Use the **tar** command to unpack and decompress the hello archive. Type

```
[root@serverA src]# tar -xvzf hello-2.1.1.tar.gz
hello-2.1.1/
hello-2.1.1/intl/
hello-2.1.1/intl/ChangeLog
hello-2.1.1/intl/Makefile.in
hello-2.1.1/intl/locale.alias
hello-2.1.1/intl/ref-add.sin
```

The **z** parameter in this **tar** command invokes **gzip** to decompress the file before the **untar** process occurs. The **v** parameter tells **tar** to show the name of the file it is **untar**ring as it goes through the process. This way you'll know the name of the directory where all the sources are being unpacked.

NOTE You might encounter files that end with the **.tar.bz2** extension. Bzip2 is a compression algorithm that is gaining popularity, and GNU **tar** does support decompressing it on the command line with the **y** or **j** option (instead of the **z** parameter).

3. A new directory called **hello-2.1.1** should have been created for you during the **untar**ring. Change to the new directory and list its contents. Type

```
[root@serverA src]# cd hello-2.1.1 ; ls
```

Looking for Documentation (Getting to Know Each Other—Again)

Okay. You have both now downloaded . . . sorry, found each other. Now is probably a good time to look around and see if either of you come with any special documentation . . . sorry, needs.

A good place to look for documentation for software will be in the root of its directory tree. Once you are inside the directory with all of the source code, begin looking for documentation. *Always read the documentation that comes with the source code!* If there are any special compile directions, notes, or warnings, they will most likely be mentioned here. You will save yourself a great deal of agony by reading the relevant files first.

So then, what are the relevant files? These files typically have names like **README** and **INSTALL**. The developer may also have put any available documentation is a directory aptly named **docs**.

The **README** file generally includes a description of the package, references to additional documentation (including the installation documentation), and references to the author of the package. The **INSTALL** file typically has directions for compiling and installing the package.

These are not, of course, absolutes. Every package has its quirks. The best way to find out is to simply list the directory contents and look for obvious signs of additional documentation. Some packages use different capitalization: **readme**, **README**, **ReadMe**, and so on. (Remember, Linux is case sensitive!) Some introduce variations on a theme, such as **README.1ST** or **README.NOW**, and so on.

While in the **/usr/local/src/hello-2.1.1** directory, use a pager to view the **INSTALL** file that comes with the hello program. Type

```
[root@serverA hello-2.1.1]# less INSTALL
```

Exit the pager by typing **q** when you are done reading the file.

TIP   Another popular pager you can use in place of **less** is called **more!** (Historical note: **more** came way before **less**.)

Configuring the Package

You both want this relationship to work and possibly last longer than the previous ones. So this is a good time to establish the guidelines and expectations.

Most packages ship with an auto-configuration script; it is safe to assume they do unless their documentation says otherwise. These scripts are typically named **configure** (or **config**), and they can accept parameters. There are a handful of stock parameters that are available across all **configure** scripts, but the interesting stuff occurs on a program-by-program basis. Each package will have a handful of features that can be enabled or disabled or that have special values set at compile time, and they must be set up via **configure**.

To see what **configure** options come with a package, simply run

```
[root@serverA hello-2.1.1]# ./configure --help
```

Yes, those are two hyphens (- -) before the word "help."

> **NOTE** One commonly available option is `--prefix`. This option allows you to set the base directory where the package gets installed. By default, most packages use **/usr/local**. Each component in the package will install into the appropriate directory in **/usr/local**.

If you are happy with the default options that the **configure** script offers, type

```
[root@serverA hello-2.1.1]# ./configure
checking for a BSD-compatible install... /usr/bin/install -c
checking whether build environment is sane... yes
checking for gawk... gawk
checking whether make sets ${MAKE}... yes
checking for gcc... gcc
checking for C compiler default output... a.out
...<OUTPUT TRUNCATED>...
config.status: executing default commands
```

With all of the options you want set up, a run of the **configure** script will create a special type of file called a *makefile*. Makefiles are the foundation of the compilation phase. Generally, if **configure** fails, you will not get a makefile. Make sure that the **configure** command did indeed complete without any errors.

Compiling the Package

This stage does not quite fit in anywhere in our dating model. But you might consider it as being similar to that period when you are so blindly in love and everything just flies by and a lot of things are just inexplicable.

All you need to do is run **make**, like so:

```
[root@serverA hello-2.1.1]# make
```

The **make** tool reads all of the makefiles that were created by the **configure** script. These files tell **make** which files to compile and the order in which to compile them—which is crucial, since there could be hundreds of source files.

Depending on the speed of your system, the available memory, and how busy it is doing other things, the compilation process could take a while to complete, so don't be surprised.

As **make** is working, it will display each command it is running and all of the parameters associated with it. This output is usually the invocation of the compiler and all of the parameters passed to the compiler—it's pretty tedious stuff that even the programmers were inclined to automate!

If the compile goes through smoothly, you won't see any error messages. Most compiler error messages are very clear and distinct, so don't worry about possibly missing an error. If you do see an error, don't panic. Most error messages don't reflect a problem with the program itself, but usually with the system in some way or another. Typically, these messages are the result of inappropriate file permissions or files that cannot be found.

In general, slow down and read the error message. Even if the format is a little odd, it may explain what is wrong in plain English, thereby allowing you to quickly fix it. If the error is still confusing, look at the documentation that came with the package to see if there is a mailing list or e-mail address you can contact for help. Most developers are more than happy to provide help, but you need to remember to be nice and to the point. (In other words, don't start an e-mail with a rant about why their software is terrible.)

Installing the Package

You've done almost everything else. You've found your partner, you've studied them, you've even compiled them, now it's time to move them in with you.

Unlike the compile stage, the installation stage typically goes smoothly. In most cases, once the compile completes successfully, all that you need to do is to run

```
[root@serverA hello-2.1.1]# make install
```

This will install the package into the location specified by the default prefix (`--prefix`) argument that was used with the **configure** script earlier.

It will start the installation script (which is usually embedded in the makefile). Because **make** displays each command as it is executing it, you will see a lot of text fly by. Don't worry about it—it's perfectly normal. Unless you see an error message, the package is installed.

If you do see an error message, it is most likely because of permissions problems. Look at the last file it was trying to install before failure, and then go check on all the permissions required to place a file there. You may need to use the **chmod**, **chown**, and **chgrp** commands for this step.

TIP If the software being installed is meant to be used and available system-wide, this is almost always the stage that needs to be performed by the superuser (i.e., root). Accordingly, most install instructions will require you to become root before performing this step. If, on the other hand, a regular user is compiling and installing a software package for his or her own personal use into a directory for which that user has full permissions (e.g., by specifying `--prefix=/home/user_name`), then there is no need to become root to do this.

Testing the Software

A common mistake administrators make is to go through all of the process of configuring and compiling and then, when they install, not to test the software to make sure that it runs as it should. Testing the software also needs be done as a regular user, if the software is to be used by nonroot users. In our example, you run the **hello** command to verify the permissions are correct and users won't have problems running the program. You will quickly change users (using the **su** command) to make sure the software is usable by everyone.

Assuming that you accepted the default installation prefix for the hello program (i.e., the relevant files will be under the **/usr/local** directory), use the full path to the program binary to execute it. Type

```
[root@serverA hello-2.1.1]$ /usr/local/bin/hello
Hello, world!
```

That's it—you're done.

Cleanup

Once the package is installed, you can do some cleanup to get rid of all the temporary files created during the installation. Since you have the original source code tarball, it is okay to simply get rid of the entire directory from which you compiled the source code. In the case of the hello program, you would get rid of **/usr/local/src/hello-2.1.1**.

Begin by going one directory level above the directory you want to remove. In this case, that would be **/usr/local/src**.

```
[root@serverA hello-2.1.1]# cd /usr/local/src
```

Now use the **rm** command to remove the actual directory, like so:

```
[root@serverA hello-2.1.1] rm -rf hello-2.1.1
```

The **rm** command, especially with the **-rf** parameter, is very dangerous. It recursively removes an entire directory without stopping to verify any of the files. It is especially potent when run by the root user—it will shoot first and leave you asking the questions later.

Be very careful and make sure you are erasing what you mean to erase. There is no easy way to undelete a file in Linux when working from the command line.

COMMON PROBLEMS IN BUILDING FROM SOURCE

The GNU hello program might not seem like a very useful tool, and for the most part, we will agree it is not. But one valuable thing it provides is the ability to test the compiler on your system. If you've just finished the task of upgrading your compiler, compiling this simple program will provide a sanity check that indeed the compiler is working.

Here are some other problems (and their solutions) you may run into when building from source.

Problems with Libraries

One problem you might run into is when the program can't find a file of the type "libsomething.so" and terminates for that reason. This file is what is called a *library*. Libraries are synonymous with DLLs in Windows. These libraries are stored in several locations on the Linux system and typically reside in **/usr/lib/** and **/usr/local/lib/**. If you have installed a software package in a different location than **/usr/local**, you will have to configure your system or shell to know where to look for those new libraries.

> **NOTE** Linux libraries can be located anywhere on your file system. You'll appreciate the usefulness of this, when for example you have to use the Network File System (NFS) to share a directory (or in our case, software) among network clients. You'll find that users or clients can easily use the software residing on the network share.

There are two methods for configuring libraries on a Linux system. One is to modify **/etc/ld.conf**, add the path of your new libraries, and use the `ldconfig -m` command to load in the new directories. You can also use the LD_LIBRARY_PATH environment variable to hold a list of library directories to look for library files. Read the man page for **ld.conf** for more information.

When There Is No configure Script

Sometimes you will download a package and instantly `cd` into a directory and run `./configure`. And you will probably be shocked when you see the message "No such file or directory." As stated earlier in the chapter, read the **README** and **INSTALL** files in the distribution. Typically, the authors of the software are courteous enough to provide at least these two files. It is very easy to want to jump right in and begin compiling something without first looking at the docs and then come back hours later to find that a step was missed. The first step you take when installing software is to read the documentation. It will probably point out the fact that you need to run `imake` first, and then `make`. You get the idea: always read the documentation first, and then proceed to compiling the software.

Broken Source Code

No matter what you do, it is possible that the source code that you have is simply broken and the only person that can get it to work or make any sense of it is its original author. A lot of times you may have already spent countless hours trying to get the application to compile and build before coming to this conclusion and throwing in the towel. It is also possible that the author of the program has left valuable/relevant information undocumented.

SUMMARY

You've explored the use of the popular RPM package manager. You used its various options to manipulate RPM packages by querying, installing, and uninstalling a sample package. You also briefly explored the other options to using `rpm` directly from the command line. The options are mostly the various GUI tools available. The GUI tools are very similar to the Windows Add/Remove Programs Control Panel applet. Just point and click. We also briefly touched on a now very popular software management system in Linux called Yum.

Using an available open-source program as an example, we described the steps involved in configuring, compiling, and building software from the raw source code.

As a bonus, you also learned a thing or two about the mechanics of relationships.

PART II

Single-Host Administration

CHAPTER 4

Managing Users

UNIX/Linux was designed from the ground up to be a multiuser operating system. A multiuser operating system will not be much good without users. And this brings us to the topic of managing users in Linux. Associated with each user is the user's baggage. This baggage might include files, processes, resources, and other information. When dealing with a multiuser system, it is necessary for a system administrator to have a good understanding of what constitutes a user (and all that user's baggage), a group, and how they interact together.

User accounts are used on computer systems to determine who has access to what. The ability of a user to access a system is determined by whether or not that user exists and has the proper permissions to use the system.

In this chapter, we will examine the technique of managing users on a single host. We'll begin by exploring the actual database files that contain information about users. From there we'll examine the system tools available to manage the files automatically.

WHAT EXACTLY CONSTITUTES A USER?

Under Linux, every file and program must be owned by a *user*. Each user has a unique identifier called a *user ID (UID)*. Each user must also belong to at least one *group*, a collection of users established by the system administrator. Users may belong to multiple groups. Like users, groups also have unique identifiers, called *group IDs (GIDs)*.

The accessibility of a file or program is based on its UIDs and GIDs. A running program inherits the rights and permissions of the user who invokes it. (SetUID and SetGID, discussed in "Understanding SetUID and SetGID Programs" later in this chapter, create an exception to this rule.) Each user's rights can be defined in one of two ways: as those of a *normal user* or the *root user*. Normal users can access only what they own or have been given permission to run; permission is granted because the user either belongs to the file's group or because the file is accessible to all users. The root user is allowed to access all files and programs in the system, whether or not root owns them. The root user is often called a *superuser*.

If you are accustomed to Windows, you can draw parallels between that system's user management and Linux's user management. Linux UIDs are comparable to Windows SIDs (system IDs), for example. In contrast to Windows NT, you may find the Linux security model maddeningly simplistic: either you're root or you're not. Normal users cannot have root privileges in the same way normal users can be granted administrator access under NT. Although this approach is a little less common, you can also implement finer-grained access control through the use of access control lists (ACLs) in Linux, as you can with Windows. Which system is better? Depends on what you want and whom you ask.

Where User Information Is Kept

If you're already used to Windows 2000 user management, you're familiar with the Active Directory tool that takes care of the nitty-gritty details of the user database. This tool is convenient, but it makes developing your own administrative tools trickier, since the only other way to read or manipulate user information is through a series of LDAP, Kerberos, or programmatic system calls.

In contrast, Linux takes the path of traditional UNIX and keeps all user information in straight text files. This is beneficial for the simple reason that it allows you to make changes to user information without the need of any other tool but a text editor such as **vi**. In many instances, larger sites take advantage of these text files by developing their own user administration tools so that they can not only create new accounts but also automatically make additions to the corporate phone book, Web pages, and so on.

However, users and groups working with UNIX style for the first time may prefer to stick with the basic user management tools that come with the Linux distribution. We'll discuss those tools in "User Management Tools" later in this chapter. For now, let's examine the text files that store user and group information in Linux.

The /etc/passwd file

The **/etc/passwd** file stores the user's login, encrypted password entry, UID, default GID, name (sometimes called GECOS), home directory, and login shell. Each line in the file represents information about a user. The lines are made up of various standard fields, with each field delimited by a colon. A sample entry from a **passwd** file with its various fields is illustrated in Figure 4-1.

The fields of the **/etc/passwd** file are discussed in detail in the sections that follow.

Username Field

This field is also referred to as the login field or the account field. It stores the name of the user on the system. The username must be a unique string and uniquely identifies a user to the system. Different sites use different methods for generating user login names. A very common method is to use the first letter of the user's first name and append that user's last name. This usually works because the chances are relatively slim that one would have users with the same first and last names. There are of course several variations of this method. For example, for a user whose first name is "Ying" and whose last name is "Yang"—a user name of "yyang" can be assigned to that user.

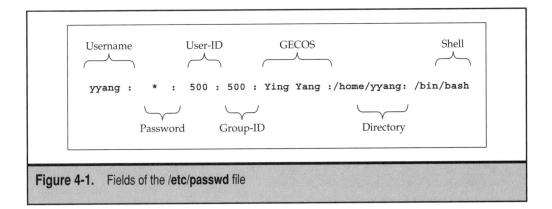

Figure 4-1.   Fields of the **/etc/passwd** file

Password Field

This field contains the encrypted password for the user. On most modern Linux systems this field contains a letter *x* to indicate that shadow passwords are being used on the system (discussed in detail later). Every user account on the system should have a password or at the very least be tagged as impossible to log in. This is crucial to the security of the system—weak passwords make compromising a system just that much simpler.

The original philosophy behind passwords is actually quite interesting, especially since we still rely on a significant part of it today. The idea is simple: instead of relying on protected files to keep passwords a secret, the system would encrypt the password using an AT&T-developed (and National Security Agency–approved) algorithm called Data Encryption Standard (DES) and leave the encrypted value publicly viewable. What originally made this secure was that the encryption algorithm was computationally difficult to break. The best most folks could do was a brute-force dictionary attack, where automated systems would iterate through a large dictionary and rely on the nature of users to pick English words for their passwords. Many people tried to break DES itself, but since it was an open algorithm that anyone could study, it was made much more bulletproof before it was actually deployed.

When users entered their passwords at a login prompt, the password they entered would be encrypted. The encrypted value would then be compared against the user's password entry. If the two encrypted values matched, the user was allowed to enter the system. The actual algorithm for performing the encryption was computationally cheap enough that a single encryption wouldn't take too long. However, the tens of thousands of encryptions that would be needed for a dictionary attack would take prohibitively long.

But then a problem occurred: Moore's Law on processor speed doubling every 18 months held true, and home computers were becoming powerful and fast enough that programs were able to perform a brute-force dictionary attack within days rather than weeks or months. Dictionaries got bigger and the software got smarter. The nature of passwords thus needed to be reevaluated. One solution has been to improve the algorithm used to perform the encryption of passwords. Some distributions of Linux have followed the path of the FreeBSD operating system and used the MD5 scheme. This has increased the complexity involved in cracking passwords, which, when used in conjunction with shadow passwords (discussed later on), works quite well. (Of course, this is assuming you make your users choose good passwords!)

TIP   Choosing good passwords is always a chore. Your users will inevitably ask, "What then, O Almighty System Administrator, makes a good password?" Here's your answer: a non-language word (not English, not Spanish, not German, not a human-language word), preferably with mixed case, numbers, and punctuation—in other words, a string that looks like line noise. Well, this is all nice and wonderful, but if a password is too hard to remember, most people will quickly defeat its purpose by writing it down and keeping it in an easily viewed place. So better make it memorable! A good technique might be to choose a phrase and then pick the first letter of every word in the phrase. Thus, the phrase "coffee is VERY GOOD for you and me" becomes ciVG4yam. The phrase is memorable even if the resulting password isn't.

User-ID Field (UID)

This field stores a unique number that the operating system and other applications use to identify the user and determine access privileges. It is the numerical equivalent of the username field. The UID must be unique for every user, with the exception of the UID 0 (zero). Any user who has a UID of 0 has root (administrative) access and thus has the full run of the system. Usually, the only user who has this specific UID has the login root. It is considered bad practice to allow any other users or usernames to have a UID of 0. This is notably different from the Windows NT and 2000 models, in which any number of users can have administrative privileges.

Different Linux distributions sometimes adopt different UID numbering schemes. For example Fedora and RHEL reserve the UID 99 for the user "nobody," while SuSE Linux uses the UID 65534 for the user "nobody."

Group-ID Field (GID)

The next field in the **/etc/passwd** file is the group-ID entry. It is the numerical equivalent of the primary group that the user belongs to. This field also plays an important role in determining user access privileges. It should be noted that besides a user's primary group, a user can belong to other groups as well (more on this in the section "The /etc/ group File").

GECOS

This field can store various pieces of information for a user. It can act as a placeholder for the user description, full name (first name and last name), telephone number, and so on. This field is optional and as result can be left blank. It is also possible to store multiple entries in this field, by simply separating the different entries with a comma.

NOTE   GECOS is an acronym for General Electric Comprehensive Operating System (now referred to as GCOS) and is a carryover from the early days of computing.

As a historical footnote, GECOS' tie to UNIX stems from the fact that GCOS machines were used for printing at Bell Labs during the creation of UNIX. To accommodate the use of the GCOS-based printing services, the extra field was added to the **/etc/passwd** file.

Directory

This is usually the user's home directory, but it can also be any arbitrary location on the system. Every user who actually logs in to the system needs a place for configuration files that are unique to the user. This place, called a *home directory*, allows each user to work in a customized environment without having to change the environment customized by another user—even if both users are logged in to the system at the same time. In this directory, users are allowed to keep not only their configuration files but their regular work files as well.

Startup Scripts

Startup scripts are not quite a part of the information stored in the users' database in Linux. But they nontheless play a very important role in determining and controlling a user's environment. In particular the startup scripts in Linux are usually stored under the user's home directory . . . and hence the need to mention them while still on the subject of the directory (home directory) field in the **/etc/passwd** file.

Linux/UNIX was built from the get-go as a multiuser environment. Each user is allowed to have his or her own configuration files; thus, the system appears to be customized for each particular user (even if other people are logged in at the same time). The customization of each individual user environment is done through the use of shell scripts, run control files, and the like. These files can contain a series of commands to be executed by the shell that starts when a user logs in. In the case of the BASH shell, for example, one of its startup files is the **.bashrc** file. (Yes, there is a period in front of the filename—filenames preceded by periods, also called dot files, are hidden from normal directory listings.) You can think of shell scripts in the same light as batch files, except shell scripts can be much more capable. The **.bashrc** script in particular is similar in nature to **autoexec.bat** in the Windows world.

Various Linux software packages use application-specific and customizable options in directories or files that begin with a . in each user's home directory. Some examples are **.mozilla** and **.kde**. Here are some common dot (.) files that are present in each user's home directory:

▼ **.bashrc/.profile**   Configuration files for BASH.

■ **.tcshrc/.login**   Configuration files for tcsh.

■ **.xinitrc**   This script overrides the default script that gets called when you log into the X Window System.

▲ **.Xdefaults**   This file contains defaults that you can specify for X Window System applications.

When you create a user's account, a set of default dot files are also created for the user; this is mostly for convenience, to help get the user started. The user creation tools discussed later on help you do this automatically. The default files are stored under the **/etc/skel** directory.

For the sake of consistency, most sites place home directories at **/home** and name each user's directory by that user's login name. Thus, if for example your login name were "yyang," your home directory would be **/home/yyang**. The exception to this is for some special system accounts, such as a root user's account or a system service. The superuser's (root's) home directory in Linux is usually set to be **/root** (but for most variants of UNIX, such as Solaris, the home directory is traditionally /). An example of a special system service that might need a specific working directory might be for a Web server whose Web pages are served from the **/var/www/** directory.

In Linux the decision to place home directories under **/home** is strictly arbitrary, but it does make organizational sense. The system really doesn't care where we place home directories, so long as the location for each user is specified in the password file.

Shell

When users log in to the system, they expect an environment that can help them be productive. This first program that users encounter is called a *shell*. If you're used to the Windows side of the world, you might equate this with command.com, Program Manager, or Windows Explorer (not to be confused with Internet Explorer, which is a Web browser).

Under UNIX/Linux, most shells are text based. A popular default user shell in Linux is the Bourne Again Shell, or BASH for short. Linux comes with several shells from which to choose—you can see most of them listed in the **/etc/shells** file. Deciding which shell is right for you is kind of like choosing a favorite beer—what's right for you isn't right for everyone, but still, everyone tends to get defensive about their choice!

What makes Linux so interesting is that you do not have to stick with the list of shells provided in **/etc/shells**. In the strictest of definitions, the password entry for each user doesn't list what shell to run so much as it lists what program to run first for the user. Of course, most users prefer that the first program run be a shell, such as BASH.

The /etc/shadow File

This is the encrypted password file. It stores the encrypted password information for user accounts. In addition to the encrypted password, the **/etc/shadow** file also stores optional password aging or expiration information. The introduction of the shadow file came about because of the need to separate encrypted passwords from the **/etc/passwd** file. This was necessary because the ease with which the encrypted passwords could be cracked was increasing with the increase in the processing power of commodity computers (home PCs). The idea was to keep the **/etc/passwd** file readable by all users without storing the encrypted passwords in it and then make the **/etc/shadow** file only readable by root or other privileged programs that require access to that information. An example of such a program would be the login program.

One might wonder, "Why not just make the regular **/etc/passwd** file readable by root only or other privileged programs?" Well, it isn't that simple. By having the password file open for so many years, the rest of the system software that grew up around it relied on the fact that the password file was always readable by all users. Changing this would simply cause software to fail.

Just as in the **/etc/passwd** file, each line in the **/etc/shadow** file represents information about a user. The lines are made up of various standard fields, with each field delimited by a colon. The fields are

▼ Login name

■ Encrypted password

■ Days since January 1, 1970, that password was last changed

■ Days before password may be changed

■ Days after which password must be changed

■ Days before password is to expire that user is warned

■ Days after password expires that account is disabled

■ Days since January 1, 1970, that account is disabled

▲ A reserved field

A sample entry from the **/etc/shadow** file is shown here for the user account mmel:

```
mmel:$1$HEWdPIJ.$qX/RbB.TPGcyerAVDlF4g.:12830:0:99999:7:::
```

The /etc/group File

The **/etc/group** file contains a list of groups, with one group per line. Each group entry in the file has four standard fields, with each field colon-delimited, as in the **/etc/passwd** and **/etc/shadow** files. Each user on the system belongs to at least one group, that being the user's default group. Users may then be assigned to additional groups if needed. You will recall that the **/etc/passwd** file contains each user's default group ID (GID). This GID is mapped to the group's name and other members of the group in the **/etc/group** file. The GID should be unique for each group.

Also like the **/etc/passwd** file, the group file must be world-readable so that applications can test for associations between users and groups. The fields of each line in the **/etc/group** file are

▼ **Group name**   The name of the group

■ **Group password**   This is optional, but if set it allows users who are not part of the group to join the group

■ **Group ID (GID)**   The numerical equivalent of the group name

▲ **Group members**   A comma-separated list

A sample group entry in the **/etc/group** file is shown here:

```
bin:x:1:root,bin,daemon
```

This entry is for the "bin" group. The GID for the group is 1, and its members are root, bin, and daemon.

USER MANAGEMENT TOOLS

The wonderful part about having password database files that have a well-defined format in straight text is that it is easy for anyone to be able to write their own management tools. Indeed, many site administrators have already done this in order to integrate their tools along with the rest of their organization's infrastructure. They can start a new user from the same form that lets them update the corporate phone and e-mail directory, LDAP servers, Web pages, and so on. Of course, not everyone wants to write their own tools, which is why Linux comes with several prewritten tools that do the job for you.

In this section, we discuss user management tools that can be used from the command-line interface, as well as graphical user interface (GUI) tools. Of course, learning how to use both is the preferred route, since they both have their advantages and place.

Command-Line User Management

You can choose from among six command-line tools to perform the same actions performed by the GUI tool: **useradd**, **userdel**, **usermod**, **groupadd**, **groupdel**, and **groupmod**. The compelling advantage of using command-line tools for user management besides speed is the fact that the tools can usually be incorporated into other automated functions (such as scripts).

NOTE Linux distributions other than Fedora and RHEL may have slightly different parameters than the tools used here. To see how your particular installation is different, read the man page for the particular program in question.

useradd

As the name implies, **useradd** allows you to add a single user to the system. Unlike the GUI tools, this tool has no interactive prompts. Instead, all parameters must be specified on the command line.

Here's how you use this tool:

```
usage: useradd  [-u uid [-o]] [-g group] [-G group,...]
                [-d home] [-s shell] [-c comment] [-m [-k template]]
                [-f inactive] [-e expire ] [-p passwd] [-M] [-n] [-r] name
        useradd  -D [-g group] [-b base] [-s shell]
                [-f inactive] [-e expire ]
```

Take note that anything in the square brackets in this usage summary is optional. Also, don't be intimidated by this long list of options! They are all quite easy to use and are described in Table 4-1.

Option	Description
-c *comment*	Allows you to set the user's name in the GECOS field. As with any command-line parameter, if the value includes a space, you will need to put quotes around the text. For example, to set the user's name to Ying Yang, you would have to specify -c "Ying Yang".
-d *homedir*	By default, the user's home directory is **/home/user_name**. When creating a new user, the user's home directory gets created along with the user account. So if you want to change the default to another place, you can specify the new location with this parameter.
-e *expire-date*	It is possible for an account to expire after a certain date. By default, accounts never expire. To specify a date, be sure to place it in *YYYY MM DD* format. For example, use -e 2009 10 28 for the account to expire on October 28, 2009.
-f *inactive-time*	This option specifies the number of days after a password expires that the account is still usable. A value of **0** (zero) indicates that the account is disabled immediately. A value of -1 will never allow the account to be disabled, even if the password has expired (for example, -f 3 will allow an account to exist for three days after a password has expired). The default value is -1.
-g *initial-group*	Using this option, you can specify the default group the user has in the password file. You can use a number or name of the group; however, if you use a name of a group, the group must exist in the **/etc/ group** file.
-G *group*[,...]	This option allows you to specify additional groups to which the new user will belong. If you use the -G option, you must specify at least one additional group. You can, however, specify additional groups by separating the elements of the list with commas. For example, to add a user to the project and admin groups, you should specify -G project,admin.

Table 4-1. Options for the useradd Command

Option	Description
-m [-k *skel-dir*]	By default, the system automatically creates the user's home directory. This option is the explicit command to create the user's home directory. Part of creating the directory is copying default configuration files into it. These files come from the **/etc/skel** directory by default. You can change this by using the secondary option **-k *skel-dir***. (You must specify **-m** in order to use **-k**.) For example, to specify the **/etc/adminskel** directory, you would use **-m -k /etc/adminskel**.
-M	If you used the **-m** option, you cannot use **-M**, and vice versa. This option tells the command *not* to create the user's home directory.
-n	Red Hat Linux creates a new group with the same name as the new user's login as part of the process of adding a user. You can disable this behavior by using this option.
-s *shell*	A user's login shell is the first program that runs when a user logs in to a system. This is usually a command-line environment, unless you are logging in from the X Window System login screen. By default, this is the Bourne Again Shell (**/bin/bash**), though some folks like other shells such as the Turbo C Shell (**/bin/tcsh**).
-u *uid*	By default, the program will automatically find the next available UID and use it. If for some reason you need to force a new user's UID to be a particular value, you can use this option. Remember that UIDs must be unique for all users.
name	Finally, the only parameter that *isn't* optional! You must specify the new user's login name.

Table 4-1.   Options for the useradd Command (*cont.*)

usermod

The **usermod** command allows you to modify an existing user in the system. It works in much the same way as **useradd**. Its usage is summarized here:

```
usage: usermod  [-u uid [-o]] [-g group] [-G group,...]
                [-d home [-m]] [-s shell] [-c comment] [-l new_name]
                [-f inactive] [-e expire ] [-p passwd] [-L|-U] name
```

Every option you specify when using this command results in that particular parameter being modified for the user. All but one of the parameters listed here are identical to the parameters documented for the **useradd** command. The one exception is **-l**.

The **-l** option allows you to change the user's login name. This and the **-u** option are the only options that require special care. Before changing the user's login or UID, you must make sure the user is not logged in to the system or running any processes. Changing this information if the user is logged in or running processes will cause unpredictable results.

userdel

The **userdel** command does the exact opposite of **useradd**—it removes existing users. This straightforward command has only one optional parameter and one required parameter:

```
usage: userdel [-r] username
```

groupadd

The group commands are similar to the user commands; however, instead of working on individual users, they work on groups listed in the **/etc/group** file. Note that changing group information does not cause user information to be automatically changed. For example, if you remove a group whose GID is 100 and a user's default group is specified as 100, the user's default group would not be updated to reflect the fact that the group no longer exists.

The **groupadd** command adds groups to the **/etc/group** file. The command-line options for this program are as follows:

```
usage: groupadd [-g gid [-o]] [-r] [-f] group
```

Table 4-2 describes command options.

groupdel

Even more straightforward than **userdel**, the **groupdel** command removes existing groups specified in the **/etc/group** file. The only usage information needed for this command is

```
usage: groupdel group
```

where **group** is the name of the group to remove.

Option	Description
-g *gid*	Specifies the GID for the new group as *gid*. This value must be unique, unless the **-o** option is used. By default, this value is automatically chosen by finding the first available value greater than or equal to 500.
-r	By default, Fedora and RHEL search for the first GID that is higher than 499. The **-r** options tell **groupadd** that the group being added is a system group and should have the first available GID under 499.
-f	This is the force flag. This will cause **groupadd** to exit without an error when the group about to be added already exists on the system. If that is the case, the group won't be altered (or added again). It is a Fedora- and RHEL-specific option.
group	This option is required. It specifies the name of the group you want to add to be *group*.

Table 4-2.   Options for the groupadd Command

groupmod

The **groupmod** command allows you to modify the parameters of an existing group. The options for this command are

```
usage: groupmod [-g gid [-o]] [-n name] group
```

where the **-g** option allows you to change the GID of the group, and the **-n** option allows you to specify a new name of a group. Additionally, of course, you need to specify the name of the existing group as the last parameter.

GUI User Managers

The obvious advantage to using the GUI tool is ease of use. It is usually just a point-and-click affair. Many of the Linux distributions come with their own GUI user managers. Fedora Core comes with a utility called **system-config-users**, RHEL comes with a utility called **redhat-config-users**, and SuSE Linux has a YaST module that can be invoked with **yast2 users**. All these tools allow you to add/edit and maintain the users on your system. These GUI interfaces work just fine—but you should be prepared to have to manually change user settings in case you don't have access to the pretty GUI front-ends. Most of these interfaces can be found in the System Settings menu within the GNOME or KDE desktop environment. They can also be launched directly from the command line. To launch Fedora's GUI user manager, you'd type

```
[root@serverA ~]# system-config-users
```

A window similar to the one in Figure 4-2 will appear.

In SuSE, to launch the user management YaST module, you'd type

```
serverA:~ # yast2 users
```

A window similar to the one in Figure 4-3 will appear.

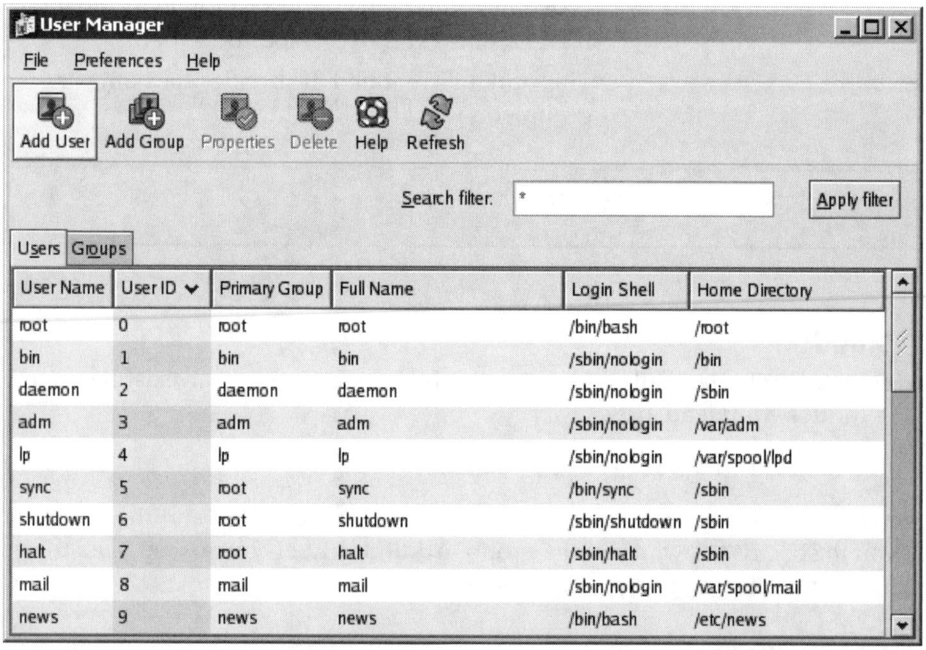

Figure 4-2. Fedora Core GUI user manager tool

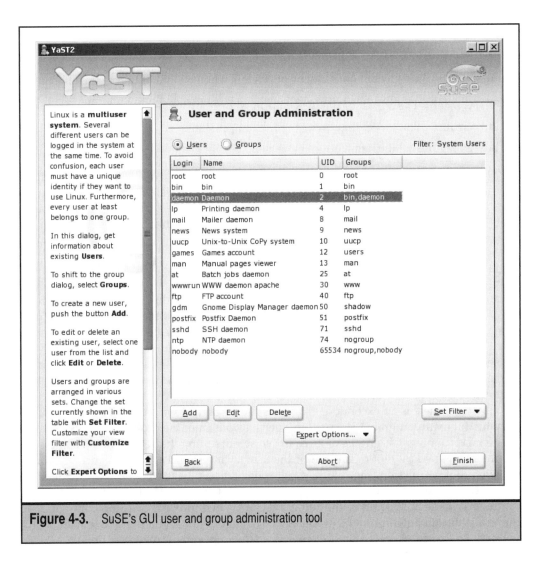

Figure 4-3.   SuSE's GUI user and group administration tool

USERS AND ACCESS PERMISSIONS

Linux determines whether or not a user or group has access to files, programs, or other resources on a system by checking the overall effective permissions on the resource. The traditional permissions model in Linux is very simple—it is based on four access types or rules. The possible access types are

▼   **(r)**   Read permission

■   **(w)**   Write permission

- ■ **(x)** Execute permission
- ▲ **(-)** No permission or no access

In addition, these permissions can be applied to three classes of users. The classes are

- ▼ **Owner** The owner of the file or application
- ■ **Group** The group that owns the file or application
- ▲ **Everyone** All users

The elements of this model can be combined in various ways to permit or deny a user (or group) access to any resource on the system. There is, however, a need for an additional type of permission-granting mechanism in Linux. This need arises because every application in Linux must run in the context of a user. This is explained in the next section, on SetUID and SetGID programs.

Understanding SetUID and SetGID Programs

Normally, when a program is run by a user, it inherits all of the rights (or lack thereof) that the user has. If the user can't read the **/var/log/messages** file, neither can the program. Note that this permission can be different than the permissions of the user who owns the program file (usually called *the binary*). For example, the **ls** program (which is used to generate directory listings) is owned by the root user. Its permissions are set so that all users of the system can run the program. Thus, if the user yyang runs **ls**, that instance of **ls** is bound by the permissions granted to the user yyang, not root.

However, there is an exception. Programs can be tagged with what's called a *SetUID bit*, which allows a program to be run with permissions from the program's owner, not the user who is running it. Using **ls** as an example again, setting the SetUID bit on it and having the file owned by root means that if the user yyang runs **ls**, that instance of **ls** will run with root permissions, not with yyang's permissions. The *SetGID bit* works the same way, except instead of applying the file's owner, it is applied to the file's group setting.

To enable the SetUID bit or the SetGID bit, you need to use the **chmod** command. To make a program SetUID, prefix whatever permission value you are about to assign it with a 4. To make a program SetGID, prefix whatever permission you are about to assign it with a 2. For example, to make **/bin/ls** a SetUID program (which is a bad idea, by the way), you would use this command:

```
[root@serverA /root]# chmod  4755  /bin/ls
```

PLUGGABLE AUTHENTICATION MODULES (PAM)

Pluggable Authentication Modules (PAM) allows the use of a centralized authentication mechanism on Linux/UNIX systems. Besides providing a common authentication scheme on a system, the use of PAM allows for a lot of flexibility and control over authentication for application developers as well as for system administrators.

Traditionally, programs that grant users access to system resources performed the user authentication through some built-in mechanism. While this worked great for a very long time, the approach was not very scalable and more sophisticated methods were required. This led to a number of very ugly hacks to abstract the authentication mechanism. Taking a cue from Solaris, Linux folks created their own implementation of Pluggable Authentication Modules (PAM).

The idea behind PAM is that instead of applications reading the password file, they would simply ask PAM to perform the authentication. PAM could then use whatever authentication mechanism the system administrator wanted. For many sites, the mechanism of choice is still a simple password file. And why not? It does what we want. Most users understand the need for it, and it's a well-tested method to get the job done.

In this section, we discuss the use of PAM under the Fedora Core version of Linux. It should be noted that while the placement of files may not be exactly the same in other distributions, the underlying configuration files and concepts still apply.

How PAM Works

PAM is to other programs as a DLL is to a Windows application—it is just a library. When programs need to perform authentication on someone, they call a function that exists in the PAM library. It provides a library of functions that an application may use to request that a user be authenticated.

When invoked, PAM checks the configuration file for that application. If there isn't a configuration file, it uses a default configuration file. This configuration file tells the library what types of checks need to be done in order to authenticate the user. Based on this, the appropriate module is called on (Fedora and RHEL folks can see these modules in the **/lib/security** directory).

This module can check any number of things. It can simply check the **/etc/passwd** file or the **/etc/shadow** file, or it can perform a more complex check like calling on an LDAP server.

NOTE The PAM Web site (http://www.kernel.org/pub/linux/libs/pam/) offers a complete list of available modules.

Once the module has made the determination, an "authenticated/not authenticated" message is passed back to the calling application.

If this feels like a lot of steps for what should be a simple check, you're almost correct. While it feels like a lot of steps, each module here is very small and does its work very quickly. From a user's point of view, there should be no noticeable performance difference between an application that uses PAM and one that does not. From a system administrator's and developer's point of view, the flexibility this scheme offers is incredible and a very welcome addition.

PAM's Files and Their Locations

On a Fedora-type system, PAM puts her configuration files in certain places. These file locations and their definitions are listed in Table 4-3.

File Location	Definition
/lib/security	Dynamically loaded authentication modules called by the actual PAM library.
/etc/security	Configuration files for the modules located in **/lib/security**.
/etc/pam.d	Configuration files for each application that uses PAM. If an application that uses PAM does not have a specific configuration file, the default is automatically used.

Table 4-3. Important PAM Directories

Looking at the list of file locations in Table 4-3, one has to ask why PAM needs so many different configuration files. "One configuration file per application? That seems crazy!" Well, maybe not. The reason PAM allows this is that not all applications are created equal. For instance, a POP mail server that uses the Qpopper mail server may want to allow all of a site's users to fetch mail, but the login program may want to allow only certain users to be able to log into the console. To accommodate this, PAM needs a configuration file for POP mail that is different from the configuration for the login program.

Configuring PAM

The configuration files that we will be discussing here are the ones located in the **/etc/pam.d** directory. If you want to change the configuration files that apply to specific modules in the **/etc/security** directory, you should consult the documentation that came with the module. (Remember, PAM is just a framework. Specific modules can be written by anyone.)

The nature of a PAM configuration file is very interesting because of its "stackable" nature. That is, every line of a configuration file is evaluated during the authentication process (with the exceptions shown next). Each line specifies a module that performs some authentication task and returns either a success or failure flag. A summary of the results is returned to the application program calling PAM.

NOTE By "failure," we do not mean the program did not work. Rather, we mean that when some process was done to verify whether a user could do something, the return value was "NO." PAM uses the terms "success" and "failure" to represent this information that is passed back to the calling application.

Each file consists of lines in the following format:

```
module_type    control_flag    module_path    arguments
```

where *module_type* represents one of four types of modules: **auth**, **account**, **session**, or **password**. Comments must begin with the hash (#) character. Table 4-4 lists these module types and their functions.

The *control_flag* allows us to specify how we want to deal with the success or failure of a particular authentication module. The control flags are described in Table 4-5.

The *module_path* specifies the actual directory path of the module that performs the authentication task. The modules are usually stored under the **/lib/security** directory. For a full list of modules, visit PAM's Web site (http://www.kernel.org/pub/linux/libs/pam).

The final entry in a PAM configuration line is *arguments*. These are the parameters passed to the authentication module. Although the parameters are specific to each module, there are some generic options that can be applied to all modules. These arguments are described in Table 4-6.

Module Type	Function
auth	Instructs the application program to prompt the user for a password and then grants both user and group privileges.
account	Performs no authentication but determines access from other factors such as time of day or location of the user. For example, the root login can be given only console access this way.
session	Specifies what, if any, actions need to be performed before or after a user is logged in (e.g., logging the connection).
password	Specifies the module that allows users to change their password (if appropriate).

Table 4-4.   PAM Module Types

Control Flag	Description
required	If this flag is specified, the module *must* succeed in authenticating the individual. If it fails, the returned summary value must be failure.
requisite	This flag is similar to **required**; however, if **requisite** fails authentication, modules listed after it in the configuration file are not called, and a failure is immediately returned to the application. This allows us to require certain conditions to hold true before even accepting a login attempt (e.g., the user is on the local area network and cannot come from over the Internet).
sufficient	If a **sufficient** module returns a success and there are no more **required** or **sufficient** control flags in the configuration file, PAM returns a success to the calling application.
optional	This flag allows PAM to continue checking other modules even if this one has failed. You will want to use this when the user is allowed to log in even if a particular module has failed.

Table 4-5.   PAM Control Flags

An Example PAM Configuration File

Let's examine a sample PAM configuration file, **/etc/pam.d/login**:

```
#%PAM-1.0
auth       required     pam_securetty.so
auth       required     pam_stack.so service=system-auth
auth       required     pam_nologin.so
account    required     pam_stack.so service=system-auth
password   required     pam_stack.so service=system-auth
# pam_selinux.so close should be the first session rule
session    required     pam_selinux.so close
session    required     pam_stack.so service=system-auth
session    optional     pam_console.so
# pam_selinux.so open should be the last session rule
session    required     pam_selinux.so multiple open
```

Argument	Description
Debug	Sends debugging information to the system logs.
no_warn	Does not give warning messages to the calling application.
use_first_pass	Does not prompt the user for a password a second time. Instead, the password that was entered in the preceding **auth** module should be reused for the user authentication. (This option is for the **auth** and **password** modules only.)
try_first_pass	This option is similar to **use_first_pass**, where the user is not prompted for a password the second time. However, if the existing password causes the module to return a failure, the user is then prompted for a password again.
use_mapped_pass	This argument instructs the module to take the clear text authentication token entered by a previous module and use it to generate an encryption/decryption key with which to safely store or retrieve the authentication token required for this module.
Expose_account	This argument allows a module to be less discrete about account information—as deemed fit by the system administrator.

Table 4-6.   PAM Configuration Arguments

We can see that the first line begins with a hash symbol and is therefore a comment. Thus we can ignore it. Let's go on to line 2:

```
auth        required     pam_securetty.so
```

Since the **module_type** is **auth**, PAM will want a password. The **control_flag** is set to **required**, so this module must return a success or the login will fail. The module itself, **pam_securetty.so**, verifies that logins on the root account can happen only on the terminals mentioned in the **/etc/securetty** file. There are no arguments on this line.

```
auth        required     pam_stack.so service=system-auth
```

Similar to the first **auth** line, line 3 wants a password for authentication, and if the password fails, the authentication process will return a failure flag to the calling application. The **pam_stack.so** module lets you call from inside the stack for a particular service or the stack defined for another service. The **service=system-auth** argument in this case tells **pam_stack.so** to execute the stack defined for the service system-auth (system-auth is also another PAM configuration under the **/etc/pam.d** directory.

```
auth          required     pam_nologin.so
```

In line 4, the **pam_nologin.so** module checks for the **/etc/nologin** file. If it is present, only root is allowed to log in; others are turned away with an error message. If the file does not exist, it always returns a success.

```
account       required     pam_stack.so service=system-auth
```

In line 5, since the **module_type** is **account**, the **pam_stack.so** module acts differently. It silently checks that the user is even allowed to log in (e.g., "has their password expired?"). If all the parameters check out okay, it will return a success.

The same concepts apply to the rest of the lines in the **/etc/pam.d/login** file (as well as other configuration files under the **/etc/pam.d** directory).

If you need more information about what a particular PAM module does or about the arguments it accepts, you may consult the man page for the module. For example, to find out more about the **pam_selinux.so** module, you would issue the command

```
[root@serverA ~]# man pam_selinux
```

The "Other" File

As we mentioned earlier, if PAM cannot find a configuration file that is specific to an application, it will use a generic configuration file instead. This generic configuration file is called **/etc/pam.d/other**. By default, the "other" configuration file is set to a paranoid setting so that all authentication attempts are logged and then promptly denied. It is recommended you keep it that way.

"DOH! I Can't Log In!"

Don't worry—screwing up a setting in a PAM configuration file happens to everyone. Consider it part of learning the ropes. First thing to do: Don't panic. Like most configuration errors under Linux, you can fix things by booting into single-user mode (see Chapter 7) and fixing the errant file.

If you've screwed up your login configuration file and need to bring it back to a sane state, here is a safe setting you can put in:

```
auth          required     pam_unix.so
account       required     pam_unix.so
password      required     pam_unix.so
session       required     pam_unix.so
```

This setting will give Linux the default behavior of simply looking into the **/etc/passwd** or **/etc/shadow** file for a password. This should be good enough to get you back in, where you can make the changes you meant to make!

NOTE The **pam_unix.so** module is what facilitates this behavior. It is the standard UNIX authentication module. According to the module's man page, it uses standard calls from the system's libraries to retrieve and set account information as well as authentication. Usually, this is obtained from the **/etc/passwd** file, and from the **/etc/shadow** file as well if shadow is enabled.

Debugging PAM

Like many other Linux services, PAM makes excellent use of the system log files (you can read more about them in Chapter 8). If things are not working the way you want them to work, begin by looking at the tail end of the log files and see if PAM is spelling out what happened. More than likely, it is. You should then be able to use this information to change your settings and fix your problem. The main system log file to monitor is the **/var/log/messages** file.

A GRAND TOUR

The best way to see many of the utilities discussed in this chapter interact with one another is to show them at work. In this section, we take a step-by-step approach to creating, modifying, and removing users and groups. Some new commands that were not mentioned but that are also useful and relevant in managing users on a system are also introduced and used.

Creating Users with useradd

Add new user accounts and assign passwords with the **useradd** and **passwd** commands.

1. Create a new user whose full name is "Ying Yang," with the login name (account name) of **yyang**. Type

   ```
   [root@serverA ~]# useradd -c  "Ying Yang"  yyang
   ```

   This command will create a new user account called yyang. The user will be created with the usual Fedora Core default attributes. The entry in the **/etc/passwd** file will be

   ```
   yyang:x:500:500:Ying Yang:/home/yyang:/bin/bash
   ```

From this entry, you can tell these things about the Fedora Core (and RHEL) default new user values:

▼ The UID number is the same as the GID number.

■ The default shell for new users is the bash shell (/bin/bash).

▲ A home directory is automatically created for all new users (e.g., **/home/ yyang**).

2. Use the **passwd** command to create a new password for the username yyang. Set the password to be **19ang19** and repeat the same password when prompted. Type

```
[root@serverA ~]# passwd  yyang
Changing password for user yyang.
New UNIX password:
Retype new UNIX password:
passwd: all authentication tokens updated successfully.
```

3. Create another user account called **mmellow** for the user with a full name of "Mel Mellow," but this time change the default Fedora behavior of creating a group having the same name as the username (i.e., this user will instead belong to the general **users** group). Type

```
[root@serverA ~]# useradd -c "Mel Mellow" -n  mmellow
```

4. Use the **id** command to examine the properties of the user mmellow. Type

```
[root@serverA ~]# id mmellow
uid=501(mmellow) gid=100(users) groups=100(users)
```

5. Again, use the **passwd** command to create a new password for the account mmellow. Set the password to be **2owl78** and repeat the same password when prompted. Type

```
[root@serverA ~]# passwd  mmellow
```

6. Create the final user account, called **bogususer**. But this time specify the user's shell to be the tcsh shell and let the user's default primary group be the system "games" group. Type

```
[root@serverA ~]# useradd -s /bin/tcsh   -g games bogususer
```

7. Examine the **/etc/passwd** file for the entry for the bogususer user. Type

```
[root@serverA ~]# grep bogususer /etc/passwd
bogususer:x:502:20::/home/bogususer:/bin/tcsh
```

From this entry, you can tell that

▼ The UID is 502.

■ The GID is 20.

■ A home directory is also created for the user under the **/home** directory.

▲ The user's shell is /bin/tcsh.

Creating Groups with groupadd

Next, create a couple of groups, nonsystem and system.

1. Create a new group called **research**. Type

   ```
   [root@serverA ~]# groupadd research
   ```

2. Examine the entry for the research group in the **/etc/group** file. Type

   ```
   [root@serverA ~]# grep research  /etc/group
   research:x:501:
   ```

   This output shows that the group ID for the research group is 501.

3. Create another group called **sales**. Type

   ```
   [root@serverA ~]# groupadd sales
   ```

4. Create the final group called **bogus** and in addition force this group to be a system group (i.e., the GID will be lower than 499). Type

   ```
   [root@serverA ~]# groupadd -r bogus
   ```

5. Examine the entry for the bogus group in the **/etc/group** file. Type

   ```
   [root@serverA ~]# grep bogus  /etc/group
   bogus:x:101:
   ```

   The output shows that the group ID for the bogus group is 101.

Modifying User Attributes with usermod

Now try using **usermod** to change user and group IDs of a couple of accounts.

1. Use the **usermod** command to change the user ID (UID) of the bogususer to 600. Type

   ```
   [root@serverA ~]# usermod -u 600  bogususer
   ```

2. Use the **id** command to view your changes. Type

   ```
   [root@serverA ~]# id bogususer
   uid=600(bogususer) gid=20(games) groups=20(games)
   ```

   The output shows the new UID (600) for the user.

3. Use the **usermod** command to change the primary group ID (GID) of the bogus-user account to that of the bogus group (GID = 101) and to also set an expiry date of 12-12-2009 for the account. Type

   ```
   [root@serverA ~]# usermod -g 101 -e 2009-12-12  bogususer
   ```

4. View your changes with the **id** command. Type

   ```
   [root@serverA ~]# id bogususer
   uid=600(bogususer) gid=101(bogus) groups=101(bogus)
   ```

5. Use the **chage** command to view the new account expiration information for the user. Type

```
[root@serverA ~]# chage  -l  bogususer
Minimum:         0
Maximum:         99999
Warning:         7
Inactive:        -1
Last Change:              Feb 18, 2007
Password Expires:         Never
Password Inactive:        Never
Account Expires:          Dec 12, 2009
```

Modifying Group Attributes with groupmod

Now try using the **groupmod** command.

1. Use the **groupmod** command to rename the bogus group to **bogusgroup**. Type

```
[root@serverA ~]# groupmod -n  bogusgroup bogus
```

2. Again use the **groupmod** command to change the group ID (GID) of the bogus-group to 600. Type

```
[root@serverA ~]# groupmod -g 600 bogusgroup
```

3. View your changes to the bogusgroup in the **/etc/group** file. Type

```
[root@serverA ~]# grep bogusgroup  /etc/group
```

Deleting Groups and Users with groupdel and userdel

Try using the **groupdel** and **userdel** commands to delete groups and users, respectively.

1. Use the **groupdel** command to delete the bogusgroup group. Type

```
[root@serverA ~]# groupdel  bogusgroup
```

You will notice that the bogusgroup entry in the **/etc/group** file will be removed accordingly.

2. Use the **userdel** command to delete the user bogususer that you created previously. At the shell prompt type

```
[root@serverA ~]# userdel  -r  bogususer
```

NOTE When you run the **userdel** command with only the user's login specified on the command line (for example, **userdel bogususer**), all of the entries in the /etc/passwd and /etc/shadow files, as well as references in the /etc/group file, are automatically removed. But if you use the optional **-r** parameter (for example, **userdel -r bogususer**), all of the files owned by the user in that user's home directory are removed as well.

SUMMARY

This chapter documents the nature of users under Linux. Much of what you read here also applies to other variants of UNIX, which makes administering users in heterogeneous environments much easier with the different *NIXs.

These are the most significant issues covered in this chapter:

▼ Each user gets a unique UID.

■ Each group gets a unique GID.

■ The **/etc/passwd** file maps UIDs to usernames.

■ Linux handles encrypted passwords in multiple ways.

■ Linux includes tools that help you administer users.

■ Should you decide to write your own tools to manage the user databases, you'll now understand the format for doing so.

▲ PAM, the Pluggable Authentication Modules, is Linux's generic way of handling multiple authentication mechanisms.

These changes are pretty significant for an administrator coming from the Windows XP/NT/200x environment and can be a little tricky at first. Not to worry, though—the Linux/UNIX security model is quite straightforward, so you should quickly get comfortable with how it all works.

If the idea of getting to build your own tools to administer users appeals to you, definitely look into books on the Perl scripting language. It is remarkably well suited for manipulating tabular data (such as the **/etc/passwd** file). With Perl's networking facilities and MS Windows support, Linux even lets you build a cross-platform **adduser** tool that can create and set up both Linux and MS Windows accounts. With so many books on Perl out there, each with a slightly different angle and assuming a slightly different level of programming background, it's tough to make a single book recommendation. Take some time and page through a few books at your local bookstore.

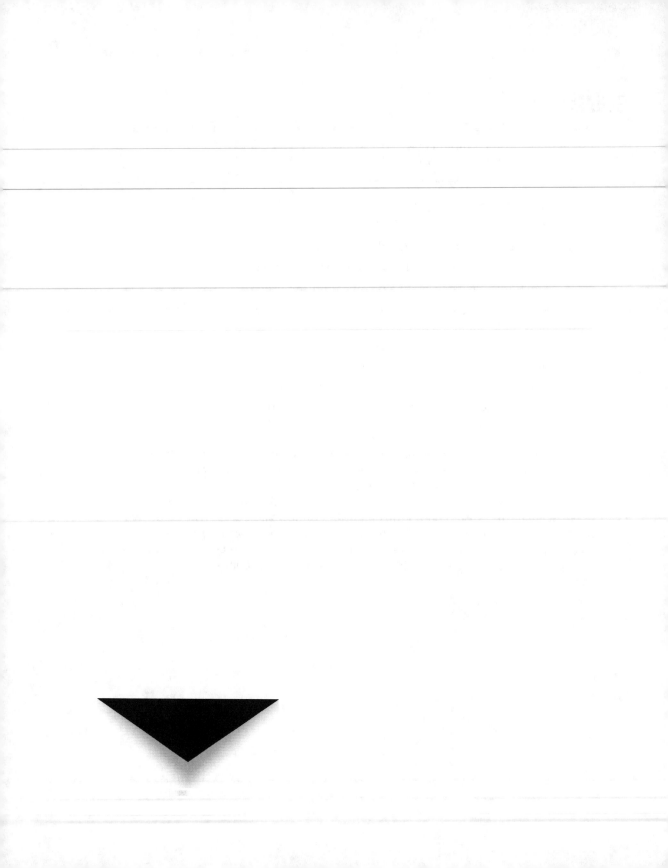

CHAPTER 5

The Command Line

The level of power, control, and flexibility that the command line offers UNIX/Linux users has been one of its most endearing and enduring qualities. There is also a flip side to this, though—for the uninitiated the command line can also produce extremes of emotions, including awe, frustration, and annoyance. Casual observers of UNIX gurus are often astounded at the results of a few carefully entered commands. Unfortunately, this power makes UNIX less intuitive to the average user. For this reason, graphical user interface (GUI) front ends for various UNIX/Linux tools, functions, and utilities have been written.

More experienced users, however, find that it is difficult for a GUI to present all of the available options. Typically, doing so would make the interface just as complicated as the command-line equivalent. The GUI design is often oversimplified, and experienced users ultimately return to the comprehensive capabilities of the command line. After all has been said and done, the fact remains that it just looks plain *cool* to do things at the command line.

Before we begin our study of the command-line interface under Linux, understand that this chapter is far from an exhaustive resource. Rather than trying to cover all the tools without any depth, we have chosen to describe thoroughly a handful of tools we believe to be most critical for day-to-day work.

NOTE For this chapter, we assume that you are logged in to the system as a regular user and that the X Window System is up and running on the system. If you are using the GNOME desktop environment, for example, you can start a virtual terminal in which to issue commands. Right-clicking on the desktop should present you with a menu that will allow you to launch a virtual terminal. The context-sensitive menu may have a menu option that reads something like "Open Terminal" or "Launch Terminal." If you don't have that particular option, look for an option in the menu that says Run Command. After the Run dialog box appears, you can then type the name of a terminal emulator (for example, xterm, gnome-terminal, or konsole) into the Run text box. All of the commands you enter in this chapter should be typed into the virtual terminal window.

AN INTRODUCTION TO BASH

In Chapter 4, you learned that one of the parameters for a user's password entry is that user's login shell, which is the first program that runs when a user logs in to a workstation. The shell is comparable to the Windows Program Manager, except that the shell program used, of course, is arbitrary.

The formal definition of a shell is: a command language interpreter that executes commands. A less formal definition might be: simply a program that provides an interface to the system. The Bourne Again Shell (BASH) in particular is a command line–only interface containing a handful of built-in commands, the ability to launch other programs, and the ability to control programs that have been launched from it (job control). It might seem simple at first, but you will begin to realize that the shell is a very powerful tool.

A variety of shells exist, most with similar features but different means of implementing them. Again for the purpose of comparison, you can think of the various shells as being like Web browsers; among several different browsers, the basic functionality is the same—displaying content from the Web. In any situation like this, everyone proclaims that their shell is better than the others, but it all really comes down to personal preference.

In this section, we'll examine some of BASH's built-in commands. A complete reference on BASH could easily be a book in itself, so we'll stick with the commands that most affect the daily operations of a system administrator. However, it is highly recommended that you eventually study BASH's other functions and operations. There's no shortage of excellent books on the topic. As you get accustomed to BASH, you can easily pick up other shells. If you are managing a large site with lots of users, it will be advantageous for you to be familiar with as many shells as possible. It is actually fairly easy to pick up another shell, as the differences between them are subtle.

Job Control

When working in the BASH environment, you can start multiple programs from the same prompt. Each program is a job. Whenever a job is started, it takes over the terminal. (This is a throwback to the days when actual dumb terminals such as VT100s and Wyse 50s were used to interface with the machine.) On today's machines, the terminal is either the straight-text interface you see when you boot the machine or the window created by the X Window System on which BASH runs. (The terminal interfaces in X Window System are called a pseudo-tty, or pty for short.) If a job has control of the terminal, it can issue control codes so that text-only interfaces (the Pine mail reader, for instance) can be made more attractive. Once the program is done, it gives full control back to BASH, and a prompt is redisplayed for the user.

Not all programs require this kind of terminal control, however. Some, including programs that interface with the user through the X Window System, can be instructed to give up terminal control and allow BASH to present a user prompt, even though the invoked program is still running.

In the following example, with the user yyang logged in to the system, the user launches the Firefox Web browser with the additional condition that the program (Firefox) give up control of the terminal (this condition is represented by the ampersand suffix):

```
[yyang@serverA ~]$ firefox &
```

Immediately after you press ENTER, BASH will present its prompt again. This is called backgrounding the task. Folks who remember Windows NT prior to version 4 will remember having to do something similar with the Start command.

If a program is already running and has control of the terminal, you can make the program give up control by pressing CTRL-Z in the terminal window. This will stop the running job (or program) and return control to BASH so that you can enter new commands.

At any given time, you can find out how many jobs BASH is tracking by typing this command:

```
[yyang@serverA ~]$ jobs
[1]+  Running                 firefox &
```

The running programs that are listed will be in one of two states: running or stopped. The preceding sample output shows that the program Firefox is in a running state. The output also shows the job number in the first column—[1].

To bring a job back to the foreground, i.e., to give it back control of the terminal, you would use the **fg** (foreground) command, like this:

```
[yyang@serverA ~]$ fg number
```

where **number** is the job number you want in the foreground. For example, to place the Firefox program (with job number 1) launched earlier in the foreground, type

```
[yyang@serverA ~]$ fg 1
firefox
```

If a job is stopped (i.e., in a stopped state), you can start it running again in the background, thereby allowing you to keep control of the terminal and resume running the job. Or a stopped job can run in the foreground, which gives control of the terminal back to that program.

To place a running job in the background, type

```
[yyang@serverA ~]$ bg number
```

where **number** is the job number you want to background.

NOTE   You can background any process if you want to. Applications that require terminal input or output will be put into a stopped state if you background them. You can, for example, try running the **top** utility in the background by typing **top &**. Then check the state of that job with the **jobs** command.

Environment Variables

Every instance of a shell, and every process that is running, has its own "environment"—settings that give it a particular look, feel, and in some cases, behavior. These settings are typically controlled by environment variables. Some environment variables have special meanings to the shell, but there is nothing stopping you from defining your own and using them for your own needs. It is through the use of environment variables that most shell scripts are able to do interesting things and remember results from user inputs as well as program outputs. If you are already familiar with the concept of environment variables in Windows NT/200x/XP, you'll find that many of the things that you know about them will apply to Linux as well; the only difference is how they are set, viewed, and removed.

Printing Environment Variables

To list all of your environment variables, use the **printenv** command. For example,

```
[yyang@serverA ~]$ printenv
HOSTNAME=serverA.example.org
SHELL=/bin/bash
TERM=xterm
HISTSIZE=1000
...<OUTPUT TRUNCATED>...
```

To show a specific environment variable, specify the variable as a parameter to **printenv**. For example, here is the command to see the environment variable TERM:

```
[yyang@serverA ~]$ printenv TERM
xterm
```

Setting Environment Variables

To set an environment variable, use the following format:

```
[yyang@serverA ~]$ variable=value
```

where **variable** is the variable name and **value** is the value you want to assign the variable. For example, to set the environment variable FOO to the value BAR, type

```
[yyang@serverA ~]$ FOO=BAR
```

Whenever you set environment variables this way, they stay local to the running shell. If you want that value to be passed to other processes that you launch, use the **export** built-in command. The format of the **export** command is as follows:

```
[yyang@serverA ~]$ export variable
```

where **variable** is the name of the variable. In the example of setting the variable FOO, you would enter this command:

```
[yyang@serverA ~]$ export  FOO
```

TIP You can combine the steps for setting an environment variable with the **export** command, like so: [yyang@serverA ~]$ **export FOO=BAR**.

If the value of the environment variable you want to set has spaces in it, surround the variable with quotation marks. Using the preceding example, to set FOO to "Welcome to the BAR of FOO.", you would enter

```
[yyang@serverA ~]$ export FOO="Welcome to the BAR of FOO."
```

You can then use the **printenv** command to see the value of the FOO variable you just set by typing

```
[yyang@serverA ~]$ printenv FOO
Welcome to the BAR of FOO.
```

Unsetting Environment Variables

To remove an environment variable, use the **unset** command. The syntax for the **unset** command is

```
[yyang@serverA ~]$ unset variable
```

where ***variable*** is the name of the variable you want to remove. For example, the command to remove the environment variable FOO is

```
[yyang@serverA ~]$ unset FOO
```

NOTE This section assumed that you are using BASH. There are many other shells to choose from; the most popular alternatives are the C shell (csh) and its brother the Tenex/Turbo/Trusted C shell (tcsh), which use different mechanisms for getting and setting environment variables. We document BASH here because it is the default shell of all new Linux accounts in most Linux distributions.

Pipes

Pipes are a mechanism by which the output of one program can be sent as the input to another program. Individual programs can be chained together to become extremely powerful tools.

Let's use the **grep** program to provide a simple example of how pipes can be used. The **grep** utility, given a stream of input, will try to match the line with the parameter supplied to it and display only matching lines. You will recall from the preceding section that the **printenv** command prints all the environment variables. The list it prints can be lengthy, so if for example, you were looking for all environment variables containing the string "TERM," you could enter this command:

```
[yyang@serverA ~]$ printenv | grep TERM
TERM=xterm
```

The vertical bar (|) character represents the pipe between **printenv** and **grep**.

The command shell under Windows also utilizes the pipe function. The primary difference is that all commands in a Linux pipe are executed concurrently, whereas Windows runs each program in order, using temporary files to hold intermediate results.

Redirection

Through *redirection*, you can take the output of a program and have it automatically sent to a file. (Remember that everything in UNIX is regarded as a file!) The shell rather than the program itself handles this process, thereby providing a standard mechanism for performing the task. (Using redirection is much easier than having to remember how to do this for every single program!)

Redirection comes in three classes: output to a file, append to a file, and send a file as input.

To collect the output of a program into a file, end the command line with the greater-than symbol (>) and the name of the file to which you want the output redirected. If you are redirecting to an existing file and you want to append additional data to it, use two > symbols (>>) followed by the filename. For example, here is the command to collect the output of a directory listing into a file called **/tmp/directory_listing**:

```
[yyang@serverA ~]$ ls > /tmp/directory_listing
```

Continuing this example with the directory listing, you could append the string "Directory Listing" to the end of the **/tmp/directory_listing** file by typing this command:

```
[yyang@serverA ~]$ echo "Directory Listing" >> /tmp/directory_listing
```

The third class of redirection, using a file as input, is done by using the less-than sign (<) followed by the name of the file. For example, here is the command to feed the **/etc/ passwd** file into the **grep** program:

```
[yyang@serverA ~]$ grep 'root' < /etc/passwd
root:x:0:0:root:/root:/bin/bash
operator:x:11:0:operator:/root:/sbin/nologin
```

COMMAND-LINE SHORTCUTS

Most of the popular UNIX/Linux shells have a tremendous number of shortcuts. Learning and getting used to the shortcuts can be a huge cultural shock for users coming from the Windows world. This section explains the most common of the BASH shortcuts and their behaviors.

Filename Expansion

Under UNIX-based shells such as BASH, wildcards on the command line are expanded before being passed as a parameter to the application. This is in sharp contrast to the default mode of operation for DOS-based tools, which often have to perform their own wildcard expansion. The UNIX method also means that you must be careful where you use the wildcard characters.

The wildcard characters themselves in BASH are identical to those in command.com: the asterisk (*) matches against all filenames, and the question mark (?) matches against single characters. If you need to use these characters as part of another parameter for whatever reason, you can escape them by preceding them with a backslash (\ ) character. This causes the shell to interpret the asterisk and question mark as regular characters instead of wildcards.

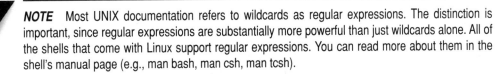

NOTE   Most UNIX documentation refers to wildcards as regular expressions. The distinction is important, since regular expressions are substantially more powerful than just wildcards alone. All of the shells that come with Linux support regular expressions. You can read more about them in the shell's manual page (e.g., man bash, man csh, man tcsh).

Environment Variables as Parameters

Under BASH, you can use environment variables as parameters on the command line. (Although the Windows command prompt can do this as well, it's not a common practice and thus is an often forgotten convention.) For example, issuing the parameter **$FOO** will cause the value of the FOO environment variable to be passed rather than the string "$FOO".

Multiple Commands

Under BASH, multiple commands can be executed on the same line by separating the commands with semicolons (;). For example, to execute this sequence of commands (**cat** and **ls**) on a single line:

```
[yyang@serverA ~]$ ls -l
[yyang@serverA ~]$ cat /etc/passwd
```

you could instead type the following:

```
[yyang@serverA ~]$ ls -l ; cat /etc/passwd
```

Since the shell is also a programming language, you can run commands serially only if the first command succeeds. For example, use the **ls** command to try to list a file that does *not* exist in your home directory and then execute the **date** command right after that on the same line. Type

```
[yyang@serverA ~]$ ls does-not-exist.txt   && date
ls: does-not-exist.txt: No such file or directory
```

This command will run the **ls** command, but that command will fail because the file it is trying to list does not exist, and so therefore the **date** command will not be executed either. But if you switch the order of commands around, you will notice that the **date** command will succeed while the **ls** command will fail. Try

```
[yyang@serverA ~]$ date && ls   does-not-exist.txt
Mon Mar  7 22:41:13 PST 2030
ls: does-not-exist.txt: No such file or directory
```

Backticks

How's this for wild: You can take the output of one program and make it the parameter of another program. Sound bizarre? Well, time to get used to it—this is one of the most useful and innovative features available in all UNIX shells.

Backticks (`) allow you to embed commands as parameters to other commands. You'll see this technique used often in this book and in various system scripts.

For example, one can pass the value of a number (a process ID number) stored in a file and pass that number as a parameter to the **kill** command. A typical instance of this occurs when the DNS server, **named**, needs to be killed. When **named** starts, it writes its process identification (PID) number into the file **/var/run/named/named.pid**. Thus, the generic way of killing the **named** process is to look at the number stored in **/var/run/named/named.pid** using the **cat** command, and then issue the **kill** command with that value. For example,

```
[yyang@serverA ~]$ cat /var/run/named/named.pid
253
[yyang@serverA ~]$ kill 253
```

One problem with killing the **named** process in this way is that it cannot be automated—we are counting on the fact that a human will read the value in **/var/run/named/named.pid** in order to kill the number. Another issue isn't so much a problem as it is a nuisance: It takes two steps to stop the DNS server.

Using backticks, however, we can combine the steps into one and do it in a way that can be automated. The backticks version would look like this:

```
[yyang@serverA ~]$ kill `cat /var/run/named/named.pid`
```

When BASH sees this command, it will first run `cat /var/run/named/named.pid` and store the result. It will then run `kill` and pass the stored result to it. From our point of view, this happens in one graceful step.

NOTE   So far in this chapter, we have looked at features that are internal to BASH (or Bash built-ins as they are sometimes called). The remainder of the chapter explores several common commands accessible outside of BASH.

DOCUMENTATION TOOLS

Linux comes with two superbly useful tools for making documentation accessible: **man** and **info**. Currently, a great deal of overlap exists between these two documentation systems because many applications are moving their documentation to the **info** format. This format is considered superior to **man** because it allows the documentation to be hyperlinked together in a Web-like way, but without actually having to be written in HTML format.

The **man** format, on the other hand, has been around for decades. For thousands of utilities, their man (short for *manual*) pages are their only documentation. Furthermore, many applications continue to utilize **man** format because many other UNIX-like operating systems (such as Sun Solaris) use **man** format.

Both the **man** and **info** documentation systems will be around for a long while to come. It is highly recommend getting comfortable with them both.

TIP   Many Linux distributions also include a great deal of documentation in the **/usr/doc** or **/usr/share/doc** directory.

The man Command

We mentioned quite early in this book that man pages are documents found online (on the local system) that cover the use of tools and their corresponding configuration files. The format of the **man** command is as follows:

```
[yyang@serverA ~]$ man program_name
```

where ***program_name*** identifies the program you're interested in. For example, to view the man page for the **ls** utility that we've been using, type

```
[yyang@serverA ~]$ man ls
```

While reading about UNIX and UNIX-related information sources (newsgroups and so forth), you may encounter references to commands followed by numbers in parentheses—for example, ls(1). The number represents the section of the manual pages (see Table 5-1). Each section covers various subject areas, to accommodate the fact that some tools (such as **printf**) are commands/functions in the C programming language as well as command-line commands.

To refer to a specific man section, simply specify the section number as the first parameter and then the command as the second parameter. For example, to get the C programmers' information on **printf**, you'd enter this:

```
[yyang@serverA ~]$ man 3 printf
```

To get the command-line information, you'd enter this:

```
[yyang@serverA ~]$ man 1  printf
```

If you don't specify a section number with the **man** command, the default behavior is that the lowest section number gets printed first.

Unfortunately, this organization can sometimes be difficult to use, and as a result, there are several other available alternatives.

Manual Section	Subject
1	User tools
2	System calls
3	C library calls
4	Device driver information
5	Configuration files
6	Games
7	Packages
8	System tools

Table 5-1.   Man Page Sections

TIP A handy option to the **man** command is **-f** preceding the command parameter. With this option, **man** will search the summary information of all the man pages and list pages matching your specified command, along with their section number. For example,

```
[yyang@serverA ~]$ man -f printf
asprintf            (3)  - print to allocated string
printf              (1)  - format and print data
printf              (3)  - formatted output conversion
```

The texinfo System

Another common form of documentation is texinfo. Established as the GNU standard, texinfo is a documentation system similar to the hyperlinked World Wide Web format. Because documents can be hyperlinked together, texinfo is often easier to read, use, and search than man pages.

To read the texinfo documents on a specific tool or application, invoke **info** with the parameter specifying the tool's name. For example, to read about the **grub** program, type

```
[yyang@serverA ~]$ info grub
```

In general, you will want to verify whether a man page exists before using **info** (there is still a great deal more information available in **man** format than in texinfo). On the other hand, some man pages will explicitly state that the texinfo pages are more authoritative and should be read instead.

UNDERSTANDING FILE LISTINGS, OWNERSHIPS, AND PERMISSIONS

Managing files under Linux is different than managing files under Windows NT/200x/XP, and radically different from managing files under Windows 95/98. In this section, we discuss basic file management tools for Linux. We'll start with specifics on some useful general-purpose commands, and then we'll step back and look at some background information.

Listing Files: ls

The **ls** command is used to list all the files in a directory. Of more than 26 available options, the ones listed in Table 5-2 are the most commonly used. The options can be used in any combination.

Option for `ls`	Description
`-l`	Long listing. In addition to the filename, shows the file size, date/time, permissions, ownership, and group information.
`-a`	All files. Shows all files in the directory, including hidden files. Names of hidden files begin with a period.
`-t`	Lists in order of last modified time.
`-r`	Reverses the listing.
`-1`	Single-column listing.
`-R`	Recursively lists all files and subdirectories.

Table 5-2.   Common ls Options

To list all files in a directory with a long listing, type this command:

```
[yyang@serverA ~]$ ls -la
```

To list a directory's nonhidden files that start with the letter A, type this:

```
[yyang@serverA ~]$ ls   A*
```

TIP   Linux/UNIX is very case sensitive. For example, a file named "**thefile.txt**" is very different from a file named "**Thefile.txt**".

If no such file exists in your working directory, `ls` prints out a message telling you so.

File and Directory Types

Under Linux (and UNIX in general), almost everything is abstracted to a file. Originally this was done to simplify the programmer's job. Instead of having to communicate directly with device drivers, special files (which look like ordinary files to the application) are used as a bridge. Several types of files accommodate all these file uses.

Normal Files

Normal files are just that—normal. They contain data or executables, and the operating system makes no assumptions about their contents.

Directories

Directory files are a special instance of normal files. Directory files list the locations of other files, some of which may be other directories. (This is similar to folders in Windows.) In general, the contents of directory files won't be of importance to your daily operations, unless you need to open and read the file yourself rather than using existing applications to navigate directories. (This would be similar to trying to read the DOS file allocation table directly rather than using command.com to navigate directories, or using the findfirst/findnext system calls.)

Hard Links

Each file in the Linux file system gets its own i-node. An i-node keeps track of a file's attributes and its location on the disk. If you need to be able to refer to a single file using two separate filenames, you can create a hard link. The *hard link* will have the same i-node as the original file and will therefore look and behave just like the original. With every hard link that is created, a reference count is incremented. When a hard link is removed, the reference count is decremented. Until the reference count reaches zero, the file will remain on disk.

NOTE   A hard link cannot exist between two files on separate partitions. This is because the hard link refers to the original file by i-node, and a file's i-node may differ among file systems.

Symbolic Links

Unlike hard links, which point to a file by its i-node, a *symbolic link* points to another file by its name. This allows symbolic links (often abbreviated symlinks) to point to files located on other partitions, even other network drives.

Block Devices

Since all device drivers are accessed through the file system, files of type *block device* are used to interface with devices such as disks. A block device file has three identifying traits:

▼   It has a major number.

■   It has a minor number.

▲   When viewed using the **ls -l** command, it shows *b* as the first character of the permissions field.

For example,

```
[yyang@serverA ~]$ ls -l /dev/hda
brw-rw----  1 root disk 3, 0 Mar  7 13:35 /dev/hda
```

Note the **b** at the beginning of the file's permissions; the **3** is the major number, and the **0** is the minor number.

A block device file's major number identifies the represented device driver. When this file is accessed, the minor number is passed to the device driver as a parameter telling it which device it is accessing. For example, if there are two serial ports, they will share the same device driver and thus the same major number, but each serial port will have a unique minor number.

Character Devices

Similar to block devices, *character devices* are special files that allow you to access devices through the file system. The obvious difference between block and character devices is that block devices communicate with the actual devices in large blocks, whereas character devices work one character at a time. (A hard disk is a block device; a modem is a character device.) Character device permissions start with a *c*, and the file has a major number and a minor number. For example,

```
[yyang@serverA ~]$ ls -l /dev/ttyS0
crw-rw----  1 root uucp 4, 64 Mar  7 21:36 /dev/ttyS0
```

Named Pipes

Named pipes are a special type of file that allows for interprocess communication. Using the **mknod** command (discussed later in this chapter), you can create a named pipe file that one process can open for reading and another process can open for writing, thus allowing the two to communicate with one another. This works especially well when a program refuses to take input from a command-line pipe, but another program needs to feed the other one data and you don't have the disk space for a temporary file.

For a named pipe file, the first character of its file permissions is a *p*. For example, if a named pipe called mypipe exists in your present working directory (pwd), a long listing of the named pipe file would show this:

```
[yyang@serverA ~]$ ls -l mypipe
prw-r--r--  1 root     root           0 Mar 16 10:47 mypipe
```

Change Ownership: chown

The **chown** command allows you to change the ownership of a file to someone else. Only the root user can do this. (Normal users may not give away file ownership or steal ownership from another user.) The format of the command is as follows:

```
[root@serverA ~]# chown [-R] username filename
```

where **username** is the login of the user to whom you want to assign ownership, and **filename** is the name of the file in question. The filename may be a directory as well.

The **-R** option applies when the specified filename is a directory name. This option tells the command to recursively descend through the directory tree and apply the new ownership not only to the directory itself, but to all of the files and directories within it.

NOTE   Linux allows you to use a special notation with **chown** to also supply the group to **chgrp** the files to. The format of the command becomes **chown username.groupname filename**.

Change Group: chgrp

The **chgrp** command-line utility lets you change the group settings of a file. It works much like **chown**. Here is the format:

```
[root@serverA ~]# chgrp [-R] groupname filename
```

where **groupname** is the name of the group to which you want to assign filename ownership. The filename may be a directory as well.

The **-R** option applies when the specified filename is a directory name. As with **chown**, the **-R** option tells the command to recursively descend through the directory tree and apply the new ownership not only to the directory itself, but also to all of the files and directories within it.

Change Mode: chmod

Directories and files within the Linux system have permissions associated with them. By default, permissions are set for the owner of the file, the group associated with the file, and everyone else who can access the file (also known as Owner, Group, Other). When you list files or directories, you see the permissions in the first column of the output. Permissions are divided into four parts. The first part is represented by the first character of the permission. Normal files have no special value and are represented with a hyphen (-) character. If the file has a special attribute, it is represented by a letter. The two special attributes we are most interested in here are directories (**d**) and symbolic links (**l**).

The second, third, and fourth parts of a permission are represented in three-character chunks. The first part indicates the file owner's permission. The second part indicates the group permission. The last part indicates the world permission. In the context of UNIX, "world" means all users in the system, regardless of their group settings.

Following are the letters used to represent permissions and their corresponding values. When you combine attributes, you add their values. The **chmod** command is used to set permission values.

Letter	Permission	Value
R	Read	4
W	Write	2
X	Execute	1

Using the numeric command mode is typically known as the *octal* permissions, since the value can range from 0–7. To change permissions on a file, you simply add these values together for each permission you want to apply.

For example, if you want to make it so that just the user (owner) can have full access (RWX) to a the file called **foo**, you would type

```
[yyang@serverA ~]$ chmod 700 foo
```

What is important to note is that using the octal mode you always *replace* any permissions that were set. So if there was a file in **/usr/local** that was SetUID and you ran the command **chmod -R 700 /usr/local**, that file will no longer be SetUID. If you want to change certain bits, you should use the symbolic mode of **chmod**. This mode turns out to be much easier to remember, and you can add, subtract, or overwrite permissions.

The symbolic form of **chmod** allows you to set the bits of either the owner, the group, or others. You can also set the bits for all. For example, if you want to change a file called **foobar.sh** so that it is executable for the owner, you can run the following command:

```
[yyang@serverA ~]$ chmod u+x foobar.sh
```

If you want to change the group's bit to execute also, use the following:

```
[yyang@serverA ~]$ chmod ug+x foobar.sh
```

If you need to specify different permissions for others, just add a comma and its permission symbols as here:

```
[yyang@serverA ~]$ chmod ug+x,o-rwx foobar.sh
```

If you do not want to add or subtract a permission bit, you can use the = sign instead of + or -. This will write the specific bits to the file and erase any other bit for that permission. In the previous examples, we used + to add the execute bit to the user and group fields. If you want *only* the execute bit, you would replace the + with =. There is also a fourth character you can use: **a**. This will apply the permission bits to all of the fields.

The following list shows the most common combinations of the three permissions. Other combinations, such as **-wx**, do exist, but they are rarely used.

Letter	Permission	Value
- - -	No permissions	0
r - -	Read only	4
rw -	Read and write	6
rwx	Read, write, and execute	7
r - x	Read and execute	5
- - x	Execute only	1

For each file, three of these three-letter chunks are grouped together. The first chunk represents the permissions for the owner of the file, the second chunk represents the permissions for file's group, and the last chunk represents the permissions for all users on the system. Table 5-3 shows some permission combinations, their numeric equivalents, and their descriptions.

Permission	Numeric Equivalent	Description
`-rw-------`	600	Owner has read and write permissions.
`-rw-r--r--`	644	Owner has read and write permissions; group and world have read-only permission.
`-rw-rw-rw-`	666	Everyone has read and write permissions. Not recommended; this combination allows the file to be accessed and changed by anyone.
`-rwx------`	700	Owner has read, write, and execute permissions. Best combination for programs or executables that the owner wishes to run.
`-rwxr-xr-x`	755	Owner has read, write, and execute permissions. Everyone else has read and execute permissions.
`-rwxrwxrwx`	777	Everyone has read, write, and execute privileges. Like the 666 setting, this combination should be avoided.
`-rwx--x--x`	711	Owner has read, write, and execute permissions; everyone else has execute-only permissions. Useful for programs that you want to let others run but not copy.
`drwx------`	700	This is a directory created with the **mkdir** command. Only the owner can read and write into this directory. Note that all directories must have the executable bit set.
`drwxr-xr-x`	755	This directory can be changed only by the owner, but everyone else can view its contents.
`drwx--x--x`	711	A handy combination for keeping a directory world-readable but restricted from access by the **ls** command. A file can be read only by someone who knows the filename.

Table 5-3.   File Permissions

FILE MANAGEMENT AND MANIPULATION

This section covers the basic command-line tools for managing files and directories. Most of this will be familiar to anyone who has used a command-line interface—same old functions, but new commands to execute.

Copy Files: cp

The **cp** command is used to copy files. It has a substantial number of options. See its man page for additional details. By default, this command works silently, only displaying status information if an error condition occurs. Following are the most common options for **cp**:

Option for cp	Description
-f	Forces copy; does not ask for verification
-I	Interactive copy; before each file is copied, verifies with user

First let's use the **touch** command to create an empty file called **foo.txt** in the user yyang's home directory. Type

```
[yyang@serverA ~]$ touch  foo.txt
```

To use the **cp** (copy) command to copy **foo.txt** to **foo.txt.html**, type

```
[yyang@serverA ~]$ cp foo.txt foo.txt.html
```

To interactively copy all files ending in **.html** to the **/tmp** directory, type this command:

```
[yyang@serverA ~]$ cp -i *.html  /tmp
```

Move Files: mv

The **mv** command is used to move files from one location to another. Files can be moved across partitions/file systems as well. Moving files across partitions involves a copy operation, and as a result the move command may take longer. But you will find that moving files within the same file system is almost instantaneous. Following are the most common options for **mv**:

Option for mv	Description
-f	Forces move
-I	Interactive move

To move a file named **foo.txt.html** from **/tmp** to your present working directory, use this command:

```
[yyang@serverA ~]$ mv  /tmp/foo.txt.html   .
```

> **NOTE**   The preceding dot (.) is not a typo—it literally means "this directory."

There is no explicit rename tool, so you can use the **mv** command. To rename the file **foo.txt.html** to **foo.txt.htm**, type

```
[yyang@serverA ~]$ mv foo.txt.html   foo.txt.htm
```

Link Files: ln

The **ln** command lets you establish hard links and soft links (see "File and Directory Types" earlier in this chapter). The general format of **ln** is as follows:

```
[yyang@serverA ~]$ ln original_file   new_file
```

Although **ln** has many options, you'll rarely need to use most of them. The most common option, **-s**, creates a symbolic link instead of a hard link.

To create a symbolic link called **link-to-foo.txt** that points to the original file called **foo.txt**, issue the command

```
[yyang@serverA ~]$ ln -s foo.txt   link-to-foo.txt
```

Find a File: find

The **find** command lets you search for files according to various criteria. Like the tools we have already discussed, **find** has a large number of options that you can read about in its man page. Here is the general format of **find**:

```
[yyang@serverA ~]$ find start_dir [options]
```

where **start_dir** is the directory from which the search should start.

To find all files in the your current directory (i.e., the "."directory) that have not been accessed in at least seven days, use the following command:

```
[yyang@serverA ~]$ find . -atime 7
```

Type this command to find all files in your present working directory whose names are **core** and then delete them (i.e., automatically run the **rm** command):

```
[yyang@serverA ~]$ find  .  -name core -exec rm {} \;
```

> **TIP**   The syntax for the **-exec** option with the **find** command as used here can be a bit trying to remember sometimes, and so you can also use the **xargs** method instead of the **exec** option used in this example. Using **xargs**, the command would then be written
>
> ```
> [yyang@serverA ~]$ find . -name 'core' | xargs rm
> ```

To find all files in your pwd whose names end in **.txt** (i.e., files that have the **txt** extension) and are also less than 100K in size, issue this command:

```
[yyang@serverA ~]$ find   .   -name '*.txt' -size  -100k
```

To find all files in your pwd whose names end in **.txt** (i.e., files that have the **txt** extension) and are also greater than 100K in size, issue this command:

```
[yyang@serverA ~]$ find   .   -name '*.txt' -size   100k
```

File Compression: gzip

In the original distributions of UNIX, the tool to compress files was appropriately called `compress`. Unfortunately, the algorithm was patented by someone hoping to make a great deal of money. Instead of paying out, most sites sought and found another compression tool with a patent-free algorithm: `gzip`. Even better, `gzip` consistently achieves better compression ratios than `compress` does. Another bonus: recent changes have allowed `gzip` to uncompress files that were compressed using the `compress` command.

> **NOTE**   The filename extension usually identifies a file compressed with `gzip`. These files typically end in **.gz** (files compressed with `compress` end in **.z**).

Note that `gzip` compresses the file in place, meaning that after the compression process, the original file is removed, and the only thing left is the compressed file.

To compress a file named **foo.txt.htm** in your pwd, type

```
[yyang@serverA ~]$ gzip  foo.txt.htm
```

And then to decompress it, use `gzip` again with the **-d** option:

```
[yyang@serverA ~]$ gzip -d foo.txt.htm.gz
```

Issue this command to compress all files ending in **.htm** in your pwd using the best compression possible:

```
[yyang@serverA ~]$ gzip  -9  *.htm
```

bzip2

If you have noticed files with a **.bz** extension, these have been compressed with the `bzip2` compression utility. The `bzip2` tool uses a different compression algorithm that usually turns out smaller files than those compressed with the `gzip` utility, but it uses semantics that are similar to `gzip`; for more information, read the man page on `bzip2`.

Create a Directory: mkdir

The **mkdir** command in Linux is identical to the same command in other flavors of UNIX, as well as in MS-DOS. An often used option of the **mkdir** command is the **-p** option. This option will force **mkdir** to create parent directories if they don't exist already. For example, if you need to create **/tmp/bigdir/subdir/mydir** and the only directory that exists is **/tmp**, using **-p** will cause **bigdir** and **subdir** to be automatically created along with **mydir**.

Create a directory tree like **bigdir/subdir/finaldir in** your pwd. Type

```
[yyang@serverA ~]$ mkdir -p  bigdir/subdir/finaldir
```

To create a single directory called **mydir**, use this command:

```
[yyang@serverA ~]$ mkdir mydir
```

Remove a Directory: rmdir

The **rmdir** command offers no surprises for those familiar with the DOS version of the command; it simply removes an existing directory. This command also accepts the **-p** parameter, which removes parent directories as well.

For example, if you want to get rid of all the directories from **bigdir** to **finaldir** that were created earlier, you'd issue this command alone:

```
[yyang@serverA ~]$ rmdir  -p   bigdir/subdir/finaldir
```

To remove a directory called **mydir**, you'd type this:

```
[yyang@serverA ~]$ rmdir mydir
```

> **TIP**   You can also use the **rm** command with the **-r** option to delete directories.

Show Present Working Directory: pwd

It is inevitable that you will sit down in front of an already logged-in workstation and not know where you are in the directory tree. To get this information, you need the **pwd** command. Its only task is to print the current working directory.

To display your current working directory, use this command:

```
[yyang@serverA ~]$ pwd
/home/yyang
```

Tape Archive: tar

If you are familiar with the PKZip program, you are accustomed to the fact that the compression tool reduces file size but also consolidates files into compressed archives. Under Linux, this process is separated into two tools: **gzip** and **tar**.

The `tar` command combines multiple files into a single large file. It is separate from the compression tool, so it allows you to select which compression tool to use or whether you even want compression. Additionally, `tar` is able to read and write to devices, thus making it a good tool for backing up to tape devices.

> **NOTE** Although the name of the `tar` program includes the word "tape," it isn't necessary to read or write to a tape drive when creating archives. In fact, you'll rarely use `tar` with a tape drive in day-to-day situations (backups aside). The reason it was named `tar` in the first place was that when it was originally created, limited disk space meant that tape was the most logical place to put archives. Typically, the `-f` option in `tar` would be used to specify the tape device file, rather than a traditional UNIX file. You should be aware, however, that you can still `tar` straight to a device.

The syntax for the `tar` command is

```
[yyang@serverA ~]$ tar  option... filename...
```

Some of the options for the `tar` command are shown here:

Option for `tar`	Description
`-c`	Creates a new archive
`-t`	Views the contents of an archive
`-x`	Extracts the contents of an archive
`-f`	Specifies the name of the file (or device) in which the archive is located
`-v`	Provides verbose descriptions during operations
`-j`	Filters the archive through the `bzip2` compression utility
`-z`	Filters the archive through the `gzip` compression utility

In order to see sample usage of the `tar` utility, first create a folder called **junk** in the pwd that contains some empty files named **1, 2, 3, 4**. Type

```
[yyang@serverA ~]$ mkdir junk ; touch junk/{1,2,3,4}
```

Now create an archive called **junk.tar** containing all the files in the folder called **junk** that you just created: type

```
[yyang@serverA ~]$ tar  -cf  junk.tar  junk
```

Create another archive called **2junk.tar** containing all the files in the **junk** folder, but this time add the **-v** (verbose) option to show what is happening as it happens. Enter the following:

```
[yyang@serverA ~]$ tar   -vcf   2junk.tar   junk
junk/
junk/4
junk/3
junk/1
junk/2
```

NOTE   You should note that the archives created in these examples are not compressed in any way. The files and directory have only been combined into a single file.

To create a **gzip**-compressed archive called **3junk.tar.gz** containing all of the files in the **junk** folder, and to show what is happening as it happens, issue this command:

```
[yyang@serverA ~]$ tar   -cvzf      3junk.tar.gz   junk
```

To extract the contents of the **gzip**ped **tar** archive created here, and be verbose about what is being done, issue the command:

```
[yyang@serverA ~]$ tar   -xvzf 3junk.tar.gz
```

TIP   The **tar** command is one of the few Linux/UNIX utilities that cares about the order with which you specify its options. If you issued the preceding **tar** command as
 # tar -xvfz 3junk.tar.gz
the command will fail because the **-f** option was not immediately followed by a filename.

If you like, you can also specify a physical device to **tar** to and from. This is handy when you need to transfer a set of files from one system to another and for some reason you cannot create a file system on the device. (Or sometimes it's just more entertaining to do it this way.) To create an archive on the first floppy device (/dev/fd0), you would enter this:

```
[yyang@serverA ~]$ tar -cvzf /dev/fd0    junk
```

NOTE   The command **tar   -cvzf   /dev/fd0** will treat the disk as a raw device and erase anything that is already on it.

To pull that archive off of a disk, you would type

```
[yyang@serverA ~]$ tar -xvzf /dev/fd0
```

Concatenate Files: cat

The **cat** program fills an extremely simple role: to display files. More creative things can be done with it, but nearly all of its usage will be in the form of simply displaying the contents of text files—much like the **type** command under DOS. Because multiple filenames can be specified on the command line, it's possible to concatenate files into a single, large continuous file. This is different from **tar** in that the resulting file has no control information to show the boundaries of different files.

To display the **/etc/passwd** file, use this command:

```
[yyang@serverA ~]$ cat  /etc/passwd
```

To display the **/etc/passwd** file and the **/etc/group** file, issue this command:

```
[yyang@serverA ~]$ cat  /etc/passwd  /etc/group
```

Type this command to concatenate **/etc/passwd** with **/etc/group** and send the output into the file **users-and-groups.txt**:

```
[yyang@serverA ~]$ cat  /etc/passwd  /etc/group  > users-and-groups.txt
```

To append the contents of the file **/etc/hosts** to the **users-and-groups.txt** file you just created, type

```
[yyang@serverA ~]$ cat  /etc/hosts  >> users-and-groups.txt
```

TIP If you want to **cat** a file in reverse, you can use the **tac** command.

Display a File One Screen at a Time: more

The **more** command works in much the same way the DOS version of the program does. It takes an input file and displays it one screen at a time. The input file can come either from its **stdin** or from a command-line parameter. Additional command-line parameters, though rarely used, can be found in the man page.

To view the **/etc/passwd** file one screen at a time, use this command:

```
[yyang@serverA ~]$ more /etc/passwd
```

To view the directory listing generated by the **ls** command one screen at a time, enter

```
[yyang@serverA ~]$ ls | more
```

Disk Utilization: du

You will often need to determine where and by whom disk space is being consumed, especially when you're running low on it! The **du** command allows you to determine the disk utilization on a directory-by-directory basis.

Following are some of the options available.

Option for du	Description
-c	Produces a grand total at the end of the run.
-h	Prints sizes in human-readable format.
-k	Prints sizes in kilobytes rather than block sizes. (Note: Under Linux, one block is equal to 1K, but this is not true for all forms of UNIX.)
-s	Summarizes. Prints only a total for each argument.

To display the total amount of space being used by all the files and directories in your pwd, in human-readable format, use this command:

```
[yyang@serverA ~]$ du -sh  .
2.2M
```

Show the Directory Location of a File: which

The **which** command searches your entire path to find the name of an executable specified on the command line. If the file is found, the command output includes the actual path to the file.

Use the following command to find out which directory the binary for the **rm** command is located in:

```
[yyang@serverA ~]$ which  rm
/bin/rm
```

You may find this similar to the **find** command. The difference here is that since **which** only searches the path, it is much faster. Of course, it is also much more limiting than **find**, but if all you're looking for is a program, you'll find it to be a better choice of commands.

Locate a Command: whereis

The **whereis** tool searches your path and displays the name of the program and its absolute directory, the source file (if available), and the man page for the command (again, if available).

To find the location of the program, source, and manual page for the command **grep**, use this:

```
[yyang@serverA ~]$ whereis  grep
grep: /bin/grep /usr/share/man/man1/grep.1.gz /usr/share/man/man1p/grep.1p.gz
```

Disk Free: df

The **df** program displays the amount of free space, partition by partition (or volume by volume). The drives/partitions must be mounted in order to get this information. NFS information can be gathered this way, as well. Some parameters for **df** are listed here; additional (rarely used) options are listed in the **df** manual page.

Option for df	Description
-h	Generates free space amount in human-readable numbers rather than free blocks.
-l	Lists only the local mounted file systems. Does not display any information about network mounted file systems.

To show the free space for all locally mounted drives, use this command:

```
[yyang@serverA ~]$ df -l
```

To show the free space in a human-readable format, for the file system in which your current working directory is located, enter

```
[yyang@serverA ~]$ df -h .
```

To show the free space in a human-readable format for the file system on which **/tmp** is located, type this command:

```
[yyang@serverA ~]$ df -h    /tmp
```

Synchronize Disks: sync

Like most other modern operating systems, Linux maintains a disk cache to improve efficiency. The drawback, of course, is that not everything you want written to disk will have been written to disk at any given moment.

To schedule the disk cache to be written out to disk, you use the **sync** command. If **sync** detects that writing the cache out to disk has already been scheduled, the kernel is instructed to immediately flush the cache. This command takes no command-line parameters.

Type this command to ensure the disk cache has been flushed:

```
yyang@serverA ~]$ sync ; sync
```

NOTE   Manually issuing this command is rarely necessary anymore, since the Linux OS does a good job of it on its own.

MOVING A USER AND ITS HOME DIRECTORY

This section will demonstrate how to put together some of the topics and utilities covered so far in this chapter. The elegant design of UNIX and Linux allows you to combine simple commands to perform advanced operations.

Sometimes in the course of administration you might have to move a user and its files around. This section will cover the process of moving a user's home directory. In this section, you are going to move the user named "project5" from his default home directory **/home/project5** to **/export/home/project5**. You will also have to set the proper permissions and ownership of the user's files and directories so that the user can access it.

Unlike the previous exercises that were being done as a regular user (the user yyang), you will need superuser privileges to perform the steps in this exercise.

1. Log in to the system as root and launch a virtual terminal.

2. Create the user that will be used for this project. The username is "project5". Type

    ```
    [root@serverA ~]# useradd project5
    ```

3. Use the **grep** command to view the entry for the user you created in the **/etc/passwd** file. Type

    ```
    [root@serverA ~]# grep project5 /etc/passwd
    project5:x:502:503::/home/project5:/bin/bash
    ```

4. Use the **ls** command to display a listing of the user's home directory. Type

    ```
    [root@serverA ~]# ls -al /home/project5
    total 56
    drwx------  3 project5 project5 4096 Mar  8 23:50 .
    drwxr-xr-x  6 root     root     4096 Mar  8 23:50 ..
    -rw-r--r--  1 project5 project5   24 Mar  8 23:50 .bash_logout
    -rw-r--r--  1 project5 project5  191 Mar  8 23:50 .bash_profile
    -rw-r--r--  1 project5 project5  124 Mar  8 23:50 .bashrc
    ```

5. Check the total disk space being used by the user. Type

    ```
    [root@serverA ~]# du -sh /home/project5
    76K     /home/project5
    ```

6. Use the **su** command to temporarily become the user. Type

    ```
    [root@serverA ~]# su - project5
    [project5@serverA ~]$
    ```

7. As user project5, view your present working directory. Type

    ```
    [project5@serverA ~]$ pwd
    /home/project5
    ```

8. As user project5, create some empty files. Type

```
[project5@serverA ~]$ touch  a b c d e
```

9. Go back to being the root user by exiting out of project5's profile. Type

```
[project5@serverA ~]$ exit
```

10. Create the **/export** directory that will house the user's new home. Type

```
[root@serverA ~]# mkdir   -p  /export
```

11. Now use the **tar** command to archive and compress project5's current home directory (**/home/project5**) and untar and decompress it into its new location. Type

```
[root@serverA ~]# tar czf  -   /home/project5    |  (cd /export ; tar  -xvzf  - )
```

TIP The dashes (-) you used here with the **tar** command force it to first send its output to stdout and then receive its input from stdin.

12. Use the **ls** command to ensure that the new home directory was properly created under the **/export** directory. Type

```
[root@serverA ~]# ls  -R /export/home/
/export/home/:
project5
/export/home/project5:
a   b   c   d   e
```

13. Make sure that project5 has complete ownership of all the files and directories in its new home. Type

```
[root@serverA ~]# chown -R  project5.project5  /export/home/project5/
```

14. Now delete project5's old home directory. Type

```
[root@serverA ~]# rm -rf   /home/project5
```

15. Good, we are almost done. Try to temporarily assume the identity of project5 again. Type

```
[root@serverA ~]# su - project5
su: warning: cannot change directory to /home/project5: No such file or directory
-bash-3.00$
```

Ah . . . one more thing left to do. We have deleted the user's home directory (**/home/project5**), as was specified in the **/etc/passwd** file, and that is why the **su** command was complaining here.

16. Exit out of project5's profile using the **exit** command. Type

```
-bash-3.00$ exit
```

17. Now we'll use the **usermod** command to automatically update the **/etc/passwd** file with the user's new home directory. Type

    ```
    [root@serverA ~]# usermod -d  /export/home/project5    project5
    ```

18. Use the **su** command again to temporarily become project5. Type

    ```
    [root@serverA ~]# su - project5
    [project5@serverA ~]$
    ```

19. While logged in as project5, use the **pwd** command to view your present working directory. Type

    ```
    [project5@serverA ~]$ pwd
    /export/home/project5
    ```

    This output shows that our migration worked out well.

20. Exit out of project5's profile to become the root user and then delete the user called project5 from the system. Type

    ```
    [root@serverA ~]# userdel -r project5
    ```

List Processes: ps

The **ps** command lists all the processes in a system, their state, size, name, owner, CPU time, wall clock time, and much more. There are many command-line parameters available; the ones most often used are described in Table 5-4.

Option for ps	Description
-a	Shows all processes with a controlling terminal, not just the current user's processes.
-r	Shows only running processes (see the description of process states later in this section).
-x	Shows processes that do not have a controlling terminal.
-u	Shows the process owners.
-f	Displays parent/child relationships among processes.
-l	Produces a list in long format.
-w	Shows a process's command-line parameters (up to half a line).
-ww	Shows all of a process's command-line parameters, despite length.

Table 5-4.   Common ps Options

The most common set of parameters used with the **ps** command is **auxww**. These parameters show all the processes (regardless of whether they have a controlling terminal), each process's owners, and all the processes' command-line parameters. Let's examine some sample output of an invocation of **ps auxww**.

```
[yyang@serverA ~]$ ps auxww
```

USER	PID	%CPU	%MEM	VSZ	RSS	TTY	STAT	START	TIME	COMMAND
root	1	0.0	0.2	2332	564	?	S	Mar07	0:12	init [3]
root	2	0.0	0.0	0	0	?	SN	Mar07	0:00	[ksoftirqd/0]
root	3	0.0	0.0	0	0	?	S<	Mar07	0:04	[events/0]
root	4	0.0	0.0	0	0	?	S<	Mar07	0:00	[khelper]
root	5	0.0	0.0	0	0	?	S<	Mar07	0:00	[kacpid]
root	1216	0.0	0.2	3004	504	?	S<s	Mar07	0:00	udevd
root	1732	0.0	0.0	0	0	?	S	Mar07	0:00	[kjournald]
root	1733	0.0	0.0	0	0	?	S	Mar07	0:00	[kjournald]
root	1734	0.0	0.0	0	0	?	S	Mar07	0:00	[kjournald]
root	2076	0.0	0.3	3284	584	?	Ss	Mar07	0:02	syslogd -m 0
root	2080	0.0	0.2	1792	468	?	Ss	Mar07	0:00	klogd -x
rpc	2108	0.0	0.3	2216	636	?	Ss	Mar07	0:00	portmap
rpcuser	2128	0.0	0.4	2496	844	?	Ss	Mar07	0:00	rpc.statd
root	2161	0.0	0.3	2972	588	?	Ss	Mar07	0:21	rpc.idmapd
root	2231	0.3	0.2	4348	572	?	Ss	Mar07	5:27	nifd -n
nobody	2261	0.0	0.5	13536	1020	?	Ssl	Mar07	0:00	mDNSResponder
root	2282	0.0	0.2	1600	532	?	Ss	Mar07	0:00	/usr/sbin/acpid
root	2357	0.0	0.8	4248	1532	?	Ss	Mar07	0:00	/usr/sbin/sshd
root	2419	0.0	0.4	5128	828	?	Ss	Mar07	0:01	crond
xfs	2445	0.0	0.7	4528	1524	?	Ss	Mar07	0:00	xfs -droppriv -
daemon	2464	0.0	0.3	2224	640	?	Ss	Mar07	0:00	/usr/sbin/atd
dbus	2474	0.0	0.6	3780	1196	?	Ss	Mar07	0:00	dbus-daemon-1 --
root	2487	0.0	0.5	3436	1032	?	Ss	Mar07	0:00	cups-config-daemon
root	2498	0.0	1.9	5836	3636	?	Ss	Mar07	1:18	hald
root	2530	0.0	0.2	2340	408	tty1	Ss+	Mar07	0:00	/sbin/mingetty tty1
root	2531	0.0	0.2	2620	408	tty2	Ss+	Mar07	0:00	/sbin/mingetty tty2
root	3196	0.0	1.1	9776	2192	?	SNs	Mar07	0:01	cupsd
root	3555	0.0	1.0	7464	2032	?	Ss	Mar07	0:00	sshd: yyang [priv]
yyang	3557	0.0	1.2	7848	2396	?	S	Mar07	0:24	sshd: yyang@pts/0
yyang	3558	0.0	0.7	6128	1444	pts/0	Ss	Mar07	0:06	-bash
yyang	3607	0.0	1.0	7176	2096	?	S	Mar07	0:02	usr/libexec/gconfd-
root	3757	0.0	1.1	7628	2124	?	Ss	Mar08	0:00	sshd: root@pts/2
root	3759	0.0	0.7	4924	1456	pts/2	Ss+	Mar08	0:00	-bash
yyang	3822	0.0	2.9	10500	5616	pts/0	S	Mar08	1:19	xterm
yyang	3824	0.0	0.7	5128	1376	pts/1	Ss	Mar08	0:00	bash
yyang	3842	0.0	0.8	4808	1648	pts/1	S+	Mar08	0:00	ssh 10.0.99.5 -l
root	5272	0.0	0.2	4524	540	?	S	00:37	0:00	sleep 1h
root	5283	0.1	0.6	5184	1152	pts/0	S	00:49	0:00	su - yyang
yyang	5284	0.2	0.7	5684	1368	pts/0	S	00:49	0:00	-bash
yyang	5310	0.0	0.4	4016	772	pts/0	R+	00:50	0:00	ps auxww

The very first line of the output provides column headers for the listing, as follows:

▼ **USER** Who owns what process.

■ **PID** Process identification number.

■ **%CPU** Percentage of the CPU taken up by a process. Note: For a system with multiple processors, this column will add up to more than 100%.

■ **%MEM** Percentage of memory taken up by a process.

■ **VSZ** The amount of virtual memory a process is taking.

■ **RSS** The amount of actual (resident) memory a process is taking.

■ **TTY** The controlling terminal for a process. A question mark in this column means the process is no longer connected to a controlling terminal.

■ **STAT** The state of the process. These are the possible states:

    ▼ **S** Process is sleeping. All processes that are ready to run (that is, being multitasked, and the CPU is currently focused elsewhere) will be asleep.

    ■ **R** Process is actually on the CPU.

    ■ **D** Uninterruptible sleep (usually I/O related).

    ■ **T** Process is being traced by a debugger or has been stopped.

    ▲ **Z** Process has gone zombie. This means either (1) the parent process has not acknowledged the death of its child using the **wait** system call; or (2) the parent was improperly **kill**ed, and until the parent is completely **kill**ed, the **init** process (see Chapter 8) cannot kill the child itself. A zombied process usually indicates poorly written software.

In addition, the STAT entry for each process can take one of the following modifiers: W = No resident pages in memory (it has been completely swapped out); < = High-priority process; N = Low-priority task; L = Pages in memory are locked there (usually signifying the need for real-time functionality).

■ **START** Date the process was started.

■ **TIME** Amount of time the process has spent on the CPU.

▲ **COMMAND** Name of the process and its command-line parameters.

Show an Interactive List of Processes: top

The **top** command is an interactive version of **ps**. Instead of giving a static view of what is going on, **top** refreshes the screen with a list of processes every two to three seconds (user adjustable). From this list, you can reprioritize processes or **kill** them. Figure 5-1 shows a **top** screen.

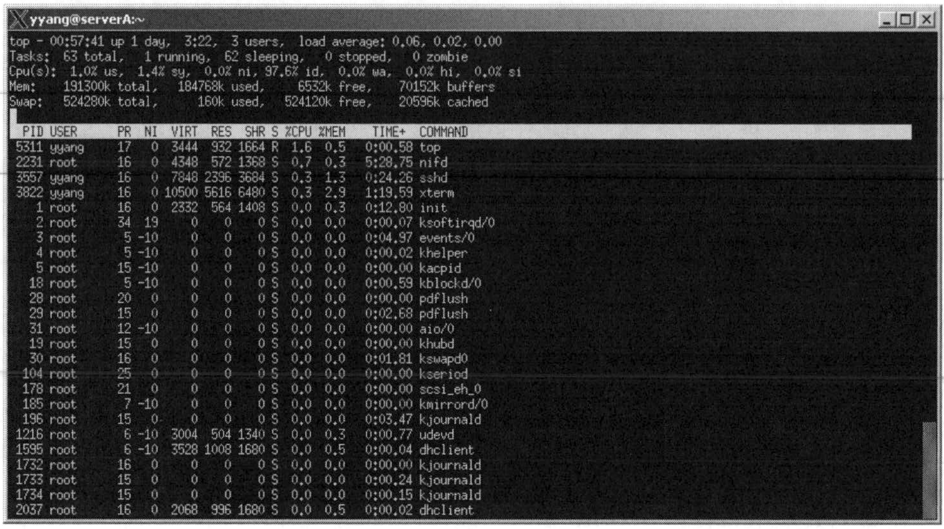

Figure 5-1. Top output

The **top** program's main disadvantage is that it's a CPU hog. On a congested system, this program tends to complicate system management issues. Users start running **top** to see what's going on, only to find several other people running the program as well, slowing down the system even more.

By default, **top** is shipped so that everyone can use it. You may find it prudent, depending on your environment, to restrict **top**'s use to root only. To do this, as root change the program's permissions with the following command:

```
[root@serverA ~]# chmod 0700    `which top`
```

Send a Signal to a Process: kill

This program's name is misleading: it doesn't really kill processes. What it does is send signals to running processes. The operating system, by default, supplies each process a standard set of *signal handlers* to deal with incoming signals. From a system administrator's standpoint, the most common handlers are for signals number 9 and 15, kill process and terminate process, respectively. When **kill** is invoked, it requires at least one parameter: the process identification number (PID) as derived from the **ps** command. When passed only the PID, **kill** sends signal 15. Some programs intercept this signal and perform a number of actions so that they can shut down cleanly. Others just stop running in their tracks. Either way, **kill** isn't a guaranteed method for making a process stop.

Signals

An optional parameter available for **kill** is **-n**, where the **n** represents a signal number. As system administrators, we are most interested in the signals 9 (kill) and 1 (hang up).

The kill signal, 9, is the impolite way of stopping a process. Rather than asking a process to stop, the operating system simply kills the process. The only time this will fail is when the process is in the middle of a system call (such as a request to open a file), in which case the process will die once it returns from the system call.

The hang-up signal, 1, is a bit of a throwback to the VT100 terminal days of UNIX. When a user's terminal connection dropped in the middle of a session, all of that terminal's running processes would receive a hang-up signal (often called a SIGHUP or HUP). This gave the processes an opportunity to perform a clean shutdown or, in the case of background processes, to ignore the signal. These days, a HUP is used to tell certain server applications to go and reread their configuration files (you'll see this in action in several of the later chapters). Most applications simply ignore the signal.

Security Issues

The ability to terminate a process is obviously a very powerful one, making security precautions important. Users may kill only processes they have permission to kill. If nonroot users attempt to send signals to processes other than their own, error messages are returned. The root user is the exception to this limitation; root may send signals to all processes in the system. Of course, this means root needs to exercise great care when using the **kill** command.

Examples Using the kill Command

> **NOTE** The following examples are very arbitrary; the PIDs used are completely fictitious and will be different on your system.

Use this command to terminate a process with PID number 205989:

```
[root@serverA ~]# kill 205989
```

For an almost guaranteed kill of process number 593999, issue this command:

```
[root@serverA ~]# kill -9 593999
```

Type the following to send the HUP signal to the **init** program (which is always PID 1):

```
[root@serverA ~]# kill -SIGHUP 1
```

This command is the same as typing

```
[root@serverA ~]# kill -1  1
```

MISCELLANEOUS TOOLS

The following tools don't fall into any specific category we've covered in this chapter. They all make important contributions to daily system administration chores.

Show System Name: uname

The **uname** program produces some system details that may be helpful in several situations. Maybe you've managed to remotely log in to a dozen different computers and have lost track of where you are! This tool is also helpful for script writers, because it allows them to change the path of a script according to the system information.

Here are the command-line parameters for **uname**:

Option for uname	Description
-m	Prints the machine hardware type (such as i686 for Pentium Pro and better architectures).
-n	Prints the machine's host name.
-r	Prints the operating system's release name.
-s	Prints the operating system's name.
-v	Prints the operating system's version.
-a	Prints all of the above.

To get the operating system's name and release, enter the following command:

```
[root@serverA ~]# uname -s -r
```

NOTE   The -s option may seem wasted (after all, we know this is Linux), but this parameter proves quite useful on almost all UNIX-like operating systems, as well. At an SGI workstation, **uname -s** will return IRIX, or SunOS at a Sun workstation. Folks who work in heterogeneous environments often write scripts that will behave differently depending on the OS, and **uname** with -s is a consistent way to determine that information.

Who Is Logged In: who

On systems that allow users to log in to other users' machines or special servers, you will want to know who is logged in. You can generate such a report by using the **who** command:

```
[yyang@serverA ~]$ who
yyang      pts/0          Mar  7 23:18  (10.45.45.2)
yyang      pts/1          Mar  8 01:12
root       pts/2          Mar  8 01:01  (10.45.45.2)
```

A Variation on who: w

The **w** command displays the same information that **who** does and a whole lot more. The details of the report include who is logged in, what their terminal is, where they are logged in from, how long they've been logged in, how long they've been idle, and their CPU utilization. The top of the report also gives you the same output as the **uptime** command.

```
[yyang@serverA ~]$ w
 01:18:44 up 1 day,  3:43,  3 users,  load average: 0.00, 0.00, 0.00
USER     TTY      FROM             LOGIN@   IDLE   JCPU   PCPU WHAT
yyang    pts/0    10.0.99.2        Mon23    0.00s  1:29   0.06s w
yyang    pts/1    -                Tue01    24:01m 0.53s  0.36s ssh 10.45.45.5 -l
root     pts/2    10.0.99.2        Tue01    1:05   0.56s  0.56s -bash
```

Switch User: su

This command was used earlier on, when we moved a user and its home directory, and now we'll discuss it briefly. Once you have logged in to the system as one user, you need not log out and back in again in order to assume another identity (root user, for instance). Instead, use the **su** command to switch. This command has very few command-line parameters.

Running **su** without any parameters will automatically try to make you the root user. You'll be prompted for the root password and, if you enter it correctly, will drop down to a root shell. If you are already the root user and want to switch to another ID, you don't need to enter the new password when you use this command.

For example, if you're logged in as the user yyang and want to switch to the root user, type this command:

```
[yyang@serverA ~]$ su
```

You will be prompted for root's password.

If you're logged in as root and want to switch to, say, user yyang, enter this command:

```
[root@serverA ~]# su  yyang
```

You will not be prompted for yyang's password.

The optional hyphen (-) parameter tells **su** to switch identities and run the login scripts for that user. For example, if you're logged in as root and want to switch over to user yyang with all of his login and shell configurations, type this command:

```
[root@serverA ~]# su - yyang
```

EDITORS

Editors are easily among the bulkiest of common tools, but they are also the most useful. Without them, making any kind of change to a text file would be a tremendous undertaking. Regardless of your Linux distribution, you will have gotten a few editors. You should take a few moments to get comfortable with them.

NOTE Not all distributions come with all of the editors listed here.

vi

The **vi** editor has been around UNIX-based systems since the 1970s, and its interface shows it. It is arguably one of the last editors to actually use a separate command mode and data entry mode; as a result, most newcomers find it unpleasant to use. But before you give **vi** the cold shoulder, take a moment to get comfortable with it. In difficult situations, you may not have a pretty graphical editor at your disposal, and **vi** is ubiquitous across all UNIX systems.

The version of **vi** that ships with Linux distributions is **vim** (VI iMproved). It has a lot of what made **vi** popular in the first place and many features that make it useful in today's typical environments (including a graphical interface if the X Window System is running).

To start **vi**, simply type

```
[yyang@serverA ~]$ vi
```

The **vim** editor has an online tutor that can help you get started with it quickly. To launch the tutor, type

```
[yyang@serverA ~]$ vimtutor
```

Another easy way to learn more about **vi** is to start it and enter **:help**. If you ever find yourself stuck in **vi**, press the ESC key several times and then type **:q!** to force an exit without saving. If you want to save the file, type **:wq**.

emacs

It has been argued that **emacs** is an operating system all by itself. It's big, feature-rich, expandable, programmable, and all-around amazing. If you're coming from a GUI background, you'll probably find **emacs** a pleasant environment to work with at first. On its face, it works like Notepad in terms of its interface. Yet underneath is a complete interface to the GNU development environment, a mail reader, a news reader, a Web browser, and even a psychiatrist (well, not exactly).

To start **emacs**, simply type

```
[yyang@serverA ~]$ emacs
```

Once **emacs** has started, you can visit the psychiatrist by pressing ESC-X and then typing **doctor**. To get help using **emacs**, press CTRL-H.

joe

Of the editors listed here, **joe** most closely resembles a simple text editor. It works much like Notepad and offers on-screen help. Anyone who remembers the original WordStar command set will be pleasantly surprised to see that all those brain cells hanging on to CTRL-K commands can be put back to use with **joe**.

To start **joe**, simply type

```
[yyang@serverA ~]$ joe
```

pico

The **pico** program is another editor inspired by simplicity. Typically used in conjunction with the Pine mail reading system, **pico** can also be used as a stand-alone editor. Like **joe**, it can work in a manner similar to Notepad, but **pico** uses its own set of key combinations. Thankfully, all available key combinations are always shown at the bottom of the screen.

To start **pico**, simply type

```
[yyang@serverA ~]$ pico
```

TIP The **pico** program will perform automatic word wraps. If you're using it to edit configuration files, for example, be careful that it doesn't word-wrap a line into two lines if it should really stay as one.

STANDARDS

One argument you hear regularly against Linux is that there are too many different distributions, and that by having multiple distributions, there is fragmentation. This fragmentation will eventually lead to different versions of incompatible Linuxes.

This is, without a doubt, complete nonsense that plays on "FUD" (Fear, Uncertainty, and Doubt). These types of arguments usually stem from a misunderstanding of the kernel and distributions. However, the Linux community has realized that it has grown past the stage of informal understandings about how things should be done. As a result, two major standards are actively being worked on.

The first standard is the File Hierarchy Standard (FHS). This is an attempt by many of the Linux distributions to standardize on a directory layout so that developers have an easy time making sure their applications work across multiple distributions without difficulty. As of this writing, Red Hat is almost completely compliant, and it is likely that most other distributions are as well.

The other standard is the Linux Standard Base Specification (LSB). Like the FHS, the LSB is a standards group that specifies what a Linux distribution should have in terms of libraries and tools.

A developer who assumes that a Linux machine complies only with the LSB and FHS is guaranteed to have an application that will work with all Linux installations. All of the major distributors have joined these standards groups. This should ensure that all desktop distributions will have a certain amount of common ground that a developer can rely on.

From a system administrator's point of view, these standards are interesting but not crucial to administering a Linux network. However, it never hurts to learn more about both. For more information on the FHS, go to their Web site at http://www.pathname .com/fhs. To find out more about the LSB, check out http://www.linuxbase.org.

SUMMARY

In this chapter, we discussed Linux's command-line interface through BASH, many command-line tools, and a few editors. As you continue through this book, you'll find many references to the information in this chapter, so be sure that you get comfortable with working at the command line. You may find it a bit annoying at first, especially if you are used to using a GUI for performing many of the basic tasks mentioned here— but stick with it. You may even find yourself eventually working faster at the command line than with the GUI!

Obviously, this chapter can't cover all the command-line tools available to you as part of your default Linux installation. It is highly recommend that you take some time to look into some of the reference books available. For a helpful but less comprehensive approach to the considerable detail of Linux systems, try the latest edition of *Linux in a Nutshell* (various editions for different systems, from O'Reilly and Associates). In addition, there are a wealth of texts on shell programming at various levels and from various points of view. Get whatever suits you; shell programming is a skill well worth learning even if you don't do system administration.

And above all else, R.T.F.M., that is, Read the *fine* manual (man pages).

CHAPTER 6

Booting and Shutting Down

A s operating systems have become more complex, the process of starting up and shutting down has become more comprehensive. Anyone who has undergone the transition from a straight DOS-based system to a Windows 2003/XP–based system has experienced this transition firsthand. Not only is the core operating system brought up and shut down, but also an impressive list of services must be started and stopped. Like Windows, Linux comprises an impressive list of services that are turned on as part of the boot procedure.

In this chapter, we discuss the bootstrapping of the Linux operating system with GRUB and LILO. We then step through the processes of starting up and shutting down the Linux environment. We discuss the scripts that automate this process as well as the parts of the process for which modification is acceptable.

NOTE Apply a liberal dose of common sense in following the practical exercises in this chapter on a real system. As you experiment with modifying startup and shutdown scripts, bear in mind that it is possible to bring your system to a nonfunctional state that cannot be recovered by rebooting. Don't mess with a production system; and if you must, first make sure that you back up all the files you wish to change; and most important, have a boot disk ready (or some other boot medium) that can help you recover.

BOOT LOADERS

For any operating system to boot on standard PC hardware you need what is called a *boot loader.* If you have only dealt with Windows on a PC, you have probably never needed to interact directly with a boot loader. The boot loader is the first software program that runs when a computer starts. It is responsible for handing over the control of the system to the operating system.

Typically, the boot loader will reside in the Master Boot Record (MBR) of the disk, and it knows how to get the operating system up and running. PartitionMagic comes with a tool called Boot Magic that supports Linux. The main choices that come with Linux distributions are GRUB (the Grand Unified Bootloader) and LILO (Linux Loader). We will mostly cover GRUB because it is the most common boot loader that ships with the newer distributions of Linux and because it also has a lot more features than LILO. A very brief mention of LILO is made for historical reasons only. Both LILO and GRUB can be configured to boot other nonnative operating systems.

GRUB

Most modern Linux distributions use GRUB as the default boot loader during installation. GRUB is the default boot loader for Fedora Core, RHEL, SuSE, Mandrake, and a host of other distributions of Linux. GRUB aims to be compliant with the Multi-boot Specification and offers many features.

> *NOTE*   You might notice that GRUB is a pre-1.0 release of software, also known as alpha software. Don't be frightened by this. Considering the fact that major Linux vendors use it in their installations, it is probably quality "alpha" code. Only bug fixes are being made to the code. The stable version of GRUB is also known as GRUB Legacy. GRUB 2 is going to be the next-generation GRUB.

The GRUB boot process happens in stages. Each stage is taken care of by special GRUB image files, with each preceding stage helping the next stage along. Two of the stages are essential, and any of the other stages are optional and dependent on the particular system setup.

Stage 1

The image file used in this stage is essential and is used for booting up GRUB in the first place. It is usually embedded in the MBR of a disk or in the boot sector of a partition. The file used in this stage is appropriately named **stage1**. A Stage 1 image can next either load Stage 1.5 or load Stage 2 directly.

Stage 2

The Stage 2 images actually consist of two types of images: the intermediate (optional image) and the actual **stage2** image file. To further blur things, the optional images are called Stage 1.5. The Stage 1.5 images serve as a bridge between Stage 1 and Stage 2. The Stage 1.5 images are file system specific; that is, they understand the semantics of one file system or the other.

The Stage 1.5 images have names of the form—*x*_stage_1_5 —where *x* can be a file system of type e2fs, reiserfs, fat, jfs, minix, xfs, etc. For example, the Stage 1.5 image that will be required to load an OS that resides on a FAT file system will have a name like **fat_stage1_5**. The Stage 1.5 images allow GRUB to access several file systems. When used, the Stage 1.5 image helps to locate the Stage 2 image as a file within the file system.

Next comes the actual **stage2** image. It is the core of GRUB. It contains the actual code to load the kernel that boots the OS, it displays the boot menu, and it also contains the GRUB shell from which GRUB commands can be entered. The GRUB shell is interactive and helps to make GRUB very flexible. For example, the shell can be used to boot items that are not currently listed in GRUB's boot menu or to bootstrap the OS from an alternate supported medium.

Other types of Stage 2 images are the **stage2_eltorito image**, the **nbgrub** image, and the **pxegrub** image. The stage2_eltorito image is a boot image for CD-ROMs. The nbgrub and **pxegrub** images are both network-type boot images that can be used to bootstrap a system over the network (using BOOTP, DHCP, PXE, Etherboot, or the like). A quick listing of the contents of the **/boot/grub** directory of most Linux distributions will show some of the GRUB images.

Conventions Used in GRUB

GRUB has its own special way of referring to devices (CD-ROM drives, floppy drives, hard disk drives, etc.). The device name has to be enclosed in parentheses, "()". GRUB starts numbering its devices and partitions from zero, *not* from one. Therefore, GRUB would refer to the master IDE hard drive on the primary IDE controller as (hd0), where "hd" means "hard disk" drive and the number zero means it is the primary IDE master.

In the same vein, GRUB will refer to the third partition on the fourth hard disk (i.e., the slave on the secondary IDE controller) as "(hd3,3)". To refer to the whole floppy disk in GRUB would mean "(fd0)"—where "fd" means "floppy disk".

Installing GRUB

Most Linux distributions will give you a choice to install and configure the boot loader during the initial operating system installation. Thus, you wouldn't normally need to manually install GRUB during normal system use.

However, there are times either by accident or by design that you don't have a boot loader. It could be by accident if you, for example, accidentally overwrite your boot sector or if another operating system accidentally wipes out GRUB. It could be by design if, for example, you want to set up your system to dual-boot with another operating system (Windows or another Linux distribution).

This section will walk you through getting GRUB installed (or reinstalled) on your system. There are several ways that this can be achieved. You can do it the easy way from within the running OS using the **grub-install** utility or using GRUB's native command-line interface. You can get to this interface using what is called a GRUB boot floppy, using a GRUB boot CD, or from a system that has the GRUB software installed.

> **NOTE**   GRUB is only installed once. Any modifications are stored in a text file, and any changes don't need to be written to the MBR or partition boot sector every time.

Backing Up the MBR

Before proceeding with the exercises that follow, it is a very good idea to make a backup of your current "known good" MBR. It is easy to do this using the **dd** command. Since the MBR of a PC's hard disk resides in the first 512 bytes of the disk, you can easily copy the first 512 bytes to a file (or to a floppy disk) by typing

```
[root@serverA ~]# dd  if=/dev/hda  of=/tmp/COPY_OF_MBR bs=512 count=1
1+0 records in
1+0 records out
```

This command will save the MBR into a file called **COPY_OF_MBR** under the **/tmp** directory.

Creating a Boot/Rescue CD

Another precautionary measure to take before performing any operation that can render a system unbootable is to create a rescue CD. The CD can then be used to boot the system in case of accidents (the CD can also be used for other purposes as well and should always be close at hand).

The boot CD is very system specific and is automatically built from current information extracted from your system. You will use the **mkbootdisk** command to generate an ISO image that can burned to a blank CD-ROM. To generate an ISO image named **BOOT-CD.iso** for your running kernel and save the image file under the **/tmp** directory, type

```
[root@serverA ~]# mkbootdisk --device /tmp/BOOT-CD.iso --iso `uname -r`
```

You will next need to find a way to burn/write the created CD image onto a blank CD. If you have a CD burner installed on the Linux box, you can use the **cdrecord** utility to achieve this by issuing the command

```
[root@serverA ~]# cdrecord speed=4 -eject --dev=/dev/hdc /tmp/BOOT-CD.iso
```

You should then date and label the disc accordingly with a descriptive name.

TIP   The **mkbootdisk** utility can also be used to create a boot floppy disk. But because of the differences between Linux kernels in the version 2.4 series and the version 2.6 series, it is no longer very straightforward to create a boot disk that will fit into the limited space (1.44MB) that a floppy disk offers. If you get your system to meet the size constraints, all you need to do to create a boot floppy is to insert a blank floppy disk into the drive and issue the command

```
[root@serverA ~]# mkbootdisk --device /dev/fd0 `uname -r`
```

Installing GRUB from the GRUB Shell

Now that we have dealt with the safety measures, we can proceed to exploring GRUB fully. In this section you will learn how to install GRUB natively using GRUB's command shell from inside the running Linux operating system. You will normally go this route if, for example, you currently have another type of boot loader (such as LILO or the NT Loader, ntldr) but you wish to replace or overwrite that boot loader with GRUB.

1. Launch GRUB's shell by issuing the **grub** command. Type

```
[root@serverA ~]# grub
GNU GRUB  version 0.95  (640K lower / 3072K upper memory)
 [ Minimal BASH-like line editing is supported.  For the first word, TAB
   lists possible command completions.  Anywhere else TAB lists the possible
   completions of a device/filename.]
grub>
```

2. Display GRUB's current root device. Type

```
grub> root
 (fd0): Filesystem type unknown, partition type 0x8e
```

The output shows that GRUB will by default use the first floppy disk drive (fd0) as its root device unless you tell it otherwise.

3. Set GRUB's root device to the partition that contains the boot directory on the local hard disk. Type

```
grub> root (hd0,0)
   Filesystem type is ext2fs, partition type 0x83
```

NOTE The boot directory may or may not be on the same partition that houses the root (/) directory. During the OS installation on our sample system, the **/boot** directory was stored on the /dev/hda1 partition, and hence we use the GRUB (hd0,0) device.

4. Make sure that the **stage1** image can be found on the root device. Type

```
grub> find  /grub/stage1
   (hd0,0)
```

The output means that the **stage1** image was located on the (hd0,0) device.

5. Finally install the GRUB boot loader directly on the MBR of the hard disk. Type

```
grub> setup (hd0)
 Checking if "/boot/grub/stage1" exists... no
 Checking if "/grub/stage1" exists... yes
 Checking if "/grub/stage2" exists... yes
 Checking if "/grub/e2fs_stage1_5" exists... yes
 Running "embed /grub/e2fs_stage1_5 (hd0)"...  16 sectors are embedded.
succeeded
 Running "install /grub/stage1 (hd0) (hd0)1+16 p (hd0,0)/grub/stage2
/grub/grub.conf"... succeeded
Done.
```

6. Quit the GRUB shell. Type

```
grub> quit
```

You are done. But you should note that you really didn't make any serious change to the system, because you simply reinstalled GRUB to the MBR (where it used to be). You would normally reboot at this point to make sure that everything is working as it should.

TIP A very simple-to-use script that can help you perform all the steps detailed in the preceding exercise with a single command is the **grub-install** script (see man grub-install). This method is not always perfect, and the authors of the GRUB software admit that it is a less safe route to take. But still—it almost always works just fine.

The GRUB Boot Floppy

Let's create a GRUB floppy. This will allow you to boot the system using the floppy disk and use GRUB to write or install itself to the MBR. This is especially useful if your system does not currently have a boot loader installed but you have access to another system that has GRUB installed.

The general idea behind using a GRUB boot floppy is that it is assumed that you currently have a system with an unbootable, or corrupt, or unwanted boot loader—and since the system cannot be booted by itself from the hard disk, you need another medium to bootstrap the system with. And so you can use a GRUB floppy disk or a GRUB CD. You want any means by which you can gain access to the GRUB shell, so that you can install GRUB into the MBR and then boot the OS.

You need to first locate the GRUB images, located by default in **/usr/share/grub/i386-redhat/** directory on a Fedora Core system (SuSE stores the GRUB image files in the **/usr/lib/grub/** directory).

Use the **dd** command to write the **stage1** and **stage2** images to the floppy disk.

1. Change to the directory that contains the GRUB images on your system. Type

   ```
   [root@serverA ~]# cd /usr/share/grub/i386-redhat/
   ```

2. Write the file **stage1** to the first 512 bytes of the floppy disk. Type

   ```
   [root@serverA i386-redhat]# dd if=stage1  of=/dev/fd0  bs=512 count=1
   1+0 records in
   1+0 records out
   ```

3. Write the **stage2** image right after the first image. Type

   ```
   [root@serverA i386-redhat]# dd if=stage2  of=/dev/fd0  bs=512 seek=1
   202+1 records in
   202+1 records out
   ```

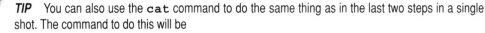

TIP You can also use the **cat** command to do the same thing as in the last two steps in a single shot. The command to do this will be

```
[root@serverA i386-redhat]# cat stage1 stage2 > /dev/fd0 .
```

Your GRUB floppy is now ready. You can now boot off of this floppy so that you can install the GRUB boot loader.

Installing GRUB on the MBR Using a GRUB Floppy

Make sure that the GRUB floppy you created is inserted into the floppy disk drive. Reboot the system and use the floppy as your boot medium (adjust the BIOS settings if necessary). After the system has booted off the GRUB floppy, you will be presented with a **grub>** prompt.

Set the root device for GRUB to your boot partition (or the partition that contains the **/boot** directory). On our sample system, the **/boot** directory resides on the /dev/hda1 (hd0,0) partition. To do this, type the following command:

```
grub> root (hd0,0)
```

Now you can write GRUB to the MBR by using the **setup** command:

```
grub> setup (hd0,0)
```

That's it, you are done. You may now reboot the system *without* the GRUB floppy. This is a good way to let GRUB reclaim management of the MBR, if it had previously been overwritten by another boot manager.

Configuring GRUB

Since you only have to install GRUB once on the MBR or partition of your choice, you have the luxury of simply editing a text file, **/boot/grub/menu.1st**. When you are done editing this file, you can simply reboot and select the new kernel that you added to the configuration. The configuration file looks like the following (please note that line numbers 1–16 have been added to the output to aid readability):

```
[root@serverA ~]# cat /etc/grub.conf
1) # grub.conf generated by anaconda
2) # Note that you do not have to rerun grub after making changes to this file
3) # NOTICE:  You have a /boot partition.  This means that
4) #          all kernel and initrd paths are relative to /boot/, eg.
5) #          root (hd0,0)
6) #          kernel /vmlinuz-version ro root=/dev/VolGroup00/LogVol00
7) #          initrd /initrd-version.img
8) #boot=/dev/had
9) default=0
10) timeout=5
11) splashimage=(hd0,0)/grub/splash.xpm.gz
12) hiddenmenu
13) title Fedora Core (2.6.11-1.1369_FC4)
14) root (hd0,0)
15) kernel /vmlinuz-2.6.11-1.1369_FC4 ro root=/dev/VolGroup00/LogVol00
16) initrd /initrd-2.6.11-1.1369_FC4.img
```

The entries in the preceding sample configuration file for GRUB are discussed here:

▼ **Lines 1–8** All lines that begin with the pound sign (#) are comments and are ignored.

■ **Line 9, default** This directive tells GRUB which entry to automatically boot. The numbering starts from zero. The preceding sample file contains only one entry—the entry titled "Fedora Core (2.6.11-1.1369_FC4)".

■ **Line 10, timeout** This means that GRUB will automatically boot the default entry after five seconds. This can be interrupted by pressing any key on the keyboard before the counter runs out.

■ **Line 11, splashimage** This line specifies the name and location of an image file to be displayed at the boot menu. This is optional and can be any custom image that fits GRUB's specifications.

- Line 12, **hiddenmenu**   This entry hides the usual GRUB menu. It is an optional entry.

- Line 13, **title**   This is used to display a short title or description for the following entry it defines. The title field marks the beginning of a new boot entry in GRUB.

- Line 14, **root**   You should notice from the preceding listing that GRUB still maintains its device naming convention (e.g., (hd0,0) instead of the usual Linux /dev/hda1).

- Line 15, **kernel**   Used for specifying the path to a kernel image. The first argument is the path to the kernel image in a partition. Any other arguments are passed to the kernel as boot parameters.

  Note that the path names are relative to the **/boot** directory, so for example, instead of specifying the path to the kernel to be "/boot/vmlinuz-2.6.11-1.1369_FC4", GRUB's configuration file references this path as "/vmlinuz-2.6.11-1.1369_FC4".

- ▲ Line 16, **initrd**   The **initrd** option allows you to load kernel modules from an image, not the modules from **/lib/modules**. See the GRUB info pages, available through the **info** command, for more information on the configuration options.

NOTE   You might be wondering what the **initrd** option is really for. Basically, this allows distributions to use a generic kernel that only supports the native Linux file system, which is currently ext3. The problem that occurs is that you might need a file system module to load all of your new modules—if you chose to install the ReiserFS file system, for example. This is a chicken and egg problem; that is, which came first. The solution is to provide the kernel with an image that contains necessary loadable modules to get the rest of the modules.

Adding a New Kernel to Boot with GRUB

In this section you will learn how to manually add a new boot entry to GRUB's configuration file. If you are compiling and installing a new kernel by hand, you will need to do this so that you can boot into the new kernel to test it or use it. If, on the other hand, you are installing or upgrading the Linux kernel using a prepackaged RPM, this is usually automatically done for you.

Because you don't have any new Linux kernel to install on the system, you will only add a dummy entry to GRUB's configuration file in this exercise. The new entry will not do anything useful—it is only being done for illustration purposes.

Here's a summary of what we will be walking you through:

You will make a copy of the current default kernel that your system uses and call the copy **duplicate-kernel**. You will also make a copy of the corresponding **initrd** image for the kernel and name the copy **duplicate-initrd**. Both files should be saved into the **/boot** directory. You will then create an entry for the supposedly new kernel and give it a descriptive title such as "**The Duplicate Kernel**."

In addition to the preceding boot entry, you will also create another entry that does nothing more than to change the foreground and background colors of GRUB's boot menu.

Let's begin:

1. Change your current working directory to the **/boot** directory. Type

   ```
   [root@serverA ~]# cd /boot
   ```

2. Make a copy of your current kernel and name the copy **duplicate-kernel**. Type

   ```
   [root@serverA ~]# cp vmlinuz-2.6.11-1.1369_FC4 duplicate-kernel
   ```

3. Make a copy of the corresponding **initrd** image and name the copy **duplicate-initrd**. Type

   ```
   [root@serverA ~]# cp initrd-2.6.11-1.1369_FC4.img duplicate-initrd.img
   ```

4. Create an entry for the new pseudo-kernels in the **/boot/grub/menu.1st** configuration file, using any text editor you are comfortable with (the **vim** editor is used in this example). Type the following text at the end of the file:

   ```
   title The Duplicate Kernel
           color yellow/black
           root (hd0,0)
           kernel /duplicate-kernel ro root=/dev/VolGroup00/LogVol00
           initrd /duplicate-initrd.img
   ```

5. Create another entry that will change the foreground and background colors of the menu when selected. The menu colors will be changed to yellow and black when this entry is selected. Enter the following text at the end of the file (beneath the entry you created in the preceding step):

   ```
   title The change color entry
           color yellow/black
   ```

6. Comment out the splashimage entry at the top of the file. The presence of the splash image will prevent your new custom foreground and background colors from displaying properly. The commented-out entry for the splash image will look like this:

   ```
   #splashimage=(hd0,0)/grub/splash.xpm.gz
   ```

7. Finally, comment out the hiddenmenu entry from the file so that the Boot menu will appear showing your new entries instead of being hidden. The commented-out entry should look like

   ```
   #hiddenmenu
   ```

8. Save the changes you made to the file and reboot the system.

The final **/boot/grub/menu.1st** file (with some of the comment fields removed) will resemble the one shown here:

```
[root@serverA boot]# cat /boot/grub/menu.1st
# grub.conf generated by anaconda
default=0
timeout=5
#splashimage=(hd0,0)/grub/splash.xpm.gz
#hiddenmenu
title Fedora Core (2.6.11-1.1369_FC4)
        root (hd0,0)
        kernel /vmlinuz-2.6.11-1.1369_FC4 ro root=/dev/VolGroup00/LogVol00
        initrd /initrd-2.6.11-1.1369_FC4.img
title The Duplicate Kernel
        color yellow/black
        root (hd0,0)
        kernel /duplicate-kernel ro root=/dev/VolGroup00/LogVol00
        initrd /duplicate-initrd.img
title The change color entry
        color yellow/black
```

When the system reboots, you should see a GRUB menu similar to the one shown here:

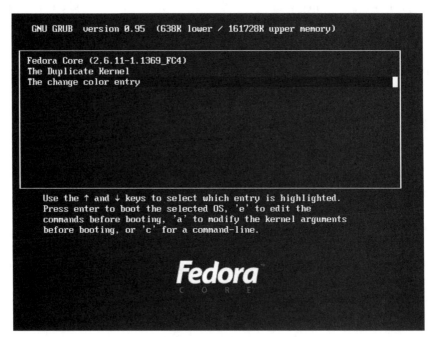

9. After the GRUB menu appears, select "The Change Color Entry" and press ENTER. The color of the menu should change to the color you specified in the **menu.1st** file using the color directive.

10. Finally, verify that you are able to boot the new kernel entry that you created, that is, the "duplicate kernel entry." Select the entry for "The Duplicate Kernel" and then press ENTER.

LILO

LILO, short for Linux Loader, is a boot manager. It allows you to boot multiple operating systems, provided each system exists on its own partition. (Under PC-based systems, the *entire* boot partition must also exist beneath the 1024-cylinder boundary.) In addition to booting multiple operating systems, with LILO you can choose various kernel configurations or versions to boot. This is especially handy when you're trying kernel upgrades before adopting them.

The big picture with LILO is straightforward: a configuration file (**/etc/lilo.conf**) specifies which partitions are bootable and, if a partition is Linux, which kernel to load. When the **/sbin/lilo** program runs, it takes this partition information and rewrites the boot sector with the necessary code to present the options as specified in the configuration file. At boot time, a prompt (usually `lilo:`) is displayed, and you have the option of specifying the operating system. (Usually, a default can be selected after a timeout period.) LILO loads the necessary code, the kernel, from the selected partition and passes full control over to it.

LILO is what is known as a two-stage boot loader. The first stage loads LILO itself into memory and prompts you for booting instructions with the `"lilo:"` prompt or a colorized boot menu. Once you select the OS to boot and press ENTER, LILO enters the second stage, booting the Linux operating system.

As was stated earlier in the chapter, LILO has somewhat fallen out of favor with most of the newer distributions of Linux. Some of the distributions do not even give you the option of selecting or choosing LILO as your boot manager!

TIP   If you are familiar with the MS Windows boot process, you can think of LILO as comparable to the OS loader (NTLDR). Similarly, the LILO configuration file, **/etc/lilo.conf**, is comparable to **BOOT.INI** (which is typically hidden from view).

Bootstrapping

In this section, I'll assume you are already familiar with the boot process of other operating systems and thus already know the boot cycle of your hardware. This section will cover the process of bootstrapping the operating system. We'll begin with the Linux boot loader (usually GRUB for PCs).

Kernel Loading

Once GRUB has started and you have selected Linux as the operating system to boot, the very first thing to get loaded is the kernel. Keep in mind that no operating system exists in memory at this point, and PCs (by their unfortunate design) have no easy way to access all of their memory. Thus, the kernel must load completely into the first megabyte of available RAM. In order to accomplish this, the kernel is compressed. The head of the file contains the code necessary to bring the CPU into protected mode (thereby removing the memory restriction) and decompress the remainder of the kernel.

Kernel Execution

With the kernel in memory, it can begin executing. It knows only whatever functionality is built into it, which means any parts of the kernel compiled as modules are useless at this point. At the very minimum, the kernel must have enough code to set up its virtual memory subsystem and root file system (usually, the ext3 file system). Once the kernel has started, a hardware probe determines what device drivers should be initialized. From here, the kernel can *mount* the root file system. (You could draw a parallel of this process to that of Windows being able to recognize and access its C drive.) The kernel mounts the root file system and starts a program called **init**, which is discussed in the next section.

THE INIT PROCESS

The **init** process is the first nonkernel process that is started, and therefore it always gets the process ID number of 1. **init** reads its configuration file, **/etc/inittab**, and determines the *runlevel* where it should start. Essentially, a runlevel dictates the system's behavior. Each level (designated by an integer between 0 and 6) serves a specific purpose. A runlevel of **initdefault** is selected if it exists; otherwise, you are prompted to supply a runlevel value.

The runlevel values are as follows:

0	Halt the system
1	Enter single-user mode (no networking is enabled)
2	Multiuser mode, but without NFS
3	Full multiuser mode (normal operation)
4	Unused
5	Same as runlevel 3, except using an X Window System login rather than a text-based login
6	Reboot the system

When it is told to enter a runlevel, **init** executes a script as dictated by the **/etc/inittab** file. The default runlevel that the system boots into is determined by the `initdefault` entry in the **/etc/inittab** file. If, for example, the entry in the file is

```
id:3:initdefault:
```

this means that the system will boot into runlevel 3. But if, on the other hand, the entry in the file is

```
id:5:initdefault:
```

this means the system will boot into runlevel 5, with the X Window subsystem running with a graphical login screen.

RC SCRIPTS

In the preceding section, we mentioned that the **/etc/inittab** file specifies which scripts to run when runlevels change. These scripts are responsible for either starting or stopping the services that are particular to the runlevel.

Because of the number of services that need to be managed, **rc** scripts are used. The main one, **/etc/rc.d/rc**, is responsible for calling the appropriate scripts in the correct order for each runlevel. As you can imagine, such a script could easily become extremely uncontrollable! To keep this from happening, a slightly more elaborate system is used.

For each runlevel, a subdirectory exists in the **/etc/rc.d** directory. These runlevel subdirectories follow the naming scheme of **rcX.d**, where X is the runlevel. For example, all the scripts for runlevel 3 are in **/etc/rc.d/rc3.d**.

In the runlevel directories, symbolic links are made to scripts in the **/etc/rc.d/init.d** directory. Instead of using the name of the script as it exists in the **/etc/rc.d/init.d** directory, however, the symbolic links are prefixed with an **S** if the script is to start a service, or with a **K** if the script is to stop (or kill) a service. Note that these two letters are case sensitive. You must use uppercase letters or the startup scripts will not recognize them.

In many cases, the order in which these scripts are run makes a difference. (For example, you can't start services that rely on a configured network interface without first enabling and configuring the network interface!) To enforce order, a two-digit number is suffixed to the **S** or **K**. Lower numbers execute before higher numbers; for example, **/etc/rc.d/rc3.d/ S10network** runs before **/etc/rc.d/rc3.d/S55sshd** (**S10network** configures the network settings, and **S55sshd** starts the SSH server).

The scripts pointed to in the **/etc/rc.d/init.d** directory are the workhorses; they perform the actual process of starting and stopping services. When **/etc/rc.d/rc** runs through a specific runlevel's directory, it invokes each script in numerical order. It first runs the scripts that begin with a **K**, and then the scripts that begin with an **S**. For scripts starting with **K,** a parameter of `stop` is passed. Likewise, for scripts starting with **S**, the parameter `start` is passed.

Let's peer into the **/etc/rc.d/rc3.d** directory and see what's there:

```
[root@serverA ~]# ls -l /etc/rc.d/rc3.d/
total 232
lrwxrwxrwx  1 root root 13 Jun 14 00:29 K01yum -> ../init.d/yum
lrwxrwxrwx  1 root root 24 Jun 14 00:29 K02NetworkManager -> ../init.d/Net..
lrwxrwxrwx  1 root root 34 Jun 14 00:29 K02NetworkManDisp.. -> ../init.d/...
lrwxrwxrwx  1 root root 19 Jun 14 00:28 K05saslauthd -> ../init.d/saslauthd
lrwxrwxrwx  1 root root 16 Jun 14 00:29 K10psacct -> ../init.d/psacct
lrwxrwxrwx  1 root root 14 Jun 14 00:29 S55sshd -> ../init.d/sshd
...<OUTPUT TRUNCATED>...
```

From the preceding sample output, you will see that "**K05saslauthd**" is one of the many files in the **/etc/rc.d/rc3.d** directory (Line 5). Thus, when the file **K05saslauthd** is executed or invoked, the command actually being executed instead is

```
#/etc/rc.d/init.d/saslauthd stop
```

By the same token, if **S55sshd** is invoked, the following command is what really gets run:

```
#/etc/rc.d/init.d/sshd start
```

Writing Your Own rc Script

In the course of keeping a Linux system running, at some point you will need to modify the startup or shutdown script. There are two roads you can take to doing this:

If your change is to take effect at boot time only, and the change is small, you may want to simply edit the **/etc/rc.d/rc.local** script. This script gets run at the very end of the boot process.

On the other hand, if your addition is more elaborate and/or requires that the shutdown process explicitly stop, you should add a script to the **/etc/rc.d/init.d** directory. This script should take the parameters **start** and **stop** and act accordingly.

Of course, the first option, editing the **/etc/rc.d/rc.local** script, is the easier of the two. To make additions to this script, simply open it in your editor of choice and append the commands you want run at the end. This is good for simple one- or two-line changes.

If you do need a separate script, however, you will need to take the second option. The process of writing an **rc** script is not as difficult as it may seem. Let's step through it using an example, to see how it works. (You can use our example as a skeleton script, by the way, changing it to add anything you need.)

Assume you want to start a special program that pops up a message every hour and reminds you that you need to take a break from the keyboard (a good idea if you don't want to get carpal tunnel syndrome!). The script to start this program will include the following:

▼ A description of the script's purpose (so that you don't forget it a year later)

■ Verification that the program really exists before trying to start it

▲ Acceptance of the **start** and **stop** parameters and performance of the required actions

NOTE Lines starting with a pound sign (#) are only comments and not part of the script's actions, *except* for the first line.

Given these parameters, let's begin creating the script.

Creating the carpald.sh Script

First we'll create the script that will perform the actual function that we want. The script is very unsophisticated, but it will serve our purpose here. A description of what the script does is embedded in its comment fields.

1. Launch any text editor of your choice and input the text that follows:

```
#!/bin/sh
#
#Description: This simple script will send a mail to any email address
#specified in ADDR variable every hour, reminding the user to take a
#break from the computer to avoid the carpal tunnel syndrome. The script
#has such little intelligence, that it will always send an email as long
#as the system is up and running - even when the user is fast asleep!!
#So don't forget to disable it after the fact.
#Author: Wale Soyinka
#
ADDR=root@localhost
while true
  do
  sleep 1h
  echo  "Get up and take a break NOW !!"  | \
      mail -s "Carpal Tunnel Warning" $ADDR
done
```

2. Save the text of the script into a file called **carpald.sh**.

3. You next need to make the script executable. Type

   `[root@serverA ~]# chmod  755   carpald.sh`

4. Copy or move the script over to the directory where our start-up scripts will find it, that is, the **/usr/local/sbin/** directory. Type

   `[root@serverA ~]# mv   carpald.sh  /usr/local/sbin/`

Creating the Startup Script

Here you will create the actual startup script that will be executed during system startup and shutdown. The file you create here will be called **carpald**. The file will be **chkconfig**-enabled. This means that if we want, we can use the **chkconfig** utility to control the runlevels at which the program starts and stops. This is a very useful and time-saving functionality.

1. Launch any text editor of your choice and input the text that follows:

```
#!/bin/sh
#Carpal          Start/Stop the Carpal Notice Daemon
#
#chkconfig:    35   99  01
# description: Carpald is a program which wakes up every 1 hour and
#                 tells us that we need to take a break from the keyboard
#                 or we'll lose all functionality of our wrists and never
#                 be able to type again as long as we live.
# Source function library.
. /etc/rc.d/init.d/functions

[ -f /usr/local/sbin/carpald.sh ] || exit 0

# See how we were called.
case "$1" in
  start)
        echo  "Starting carpald: "
        /usr/local/sbin/carpald.sh &
        echo  "done"
        touch /var/lock/subsys/carpald
        ;;
  stop)
        echo -n "Stopping carpald services: "
        echo "done"
        killall -q -9  carpald &
        rm -f /var/lock/subsys/carpald
        ;;
  status)
        status carpald
        ;;
  restart|reload)
        $0 stop
        $0 start
        ;;
  *)
        echo "Usage: carpald start|stop|status|restart|reload"
        exit 1
esac
exit 0
```

A few comments about the preceding startup script:

▼ Even though the very first line of the script begins with "#!/bin/sh", it should be noted that **/bin/sh** is a symbolic link to **/bin/bash**. This is not the case on other UNIX systems.

■ The line "chkconfig: 35 99 01" is actually very important to the **chkconfig** utility that we want to use. The numbers "35" means that **chkconfig** should create startup and stop entries for programs in runlevels 3 and 5 by default, i.e., entries will be created in the **/etc/rc.d/rc3.d** and **/etc/rc.d/rc5.d** directories.

▲ The fields "99" and "01" means that **chkconfig** should set the startup priority of our program to be 99 and the stop priority to be 01, i.e., start up late and end early.

2. Save the text of the script into a file called **carpald**.

3. You next need to make the file executable. Type

```
[root@serverA ~]# chmod  755   carpald
```

4. Copy or move the script over to the directory where startup scripts are stored, i.e., the **/etc/rc.d/init.d/** directory. Type

```
[root@serverA ~]# mv   carpald  /etc/rc.d/init.d/
```

5. Now you need to tell **chkconfig** about the existence of this new start/stop script and what we want it to do with it. Type

```
[root@serverA ~]# chkconfig  --add carpald
```

This will automatically create the symbolic links listed for you here:

```
lrwxrwxrwx  1 root root   17 Dec  4 09:37 /etc/rc.d/rc0.d/K01carpald -> ../init.d/carpald
lrwxrwxrwx  1 root root   17 Dec 4 09:37 /etc/rc.d/rc1.d/K01carpald -> ../init.d/carpald
lrwxrwxrwx  1 root root   17 Dec 4 09:37 /etc/rc.d/rc2.d/K01carpald -> ../init.d/carpald
lrwxrwxrwx  1 root root   17 Dec 4 09:37 /etc/rc.d/rc3.d/S99carpald -> ../init.d/carpald
lrwxrwxrwx  1 root root   17 Dec 4 09:37 /etc/rc.d/rc4.d/K01carpald -> ../init.d/carpald
lrwxrwxrwx  1 root root   17 Dec 4 09:37 /etc/rc.d/rc5.d/S99carpald -> ../init.d/carpald
lrwxrwxrwx  1 root root   17 Dec 4 09:37 /etc/rc.d/rc6.d/K01carpald -> ../init.d/carpald
```

(The meaning and significance of the **K** (kill) and **S** (start) prefixes in the preceding listing was explained earlier.)

This may all appear rather elaborate, but the good news is that because you've set up this **rc** script, you won't ever need to do it again. More important, the script will automatically run during startup and shutdown and be able to manage itself. The overhead up front is well worth the long-term benefits of avoiding carpal tunnel syndrome!

6. Use the **service** command to find out the status of the **carpald.sh** program. Type

```
[root@serverA ~]# service carpald status
carpald is stopped
```

7. Manually start the **carpald** program to make sure that it will indeed start up correctly upon system startup. Type

```
[root@serverA ~]# service carpald start
Starting carpald:
done
```

TIP   If you wait about an hour, you should see a mail message from the **carpald.sh** script. You can use the **mail** program from the command line by typing:

```
[root@serverA ~]# mail
Mail version 8.1 6/6/93. Type ? for help.
"/var/spool/mail/root": 1 message 1 new
>N 1 root@serverA.example Fri Dec 4 11:49 16/677 "Carpal Tunnel Warning"
&
```

Type **q** at the ampersand (&) prompt to quit the mail program.

8. Next stop the program. Type

```
[root@serverA ~]# service carpald stop
Stopping carpald services: done
```

9. We are done. Now is a good time to prevent the **carpald** script from starting up with the system in the future. Type

```
[root@serverA ~]# chkconfig  --del carpald
```

ENABLING AND DISABLING SERVICES

At times, you may find that you simply don't need a particular service to be started at boot time. This is especially true if you are considering Linux as a replacement for a Windows NT file and print server and you need only very specific services and nothing else.

As described in the preceding sections, you can cause a service not to be started by simply renaming the symbolic link in a particular runlevel directory; rename it to start with a **K** instead of an **S**. Once you are comfortable working with the command line, you'll quickly find that it is very easy to enable or disable a service.

The startup runlevels of the service/program can also be managed using the **chkconfig** utility. To view all the runlevels in which the **carpald.sh** program is configured to start up, type

```
[root@serverA ~]# chkconfig --list carpald
carpald           0:off    1:off    2:off    3:on    4:off    5:on     6:off
```

To make the **carpald.sh** program start up automatically in runlevel 2, type

```
[root@serverA ~]# chkconfig --level 2 carpald  on
```

If you check the list of runlevels for the **carpald.sh** program again, you will see that the field for runlevel 2 has been changed from 2:off to 2:on. Type

```
[root@serverA ~]# chkconfig --list carpald
carpald          0:off   1:off   2:on    3:on    4:off   5:on    6:off
```

There are also GUI tools available that will help you manage which services start up at any given runlevel. In Fedora and other Red Hat–type systems (including RHEL), one such tool is the **system-config-services** utility (see Figure 6-1). To launch the program, type

```
[root@serverA ~]# system-config-services
```

On a system running SuSE Linux, the equivalent GUI program (see Figure 6-2) can be launched by typing

```
serverA:~ yast2  runlevel
```

or

```
serverA:~ yast   runlevel
```

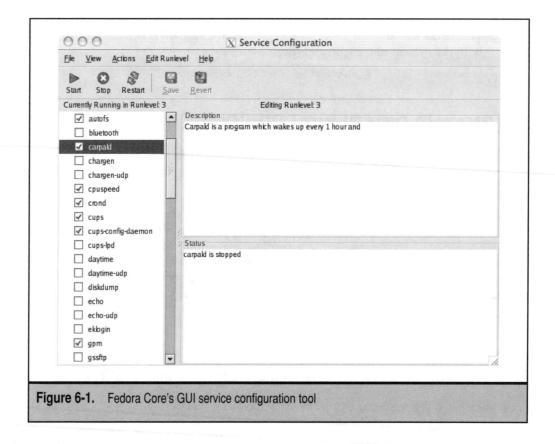

Figure 6-1. Fedora Core's GUI service configuration tool

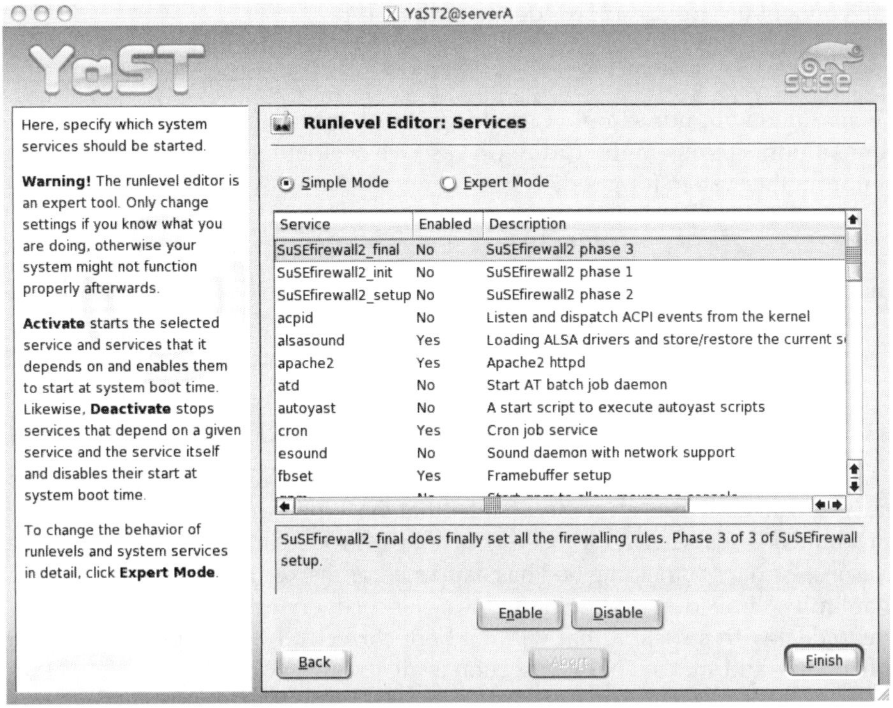

Figure 6-2.   SuSE's GUI runlevel editor

Although a GUI tool is a nice way to do this task, you may find yourself in a situation where it is just not convenient or available.

Disabling a Service

To completely disable a service, you must at a minimum know the name of the service. You can then use the **chkconfig** tool to permanently turn it off from starting in all run-levels.

For example, to disable our "life saving" **carpald.sh** program, you could type

```
[root@serverA ~]# chkconfig  carpald off
```

If you check the list of runlevels for the **carpald.sh** program again, you will see that it has been turned off for all runlevels. Type

```
[root@serverA ~]# chkconfig --list carpald
carpald          0:off    1:off    2:off    3:off    4:off    5:off    6:off
```

To permanently remove the **carpald.sh** program from under the **chkconfig** utility's control, you will use **chkconfig**'s delete option. Type

```
[root@serverA ~]# chkconfig --del carpald
```

We are done with our sample **carpald.sh** script, and to prevent it from flooding us with e-mail notifications in the future (in case we accidentally turn it back on), we can delete it from the system for good. Type

```
[root@serverA ~]# rm -f /usr/local/sbin/carpald.sh
```

And those are the ABC's of how services start up and shut down automatically in Linux. Now go out and take a break.

ODDS AND ENDS OF BOOTING AND SHUTTING DOWN

Most Linux administrators do not like to shut down their Linux servers. It spoils their uptime (you will recall from an earlier chapter that the "uptime" is a thing of pride for Linux system admins). Thus when a Linux box has to be rebooted, it is usually for very unavoidable reasons. Perhaps something bad has happened or the kernel has been upgraded.

Thankfully, Linux does an excellent job of self-recovery even during reboots. It is rare to have to deal with a system that will not boot correctly, but that is not to say that it'll never happen—and that's what this section is all about.

fsck!

Making sure that data on a system's hard disk is in a consistent state is a very important function. This function is partly controlled by a runlevel script and another file called the **/etc/fstab** file. The File System Check (**fsck**) tool is automatically run as necessary on every boot as specified by the presence or absence of a file named **/.autofsck** and also as specified by the **/etc/fstab** file. The purpose of the **fsck** program is similar to that of Windows Scandisk: to check and repair any damage on the file system before continuing the boot process. Because of its critical nature, **fsck** is traditionally placed very early in the boot sequence.

If you were able to do a clean shutdown, the **/.autofsck** file will be deleted and **fsck** will run without incident as specified in the **/etc/fstab** file (as specified in the sixth field— see the fstab manual page at man fstab). However, if for some reason you had to perform a hard shutdown (such as having to press the reset button), **fsck** will need to run through all of the local disks listed in the **/etc/fstab** file and check them. (And it isn't uncommon for the system administrator to be cursing through the process.)

If **fsck** does need to run, don't panic. It is unlikely you'll have any problems. However, if something does arise, **fsck** will prompt you with information about the problem and ask whether you want to repair it. In general, you'll find that answering "yes" is the right thing to do.

Most of the newer distributions of Linux use what is called a journaling file system, and this makes it easy and quicker to recover from file system inconsistencies that might arise from unclean shutdowns and other minor software errors. Examples of file systems with this journaling capability are ext3, ReiserFS, jfs, and xfs.

If you are running the new ext3 or ReiserFS file system, for example, you will notice that recovering from unclean system resets will be much quicker and easier. The only tradeoff with running a journaled file system is the overhead involved in keeping the journal, and even this depends on the method by which the file system implements its journaling.

Booting into Single-User ("Recovery") Mode

Under Windows, the concept of "Recovery Mode" was borrowed from a long-time UNIX feature of booting into single-user mode. What this means for you under Linux is that if something gets broken in the startup scripts that affects the booting process of a host, it is possible for you to boot into this mode, make the fix, and then allow the system to boot into complete multiuser mode (normal behavior).

If you are using the GRUB boot loader, these are the steps:

1. First you need to select the GRUB entry that you want to boot from the GRUB menu and then press the E key. You will next be presented with a submenu with various directives (directives from the **/boot/grub/menu.1st** file).

2. Select the entry label kernel and press E again. Now you can add the keyword `single` (or the letter s) to the end of the line. Press ENTER to go back to the GRUB boot menu, then press B to boot the kernel into single-user mode.

3. When you boot into single-user mode, the Linux kernel will boot as normal, except when it gets to the point where it starts the **init** program, it will only go through runlevel 1 and then stop. (See previous sections in this chapter for a description of all the runlevels.) Depending on the system configuration, you will either be prompted for the root password or simply given a shell prompt. If prompted for a password, type in the root password and press ENTER, and you will get the shell prompt.

4. In this mode, you'll find that almost all the services that are normally started are not running. This includes network configuration. So if you need to change the IP address, gateway, netmask, or any network-related configuration file, you can. This is also a good time to run `fsck` manually on any partitions that could not be automatically checked and recovered. (The `fsck` program will tell you which partitions are misbehaving, if any).

TIP In single-user mode of many Linux distributions, only the root partition will be automatically mounted for you. If you need to access any other partitions, you will need to mount them yourself using the `mount` command. You can see all of the partitions that you can mount in the **/etc/fstab** file.

5. Once you have made any changes you need to make, simply press CTRL-D. This will exit single-user mode and continue with the booting process, or you can just issue the reboot command to reboot the system.

SUMMARY

This chapter looked at the various aspects involved with starting up and shutting down a typical Linux system. We started our exploration with the almighty boot loader. We looked at GRUB in particular as a sample boot loader/manager because it is the boot loader of choice among the popular Linux distributions. Next we explored how things (or services) typically get started and stopped in Linux and how Linux decides what to start and stop and at which runlevel it is supposed to do this. We even wrote a little shell program, as a demonstration, that helps us to avoid carpal tunnel syndrome. We then went ahead and configured the system to automatically start up the program at specific runlevels.

CHAPTER 7

File Systems

File systems are the mechanisms by which the data on a storage medium gets organized. They provide all of the abstraction layers above sectors and cylinders of disks. In this chapter, we'll discuss the composition and management of these abstraction layers supported by Linux. Particular attention will be given to the default Linux file system, ext2/ext3.

We will also cover the many aspects of managing disks. This includes creating partitions and volumes, establishing file systems, automating the process by which they are mounted at boot time, and dealing with them after a system crash. We will also touch on Logical Volume Management (LVM) concepts.

> **NOTE** Before beginning your study of this chapter, you should already be familiar with files, directories, permissions, and ownership in the Linux environment. If you haven't yet read Chapter 5, it's best to read that chapter before continuing.

THE MAKEUP OF FILE SYSTEMS

Let's begin by going over the structure of file systems under Linux. It will help to clarify your understanding of the concept and let you see more easily how to take advantage of the architecture.

i-Nodes

The most fundamental building block of many UNIX file systems (including Linux's ext2) is the *i-node*. An i-node is a control structure that points either to other i-nodes or to data blocks.

The control information in the i-node includes the file's owner, permissions, size, time of last access, creation time, group ID, and so on. (For the truly curious, the entire kernel data structure is available in **/usr/src/linux/include/linux/ext2_fs.h**—assuming, of course, that you have the source tree installed in the **/usr/src** directory.) The one thing an i-node *does not* keep is the file's name.

As mentioned in Chapter 5, directories themselves are special instances of files. This means each directory gets an i-node, and the i-node points to data blocks containing information (filenames and i-nodes) about the files in the directory. Figure 7-1 illustrates the organization of i-nodes and data blocks in the ext2 file system.

As you can see in Figure 7-1, the i-nodes are used to provide *indirection* so that more data blocks can be pointed to—which is why each i-node does not contain the filename. (Only one i-node works as a representative for the entire file; thus, it would be a waste of space if every i-node contained filename information.) Take for example a 6GB disk that contains 1,079,304 i-nodes. If every i-node consumed 256 bytes to store the filename, a total of about 33MB would be wasted in storing filenames, even if they weren't being used!

Each indirect block can point in turn to other indirect blocks if necessary. With up to three layers of indirection, it is possible to store files with very large sizes on a Linux file system.

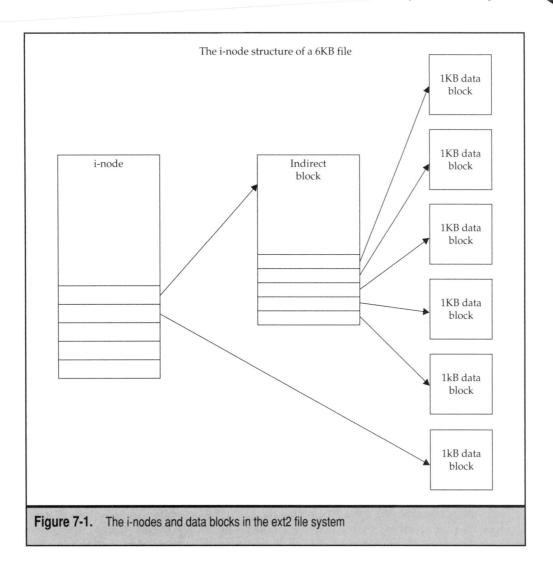

The i-node structure of a 6KB file

i-node

Indirect block

1KB data block

1KB data block

1KB data block

1KB data block

1kB data block

1kB data block

Figure 7-1.   The i-nodes and data blocks in the ext2 file system

Superblocks

The very first piece of information read from a disk is its *superblock*. This small data structure reveals several key pieces of information, including the disk's geometry, the amount of available space, and, most important, the location of the first i-node. Without a superblock, an on-disk file system is useless.

Something as important as the superblock is not left to chance. Multiple copies of this data structure are scattered all over the disk to provide backup in case the first one is damaged. Under Linux's ext2 file system, a superblock is placed after every *group* of blocks, which contains i-nodes and data. One group consists of 8192 blocks; thus, the first redundant superblock is at 8193, the second at 16385, and so on. The designers of most Linux file systems intelligently included this superblock redundancy into the file system design.

ext3 and ReiserFS

Ext3 and ReiserFS are two popular Linux file systems, used by the major Linux distributions. The ext3 file system is an enhanced extension of the ext2 file system. As of this writing, the ext2 file system is somewhere around 14 years old. This means two things for us as system administrators. First and foremost, ext2 is rock solid. It is a well-tested subsystem of Linux and has had the time to be very well optimized. Second, other file systems that were considered experimental when ext2 was created have matured and become available to Linux.

The two file systems that are popular replacements for ext2 are the ext3 and ReiserFS file systems. Both offer significant improvements in performance and stability, but the most important component of both of them is that they have moved to a new method of getting the data to the disk. This new method is called *journaling*. Traditional file systems (such as ext2) must search through the directory structure, find the right place on disk to lay out the data, and then lay out the data. (Linux can also cache the whole process, including the directory updates, thereby making the process appear faster to the user.) Almost all new versions of Linux distributions now all make use of one journaling file system or the other by default. Fedora Core and the various RHEL products, for example, use ext3 by default, and SuSE uses ReiserFS.

The problem with not having a journaling file system is that in the event of an unexpected crash, the file system checker or file system consistency checker (**fsck**) program has to follow up on all of the files on the disk to make sure they don't contain any dangling references (for example, i-nodes that point to other, invalid i-nodes or data blocks). As disks expand in size and shrink in price, the availability of these large-capacity disks means more of us will have to deal with the aftermath of having to **fsck** a large disk. And as anyone who has had to do that before can tell you, it isn't fun. The process can take a long time to complete, and that means downtime for your users.

Journaling file systems work by first creating an entry of sorts in a log (or journal) of changes that are about to be made before actually committing the changes to disk. Once this transaction has been committed to disk, then the file system goes ahead to modify the actual data or metadata. This results in an all-or-nothing situation; that is, either all or none of the file system changes get done.

One of the benefits of using a journaling type file system is the greater assurance that data integrity will be preserved, and in the unavoidable situations where problems arise, speed, ease of recovery, and likelihood of success are vastly increased. One such unavoidable situation might be in the event of a system crash. Here you may not need to run **fsck**. Think how much faster you could recover a system if you didn't have to run **fsck** on a 200GB disk! (Haven't had to run **fsck** on a big disk before? Think about how long it takes to run Scandisk under Windows on large disks). Other benefits of using journaling-type file systems are that system reboots are simplified, disk fragmentation is reduced, and input/output (I/O) operations can be accelerated (this depends on the journaling method used).

If you want to learn more about the ext2 file system, we recommend that you read the latest edition of the book titled *Linux Kernel Internals,* edited by Michael Beck (Addison-Wesley, 1998). Although the book is very dated in many aspects in terms of the kernel (it was written for the 2.0 series), the parts about the ext2 file system still hold true, since ext2 is the base of the ext3 file system.

Which File System to Use?

You might be asking by now, which file system should I use? As of this writing, the current trend is to shift toward any file system with journaling capabilities. As with all things Linux, the choice is yours. Your best bet is to try many file systems and see how they perform with the application you are using the system for. Just keep in mind that journaling has its own overhead.

MANAGING FILE SYSTEMS

The process of managing file systems is trivial—that is, the management becomes trivial *after* you have memorized all aspects of your networked servers, disks, backups, and size requirements with the condition that they will never again have to change. In other words, managing file systems isn't trivial at all.

Once the file systems have been created, deployed, and added to the backup cycle, they do tend to take care of themselves for the most part. What makes them tricky to manage are the administrative issues—such as users who refuse to do housekeeping on their disks, and cumbersome management policies dictating who can share what disk and under what conditions, depending, of course, on the account under which the storage/disk was purchased, and . . . . (It sounds frighteningly like a *Dilbert* cartoon strip, but there is a good deal of truth behind that statement.)

Unfortunately, there's no cookbook solution available for dealing with office politics, so in this section we'll stick to the technical issues involved in managing file systems— that is, the process of mounting and unmounting partitions, dealing with the **/etc/fstab** file, and performing file-system recovery with the **fsck** tool.

Mounting and Unmounting Local Disks

Linux's strong points include its flexibility and the way it lends itself to seamless management of file locations. Partitions need to be mounted so that their contents can be accessed. (In actuality, it is the file system on a partition or volume that is mounted.) The file systems are mounted so that they appear as just another subdirectory on the system. This helps to promote the illusion of one large directory tree structure, even though there may be several different file systems in use. This characteristic is especially helpful to the administrator, who can relocate data stored on a physical partition to a new location (possibly a different partition) under the directory tree with the system users being none the wiser.

The file system management process begins with the root directory. This partition is also called slash and likewise symbolized by a slash(/). The partition containing the kernel and core directory structure is mounted at boot time. It is possible and usual for the physical partition that houses the Linux kernel to be on a separate file system such as **/boot**. It is also possible for the root file system ("/") to house both the kernel and other required utilities and configuration files to bring the system up to single-user mode.

As the boot scripts run, additional file systems are mounted, adding to the structure of the root file system. The mount process overlays a single subdirectory with the directory tree of the partition it is trying to mount. For example, let's say that /dev/hda2 is the root partition. It has the directory **/usr,** which contains no files. The partition /dev/hda3 contains all the files that you want in **/usr,** so you mount /dev/hda3 to the directory **/usr.** Users can now simply change directories to **/usr** to see all the files from that partition. The user doesn't need to know that **/usr** is actually a separate partition.

> **NOTE** In this and other chapters we might inadvertently say that a partition is being mounted at such and such a directory. Please note that it is actually the file system on the partition that is being mounted. For the sake of simplicity and in keeping with everyday verbiage, we might interchange these two meanings.

Keep in mind that when a new directory is mounted, the **mount** process hides all the contents of the previously mounted directory. So in our **/usr** example, if the root partition did have files in **/usr** before mounting /dev/hda3, those **/usr** files would no longer be visible. (They're not erased, of course—once /dev/hda3 were unmounted, the **/usr** files would become visible again.)

Using the mount Command

Like many command-line tools, the **mount** command has a plethora of options, most of which you won't be using in daily work. You can get full details on these options from the **mount** man page. In this section, we'll explore the most common uses of the command.

The structure of the **mount** command is as follows:

```
mount [options] device directory
```

where **options** may be any of those shown in Table 7-1.

The options available for use with the **mount -o** flag are shown in Table 7-2.

Issuing the **mount** command without any options will list all the currently mounted file systems. For example, type

```
[root@serverA ~]# mount
/dev/mapper/VolGroup00-LogVol00 on / type ext3 (rw)
none on /proc type proc (rw)
none on /sys type sysfs (rw)
...(OUTPUT TRUNCATED)...
/dev/mapper/VolGroup00-LogVol03 on /tmp type ext3 (rw)
none on /proc/sys/fs/binfmt_misc type binfmt_misc (rw)
sunrpc on /var/lib/nfs/rpc_pipefs type rpc_pipefs (rw)
```

Option for `mount`	Description
`-a`	Mounts all the file systems listed in **/etc/fstab** (this file is examined later in this section).
`-t fstype`	Specifies the type of file system being mounted. Linux can mount file systems other than the ext2 standard, most notably FAT, VFAT, and FAT32. The **mount** command can usually sense this information on its own.
`-o options`	Specifies options applying to this **mount** process. These are usually options specific to the file system type (options for mounting network file systems may not apply to mounting local file systems).

Table 7-1. Options Available for the `mount` Command

Option for the `mount -o` Parameter (for Local Partitions)	Description
`ro`	Mounts the partition as read-only.
`rw`	Mounts the partition as read/write (default).
`exec`	Permits the execution of binaries (default).
`noatime`	Disables update of the access time on i-nodes. For partitions where the access time doesn't matter, enabling this improves performance.
`noauto`	Disables automatic mount of this partition when the `-a` option is specified (applies only to the **/etc/fstab** file).
`nosuid`	Disallows application of SetUID program bits to the mounted partition.
`sb=n`	Tells **mount** to use block **n** as the superblock. This is useful when the file system might be damaged.

Table 7-2. Options Available for Use with the `mount -o` Parameter

The following **mount** command mounts the /dev/hda3 partition onto the **/bogus-directory** directory with read-only privileges:

```
[root@serverA ~]# mount -o ro  /dev/hda3  /bogus-directory
```

Unmounting File Systems

To unmount a file system, use the **umount** command (note that the command is *not* **unmount**). Here's the command format:

```
umount [-f] directory
```

where **directory** is the directory to be unmounted. For example,

```
[root@serverA ~]# umount /bogus-directory
```

unmounts the partition mounted on the **/bogus-directory** directory.

When the File System Is in Use   There's a catch to **umount**: if the file system is in use (that is, when someone is currently accessing the contents of file system or has a file open on the file system), you won't be able to unmount that file system. To get around this, you have the following choices:

- ▼   You can use the **lsof** or **fuser** program to determine which processes are keeping the files open, and then kill them off or ask the process owners to stop what they're doing. (Read about the **kill** parameter in **fuser** in the **fuser** man page.) If you choose to kill the processes, be sure you understand the repercussions of doing so (read: don't get fired for doing this).

- ■   You can use the **-f** option with **umount** to force the unmount process. It is especially useful for NFS-type file systems that are no longer available.

- ■   Use the Lazy unmount. This is specified with the **-l** option. This option almost always works even when others fail. It detaches the file system from the file-system hierarchy immediately, and it cleans up all references to the file system as soon as it stops being busy.

- ▲   The safest and most proper alternative is to bring the system down to single-user mode and then unmount the file system. In reality, of course, you don't always get this luxury.

The /etc/fstab File

As mentioned earlier, **/etc/fstab** is a configuration file that **mount** can use. This file contains a list of all partitions known to the system. During the boot process, this list is read and the items in it are automatically mounted with the options specified therein.

Here's the format of entries in the **/etc/fstab** file:

```
/dev/device /dir/to/mount      fstype   parameters   fs_freq      fs_passno
```

Following is a sample **/etc/fstab** file:

```
1.  /dev/VolGroup00/LogVol00 /                    ext3    defaults       1 1
2.  LABEL=/boot               /boot               ext3    defaults       1 2
3.  none                      /dev/pts            devpts  gid=5,mode=620 0 0
4.  none                      /dev/shm            tmpfs   defaults       0 0
5.  /dev/VolGroup00/LogVol02 /home                ext3    defaults       1 2
6.  none                      /proc               proc    defaults       0 0
7.  none                      /sys                sysfs   defaults       0 0
8.  /dev/VolGroup00/LogVol03 /tmp                 ext3    defaults       1 2
9.  /dev/VolGroup00/LogVol01 swap                 swap    defaults       0 0
10. /dev/hdc     /media/cdrom     auto
pamconsole,fscontext=system_u:object_r:removable_t,ro,exec,noauto,managed 0 0
11. /dev/fd0     /media/floppy    auto
pamconsole,fscontext=system_u:object_r:removable_t,exec,noauto,managed 0 0
```

Let's take a look at some of the entries in the **/etc/fstab** file that haven't yet been discussed. Please note that line numbers have been added to the preceding output to aid readability.

Line 1 The first entry in our sample **/etc/fstab** file is the entry for the root volume. The first column shows the device that the houses the file system, i.e., the /dev/VolGroup00/ LogVol00 logical volume (more on volumes later on). The second column shows the mount point, i.e., the "/" directory. The third column shows the file system type, i.e., ext3 in this case. The fourth column shows the options with which the file system should be mounted—only the default options are required in this case. The fifth field is used by the **dump** utility (a simple backup tool discussed in Chapter 28) to determine which file systems need to be backed up. And the sixth and final field is used by the **fsck** program to determine if the file system needs to be checked and also to determine the order in which the checks are done.

Line 2 The next entry in our sample file is the /boot mount point. The first field of this entry shows the device—in this case, it points to any device with the /boot label. The other fields mean basically the same thing as the field for the root mount point discussed previously.

Note that in the case of the /boot mount point, you might notice the field for the device looks a little different from the usual */dev/<path-to-device>* convention. The use of labels helps to hide the actual device (partition) that the file system is being mounted from. The device has been replaced with a token that looks like the following: **LABEL=/boot**. During the initial installation, the partitioning program of the installer automatically set the label on the partition. Upon bootup, the system scans the partition tables and looks for these labels. This is especially useful when SCSI disks are being used. Typically, SCSI has a set SCSI ID. Using labels allows you to move the disk around and change the SCSI ID, and the system will still know how to mount the file system even though the device might have changed from for example /dev/sda10 to /dev/sdb10 (See the section "Disk and Partition Naming Conventions" further on).

Line 4   Next comes the tmpfs file system, also known as a virtual memory (VM) file system. It uses both the system RAM and swap area. It is not a typical block device, because it does not exist on top of an underlying block device; it sits directly on top of VM. It is used to request pages from the VM subsystem to store files. The first field—**none**—means that this entry deals with a VM and as such is not associated with any regular UNIX/Linux device file. The second entry shows the mount point, /dev/shm. The third field shows the file system type, i.e., tmpfs. The fourth field shows that this file system should be mounted with the default options. The fifth and sixth fields have the same meanings as the ones for the previous entries discussed. Note especially that the values are zero in this case, which makes perfect sense because there is no reason to run a dump on a temporary file system at boot and there is also no reason to run **fsck** on it, since it does not contain an ext2/3-type file system.

Line 6   The next notable entry is for the proc-type file system. Information concerning the system processes (hence the abbreviation proc) are dynamically maintained in this file system. The **none** in the first field of the proc entry in the **/etc/fstab** file has the same implication as that of the tmpfs file system entry. The proc file system is a special file system that provides an interface to kernel parameters through what looks like any other file system; that is, it provides an almost human-readable look to the kernel. Although it appears to exist on disk, it really doesn't—all the files represent something that is in the kernel. Most notable is **/dev/kcore**, which is the system memory abstracted as a file. People new to the proc file system often mistake this for a large, unnecessary file and accidentally remove it, which will cause the system to malfunction in many glorious ways. Unless you are sure you know what you are doing, it's a safe bet to leave all the files in the **/proc** directory alone (more details of **/proc** appear in Chapter 10).

Line 7   Next comes the entry for the sysfs file system. This is new and necessary in the Linux 2.6 kernels. Again it is temporary and special, just like the tmpfs and proc file systems. It serves as an in-memory repository for system and device status information. It provides a structured view of a system's device tree. This is akin to viewing the devices in Windows Device Manager as a series of files and directories instead of through the Control Panel view.

Line 8   The next entry is for the /tmp mount point. This refers to an actual physical entity or device on the system just like the root ("/") mount point and the /boot mount point.

Line 9   This is the entry for the system swap partition. It is where virtual memory resides. In Linux, the virtual memory can be kept on a separate partition from the root partition

(It should be noted that a regular file can also be used for swap purposes in Linux.) Keeping the swap space on a separate partition helps to improve performance, since the swap partition can obey rules differently than a normal file system. Also, since the partition doesn't need to be backed up or checked with **fsck** at boot time, the last two parameters on it are zeroed out. (Note that a swap partition can be kept in a normal disk file as well. See the man page on **mkswap** for additional information.)

Line 10 The last entry in the **fstab** file that is perhaps worthy of mentioning is the entry for the removable media. In this example, the device field points to the device file that represents the cdrom device. The CD-ROM drive here is the master of the secondary IDE controller (/dev/hdc). The mount point is /media/cdrom, and so when a CD-ROM is inserted and mounted on the system, the content of the CD can be accessed from the **/media/cdrom** directory. The **auto** in the third field means that system will automatically try to probe/detect the correct file system type for the device. For CD-ROMs, this is usually the iso9660 file system. The fourth field lists the mount options. These particular options are relevant on a system with an SELinux-enabled kernel.

> **NOTE** When mounting partitions with the **/etc/fstab** file configured, you can run the **mount** command with only one parameter: the directory you wish to mount to. The **mount** command checks **/etc/fstab** for that directory; if found, **mount** will use all parameters that have already been established there. For example, here's the short command to mount a CD-ROM given the **/etc/fstab** file shown earlier:

```
[root@serverA ~]# mount /media/cdrom/
```

Using fsck

The **fsck** tool (short for File System Check), is used to diagnose and repair file systems that may have become damaged in the course of daily operations. Such repairs are usually necessary after a system crash in which the system did not get a chance to fully flush all of its internal buffers to disk. (Although this tool's name bears a striking resemblance to one of the expressions often uttered after a system crash, that this tool is part of the recovery process is *strictly* coincidental.)

Usually, the system runs the **fsck** tool automatically during the boot process as it deems necessary (much in the same way Windows runs Scandisk). If it detects a file system that was not cleanly unmounted, it runs the utility. Linux makes an impressive effort to automatically repair any problems it runs across and, in most instances, does take care of itself. The robust nature of the Linux file system helps in such situations. Nevertheless, it may happen that you get this message:

```
*** An error occurred during the file system check.
*** Dropping you to a shell; the system will reboot
*** when you leave the shell.
```

At this point, you need to run **fsck** by hand and answer its prompts yourself.

If you do find that a file system is not behaving as it should (log messages are an excellent hint of this type of anomaly), you may want to run **fsck** yourself on a running system. The only downside is that the file system in question must be unmounted in order for this to work. If you choose to take this path, be sure to remount the file system when you are done.

The name **fsck** isn't the proper title for the ext3 repair tool; it's actually just a wrapper. The **fsck** wrapper tries to determine what kind of file system needs to be repaired and then runs the appropriate repair tool, passing any parameters that were passed to **fsck**. In ext2, the real tool is called **fsck.ext2**. For the ext3 file system, the real tool is **fsck.ext3**, for the VFAT file system, the tool is **fsck.vfat**, and for a ReiserFS file system, the utility is called **fsck.reiserfs**. When a system crash occurs, for example, on an ext2-formatted partition, you may need to call **fsck.ext2** directly rather than relying on other applications to call it for you automatically.

For example, to run **fsck** on the /dev/mapper/VolGroup00-LogVol02 file system mounted at the **/home** directory, you will run the following commands. First, to unmount the file system, type

```
[root@serverA ~]# umount /home
```

NOTE   The preceding step assumes that the **/home** file system is not currently being used or accessed by any process.

Since we know that this particular file system is ext3, we can call the correct utility (**fsck.ext3**) directly or simply use the **fsck** utility. Type

```
[root@serverA ~]# fsck    /dev/mapper/VolGroup00-LogVol02
fsck 1.35 (28-Feb-2024)
e2fsck 1.35 (28-Feb-2024)
/dev/mapper/VolGroup00-LogVol02: clean, 11/393216 files, 21703/786432 blocks
```

The preceding output shows that the file system is marked clean. To forcefully check the file system and answer yes to all questions in spite of what your OS thinks, type

```
[root@serverA ~]# fsck.ext3 -f  -y /dev/mapper/VolGroup00-LogVol02
```

What If I Still Get Errors?

First, relax. The **fsck** check rarely finds problems that it cannot correct by itself. When it does ask for human intervention, telling **fsck** to execute its default suggestion is often enough. Very rarely does a single pass of **e2fsck** not clear up all problems.

On the rare occasions when a second run is needed, it *should not* turn up any more errors. If it does, you are most likely facing a hardware failure. Remember to start with the obvious: check for reliable power and well-connected cables. Anyone running SCSI systems should verify that they're using the correct type of terminator, that cables aren't too long, that SCSI IDs aren't conflicting, and that cable quality is adequate. (SCSI is especially fussy about the quality of the cables.)

The lost+found Directory

Another rare situation is when `fsck` finds segments of files that it cannot rejoin with the original file. In those cases, it will place the fragment in the partition's **lost+found** directory. This directory is located where the partition is mounted, so if /dev/mapper/ VolGroup00-LogVol02 is mounted on **/home**, for example, then **/home/lost+found** correlates to the **lost+found** directory for that particular file system.

Anything can go into a **lost+found** directory—file fragments, directories, and even special files. When normal files wind up there, a file owner should be attached, and you can contact the owner and see if they need the data (typically, they won't). If you encounter a directory in **lost+found**, you'll most likely want to try to restore it from the most recent backups rather than trying to reconstruct it from **lost+found**.

At the very least, **lost+found** tells you if anything became dislocated. Again, such errors are extraordinarily rare.

ADDING A NEW DISK

The process of adding a disk under Linux on the Intel (*x86*) platform is relatively easy. Assuming you are adding a disk that is of similar type to your existing disks (for example, adding an IDE disk to a system that already has IDE drives or adding a SCSI disk to a system that already has SCSI drives), the system should automatically detect the new disk at boot time. All that is left is partitioning it and creating a file system on it.

If you are adding a new type of disk (like a SCSI disk on a system that only has IDE drives), you may need to ensure that the your kernel supports the new hardware. This support can either be built directly into the kernel or be available as a loadable module (driver). Note that the kernels of most Linux distributions come with support for many popular SCSI controllers, but you will occasionally come across very troublesome kernel and hardware combinations, especially with the very new motherboards that have very exotic chipsets.

Once the disk is in place, simply boot the system and you're ready to go. If you aren't sure about whether the system can see the new disk, run the **dmesg** command and see whether the driver loaded and was able to find your disk. For example,

```
[root@serverA ~]# dmesg | less
```

Overview of Partitions

For the sake of clarity, and in case you need to know what a partition is and how it works, let's do a brief review of this subject. Every disk must be *partitioned. Partitions* divide the disk into segments, and each segment acts as a complete disk by itself. Once a partition is filled, it cannot automatically overflow onto another partition. Various things can be done with a partitioned disk, such as installing an OS into a single partition that spans the entire disk, installing several different OSes into their own separate partitions in what is commonly called a "dual boot" configuration, and using the different partitions to separate and restrict certain system functions into their own work areas.

This last reason is especially relevant on a multiuser system, where the content of users' home directories should not be allowed to overgrow and disrupt important OS functions.

Disk and Partition Naming Conventions

Under Linux, each disk is given its own device name. The device files are stored under the **/dev** directory. IDE disks start with the name hd*X*, where *X* can range from *a* through *z*, with each letter representing a physical device. For example, in an IDE-only system with one hard disk and one CD-ROM, both on the same IDE chain, the hard disk would be /dev/hda and the CD-ROM would be /dev/hdb. Disk devices are automatically created during system installation.

When partitions are created, new devices are used. They take the form of /dev/hd*XY*, where *X* is the device letter (as described in the preceding paragraph), and *Y* is the partition number. Thus, the first partition on the /dev/hda disk is /dev/hda1, the second partition would be /dev/hda2, and so on.

SCSI disks follow the same basic scheme as IDE, except instead of starting with hd, they start with sd. Therefore, the first partition on the first SCSI disk would be /dev/sda1, the second partition on the third SCSI disk would be /dev/sdc2, and so on.

VOLUME MANAGEMENT

You may have noticed earlier that we use the terms partition and volume interchangeably in parts of the text. While they are not exactly the same things, the concepts carry over. Volume management is a new approach to dealing with disks and partitions. Instead of viewing a disk or storage entity along partition boundaries, the boundaries are no longer there and everything is now seen as volumes.

Did your head just spin? Don't worry if it did; this is a tricky concept. Let's try this again with more detail.

This new approach to dealing with partitions is called Logical Volume Management (LVM) in Linux. It lends itself to several benefits and removes the restrictions, constraints, and limitations that the concept of partitions imposes. Some of the benefits are

▼ Greater flexibility for disk partitioning

■ Easy online resizing of volumes

■ Easy increases in storage space by simply adding new disks to the storage pool

▲ Use of snapshots

Following are some important volume management terms.

Physical Volume (PV)   This typically refers to the physical hard disk(s) or other physical storage entity, such as a hardware RAID array or software RAID device(s). There can be only a single storage entity (e.g., one partition) in a PV.

Volume Group (VG)   Volume groups are used to house one or more physical volumes and logical volumes into a single administrative unit. A volume group is created out of physical volumes. VGs are simply a collection of PVs; however, VGs are not mountable. They are more like virtual raw disks.

Logical Volume (LV)   This perhaps is the trickiest LVM concept to grasp, because logical volumes (LVs) are the equivalent of disk partitions in a non-LVM world. The LV appears as a standard block device. It is on the LV that we put file systems. It is the LV that gets mounted. It is the LV that gets **fsck**ed if necessary.

   LVs are created out of the space available in VGs. To the administrator, an LV appears as one contiguous partition independent of the actual PVs that make it up.

Extents   There are two kinds of extents: physical extents and logical extents. Physical volumes (PVs) are said to be divided into chunks or units of data called "physical extents." And logical volumes (LVs) are said to be divided into chunks or units of data called "logical extents."

Creating Partitions and Logical Volumes

During the installation process, you probably used a "pretty" tool with a nice GUI front end to create partitions. The GUI tools available across the various Linux distributions vary greatly in looks and usability. One tool that can be used to perform most partitioning tasks, and that has a unified look and feel regardless of the Linux flavor, is the venerable **fdisk** utility. Though it's small and somewhat awkward, it's a reliable partitioning tool. Furthermore, in the event you need to troubleshoot a system that has gone really wrong, you should be familiar with basics such as **fdisk**. Other very powerful command-line utilities for managing partitions are **sfdisk**, **cfdisk**, and the much newer **parted** utility: **parted** is much more user friendly and has a lot more built-in functionalities than the other tools have. In fact, a lot of the GUI partitioning tools call the **parted** program in their back end.

   During the installation of the OS as covered in Chapter 2, you were asked to leave some free, unpartitioned space. We will now use that free space to demonstrate some LVM concepts by walking through the steps required to create a logical volume.

   In particular, we will create a logical volume that will house the contents of our current **/var** directory. Because a separate "/var" volume was *not* created during the OS installation, the contents of the **/var** directory are currently stored under the volume that holds the root ("/") tree. The general idea is that, because the **/var** directory is typically used to hold frequently changing and growing data (such as log files), it is prudent to put its content on its own separate file system.

   The steps involved with creating a logical volume can be summarized this way:

   1. Initialize a regular partition for use by the LVM system (or simply create a partition of the type Linux LVM (0x8e).

   2. Create physical volumes from the hard disk partition.

   3. Assign the physical volume(s) to volume group(s).

   4. Finally, create logical volumes within the volume groups and assign mount points to the logical volumes after formatting.

The following illustration shows the relationship between disks, physical volumes (PVs), volume groups (VGs), and logical volumes (LVs) in LVM:

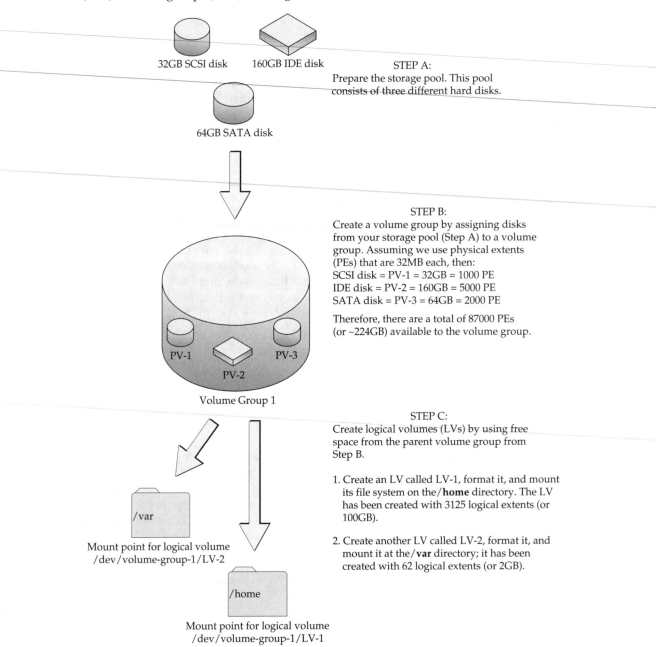

32GB SCSI disk   160GB IDE disk

64GB SATA disk

STEP A:
Prepare the storage pool. This pool consists of three different hard disks.

STEP B:
Create a volume group by assigning disks from your storage pool (Step A) to a volume group. Assuming we use physical extents (PEs) that are 32MB each, then:
SCSI disk = PV-1 = 32GB = 1000 PE
IDE disk = PV-2 = 160GB = 5000 PE
SATA disk = PV-3 = 64GB = 2000 PE

Therefore, there are a total of 87000 PEs (or ~224GB) available to the volume group.

PV-1   PV-3
PV-2

Volume Group 1

STEP C:
Create logical volumes (LVs) by using free space from the parent volume group from Step B.

1. Create an LV called LV-1, format it, and mount its file system on the/**home** directory. The LV has been created with 3125 logical extents (or 100GB).

2. Create another LV called LV-2, format it, and mount it at the/**var** directory; it has been created with 62 logical extents (or 2GB).

/var

Mount point for logical volume
/dev/volume-group-1/LV-2

/home

Mount point for logical volume
/dev/volume-group-1/LV-1

CAUTION   The process of creating partitions is irrevocably destructive to the data already on the disk. Before creating, changing, or removing partitions on any disk, you must be very sure of what you are doing and its consequences.

The following section will be broken down into several parts:

▼   Creating a partition

■   Creating a physical volume

■   Assigning a physical volume to a volume group

▲   Creating a logical volume

The entire process from start to finish may appear a bit lengthy. It is actually a very simple process in itself, but we intersperse the steps with some *extra steps,* along with some notes and explanations.

Let's begin the process. Note that some LVM utilities that we'll be using during the process are listed in Table 7-3.

LVM Command	Description
`lvcreate`	Used for creating a new logical volume in a volume group, by allocating logical extents from the free physical extent pool of that volume group.
`lvdisplay`	Displays the attributes of a logical volume, such as read/write status, size, and snapshot information.
`pvcreate`	Initializes a physical volume for use with the LVM system.
`pvdisplay`	Displays the attributes of physical volumes, such as size and PE size.
`vgcreate`	Used for creating new volume groups from block devices created using the `pvcreate` command.
`vgextend`	Used for adding one or more physical volumes to an existing volume group to extend its size.
`vgdisplay`	Displays the attributes of volume groups.

Table 7-3.   LVM Utilities

Creating a Partition

We will be using the free unpartitioned space on the main system disk, /dev/hda.

1. Begin by running **fdisk** with the **-l** parameter to list the current partition table. Type

```
[root@serverA ~]# fdisk -l
Disk /dev/hda: 10.7 GB, 10737418240 bytes
...(OUTPUT TRUNCATED)...
/dev/hda2                26       1200      9438187+  8e  Linux LVM
```

2. Next, we begin the actual repartitioning process using **fdisk** again. Type

```
[root@serverA ~]# fdisk  /dev/hda
The number of cylinders for this disk is set to 1305.
...(OUTPUT TRUNCATED)...
2) booting and partitioning software from other OSs
   (e.g., DOS FDISK, OS/2 FDISK)
Command (m for help):
```

You will be presented with a simple **fdisk** prompt "Command (m for help):"

3. Print the partition table again while inside the **fdisk** program. Type **p** at the **fdisk** prompt to print the partition table.

```
Command (m for help): p
Disk /dev/hda: 10.7 GB, 10737418240 bytes
255 heads, 63 sectors/track, 1305 cylinders
Units = cylinders of 16065 * 512 = 8225280 bytes
 Device   Boot   Start       End      Blocks   Id  System
/dev/hda1   *       1         25      200781   83  Linux
/dev/hda2          26       1200     9438187+  8e  Linux LVM
```

A few facts worthy of note regarding this output:

▼ The total disk size is approximately 10.7GB.

■ There are currently two partitions defined on the sample system. The partitions are /dev/hda1 and /dev/hda2.

■ The /dev/hda1 partition is of type "Linux" (0x83), and the /dev/hda2 partition is of the type "Linux LVM" (0x8e).

■ From the partitioning scheme we chose during the OS installation, we can deduce that /dev/hda1 houses the /boot file system and /dev/hda2 houses everything else (see the output of the **df** command for reference).

■ The entire disk spans 1305 cylinders.

▲ The last partition, i.e., /dev/hda2, ends at the 1200-cylinder boundary. Therefore, there is room to create a partition that will occupy the space from cylinder 1201 to the last cylinder on the disk (i.e., 1305).

4. Type **n** at the prompt to create a new partition.

```
Command (m for help): n
```

NOTE   If you are curious about the other things you can do at the **fdisk** prompt, type **m** to display a help menu.

5. Type **p** to select a primary partition type.

```
e    extended
p    primary partition (1-4)
p
```

6. We want to create the third primary partition. Type **3** when prompted for a partition number:

```
Partition number (1-4): 3
```

7. The next step is to specify the partition size. First we choose the lower limit. Accept the default value for the first cylinder. Type **1201**.

```
First cylinder (1201-1305, default 1201): 1201
```

8. Instead of designating a megabyte value for the size of this partition, we enter the last cylinder number, thus taking up the remainder of the disk. Accept the default suggested for the last cylinder. On our sample system this value is 1305. Type **1305**.

```
Last cylinder or +size or +sizeM or +sizeK (1201-1305, default 1305): 1305
```

9. By default, **fdisk** creates ext2-type partitions (i.e., 0x83). But we want to create a partition of type "Linux LVM." Change the partition type from the default Linux (0x83) to the "Linux LVM" type. To do this, we use the **t** (change partition type) command. Type **t**.

```
Command (m for help): t
```

10. Enter the partition number whose type you want to change. We want to change the type for the /dev/hda3 partition that was just created, so type **3** when prompted for a partition number.

```
Partition number (1-4): 3
```

11. Enter the partition type for "Linux LVM". Type **8e** at the prompt:

```
Hex code (type L to list codes): 8e
```

NOTE   You can list the hex codes for the available partition types by typing **L**.

12. View the changes you've made by viewing the partition table. Type **p**.

```
Command (m for help): p
Disk /dev/hda: 10.7 GB, 10737418240 bytes
255 heads, 63 sectors/track, 1305 cylinders
Units = cylinders of 16065 * 512 = 8225280 bytes
Device     Boot    Start      End      Blocks   Id  System
/dev/hda1   *          1       25      200781   83  Linux
/dev/hda2             26     1200     9438187+  8e  Linux LVM
/dev/hda3           1201     1305      843412+  8e  Linux LVM
```

13. Once you are satisfied with your changes, commit or write the changes you've made to the disk's partition table using the **w** (write table to disk) command:

```
Command (m for help): w
```

14. Quit the **fdisk** utility. Type **q**.

```
Command (m for help): q
```

15. When you are back at the shell prompt, reboot the system to allow the Linux kernel to properly recognize the new partition table. Type

```
[root@serverA ~]# reboot
```

Creating a Physical Volume

Next, create the physical volume itself.

1. After the system comes back up from the reboot, log back in as the superuser.

2. First let's view the current physical volumes defined on the system. Type

```
[root@serverA ~]# pvdisplay
  --- Physical volume ---
  PV Name               /dev/hda2
  VG Name               VolGroup00
  PV Size               9.00 GB / not usable 0
...(OUTPUT TRUNCATED)...
```

Take note of the physical volume name field (PV Name).

3. Use the **pvcreate** command to initialize the partition we created earlier as a physical volume. Type

```
[root@serverA ~]# pvcreate  /dev/hda3
  Physical volume "/dev/hda3" successfully created
```

4. Use the **pvdisplay** command to view your changes again. Type

```
[root@serverA ~]# pvdisplay
  --- Physical volume ---
  PV Name               /dev/hda2
  VG Name               VolGroup00
...(OUTPUT TRUNCATED)...
```

```
--- NEW Physical volume ---
PV Name                /dev/hda3
VG Name
PV Size                823.46 MB
...(OUTPUT TRUNCATED)...
```

Assigning a Physical Volume to a Volume Group

Here we will assign the physical volume created earlier to a volume group (VG).

1. First use the **vgdisplay** command to view the current volume groups that might exist on your system. Type

```
[root@serverA ~]# vgdisplay
   --- Volume group ---
   VG Name                VolGroup00
   Format                 lvm2
...(Output truncated)...
   VG Size                9.00 GB
   PE Size                32.00 MB
   Total PE               288
   Alloc PE / Size        286 / 8.94 GB
   Free  PE / Size        2 / 64.00 MB
   VG UUID                JgPahd-1TBY-L5sT-tqho-KCk6-HxTy-rNCdz8
```

From the preceding output, we can tell that

▼ The volume group name (VG Name) is VolGroup00.

■ The current size of the VG is 9.00GB (this should increase by the time we are done).

■ The physical extent size is 32MB, and there are a total of 288 PEs.

▲ There are only two physical extents that are free in the VG. They are equivalent to 64MB of space.

2. Assign the PV to the volume group using the **vgextend** command. The syntax for the command is

```
Vgextend   [options] VolumeGroupName PhysicalDevicePath
```

Substituting the correct values in this command, type

```
[root@serverA ~]# vgextend VolGroup00  /dev/hda3
Volume group "VolGroup00" successfully extended
```

3. View your changes with the **vgdisplay** command. Type

```
[root@serverA ~]# vgdisplay
   --- Volume group ---
   VG Name                VolGroup00
   ...(Output truncated)...
```

```
Act PV                 2
VG Size                9.78 GB
PE Size                32.00 MB
Total PE               313
Alloc PE / Size        286 / 8.94 GB
Free  PE / Size        27 / 864.00 MB
```

Note that the VG Size, Total PE, and Free PE values have dramatically increased. We now have a total of 27 free PEs (or 864MB).

Creating a Logical Volume (LV)

Now that we have some room in the VG, we can go ahead and create the final logical volume (LV).

1. First view the current LVs on the system. Type

```
[root@serverA ~]# lvdisplay
--- Logical volume ---
  LV Name                /dev/VolGroup00/LogVol00
  VG Name                VolGroup00
...(Output truncated)...
--- Logical volume ---
  LV Name                /dev/VolGroup00/LogVol02
  VG Name                VolGroup00
...(Output truncated)...
--- Logical volume ---
  LV Name                /dev/VolGroup00/LogVol03
  VG Name                VolGroup00
...(Output truncated)...
--- Logical volume ---
  LV Name                /dev/VolGroup00/LogVol01
  VG Name                VolGroup00
```

The preceding output shows the current LVs—/dev/VolGroup00/LogVol00, /dev/VolGroup00/LogVol02, /dev/VolGroup00/LogVol03, and so on.

2. With the background information that we now have, we will create an LV using the same naming convention that is currently used on the system. We will create a fourth LV called "LogVol04." The full path to the LV will be /dev/VolGroup00/LogVol04. Type

```
[root@serverA ~]# lvcreate -l 27  --name  LogVol04     VolGroup00
  ...(OUTPUT TRUNCATED)...
  Logical volume "LogVol04" created
```

NOTE   You can actually name your LV any way you want. We named ours **LogVol04** for consistency only. We could have replaced LogVol04 with another name like "my-volume" if we wanted to. The value for the `--name` `(-n)` options determines the name of the LV. The `-l` option specifies the size in physical extents units (see Step 1 under "Assigning a Physical Volume to a Volume Group"). We could have also specified the size in megabytes, by using an option like `-L 864M`.

3. View the LV you created. Type

```
[root@serverA ~]# lvdisplay /dev/VolGroup00/LogVol04
   --- Logical volume ---
   LV Name                /dev/VolGroup00/LogVol04
   VG Name                VolGroup00
   ...(Output truncated)...
   LV Size                864.00 MB
   Current LE             27
```

Fedora and RHEL distributions of Linux have a GUI tool that can greatly simplify the entire management of an LVM system. The command **system-config-lvm** will launch the tool, as shown here:

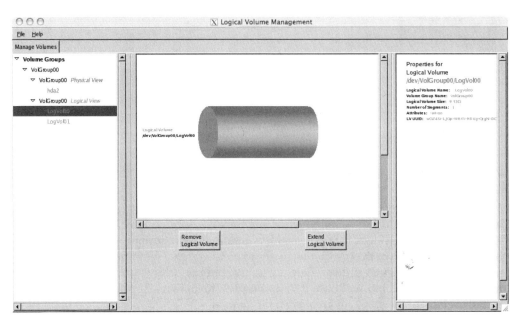

SuSE Linux also has a very capable GUI tool for managing disks, partitions, and the LVM. Issue the command `yast2 lvm_config` to launch the utility, shown here:

CREATING FILE SYSTEMS

With the volumes created, you need to put file systems on them. (If you're accustomed to Microsoft Windows, this is akin to formatting the disk once you've partitioned it.)

The type of file system that you want to create will determine the particular utility that you should use. In this project we want to create an ext3-type file system; therefore, we'll use the `mkfs.ext3` utility. There are many command-line parameters available for the `mkfs.ext3` tool, but we'll use it in its simplest form here.

Following are the steps for creating a file system:

1. The only command-line parameter you'll usually have to specify is the partition (or volume) name onto which the file system should go. To create a file system on the /dev/VolGroup00/LogVol04, you would issue the following command:

```
[root@serverA ~]# mkfs.ext3   /dev/VolGroup00/LogVol04
mke2fs 1.35 (28-Feb-2004)
max_blocks 226492416, rsv_groups = 6912, rsv_gdb = 53
OS type: Linux
Block size=4096 (log=2)
  ...(Output truncated)...
110656 inodes, 221184 blocks
Superblock backups stored on blocks:
        32768, 98304, 163840
Writing inode tables: done
inode.i_blocks = 1704, i_size = 4243456
Creating journal (4096 blocks): done
Writing superblocks and file system accounting information: done
This file system will be automatically checked every 38 mounts or
180 days, whichever comes first.  Use tune2fs -c or -i to override
```

Once the preceding command runs to completion, you are done with creating the file system. We will next begin the process of trying to restore the contents of the /var file system.

2. Create a temporary folder that will be used as the mount point for the new file system. Create it under the root folder. Type

```
[root@serverA ~]# mkdir  /new_var
```

3. Mount the LogVol04 logical volume at the **/new_var** directory. Type

```
[root@serverA ~]# mount  /dev/VolGroup00/LogVol04   /new_var
```

4. Copy the content of the current **/var** directory to the **/new_var** directory. Type

```
[root@serverA ~]# cp -rp   /var/*   /new_var/
```

5. In order to avoid taking down the system into single-user mode to perform the following sensitive steps, we have to use a few old military tricks. Type

```
[root@serverA ~]# mount --bind /var/lib/nfs/rpc_pipefs \
/new_var/lib/nfs/rpc_pipefs
```

The preceding step is necessary because the rpc_pipefs pseudo–file system happens to be mounted under a subfolder in the **/var** directory.

6. Now you can rename the current **/var** to **/old_var**. Type

```
[root@serverA ~]# mv  /var   /old_var
```

7. Create a new and empty **/var** directory. Type

```
[root@serverA ~]# mkdir /var
```

8. Restore the security contexts for the new **/var** folder so that the daemons that need it can use it. Type

```
[root@serverA /]# restorecon -R  /var
```

> *NOTE* The preceding step is only necessary on a system running an SELinux-enabled kernel, like Fedora or RHEL.

We are almost done now. We need to create an entry for the new file system in the **/etc/fstab** file. To do so, we must edit the **/etc/fstab** file so that our changes can take effect the next time the system is rebooted. Open up the file for editing with any text editor of your choice and add the following entry into the file:

```
/dev/VolGroup00/LogVol04   /var                    ext3    defaults        1  2
```

> *TIP* You can also use the **echo** command to append the preceding text to the end of the file. The command is

```
echo "/dev/VolGroup00/LogVol04 /var ext3 defaults 1 2" >> /etc/fstab.
```

9. This will be a good time to reboot the system. Type

```
[root@serverA /]# reboot
```

10. Hopefully the system came back up fine. After the system boots, delete the **/old_var** and **/new_var** folders using the **rm** command.

> *NOTE* If, during system bootup, the boot process was especially slow starting the system "logger service," don't worry too much—it will time out eventually and continue with the boot process. But you will need to set the proper security contexts for the files now under the /**var** folder, by running the **restorecon -R /var** command again, with the actual files now in the directory. And then reboot the system one more time.

SUMMARY

In this chapter, we covered the process of administering your file systems, from creating partitions to creating physical volumes, to extending an existing volume group and then creating the final logical volume. We also went through the process of moving a very sensitive system directory onto its own separate file system. The exercise detailed what you might need to do while managing a Linux server in the real world. With this information, you're armed with what you need in order to manage a commercial-level Linux server in a variety of environments.

Like any operating system, Linux undergoes changes from time to time. Although the designers and maintainers of the file systems go to great lengths to keep the interface the same, you'll find some alterations cropping up from time to time. Sometimes they'll be interface simplifications. Others will be dramatic improvements in the file system itself. Keep your eyes open for these changes. Linux provides a superb file system that is robust, responsive, and in general a pleasure to use. Take the tools we have discussed in this chapter and find out for yourself.

CHAPTER 8

Core System Services

Regardless of distribution, network configuration, and overall system design, every Linux system ships with some core services. Some of these services include **init**, **syslogd**, **cron**, and others. The functions performed by these services may be simple, but they are also fundamental. Without their presence, a great deal of Linux's power would be missed.

In this chapter, we'll discuss each one of the core services, in addition to another very useful system service called **xinetd**. We'll also discuss each service's corresponding configuration file, and the suggested method of deployment (if appropriate). You'll find that the sections covering these simple services are not terribly long, but don't neglect this material. We highly recommend taking some time to get familiar with their implications. Many creative solutions have been realized through the use of these services. Hopefully, this chapter will inspire a few more.

THE INIT SERVICE

The **init** process is the patron of all processes. *Always* the first process that gets started in any UNIX-based system (such as Linux), **init**'s process ID is always 1. Should **init** ever fail, the rest of the system will most likely follow suit.

> **NOTE**   If one wants to be strictly technically correct, **init** is not actually the very, very first process that gets run. But in order to remain politically correct, we'll assume that it is! You should also keep in mind that some so-called security-hardened Linux systems deliberately randomize the PID of **init**, so don't be surprised if you ever find yourself on such a system and notice that the PID of **init** is *not* one (1).

The **init** process serves two roles. The first is being the ultimate parent process. Because **init** never dies, the system can always be sure of its presence and, if necessary, make reference to it. The need to refer to **init** usually happens when a process dies before all of its spawned child processes have completed. This causes the children to inherit **init** as their parent process. A quick execution of the `ps -af` command will show a number of processes that will have a parent process ID (PPID) of 1.

The second job for **init** is to handle the various runlevels by executing the appropriate programs when a particular runlevel is reached. This behavior is defined by the **/etc/inittab** file.

The /etc/inittab File

The **/etc/inittab** file contains all the information **init** needs for starting runlevels. The format of each line in this file is as follows:

```
id:runlevels:action:process
```

TIP   Lines beginning with the pound symbol (#) are comments. Take a peek at your own **/etc/inittab**, and you'll find that it's already liberally commented. If you ever do need to make a change to **/etc/inittab**, you'll do yourself a favor by including liberal comments to explain what you've done.

Table 8-1 explains the significance of each of the four fields of an entry in the **/etc/inittab** file, while Table 8-2 defines some common options available for the **action** field in this file.

Now let's look at a sample entry from an **/etc/inittab** file:

```
# If power was restored before the shutdown kicked in, cancel it.
pr:12345:powerokwait:/sbin/shutdown -c "Power Restored; Shutdown Cancelled"
```

In this case:

▼   The first line, which begins with the pound sign (#), is a comment entry and is ignored.

■   **pr** is the unique identifier.

■   **1, 2, 3, 4,** and **5** are the runlevels at which this process can be activated.

■   **powerokwait** is the condition under which the process is run.

▲   The **/sbin/shutdown** . . . command is the process.

/etc/inittab Item	Description
id	A unique sequence of 1–4 characters that identifies this entry in the **/etc/inittab** file.
runlevels	The runlevels at which the process should be invoked. Some events are special enough that they can be trapped at all runlevels (for instance, the CTRL-ALT-DEL key combination to reboot). To indicate that an event is applicable to all runlevels, leave **runlevels** blank. If you want something to occur at multiple runlevels, simply list all of them in this field. For example, the **runlevels** entry **123** specifies something that runs at runlevels 1, 2, or 3.
action	Describes what action should be taken. Options for this field are explained in the next table.
process	Names the process (or program) to execute when the runlevel is entered.

Table 8-1.   /etc/inittab Entries

action Field in /etc/inittab	Description
`respawn`	The process will be restarted whenever it terminates.
`wait`	The process will be started once when the runlevel is entered, and **init** will wait for its completion.
`once`	The process will be started once when the runlevel is entered; however, **init** won't wait for termination of the process before possibly executing additional programs to be run at that particular runlevel.
`boot`	The process will be executed at system boot. The *runlevels* field is ignored in this case.
`bootwait`	The process will be executed at system boot, and **init** will wait for completion of the boot before advancing to the next process to be run.
`ondemand`	The process will be executed when a specific runlevel request occurs. (These runlevels are **a**, **b**, and **c**.) No change in runlevel occurs.
`initdefault`	Specifies the default runlevel for **init** on startup. If no default is specified, the user is prompted for a runlevel on console.
`sysinit`	The process will be executed during system boot, before any of the **boot** or **bootwait** entries.
`powerwait`	If **init** receives a signal from another process that there are problems with the power, this process will be run. Before continuing, **init** will wait for this process to finish.
`powerfail`	Same as **powerwait**, except that **init** will not wait for the process to finish.

Table 8-2.   Options Available for the *action* Field in the /etc/inittab File

$action$ Field in /etc/inittab	Description
`powerokwait`	This process will be executed as soon as **init** is informed that the power has been restored.
`ctrlaltdel`	The process is executed when **init** receives a signal indicating that the user has pressed the CTRL-ALT-DELETE key combination. Keep in mind that most X Window System servers capture this key combination, and thus **init** may not receive this signal if the X Window System is active.

Table 8-2.   Options Available for the $action$ Field in the /etc/inittab File (*cont.*)

The telinit Command

It's time to 'fess up: the mysterious force that tells **init** when to change runlevels is actually the `telinit` command. This command takes two command-line parameters. One is the desired runlevel that **init** needs to know about, and the other is **-t** *sec*, where *sec* is the number of seconds to wait before telling **init**.

NOTE   Whether **init** actually changes runlevels is its decision. Obviously, it usually does, or this command wouldn't be terribly useful.

It is extremely rare that you'll ever have to run the `telinit` command yourself. Usually, this is all handled for you by the startup and shutdown scripts.

NOTE   Under most UNIX implementations (including Linux), the `telinit` command is really just a symbolic link to the **init** program. Because of this, some folks prefer running **init** with the runlevel they want rather than using `telinit`.

XINETD AND INETD

The **xinetd** and **inetd** programs are two popular services on Linux systems; **xinetd** is the more modern incarnation of the older **inetd**. Strictly speaking, a Linux system can run effectively without the presence of either of them. But some daemons rely solely on the functionality they provide, So if you need either **xinetd** or **inetd**, then you need it and there are no two ways about it.

The **inetd** and **xinetd** programs are daemon processes. You probably know that daemons are special programs that, after starting, voluntarily release control of the terminal from which they started. The main mechanism by which daemons can interface with the rest of the system is through interprocess communication (IPC) channels, by sending messages to the system-wide log file, or by appending to a file on disk.

The role of **inetd** is to function as a "super-server" to other network server–related processes, such as **telnet, ftp, tftp**, etc.

It's a simple philosophy: Not all server processes (including those that accept new connections) are called upon so often that they require a program to be running in memory all the time. The main reason for the existence of a super-server is to conserve system resources. So instead of constantly maintaining potentially dozens of services loaded in memory waiting to be used, they are all listed in **inetd**'s configuration file, **/etc/inetd .conf**. On their behalf, **inetd** listens for incoming connections. Thus only a single process needs to be in memory.

A secondary benefit of **inetd** falls to those processes needing network connectivity but whose programmers do not want to have to write it into the system. The **inetd** program will handle the network code and pass incoming network streams into the process as its standard input (**stdin**). Any of the process's output (**stdout**) is sent back to the host that has connected to the process.

> **NOTE**   Unless you are programming, you don't have to be concerned with **inetd**'s **stdin/ stdout** feature. On the other hand, for someone who wants to write a simple script and make it available through the network, it's worth exploring this very powerful tool.

As a general rule of thumb, low-volume services (such as **tftp**) are usually best run through the **inetd**, whereas higher-volume services (such as Web servers) are better run as a standalone process that is always in memory ready to handle requests.

Current versions of Fedora, RHEL, SuSE, Mandrake, and even Mac OS X ship with a newer incarnation of **inetd** called **xinetd**—the name is an acronym for "extended Internet services daemon." The **xinetd** program accomplishes the same task as the regular **inetd** program: it helps to start programs that provide Internet services. Instead of having such programs automatically start up during system initialization and remain unused until a connection request arrives, **xinetd** instead stands in the gap for those programs and listens on their normal service ports. As a result, when **xinetd** hears a service request meant for one of the services it manages, it then starts or spurns the appropriate service.

Inasmuch as **xinetd** is similar to **inetd** in function, it should be noted that it includes a new configuration file format and a lot of additional features. The **xinetd** daemon uses a configuration file format that is very different from the classic **inetd** configuration file format. (Most other variants of UNIX, including Solaris and FreeBSD, use the classic **inetd** format.) This means that if you have an application that relies on **inetd**, you may need to provide some hand adjustments to make it work. Of course, you should definitely contact the developers of the application and let them know of the change so that they can release a newer version that works with the new **xinetd** configuration format, as well.

In this section, we will cover the new **xinetd** daemon. If your system uses **inetd**, you should be able to view the **/etc/inetd.conf** file and see the similarities between **inetd** and **xinetd**.

The /etc/xinetd.conf File

The **/etc/xinetd.conf** file consists of a series of blocks that take the following format:

```
blockname
{
    variable = value
}
```

where **blockname** is the name of the block that is being defined, **variable** is the name of a variable being defined within the context of the block, and **value** is the value assigned to the **variable**. Every block can have multiple variables defined within.

One special block is called **defaults**. Whatever variables are defined within this block are applied to all other blocks that are defined in the file.

An exception to the block format is the **includedir** directive, which tells **xinetd** to go read all the files in a directory and consider them to be part of the **/etc/xinetd.conf** file.

Any line that begins with a pound sign (#) is the start of a comment. The stock **/etc/xinetd.conf** file that ships with Fedora Core looks like this:

```
# Simple configuration file for xinetd
# Some defaults, and include /etc/xinetd.d/

defaults
{
        instances            = 60
        log_type             = SYSLOG authpriv
        log_on_success       = HOST PID
        log_on_failure       = HOST
        cps                  = 25 30
}

includedir /etc/xinetd.d
```

Don't worry if all of the variables and values aren't familiar to you yet; we will go over those in a moment. Let's first make sure you understand the format of the file.

In this example, the first two lines of the file are comments explaining what the file is and what it does. After the comments, you see the first block: **defaults**. The first variable that is defined in this block is **instances**, which is set to the value of 60. Five variables in total are defined in this block, the last one being **cps**. Since this block is titled **defaults**, the variables that are set within it will apply to all future blocks that are defined. Finally, the last line of the file specifies that the **/etc/xinetd.d** directory must be examined for other files that contain more configuration information. This will cause **xinetd** to read all of the files in that directory and parse them as if they were part of the **/etc/xinetd.conf** file.

Variables and Their Meanings

Table 8-3 lists some of the variable names that are supported in the **/etc/xinetd.conf** file.

You do not need to specify all of the variables when defining a service. The only required ones are

▼   `socket_type`

■   `user`

■   `server`

▲   `wait`

Variable	Description
`id`	This attribute is used to uniquely identify a service. This is useful because services exist that can use different protocols and need to be described with different entries in the configuration file. By default, the service ID is the same as the service name.
`type`	Any combination of the following values may be used: **RPC** if this is an RPC service, **INTERNAL** if this service is provided by **xinetd**, or **UNLISTED** if this is a service not listed in the **/etc/services** file.
`disable`	This is either the value **yes** or **no**. A **yes** value means that although the service is defined, it is not available for use.
`socket_type`	Valid values for this variable are **stream** to indicate that this service is a stream-based service, **dgram** to indicate that this service is a datagram, or **raw** to indicate that this service uses raw IP datagrams. The **stream** value refers to connection-oriented (TCP) data streams (for example, Telnet and FTP). The **dgram** value refers to datagram (UDP) streams (for example, the TFTP service is a datagram-based protocol). Other protocols outside the scope of TCP/IP do exist; however, you'll rarely encounter them.
`protocol`	Determines the type of protocol (either **tcp** or **udp**) for the connection type.
`wait`	If this is set to **yes**, only one connection will be processed at a time. If this is set to **no**, multiple connections will be allowed by running the appropriate service daemon multiple times.

Table 8-3.   xinetd Configuration File Variables

Variable	Description
user	Specifies the username under which this service will run. The username must exist in the **/etc/passwd** file.
group	Specifies the group name under which this service will run. The group must exist in the **/etc/group** file.
instances	Specifies the maximum number of concurrent connections this service is allowed to handle. The default is no limit if the **wait** variable is set to **nowait**.
server	The name of the program to run when this service is connected.
server_args	The arguments passed to the server. In contrast to **inetd**, the name of the server should not be included in *server_args*.
only_from	Specifies the networks from which a valid connection may arrive. (This is the built-in TCP Wrappers functionality.) You can specify this in one of three ways: as a numeric address, a host name, or a network address with netmask. The numeric address can take the form of a complete IP address to indicate a specific host (such as 192.168.1.1). However, if any of the ending octets are zeros, the address will be treated like a network where all of the octets that are zero are wildcards (for instance, 192.168.1.0 means any host that starts with the numbers 192.168.1). Alternatively, you can specify the number of bits in the netmask after a slash (for example, 192.168.1.0/24 means a network address of 192.168.1.0 with a netmask of 255.255.255.0).
no_access	The opposite of *only_from* in that instead of specifying the addresses from which a connection is valid, this variable specifies the addresses from which a connection is invalid. It can take the same type of parameters as *only_from*.
log_type	Determines where logging information for that service will go. There are two valid values: **SYSLOG** and **FILE**. If **SYSLOG** is specified, you must specify to which **syslog** facility to log as well (see "The syslogd Daemon," later in this chapter, for more information on facilities). For example, you can specify: `>log_type = SYSLOG local0`

Table 8-3.   xinetd Configuration File Variables (*cont.*)

Variable	Description
	Optionally, you can include the log level, as well. For example:
	`>log_type = SYSLOG local0 info`
	If **FILE** is specified, you must specify which filename to log. Optionally, you can also specify the soft limit on the file size. The soft limit on a file size is where an extra log message indicating that the file has gotten too large will be generated. If the soft limit is specified, a hard limit can also be specified. At the hard limit, no additional logging will be done. If the hard limit is not explicitly defined, it is set to be 1% higher than the soft limit. An example of the **FILE** option is as follows:
	`log_type = FILE /var/log/mylog`
log_on_ success	Specifies which information is logged on a connection success. The options include **PID** to log the process ID of the service that processed the request, **HOST** to specify the remote host connecting to the service, **USERID** to log the remote username (if available), **EXIT** to log the exit status or termination signal of the process, or **DURATION** to log the length of the connection.
port	Specifies the network port under which the service will run. If the service is listed in **/etc/services**, this port number must equal the value specified there.
interface	Allows a service to bind to a specific interface and only be available there. The value is the IP address of the interface that you wish this service to be bound to. An example of this is binding less secure services (such as Telnet) to an internal and physically secure interface on a firewall and not allowing it the external, more vulnerable interface outside the firewall.
cps	The first argument specifies the maximum number of connections per second this service is allowed to handle. If the rate exceeds this value, the service is temporarily disabled for the second argument number of seconds. For example:
	`>cps = 10 30`
	This will disable a service for 30 seconds if the connection rate ever exceeds 10 connections per second.

Table 8-3.   xinetd Configuration File Variables (*cont.*)

Examples: A Simple Service Entry and Enabling/Disabling a Service

Using the **finger** service as an example, let's take a look at one of the simplest entries possible with **xinetd**:

```
# default: on
# description: The finger server answers finger requests. Finger is \
#        a protocol that allows remote users to see information such \
#        as login name and last login time for local users.
service finger
{
        socket_type     = stream
        wait            = no
        user            = nobody
        server          = /usr/sbin/in.fingerd

}
```

As you can see, the entry is self-explanatory. The service name is **finger**, and because of the *socket_type* we know this is a TCP service. The *wait* variable tells us that there can be multiple **finger** processes running concurrently. The *user* variable tells us that "**nobody**" will be the process owner. Finally, the name of the process being run is **/usr/sbin/in.fingerd**.

With our understanding of an **xinetd** service entry, let's try to enable and disable a service.

Enabling/Disabling the Echo Service

If you want a secure system, chances are you will run with very few services—there are some people who don't even run **xinetd** at all! It takes very few steps to enable or disable a service. For example, to enable a service you would first enable the service in the **xinetd** configuration file (or **inetd.conf** if you are using **inetd** instead), restart the **xinetd** service, and finally test things out to make sure you have the behavior you expect. To disable a service is just the opposite procedure.

> **NOTE**   The service we will be exploring is the **echo** service. This service is internal to **xinetd**; i.e., it is not provided by any external daemon.

Let's step through this process:

1. Use any plain text editor to edit the file **/etc/xinetd.d/echo** and change the variable *disable* to **no**:

```
# default: off
# description: An xinetd internal service which echo's characters back
to #clients. This is the tcp version.
service echo
```

```
{
        disable = no
        type            = INTERNAL
        id              = echo-stream
        socket_type     = stream
        protocol        = tcp
        user            = root
        wait            = no
}
```

2. Save your changes to the file and exit the editor.

3. Restart the **xinetd** service. Under Fedora Core or RHEL, type

   ```
   [root@serverA ~]# service xinetd restart
   ```

   Note that for other distributions that don't have the **service** command available, we can send a HUP signal to **xinetd** instead. First find **xinetd**'s process ID (PID) using the **ps** command. Then use the **kill** command to send the HUP signal to **xinetd**'s process ID. We can verify that the restart worked by using the **tail** command to view the last few messages of the **/var/log/messages** file. The commands to find **xinetd**'s PID, kill **xinetd**, and view the log files are

   ```
   [root@serverA ~]# ps -C xinetd
     PID TTY          TIME CMD
   31430 ?        00:00:00 xinetd
   [root@serverA ~]# kill -1 31430
   [root@serverA ~]# tail /var/log/messages
   Jun  2 08:49:36 serverA xinetd[31430]: xinetd Version 2009.03.28 started with
   libwrap options compiled in.
   Jun  2 08:49:36 serverA xinetd[31430]: Started working: 1 available service
   Jun  2 08:50:22 serverA xinetd[31430]: Starting reconfiguration
   Jun  2 08:50:22 serverA xinetd[31430]: readjusting service echo
   Jun  2 08:50:22 serverA xinetd[31430]: Reconfigured: new=0 old=1 dropped=0
   ```

4. Telnet to the port (port 7) of the **echo** service and see if the service is indeed running. Type

   ```
   [root@serverA ~]# telnet localhost 7
   Trying 127.0.0.1...
   Connected to localhost.localdomain (127.0.0.1).
   Escape character is '^]'.
   ```

   Your output should be similar to the preceding, if the **echo** service has been enabled.

   You can type any character on your keyboard at the Telnet prompt and watch the character get echoed (repeated) back to you.

As you can see, the **echo** service is one of those terribly useful and life-saving services that users and system administrators *cannot* do without.

This exercise walked you through enabling a service by directly editing its **xinetd** configuration file. It is a simple process to enable or disable a service. But you should actually go back and make sure that the service is indeed disabled (if that is what you want) by actually testing it. You don't want to think that you have disabled Telnet and have it still be running.

TIP   You can also quickly enable or disable a service that runs under **xinetd** by using the `chkconfig` utility, which is available in Fedora Core, RHEL, SuSE, and most other flavors of Linux. For example, to disable the **echo** service that you manually enabled, just issue the command `chkconfig echo off`.

THE SYSLOGD DAEMON

With so much going on at any one time, especially with services that are disconnected from a terminal window, it's necessary to provide a standard mechanism by which special events and messages can be logged. Linux uses the **syslogd** daemon to provide this service.

The **syslogd** daemon provides a standardized means of performing logging. Many other UNIX systems employ a compatible daemon, thus providing a means for cross-platform logging over the network. This is especially valuable in a large heterogeneous environment where it's necessary to centralize the collection of log entries to gain an accurate picture of what's going on. You could equate this system of logging facilities to the Windows NT System Logger.

The log files that **syslogd** writes to are straight text files, usually stored in the **/var/log** directory. Each log entry consists of a single line containing the date, time, host name, process name, PID, and the message from that process. A system-wide function in the standard C library provides an easy mechanism for generating log messages. If you don't feel like writing code but want to generate entries in the logs, you have the option of using the `logger` command.

As you can imagine, a tool with **syslogd**'s importance is something that gets started as part of the boot scripts. Every Linux distribution you would use in a server environment will already do this for you.

Invoking syslogd

If you do find a need to either start **syslogd** manually or modify the script that starts it up at boot, you'll need to be aware of **syslogd**'s command-line parameters, shown in Table 8-4.

The /etc/syslog.conf File

The **/etc/syslog.conf** file contains the configuration information that **syslogd** needs to run. The file's format is a little unusual, but the default configuration file you have will probably suffice unless you need to send specific information into specific files or perhaps want to send local logging messages to remote logging machines that can accept.

Parameter	Description
`-d`	Debug mode. Normally, at startup, **syslogd** detaches itself from the current terminal and starts running in the background. With the **-d** option, **syslogd** retains control of the terminal and prints debugging information as messages are logged. It's extremely unlikely that you'll need this option.
`-f config`	Specifies a configuration file as an alternative to the default **/etc/syslog.conf**.
`-h`	By default, **syslogd** does not forward messages sent to it that were really destined for another host. Caution: If you use this parameter, you run the risk of being used as part of a denial-of-service attack.
`-l hostlist`	This option lets you list the hosts for which you are willing to perform logging. Each host name should be its simple name, not its fully qualified domain name (FQDN). You can list multiple hosts, as long as they are separated by a colon; for example, `-l toybox:serverB`
`-m interval`	By default, **syslogd** generates a log entry every 20 minutes as a "just so you know I'm running" message. This is for systems that may not be busy. (If you're watching the system log and don't see a single message in over 20 minutes, you'll know for a fact that something has gone wrong.) By specifying a numeric value for **interval**, you can indicate the number of minutes **syslogd** should wait before generating another message.
`-r`	By default, as a security precaution, the **syslogd** daemon refuses messages sent to it from the network. This command-line parameter enables this feature.
`-s domainlist`	If you are receiving **syslogd** entries that show the entire FQDN, you can have **syslogd** strip off the domain name and leave just the host name. Simply list the domain names to remove in a colon-separated list as the parameter to the **-s** option. For example: `-s conspiracy.com:wealthy.com`

Table 8-4. syslogd Command-Line Parameters

Log Message Classifications

Before you can understand the **/etc/syslog.conf** file format itself, you have to understand how log messages get classified. Each message has a *facility* and a *priority*. The facility tells you from which subsystem the message originated, and the priority tells you how important the message is. These two values are separated by a period.

Both values have string equivalents, making them easier to remember. The string equivalents for facility and priority are listed in Tables 8-5 and 8-6, respectively.

NOTE The priority levels are in the order of severity according to **syslogd**. Thus **debug** is not considered severe at all, and **emerg** is the most crucial. For example, the combination facility-and-priority string **mail.crit** indicates there is a critical error in the mail subsystem (for example, it has run out of disk space). **syslogd** considers this message more important than **mail.info**, which may simply note the arrival of another message.

Facility String Equivalent	Description
`auth`	Authentication messages
`authpriv`	Essentially the same as **auth**
`cron`	Messages generated by the **cron** subsystem
`daemon`	Generic classification for service daemons
`kern`	Kernel messages
`Lpr`	Printer subsystem messages
`Mail`	Mail subsystem messages (including per mail logs)
`Mark`	Obsolete, but you may find some books that discuss it; **syslogd** simply ignores it
`News`	Messages through the NNTP subsystem
`security`	Same thing as **auth**; should not be used
`syslog`	Internal messages from **syslog** itself
`User`	Generic messages from user programs
`Uucp`	Messages from the UUCP (UNIX to UNIX copy) subsystem
`Local0-local9`	Generic facility levels whose importance can be decided based on your needs

Table 8-5. String Equivalents for the Facility Value in /etc/syslog.conf

Priority String Equivalent	Description
debug	Debugging statements
info	Miscellaneous information
notice	Important statements, but not necessarily bad news
warning	Potentially dangerous situation
warn	Same as **warning**; should not be used
err	An error condition
error	Same as **err**; should not be used
crit	Critical situation
alert	A message indicating an important occurrence
emerg	An emergency situation

Table 8-6.   String Equivalents for Priority Levels in /etc/syslog.conf

In addition to the priority levels in Table 8-6, **syslogd** also understands wildcards. Thus, you can define a whole class of messages; for instance, **mail.*** refers to all messages related to the mail subsystem.

Format of /etc/syslog.conf

Here is the format of each line in the configuration file:

```
facility/priority combinations separated by semicolons        file/process/host
to log to
```

For example:

```
kern.info; kern.err        /var/log/kernel-info
```

The location to which **syslogd** can send log messages is also quite flexible. It can save messages to files and send messages to FIFOs, to a list of users, or (in the case of centralized logging for a large site) to a master log host. To differentiate these location elements, the following rules are applied to the location entry:

▼   If the location begins with a slash (/), the message is going to a file.

■   If the location begins with a pipe (|), the message is going to a named pipe (FIFO).

▲   If the location begins with an @, the message is going to a host.

Table 8-7 shows examples of location entries.

Location Style	Description
Regular file (e.g., /var/log/messages)	A file. Note that if you prefix the filename with a dash, **syslogd** will not synchronize the file system after the write. This means you run the risk of losing some data if there is a crash before the system gets a chance to flush its buffers. On the other hand, if an application is being overly verbose about its logging, you'll gain performance using this option. Remember: If you want messages sent to the console, you need to specify /dev/console.
|/tmp/mypipe	A named pipe. This type of file is created with the **mknod** command. With **syslogd** feeding one side of the pipe, you can have another program running that reads the other side of the pipe. This is an effective way to have programs parsing log output, looking for critical situations, so that you can be paged if necessary.
@loghost	A host name. This example will send the message to **loghost**. The **syslogd** daemon on **loghost** will then record the message.

Table 8-7. Location Entry Examples

If you enter no special character before the location entry, **syslogd** assumes that the location is a comma-separated list of users who will have the message written to their screen. If you use an asterisk (*), **syslogd** will send the message to all of the users who are logged in.

As usual, any line that begins with a pound symbol (#) is a comment. Now let's look at some examples of configuration file entries:

```
# Log all the mail messages in one place.
mail.* /var/log/maillog
```

This example shows that all priorities in the mail facility should have their messages placed in the **/var/log/maillog** file.

Consider the next example:

```
# Listed users get emergency messages, plus logging those messages to remote
#system
*.emerg        @loghost,yyang,root,dude
```

In this example, you see that any facility with a log level of **emerg** is sent to another system running **syslogd** called `loghost`. Also, if the user yyang, root, or dude is logged in, the message being logged is written to the user's console.

You can also specify multiple selectors on a single line for a single event. For example:

```
*.info;mail.none;authpriv.none              /var/log/messages
```

Sample /etc/syslog.conf File

Following is a complete **syslog.conf** file:

```
# Log all kernel messages to the console.
# Logging much else clutters up the screen.
#kern.*                                      /dev/console
# Log anything (except mail) of level info or higher.
# Don't log private authentication messages!

*.info;mail.none;authpriv.none;cron.none     /var/log/messages
# The authpriv file has restricted access.
authpriv.*                                   /var/log/secure

# Log all the mail messages in one place.
mail.*                                       -/var/log/maillog

# Log cron stuff
cron.*                                       /var/log/cron

# Everybody gets emergency messages
*.emerg                                      *

# Save news errors of level crit and higher in a special file.
uucp,news.crit                               /var/log/spooler

# Save boot messages also to boot.log
local7.*                                     /var/log/boot.log
```

CRON

The **cron** program allows any user in the system to schedule a program to run on any date, at any time, or on a particular day of week, down to the minute. Using **cron** is an extremely efficient way to automate your system, generate reports on a regular basis, and perform other periodic chores. (Not-so-honest uses of **cron** include having it invoke a system to have you paged when you want to get out of a meeting!)

Like the other services we've discussed in this chapter, **cron** is started by the boot scripts and is most likely already configured for you. A quick check of the process listing should show it quietly running in the background:

```
[root@serverA ~]# ps aux | grep crond | grep -v grep
root      2422  0.0  0.3  2256  764 ?        Ss   Mar17   0:25 crond
```

The **cron** service works by waking up once a minute and checking each user's **crontab** file. This file contains the user's list of events that they want executed at a particular date and time. Any events that match the current date and time are executed.

The **crond** command itself requires no command-line parameters or special signals to indicate a change in status.

The crontab File

The tool that allows you to edit entries to be executed by **crond** is **crontab**. Essentially, all it does is verify your permission to modify your **cron** settings and then invoke a text editor so you can make your changes. Once you're done, **crontab** places the file in the right location and brings you back to a prompt.

Whether or not you have appropriate permission is determined by **crontab** by checking the **/etc/cron.allow** and **/etc/cron.deny** files. If either of these files exists, you must be explicitly listed there for your actions to be effected. For example, if the **/etc/cron.allow** file exists, your username must be listed in that file in order for you to be able to edit your **cron** entries. On the other hand, if the only file that exists is **/etc/cron.deny**, unless your username is listed there, you are implicitly allowed to edit your **cron** settings.

The file listing your **cron** jobs (often referred to as the **crontab** file) is formatted as follows. All values must be listed as integers.

Minute Hour Day Month DayOfWeek Command

If you want to have multiple entries for a particular column (for instance, you want a program to run at 4:00 A.M., 12:00 P.M., and 5:00 P.M.), then you need to have each of these time values in a comma-separated list. Be sure not to type any spaces in the list. For the program running at 4:00 A.M., 12:00 P.M., and 5:00 P.M., the *Hour* values list would read **4,12,17**. Newer versions of **cron** allow you to use a shorter notation for supplying fields. For example, if you want to run a process every two minutes, you just need to put **/2** as the first entry. Notice that **cron** uses military time format.

For the *DayOfWeek* entry, 0 represents Sunday, 1 represents Monday, and so on, all the way to 6 representing Saturday.

Any entry that has a single asterisk (*) wildcard will match any minute, hour, day, month, or day of week when used in the corresponding column.

When the dates and times in the file match the current date and time, the command is run as the user who set the **crontab**. Any output generated is e-mailed back to the user.

Obviously, this can result in a mailbox full of messages, so it is important to be thrifty with your reporting. A good way to keep a handle on volume is to output only error conditions and have any unavoidable output sent to **/dev/null**.

Let's look at some examples. The following entry runs the program **/bin/ping -c 5 serverB** every four hours:

```
0 0,4,8,12,16,20 * * * /bin/ping -c 5 serverB
```

or using the shorthand method:

```
0 */4 * * * /bin/ping -c 5 serverB
```

Here is an entry that runs the program **/usr/local/scripts/backup_level_0** at 10:00 P.M. every Friday night:

```
0 22 * * 5 /usr/local/scripts/backup_level_0
```

And finally, here's a script to send out an e-mail at 4:01 A.M. on April 1 (whatever day that may be):

```
1 4 1 4 * /bin/mail dad@domain.com < /home/yyang/joke
```

NOTE   When **crond** executes commands, it does so with the **sh** shell. Thus, any environment variables that you might be used to may not work within **cron**.

Editing the crontab File

Editing or creating a **cron** job is as easy as editing a regular text file. But you should be aware of the fact that the program will by default use an editor specified by the EDITOR or VISUAL environment variable. On most Linux systems the default editor is usually **vi**. But you can always change this default to any editor you are comfortable with by setting the EDITOR or VISUAL environment variable.

Now that you know the format of the **crontab** configuration file, you need to edit the file. You don't do this by editing the file directly; you use the **crontab** command to edit your **crontab** file:

```
[yyang@serverA ~]$ crontab -e
```

To list what is in your current **crontab** file, just give **crontab** the **-l** argument to display the content. Type

```
[yyang@serverA ~]$ crontab -l
no crontab for yyang
```

According to this output, the user yyang does not currently have anything in the **crontab** file.

SUMMARY

In this chapter, we discussed some important system services that come with most Linux systems. These services do not require network support and can vary from host to host, making them very useful, since they can work whether or not the system is in multiuser mode.

A quick recap of the chapter:

▼   **init** is the mother of all processes in the system, with a PID of 1. It also controls runlevels and can be configured through the **/etc/inittab** file.

■   **inetd**, although barely used anymore, is the original super-server that listens to server requests on behalf of a large number of smaller, less frequently used services. When it accepts a request for one of those services, **inetd** starts the actual service and quietly forwards data between the network and actual service. Its configuration file is **/etc/inetd.conf**.

■   **xinetd** is the "new" version of the classic **inetd** super-server that offers more configuration options and better built-in security. Its main configuration file is **/etc/xinetd.conf**.

■   **syslog** is the system-wide logging daemon. Along with log entries generated by the system, **syslog** can accept log messages over the network (so long as you enable that feature). Its configuration file is **/etc/syslog.conf**.

▲   Finally, the **cron** service allows you to schedule events to take place at certain dates and times, which is great for periodic events like backups and e-mail reminders. All the configuration files on which it relies are handled via the `crontab` program.

In each section of this chapter, we discussed how to configure a different service and even suggested some uses beyond the default settings that come with the system. It is recommended that you poke around these services and familiarize yourself with what can be accomplished with them. Many powerful automation, data collection, and analysis tools have been built around these basic services—as well as many wonderfully silly and useless things. Don't be afraid to have fun with it!

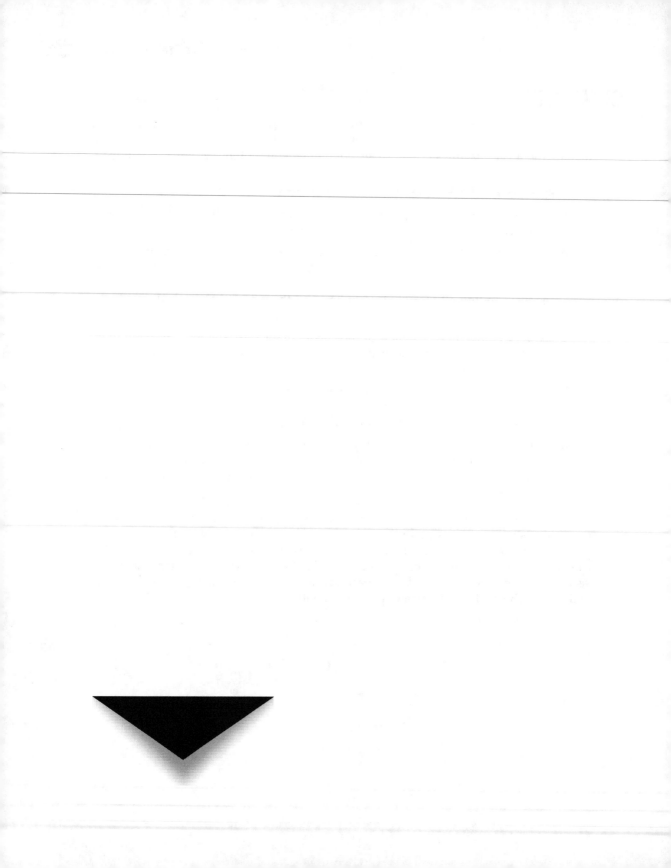

CHAPTER 9

Compiling the
Linux Kernel

One of Linux's greatest strengths is that its source code is available to anyone who wants it. The GNU GPL (General Public License) under which Linux is distributed even allows you to tinker with the source code and distribute your changes! Real changes to the source code (at least, those to be taken seriously) go through the process of joining the official kernel tree. This requires extensive testing and proof that the changes will benefit Linux as a whole. At the very end of the approval process, the code gets a final yes or no from a core group of the Linux project's original developers. It is this extensive review process that keeps the quality of Linux's code so noteworthy.

For system administrators who have used other proprietary operating systems, this approach to code control is a significant departure from the philosophy of waiting for the company to release a patch, a service pack, or some sort of "hot fix." Instead of having to wade through public relations, sales engineers, and other front-end units, you have the option of contacting the author of the subsystem directly and explaining your problem. A patch can be created and sent to you before the next official release of the kernel, and get you up and running.

Of course, the flip side of this working arrangement is that you need to be able to compile a kernel yourself rather than rely on someone else to supply precompiled code. And, of course, you won't have to do this often, because production environments, once stable, rarely need a kernel compile. But if need be, you should know what to do. Luckily, it's not difficult.

In this chapter, we'll walk through the process of acquiring a kernel source tree, configuring it, compiling it, and finally, installing the end result.

> **CAUTION** The kernel is the first thing that loads when a Linux system is booted (after the boot loader of course!). If the kernel doesn't work right, it's unlikely that the rest of the system will boot. Be sure to have an emergency or rescue boot medium handy in case you need to revert to an old configuration. (See the section on GRUB in Chapter 6).

WHAT EXACTLY IS A KERNEL?

Before we jump into the process of compiling, let's back up a step and make sure you're clear on the concept of what a kernel is and the role it plays in the system. Most often, when people say "Linux" they are usually referring to a "Linux distribution." As discussed in Chapter 1, a distribution comprises everything necessary to get Linux to exist as a functional operating system. (For example, SuSE Linux is a type of Linux distribution.) Distributions make use of code from various open source projects that are independent of Linux; in fact, many of the software packages maintained by these projects are used extensively on other UNIX-like platforms as well. The GNU C Compiler, for example, which comes with most Linux distributions, also exists on many other operating systems (probably more systems than most people realize exist).

So, then, what *does* make up the pure definition of Linux? The *kernel*. The kernel of any operating system is the core of all the system's software. The only thing more fundamental than the kernel is the hardware itself.

The kernel has many jobs. The essence of its work is to abstract the underlying hardware from the software and provide a running environment for application software, through system calls. Specifically, the environment must handle issues such as networking, disk access, virtual memory, and multitasking—a complete list of these tasks would take up an entire chapter in itself! Today's Linux kernel (version 2.6.*) contains almost six million lines of code (including device drivers). By comparison, the sixth edition of UNIX from Bell Labs in 1976 had roughly 9000 lines. Figure 9-1 illustrates the kernel's position in a complete system.

Although the kernel is a small part of a complete Linux system, it is by far the most critical element. If the kernel fails or crashes, the rest of the system goes with it. Happily, Linux can boast its kernel stability. *Uptimes* (the length of time in between reboots) for Linux systems are often expressed in years. Indeed, UNIX systems in general regularly claim significantly long uptimes.

FINDING THE KERNEL SOURCE CODE

Your distribution of Linux probably has the source code to the specific kernel version(s) it supports available in one form or the other. These could be in the form of a compiled binary (*.src.rpm), a source rpm (*.srpm), or the like.

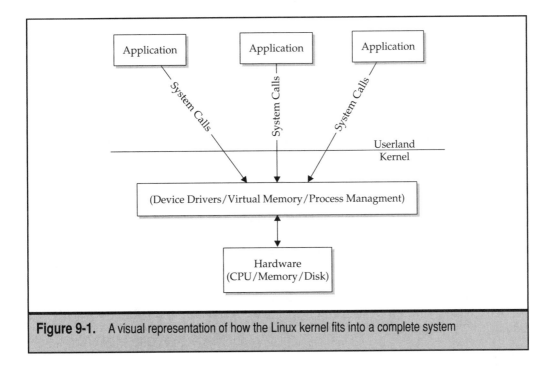

Figure 9-1.   A visual representation of how the Linux kernel fits into a complete system

If you find a need to download a different (possibly newer) version than the one that your particular Linux distribution provides, the first place to look for the source code is at the official kernel Web site: http://www.kernel.org/. The kernel.org tree represents the "Linus Tree." This site maintains a listing of Web sites mirroring the kernel source as well as tons of other open source software and general-purpose utilities.

Under the site's link for downloading the kernel, you'll find a list of mirror Web sites based on country codes. Although you can connect to any of them, you'll most likely get the best performance by sticking to your own country. Go to http://www.*xx*.kernel.org/, where *xx* is the Internet country code for your country. For the United States, this address is http://www.us.kernel.org/.

NOTE There is a common tendency for people to want to download the most pristine source possible, and where else would one get the most pristine source possible but from kernel.org itself! But there are several reasons that it is probably okay to get the sources from other locations than kernel.org. For one thing, you can always check the signature or md5sum of the file you download and compare it with the official signature. Most of the sites that mirror kernel.org regularly synchronize their sites with that of kernel.org on a frequent basis. With all this in mind, it is probably okay for you to download the source tree from a mirror that is geographically closest to you.

Getting the Correct Kernel Version

The Web site listing of kernels available will contain folders for v1.0, v1.1, and so forth, and v2.5, v2.6, and so forth. Before you follow your natural inclination to get the latest version, make sure you understand how the Linux kernel versioning system works.

Because Linux's development model encourages public contributions, the latest version of the kernel must be accessible to everyone, all the time. This presents a problem, however: software that is undergoing significant updates may be unstable and not of production quality.

To circumvent this problem, early Linux developers adopted a system of using odd-numbered kernels (1.1, 1.3, 2.1, 2.3, and so on) to indicate a design-and-development cycle. Thus, the odd-numbered kernels carry the disclaimer that they may not be stable and should not be used for situations for which reliability is a must. These development kernels are typically released at a very high rate, since there is so much activity around them—new versions of development kernels can be released as often as twice a week!

On the other hand, even-numbered kernels (1.0, 1.2, 2.0, 2.2, 2.4, 2.6, and so on) are considered ready-for-production systems. They have been allowed to mature under the public's usage (and scrutiny). Unlike development kernels, production kernels are released at a much slower rate and contain mostly bug fixes.

The version of the kernel that we are going to work with in the following section is version 2.6.12.1, which is available at http://www.kernel.org/pub/linux/kernel/v2.6/linux-2.6.12.1.tar.gz.

TIP You can use the `wget` utility to quickly download the kernel source into your current working directory by typing

```
# wget http://www.kernel.org/pub/linux/kernel/v2.6/linux-
2.6.12.1.tar.gz
```

Unpacking the Kernel Source Code

Most of the software packages you have dealt with so far have probably been RPM packages, and you're most likely accustomed to using the tools that came with the system (such as RPM or Yast) to manage the packages. Kernel source code is a little different and requires some user participation. Let's go through the steps to unpack the kernel.

The kernel source consists of a bunch of different files, and because of the sheer number and size of these files collectively, it is useful to compress the files and put them all in a single directory structure. The kernel source that you will download from the Internet is a file that has been compressed and tarred. Therefore, to use the source, you need to decompress and untar the source file. This is what it means to unpack the kernel. Overall, it's really a straightforward process.

The traditional location for the kernel source tree on the local file system is the **/usr/src** directory. For the remainder of this chapter, we'll assume you are working out of the **/usr/src** directory.

NOTE Some Linux distributions sometimes have a symbolic link under the **/usr/src** directory. This symbolic link is usually named "linux" and is usually a link to a default or the latest kernel source tree. Some third-party software packages rely on this link in order to compile or build properly!

Copy the kernel tarball that you downloaded earlier into the **/usr/src** directory. Use the **tar** command to unpack and decompress the file. Type

```
[root@serverA src]# tar xvzf linux-2.6.12.1.tar.gz
```

You'll hear your hard disk whir for a bit as this command runs—the kernel source is, after all, a large file!

TIP Take a moment to check out what's inside of the kernel source tree. At the very least, you'll get a chance to see what kind of documentation ships with a stock kernel. A good portion of the kernel documentation is conveniently stored in the **Documentation** directory at the root of the kernel source tree.

BUILDING THE KERNEL

So now you have an unpacked kernel tree just waiting to be built. In this section, we're going to review the process of configuring and building a kernel. This is in contrast to operating systems such as Windows 2000, which come preconfigured and therefore contain support for many features you may or may not want.

The Linux design philosophy allows the individual to decide about the important parts of the kernel. (For example, if you don't have a SCSI subsystem, what's the point in wasting memory to support it?) This individualized design has the important benefit of letting you thin down the feature list so that Linux can run as efficiently as possible. This is also one of the reasons why it is possible to run Linux in various hardware setups, from low-end systems, to embedded systems, to really high-end systems. You may find that a box incapable of supporting a Windows-based server is more than capable of supporting a Linux-based OS.

Two steps are required in building a kernel: configuring and compiling. We won't get into the specifics of configuration in this chapter, which would be difficult because of the fast-paced evolution of the Linux kernel. However, once you understand the basic process, you should be able to apply it from version to version. For the sake of discussion, we'll cite examples from the v2.6.* kernel that we unpacked in the previous section.

The first step in building the kernel is configuring its features. Usually your desired feature list will be based on whatever hardware you need to support. This, of course, means that you'll need a list of that hardware.

On a system that is already running Linux, the following command will list all hardware connected to the system via the PCI bus:

```
[root@serverA ~]# lspci
```

With this list of hardware, you're ready to start configuring the kernel.

Avoid Needless Upgrades

Bear in mind that, if you have a working system that is stable and well behaved, there is little reason to upgrade the kernel unless one of these conditions holds for you:

- ▼ There is a security fix that you must apply.
- ■ There is a specific new feature in a stable release that you need.
- ▲ There is a specific bug fix that impacts you.

In the case of a security fix, decide whether the risk really impacts you; e.g., if the security issue is found in a device driver that you don't use, then there is no reason to upgrade. In the case of a bug fix release, read carefully through the release notes and decide if the fixes really impact you—if you have a stable system, upgrading the kernel with patches you never use is just introducing risk for no reason. On production systems, the kernel shouldn't simply be upgraded just to have "the latest kernel"; there should be a truly compelling reason to upgrade.

Preparing to Configure the Kernel

Now that we have a rough idea of the types of hardware and features that our new kernel needs to support, we can begin the actual configuration. But first some background information:

The Linux kernel source tree contains several files named **Makefile** (a makefile is simply a text file that describes the relationships among the files in a program). These makefiles help to glue the thousands of other files that make up the kernel source together. What is more important to us here—the makefiles also contain targets. The targets are the commands or directives that are executed by the **make** program.

The **Makefile** in the root of the kernel source tree contains specific targets that can be used in prepping the kernel build environment, configuring the kernel, compiling the kernel, installing the kernel, and so on. Some of the targets are discussed in more detail here:

▼ **make mrproper**   This target cleans up the build environment of any stale files and dependencies that might have been left over from a previous kernel build. All previous kernel configurations will be cleaned (deleted) from the build environment.

■ **make clean**   This target does not do as thorough a job as the "mrproper" target. It only deletes most generated files. It does not delete the kernel configuration file (**.config**).

■ **make menuconfig**   This target invokes a text-based editor interface with menus, radio lists, and text-based dialog boxes for configuring the kernel.

■ **make xconfig**   This is an X Window–based kernel configuration tool that relies on the Qt graphical development libraries. These libraries are used by KDE-based applications.

■ **make gconfig**   This target also invokes an X Window-based kernel configuration tool. But it relies on the GTK2 (GIMP) toolkit. This GTK2 toolkit is heavily used in the GNOME desktop world.

▲ **make help**   This target will show you all the other possible make targets and also serves as a source of quick online help system.

To configure the kernel in this section, we will make use of only one of the targets. In particular, we will use the **make xconfig** command. The **xconfig** kernel config editor is one of the more popular tools for configuring the Linux 2.6–series kernels. The graphical editor has a simple and clean interface and is *almost* intuitive to use.

But before beginning the actual kernel configuration, you should clean (prepare) the kernel build environment by using the **make mrproper** command. Type

```
[root@serverA linux-2.6.12.1]# make mrproper
```

Kernel Configuration

Next, we will step through the process of configuring a Linux 2.6.* series kernel. In order to explore some of the innards of this process, we will enable the support of a very specific feature that we'll pretend must be supported on the system. Once you understand how this works, you can apply the same procedure to add support for any other new kernel feature that you want. Specifically we'll enable support for the NTFS file system into our custom kernel.

Most modern Linux distros that ship with the 2.6.* series kernels (where the asterisk is a wildcard that represents the complete version number of the kernel) also have a kernel configuration file for the running kernel available on the local file system as a compressed or regular file. On our sample system that runs the Fedora Core Linux, this file resides in the **/boot** directory and is usually named something like "config-2.6.*." The configuration file contains a list of the options and features that were enabled for the particular kernel it represents. A config file similar to this one is what we aim to create through the process of configuring the kernel. The only difference between the file we'll create and the ready-made one is that we have added further customization to ours.

Using a known, preexisting config file as a framework for creating our own custom file helps us to ensure we don't waste too much time duplicating the effort that other people have already put into finding what works and what doesn't work!

The following steps will cover how to compile the kernel after you have first gone through the configuration of the kernel. We will be using the Graphical Kernel configuration utility, so your X Window System needs to be up and running.

1. To begin with, we'll copy over and rename the preexisting config file from the **/boot** directory into our kernel build environment. Type

   ```
   [root@serverA linux-2.6.12.1]# cp /boot/config-`uname -r`  .config
   ```

   We use **uname -r** here to help us obtain the configuration file for the running kernel. The **uname -r** command prints the running kernel's release. Using it here helps ensure that we are getting the exact version that we want, just in case there are other versions present. On our sample Fedora system, the command is the equivalent of manually typing

   ```
   [root@serverA linux-2.6*]# cp /boot/config-2.6.11-1.1369_FC4 .config
   ```

NOTE The Linux kernel configuration editor specifically looks for and generates a file named **.config** at the root of the kernel source tree. This file is hidden.

2. Launch the graphical kernel configuration tool. Type

   ```
   [root@serverA linux-2.6.12.2]# make xconfig
   ```

A window similar to this will appear:

If the preceding command complains about some missing dependencies, it is probably saying that you don't have the appropriate Qt development environment. Assuming that you are connected to the Internet, you can take care of its whining by using Yum to install the proper packages over the Net, by typing

```
[root@serverA ~]# yum install qt-devel
```

Or on a SuSE system, use Yast to install the required dependencies. Type

```
# yast -i  qt3-devel
```

The kernel configuration window (titled qconf) that appears is divided into three panes. The left pane shows an expandable tree-structured list of the overall configurable kernel options. The top-right pane displays the detailed configurable options of the parent option that currently has the focus in the left pane. Finally, the bottom-right pane displays help information that is available for the currently selected configuration item. This pane displays very useful information.

3. Now let us examine one very important option a little more closely by selecting it in the left pane. Use your mouse to click the Loadable Module Support item in the left pane. On almost all Linux distributions you will see that the support for this feature is enabled. In the top-right pane, select the Enable Loadable Module Support option and then study the inline help information that appears in the bottom-right pane, as shown in the following illustration.

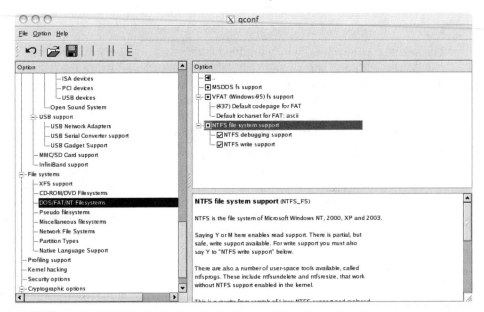

4. Next, we'll add support for the NTFS file system into our custom kernel. In the left pane, scroll through the list of available sections, and then select the File Systems section. Then select DOS/FAT/NT Filesystems under that section.

5. In the top-right pane, click the box next to the NTFS File System Support option until a little dot appears in the box. Then click the boxes beside the NTFS Debugging Support and NTFS Write Support options. A check mark should appear in each box like the ones shown here when you are done:

A Quick Note on Kernel Modules

Loadable module support is a kernel feature that allows the dynamic loading (or removal) of kernel modules. Kernel modules are small pieces of compiled code that can be dynamically inserted into the running kernel, rather than being permanently built into the kernel. Features not often used can thus be enabled but won't occupy any room in memory when they aren't being used. Thankfully, the kernel can automatically determine what to load and when. Naturally, not every feature is eligible to be compiled as a module. The kernel must know a few things before it can load and unload modules, such as how to access the hard disk and parse through the file system where the loadable modules are stored. Some kernel modules are also commonly referred to as drivers.

NOTE   For each option, in the top-right pane, a blank box indicates that the feature in question is disabled. A box with a check mark indicates that the feature is enabled. A box with a dot indicates that the feature is to be compiled as a module. Clicking the box will cycle through the three states.

6.   Finally, save your changes to the **.config** file in the root of your kernel source tree. Click File in the menu bar of the qconf window and select the Save option.

TIP   To view the results of the changes you made using the qconf GUI tool, use the `grep` utility to directly view the **.config** file that you saved. Type

```
[root@serverA linux-2.6.12.1]# grep NTFS .config
CONFIG_NTFS_FS=m
CONFIG_NTFS_DEBUG=y
CONFIG_NTFS_RW=y
```

7.   Close the qconf window when you are done.

Compiling the Kernel

In the previous section, we stepped through the process of creating a configuration file for the custom kernel that we want to build. In this section we will now perform the actual build of the kernel. But before doing this, we will add one more simple customization to the entire process.

The final customization will be to add an extra piece of information used in the final name of our kernel. This will help us be able to absolutely differentiate this kernel from any other kernel with the same version number. We will add the tag "custom" to the kernel version info. This can be done by editing the main **Makefile** and appending the tag that we want to the EXTRAVERSION variable.

This stage of the kernel-building process is by far the easiest, but it also takes the most time. All that is needed at this point is to simply execute the **make** command, which will then automatically generate and take care of any dependency issues, compile the kernel itself, and compile any features (or drivers) that were enabled as loadable modules.

Because of the amount of code that needs to be compiled, be ready to wait a few minutes at the very least—depending on the processing power of your system.

Let's dig into the specific steps required to compile your new kernel:

1. First we'll add an extra piece to the identification string for the kernel we are about to build. While still in the root of the kernel source tree, open up the **Makefile** for editing with any text editor. The variable we want to change is very close to the top of the file. Change the line in the file that looks like

   ```
   EXTRAVERSION = .1
   ```

   to

   ```
   EXTRAVERSION = .1-custom
   ```

2. Save your changes to the file and exit the text editor.

3. The only command that is needed here in order to compile the kernel is the **make** command. Type

   ```
   [root@serverA linux-2.6.12.1]# make
     CHK     include/linux/version.h
     SPLIT   include/linux/autoconf.h -> include/config/*
   ...<OUTPUT TRUNCATED>...
     CC      sound/usb/usx2y/snd-usb-usx2y.mod.o
     LD [M]  sound/usb/usx2y/snd-usb-usx2y.ko
   ```

4. The end product of this command (i.e., the kernel) is sitting pretty and waiting in the path: **<kernel-source-tree>/arch/i386/boot/bzImage**.

5. Because we compiled portions of the kernel as modules (e.g., the NTFS module), we need to install the modules. Type

   ```
   [root@serverA linux-2.6.12.1]# make modules_install
   ```

   On a Fedora system, this command will install all the compiled kernel modules into the **/lib/modules/<new_kernel-version>** directory. In this example this path will translate to the **/lib/modules/2.6.12.1-custom/** directory. This is the path from which the kernel will load all loadable modules, as needed.

Installing the Kernel

So now you have a fully compiled kernel just waiting to be installed. You probably have a couple of questions: Just where *is* the compiled kernel, and where the heck do I install it?

The first question is easy to answer. Assuming you have a PC and are working out of the **/usr/src/<kernel-source-tree>/** directory, the compiled kernel that was created in the previous exercise will be called **/usr/src/<kernel-source-tree>/arch/i386/boot/bzImage**, or to be precise **/usr/src/linux-2.6.12.1/arch/i386/boot/bzImage.**

The corresponding map file for this will be located at **/usr/src/<kernel-source-tree>/ System.map** or—as in our example—/**usr/src/linux-2.6.12.1/System.map.** You'll need both files for the install phase.

The **System.map** file is useful when the kernel is misbehaving and generating "Oops" messages. An "Oops" is generated on some kernel errors. It may be due to kernel bugs or faulty hardware. The "Oops" error is akin to the Blue Screen of Death (BSOD) in MS Windows. These messages include a lot of detail about the current state of the system, including a lot of hexadecimal numbers. **System.map** gives Linux a chance to turn those hexadecimal numbers into readable names, making debugging easier. Though this is mostly for the benefit of developers, it can be handy when you're reporting a problem.

Let's go through the steps required to install the new kernel image.

1. While in the root of your kernel build directory, copy and rename the **bzImage** file into the **/boot** directory:

   ```
   [root@serverA linux-2.6.12.1]# cp arch/i386/boot/bzImage \
    /boot/vmlinuz-<kernel-version>
   ```

   where **kernel-version** is the version number of the kernel. For the sample kernel we are using in this exercise, the filename would be **vmlinuz-2.6.12.1-custom**. So the exact command for this example is

   ```
   # cp arch/i386/boot/bzImage /boot/vmlinuz-2.6.12.1-custom
   ```

NOTE The decision to name the kernel image **vmlinuz-2.6.12.1-custom** is somewhat arbitrary. It's convenient because kernel images are commonly referred to as **vmlinuz**, and the suffix of the version number is useful when you have multiple kernels available. Of course, if you want to have multiple versions of the same kernel (for instance, one with SCSI support and the other without it), then you will need to design a more representative name. For example, you can choose a name like **vmlinuz-2.8.50-wireless** for the kernel for a laptop running Linux that has wireless capabilities.

2. Now that the kernel image is in place, copy over and rename the corresponding **System.map** file into the **/boot** directory using the same naming convention. Type

   ```
   [root@serverA linux-2.6.12.1]# cp  System.map \
    /boot/System.map-2.6.12.1-custom
   ```

3. With the kernel in place, the **System.map** file in place, and the modules in place, we are now ready to for the final step. Type

   ```
   [root@serverA linux-2.6.12.1]# new-kernel-pkg -v --mkinitrd --depmod \
   --install  <kernel-version>
   ```

where ***kernel-version*** is the version number of the kernel. For the sample kernel we are using in this exercise, the kernel version is 2.6.12.1-custom. So the exact command for this example is

```
# new-kernel-pkg -v --mkinitrd --depmod --install  2.6.12.1-custom
```

The **new-kernel-pkg** command used here is a very nifty little shell script. It may not be available in every Linux distribution, but it is available in Fedora, RHEL, and SuSE. It automates a lot of the final things we'd ordinarily have to do manually to set up the system to boot the new kernel we just built. In particular, it does the following:

▼   It creates the appropriate initial RAM disk image (the initrd image, i.e., the **/boot/ initrd-<kernel-version>.img** file). The command to do this manually on systems where **new-kernel-pkg** is not available is the **mkinitrd** command.

■   It runs the **depmod** command (which creates a list of module dependencies).

▲   And finally, it updates the boot loader configuration (in our case, it updates the **/boot/grub/grub.conf** file).

The new entry that was automatically added to the **grub.conf** file after running the preceding command on our sample system was

```
title Fedora Core (2.6.12.1-custom)
  root (hd0,0)
  kernel /vmlinuz-2.6.12.1-custom ro root=/dev/VolGroup00/LogVol00 rhgb quiet
  initrd /initrd-2.6.12.1-custom.img
```

NOTE   The one thing that the **new-kernel-pkg** command does not do is that it does not automatically make the most recent kernel installed the default kernel to boot. And so, you may have to manually select the kernel that you want to boot from the boot loader menu while the system is booting up. Of course, you can change this behavior by manually editing the **/boot/grub/grub .conf** file using any text editor (see Chapter 6).

Booting the Kernel

The next stage is to test the new kernel to make sure that your system can indeed boot with it.

1. Assuming you did everything the exact way that the doctor prescribed and that everything worked out the exact way that the doctor said it would, you can safely reboot the system and select the new kernel from the boot loader menu during system bootup. Type

```
[root@serverA ~]# reboot
```

2. After the system boots up, you can use the **uname** command to find out the name of the current kernel. Type

```
[root@serverA ~]# uname -r
2.6.12.1-custom
```

3. You will recall that one of the features that we added to our new kernel was to enable support for the NTFS file system. Make sure that the new kernel does indeed have support for the NTFS file system, by displaying information about the NTFS module. Type

```
[root@serverA ~]# modinfo  ntfs
filename:        /lib/modules/2.6.12.1-custom/kernel/fs/ntfs/ntfs.ko
description: NTFS 1.2/3.x driver - Copyright (c) 2001-2006 Anton
Altaparmakov
...<OUTPUT TRUNCATED>...
vermagic:        2.6.12.1-custom 686 REGPARM gcc-4.0
srcversion:      CFCABE9B21AEE7D9CA662A2
```

TIP Assuming you indeed have an NTFS-formatted file system that you want to access, you can manually load the NTFS module by typing

```
[root@serverA ~]# modprobe ntfs
```

The Author Lied—It Didn't Work!

The kernel *didn't* fly, you say? It froze in the middle of booting? Or it booted all the way and then nothing worked right? First and foremost, *don't panic.* This kind of problem happens to everyone, even the pros. After all, they're more likely to try untested software first. So don't worry, the situation is most definitely reparable.

First, notice that a new entry was added to the **/boot/grub/grub.conf** file (or the **/boot/grub/menu.1st**) file, and the previous entry was *not removed.* You can safely fall back to the old kernel that you know works and boot into it. Reboot, and at the GRUB menu, select the name of the previous kernel that was known to work. This action should bring you back to a known system state.

Now go back to the kernel configuration and verify that all the options you selected will work for your system. For example, did you accidentally enable support for the Sun UFS file system instead of Linux's ext2 file system? Did you set any options that depended on other options being set? Remember to view the informative Help screen for each kernel option in the configuration interface, making sure that you understand what each option does and what you need to do to make it work right.

When you're sure you have your settings right, step through the compilation process again and reinstall the kernel. Creating an appropriate initial RAM disk image (**initrd** file) is also very important (see man mkinitrd). If you are running GRUB, you simply need to edit the **/boot/grub/menu.1st** file, create an appropriate entry for your new kernel, and then reboot and try again.

Don't worry, each time you compile a kernel, you'll get better at it. When you do make a mistake, it'll be easier to go back, find it, and fix it.

PATCHING THE KERNEL

Like any other operating system, Linux periodically requires upgrades to fix bugs, improve performance, and add new features. These upgrades come out in two forms: in the form of a complete new kernel release and in the form of a patch. The complete new kernel works well for people who don't have at least one complete kernel already downloaded. For those who do have a complete kernel already downloaded, patches are a much better solution because they contain only the changed code and as such are much quicker to download.

Think of a patch as comparable to a Windows HotFix or service pack. By itself, it's useless; but when added to an existing version of Windows, you (hopefully) get an improved product. The key difference between HotFixes and patches is that patches contain the changes in the source code that need to be made. This allows you to review the source code changes before applying them. This is much nicer than guessing whether or not a fix will break the system!

You can find out about new patches to the kernel at many Internet sites. Your distribution vendor's Web site is a good place to start; it'll list not only kernel updates but also patches for other packages as well. A major source is the official Linux Kernel Archive at http://www.kernel.org. (That's where we got the complete kernel to use as the installation section's example.)

In this section, we'll demonstrate how to apply a patch to update a Linux kernel source version 2.6.11 to version 2.6.12. The exact patch file that we will use is named **patch-2.6.12.bz2**.

> **NOTE** You might sometimes see kernel patch files with names like "patch-2.6.12-rc2.bz2" available at the kernel.org Web site. The "rc2" in this example, which makes up part of the patch name and version (and hence the final kernel version), means that the patch in question is the "release candidate 2" patch that can be used to upgrade the appropriate kernel source tree to Linux kernel version 2.6.12-rc2. The same goes for a patch file named "patch-2.6.12-rc6.bz2"—which will be a "release candidate 6"—and so on.

Downloading and Applying Patches

Patch files are located in the same directory from which the kernel is downloaded. This applies to each major release of Linux; so for example the patch to update Linux version 2.6.49 to Linux version 2.6.50 may be located at http://www.kernel.org/pub/linux/kernel/v2.6/patch-2.6.50.bz2. The test patches (or point release candidates) are stored at the kernel.org Web site under the **/pub/linux/kernel/v2.6/testing/** directory.

Each patch filename is prefixed with the string "patch" and suffixed with the Linux version number being installed by the patch. Note that each patch brings Linux up by only one version; thus the **patch-2.6.50** file can only be applied to linux-2.6.49. Thus if you have linux-2.6.48 and wish to bring it up to version 2.6.50, you'll need two patches, **patch-2.6.49** and **patch-2.6.50**.

Patch files are stored on the server in a compressed format. In this example, we'll be using **patch-2.6.13.bz2** (from http://www.kernel.org/pub/linux/kernel/v2.6/patch-2.6.13.bz2). You will also need the actual kernel source tarball that you want to upgrade. In this example we'll use the kernel source that was downloaded from http://www.kernel.org/pub/linux/kernel/v2.6/linux-2.6.12.tar.gz.

Once you have the files from the kernel.org site (or mirror), move them to the **/usr/src** directory. We'll assume that you unpacked the kernel source that you want to upgrade into the **/usr/src/linux-2.6.12** directory. You will next decompress the patch using the **bzip2** utility and then pipe the resulting output to the patch program, which will then do the actual work of patching/updating your kernel.

1. Copy the compressed patch file that you downloaded into a directory one level above the root of your target kernel source tree. Assuming for example that the kernel you want to patch has been untarred into the **/usr/src/linux-2.6.12/** directory, you would copy the patch file into the **/usr/src/** directory.

2. First change your current working directory to the top level of the kernel source tree. This directory in our example is **/usr/src/linux-2.6.12/**. Type

   ```
   [root@serverA ~]# cd /usr/src/linux-2.6.12/
   ```

3. It is a good idea to do a test run of the patching process to make sure that there are no errors and to make sure that the new patch will indeed apply cleanly. Type

```
[root@serverA linux-2.6.12]# bzip2 -dc ../patch-2.6.13.bz2|patch -p1 --dry-run
```

4. Assuming the preceding command ran successfully without any errors, you're now ready to apply the patch. Run this command to decompress the patch and apply it to your kernel:

```
[root@serverA linux-2.6.12]# bzip2 -dc ../patch-2.6.13.bz2 | patch -p1
```

   where **../patch-2.6.13.bz2** is the name and path to the patch file. A stream of filenames is printed out to your screen. Each of those files has been updated by the patch file. If there were any problems with the upgrade, you will see them reported here.

If the Patch Worked . . .

If the patch worked and you received no errors, you're just about done! All that needs to be done is to recompile the kernel. Just follow the steps in the section "Installing the Kernel" earlier in this chapter.

If the Patch Didn't Work . . .

If you had errors during the process of patching the kernel, don't despair. This probably means one of two things:

▼ The patch version number cannot be applied to the kernel version number (for instance, you've tried to apply **patch-2.6.50.bz2** to **Linux-2.6.60**).

▲ The kernel source itself has changed. (This happens to developers who forget that they made changes!)

The easiest way to fix either situation is to erase the kernel located in the directory where you unpacked it and then unpack the full kernel there again. This will ensure you have a pristine kernel. Then apply the patch. It's tedious, but if you've done it once, it's easier and faster the second time.

TIP   You can usually back out of (remove) any patch that you apply by using the `-R` option with the `patch` command. For example, to back out of a patch version 2.6.20 that was applied to Linux kernel version 2.6.19, while in the root of the kernel source tree you would type
`# bzip2 -dc ../patch-2.6.20.bz2 | patch -p1 -R`
Backing out of a patch can be risky at times, and it doesn't always work—that is, your mileage may vary!

SUMMARY

In this chapter, we discussed the process of configuring and compiling the Linux kernel. This isn't exactly a trivial process, but doing it gives you the power to have a fine-grained control of your computer that simply isn't possible with most other operating systems. Compiling the kernel is pretty much a straightforward process. The Linux development community has provided excellent tools that make the process as painless as possible.

In addition to compiling kernels, we walked through the process of upgrading kernels using the patches available from the Linux Kernel Web site, http://www.kernel.org.

When you compile a kernel for the first time, do it on a nonproduction machine, if possible. This gives you a chance to take your time and fiddle with the many operational parameters that are available. It also means you won't annoy your users if something goes wrong!

For programmers curious about the kernel's innards, many references are available in the form of books and Web sites, and of course, the source code itself is the ultimate documentation.

CHAPTER 10

Knobs and Dials:
The proc File System

M ost operating systems offer a mechanism by which the insides of the operating system can be probed and by which operational parameters can be set when needed. In Linux, this mechanism is provided by the proc file system. Microsoft Windows operating systems allow this to some degree through the Registry, and Solaris allows this through the **ndd** tool. (Solaris has a proc file system, as well.) The **/proc** directory is the mount point for the proc file system, and so the two terms are often used interchangeably. The proc file system is also often referred to as a virtual file system.

In this chapter, we discuss the proc file system and how it works under Linux. We'll step through some overviews and study some interesting entries in **/proc**, and then we'll demonstrate some common administrative tasks using **/proc**. We'll end with a brief mention of the system file system (SysFS).

WHAT'S INSIDE THE /PROC DIRECTORY?

Since the Linux kernel is such a key component in server operations, it's important that there be a method for exchanging information with the kernel. Traditionally, this is done through *system calls*—special functions written for programmers to use in requesting the kernel to perform functions on their behalf. In the context of system administration, however, system calls mean a developer needs to write a tool for us to use (unless, of course, you like writing your own tools). When all you need is a simple tweak or to extract some statistics from the kernel, having to write a custom tool is a lot more effort than should be necessary.

To improve communication between users and the kernel, the proc file system was created. The entire file system is especially interesting because it doesn't really exist on disk anywhere; it's purely an abstract of kernel information. All of the files in the directory correspond to either a function in the kernel or to a set of variables in the kernel.

> **NOTE** That proc is abstract doesn't mean it isn't a file system. It does mean that a special file system had to be developed to treat proc differently than normal disk-based file systems.

For example, to see a report on the type of processor on a system, we can consult one of the files under the **/proc** directory. The particular file that holds this information is the **/proc/cpuinfo** file. The file can be viewed with this command:

```
[root@serverA ~]# cat /proc/cpuinfo
```

The kernel will dynamically create the report showing processor information and hand it back to **cat** so that we can see it. This is a simple yet powerful way for us to examine the kernel. The **/proc** directory supports an easy-to-read hierarchy using subdirectories, and as such finding information is easy. The directories under **/proc** are also organized such that files containing information about similar topics are grouped together. For example, the **/proc/scsi** directory offers reports about the SCSI subsystem.

Even more of an advantage is that the flow of information goes both ways: The kernel can generate reports for us, and we can easily pass information back into the kernel. For instance, performing an **ls -l** in the **/proc/sys/net/ipv4** directory will show us a lot of files that are not read-only, but read/write, which means some of the values stored in those files can be altered on the fly.

"Hey! Most the **/proc** files have zero bytes, and one is HUGE! What gives?" Don't worry if you've noticed all those zero-byte files—most of the files in **/proc** are zero bytes because **/proc** doesn't really exist on disk. When you use **cat** to read a **/proc** file, the content of the file is dynamically generated by a special program inside the kernel. As a result, the report is never saved back to disk and thus does not take up space. Think of it in the same light as CGI scripts for Web sites, where a Web page generated by a CGI script isn't written back to the server's disk but regenerated every time a user visits the page.

CAUTION   That one huge file you see in /**proc** is /**proc/kcore**, which is really a pointer to the contents of RAM. So if you have 128MB of RAM, the /**proc/kcore** file is also 128MB. Reading /**proc/ kcore** is like reading the raw contents of memory (and, of course, requires root permissions).

Tweaking Files Inside of /proc

As was mentioned in the preceding section, some of the files under the **/proc** directory (and subdirectories) have a read-write mode. Let us examine one of such directories a little more closely. The files in **/proc/sys/net/ipv4** represent parameters in the TCP/IP stack that can be "tuned" dynamically. Use the **cat** command to look at a particular file, and you'll see that most of the files contain nothing but a single number. But by changing these numbers, you can affect the behavior of the Linux TCP/IP stack!

For example, the file **/proc/sys/net/ipv4/ip_forward** contains a 0 (Off) by default. This tells Linux not to perform IP forwarding when there are multiple network interfaces. But if you want to set up something like a Linux router, you need to allow forwarding to occur. In this situation, you can edit the **/proc/sys/net/ipv4/ip_forward** file and change the number to 1 (On).

A quick way to make this change is by using the **echo** command like so:

```
[root@serverA ~]# echo "1" > /proc/sys/net/ipv4/ip_forward
```

CAUTION   Be very careful when tweaking parameters in the Linux kernel. There is no safety net to keep you from making the wrong settings for critical parameters, which means it's entirely possible that you can crash your system. If you aren't sure about a particular item, it's safer to leave it be until you've found out for sure what it's for.

SOME USEFUL /PROC ENTRIES

Table 10-1 lists some **/proc** entries that you may find useful in managing your Linux system. Note that this is a far cry from an exhaustive list. For more detail, peruse the directories yourself and see what you find. Or you can also read the **proc.txt** file in the Documentation directory of the Linux kernel source code.

Unless otherwise stated, you can simply use the **cat** program to view the contents of a particular file in the **/proc** directory.

Filename	Contents
/proc/cpuinfo	Information about the CPU(s) in the system.
/proc/interrupts	IRQ usage in your system.
/proc/ioports	Displays a listing of the registered port regions used for input or output (I/O) communication with devices.
/proc/iomem	Displays the current map of the system's memory for each physical device.
/proc/mdstat	Status of RAID configuration.
/proc/meminfo	Status of memory usage.
/proc/kcore	This file represents the physical memory of the system. Unlike the other files under **/proc**, this file has a size associated with it. Its size is usually equal to the total amount of physical RAM available.
/proc/modules	Same information produced as output from **lsmod**.
/proc/pci	Report of all known PCI devices in a system.
/proc/buddyinfo	Information stored in this file can be used for diagnosing memory fragmentation issues.
/proc/cmdline	Displays the parameters passed to the kernel when the kernel started up (boot time parameters)
/proc/swaps	Status of swap partitions, volume, and/or files.
/proc/version	Current version number of the kernel, the machine on which it was compiled, and the date and time of compilation.
/proc/ide/*	Information about all of the IDE devices.
/proc/scsi/*	Information about all of the SCSI devices.
/proc/net/arp	ARP table (same as output from **arp -a**).
/proc/net/dev	Information about each network device (packet counts, error counts, and so on).
/proc/net/snmp	SNMP statistics about each protocol.

Table 10-1. Useful Entries under /proc

Filename	Contents
/proc/net/sockstat	Statistics on network socket utilization.
/proc/sys/fs/*	Settings for file system utilization by the kernel. Many of these are writable values; be careful about changing them unless you are sure of the repercussions of doing so.
/proc/sys/net/core/netdev_ max_backlog	When the kernel receives packets from the network faster than it can process them, it places them on a special queue. By default, a maximum of 300 packets is allowed on the queue. Under extraordinary circumstances, you may need to edit this file and change the value for the allowed maximum.
/proc/sys/net/ipv4/icmp_ echo_ignore_all	Default = 0, meaning that the kernel will respond to ICMP echo-reply messages. Set this to 1 to tell the kernel to stop replying to those messages.
/proc/sys/net/ipv4/icmp_ echo_ignore_broadcasts	Default = 0, meaning that the kernel will allow ICMP responses to be sent to broadcast or multicast addresses.
/proc/sys/net/ipv4/ip_ forward	Default = 0, meaning the kernel will not forward packets between network interfaces. To allow forwarding (e.g., for routing), change this to 1.
/proc/sys/net/ipv4/ip_ local_port_range	Range of ports Linux will use when originating a connection. Default = 32768–61000.
/proc/sys/net/ipv4/tcp_ syn_cookies	Default = 0 (Off). Change to 1 (On) to enable protection for the system against SYN flood attacks.

Table 10-1.   Useful Entries under /proc (*cont.*)

Enumerated /proc Entries

A listing of the **/proc** directory will reveal a large number of directories whose names are just numbers. These numbers are the PIDs for each running process in the system. Within each of the process directories are several files describing the state of the process. This information can be useful in finding out how the system perceives a process and what sort of resources the process is consuming. (From a programmer's point of view, the process files are also an easy way for a program to get information about itself.)

For example, a long listing of some of the files under **/proc** shows

```
[root@serverA ~]# ls -l /proc
dr-xr-xr-x    3 root     root               0 Apr 10 04:12 1
dr-xr-xr-x    3 root     root               0 Apr 10 04:12 11068
dr-xr-xr-x    3 root     root               0 Apr 10 04:12 11117
...<OUTPUT TRUNCATED>...
```

If you look a little closer at the folder named "1" in the preceding output, you will notice that this particular folder represents the information about the "init" process. (PID=1). A listing of the files under **/proc/1/** shows

```
[root@serverA ~]# ls -l /proc/1/
dr-xr-xr-x  2 root root 0 Apr 10 04:12 attr
-r--------  1 root root 0 Apr 10 04:12 auxv
-r--r--r--  1 root root 0 Apr 10 04:12 cmdline
...<OUTPUT TRUNCATED>...
lrwxrwxrwx  1 root root 0 Apr 10 04:12 exe -> /sbin/init
```

Again, as you can see from the output, the "/proc/1/exe" file is a soft link that points to the actual executable for the **init** program (**/sbin/init**).

The same logic applies to the other numeric named directories that are under **/proc**—i.e., they represent processes.

COMMON REPORTS AND SETTINGS DONE WITH PROC

As was already mentioned, the proc file system is a virtual file system, and as a result, changes to default settings in **/proc** do not survive reboots. If you need a change to a value under **/proc** to be automatically set/enabled between system reboots, you can either edit your boot scripts so that the change is made at boot time or use the **sysctl** tool. The former approach can, for example, be used to enable IP packet forwarding functionality in the kernel every time the system is booted. To do this, you can add the following line to the end of your **/etc/rc.d/rc.local** file:

```
echo "1" > /proc/sys/net/ipv4/ip_forward
```

Most Linux distributions now have a more graceful way of making persistent changes to the proc file system.

In this section we'll look at a tool that can be used to interactively make changes in real time to some variables stored in the proc file system.

The **sysctl** utility is used for displaying and modifying kernel parameters in real time. Specifically, it is used to tune parameters that are stored under the **/proc/sys/** directory of the proc file system. A summary of its usage and options is shown here:

```
sysctl  [options] variable[=value]
```

where these are the possible options:

Options	Explanation
`variable[=value]`	Used to set or display the value of a key, where `variable` is the key and `value` is the value to set the key to. For instance, a certain key is called "kernel.hostname" and a possible value for that key may be "serverA.example.com".
`-n`	Disables printing of the key name when printing values.
`-e`	This option is used to ignore errors about unknown keys.
`-w`	Use this option when you want to change a `sysctl` setting.
`-p <filename>`	Load in `sysctl` settings from the file specified or **/etc/sysctl.conf** if no filename is given.
`-a`	Display all values currently available.

We will use actual examples to demonstrate how to use the **sysctl** tool. The examples demonstrate a few of the many things you can do with proc to complement day-to-day administrative tasks. Reports and tunable options available through proc are especially useful in network-related tasks. The examples also provide some background information about the proc setting that we want to tune.

SYN Flood Protection

When TCP initiates a connection, the very first thing it does is send a special packet to the destination, with the flag set to indicate the start of a connection. This flag is known as the SYN flag. The destination host responds by sending an acknowledgment packet back to the source, called (appropriately) a SYNACK. Then the destination waits for the source to return an acknowledgment showing that both sides have agreed on the parameters of their transaction. Once these three packets are sent (this process is called the "three-way handshake"), the source and destination hosts can transmit data back and forth.

Because it's possible for multiple hosts to simultaneously contact a single host, it's important that the destination host keep track of all the SYN packets it gets. SYN entries are stored in a table until the three-way handshake is complete. Once this is done, the connection leaves the SYN tracking table and moves to another table that tracks established connections.

A SYN flood occurs when a source host sends a large number of SYN packets to a destination with no intention of responding to the SYNACK. This results in overflow of the destination host's tables, thereby making the operating system unstable. Obviously, this is not a good thing.

Linux can prevent SYN floods by using a *syncookie*, a special mechanism in the kernel that tracks the rate at which SYN packets arrive. If the syncookie detects the rate going above a certain threshold, it begins to aggressively get rid of entries in the SYN table that don't move to the "established" state within a reasonable interval. A second layer of protection is in the table itself: If the table receives a SYN request that would cause the table to overflow, the request is ignored. This means it may happen that a client will be temporarily unable to connect to the server—but it also keeps the server from crashing altogether and kicking *everyone* off!

First use the **sysctl** tool to display the current value for tcp_syncookie setting. Type

```
[root@serverA ~]# sysctl net.ipv4.tcp_syncookies
net.ipv4.tcp_syncookies = 0
```

The output shows that this setting is currently disabled (value=0). To turn on tcp_syncookie support, enter this command:

```
[root@serverA ~]# sysctl -w net.ipv4.tcp_syncookies=1
net.ipv4.tcp_syncookies = 1
```

Because **/proc** entries do not survive system reboots, you should add the following line to the end of your **/etc/sysctl.conf** configuration file. To do this using the **echo** command, type

```
echo "net.ipv4.tcp_syncookies = 1" >> /etc/sysctl.conf
```

NOTE You should, of course, first make sure that the **/etc/sysctl.conf** file does not already contain an entry for the key that you are trying to tune. If it does, you can simply hand-edit the file and change the value of the key to the new value.

Issues on High-Volume Servers

Like any operating system, Linux has finite resources. If the system begins to run short of resources while servicing requests (such as Web access requests), it will begin refusing new service requests.

The **/proc** entry **/proc/sys/fs/file-max** specifies the maximum number of open files that Linux can support at any one time. The default value on our Fedora system was 12094, but this may be quickly exhausted on a very busy system with a lot of network connections. Raising it to a larger number, such as 20480, may be necessary. Using the **sysctl** command again, type

```
[root@serverA ~]# sysctl -w fs.file-max=20480
fs.file-max = 20480
```

Don't forget to append your change to the **/etc/sysctl.conf** file if you want the change to be persistent.

Debugging Hardware Conflicts

Debugging hardware conflicts is always a chore. You can ease the burden by using some of the entries in **/proc**. These three entries are specifically designed to tell you what's going on with your hardware:

▼   **/proc/pci** details all the PCI devices in your system; it is very handy when you don't know the make and model of a device—and you don't want to have to open the machine!

■   **/proc/ioports** tells you the relationships of devices to I/O ports, and whether there are any conflicts. With PCI devices becoming dominant, this isn't as big an issue. Nevertheless, as long as you can buy a new motherboard with ISA slots, you'll always want to have this option.

▲   **/proc/interrupts** shows you the association of interrupt numbers to hardware devices. Again, like **/proc/ioports**, PCI is making this less of an issue.

SysFS

SysFS (short for system file system) is similar to the proc file system previously discussed in this chapter. The major similarities between the two are that they are both virtual file systems and they both provide a means for information (data structures, actually) to be exported from within the kernel to the user space. SysFS is usually mounted at the **/sys** mount point.

The SysFS file system can be used to obtain information about kernel objects such as devices, modules, the system bus, firmware, and so on. This file system provides a view of the device tree (among other things) as the kernel sees it. This view displays most of the known attributes of detected devices, such as the device name, vendor name, PCI class, IRQ and DMA resources, and power status. Some of the information that used to be available (in the Linux 2.4 series kernel versions) under the proc file system can now be found under SysFS.

Another purpose of SysFS is that it provides a uniform view of the device space, providing a sharp contrast to what is currently seen in the **/dev** directory, which has no fixed naming scheme, allowing anyone to name any device anything. Administrators familiar with Solaris will find themselves at home with the naming conventions used. The key difference between Solaris and Linux, however, is that the representations under SysFS do not provide means to access the device through the device driver. For device driver–based access, administrators will need to continue using the appropriate **/dev** entry.

A listing of the top level of the **sysfs** directory shows these directories:

```
[root@serverA ~]# ls /sys/
block  bus  class  devices  firmware  kernel  module  power
```

A deeper look into the **/sys/devices** directory reveals this listing:

```
[root@serverA ~]# ls -1 /sys/devices/
pci0000:00
platform
pnp0
pnp1
system
```

If we look at a sample representation of a device connected to the PCI bus on our system, we'll see these elements:

```
[root@serverA ~]# ls -1 /sys/devices/pci0000:00/0000:00:00.0/
class
config
detach_state
device
driver
irq
local_cpus
resource
resource0
vendor
```

The topmost element under the **devices** directory in the preceding output describes the PCI domain and bus number. The particular system bus here is the "pci0000:00" PCI bus, where "0000" is the domain number and the bus number is "00". The functions of the other files are listed here:

File	Function
class	PCI class
config	PCI config space
detach_state	Connection status
device	PCI device
irq	IRQ number
local_cpus	Nearby CPU mask
resource	PCI resource host addresses
resource0 (resource0 . . . n)	PCI resource zero (or PCI resource *n* if present)
vendor	PCI vendor ID (a list of vendor IDs can be found in the **/usr/share/hwdata/pci.ids** file)

SUMMARY

In this chapter, you learned about the proc file system and how you can use it to get a peek inside the Linux kernel as well as to influence the kernel's operation. The tools used to accomplish these tasks are relatively trivial (**echo** and **cat**), but the concept of a pseudo-file system that doesn't exist on disk can be a little difficult to grasp.

Looking at proc from a system administrator's point of view, you learned to find your way around the proc file system and how to get reports from various subsystems (especially the networking subsystem). You learned how to set kernel parameters to accommodate possible future enhancements. Finally, brief mention was also made of the SysFS virtual file system.

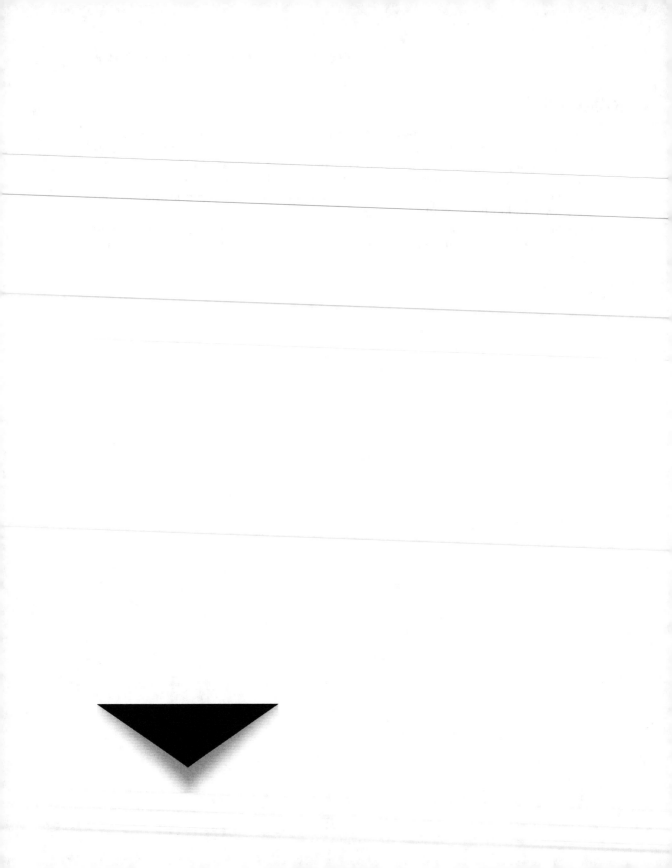

PART III

Security and Networking

CHAPTER 11

TCP/IP for System Administrators

For the last 20 years, a key feature of UNIX has been network awareness. To imagine a UNIX system that is not connected to a network is to imagine a sports car without a race track. Linux inherits that legacy and keeps it going in full strength.

To be a system administrator today is to also have a reasonably strong understanding of the network and the protocols used to communicate over it. After all, if your server is receiving or sending any information, you are responsible for your server's actions.

This chapter is an introduction to the guts of the Transmission Control Protocol/Internet Protocol, better known as TCP/IP. We'll tackle the contents in two parts: first, we will walk through the details of packets, Ethernet, TCP/IP, and some related protocol details. This part may seem a little tedious at first, but perseverance will pay off in the second part. The second part will walk through several examples of common problems and how you can quickly identify them with your newfound knowledge of TCP/IP. Along the way we will use a wonderful tool called **tcpdump**, a tool that you'll find indispensable by the end of the chapter.

Please note that the intent of this chapter is not to be a complete replacement for the many books on TCP/IP, but rather an introduction from the standpoint of someone who needs to worry about system administration. If you want a more complete discussion on TCP/IP, we highly recommend *TCP/IP Illustrated Vol. 1,* by Richard Stevens (Addison-Wesley, 1994).

THE LAYERS

TCP/IP is built in layers, thus the references to TCP/IP *stacks.* In this section, we take a look at what the TCP/IP layers are, their relationship to one another, and finally, why they really don't match the International Organization for Standardization (ISO) seven-layer Open Systems Interconnection (OSI) model. We'll also translate the OSI layers into meanings that are relevant to your network.

Packets

At the very bottom of the layering system is the smallest unit of data that networks like dealing with: *packets.* Packets contain both the data that we want to transmit between our systems as well as some control information that helps networking gear determine where the packet should go.

NOTE   The terms "packet" and "frame" are often interchanged when discussing networks. In these situations, people referring to a frame often mean a packet. The difference is subtle. A frame is the space in which packets go on a network. At the hardware level, frames on a network are separated by preambles and postambles that tell the hardware where one frame begins and ends. A packet is the data that is contained within the frame.

A typical TCP/IP packet flowing in an Ethernet network looks like Figure 11-1.

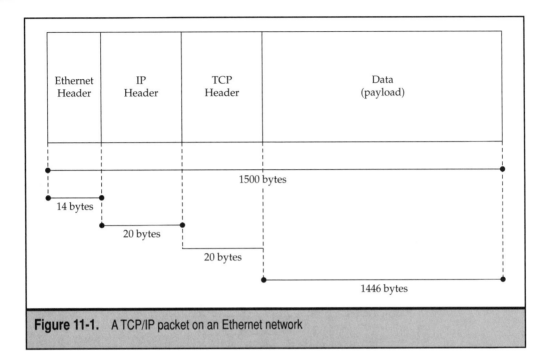

Figure 11-1.   A TCP/IP packet on an Ethernet network

Frames under Ethernet

In the last few years, the Ethernet specification has been updated to allow frames larger than 1518 bytes. These frames, appropriately called jumbo frames, can hold up to 9000 bytes. This, conveniently, is enough space for a complete set of TCP/IP headers, Ethernet headers, NFS control information, and one page of memory (4K to 8K, depending on your system's architecture; Intel uses 4K pages). Because servers can now push one complete page of memory out of the system without having to break it up into tiny packets, throughput on some applications (such as remote disk service) can go through the roof!

The downside to this is that very few people use jumbo frames, so you need to make sure your network cards are compatible with your switches, etc. Furthermore, jumbo frames are only used in Gigabit Ethernet environments. Linux supports the use of jumbo frames with several of the Gigabit Ethernet drivers, including acenic.o (Alteon's Tigon chipset, now part of the Broadcom family).

An important detail: In older machines, jumbo frames were necessary in order to achieve 100% utilization of gigabit links from PC servers. This is no longer true. Performance of server-class PCs has risen enough to allow them to achieve gigabit performance on 1518-byte frames. More often than not, performance bottlenecks stem from application limitations, not kernel or hardware limitations.

As we can see in Figure 11-1, packets are layered by protocol, with the lowest layers coming first. Each protocol uses a *header* to describe the information needed to move data from one host to the next. Packet headers tend to be small—the headers for TCP, IP, and Ethernet in their simplest and most common combined form only take 54 bytes of space from the packet. This leaves the rest of the 1446 bytes of the packet to data.

Figure 11-2 illustrates how a packet is passed up the protocol stack. Let's look into this process a little more closely.

When a host's network card receives a packet, it first checks to see if it is supposed to accept the packet. This is done by looking at the destination addresses located in the packet's headers. (More about that in "Headers," later in the chapter.) If the network card thinks that it should accept the packet, it keeps a copy of it in its own memory and generates an interrupt to the operating system.

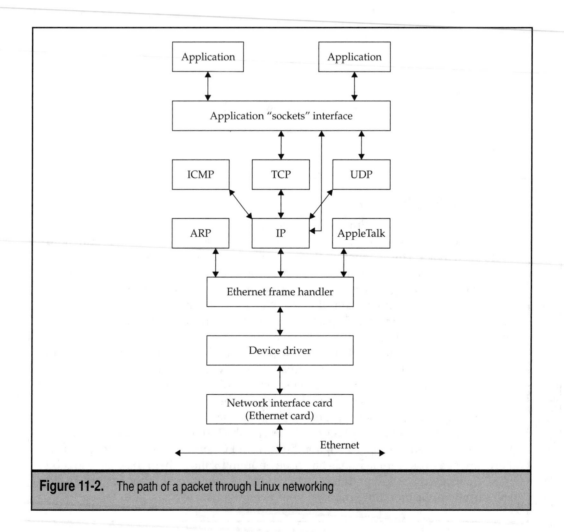

Figure 11-2.   The path of a packet through Linux networking

Upon receiving this interrupt, the operating system calls on the device driver of the network interface card (NIC) to process the new packet. The device driver copies the packet from the NIC's memory to the system's memory. Once it has a complete copy, it can examine the packet and determine what type of protocol is being used. Based on the protocol type, the device driver makes a note to the appropriate handler for that protocol that it has a new packet to process. The device driver then puts the packet in a place where the protocol's software ("the stack") can find it and returns to the interrupt processing.

Note that the stack does not begin processing the packet immediately. This is because the operating system may be doing something important that it needs to finish before letting the stack process the packet. Since it is possible for the device driver to receive many packets from the NIC quickly, a *queue* exists between the driver and the stack software. The queue simply keeps track of the order in which packets arrive and notes where they are in memory. When the stack is ready to process those packets, it grabs them from the queue in the appropriate order.

As each layer processes the packet, appropriate headers are removed. In the case of a TCP/IP packet over Ethernet, the driver will strip the Ethernet headers, IP will strip the IP header, and TCP will strip the TCP header. This will leave just the data that needs to be delivered to the appropriate application.

TCP/IP and the OSI Model

The ISO's OSI reference model is a well-known model for describing the various abstraction layers in networking. The OSI model has seven layers (see Figure 11-3) that unfortunately don't map to TCP/IP very well. However, network vendors managed to make a mapping, and a general understanding of what each layer of OSI represents in each layer of TCP/IP has emerged.

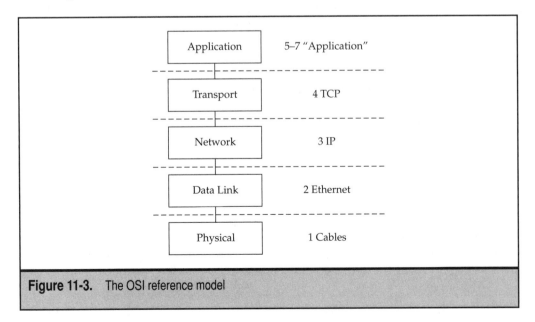

Figure 11-3.   The OSI reference model

Layer 1

Layer 1, the physical layer, describes the actual medium on which the data flows. In a network infrastructure, a pile of Cat 5 Ethernet cable and the signaling protocol are considered the physical layer.

Ethernet and Layer 2

Layer 2, the data link layer, is used to describe the Ethernet protocol. The difference between the OSI's view of layer 2 and Ethernet is that Ethernet only concerns itself with sending frames and providing a valid *checksum* for them. The purpose of the checksum is to allow the receiver to validate whether the data arrived as it was sent. This is done by computing the CRC of the packet contents and comparing them against the checksum that was provided by the sender. If the receiver gets a corrupted frame (that is, the checksums do not match), the packet is dropped here. From Linux's point of view, it should not receive a packet that the network interface card knows is corrupted.

Although the OSI model formally specifies that layer 2 should handle the automatic retransmission of a corrupted packet, Ethernet does not do this. Instead, Ethernet relies on higher-level protocols (TCP in this case) to handle retransmission.

Ethernet's primary responsibility is simple: get the packet from one host on a LAN (local area network) to another host on a LAN. Ethernet has no concept of a global network because of limitations on the timing of packets, as well as the number of hosts that can exist on a single network segment. You'll be pressed to find more than 200 or so hosts on any given segment due to bandwidth issues and simple management issues. It's easier to manage smaller groups of machines.

NOTE   Ethernet is increasingly used in metro area networks (MANs) and wide area networks (WANs) as a framing protocol for connectivity. Although the distance may be great between two endpoints, these networks are not the standard broadcast-style Ethernet that you see in a typical switch or hub. Rather, networking vendors have opted to maintain the layer 2 framing information as Ethernet so that routers don't need to fragment packets between networks. From a system administrator's point of view, don't be concerned if your network provider says they use Ethernet in their WAN/MAN—they haven't strung together hundreds of switches to make the distance!

IP and Layer 3

The Internet Protocol (IP) is wiser to the world around it than Ethernet. IP understands how to communicate with both hosts inside the immediate LAN as well as with hosts that are connected to you via routers (for example, hosts on other subnets, the Internet, etc.). This means that an IP packet can make its way to any other host connected to the same IP network so long as a route exists to the destination host.

Layer 3, by comparison, is the network layer. IP doesn't live up to the formal definition of layer 3. The formal definition calls for accounting and congestion control, neither of which IP is capable of. IP will of course try to get a packet to its destination. This means that packets can be delivered out of order, sent after a long delay, or even dropped along the way. Furthermore, IP only understands how to get a packet to another host. Once a packet arrives at the host, there is no information in the IP header to tell it which application to deliver the data to.

The reason why IP does not provide any more features than those of a simple transport protocol is that it was meant to be a foundation for other protocols to rest on. Of the protocols that use IP, not all of them need reliable connections or guaranteed packet order. Thus, it is the responsibility of higher-level protocols to provide additional features if needed.

TCP, UDP, and Layer 4

TCP (Transmission Control Protocol) and UDP (User Datagram Protocol) are mapped to layer 4, the transport layer. TCP actually maps to this OSI layer quite well by providing a reliable transport for one *session*, that is, a single connection from a client program to a server program. For example, using ssh to connect to a server creates a session. You can have multiple windows running ssh from the same client to the same server and each instance of ssh will have its own session.

In addition to sessions, TCP also handles the ordering and retransmission of packets. If a series of packets arrive out of order, the stack will put them back into order before passing them up to the application. If a packet arrives with any kind of problem or goes missing altogether, TCP will automatically request the sender to retransmit.

Finally, TCP connections are also bidirectional. This means that the client and server can send and receive data on the same connection.

UDP, by comparison, doesn't map quite as nicely to OSI. While UDP understands the concept of sessions and is bidirectional, it does not provide reliability. In other words, UDP won't detect lost or duplicate packets the way TCP does.

Why Use UDP at All?

UDP's limitations, however, are also its strengths. UDP is a good choice for two types of traffic: short request/response transactions that fit in one packet (like DNS) and streams of data that are better off skipping lost data and moving on (like streaming audio and video). In the first case, UDP is better because a short request/response usually doesn't merit the overhead that TCP requires in order to guarantee reliability. The application is usually better off adding additional logic to retransmit on its own in the event of lost packets.

In the case of streaming data, developers actually don't want TCP's reliability. They would prefer that lost packets are simply skipped on the (reasonable) assumption that most packets will arrive in the desired order. This is because human listeners/viewers are much better at handling (and much less annoyed by!) short drops in audio than they are in delays.

HTTP, SSL, XML, and Layers 5 Through 7

Technically, OSI's layers 5–7 each have a specific purpose, but in TCP/IP lingo, they're all clumped together into the application layer. Technically, all applications that use TCP or UDP sit here; however, the marketplace generally calls HTTP traffic layer 7. Some vendors refer to it as layer 5, but from our point of view they are both the same.

SSL is a bit of an odd bird, which is not commonly associated with any layer. It sits squarely between layer 4 (TCP) and layer 7 (application, typically HTTP) and can be used to encrypt arbitrary TCP streams. In general, SSL is not referred to as a layer. You should note, however, that SSL can encrypt arbitrary TCP connections, not just HTTP. Many protocols like POP and IMAP offer SSL as an encryption option, and the emergence of SSL-VPN technology shows how SSL can be used as an arbitrary tunnel.

XML data can also be confusing. To date, there is no framing protocol for XML that runs on top of TCP directly. Instead, XML data uses existing protocols like HTTP, DIME, and SMTP. (DIME was created specifically for transmitting XML.) For most applications, XML uses HTTP, which from a layering point of view looks like this: Ethernet -> IP -> TCP -> HTTP -> XML. XML can wrap other XML documents within it. For example, SOAP can wrap digital signatures within it. For additional information on XML itself, take a look at http://www.oasis.org and http://www.w3c.org.

ICMP

The Internet Control Message Protocol (ICMP) was especially designed for one host to communicate to another host on the state of the network. Since the data is used only by the operating system and not by users, ICMP does not support the concept of port numbers, reliable delivery, or guaranteed order of packets.

Every ICMP packet contains a *type* that tells the recipient what the nature of the message is. The most popular type is "Echo-Request," which is used by the infamous ping program. When a host receives the ICMP "Echo-Request" message, it responds with an ICMP "Echo-Reply" message. This allows the sender to confirm that the other host is up, and since we can see how long it takes the message to be sent and replied to, we get an idea of the latency of the network between the two hosts.

NOTE   You may hear references to "layer 8" from time to time. Typically this is in reference to American sarcasm. Layer 8 typically refers to the "political" or "financial" layer, meaning that above all networks there are people. And people, unlike networks, are nondeterministic. What may make sense for the network doesn't make sense politically, and thus seemingly arbitrary infrastructure is built. A simple example: two department heads within the same company refuse to acknowledge each other. When they find out they share the network, they demand to get their own infrastructure (routers, switches, etc.) and get placed on different networks, yet at the same time be able to communicate with each other—through secure firewalls only. What may have been a nice, simple (and functional) network is now much more complex than it needs to be, all because of layer 8 . . . . (This may sound like a Dilbert cartoon, but remember that Dilbert's creator uses a lot of true stories from his readers!)

HEADERS

Earlier in the chapter, we learned that a TCP/IP packet over Ethernet was a series of *headers* for each protocol followed by the actual data being sent. "Packet headers," as they are typically called, are simply those pieces of information that tell the protocol how to handle the packet.

In this section we look at each of these headers using the **tcpdump** tool. All common Linux distributions have it preinstalled; however, if you want to see what the latest status of it is, you can visit the **tcpdump** Web site at http://www.tcpdump.org. After reading this chapter, you may find it handy to read the complete manual page for **tcpdump**.

NOTE You must be root in order to run the `tcpdump` command.

Ethernet

Ethernet has a very interesting history. As a result, there are two types of Ethernet headers: 802.3 and Ethernet II. Thankfully, although they both look similar, there is a simple test to tell them apart. Let's begin by looking at the contents of the Ethernet header (see Figure 11-4).

The Ethernet header contains three entries: the destination address, the source address, and the packet's protocol type.

Ethernet addresses—also called MAC (Media Access Control) addresses; no relation to the Apple Macintosh—are 48-bit (six-byte) numbers that uniquely identify every Ethernet card in the world. Although it is possible to change the MAC address of an interface, this is not recommended, as the default is guaranteed to be unique and all MAC addresses on a LAN segment must be unique.

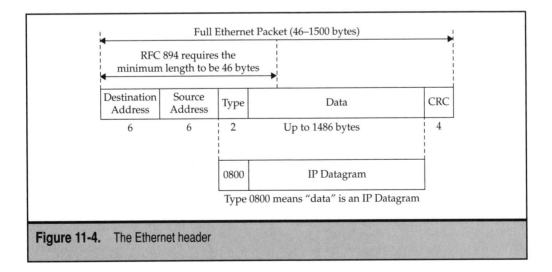

Figure 11-4. The Ethernet header

NOTE   A packet that is sent as a broadcast (meaning all network cards should accept this packet) has the destination address set to ff:ff:ff:ff:ff:ff.

The packet's protocol type is a two-byte value that tells us what protocol this packet should be delivered to on the receiver's side. For IP packets, this value is hex 0800 (decimal 2048).

The packet we have just described here is an Ethernet II packet. (Typically, it is just called *Ethernet*.) In 802.3 packets the destination and source MAC addresses remain in place; however, the next two bytes represent the length of the packet. The way you can tell the difference between the two types of Ethernet is that there is no protocol type with a value of less than 1500. Thus, any Ethernet header where the protocol type is less than 1500 is really an 802.3 packet. Realistically, you probably won't see many (if any) 802.3 packets anymore.

Viewing Ethernet Headers

To see the Ethernet headers on your network, run the following command:

```
[root@hostA ~]# tcpdump -e
```

This tells **tcpdump** to dump the Ethernet headers along with the TCP and IP headers.

Now generate some traffic by visiting a Web site or use ssh to communicate with another host. Doing so will generate output like this:

```
15:46:08.026966 0:d0:b7:6b:20:17 0:10:4b:cb:15:9f ip 191: hostA.ssh >
10.2.2.2.4769: P 5259:5396(137) ack 1 win 17520 (DF) [tos 0x10]

15:46:08.044151 0:10:4b:cb:15:9f 0:d0:b7:6b:20:17 ip 60: 10.2.2.2.4769 >
hostA.ssh: . ack 5396 win 32120 (DF)
```

The start of each line is a timestamp of when the packet was seen. The next two entries in the lines are the source and destination MAC addresses, respectively, for the packet. In the first line, the source MAC address is 0:d0:b7:6b:20:17, and the destination MAC address is 0:10:4b:cb:15:9f.

After the MAC address is the packet's type. In this case, **tcpdump** saw **0800** and automatically converted it to **ip** for us so that it would be easier to read. If you don't want **tcpdump** to convert numbers to names for you (especially handy when your DNS resolution isn't working), you can run

```
[root@hostA ~]# tcpdump -e -n
```

where the **-n** option tells **tcpdump** to not do name resolution. The same two preceding lines without name resolution would look like this:

```
15:46:08.026966 0:d0:b7:6b:20:17 0:10:4b:cb:15:9f 0800 191: 10.2.2.1.22 >
10.2.2.2.4769: P 5259:5396(137) ack 1 win 17520 (DF) [tos 0x10]

15:46:08.044151 0:10:4b:cb:15:9f 0:d0:b7:6b:20:17 0800 60: 10.2.2.2.4769 >
10.2.2.1.22: . ack 5396 win 32120 (DF)
```

Notice that in each line, the `ip` became `0800`, the host name `hostA` became `10.2.2.1`, and the port number `ssh` became `22`. We will discuss the meaning of the rest of the lines in the section "TCP" later in this chapter.

IP

The Internet Protocol has a slightly more complex header than Ethernet, as we can see in Figure 11-5. Let's step through what each of the header values signifies.

The first value in the IP header is the version number. The version of IP that is in most common use today is version 4 (IPv4); however, you will be seeing more of version 6 over the next few years. Version 6 offers many improvements (and changes) to version 4 that are best left to books dedicated to the subject. (Version 5, by the way, was an experimental version designed for multimedia that never made it outside of the lab.)

The next value is the length of the IP header itself. We need to know how long the header is because there may be optional parameters appended to the end of the base header. The header length tells us how many, if any, options are there. To get the byte count of the total IP header length, multiply this number by 4. Typical IP headers will have the header length value set to 5, indicating that there are 20 bytes in the complete header.

The Type of Service (ToS) header tells IP stacks what kind of treatment should be given to the packet. As of this writing, the only defined values are minimized delay, maximized throughput, maximized reliability, and minimized cost. See RFCs 1340 (ftp://ftp.isi.edu/in-notes/rfc1340.txt) and 1349 (ftp://ftp.isi.edu/in-notes/rfc1349.txt) for more details. The use of ToS bits is sometimes referred to as "packet coloring"; they are used by networking devices for the purpose of rate shaping and prioritization.

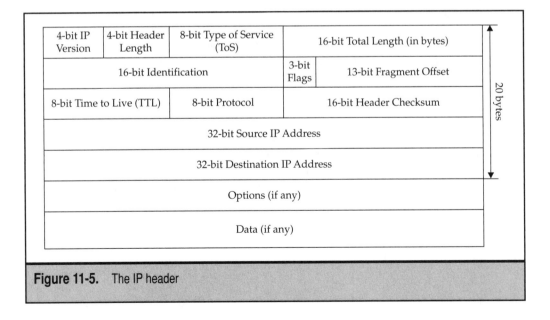

Figure 11-5. The IP header

The total length value tells us how long the complete packet is, including the IP and TCP headers, but not including the Ethernet headers. This value is represented in bytes. An IP packet cannot be longer than 65,535 bytes.

The identification number is supposed to be a unique number used by a host to identify a particular packet. Note that some security scanning tools identify "IP ID Randomization" as a possible security issue, but this is not quite true. If the IP ID is not fully randomized, it is possible to use that as a means to determine the operating system. An attacker can use that information to narrow the search for possible attack vectors; however, most TCP/IP stacks give up their identity in a number of ways. Don't focus too hard on this issue; there are far more important attack vectors to concern yourself with.

The flags in the IP packet tell us whether the packet is fragmented or not. Fragmentation occurs when an IP packet is larger than the smallest *MTU* (maximum transmission unit) between two hosts. MTU defines the largest packet that can be sent over a particular network. For example, Ethernet's MTU is 1500 bytes. Thus, if we have a 4000-byte IP packet that needs to be sent over Ethernet, the packet will be fragmented into three smaller packets. The first two packets will be 1500 bytes, and the last packet will be 1000 bytes.

The fragment offset value tells us which part of the complete packet we are receiving. Continuing with the 4000-byte IP packet example, the first fragment offset we'll receive will be 0. The second will be 1500, and the third will be 3000. The receiving IP stack will take these three packets and reassemble them into one large packet before passing it up the stack.

> **NOTE** IP fragments don't happen too frequently over the Internet anymore. Thus, many firewalls take a very paranoid approach about dealing with IP fragments, since they are the source of denial of service (DoS) attacks.
>
> The reason why DoS attacks use IP fragments is that many IP stacks don't handle them very well, thereby causing the system to crash. Linux handles IP fragments correctly, which makes it a great candidate for being a firewall. If you choose to go with a commercial firewall package, you may find it a good exercise to look for a tool that can send a large number of broken IP fragments and let it loose on the firewall to verify that it'll handle the attack.

The time-to-live field (TTL) is a number between 0 and 255 that signifies how much time a packet is allowed to have on the network before being dropped. The idea behind this is that in the event of a routing error where the packet is going around in a circle (also known as a "routing loop"), the TTL would cause the packet to eventually time out and be dropped, thus keeping the network from becoming completely congested with circling packets. As each router processes the packet, the TTL value is decreased by one. When the TTL reaches zero, the router at which this happens sends a message via the ICMP protocol (refer to "ICMP" earlier in the chapter), informing the sender of this.

> *NOTE*   Layer 2 switches do not decrement the TTL, only routers. Layer 2 switch loop detection does not rely on tagging packets but instead uses the switches' own protocol for communicating with other layer 2 switches to form a "spanning tree." In essence, a layer 2 switch maps all adjacent switches and sends test packets (bridge protocol data units, BPDUs) and looks for test packets generated by itself. When a switch sees a packet return to it, a loop is found and the offending port is automatically shut down to normal traffic. Tests are constantly run so that if the topology changes or the primary path for a packet fails, ports that were shut down to normal traffic may be reopened.

The protocol field in the IP header tells us which higher-level protocol this packet should be delivered to. Typically this has a value for TCP, UDP, or ICMP. In the **tcpdump** output we've seen, it is this value that determines whether the output reads **udp** or **tcp** after displaying the source and destination IP/port combination.

The last small value in this IP header is the checksum. This field holds the sum of every byte in the IP header, including any options. When a host builds an IP packet to send, it computes the IP checksum and places it into this field. The receiver can then do the same math and compare values. If the values mismatch, the receiver knows that the packet was corrupted during transmission. (For example, a lightning strike creating an electrical disturbance might create packet corruption.)

Finally, the numbers that matter the most in an IP header: the source and destination IP addresses. These values are stored as 32-bit integers instead of the more human-readable dotted-decimal notation. For example, instead of 192.168.1.1, the value would be hexadecimal c0a80101 or decimal 3232235777.

tcpdump and IP

By default, **tcpdump** doesn't dump all of the details of the IP header. To see everything, you need to specify the **-v** option. The **tcpdump** program will continue displaying all matching packets until you press CTRL-C to stop the output. You can ask **tcpdump** to automatically stop after a fixed number of packets with the **-c** parameter followed by the number of packets to look for. Finally, we can remove the timestamp for brevity by using the **-t** parameter. Assuming we want to see the next two IP packets without any DNS decoding, we would use the following parameters:

```
[root@hostA:~]# tcpdump -v -t -n -c 2 ip
68.121.105.169 > 68.121.105.170: icmp: echo request (ttl 127, id 21899, len 60)
68.121.105.170 > 68.121.105.169: icmp: echo reply (ttl 64, id 35004, len 60)
```

In the output we see a ping packet sent and returned. The format of this output is

```
src > dest: [deeper protocols] (ttl, id, length)
```

where *src* and *dest* refer to the source and destination of the packet, respectively. For TCP and UDP packets, the source and destination will include the port number after the IP address. The tail end of the line shows the TTL, IP ID, and length, respectively. Without the **-v** option, the TTL is shown only when it is equal to 1.

TCP

The TCP header is similar to the IP header in that it packs quite a bit of information into a little bit of space. Let's start by looking at Figure 11-6.

The first two pieces of information in a TCP header are the source and destination port numbers. Because these are only 16-bit values, their range is 0 to 65535. Typically, the source port is a value greater than 1024, since ports 1 to 1023 are reserved for system use on most operating systems (including Linux, Solaris, and the many variants of MS Windows). On the other hand, the destination port is typically low; most of the popular services reside there, although this is not a requirement.

In **tcpdump**'s output, we see port numbers immediately after the IP address. For example, in the output from **tcpdump -n -t**

```
192.168.1.1.2046 > 192.168.1.12.79:  . 1:1(0) ack 1 win 32120 (DF)
```

the source port number is 2046, and the destination port number is 79.

The next two numbers in the TCP header are the sequence and acknowledgment numbers. These values are used by TCP to ensure the order of packets is correct and to let the sender know which packets have been properly received. In day-to-day administrative tasks, you shouldn't have to deal with them.

In **tcpdump**'s output, we see sequence numbers in packets containing data. The format is *starting number:ending number.* Look at the following **tcpdump** output from **tcpdump -n -t**:

```
192.168.1.1.2046 > 192.168.1.12.79:  P 1:6(5) ack 1 win 32120 (DF)
```

We see that the sequence numbers are 1:6, meaning that the data started at sequence number 1 and ended at sequence number 6. In the parenthesized number immediately following the sequence numbers, we can see the length of the data being sent (five bytes in this example).

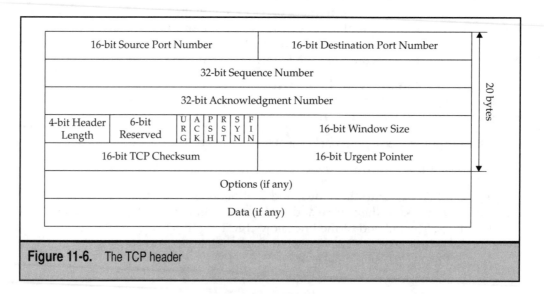

Figure 11-6. The TCP header

In this sample output, we also see the acknowledgment number. Whenever the packet has the acknowledgment flag set, it can be used by the receiver to confirm how much data has been received from the sender (refer to the discussion of the ACK flag later in this section). **tcpdump** prints **ack** followed by the acknowledgment number when it sees a packet with the acknowledgment bit set. In this case, the acknowledgment number is 1, meaning that 192.168.1.1 is acknowledging the first byte sent to it by 192.168.1.12 in the current connection.

> **NOTE** In order to make the output more readable, **tcpdump** uses relative values. Thus a sequence number of 1 really means that the data contained within the packet is the first byte being sent. If you want to see the actual sequence number, use the -**s** option.

Similar to IP's header length, TCP's header length tells us how long the header is, including any TCP options. Whatever value is in the header length field is multiplied by 4 to get the byte value.

This next part is a bit tricky. TCP uses a series of flags to indicate whether the packet is supposed to initiate a connection, contain data, or terminate a connection. The flags (in the order they appear) are: Urgent (URG), Acknowledge (ACK), Push (PSH), Reset (RST), Synchronize (SYN), and Finish (FIN). Their meanings are as follows:

Flag	Meaning
URG	Message that there is urgent data in the packet that should receive priority processing. There isn't a valid reason for modern operating systems to use this bit.
ACK	Acknowledgment of successfully received data.
PSH	Request to immediately process any received data.
RST	Immediately terminates the connection.
SYN	Request to start a new connection.
FIN	Request to finish a connection.

These flags are typically used in combination with one another. For example, it is common to see PSH and ACK together. Using this combination, the sender essentially tells the receiver two things:

▼ There is data in this packet that needs to be processed.

▲ I am acknowledging that I have received data from you successfully.

You can see which flags are in a packet in **tcpdump**'s output immediately after the destination IP address and port number. For example,

```
192.168.1.1.2046 > 192.168.1.12.79: P 1:6(5) ack 1 win 32120 (DF)
```

In the preceding line, we see the flag is P for PSH. **tcpdump** uses the first character of the flag's name to indicate the flag's presence (such as S for SYN or F for FIN). The only exception to this is ACK, which is actually spelled out as **ack** later in the line. (If the packet has only the ACK bit set, a period is used as a placeholder where the flags are usually printed.) ACK is an exception because it makes it easier to find what the acknowledgment number is for that packet. (See the discussion on acknowledgment numbers earlier in this section; we will discuss flags in greater detail when we discuss connection establishment and tear down.)

The next entry in the header is the window size. TCP uses a technique called *sliding window*, which allows each side of a connection to tell the other how much buffer space it has available for dealing with connections. When a new packet arrives on a connection, the available window size decreases by the size of the packet until the operating system has a chance to move the data from TCP's input buffer to the receiving application's buffer space. Window sizes are computed on a connection-by-connection basis. Let's look at some output from **tcpdump -n -t** as an example:

```
192.168.1.1.2046 > 192.168.1.12.79:  . 6:8(2) ack 1 win 32120 (DF)
192.168.1.12.79 > 192.168.1.1.2046:  . 1:494(493) ack 8 win 17520 (DF)
192.168.1.1.2046 > 192.168.1.12.79:  . 8:8(0) ack 495 win 31626 (DF)
192.168.1.1.2046 > 192.168.1.12.79:  . 8:8(0) ack 495 win 32120 (DF)
```

In the first line, we can see that 192.168.1.1 is telling 192.168.1.12 that it currently has 32,120 bytes available in its buffer for this particular connection. In the second packet, 192.168.1.12 sends 493 bytes to 192.168.1.1. (At the same time, 192.168.1.12 tells 192.168.1.1 that its available window is 17520 bytes.) 192.168.1.1 responds to 192.168.1.12 with an acknowledgment saying it has properly accepted everything up to the 495th byte in the stream, which in this case includes all of the data that has been sent by 192.168.1.12. It's also acknowledging that its available window is now 31626, which is exactly the original window size (32120) minus the amount of data that has been received (493 bytes). A few moments later, in the fourth line, 192.168.1.1 sends a note to 192.168.1.12 stating that it has successfully transferred the data to the application's buffer and that its window is back to 32120.

A little confusing? Don't worry too much about it. As a system administrator, you shouldn't have to deal with this level of detail, but it is helpful to know what the numbers mean.

NOTE   You may have noticed an off-by-one error in my math here. 32120 – 493 is 31627, not 31626. This has to do with the nuances of sequence numbers, calculations of available space, etc. For the full ugliness of how the math works, read RFC 793 (ftp://ftp.isi.edu/in-notes/rfc793.txt).

The next element in the TCP header is the checksum. This is similar to the IP checksum in that its purpose is to provide the receiver a way of verifying that the data received isn't corrupted. Unlike the IP checksum, the TCP checksum actually takes into account both the TCP header as well as the data being sent. (Technically, it also includes the TCP pseudo-header, but being system administrators, that's another mess we can skip over.)

Finally, the last piece of the TCP header is the *urgent pointer*. This value is observed when the URG flag is set and tells the receiving TCP stack that some very important data starts at the offset pointed to by the urgent pointer, relative to the sequence number. The TCP stack is supposed to relay this information to the application so that it knows it should treat that data with special importance.

In reality, you'll be pressed to see a packet that uses the URG bit. Ever. Most applications have no way of knowing whether data sent to them is urgent or not, and most applications don't really care. As a result, a small chord of paranoia should strike you if you do see urgent flags in your network. Make sure it isn't part of a probe from the outside trying to exploit bugs in your TCP stack and cause your servers to crash. (Don't worry about Linux—it knows how to handle the urgent bit correctly.)

UDP

In comparison to TCP headers, UDP headers are much simpler. Let's start by looking at Figure 11-7.

The first fields in the UDP header are the source and destination ports. These are conceptually the same thing as the TCP port numbers. In **tcpdump** output, they appear in a very similar manner. Let's look at a DNS query to resolve www.djdan.com into an IP address as an example with the command **tcpdump -n -t port 53**:

```
192.168.1.1.1096 > 192.168.1.8.53: 25851+ A? www.djdan.com. (31)
```

In this output, we can see that the source port of this UDP packet is 1096, and the destination port is 53. The rest of the line is the DNS request broken up into a human-readable form.

The next field in the UDP header is the length of the packet. **tcpdump** does not display this information.

Finally, the last field is the UDP checksum. This is used by UDP to validate that the data has arrived to its destination without corruption. If the checksum is corrupted, **tcpdump** will tell you.

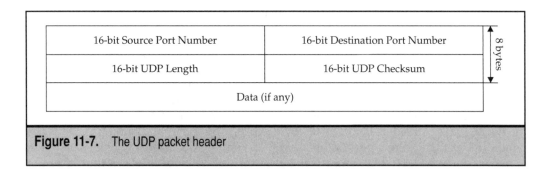

16-bit Source Port Number	16-bit Destination Port Number	8 bytes
16-bit UDP Length	16-bit UDP Checksum	
Data (if any)		

Figure 11-7. The UDP packet header

A COMPLETE TCP CONNECTION

As we discussed earlier, TCP supports the concept of a *connection*. Each connection must go through a sequence to get established; once both sides are done sending data, they must go through another sequence to close the connection.

In this section, we review the complete process of a simple HTTP request and view the process as seen by **tcpdump**. Note that all of the **tcpdump** logs in this section were generated with the **tcpdump -n -t port 80** command. Unfortunately, because of the complex nature of TCP, we cannot cover every possible scenario that a TCP connection can take. However, the coverage given here should be enough to help you determine when things are going wrong at the network level rather than at the server level.

Opening a Connection

TCP goes through a *three-way handshake* for every connection that it opens up. The reason for this is to allow both sides to send each other their state information and give each other a chance to acknowledge the receipt of that data.

The first packet is sent by the host that wants to open the connection with a server. For this discussion, we will call this host the *client*. The client sends a TCP packet over IP and sets the TCP flag to SYN. The sequence number is the initial sequence number that the client will use for all of the data it will send to the other host (which we'll call the *server*).

The second packet is sent from the server to the client. This packet contains two TCP flags set: SYN and ACK. The purpose of the ACK is to tell the client that it has received the first (SYN) packet. This is double-checked by placing the client's sequence number in the acknowledgment field. The purpose of the SYN is to tell the client with which sequence number the server will be sending its responses.

Finally, the third packet goes from the client to the server. It has only the ACK bit set in the TCP flags for the purpose of acknowledging to the server that it received its SYN. This ACK packet has the client's sequence number in the sequence number field and the server's sequence number in the acknowledgment field.

Sound a little confusing? Don't worry—it is. Let's try to clarify it with a real example from **tcpdump**. The first packet is sent from 192.168.1.1 to 207.126.116.254, and it looks like this (note that both lines are actually one very long line):

```
192.168.1.1.1367 > 207.126.116.254.80: S 2524389053:2524389053(0)
win 32120 <mss 1460,sackOK,timestamp 26292983 0,nop,wscale 0> (DF)
```

We can see the client's port number is 1367 and the server's port number is 80. The **S** means that the SYN bit is set and that the sequence number is 2524389053. The 0 in the parentheses after the sequence number means that there is no data in this packet. After the window is specified as being 32,120 bytes large, we see that **tcpdump** has shown us which TCP options were a part of the packet. The only option worth noting as a system administrator is the MSS (Maximum Segment Size) value. This value tells us the maximum size that TCP is tracking for a nonsegmented packet for that given connection. Connections that require small MSS values because of the networks that are being traversed typically require more packets to transmit the same amount of data. More packets means more overhead, and that means more CPU required to process a given connection.

Notice that there is no acknowledgment bit set and no acknowledgment field to print. This is because the client has no sequence number to acknowledge yet! Time for the second packet from the server to the client:

```
207.126.116.254.80 > 192.168.1.1.1367: S 1998624975:1998624975(0)
ack 2524389054 win 32736 <mss 1460>
```

Like the first packet, the second packet has the SYN bit set, meaning that it is telling the client what it will start its sequence number with (in this case, 1998624975). It's okay that the client and server use different sequence numbers. What's important, though, is that the server acknowledges receiving the client's first packet by turning the ACK bit on and setting the acknowledgment field to 2524389054 (the sequence number that the client used to send the first packet plus one).

Now that the server has acknowledged receiving the client's SYN, the client needs to acknowledge receiving the server's SYN. This is done with a third packet that has only the ACK bit set in its TCP flags. This packet looks like this:

```
192.168.1.1.1367 > 207.126.116.254.80: . 1:1(0) ack 1 win 32120 (DF)
```

We can clearly see that there is only one TCP bit set: ACK. The value of the acknowledgment field is shown as a 1. But wait! Shouldn't it be acknowledging 1998624975? Well, don't worry—it is. **tcpdump** has been kind enough to automatically switch into a mode that prints out the relative sequence and acknowledgment numbers instead of the absolute numbers. This makes the output much easier to read. So in this packet, the acknowledgment value of 1 means that it is acknowledging the server's sequence number plus one.

We now have a fully established connection.

So why all the hassle to start a connection? Why can't the client just send a single packet over to the server stating "I want to start talking, okay?" and have the server send back an "okay"? The reason is that without all three packets going back and forth, neither side is sure that the other side received the first SYN packet—and that packet is crucial to TCP's ability to provide a reliable and in-order transport.

Transferring Data

With a fully established connection in place, both sides are able to send data. Since we are using an HTTP request as an example, we will first see the client generate a simple request for a Web page. The **tcpdump** output looks like this:

```
192.168.1.1.1367 > 207.126.116.254.80: P 1:8(7) ack 1 win 32120 (DF)
```

Here we see the client sending 7 bytes to the server with the PSH bit set. The intent of the PSH bit is to tell the receiver to immediately process the data, but because of the nature of the Linux network interface to applications (sockets), setting the PSH bit is unnecessary. Linux (like all socket-based operating systems) automatically processes the data and makes it available for the application to read as soon as it can.

Along with the PSH bit is the ACK bit. This is because TCP always sets the ACK bit on outgoing packets. The acknowledgment value is set to 1, which, based on the connection setup we observed in the previous section, means that there has been no new data that needs acknowledging.

Given that this is an HTTP transfer, it is safe to assume that since it is the first packet going from the client to the server, it is probably the request itself.

Now the server sends a response to the client with this packet:

```
207.126.116.254.80 > 192.168.1.1.1367: P 1:767(766) ack 8 win 32736 (DF)
```

Here the server is sending 766 bytes to the client and acknowledging the first 8 bytes that the client sent to the server. This is probably the HTTP response. Since we know that the page we requested is very small, this is probably all of the data that is going to be sent in this request.

The client acknowledges this data with the following packet:

```
192.168.1.1.1367 > 207.126.116.254.80: . 8:8(0) ack 767 win 31354 (DF)
```

This is a *pure acknowledgment*, meaning that the client did not send any data, but it did acknowledge up to the 767th byte that the server sent.

The process of the server sending some data and then getting an acknowledgment from the client can continue as long as there is data that needs to be sent.

Closing the Connection

TCP connections have the option of ending ungracefully. That is to say, one side can tell the other "stop *now!*" Ungraceful shutdowns are accomplished with the RST (reset) flag, which the receiver does not acknowledge upon receipt. This is to keep both hosts from getting into a "RST war" where one side resets and the other side responds with a reset, thus causing a never-ending ping-pong effect.

Let's start with examining a clean shutdown of the HTTP connection we've been observing so far. In the first step in shutting down a connection, the side that is ready to close the connection sends a packet with the FIN bit set, indicating that it is finished. Once a host has sent a FIN packet for a particular connection, it is not allowed to send anything other than acknowledgments. This also means that even though it may be finished, the other side may still send it data. It is not until both sides send a FIN that both sides are finished. And like the SYN packet, the FIN packet must receive an acknowledgment.

In the next two packets, we see the server tell the client that it is finished sending data, and the client acknowledges this:

```
207.126.116.254.80 > 192.168.1.1.1367: F 767:767(0) ack 8 win 32736
192.168.1.1.1367 > 207.126.116.254.80: . 8:8(0) ack 768 win 31353 (DF)
```

We then see the reverse happen. The client sends a FIN to the server, and the server acknowledges it:

```
192.168.1.1.1367 > 207.126.116.254.80: F 8:8(0) ack 768 win 32120 (DF)
207.126.116.254.80 > 192.168.1.1.1367: . 768:768(0) ack 9 win 32735 (DF)
```

And that's all there is to a graceful connection shutdown.

As we indicated earlier, an ungraceful shutdown is simply one side sending another the RST packet, which looks like this:

```
192.168.1.1.1368 > 207.126.116.254.80: R 93949335:93949349(14) win 0
```

In this example, 192.168.1.1 is ending a connection with 207.126.116.254 by sending a reset. After receiving this packet, running **netstat** on 207.126.116.254 (which happens to be another Linux server) affirmed the connection was completely closed.

HOW ARP WORKS

The Address Resolution Protocol (ARP) is a mechanism that allows IP to map Ethernet addresses to IP addresses. This is important because when you send a packet on an Ethernet network, it is necessary to put in the Ethernet address of the destination host.

The reason we separate ARP from Ethernet, IP, TCP, and UDP is that ARP packets do not go up the normal packet path. Instead, because ARP has its own Ethernet header type (0806), the Ethernet driver sends the packet to the ARP handler subsystem, which has nothing to do with TCP/IP.

The basic steps of ARP are as follows:

1. The client looks in its ARP cache to see if it has a mapping between its IP address and its Ethernet address. (You can see your ARP cache by running **arp -a** on your system.)

2. If an Ethernet address for the requested IP address is not found, a broadcast packet is sent out requesting a response from the person with the IP we want.

3. If the host with that IP address is on the LAN, it will respond to the ARP request, thereby informing the sender of what its Ethernet address/IP address combination is.

4. The client saves this information in its cache and is now ready to build a packet for transmission.

We can see an example of this from **tcpdump** with the command **tcpdump -e -t -n arp**:

```
0:a0:cc:56:fc:e4 0:0:0:0:0:0 arp 60: arp who-has 192.168.1.1 tell 192.168.1.8
0:10:4b:cb:15:9f 0:a0:cc:56:fc:e4 arp 42: arp reply 192.168.1.1 (0:10:4b:cb:15:9f)
is-at 0:10:4b:cb:15:9f
```

The first packet is a broadcast packet asking all of the hosts on the LAN for 192.168.1.1's Ethernet address. The second packet is a response from 192.168.1.1 giving its IP/MAC address mapping.

This, of course, begs the question: "If we can find the MAC address of the destination host using a broadcast, why can't we just send all packets to the broadcast?" The answer has two parts. The first is that the broadcast packet requires that hosts on the LAN receiving the packet take a moment and process it. This means that if two hosts are having a very intense conversation (such as a large file transfer), all of the other hosts on the same LAN would incur a lot of overhead checking on packets that don't belong to them. The second reason is that networking hardware (such as switches) relies on Ethernet addresses in order to quickly forward packets to the right place and to minimize network congestion. Any time a switch sees a broadcast packet, it must forward that packet to *all* of its ports. This makes a switch no better than a hub.

"Now, if I need the MAC address of the destination host in order to send a packet to it, does that mean I have to send an ARP request to hosts that are sitting across the Internet?" The answer is a reassuring *no*.

When IP figures out where a packet should head off to, it first checks the routing table. If it can't find the appropriate route entry, IP looks for a *default route*. This is the path that, when all else fails, should be taken. Typically, the default route points to a router or firewall that understands how to forward packets to the rest of the world.

This means that when a host needs to send something to another server across the Internet, it only needs to know how to get the packet to the router, and therefore, it only needs to know the MAC address of the router.

To see this happen on your network, do a **tcpdump** on your host and then visit a Web site that is elsewhere on the Internet, such as www.yahoo.com. You will see an ARP request from your machine to your default route, a reply from your default route, and then the first packet from your host with the destination IP of the remote Web server.

The ARP Header: ARP Works with Other Protocols, Too!

The ARP protocol is not specific to Ethernet and IP. To see why, let's take a quick peek at the ARP header (see Figure 11-8).

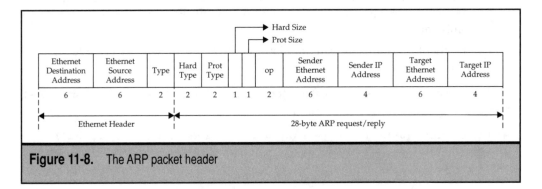

Figure 11-8. The ARP packet header

The first field that we see in the ARP header is the hard type. The hard type field specifies the type of hardware address. (Ethernet has the value of 1.)

The next field is the prot type. This specifies the protocol address being mapped. In the case of IP, this is set to 0800 (hexadecimal).

The hard size and prot size fields that immediately follow tell ARP how large the addresses it is mapping are. Ethernet has a size of 6, and IP has a size of 4.

The op field tells ARP what needs to be done. ARP requests are 1, and ARP replies are 2.

> **NOTE**   There is a variant of ARP called RARP (which stands for Reverse ARP). RARP has different values for the op field.

Finally, there are the fields that we are trying to map. A request has the sender's Ethernet and IP addresses as well as the destination IP address filled in. The reply fills in the destination Ethernet address and responds to the sender.

BRINGING IP NETWORKS TOGETHER

Now that we have some of the fundamentals of TCP/IP under our belt, let's take a look at how they work to let us glue networks together. In this section, we cover the differences between hosts and networks, netmasks, static routing, and some basics in dynamic routing.

The purpose of this section is not to show you how to configure a Linux router, but to introduce the concepts. Although you may find it less exciting than actually playing, you'll find that understanding the basics makes playing a little more interesting. More important, should you be looking to apply for a Linux system administrator's job, these could be things that pop up as part of the interview questions. Well, if you ever get interviewed by me, you can *expect* it!

Hosts and Networks

The Internet is a large group of interconnected networks. All of these networks have agreed to connect with some other network, thus allowing everyone to connect to one another. Each of these component networks is assigned a network address.

Traditionally, in a 32-bit IP address, the network component typically takes up 8, 16, or 24 bits to encode a class A, B, or C network, respectively. Since the remainder of the bits in the IP address are used to enumerate the host within the network, the fewer bits that are used to describe the network, the more bits are available to enumerate the hosts. For example, class A networks have 24 bits left for the host component, which means there can be upward of 16,777,214 hosts within that network. (Classes B and C have 65,534 and 254 nodes, respectively.)

> **NOTE**   There are also class D and class E ranges. Class D is used for multicast, and class E is reserved for experimental use.

To better organize the various classes of networks, it was decided early in IP's life that the first few bits would decide to which class the address belonged. For the sake of readability, the first *octet* of the IP address specifies the class.

NOTE   An octet is 8 bits, which in the typical dotted decimal notation of IP means the number before a dot. For example, in the IP address 192.168.1.42, the first octet is 192, the second octet is 168, and so on.

The ranges are as follows:

Class	Octet Range
A	0–126
B	128–192.167
C	192.169–223

You probably noted some gaps in the ranges. This is because there are some special addresses that are reserved for special uses. The first special address is one you are likely to be familiar with: 127.0.0.1. This is also known as the *loopback address.* It is set up on every host using IP so that it can refer to itself. It seems a bit odd to do it this way, but just because a system is capable of speaking IP doesn't mean it has an IP address allocated to it! On the other hand, the 127.0.0.1 address is virtually guaranteed. (If it isn't there, more likely than not, something has gone wrong.)

Three other ranges are notable: Every IP in the 10.0.0.0 network, the 172.16–172.31 networks, and the 192.168 network is considered a *private IP.* These ranges are not allowed to be allocated to anyone on the Internet, and therefore, you may use them on your internal networks.

NOTE   We define internal networks as networks that are behind a firewall—not really connected to the Internet—or that have a router performing network address translation at the edge of the network connecting to the Internet. (Most firewalls perform this address translation as well.)

Subnetting

Imagine a network with a few thousand hosts on it, which is not unreasonable in a medium-sized company. Trying to tie them all together into a single large network would probably lead you to pull out all your hair, beat your head into a wall, or possibly both. And that's just the figurative stuff.

The reasons for not keeping a network as a single large entity range from very technical issues to very political ones. On the technical front, there are limitations to every technology on how large a network can get before it becomes too large. Ethernet, for instance, cannot have more than 1024 hosts on a single collision domain. Realistically, having more than a dozen on an even mildly busy network will cause serious performance issues. Even migrating hosts to switches doesn't solve the entire problem, since switches, too, have limitations on how many hosts they can deal with.

Of course, you're likely to run into management issues before you hit limitations of switches; managing a single large network is very difficult. Furthermore, as an organization grows, individual departments will begin compartmentalizing. Human Resources is usually the first candidate to need a secure network of their own so that nosy engineers don't peek into things they shouldn't. In order to support a need like that, you need to create subnetworks, a task more commonly referred to as *subnetting*.

Assuming our corporate network is 10.0.0.0, we could subnet it by setting up smaller class C networks within it, such as 10.1.1.0, 10.1.2.0, 10.1.3.0, and so on. These smaller networks would have 24-bit network components and 8-bit host components. Since the first 8 bits would be used to identify our corporate network, we could use the remaining 16 bits of the network component to specify the subnet, giving us 65,534 possible subnetworks. Of course, you don't have to use all of them!

> **NOTE** As we've seen earlier in this chapter, network addresses have the host component of an IP address typically set to all zeros. This convention makes it easy for other humans to recognize which addresses correspond to entire networks and which addresses correspond specifically to hosts.

Netmasks

The purpose of a *netmask* is to tell the IP stack which part of the IP address is the network and which part is the host. This allows the stack to determine whether a destination IP address is on the LAN or if it needs to be sent to a router for forwarding elsewhere.

The best way to start looking at netmasks is to look at IP addresses and netmasks in their binary representations. Let's look at the 192.168.1.42 address with the netmask 255.255.255.0:

Dotted Decimal	Binary
192.168.1.42	11000000 10101000 00000001 00101010
255.255.255.0	11111111 11111111 11111111 00000000

In this example, we want to find out what part of the IP address 192.168.1.42 is network and what part is host. Now, according to the definition of netmask, those bits that are zero are part of the host. Given this definition, we see that the first three octets make up the network address and the last octet makes up the host.

In discussing network addresses with other people, it's often handy to be able to state the network address without having to give the original IP address and netmask. Thankfully, this network address is computable, given the IP address and netmask, using a bitwise AND operation.

The way the bitwise AND operation works can be best explained by observing the behavior of two bits being ANDed together. If both bits are 1, then the result of the AND is also 1. If either bit (or both bits) is zero, the result is zero. We can see this more clearly in this table:

Bit 1	Bit 2	Result of Bitwise AND
0	0	0
0	1	0
1	0	0
1	1	1

So computing the bitwise AND operation on 192.168.1.42 and 255.255.255.0 yields the bit pattern 11000000 10101000 00000001 00000000. Notice that the first three octets remained identical and the last octet became all zeros. In dotted decimal notation, this reads 192.168.1.0.

NOTE   Remember that we need to give up one IP to the network address and one IP to the broadcast address. In this example, the network address is 192.168.1.0, and the broadcast address is 192.168.1.255.

Let's walk through another example. This time, we want to find the address range available to us for the network address 192.168.1.176 with a netmask of 255.255.255.240. (This type of netmask is commonly given by ISPs to business DSL and T1 customers.)

A quick breakdown of the last octet in the netmask shows us that the bit pattern for 240 is 11110000. This means that the first three octets of the network address plus four bits into the fourth octet are held constant (255.255.255.240 in binary is 11111111 11111111 11111111 11110000). Since the last four bits are variable, we know we have 16 possible addresses ($2^4 = 16$). Thus, our range goes from 192.168.1.176 to 192.168.1.192 (192 − 176 = 16).

Because it is so tedious to type out complete netmasks, many people have started using an abbreviated format where the network address is followed by a slash and the number of bits in the netmask. So the network address 192.168.1.0 with a netmask of 255.255.255.0 would be abbreviated to 192.168.1.0/24.

NOTE   The process of using netmasks that do not fall on the class A, B, or C boundaries is also known as classless interdomain routing (CIDR). You can read more about CIDR in RFC 1817 (http://www.rfc-editor.org/rfc/rfc1817.txt).

Static Routing

When two hosts on the same LAN want to communicate, it is quite easy for them to find each other: Simply send out an ARP message, get the other host's MAC address, and you're off. But when the second host is not local, things become trickier.

In order to get two or more LANs to communicate with one another, a router needs to be put into place. The purpose of the router is to know about the topology of multiple networks. When you want to communicate with another network, your machine will set the destination IP as the host on the other network, but the destination MAC address will be for the router. This allows the router to receive the packet and examine the destination IP, and since it knows that IP is on the other network, it will forward the packet. The reverse is also true for packets that are coming from the other network to my network (see Figure 11-9).

The router must in turn know what networks are plugged into it. This information is called a *routing table*. When the router is manually informed about what paths it can take, the table is called *static*, thus the term *static routing*. Once routes are plugged into the routing table by a human, they cannot be changed until a human operator comes back to change them.

Unfortunately, routers are rather expensive devices. They are typically dedicated pieces of hardware that are highly optimized for the purpose of forwarding packets from one interface to another. You can, of course, make a Linux-based router (we discuss this in Chapter 12) using a stock PC that has two or more network cards. Such configurations are fast and cheap enough for smaller networks. In fact, many companies are already starting to do this, since older PCs that are too slow to run the latest Web browsers and word processing applications are still plenty fast to perform routing. (A low-end Pentium-class machine is fast enough to keep a 100Mb Ethernet connection full! Many dedicated routers use even simpler, slower hardware.)

The downside to Linux-based routers has more to do with PC hardware than Linux. By their nature, PCs are built to be less robust than dedicated network hardware. Furthermore, having an operating system that allows users to log in to do things other than routing means you run the risk of junior administrators adding load to a router that they shouldn't be touching. (This problem is independent of your operating system. Watch any server's or router's performance drop through the floor when someone thinks that an OpenGL-based screen saver would be a cute addition!)

As with any advice, take it within the context of your requirements, budget, and skills. Open source and Linux are great tools, but like anything else, make sure you're using the right tool for the job.

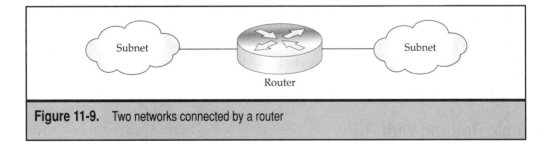

Figure 11-9.   Two networks connected by a router

Routing Tables

As mentioned earlier, routing tables are lists of network addresses, netmasks, and destination interfaces. A simplified version of a table might look like this:

Network Address	Netmask	Destination Interface
192.168.1.0	255.255.255.0	Interface 1
192.168.2.0	255.255.255.0	Interface 2
192.168.3.0	255.255.255.0	Interface 3
Default	0.0.0.0	Interface 4

When a packet arrives at a router that has a routing table like this, it will go through the list of routes and apply each netmask to the destination IP address. If the resulting network address is equal to the network address in the table, the router knows to forward the packet on to that interface.

So let's say that the router receives a packet with the destination IP address set to 192.168.2.233. The first table entry has the netmask 255.255.255.0. When this netmask is applied to 192.168.2.233, the result is not 192.168.1.0, so the router moves on to the second entry. Like the first table entry, this route has the netmask of 255.255.255.0. The router will apply this to 192.168.2.233 and find that the result network address is equal to 192.168.2.0. So now the appropriate route is found. The packet is forwarded out of interface 2.

If a packet arrives that doesn't match the first three routes, it will match the default case. In our sample routing table, this will cause the packet to be forwarded to interface 4. More than likely, this is a gateway to the Internet.

Limitations of Static Routing

The example of static routing we've used is typical of smaller networks. There are only a handful of networks that need to communicate with one another, and they aren't going to change often.

However, there are limitations to this technique. The biggest limitation is human—you are responsible for updating all of your routers with new information whenever you make any changes. Although this is usually very easy to do in a small network, it means that there is room for error. Furthermore, as your network grows and more routes get added, it is more likely that the routing table will become trickier to manage this way.

The second—but almost as significant—limitation is that the time it takes the router to process a packet can increase to the number of routes there are. With only three or four routes, this isn't a big deal. But as you start getting into dozens of routes, the overhead can become noticeable.

Given these two limitations, it is best to use static routes only in small networks.

Dynamic Routing with RIP

As networks grow, the need to subnet them grows, too. Eventually, you'll find that you have a lot of subnets that can't all be tracked easily, especially if they are being managed by different administrators. One subnet, for instance, may need to break their network in half for security reasons. In a situation this complex, going around and telling everyone to update their routing tables would be a real nightmare and would lead to all sorts of network headaches.

The solution to this problem is to use *dynamic routing*. The idea behind dynamic routing is that each router only knows immediately adjacent networks when it starts up. It then announces to other routers connected to it what it knows, and the other routers reply back with what they know. Think of it as "word of mouth" advertising for your network. You tell the people around you about your network, they then tell their friends, and their friends tell their friends, and so on. Eventually, everyone connected to the network knows about your new network.

On campus-wide networks (such as a large company with many departments) you'll typically see this method of announcing route information. As of this writing, the two most commonly used routing protocols are RIP and OSPF.

RIP (short for Routing Information Protocol) is currently up to version 2. It is a very simple protocol that is easy to configure. Simply tell the router information about one network (making sure each subnet in the company has a connection to a router that knows about RIP), and then have the routers connected to one another. RIP broadcasts happen at regular time intervals (usually less than a minute), and in only a few minutes, the entire campus network knows about you.

Let's see how a smaller campus network with four subnets would work with RIP. Figure 11-10 shows how the network is connected.

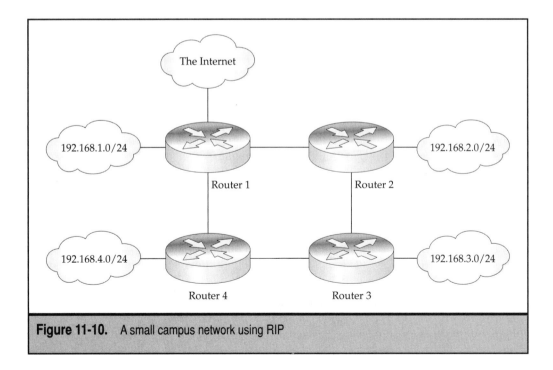

Figure 11-10.   A small campus network using RIP

NOTE For the sake of simplicity, we're serializing the events. In reality, many of these events would happen in parallel.

As illustrated in this figure, router 1 would be told about 192.168.1.0/24 and about the default route to the Internet. Router 2 would be told about 192.168.2.0/24, router 3 would know about 192.168.3.0/24, and so on. At startup, each router's table looks like this:

Router	Table
Router 1	192.168.1.0/24
	Internet gateway
Router 2	192.168.2.0/24
Router 3	192.168.3.0/24
Router 4	192.168.4.0/24

Router 1 then makes a broadcast stating what routes it knows about. Since routers 2 and 4 are connected to it, they update their routes. This makes the routing table look like this (new routes in *italics*):

Router	Table
Router 1	192.168.1.0/24
	Internet gateway
Router 2	192.168.2.0/24
	192.168.1.0/24 via router 1
	Internet gateway via router 1
Router 3	192.168.3.0/24
Router 4	192.168.4.0/24
	192.168.1.0/24 via router 1
	Internet gateway via router 1

Router 2 then makes its broadcast. Routers 1 and 3 see these packets and update their tables as follows (new routes in *italics*):

Router	Table
Router 1	192.168.1.0/24
	Internet Gateway
	192.168.2.0/24 via router 2

Router 2	192.168.2.0/24
	192.168.1.0/24 via router 1
	Internet gateway via router 1
Router 3	192.168.3.0/24
	192.168.2.0/24 via router 2
	192.168.1.0/24 via router 2
	Internet gateway via router 2
Router 4	192.168.4.0/24
	192.168.1.0/24 via router 1
	Internet gateway via router 1

Router 3 then makes its broadcast, which routers 2 and 4 hear. This is where things get interesting, since this introduces enough information for there to be multiple routes to the same destination. The routing tables now look like this (new routes in *italics*):

Router	Table
Router 1	192.168.1.0/24
	Internet gateway
	192.168.2.0/24 via router 2
Router 2	192.168.2.0/24
	192.168.1.0/24 via router 1
	Internet gateway via router 1
	192.168.3.0/24 via router 3
Router 3	192.168.3.0/24
	192.168.2.0/24 via router 2
	192.168.1.0/24 via router 2
	Internet gateway via router 2
Router 4	192.168.4.0/24
	192.168.1.0/24 via router 1 *or 3*
	Internet gateway via router 1 *or 3*
	192.168.3.0/24 via router 3
	192.168.2.0/24 via router 3

Next, router 4 makes its broadcast. Routers 1 and 3 hear this and update their tables to the following (new routes in *italics*):

Router	Table
Router 1	192.168.1.0/24
	Internet gateway
	192.168.2.0/24 via router 2 *or 4*
	192.168.3.0/24 via router 4
	192.168.4.0/24 via router 4
Router 2	192.168.2.0/24
	192.168.1.0/24 via router 1
	Internet gateway via router 1
	192.168.3.0/24 via router 3
Router 3	192.168.3.0/24
	192.168.2.0/24 via router 2
	192.168.1.0/24 via router 2 *or 4*
	Internet gateway via router 2 *or 4*
	192.168.4.0/24 via router 4
Router 4	192.168.4.0/24
	192.168.1.0/24 via router 1
	Internet gateway via router 1
	192.168.3.0/24 via router 3
	192.168.2.0/24 via router 3

Once all the routers go through another round of broadcasts, the complete table would look like this:

Router	Table
Router 1	192.168.1.0/24
	Internet gateway
	192.168.2.0/24 via router 2 or 4
	192.168.3.0/24 via router 4 or 2
	192.168.4.0/24 via router 4 or 2
Router 2	192.168.2.0/24
	192.168.1.0/24 via router 1 or 3
	Internet gateway via router 1 or 3
	192.168.3.0/24 via router 3 or 1

Router 3	192.168.3.0/24
	192.168.2.0/24 via router 2 or 4
	192.168.1.0/24 via router 2 or 4
	Internet gateway via router 2 or 4
	192.168.4.0/24 via router 4 or 2
Router 4	192.168.4.0/24
	192.168.1.0/24 via router 1 or 3
	Internet gateway via router 1 or 3
	192.168.3.0/24 via router 3 or 1
	192.168.2.0/24 via router 3 or 1

Why is this mesh important? Let's say router 2 fails. If router 3 was relying on router 2 to send packets to the Internet, it can immediately update its tables, reflecting that router 2 is no longer there and then forward Internet-bound packets through router 4.

RIP's Algorithm (and Why You Should Use OSPF Instead)

Unfortunately, when it comes to figuring out the most optimal path from one subnet to another, RIP is not the smartest protocol. Its method of determining which route to take is based on the fewest number of routers (hops) between it and the destination. Although that sounds optimal, what this algorithm doesn't take into account is how much traffic is on the link or how fast the link is.

Looking back at Figure 11-10, we can see where this situation might play itself out. Let's assume that the link between routers 3 and 4 becomes very congested. Now if router 3 wants to send a packet out to the Internet, RIP will still evaluate the two possible paths (3 to 4 to 1 and 3 to 2 to 1) as being equidistant. As a result, the packet may end up going via router 4 when clearly the path through router 2 (whose links are not congested) would be much faster.

OSPF (Open Shortest Path First) is very similar to RIP in how it broadcasts information to other routers. What makes it different is that instead of keeping track of how many hops it takes to get from one router to another, it keeps track of how quickly each router is talking to the others. Thus, in our example where the link between routers 3 and 4 becomes congested, OSPF will realize that and be sure to route a packet destined to router 1 via router 2.

Another feature of OSPF is its ability to realize when a destination address has two possible paths that would take an equal amount of time. When it sees this, OSPF will share the traffic across both links—a process called *equal-cost multipath*—thereby making optimal use of available resources.

There are two "gotchas" with OSPF. Older networking hardware and some lower-end networking hardware may not have OSPF available or have it at a substantially higher cost. The second gotcha is complexity: RIP is much simpler to set up than OSPF. For a small network, RIP may be a better choice at first.

DIGGING INTO TCPDUMP

The **tcpdump** tool is truly one of the more powerful tools you will use as a system administrator. The GUI version of it, Ethereal (http://www.ethereal.com), is an even better choice when a graphical front end is available. Ethereal offers all of the power of **tcpdump** with the added bonus of richer filters, additional protocol support, the ability to quickly follow TCP connections, and some handy statistics.

In this section, we walk through a few examples of how you can use **tcpdump**.

A Few General Notes

Here are a few quick tips regarding these tools before you jump into more advanced examples.

Ethereal

Ethereal is a graphical tool for taking packet traces and decoding them. It offers a lot more features than **tcpdump** and is a great way to peer inside of various protocols. You can download the latest version of Ethereal at http://www.ethereal.com.

An extra nice feature of Ethereal is that it can work under the native Windows environment, so you if you have a Windows desktop and a lot of Linux servers, you can take a packet capture on the server, pull the capture back, and then view it from your desktop without needing to start an X Window session on a remote Linux system.

Before you get too excited about Ethereal, don't forget to get your hands dirty with **tcpdump** too. In troubleshooting sessions, you don't always have the time or luxury of pulling up Ethereal, and if you're just looking for a quick validation that packets are moving, starting up a GUI tool may be a bit more than you need. The **tcpdump** tool offers a quick way to get a handle on the situation. Learning it will get you a quick handle on a lot of situations.

> **TIP**   Your Sun Solaris friends may have spoken about **snoop**. The **tcpdump** tool and **snoop**, while not identical, have a lot of similarities. Learn one and you'll have a strong handle on the other.

Reading and Writing Dumpfiles

If you need to capture a lot of data and save it, you'll want to use the **-w** option to write all the packets to disk for later processing. Here is a simple example:

```
[root@hostA:~]# tcpdump -w /tmp/trace.pcap -i eth0
```

The **tcpdump** tool will continue capturing packets seen on the eth0 interface until the terminal is closed, the process is killed, or CTRL-C is pressed. The resulting file can be loaded by Ethereal or read by any number of other programs that can process **tcpdump**-formatted captures. (The packet format itself is referred to as "pcap.")

NOTE When the **-w** option is used with **tcpdump**, it is not necessary to issue the **-n** option to avoid DNS lookups for each IP address seen.

To read back the packet trace using **tcpdump**, use the **-r** option. When reading a packet trace back, additional filters and options can be applied to affect how the packets will be displayed. For example, to show only ICMP packets from a trace file and avoid DNS lookups as the information is displayed, do the following:

```
[root@hostA:~]# tcpdump -r /tmp/trace.pcap -n icmp
```

Capturing More per Packet

By default, **tcpdump** limits itself to capturing the first 68 bytes of a packet. If you're just looking to track some flows and see what's happening on the wire, this is usually good enough. However, if you need to capture the entire packet for further decoding, you'll need to increase this value. To do so, use the **-s** (snaplen) option. For example, to capture a full 1500-byte packet and write it to disk, you could use

```
[root@hostA:~]# tcpdump -w /tmp/dump.pcap -i eth0 -s 1500
```

Performance Impact

Taking a packet trace can have a performance impact, especially on a heavily loaded server. There are two parts to the performance piece: the actual capture of packets and the decoding/printing of packets.

The actual capture of packets, while somewhat costly, can actually be minimized with a good filter. In general, unless your server load is extremely high or you're moving a lot of traffic, (a lot being hundreds of megabits/sec), this penalty is not too significant. The cost that is there comes from the penalty of moving packets from the kernel up to the **tcpdump** application, which requires both a buffer copy and a context switch.

The decoding/printing of packets, by comparison, is substantially more expensive. The decode itself is a small fraction of the cost, but the printing is very high. If your server is loaded, you want to avoid printing for two reasons: it generates load to format the strings that are output, and it generates load to update your screen. The latter factor can be especially costly if you're using a serial console, since each byte sent over the serial port generates a high-priority interrupt (higher than the network cards) that takes a long time to process because serial ports are comparatively so much slower than everything else. Printing decoded packets over a serial port can generate enough interrupt traffic to cause network cards to drop packets as they are starved for attention by the main CPU.

To alleviate the stress of the decode/print process, use the **-w** option to write raw packets to disk. The process of writing raw packets is much faster and lower in cost than printing them. Furthermore, writing raw packets means you skip the entire decode/ print step, since that is only done when you need to see the packets.

In short, if you're not sure, use the **-w** option to write the packets to disk, copy them off to another machine, and then read them there.

Don't Capture Your Own Network Traffic

A common mistake made when using **tcpdump** is to log in via the network and then start a capture. Without the appropriate filter, you'll end up capturing your session packets, which in turn, if you're printing them to the screen, may generate new packets, which get captured again, and so on. A quick way to skip your own traffic (and that over other administrators) is to simply skip port 22 (the ssh port) in the capture like so:

```
[root@hostA:~]# tcpdump not tcp port 22
```

If you want to see what other people are doing on that port, add a filter that applies only to your host. For instance, if you're coming from 192.168.1.8, you can write

```
root@hostA:~]# tcpdump "not (host 192.168.1.8 and tcp port 22)"
```

Note the addition of the quote marks. This was done so as not to confuse the shell with the added parentheses, which are for **tcpdump**.

Read the Man Page

To see the full power of **tcpdump**, take some time to read its complete man page. You can see the latest version of **tcpdump** at http://www.tcpdump.org and the latest version of the man page at http://www.tcpdump.org/tcpdump_man.html.

Using tcpdump to Watch a Traceroute

The **traceroute** program works by initially setting the TTL value of a UDP packet to 1 and then sending it off to the destination host. This causes the first router along the path to drop the packet and send back an ICMP message. **traceroute** sees the ICMP message and now knows the first router in the path between the source host and the destination host. Another packet is built, this time with a TTL value of 2, and sent off. Of course, this packet causes the second router along the path to announce itself by means of an ICMP message.

The **traceroute** program repeats this process until the destination host itself generates an ICMP message about the packet having a TTL of 0. Having received an ICMP message from every router in between two hosts, it can display this list to you. For example, if we want to see every router between hostA.planetoid.org and 68.121.104.1, we would see the following **traceroute** output:

```
[sshah@hostA:~]$ traceroute -n 68.121.104.1
traceroute to 68.121.104.1 (68.121.104.1), 64 hops max, 44 byte packets
 1   68.121.105.174   7.689 ms   8.471 ms   8.556 ms
 2   64.164.97.67   9.304 ms   9.494 ms   9.541 ms
 3   64.164.97.142   12.532 ms   12.978 ms   12.928 ms
```

The end point in this case is likely to be a router that has multiple IP addresses assigned to it; thus, the last hop is showing a different IP address than the one we choose in the `traceroute` command. So what then did the actual packet trace look like?

To make the **tcpdump** output more concise, let's add the **-t** option, which will not print the timestamp, and use the filter **udp or icmp**. The **tcpdump** command used to capture this traceroute is

```
[root@hostA:~]# tcpdump -t -n udp or icmp
68.121.105.170.47762 > 68.121.104.1.33435: udp 16 [ttl 1]
68.121.105.174 > 68.121.105.170: icmp: time exceeded in-transit
68.121.105.170.47762 > 68.121.104.1.33436: udp 16 [ttl 1]
68.121.105.174 > 68.121.105.170: icmp: time exceeded in-transit
68.121.105.170.47762 > 68.121.104.1.33437: udp 16 [ttl 1]
68.121.105.174 > 68.121.105.170: icmp: time exceeded in-transit
68.121.105.170.47762 > 68.121.104.1.33438: udp 16
64.164.97.67 > 68.121.105.170: icmp: time exceeded in-transit [tos 0xc0]
68.121.105.170.47762 > 68.121.104.1.33439: udp 16
64.164.97.67 > 68.121.105.170: icmp: time exceeded in-transit [tos 0xc0]
68.121.105.170.47762 > 68.121.104.1.33440: udp 16
64.164.97.67 > 68.121.105.170: icmp: time exceeded in-transit [tos 0xc0]
68.121.105.170.47762 > 68.121.104.1.33441: udp 16
64.164.97.142 > 68.121.105.170: icmp: 68.121.104.1 udp port 33441 unreachable
68.121.105.170.47762 > 68.121.104.1.33442: udp 16
64.164.97.142 > 68.121.105.170: icmp: 68.121.104.1 udp port 33442 unreachable
68.121.105.170.47762 > 68.121.104.1.33443: udp 16
64.164.97.142 > 68.121.105.170: icmp: 68.121.104.1 udp port 33443 unreachable
```

In the trace we can see host A (68.121.105.170) sending a UDP packet to the destination with a TTL of 1. The next-hop router, 68.121.105.174, decrements the TTL on the packet, finds it is zero, and shoots back an "icmp: time exceeded in-transit" message. This is done three times by host A, so three different timestamps (7.689 ms, 8.471 ms, and 8.556 ms) can be seen. With all three responses back, host A tries again with another UDP packet to the destination, this time with a TTL of 2. (Using a **-v** option in the **tcpdump** line would have shown this.) The 68.121.105.174 hop makes the TTL 1, which means that the second hop, 64.164.97.67, sends back the ICMP message. This is repeated until we see an "unreachable" ICMP message that tells us we've found our end point.

Why Is DNS Slow?

Odd or intermittent problems are great candidates for using **tcpdump**. Using a trace of the packets themselves, you can look at activity over a period of time and identify issues that may be masked by other activity on the system or a lack of debugging tools.

Let's assume for a moment that you are using the DNS server managed by your DSL provider. Everything is working until one day things seem to be acting up. Specifically, when you visit a Web site, the first connection seems to take a long time, but once connected, the system seems to run pretty quickly. Every couple of sites, the connection doesn't even work, but clicking "Reload" seems to do the trick. That means that DNS is working and connectivity is there. What gives?

Time to take a packet trace. Since this is Web traffic, we know that there are two protocols at work: DNS for the host name resolution and TCP for connection setup. That means we want to filter all the other noise out and focus on those two protocols. Since there seems to be some kind of speed issue, getting the packet timestamps is necessary, so we don't want to use the **-t** option. The result is

```
[root@hostA:~]# tcpdump -n port 80 or port 53
```

Now visit the desired Web site. For this example, we'll go to www.rondcore.com.
Let's look at the first few UDP packets:

```
21:27:40 68.12.10.17.4102 > 206.13.31.12.53: A? rondcore.com (31)
21:27:50 68.12.10.17.4103 > 206.13.31.12.53: A? rondcore.com (31)
21:27:58 206.13.31.12.53 > 68.12.10.17.4102: 1/4/4 A 67.43.6.47 (206)
```

That's interesting . . . we needed to retransmit the DNS request to get the IP address for the host name. Looks like there is some kind of connectivity problem here, since we do eventually get the response back. What about the rest of the connection? Does the connectivity problem impact other activity?

```
21:27:58 68.12.10.17.3013 > 67.43.6.47.80: S 1031:1031(0) win 57344 (DF)
21:27:58 67.43.6.47.80 > 68.12.10.17.3013: S 192:192(0) ack 1031 win 5840 (DF)
21:27:58 68.12.10.17.3013 > 67.43.6.47.80: . ack 1 win 58400 (DF)
21:27:58 68.12.10.17.3013 > 67.43.6.47.80: P 1:17(16) ack 1 win 58400 (DF)
21:27:58 67.43.6.47.80 > 68.12.10.17.3013: . ack 17 win 5840 (DF)
21:27:58 68.12.10.17.3013 > 67.43.6.47.80: P 17:94(77) ack 1 win 58400 (DF)
21:27:58 67.43.6.47.80 > 68.12.10.17.3013: . ack 94 win 5840 (DF)
21:27:58 67.43.6.47.80 > 68.12.10.17.3013: . 1:1461(1460) ack 94 win 5840 (DF)
21:27:58 67.43.6.47.80 > 68.12.10.17.3013: F 2155:2155(0) ack 94 win 5840 (DF)
21:27:58 68.12.10.17.3013 > 67.43.6.47.80: . ack 1461 win 56940 (DF)
21:27:58 67.43.6.47.80 > 68.12.10.17.3013: P 1461:2155(694) ack 94 win 5840 (DF)
21:27:58 68.12.10.17.3013 > 67.43.6.47.80: . ack 2156 win 56511 (DF)
21:27:58 68.12.10.17.3013 > 67.43.6.47.80: F 94:94(0) ack 2156 win 58400 (DF)
21:27:58 67.43.6.47.80 > 68.12.10.17.3013: . ack 95 win 5840 (DF)
```

Clearly the rest of the connection went quickly. Time to poke at the DNS server . . .

```
[sshah@hostA:~]$ ping 206.13.28.12
PING 206.13.28.12 (206.13.28.12) from 192.168.1.15 : 56(84) bytes of data.
64 bytes from 206.13.28.12: icmp_seq=1 ttl=247 time=213.0 ms
64 bytes from 206.13.28.12: icmp_seq=3 ttl=247 time=477.0 ms
64 bytes from 206.13.28.12: icmp_seq=4 ttl=247 time=177.5 ms
```

Yikes! We're losing packets and the jitter on the wire is very bad. This explains the odd DNS behavior. Time to look for another DNS server while this issue is resolved.

Graphing Odds and Ends

As administrators, we sometimes have questions about the system that are, well, just for the heck of asking. When it comes to collecting network information, **tcpdump** is a gold mine. Here are a few examples of things you can do.

Graphing Initial Sequence Numbers

The Initial Sequence Number (ISN) in a TCP connection is the sequence number specified in the SYN packet that starts a connection. For security reasons, it is important to have a sufficiently random ISN so that others can't spoof connections to your server. To see a graph of the distribution of ISNs that your server is generating, let's use **tcpdump** to capture SYN/ACK packets sent from the Web server. To capture the data, we use the following bit of **tcpdump** piped to Perl:

```
[root@hostA:~]# tcpdump -l -n -t "tcp[13] == 18" | perl -ane
'($s,$j)=split(/:/,$F[4],2 ); print "$s\n";' > graphme
```

The **tcpdump** command introduces a new parameter, **-l**. This parameter tells **tcpdump** to line buffer its output. This is necessary when piping **tcpdump**'s output to another program such as Perl. We also introduce a new trick, whereby we look into a specific byte offset of the TCP packet and check for a value. In this case, we used the figure of the TCP header to determine that the 13th byte holds the TCP flags. For SYN/ACK, the value is 18. The resulting line is piped into a Perl script that pulls the sequence number out of the line and prints it. The resulting file **graphme** will simply be a string of numbers that looks something like this:

```
803950992
1953034072
3833050563
3564335347
2706314477
```

We now use **gnuplot** (http://www.gnuplot.info) to graph these. You could use another spreadsheet to plot these, but depending on how many entries you have, that could be an issue. The **gnuplot** program works well with very large data sets and is free.

We start **gnuplot** and issue the following commands:

```
[sshah@hostA:~]$ gnuplot
gnuplot> set terminal png
Terminal type set to 'png'
Options are 'small monochrome'
gnuplot> set output 'syns.png'
gnuplot> plot 'graphme'
gnuplot> quit
```

Taking a look at the **syns.png** file, we see the following graph:

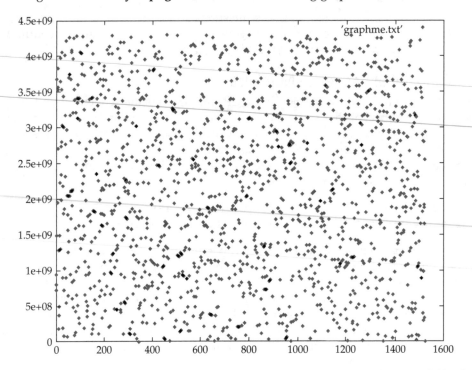

The graph shows a good distribution of ISN values. This implies that it is difficult to spoof TCP connections to this host. Clearly, the more data you have to graph here, the more sure you can be of this result. Taking the data to a statistics package to confirm the result can be equally interesting.

What's My Average Packet Size?

The amount of throughput a network gets has a lot to do with packet sizes. The more that gets stuffed into a packet, the more efficient it is, due to the fixed costs of dealing with a packet. Academics have found that the distribution of packet sizes is typically bimodal, with a spike around small 64-byte packets (usually due to TCP acknowledgments) and large packets (TCP packets pushing real data).

The academics may have done their own research, but it's always good fun to find out whether it applies to your server. To get the same information, we use **tcpdump**, and a little bit of **awk**. For the uninitiated, **awk** is another scripting language that comes standard with most UNIX and Linux systems. For non-Linux machines, Perl is often optional; however, **awk** is guaranteed to be there. For more information on **awk**, visit http://www.gnu.org/software/gawk/gawk.html.

Let's start with the **tcpdump** command to collect the data. As in the previous section, we use the **-l** parameter to make the output line buffered and pipe the output. However, this time, the choice of **awk** is out of laziness—it takes fewer characters to express what we want with **awk** than with Perl.

```
[root@hostA:~]# tcpdump -l -q -t -n | awk '{print $5}' > psize
```

Depending on what you're looking for, you may want to alter the filter on **tcpdump** to isolate the individual types of traffic. For example, if you're only interested in Web traffic, applying a filter "port 80" will do the trick. This is also an excellent example of where using the **-w** parameter instead to write all traffic down would be a good choice. With the raw packets stored on disk, you can go back and apply different filters on the same data multiple times to get different kinds of graphs. For instance, is the distribution any different between Web and mail traffic? What about non-TCP traffic vs. TCP traffic? For the moment, let's assume we want to see all traffic and look at the **packet_size.txt** file.

What we'll see is a list of numbers between 0 and 1460 showing how much data is in each packet. Why 1460? Because the output is not accounting for the packet headers themselves and TCP + IP headers are 40 bytes at a minimum. With the list in hand, we need to sort and count them. To do this, we use the **sort** and **uniq** commands like so:

```
[sshah@hostA:~]$ sort -n psize | uniq -c | awk '{print $2,$1}' > psize2
```

The **sort** command does a numerical sort of all the numbers, so all the 0's get grouped together, 1's together, and so on. This is piped to **uniq**, which counts how many of each number is there and displays the count followed by the number. In order to get our axis correct, this output is piped to **awk** so the numbers are reversed. The x-axis value (the first number) is the packet size, followed by how many are there.

A quick trip through **gnuplot** would be

```
[sshah@hostA:~]$ gnuplot
gnuplot> set terminal png
Terminal type set to 'png'
Options are 'small monochrome'
gnuplot> set output 'packet_size.png'
gnuplot> plot 'psize2'
gnuplot> quit
```

For my particular test server, running a load generation tool (Apache Benchmark, see the man page for "ab") against a small home page produced a lot of small packets. Clearly, most of the packets were zero bytes in length, which meant that a lot of overhead was present in connection setup and tear down. The result is shown here (your graph should be quite a bit different):

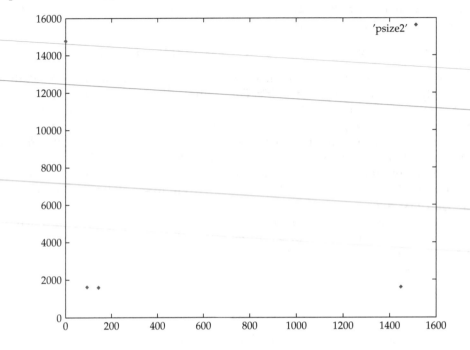

SUMMARY

This chapter covered the fundamentals of TCP/IP and other protocols, ARP, subnetting and netmasks, and routing. It's a lot to digest, but hopefully this simplified version should make it easier to understand. Specifically, we discussed:

▼ How TCP/IP relates to the ISO OSI seven-layer model

■ The composition of a packet

■ The specifications of packet headers and how to get them using the **tcpdump** tool

■ The complete process of a TCP connection setup, data transfer, and connection tear down

■ How to calculate netmasks

■ How static routing works

■ How dynamic routing works with RIP

▲ Several examples of using **tcpdump**

Because the information here is (substantially) simplified from the real deal, you may want to take a look at some other books for more information regarding this topic. This is especially important if you have complex networks that your machines need to live in or if you need to understand the operation of your firewall.

One book we recommend to everyone is *TCP/IP Illustrated, Volume 1* by Richard Stevens (Addison-Wesley, 1994). This book covers TCP/IP in depth and several popular protocols that send their data over IP. Stevens does a fantastic job of explaining this complex subject in a very clear and methodical manner. We have yet to meet a single person who read this and didn't understand what he said. A system administrator who has read this book can easily make him/herself much more valuable in the job market.

If you need to start out with something a little less meaty, try *TCP/IP for Dummies, Fifth Edition* by Candace Leiden, et al. (Hungry Minds, 2003). Although it is a "dummies" book, you'll be pleased to see that the coverage does get deep, just at a much slower rate. And thankfully, the authors didn't slip on correctness to make it simpler. (Marketing and sales folk who need to sell networking hardware should be required to read this book!)

My last recommendation is specific to those who need to configure Cisco equipment (which according to Cisco's sales figures, is a lot of you!): the *Cisco TCP/IP Routing Professional Reference* by Chris Lewis (McGraw-Hill/Osborne, 2000). Chris does a solid job at explaining both the protocols as well as configuration issues for Cisco equipment.

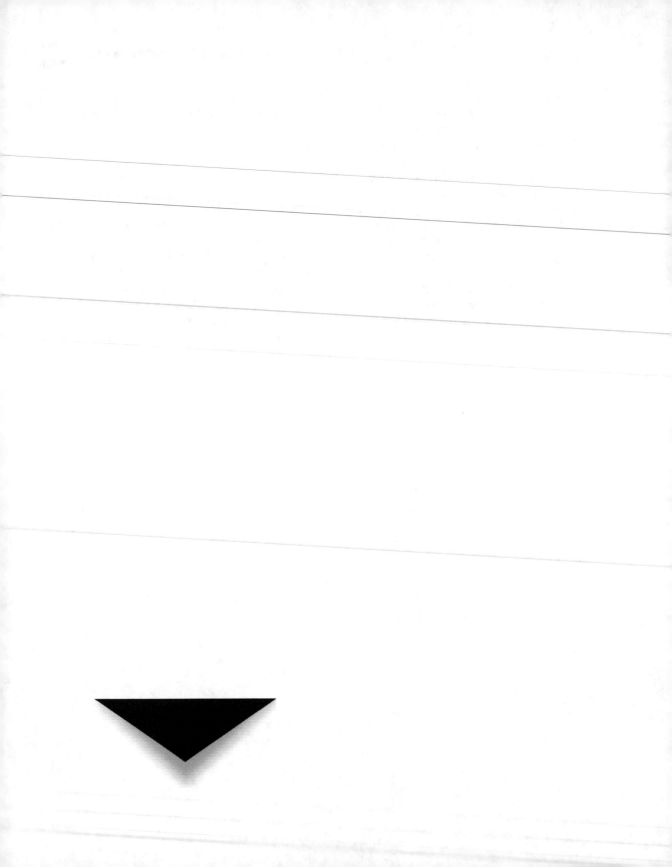

CHAPTER 12

Network Configuration

K nowing how to configure your network services by hand can be terribly important for several reasons. First and foremost is that when things are breaking and you can't start your favorite GUI, being able to handle network configuration from the command line is crucial. Another reason is remote administration: you may not be able to run a graphical configuration tool from a remote site. Issues such as firewalls and network latency will probably restrict your remote administration to the command line only. Finally, it's always nice to be able to perform network configuration through scripts, and command-line tools are best suited for scriptability.

In this chapter, we will tackle an overview of network interface drivers, the two tools necessary for performing command-line administration of your network interface: `ifconfig` and `route`.

MODULES AND NETWORK INTERFACES

Network devices under Linux break the tradition of accessing all devices through the file metaphor. Not until the network driver initializes the card and registers itself with the kernel does there exist a mechanism for anyone to access the card. Typically, Ethernet devices register themselves as being eth$X$, where X is the device number. The first Ethernet device is eth0, the second is eth1, and so on.

Depending on how your kernel was compiled, the device drivers for your network interface cards may have been compiled as a module. For most distributions, this is the default mechanism for shipping, since it makes it much easier to probe for hardware.

If the driver is configured as a module, and you have autoloading modules set up, you will need to tell the kernel the mapping between device names and the module to load in the **/etc/modprobe.conf** file. For example, if your eth0 device is an Intel PRO/1000 card, you would add the following line to your **/etc/modprobe.conf** file:

```
alias eth0 e1000
```

where **e1000** is the name of the device driver.

You will need to set this up for every network card you have in the same system. For example, if you have two network cards, one based on the DEC Tulip chipset and another on the RealTek 8169 chipset, you would need to make sure your **/etc/modprobe .conf** file includes these lines:

```
alias eth0 tulip
alias eth1 r8169
```

where **tulip** refers to the network card with the Tulip chip on it, and **r8169** refers to the RealTek 8169 card.

NOTE   These alias commands will not be the only entries in the **/etc/modprobe.conf** file.

One of the goals of this book is to provide a way for Windows administrators to become comfortable with Linux by demonstrating system parallels. This section visualizes some of the most important concepts for both operating systems so that you can see how their foundations are established. In addition to comparisons, we have visualized two common processes in a Linux system: processing of Web requests and processing of new e-mail.

Linux Administration Blueprints

Table of Contents

Linux vs. Windows Server 2003 Boot Process

The Linux Boot Process

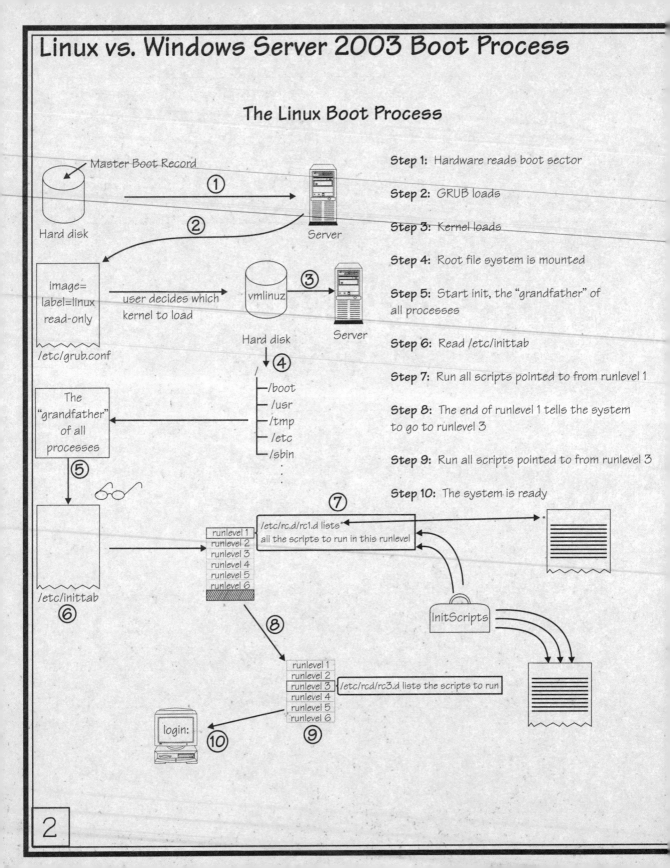

Master Boot Record

Hard disk

Server

image=
label=linux
read-only

/etc/grub.conf

user decides which kernel to load

vmlinuz

Hard disk

Server

The "grandfather" of all processes

/
— /boot
— /usr
— /tmp
— /etc
— /sbin
:

Step 1: Hardware reads boot sector

Step 2: GRUB loads

Step 3: Kernel loads

Step 4: Root file system is mounted

Step 5: Start init, the "grandfather" of all processes

Step 6: Read /etc/inittab

Step 7: Run all scripts pointed to from runlevel 1

Step 8: The end of runlevel 1 tells the system to go to runlevel 3

Step 9: Run all scripts pointed to from runlevel 3

Step 10: The system is ready

/etc/inittab

runlevel 1
runlevel 2
runlevel 3
runlevel 4
runlevel 5
runlevel 6

/etc/rc.d/rc1.d lists all the scripts to run in this runlevel

InitScripts

runlevel 1
runlevel 2
runlevel 3
runlevel 4
runlevel 5
runlevel 6

/etc/rcd/rc3.d lists the scripts to run

login:

2

The Windows Server 2003 Boot Process

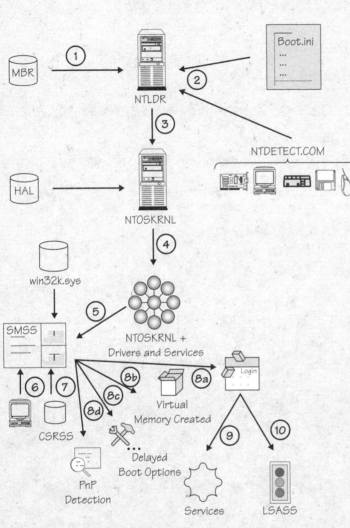

Step 1: Master Boot Record (MBR) loads and starts NTLDR (NT Loader)

Step 2: NTLDR reads BOOT.INI and the results from NTDETECT.COM

Step 3: NTOSKRNL.EXE is loaded with appropriate HAL.DLL

Step 4: Drivers and kernel services are loaded

Step 5: SMSS.EXE (Session Manager) starts and creates the environment, invokes kernel mode (Win32.sys)

Step 6: Kernel mode starts graphics subsystem

Step 7: CSRSS.EXE (User mode) is started

Step 8a: Winlogon is started

Step 8b: Virtual memory is created

Step 8c: Other delayed boot options are started (e.g., remaining components of an installation process)

Step 8d: PnP detection occurs

Step 9: Services.exe (Service Control Manager) is started

Step 10: lsass.exe (Local Security Authority) is started

While the names and the exact order of the steps are different than Linux's boot process, the principle remains the same in Windows: start a boot loader, start a kernel, start services, and get a login prompt up. When a user logs in, start user-specific programs. One key difference is the approach to controlled boots, where the administrator wishes to tightly control what gets started during trouble-shooting sessions. Linux implements this using runlevels and kernel parameters. Windows implements this concept using "Safe Mode."

3

Linux vs. Windows Server 2003 Based Network

Linux Network

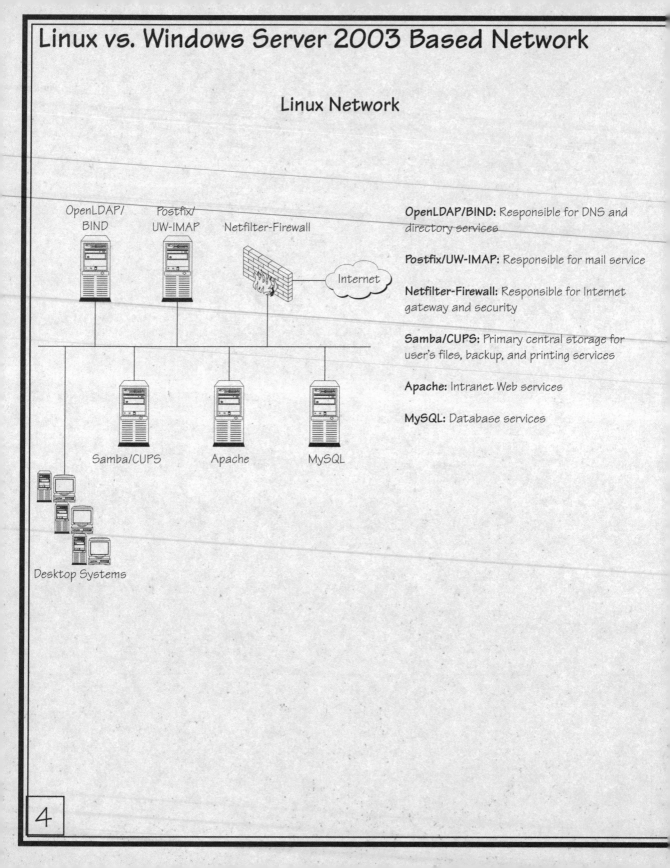

OpenLDAP/BIND: Responsible for DNS and directory services

Postfix/UW-IMAP: Responsible for mail service

Netfilter-Firewall: Responsible for Internet gateway and security

Samba/CUPS: Primary central storage for user's files, backup, and printing services

Apache: Intranet Web services

MySQL: Database services

Windows Server 2003 Based Network

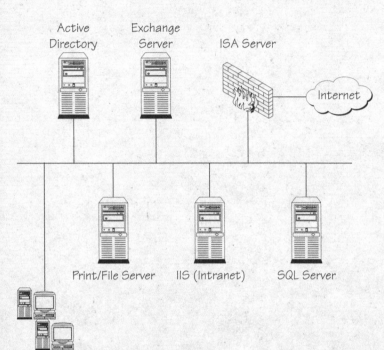

Active Directory

Exchange Server

ISA Server

Internet

Print/File Server

IIS (Intranet)

SQL Server

Desktop Systems

Active Directory: Responsible for AAA, DNS, and directory services

Exchange Server: Responsible for mail service

ISA Server: Responsible for Internet gateway and security

Print/File Server: Primary central storage for user files, backup, and printing services

IIS Server: Internet Web services

SQL Server: Database services

Both networks are functionally equivalent: whatever Windows can do, Linux can do also. The key difference is how Linux breaks key components down into smaller functional pieces. From a system administrator's point of view, the difference means that Linux services can be separated onto smaller, independent servers for specific tasks. Keep in mind that it is possible to consolidate functions on both Linux and Windows. For a small enough office environment, it is possible to merge many of these functions onto one server.

Web Request vs. E-mail Processing Pipeline

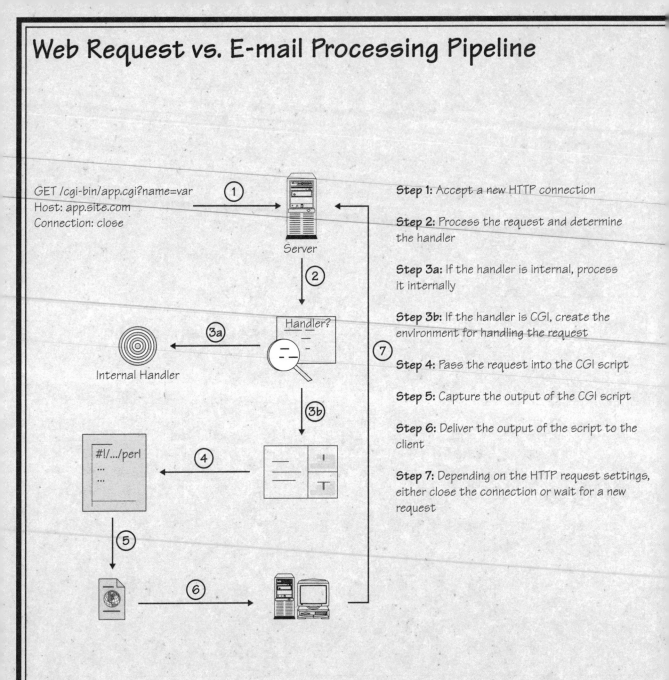

GET /cgi-bin/app.cgi?name=var
Host: app.site.com
Connection: close

① Server

②

Handler?

③a Internal Handler

③b

#!/.../perl
...
...

④

⑤

⑥

⑦

Step 1: Accept a new HTTP connection

Step 2: Process the request and determine the handler

Step 3a: If the handler is internal, process it internally

Step 3b: If the handler is CGI, create the environment for handling the request

Step 4: Pass the request into the CGI script

Step 5: Capture the output of the CGI script

Step 6: Deliver the output of the script to the client

Step 7: Depending on the HTTP request settings, either close the connection or wait for a new request

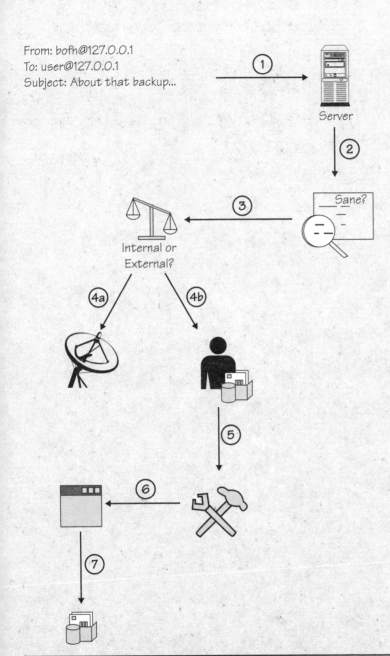

From: bofh@127.0.0.1
To: user@127.0.0.1
Subject: About that backup...

Server

Sane?

Internal or
External?

Step 1: E-mail arrives to the server

Step 2: Initial sanity checks for correctness, relaying, etc.

Step 3: Internal or external delivery?

Step 4a: If external delivery, forward mail to appropriate mail server

Step 4b: If internal delivery, find appropriate user's mailbox

Step 5: Apply all appropriate filters (spam, mailing lists, etc.)

Step 6: Pass message to delivery agent

Step 7: Delivery agent appends e-mail to the appropriate mailbox

Processing Web and e-mail traffic, two very common practices with Linux, are actually quite complex processes. A lot of activity is going on under the hood. Becoming familiar with these steps will make troubleshooting the process a little easier the next time you need to dig into a tricky problem.

7

Linux vs. Windows Server 2003 Shutdown Process

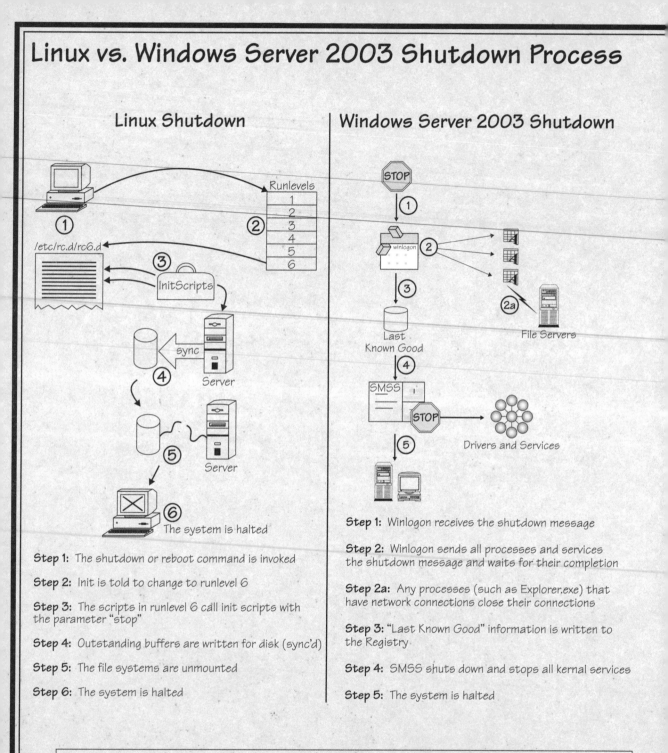

Linux Shutdown

Runlevels
1
2
3
4
5
6

/etc/rc.d/rc6.d

InitScripts

sync

Server

Server

The system is halted

Step 1: The shutdown or reboot command is invoked

Step 2: Init is told to change to runlevel 6

Step 3: The scripts in runlevel 6 call init scripts with the parameter "stop"

Step 4: Outstanding buffers are written for disk (sync'd)

Step 5: The file systems are unmounted

Step 6: The system is halted

Windows Server 2003 Shutdown

STOP

winlogon

File Servers

Last Known Good

SMSS
STOP

Drivers and Services

Step 1: Winlogon receives the shutdown message

Step 2: Winlogon sends all processes and services the shutdown message and waits for their completion

Step 2a: Any processes (such as Explorer.exe) that have network connections close their connections

Step 3: "Last Known Good" information is written to the Registry

Step 4: SMSS shuts down and stops all kernal services

Step 5: The system is halted

Although it may seem that the shutdown processes don't share a lot in common, their principles do. Where Linux uses runlevels to issue stop signals to all of its services, Windows issues stop signals across the board. Both then do general housekeeping before finally shutting down kernel services.

You can find a listing of all of the device drivers that are installed for your kernel in the **/lib/modules/`uname -r`/kernel/drivers/net** directory like so:

```
[root@hostA etc]# cd /lib/modules/`uname -r`/kernel/drivers/net
[root@hostA net]#
```

Note that there are backticks (versus single quotes) surrounding the embedded **uname -r** command. This will let you be sure you are using the correct driver version for your current kernel version. If you are using a standard installation of your distribution, you'll find that there should be only one subdirectory name in the **/lib/modules** directory.

If you want to see a driver's description without having to load the driver itself, use the **strings** command on the **.ko** file. For example, to see the description of the **yellowfin.ko** driver, type

```
[root@hostA net]# strings yellowfin.ko | grep description=
description=Packet Engines Yellowfin G-NIC Gigabit Ethernet driver
```

To get a listing of all the driver descriptions, you can use the following shell script:

```
#!/bin/sh
KERNEL=`uname -r`
for i in `find /lib/modules/$KERNEL/kernel/drivers/net -name "*.ko" -print`
do
   DESCRIPTION=`strings $i | grep 'description=' | sed 's/description=/ /'`
   echo $i "-" $DESCRIPTION
done
```

Keep in mind that not all drivers have descriptions associated with them, but most do. When copying this script, take careful notice of single quotes, double quotes, spaces, and backticks.

USING IFCONFIG TO CONFIGURE SET IP ADDRESSES

The **ifconfig** program is responsible for setting up your network interface cards (NICs). All of its operations can be performed through command-line options, as its native format has no menus or graphical interface. Administrators that have used the Windows **ipconfig** program may see some similarities, as Microsoft implemented some CLI networking tools that mimicked functional subsets of their UNIX brothers.

TIP Administrators still dealing with Windows may find the **%SYSTEMROOT%\system32\netsh .exe** program a handy tool for exposing the details of Windows networking via the CLI by means of a Cisco-like interface.

NOTE   The `ifconfig` program typically resides in the /**sbin** directory and must be run as root. Some login scripts, such as those in Fedora, do not include /**sbin** in the PATH by default. Thus, you may need to invoke /**sbin**/**ifconfig** when calling on it. If you expect to be a frequent user of /**sbin** commands, you may find it prudent to add /**sbin** to your PATH.

A number of tools have been written to wrap around `ifconfig`'s command-line interface to provide menu-driven or graphical interfaces, and many of these tools are shipped with distributions of Linux. Fedora, for example, has a GUI tool under the Applications | System Settings menu.

As an administrator, you should at least know how to configure the network interface by hand; knowing how is invaluable, as many additional options not shown in GUIs are exposed in the CLI. For that reason, this section will cover the use of the `ifconfig` command-line tool.

Simple Usage

In its simplest usage, all you need to do is provide the name of the interface being configured and the IP address. The **ifconfig** program will deduce the rest of the information from the IP address. Thus, you could enter

```
[root@hostA /root]# ifconfig eth0 192.168.1.42
```

to set the eth0 device to the IP address 192.168.1.42. Because 192.168.1.42 is a class C address, the calculated netmask will be 255.255.255.0, and the broadcast address will be 192.168.1.255.

If the IP address you are setting is a class A or class B address that is subnetted differently, you will need to explicitly set the broadcast and netmask addresses on the command line, like so:

```
[root@hostA /root]# ifconfig dev ip netmask nmask broadcast bcast
```

where **dev** is the network device you are configuring, **ip** is the IP address you are setting it to, **nmask** is the netmask, and **bcast** is the broadcast address. For example, the following will set the eth0 device to the IP address 1.1.1.1 with a netmask of 255.255.255.0 and a broadcast address of 1.1.1.255:

```
[root@hostA /root]# ifconfig eth0 1.1.1.1 netmask 255.255.255.0 broadcast
1.1.1.255
```

TIP   You can list all of the active devices by running `ifconfig` with no parameters. You can list all devices, regardless of whether they are active, by running `ifconfig -a`.

IP Aliasing

In some instances, it is necessary for a single host to have multiple IP addresses. Linux can support this by using IP aliases.

Each interface in the Linux system can have multiple IP addresses assigned. This is done by enumerating each instance of the same interface with a colon followed by a number. For example, eth0 is the main interface, eth0:0 is an aliased interface, eth0:1 is an aliased interface, and so on.

Configuring an aliased interface is just like configuring any other interface: simply use `ifconfig`. For example, to set eth0:0 with the address 10.0.0.2 and netmask 255.255.255.0, we would do the following:

```
[root@hostA /root]# ifconfig eth0:0 10.0.0.2 netmask 255.255.255.0
[root@hostA /root]# ifconfig eth0:0
eth0:0    Link encap:Ethernet   HWaddr 00:30:48:21:2A:36
          inet addr:10.0.0.2  Bcast:10.255.255.255  Mask:255.255.0.0
          UP BROADCAST RUNNING MULTICAST  MTU:1500  Metric:1
          Interrupt:9 Base address:0xd000
```

Note that network connections made *to* the aliased interface will communicate on the aliased IP address; however, in most circumstances any connection originating from the host to another host will use the first assigned IP of the interface. For example, if eth0 is 192.168.1.15 and eth0:0 is 10.0.0.2, a connection from the machine that is routed through eth0 will use the IP address 192.168.1.15. The exception to this behavior is for applications that bind themselves to a specific IP address. In those cases, it is possible for the application to originate connections from the aliased IP address. In the case that a host has multiple interfaces, the route table will decide which interface to use. Based on the routing information, the first assigned IP address of the interface will be used.

Confusing? Don't worry, it's a little odd to get the idea at first. The choice of source IP is associated to routing as well so we'll revisit this concept later in the chapter.

Setting Up NICs at Boot Time

Unfortunately, each distribution has taken to automating their setup process for network cards a little differently. We will cover the Fedora Core 3 specifics in the next section. For other distributions, you need to handle this procedure in one of two ways:

▼   Use the administrator tool that comes with that distribution to add network card support. This is probably the easiest and most reliable method.

▲   Find the startup script that is responsible for configuring network cards. (Using the `grep` tool to find which script runs `ifconfig` works well.) At the end of the script, add the necessary `ifconfig` statements. Another place to add `ifconfig` statements is in the **rc.local** script—not as pretty, but it works equally well.

Setting Up NICs under Fedora Core 3 and Red Hat Enterprise

Fedora Core and Red Hat Enterprise have a system setup that makes it easy to configure network cards at boot time. It is done through the creation of files in the **/etc/sysconfig/ network-scripts** directory that are read at boot time. All of the graphical tools under

Linux create these files for you, but for the power user inside of you just dying to edit the files by hand, the following is what you need to know.

For each network interface, there is an **ifcfg** file in **/etc/sysconfig/network-scripts**. This filename is suffixed by the name of the device; thus **ifcfg-eth0** is for the eth0 device, **ifcfg-eth1** is for the eth1 device, and so on.

If you choose a static IP at installation time, the format of each of these files will be as follows:

```
DEVICE="eth0"
IPADDR="192.168.1.1"
NETMASK="255.255.255.0"
NETWORK=192.168.1.0
BROADCAST=192.168.1.255
ONBOOT="yes"
BOOTPROTO="static"
```

TIP Sometimes if you are running other protocols, IPX, for instance, you might see variables that start with IPX. If you don't have to run IPX (which is typical), you can safely remove the lines that have IPX in them.

If you choose to use DHCP at installation time, your file will look as follows:

```
DEVICE=eth0
BOOTPROTO=dhcp
ONBOOT=yes
TYPE=Ethernet
```

These fields determine the IP configuration information for the eth0 device. Note how each of these values corresponds to the parameters in **ifconfig**. To change the configuration information for this device, simply change the information in the **ifcfg** file and run

```
[root@hostA /root]# cd /etc/sysconfig/network-scripts
[root@hostA network-scripts]# ./ifdown eth0
[root@hostA network-scripts]# ./ifup eth0
```

If you are changing from DHCP to a static IP address, simply change BOOTPROTO to equal "yes" and add lines for IPADDR, NETWORK, and BROADCAST. If you need to configure a second network interface card, copy the **ifcfg-eth0** file to **ifcfg-eth1** and change the information in **ifcfg-eth1** to reflect the second network card's information. Once there, Red Hat and Fedora Core will automatically configure it during the next boot.

If you need to activate the card immediately, run

```
[root@hostA /root]# cd /etc/sysconfig/network-scripts
[root@hostA network-scripts]# ./ifup eth1
```

NOTE   It is possible to configure aliased IP addresses using this method as well.

Additional Parameters

The format of the `ifconfig` command is as follows:

```
[root@hostA /root]# ifconfig device address options
```

where **device** is the name of the Ethernet device (for instance, eth0), **address** is the IP address you wish to apply to the device, and **options** are one of the following:

Option	Description
`up`	Enables the device. This option is implicit.
`down`	Disables the device.
`arp`	Enables this device to answer `arp` requests (default).
`-arp`	Disables this device from answering `arp` requests.
`mtu value`	Sets the maximum transmission unit (MTU) of the device to **value**. Under Ethernet, this defaults to 1500. (See the Note following the table regarding certain Gigabit Ethernet cards.)
`netmask address`	Sets the netmask to this interface to **address**. If a value is not supplied, `ifconfig` calculates the netmask from the class of the IP address. A class A address gets a netmask of 255.0.0.0, class B gets 255.255.0.0, and class C gets 255.255.255.0.
`broadcast address`	Sets the broadcast address to this interface to **address**. If a value is not supplied, `ifconfig` calculates the broadcast address from the class of the IP address in a similar manner to netmask.
`pointtopoint address`	Sets up a point-to-point connection (PPP) where the remote address is **address**.

NOTE   Many Gigabit Ethernet cards now support jumbo Ethernet frames. A jumbo frame is 9000 bytes in length, which (conveniently) holds one complete NFS packet. This allows file servers to perform better, since they have to spend less time fragmenting packets to fit into 1500-byte Ethernet frames. Of course, your network infrastructure as a whole must support this in order to benefit. If you have a network card and appropriate network hardware to set up jumbo frames, it is very much worth looking into how to toggle those features on. If your Gigabit Ethernet card supports it, you can set the frame size to 9000 bytes by changing the MTU setting when configured with `ifconfig` (for example, `ifconfig eth0 192.168.1.1 mtu=9000`).

There are many more options to `ifconfig`; however, you'll find that it is unusual to need more of them. For the curious, simply read the manual page for `ifconfig` to see the complete list of options with their descriptions.

USING ROUTES

If your host is connected to a network with multiple subnets, you need a *router* or *gateway*. This device, which sits between networks, redirects packets toward their actual destination. (Typically, most hosts don't know the correct path to a destination; they only know the destination itself.)

In the case where a host doesn't even have the first clue about where to send a packet, it uses its *default route*. This path points to a router, which ideally does have an idea of where the packet should go, or at least knows of another router that can make smarter decisions.

▼ **NOTE** On Red Hat and Fedora Core systems, the default route is typically stored as the variable GATEWAY in the appropriate interface file in **/etc/sysconfig/network**.

A typical Linux host knows of three routes: the first is the loopback route, which simply points toward the loopback device. The second is the route to the local area network so that packets destined to hosts within the same LAN are sent directly to them. Finally, the third route is the default route. This route is used for packets that need to leave the local area network to communicate with other networks.

If you set up your network configuration at install time, this setting is most likely already taken care of for you, so you don't need to change it. However, this doesn't mean you can't.

▼ **NOTE** There are actually instances where you will need to change your routes by hand. Typically, this is necessary when multiple network cards are installed into the same host, where each NIC is connected to a different network. You should know how to add a route so that packets can be sent to the appropriate network for a given destination address.

Simple Usage

The typical **route** command is structured as follows:

```
[root@hostA /root]# route cmd type addy netmask mask gw gway dev dn
```

The parameters are as follows:

Parameter	Description
cmd	Either **add** or **del** depending on whether you are adding or deleting a route. If you are deleting a route, the only other parameter you need is **addy**.
type	Either **-net** or **-host** depending on whether **addy** represents a network address or a router address.
addy	The destination network to which you want to offer a route.
netmask *mask*	Sets the netmask of the **addy** address to *mask*.
gw *gway*	Sets the router address for **addy** to *gway*. Typically used for the default route.
dev *dn*	Sends all packets destined to **addy** through the network device *dn* as set by **ifconfig**.

Here's how to set the default route on a sample host, which has a single Ethernet device and a router of 192.168.1.1:

```
[root@hostA /root]# route add -net default gw 192.168.1.1 dev eth0
```

This command line sets up a system so that all packets destined to 192.168.1.42 are sent through the first PPP device:

```
[root@hostA /root]# route add -host 192.168.1.42 netmask 255.255.255.255 dev ppp0
```

Here's how to delete the route destined to 192.168.1.42:

```
[root@hostA /root]# route del 192.168.1.42
```

NOTE   If you are using a gateway, you need to make sure a route exists to the gateway before you reference it for another route. For example, if your default route uses the gateway at 192.168.1.1, you need to be sure you have a route to get to the 192.168.1.0 network first.

Displaying Routes

There are two ways you can display your route table: the **route** command and **netstat**.

Route

Using **route** is the easiest way to display your route table—simply run **route** without any parameters. Here is a complete run, along with the output:

```
[root@hostA /root]# route
Kernel IP routing table
Destination     Gateway      Genmask           Flags Metric Ref Use Iface
10.10.2.0       *            255.255.255.0     UH    0      0   0   eth1
192.168.1.0     *            255.255.255.0     U     0      0   0   eth0
127.0.0.0       *            255.0.0.0         U     0      0   0   lo
default         firewall     0.0.0.0           UG    0      0   0   eth1
```

You see two networks. The first is the 192.168.1.0 network, which is accessible via the first Ethernet device, eth0. The second is the 10.10.2.0 network, which is connected via the second Ethernet device, eth1. The default route is 10.10.2.4; however, because the IP address resolves to the host name firewall in DNS, **route** prints its host name instead of the IP address.

We have already discussed the destination, gateway, netmask (referred to as **genmask** in this table), and **iface** (interface, set by the **dev** option on **route**). The other entries in the table have the following meanings:

Entry	Description
flags	A summary of connection status, where each letter has a significance: **U** The connection is up. **H** The destination is a host. **G** The destination is a gateway.
metric	The cost of a route, usually measured in hops. This is meant for systems that have multiple paths to get to the same destination, but one path is preferred over the other. A path with a lower metric is typically preferred. The Linux kernel doesn't use this information, but certain advanced routing protocols do.
ref	The number of references to this route. This is not used in the Linux kernel. It is here because the route tool itself is cross-platform. Thus it prints this value, since other operating systems do use it.
use	The number of successful route cache lookups. To see this value, use the **-F** option when invoking **route**.

Note that **route** displayed the host names to any IP addresses it could look up and resolve. While this is nice to read, it presents a problem when there are network difficulties, and DNS or NIS servers become unavailable. The **route** command will hang on, trying to resolve host names and waiting to see if the servers come back and resolve them. This wait will go on for several minutes until the request times out.

To get around this, use the -n option with **route** so that the same information is shown, but **route** will make no attempt to perform host name resolution on the IP addresses.

netstat

Normally, the **netstat** program is used to display the status of all of the network connections on a host. However, with the -r option, it can also display the kernel routing table. You should note that most other UNIX-based operating systems require that you use this method of viewing routes.

Here is an example invocation of **netstat -r** and its corresponding output:

```
[root@hostA /root]# netstat -r
Kernel IP routing table
Destination     Gateway       Genmask         Flags MSS Window irtt Iface
192.168.1.0     0.0.0.0       255.255.255.0 U     0   0        0    eth0
127.0.0.0       0.0.0.0       255.0.0.0     U     0   0        0    lo
default         192.168.1.1 0.0.0.0         UG    0   0        0    eth0
```

In this example, you see a simple configuration. The host has a single network interface card, is connected to the 192.168.1.0 network, and has a default gateway set to 192.168.1.1.

Like the **route** command, **netstat** can also take the -n parameter so that it does not perform host name resolution.

A SIMPLE LINUX ROUTER

Linux has an impressive number of networking features, including the ability to act as a full-featured router. For small networks that need a low-cost network where extremely high performance is not required, a low-cost PC with a few network cards can work quite nicely.

Realistically, a Linux router is able to move a few hundred megabits/sec, depending on the speed of the PC, the CPU cache, the type of NIC, PCI interfaces, and the speed of the front side bus. While this is no replacement for a full-blown Cisco-class router, it can serve the needs of smaller environments where a lot of traffic doesn't move through the router and cost is a significant consideration. (Full-blown UNIX systems were known to act as full-blown routers in early Internet data centers before layer 3 processing was moved to hardware.)

Routing with Static Routes

Let us assume that we want to configure a dual-homed Linux system as a router as shown in Figure 12-1.

In this network we want to route packets between the 192.168.1.0/24 network and the 192.168.2.0/24 network. The default route is through the 192.168.1.8 router, which is performing NAT to the Internet. (We discuss NAT in further detail in Chapter 13.) For all the machines on the 192.168.2.0/24 network, we want to simply set their default route

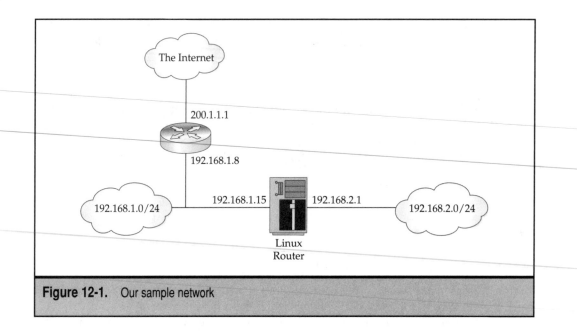

Figure 12-1. Our sample network

to 192.168.2.1 and let the Linux router figure out how to forward on to the Internet and the 192.168.1.0/24 network. For the systems on the 192.168.1.0/24 network, we want to configure 192.168.1.15 as the default route so that all the machines can see the Internet and the 192.168.2.0/24 network.

This requires that our Linux system have two network interfaces: eth0 and eth1. We configure them as follows:

```
[root@hostA /root]# ifconfig eth0 192.168.1.15 netmask 255.255.255.0
[root@hostA /root]# ifconfig eth1 192.168.2.1 netmask 255.255.255.0
```

The result looks like this:

```
[root@hostA /root]# ifconfig -a
eth0      Link encap:Ethernet  HWaddr 00:30:48:21:2A:36
          inet addr:192.168.1.15  Bcast:192.168.1.255  Mask:255.255.255.0
          UP BROADCAST RUNNING MULTICAST  MTU:1500  Metric:1
          RX packets:0 errors:0 dropped:0 overruns:0 frame:0
          TX packets:0 errors:0 dropped:0 overruns:0 carrier:0
          collisions:0 txqueuelen:1000
          RX bytes:0 (0.0 b)  TX bytes:0 (0.0 b)
          Interrupt:9 Base address:0xd000

eth1      Link encap:Ethernet  HWaddr 00:02:B3:AC:5E:AC
          inet addr:192.168.2.1  Bcast:192.168.2.255  Mask:255.255.255.0
```

```
             UP BROADCAST MULTICAST  MTU:1500  Metric:1
             RX packets:0 errors:0 dropped:0 overruns:0 frame:0
             TX packets:0 errors:0 dropped:0 overruns:0 carrier:0
             collisions:0 txqueuelen:1000
             RX bytes:0 (0.0 b)  TX bytes:0 (0.0 b)
             Base address:0xef80 Memory:febe0000-fec00000

lo           Link encap:Local Loopback
             inet addr:127.0.0.1  Mask:255.0.0.0
             UP LOOPBACK RUNNING  MTU:16436  Metric:1
             RX packets:2173386 errors:0 dropped:0 overruns:0 frame:0
             TX packets:2173386 errors:0 dropped:0 overruns:0 carrier:0
             collisions:0 txqueuelen:0
             RX bytes:164613316 (156.9 Mb)  TX bytes:164613316 (156.9 Mb)
```

NOTE It is possible to configure a one-armed router where the eth0 interface is configured with 192.168.1.15 and eth0:0 is configured with 192.168.2.1. However, doing this will eliminate any benefits of network segmentation. In other words, any broadcast packets on the wire will be seen by both networks. Thus, it is usually preferred to put each network on its own physical interface.

When **ifconfig** adds an interface, it also creates a route entry for that interface based on the netmask value. Thus, in the case of 192.168.1.0/24, a route is added on eth0 that sends all 192.168.1.0/24 traffic to it. With the two network interfaces present, let's take a look at the routing table:

```
[root@hostA /root]# route -n
Kernel IP routing table
Destination     Gateway         Genmask         Flags Metric Ref    Use Iface
192.168.2.0     0.0.0.0         255.255.255.0   U     0      0        0 eth1
192.168.1.0     0.0.0.0         255.255.255.0   U     0      0        0 eth0
127.0.0.0       0.0.0.0         255.0.0.0       U     0      0        0 lo
```

All that is missing here is the default route to 192.168.1.8. Let's add that using the **route** command.

```
[root@hostA /root]# route add default gw 192.168.1.8
[root@hostA /root]# route -n
Kernel IP routing table
Destination     Gateway         Genmask         Flags Metric Ref    Use Iface
192.168.2.0     0.0.0.0         255.255.255.0   U     0      0        0 eth1
192.168.1.0     0.0.0.0         255.255.255.0   U     0      0        0 eth0
127.0.0.0       0.0.0.0         255.0.0.0       U     0      0        0 lo
0.0.0.0         192.168.1.8     0.0.0.0         UG    0      0        0 eth0
```

A quick check with **ping** verifies that we have connectivity through each route:

```
[root@hostA /root]# ping -c 1 4.2.2.1
PING 4.2.2.1 (4.2.2.1) from 192.168.1.15 : 56(84) bytes of data.
64 bytes from 4.2.2.1: icmp_seq=1 ttl=245 time=15.2 ms

--- 4.2.2.1 ping statistics ---
1 packets transmitted, 1 received, 0% loss, time 0ms
rtt min/avg/max/mdev = 15.277/15.277/15.277/0.000 ms

[root@hostA /root]# ping -c 1 192.168.1.30
PING 192.168.1.30 (192.168.1.30) from 192.168.1.15 : 56(84) bytes of data.
64 bytes from 192.168.1.30: icmp_seq=1 ttl=64 time=0.233 ms

--- 192.168.1.30 ping statistics ---
1 packets transmitted, 1 received, 0% loss, time 0ms
rtt min/avg/max/mdev = 0.233/0.233/0.233/0.000 ms

[root@hostA /root]# ping -c 1 192.168.2.2
PING 192.168.2.2 (192.168.2.2) from 192.168.2.1 : 56(84) bytes of data.
64 bytes from 192.168.2.2: icmp_seq=1 ttl=64 time=0.192 ms

--- 192.168.2.2 ping statistics ---
1 packets transmitted, 1 received, 0% loss, time 0ms
rtt min/avg/max/mdev = 0.192/0.192/0.192/0.000 ms
```

Looks good. Now it's time to enable IP forwarding. This tells the Linux kernel that it is allowed to forward packets that are not destined to it, if it has a route to the destination. This is done by setting **/proc/sys/net/ipv4/ip_forward** to 1 as follows:

```
[root@hostA /root]# echo "1" > /proc/sys/net/ipv4/ip_forward
```

Hosts on the 192.168.1.0/24 network should set their default route to 192.168.1.15, and hosts on 192.168.2.0/24 should set their default route to 192.168.2.1. Most important, don't forget to make the route additions and the enabling of **ip_forward** part of the startup scripts.

> **TIP**   Need a DNS server off the top of your head? For a quick query against an external DNS server, try 4.2.2.1, which is currently owned by Verizon. The address has been around for a long time (originally belonging to GTE Internet) and has numbers that are easy to remember. However, be nice about it—a quick query or two to test connectivity is fine, but making it your primary DNS server isn't.

HOW LINUX CHOOSES AN IP ADDRESS

Now that host A has two interfaces (192.168.1.15 and 192.168.2.1) in addition to the loopback interface (127.0.0.1), we can observe how Linux will choose a source IP address to communicate with.

When an application starts, it has the option to bind to an IP address. If the application does not explicitly do so, Linux will automatically choose the IP address on behalf of the application on a connection-by-connection basis. When Linux is making the decision, it examines a connection's destination IP address, makes a routing decision based on the current route table, and then selects the IP address corresponding to the interface that the connection will go out of. For example, if an application on host A makes a connection to 192.168.1.100, Linux will find that the packet should go out of the eth0 interface, and thus the source IP address for the connection will be 192.168.1.15.

Let us assume that the application does choose to bind to an IP address. If the application were to bind to 192.168.2.1, Linux will source that as the source IP address regardless of which interface the connection will leave from. For example, if the application is bound to 192.168.2.1 and a connection is made to 192.168.1.100, the connection will leave out of eth0 (192.168.1.15) with the source IP address of 192.168.2.1. It is now the responsibility of the remote host (192.168.1.100) to know how to send a packet back to 192.168.2.1. (Presumably, the default route for 192.168.1.100 will know how to deal with that case.)

For hosts that have aliased IP address, a single interface may have many IP addresses. For example, we can assign eth0:0 to 192.168.1.16, eth0:1 to 192.168.1.17, and eth0:2 to 192.168.1.18. In this case, if the connection leaves from the eth0 interface and the application did not bind to a specific interface, Linux will always choose the non-aliased IP address, that is, 192.168.1.15 for eth0. If the application did choose to bind to an IP address, say, 192.168.1.17, Linux will use that IP address as the source IP regardless of whether the connection leaves from eth0 or eth1.

SUMMARY

In this chapter we have seen how the **ifconfig** and **route** commands are used to configure the IP addresses and route entries, respectively. We have also seen how to use these commands together to build a simple Linux router.

Although we covered kernel modules earlier in the book, we brought them up again in the specific context of network drivers. Remember that network interfaces don't follow the same method of access as most devices with a /dev entry.

Finally, remember that when making IP address and routing changes, be sure to add any and all changes to the startup scripts. You may want to schedule a reboot if you're on a production system to make sure that the changes work as expected so that you don't get caught off guard later on.

If you're interested in more details on routing, it is worth taking a closer look at the next chapter and some of the advanced Linux routing features. Linux offers a rich set of functions that, while not typically used in server environments, can lead to a powerful routing system. For anyone interested in dynamic routing using RIP, OSPF, or BGP, be sure to look into Zebra (http://www.zebra.org). With Zebra you can run a highly configurable dynamic routing system that can share route updates with any standard router, including big Cisco equipment.

CHAPTER 13

Configuring the
Linux Firewall

I n what feels like a long, long time ago, the Internet was a pretty friendly place. The users of the network had research to do and thus had better things to do than to waste their time poking at other people's infrastructure. To the extent security was in place, it was largely to keep practical jokers from doing silly things. Many administrators made no serious effort to secure their systems, often leaving default administrator passwords in place.

Unfortunately, as the population grew, so did the threat from the bored and malicious. The need for putting up barriers between the Internet and private networks started becoming increasingly commonplace in the early 1990s. Papers such as "An Evening with Berferd" and "Design of a Secure Internet Gateway" by Bill Cheswick signified the first popular idea of what has become a firewall. (Both papers are available on Bill's Web site at http://www.cheswick.com/ches.)

Since then, firewall technology has been through a lot of changes.

The Linux firewall and packet filtering system has come a long way with these changes as well; from an initial implementation borrowed from BSD, through four major rewrites (kernels 2.0, 2.2, 2.4, and 2.6), and three user-level interfaces (ipfwadm, ipchains, and iptables). The current Linux packet filter and firewall infrastructure (both kernel and user tools) is referred to as "Netfilter."

In this chapter, we start with a discussion of how Linux Netfilter works, follow up with how those terms are applied in the Linux 2.6 toolkit, and finish up with several configuration examples.

NOTE Do not assume that by reading this chapter you are a firewall expert! This chapter provides an introduction to the Netfilter system and how firewalls work with enough guidance to secure a simple network. Entire volumes have been written about how firewalls work, how they should be configured, and the intricacies of how they should be deployed. If you are interested in security beyond the scope of a simple configuration, you should pick up some of the books recommended at the end of the chapter.

HOW NETFILTER WORKS

The principle behind Netfilter is simple: provide simple means of making decisions on how a packet should flow. In order to make configuration easier, Netfilter provides a tool called **iptables** that can be run from the command line. The **iptables** tool makes it easy to list, add, and remove rules as necessary from the system. All of the actual code that processes packets according to your configuration is actually run inside of the kernel.

To accomplish this, the Netfilter infrastructure breaks the task down into three distinct types of operations: *NAT, mangle,* and *filter.* Each operation has its own table of operations that can be performed based on administrator-defined rules. The NAT table is responsible for handling *Network Address Translation,* that is, making or changing IP addresses to a particular source or destination IP address. The most common use for this is to allow multiple systems to access another network (typically the Internet) from a single IP address. When combined with connection tracking, this is the essence of the Linux firewall.

The mangle table is responsible for altering or marking the packets. The number of possible uses of the mangle table is enormous; however, it is also infrequently used. An example of its usage would be to change the ToS (Type of Service) bits in the TCP header so that Quality of Service (QoS) mechanisms can be applied to a packet either later in the routing or in another system.

Finally, the filter table is responsible for providing basic packet filtering. This can be used to selectively allow or block traffic according to whatever rules you apply to the system. An example of filtering is blocking all traffic except for that destined to port 22 (ssh) or port 25 (SMTP).

A NAT Primer

Network Address Translation (NAT) allows administrators to hide hosts on both sides of a router so that both sides can, for whatever reason, remain blissfully unaware of the other. NAT under Netfilter can be broken down into three categories: Source NAT (SNAT), Destination NAT (DNAT), and Masquerading.

SNAT is responsible for changing what the source IP address and port is so that a packet appears to be coming from an administrator-defined IP. This is most commonly used in the case where a private network needs to use an externally visible IP address. To use a SNAT, the administrator must know what the new source IP address is when the rule is being defined. In the case where it is not known (e.g., the IP address is dynamically defined by an ISP), the administrator should use Masquerading (defined shortly). Another example of using SNAT is when an administrator wants to make a specific host on one network (typically private) appear as another IP address (typically public). SNAT, when done, needs to be done late in the packet processing stages so that all of the other parts of Netfilter see the original source IP address before the packet leaves the system.

DNAT is responsible for changing the destination IP address and port so that a packet is redirected to another IP address. This is useful for situations where administrators wish to hide servers in a private network (typically referred to as a DMZ in firewall parlance) and map select external IP addresses to an internal address for incoming traffic. From a management point of view, doing DNAT makes it easier to manage policies, since all externally visible IP addresses are visible from a single host (also known as a *choke point*) in the network.

Finally, *Masquerading* is simply a special case of SNAT. This is useful in situations when there are multiple systems inside of a private network that need to share a single dynamically assigned IP address to the outside world and is the most common use of Linux-based firewalls. In such a case, Masquerading will make all of the packets appear as if they have originated from the NAT device's IP address, thus hiding the structure of your private network. Using this method of NAT also allows your private network to use the RFC 1918 private IP spaces as shown in Chapter 11 (192.168.0.0/16, 172.16.0.0/12, and 10.0.0.0/8).

Examples of NAT

Figure 13-1 shows a simple example where a host (192.168.1.2) is trying to connect to a server (200.1.1.1). Using SNAT or Masquerading in this case would apply a transformation to the packet so that the source IP address is changed to the NAT's external

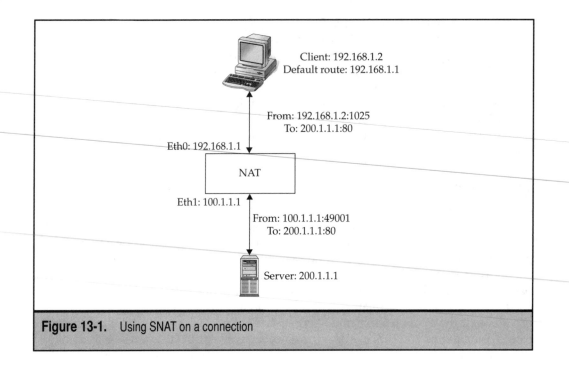

Figure 13-1. Using SNAT on a connection

IP address (100.1.1.1). From the server's point of view, it is communicating with the NAT device, not the host directly. From the host's point of view, it has unobstructed access to the public Internet. If there were multiple clients behind the NAT device (say, 192.168.1.3 and 192.168.1.4), the NAT would transform all of their packets to appear as if they originated from 100.1.1.1 as well.

Alas, this raises a small problem. The server is going to send some packets back—but how is the NAT device going to know who to send what packet to? Herein lies the magic: the NAT device maintains an internal list of client connections and associated server connections called *flows*. Thus, in the first example, the NAT is maintaining a record that "192.168.1.1:1025 converts to 100.1.1.1:49001, which is communicating with 200.1.1.1:80," When 200.1.1.1:80 sends a packet back to 100.1.1.1:49001, the NAT device automatically alters the packet so that the destination IP is set to 192.168.1.1:1025 and then passes it back to the client on the private network.

In its simplest form, a NAT device is only tracking flows. Each flow is kept open so long as it sees traffic. If the NAT does not see traffic on a given flow for some period of time, the flow is automatically removed. These flows have no idea about the content of the connection itself, only that traffic is passing between two endpoints and it is the job of the NAT to ensure the packets arrive as each endpoint expects.

Now let's look at the reverse case as shown in Figure 13-2: A client from the Internet wants to connect to a server on a private network through a NAT. Using DNAT in this situation, we can make it the NAT's responsibility to accept packets on behalf of the server, transform the destination IP of the packets, and then deliver them to the server.

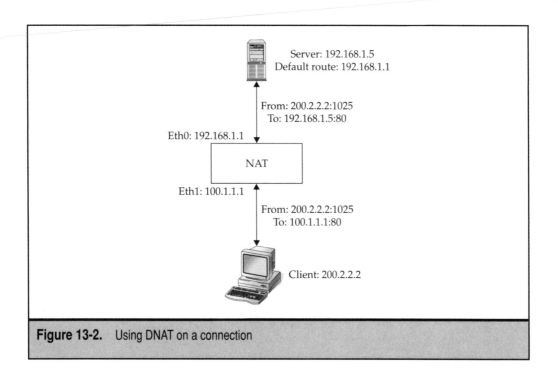

Figure 13-2.   Using DNAT on a connection

When the server returns packets to the client, the NAT must look up the associated flow and change the packet's source IP address so that it reads from the NAT device rather than from the server itself. Turning this into the IP addresses shown in Figure 13-2, we see a server on 192.168.1.5:80 and a client on 200.2.2.2:1025. The client connects to the NAT IP address, 100.1.1.1:80, and the NAT transforms the packet so that the destination IP address is 192.168.1.5. When the server sends a packet back, the NAT device does the reverse, so the client thinks that it is talking to 100.1.1.1. (Note that this particular form of NAT is also referred to as Port Address Translation, or PAT.)

Connection Tracking and NAT

While NAT appears to be a great way to provide security on the surface, it is unfortunately not enough. The problem with NAT is that it doesn't understand the contents of the flows and whether a packet should be blocked because it is in violation of the protocol. For example, let us assume that we have a network set up as in Figure 13-2. When a new connection arrives for the Web server, we know that it must be a TCP SYN packet. There is no other valid packet for the purpose of establishing a new connection. With a blind NAT, however, the packet will be forwarded regardless of whether it is a TCP SYN or not.

In order to make NAT more useful, Linux offers *stateful connection tracking*. This feature allows NAT to intelligently examine a packet's header and determine whether it makes sense from a TCP protocol level. Thus, if a packet arrives for a new TCP connection that is not a TCP SYN, stateful connection tracking will reject the packet without putting the server itself at risk. Even better, if a valid connection is established and a malicious person tries to spoof a random packet into the flow, stateful connection tracking will drop the packet unless it matches all of the criteria to be a valid packet between the two endpoints (a very difficult feat unless the attacker is able to sniff the traffic ahead of time).

As we discuss NAT throughout the remainder of this chapter, keep in mind that wherever NAT can occur, stateful connection tracking can occur.

NAT-Friendly Protocols

As we cover NAT in deeper detail, you may have noticed that we always seem to be talking about single connections traversing the network. For protocols that need only a single connection to work (like HTTP), and for protocols that don't rely on communicating the client's or server's real IP address (like SMTP), this is great. But what happens when you do have a protocol that needs multiple connections or passes real IP addresses? Well, you have a problem.

There are two solutions to handling these protocols: Use an application-aware NAT or a full application proxy. In the former case, the NAT will generally do the least possible work to make the protocol correctly traverse the NAT, such as IP address fixes in the middle of a connection and logically group multiple connections together because they are related to one another. The FTP NAT is an example of both: the NAT must alter an active FTP stream so that the IP address that is embedded in the packet is fixed to show the IP address of the NAT itself, and the NAT will know to expect a connection back from the server and know to redirect it back to the appropriate client.

For more complex protocols or protocols where full application awareness is necessary to correctly secure them, an application-level proxy is typically required. The application proxy would have the job of terminating the connection from the inside network and initiating it on behalf of the client on the outside network. Any return traffic would have to traverse the proxy before going back to the client.

From a practical point of view, there are very few protocols that actually need to traverse a NAT, and these protocols are typically NAT-friendly already, in that they require a single client-to-server connection only. Active FTP is the only protocol that is frequently needed that needs a special module in Netfilter. An increasing number of complex protocols are offering simple, NAT-friendly fallbacks that make them easier to deploy. For example, most instant messenger, streaming media, and IP telephony applications are offering NAT-friendly fallbacks.

As we cover different Netfilter configurations, we will introduce some of the modules that support other protocols.

Chains

For each table, there exists a series of *chains* that a packet goes through. A chain is simply a list of rules that act on a packet flowing through the system. There are five predefined chains in Netfilter: PREROUTING, FORWARD, POSTROUTING, INPUT, and OUTPUT.

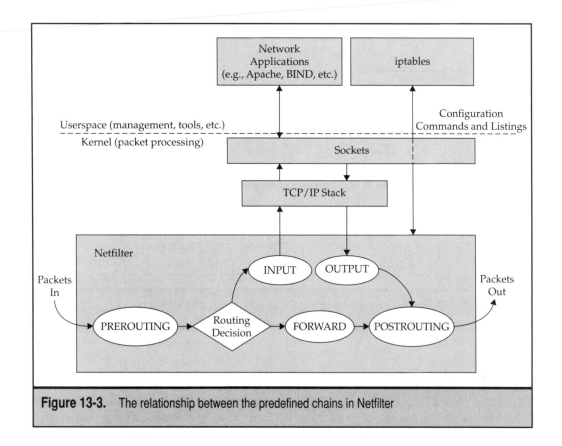

Figure 13-3.   The relationship between the predefined chains in Netfilter

Their relationship to each other is shown in Figure 13-3. You should note, however, that the relationship between TCP/IP and Netfilter as shown in the figure is logical.

Each of the predefined chains can invoke rules that are in one of the predefined tables (NAT, mangle, or filter). Not all chains can invoke any rule in any table; each chain can only invoke rules in a defined list of tables. We will discuss what tables can be used from each chain when we explain what each of the chains do in the sections that follow.

Administrators can add more chains to the system if they wish. A packet matching a rule can then in turn invoke another administrator-defined chain of rules. This makes it easy to repeat a list of rules multiple times from different chains. We will see examples of this kind of configuration later in the chapter.

All of the predefined chains are a member of the mangle table. This means that at any point along the path, it is possible to mark or alter the packet in an arbitrary way. The relationship between the other tables and each chain, however, varies by chain. A visual representation of all of the relationships can be seen in Figure 13-4.

Let's step through each of these chains to understand these relationships.

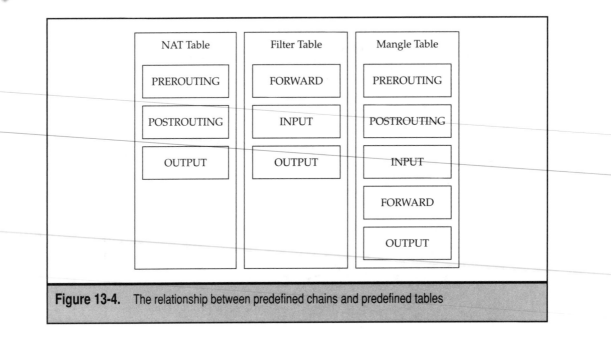

Figure 13-4. The relationship between predefined chains and predefined tables

PREROUTING

The PREROUTING chain is the very first thing a packet hits when entering the system. This chain can invoke rules in one of two tables: NAT and mangle. From a NAT perspective, this is the ideal point at which to do a Destination NAT (DNAT), which changes the destination IP address of a packet.

Administrators looking to track connections for the purpose of a firewall should start the tracking here, since it is important to track the original IP addresses along with any NAT address from a DNAT operation.

FORWARD

The FORWARD chain is invoked only in the case when IP forwarding is enabled *and* the packet is destined for a system other than the host itself. If for example the Linux system has the IP address 172.16.1.1 and is configured to route packets between the Internet and the 172.16.1.0/24 network, and a packet from 1.1.1.1 is destined to 172.16.1.10, the packet will traverse the FORWARD chain.

The FORWARD chain calls rules in the filter and mangle tables. This means that the administrator can define packet filtering rules at this point that will apply to any packets to or from the routed network.

INPUT

The INPUT chain is invoked only when a packet is destined for the host itself. The rules that are run against a packet are done before the packet goes up the stack and arrives at the application. For example, if the Linux system has the IP address 172.16.1.1, the packet has to be destined to 172.16.1.1 in order for any of the rules in the INPUT chain to apply. If a rule drops all packets destined to port 80, any application listening for connections on port 80 will never see any.

The INPUT chain calls on rules in the filter and mangle tables.

OUTPUT

The OUTPUT chain is invoked when packets are sent from applications running on the host itself. For example, if an administrator on the CLI tries to use ssh to connect to a remote system, the OUTPUT chain will see the first packet of the connection. The packets that return from the remote host will come in through PREROUTING and INPUT.

In addition to the filter and mangle tables, the OUTPUT chain can call on rules in the NAT table. This allows administrators to configure NAT transformations to occur on outgoing packets that are generated from the host itself. While this is atypical, the feature does enable administrators to do PREROUTING-style NAT operations on packets. (Remember, if the packet originates from the host, it never has a chance to go through the PREROUTING chain.)

POSTROUTING

The POSTROUTING chain can call on the NAT and mangle tables. In this chain, administrators can alter source IP address for the purposes of Source NAT (SNAT). This is also another point at which connection tracking can happen for the purpose of building a firewall.

INSTALLING NETFILTER

The good news is that if you have a modern distribution of Linux, you probably already have Netfilter installed, compiled, and working. A quick check is to simply try running the **iptables** command like so:

```
[root@hostA:/root]# iptables -L
```

Note that some distributions do not include the **/sbin** directory in the path and there is a good chance that the **iptables** program lives there. If you aren't sure, try using one of the following full paths: **/sbin/iptables**, **/usr/sbin/iptables**, **/usr/local/bin/iptables**, or **/usr/local/sbin/iptables**. The **/bin** and **/usr/bin** directories should already be in your path and should have been checked when you tried **iptables** without an absolute path.

If the command gave you a list of chains and tables, then you've already got Netfilter installed. In fact, there is a good chance the installation process enabled some filters already! Fedora Core, for example, gives an option to configure a low-, medium-, or high-security system at installation time. That preference defined what Netfilter configuration to use.

With Netfilter already present, you can skip this section if you aren't interested in how to install Netfilter by hand.

TIP As an administrator, you never know when you'll find yourself faced with getting Netfilter installed by hand. Taking a skim of this section may still be a good idea, even if you don't need to install it right now.

The complete process of installing Netfilter is actually two parts: enabling features during the kernel compilation process and compiling the administration tools. Let's start with the first.

Enabling Netfilter in the Kernel

Most of Netfilter's code actually lives inside of the kernel and ships with the standard kernel.org distribution of Linux. In order to enable Netfilter, you simply need to enable the right options during the kernel configuration step of compiling a kernel. If you are not familiar with the process of compiling a kernel, see Chapter 9 for details.

Netfilter, however, has a lot of options. In this section, we cover what those options are and which ones you want to select.

Required Kernel Options

There are three required modules that must be supported: Network Packet Filtering, IP Tables, and Connection Tracking.

The first is found under the Networking Support | Networking Options menu when compiling the kernel. This provides the basic Netfilter framework functionality in the kernel. Without this option enabled, none of the other options listed will work. Note that this feature cannot be compiled as a kernel module; it is either in or out.

The second, IP Tables, is found under Networking Support | Networking Options | Network Packet Filtering | IP: Netfilter Configuration. The purpose of this module is to provide the IP Tables interface and management to the Netfilter system. Technically, this module is optional, as it is possible to use the older ipchains or ipfwadm interfaces; however, unless you have a specific reason to stick to the old interface, you should use IP Tables instead. If you are in the process of migrating from your old ipchains/ipfwadm configuration to IP Tables, you will want all of the modules compiled and available to you.

Finally, the Connection Tracking option (which can be found in the same place as the IP Tables option) offers the ability to add support for intelligent TCP/IP connection tracking and specific support for key protocols like FTP. Like the IP Tables option, this can be compiled as a module.

Optional but Sensible Kernel Options

With the options just named compiled into the kernel, you technically have enough together to make Netfilter work for most applications. There are, however, a few options that make life easier, provide additional security, and support some common protocols. For all practical purposes, you should consider these options as requirements. All of the following options can be compiled as modules so that only those in active use are loaded into memory. Let's step through them.

▼   **FTP Protocol Support**   This option is available once Connection Tracking is selected. With it, you can correctly handle active FTP connections through the NAT. This is necessary because, as Chapter 17 will cover, active FTP requires that a separate connection from the server be made back to the client when transferring data (e.g., directory listings, file transfers, etc.) By default, NAT will not know what to do with the server-initiated connection. With the FTP module, NAT will be given the intelligence to correctly handle the protocol and make sure that the associated connection makes it back to the appropriate client.

■   **IRC Protocol Support**   This option is available once Connection Tracking is selected. If you expect that users behind the NAT will want to use IRC to communicate with others on the Internet, this module will be required to correctly handle connectivity, IDENT requests, and file transfers.

■   **Connection State Match**   This option is available once IP Tables Support is enabled. With it, connection tracking gains the stateful functionality that was discussed in the section "Connection Tracking and NAT" earlier in the chapter. This should be considered a requirement for anyone configuring their system as a firewall.

■   **Packet Filtering**   This option is required if you want to provide packet filter options. This should be considered a requirement.

■   **REJECT Target Support**   This option is related to the Packet Filtering option in that it provides a way of rejecting a packet based on the packet filter by sending an ICMP error back to the source of a packet instead of just dropping it. Depending on your network, this may be useful; however, if your network is facing the Internet, the REJECT option is not a good idea. It is better to silently drop packets you do not want rather than generate more traffic.

■   **LOG Target Support**   With this option, you can configure the system to log a packet that matches a rule. For example, if you want to log all packets that are dropped, this option makes it possible.

■   **Full NAT**   This option is a requirement to provide NAT functionality in Netfilter. You should consider this option a requirement.

■   **MASQUERADE Target Support**   This option is a requirement to provide an easy way to hide a private network through NAT. This module internally creates a NAT entry.

■ **REDIRECT Target Support** This option allows the system to redirect a packet to the NAT host itself. Using this option allows you to build transparent proxies, which are useful when it is not feasible to configure every client in your network with proper proxy settings or if the application itself is not conducive to connecting to a proxy server.

■ **NAT of Local Connections** This option allows you to apply DNAT rules to packets that originate from the NAT system itself. If you are not sure if you'll need this later on, go ahead and compile it in.

▲ **Packet Mangling** This option adds the mangle table. If you think you'll want the ability to manipulate or mark individual packets for options like Quality of Service, you will want to enable this module.

Other Options

There are many additional options that can be enabled with Netfilter. Most of them are set to compile as modules by default, which means you can compile them now and decide whether you want to actually use them later without taking up precious memory.

As you go through the compilation process, take some time to look at the other modules and read their help sections. Many modules offer interesting little functions that you may find handy for doing offbeat things that are typically not possible with firewalls. In other words, these functions allow you to really show off the power of Netfilter and Linux.

Of course, there is a trade-off with the obscure. When a module is not heavily used, it doesn't get as heavily tested. If you're expecting to run this NAT as a production system, you may want to stick to the basics and keep things simple. Simple is easier to troubleshoot, maintain, and of course, secure.

Compiling IPTables

Once you have your kernel compiled and installed, you are ready to install the second part of Netfilter: the IPTables tool. This tool is responsible for providing an interface to creating, managing, and troubleshooting the Netfilter rules. As your interface, it is built as an application that runs on the CLI and thus is separate from the kernel package itself.

Start by downloading the latest **iptables** package from http://www.netfilter.org/. As of this writing, that is netfilter-1.3.0.

Once you have the **iptables** package, save and unpack it into **/usr/local/src**.

```
[root@hostA src]# tar -xvjf iptables-1.3.0.tar.bz2
```

This will create the **iptables-1.3.0** directory in which the source code will be unpacked. Move into the **iptables** directory.

```
[root@hostA src]# cd iptables-1.3.0
```

Take a moment to view the **INSTALL** file that comes with the package. It will list the latest news on the installation process, any caveats, and some troubleshooting tips for common problems. In most cases, you will only need to invoke the **make** command with a parameter specifying the location of the current kernel.

To build **iptables**, run

```
[root@hostA iptables-1.3.0]# make KERNEL_DIR=/usr/src/kernel
```

If your kernel is in a different location, change the KERNEL_DIR setting to reflect that.

NOTE   "What if I don't have the kernel source code installed?" If you are updating the **iptables** command but are using the kernel that came with your Linux distribution, the kernel source may not be installed on the system. (Fedora Core, for instance, doesn't install the kernel source by default.) Don't worry, **iptables** isn't interested in a complete copy of the current kernel but only in where it can find the current kernel's *include* files. These files are used by developers to share common bits of code. To get around that, simply set the KERNEL_DIR setting to **/usr/include**.

Once you have the **iptables** tool built, install it and you're done!

```
[root@hostA iptables-1.3.0]# make install
```

CONFIGURING NETFILTER

There is a good chance that your installation of Linux has already configured some Netfilter settings for you, especially if you are using a relatively recent distribution. The graphical desktops that automatically start may have already let you play with some of the settings on Netfilter in the form of security policies for network connectivity.

From an administrative point of view, this gives you three choices: stick to the GUI for configuring Netfilter, learn how to manage the system using the existing set of scripts, or move to the command line.

If you choose to stick with a GUI, be aware of the fact that there are multiple GUIs available for Linux in addition to the one that may have shipped with your system. The key to your decision, however, is that once you have made up your mind, you're going to want to stick to it. While it is possible to switch between the GUI and CLI, it is not recommended unless you know how to manage the GUI configuration files by hand.

Managing the system using the existing set of scripts requires the least amount of changing from a startup/shutdown script point of view, since you are using the existing framework; however, it also means getting to know how the current framework is configured and learning how to edit those files.

Finally, ignoring the existing scripts and going with your own means you need to start from scratch, but you will have the benefit of knowing exactly how it works, when it starts, and how to manage it. The downside is that that you will need to create all of the start and stop infrastructure as well. Because of the importance of the firewall functionality, it is not acceptable to simply add the configuration to the end of the **/etc/rc.d/rc.local** script, as it runs at the very end of startup. Because of the time to boot, the window between starting a service and starting the firewall offers too much time for an attack to potentially happen.

Saving Your Netfilter Configuration

At the end of this chapter, you will have some mix of rules defined with `iptables` commands, possibly a setting in the /proc file system, and the need to load additional kernel modules at boot time. In order to make these changes persistent across multiple reboots, you will need to save each of these components so that they start as you expect them to at boot time.

Saving under Fedora Core and Red Hat is quite straightforward. Simply take the following steps:

1. Save your Netfilter rules using the following command:

   ```
   [root@hostA ~]# /etc/rc.d/init.d/iptables save
   ```

2. Add the appropriate modules to the IPTABLES_MODULES variable in the **/etc/sysconfig/iptables-config** file. For example, to add ip_conntrack_ftp and ip_nat_ftp, make the IPTABLES_MODULES line read as follows:

   ```
   IPTABLES_MODULES="ip_conntrack_ftp ip_nat_ftp"
   ```

3. Add any changes to the proc file system to the **/etc/rc.d/rc.local** file. For example, to enable IP forwarding, you would need to add the following line:

   ```
   echo "1" > /proc/sys/net/ipv4/ip_forward
   ```

For other distributions, methods will vary. If you aren't sure about how your distribution works or it's proving to be more headache than it is worth, simply disable the built-in scripts from the startup sequence and add your own. In the case you write your own script, you can use the following outline:

```
#!/bin/sh
## Define where iptables and modprobe is located
IPT="/sbin/iptables"
MODPROBE="/sbin/modprobe"

## Add your insmod/depmod lines here.
$MODPROBE ip_tables
$MODPROBE ipt_state
$MODPROBE iptable_filter
$MODPROBE ip_conntrack
$MODPROBE ip_conntrack_ftp
$MODPROBE iptable_nat
$MODPROBE ip_nat_ftp
```

```
## Flush the current chains, remove non-standard chains, and zero counters
$IPT -t filter -F
$IPT -t filter -X
$IPT -t filter -Z
$IPT -t mangle -F
$IPT -t mangle -X
$IPT -t mangle -Z
$IPT -t nat -F
$IPT -t nat -X
$IPT -t nat -Z

## Add your rules here. Here is a sample one to get you started.
$IPT -A INPUT -i lo -j ACCEPT

## Add any /proc settings here.
echo "1" > /proc/sys/net/ipv4/tcp_syncookies
```

The iptables Command

The **iptables** command is the key to configuring the Netfilter system. A quick glance at its online help with the **iptables -h** command shows an impressive number of configuration options. In this section, we will walk through those options and learn how to use them.

At the heart of the command is the ability to define individual rules that are made a part of a rule chain. Each individual rule has a packet-matching criterion and a corresponding action. As a packet traverses a system, it will traverse the appropriate chains as we saw in Figure 13-3 earlier in the chapter. Within each chain, each rule will be executed on the packet in order. When a rule matches a packet, the specified action is taken on the packet. These individual actions are referred to as *targets*.

Managing Chains

The format of the command varies by the desired action on the chain. These are the possible actions:

`iptables -t table -A chain rule-spec [options]`	Append *rule-spec* to *chain*
`iptables -t table -D chain rule-spec`	Delete *rule-spec* from *chain*
`iptables -t table -I chain [rulenum] rule-spec [options]`	Insert *rule-spec* at rule number *rulenum*. If no rule number is specified, the rule is inserted at the top of the chain

`iptables -t table -R chain` `rulenum rule-spec [options]`	Replace *rulenum* with *rule-spec* on *chain*
`iptables -t table -L chain` `[options]`	List the rules on *chain*
`iptables -t table -F chain` `[options]`	Flush (remove all) the rules on *chain*
`iptables -t table -Z chain` `[options]`	Zero all the counters on *chain*
`iptables -t table -N chain`	Define a new chain called *chain*
`iptables -t table -X [chain]`	Delete *chain*. If no chain is specified, all nonstandard chains are deleted
`iptables -t table -P chain` `target`	Define the default policy for a chain. If no rules are matched for a given chain, the default policy sends the packet to *target*
`iptables -t table -E chain` `[new-chain]`	Rename *chain* to *new-chain*

Recall that there are three built-in tables (NAT, filter, and mangle) and five built-in chains (PREROUTING, POSTROUTING, INPUT, FORWARD, and OUTPUT). Recall that Figure 13-4 shows their relationships.

However, as rules become more complex, it is sometimes necessary to break them up into smaller groups. Netfilter lets you do this by defining your own chain and place it within the appropriate table.

When traversing the standard chains, a matching rule can trigger a jump to another chain in the same table. For example, let's create a chain called "to_net10" that handles all the packets destined to the 10.0.0.0/8 network that is going through the FORWARD chain.

```
[root@hostA ~]# iptables -t filter -N to_net10
[root@hostA ~]# iptables -t filter -A FORWARD -d 10.0.0.0/8 -j to_net10
[root@hostA ~]# iptables -t filter -A to_net10 -j RETURN
```

In this example, the to_net10 chain doesn't do anything but return control back to the FORWARD chain.

TIP Every chain should have a default policy. That is, it must have a default action to take in the event a packet fails to meet any of the rules. When designing a firewall, the safe approach is to set the default policy (using the `-P` option in `iptables`) for each chain to be DROP and then explicitly insert ALLOW rules for the network traffic that you do want to allow.

Defining the Rule-Spec

In the preceding section, we made mention of the *rule-spec*. The rule-spec is the list of rules that are used to by Netfilter to match on a packet. If the specified rule-spec matches a packet, Netfilter will apply the desired action on it.

Following are the built-in rules:

▼   **p [!] *protocol***   This specifies the IP protocol to compare against. You can use any protocol defined in the **/etc/protocols** file, such as "tcp," "udp," or "icmp." A built-in value for "all" indicates that all IP packets will match. If the protocol is not defined in **/etc/protocols**, you can use the protocol number here. For example, 47 represents "gre." The exclamation mark (!) negates the check. Thus, specifying **-p ! tcp** means all packets that are not TCP. If this option is not provided, Netfilter will assume "all." The **--protocol** option is an alias for this option. An example of its usage is

```
[root@hostA ~]# iptables -t filter -A INPUT -p tcp --dport 80 -j ACCEPT
```

This rule will accept all packets destined to TCP port 80 on the INPUT chain.

■   **s [!] address[/mask]**   This option specifies the source IP address to check against. When combined with an optional netmask, the source IP can be compared against an entire netblock. As with **-p**, the use of the exclamation mark (!) inverts the meaning of the rule. Thus, specifying **-s ! 10.13.17.2** means all packets not from 10.13.17.2. Note that the *address* and *netmask* can be abbreviated. An example of its usage is

```
[root@hostA ~]# iptables -t filter -A INPUT -s 172.16/16 -j DROP
```

This rule will drop all packets from the 172.16.0.0/16 network. This is the same network as 172.16.0.0/255.255.0.0.

■   **d [!] address[/mask]**   This option specifies the destination IP address to check against. When combined with an optional netmask, the destination IP can be compared against an entire netblock. As with **-s**, the exclamation mark negates the rule and the *address* and *netmask* can be abbreviated. An example of its usage is

```
[root@hostA ~]# iptables -t filter -A FORWARD -d 10.100.93.0/24 -j ACCEPT
```

This rule will allow all packets going through the FORWARD chain that are destined to the 10.100.93.0/24 network.

▲   **j target**   This option specifies an action to "jump" to. These actions are referred to as *targets* in **iptables** parlance. The targets that we've seen so far have been ACCEPT, DROP, and RETURN. The first two accept and drop packets respectively. The third is related to the creation of additional chains.

As we saw in the preceding section, it is possible for you to create your own chains to help keep things organized and to accommodate more complex rules. If **iptables** is evaluating a set of rules in a chain that is not built-in, the RETURN target will tell **iptables** to return back to the parent chain. Using the to_net10 example from earlier, when **iptables** reaches the **-j RETURN**, it goes back to processing the FORWARD chain where it left off. If **iptables** sees the RETURN action in one of the built-in chains, it will execute the default rule for the chain.

Additional targets can be loaded via Netfilter modules. For example, the REJECT target can be loaded with ipt_REJECT, which will drop the packet and return an ICMP error packet back to the sender. Another useful target is ipt_REDIRECT, which can make a packet be destined to the NAT host itself even if the packet is destined to somewhere else.

▼ **i interface** This option specifies the name of the interface on which a packet was received. This is handy for instances where special rules should be applied if a packet arrives from a physical location such as a DMZ interface. For example, if eth1 is your DMZ interface and you want to allow it to send packets to the host at 10.4.3.2, you can use

```
[root@hostA ~]# iptables -t filter -A FORWARD -i eth1 -d 10.4.3.2 -j ACCEPT
```

■ **o interface** This option specifies the name of the interface on which a packet will leave the system. For example,

```
[root@hostA ~]# iptables -t filter -A FORWARD -i eth0 -o eth1 -j ACCEPT
```

In this example, any packets coming in from eth0 and going out to eth1 are accepted.

■ **[!] -f** This option specifies whether a packet is an IP fragment or not. The exclamation mark negates this rule. For example,

```
[root@hostA ~]# iptables -t filter -A INPUT -f -j DROP
```

In this example, any IP fragments coming in on the INPUT chain are automatically dropped. The same rule with negative logic would be

```
[root@hostA ~]# iptables -t filter -A INPUT ! -f -j ACCEPT
```

■ **c PKTS BYTES** This option allows you to set the counter values for a particular rule when inserting, appending, or replacing a rule on a chain. The counters correspond to the number of packets and bytes that have traversed the rule, respectively. For most administrators, this is a rare need. An example of its usage is

```
[root@hostA ~]# iptables -t filter -I FORWARD -f -j ACCEPT -c 10 10
```

In this example, a new rule allowing packet fragments is inserted into the FORWARD chain and the packet counters are set to 10 packets and 10 bytes.

■ **v** This option will display any output of **iptables** (usually specified with **-L**) to show additional data. For example,

```
[root@hostA ~]# iptables -L -v
```

■ **n** This option will display any host names or port names in their numeric form. Normally, **iptables** will do DNS resolution for you and show host names instead of IP addresses and protocol names (like smtp) instead of port numbers (25). If your DNS system is down or you do not want to generate any additional packets, this is a useful option.

An example of this is

```
[root@hostA ~]# iptables -L -n
```

■ **x** This option will show the exact values of a counter. Normally, **iptables** will try to print values in "human friendly" terms and thus perform rounding in the process. For example, instead of showing "10310," **iptables** will show "10k."

An example of this is

```
[root@hostA ~]# iptables -L -x
```

▲ **line-numbers** This option will display the line numbers next to each rule in a chain. This is useful when you need to insert a rule in the middle of a chain and need a quick list of the rules and their corresponding rule numbers.

An example of this is

```
[root@hostA ~]# iptables -L --line-numbers
```

Rule-Spec Extensions with Match

One of the most powerful aspects of Netfilter is the fact that it offers a "pluggable" design. For developers, this means that it is possible to make extensions to Netfilter using an API rather than having to dive deep into the kernel code and hack away. For users of Netfilter, this means a wide variety of extensions are available beyond the basic feature set.

These extensions are accomplished with the Match feature in the **iptables** command line tool. By specifying a desired module name after the **-m** parameter, **iptables** will take care of loading the necessary kernel modules and then offer an extended command-line parameter set. These parameters are used to offer richer packet-matching features.

In this section, we discuss the use of a few of these extensions that have, as of this writing, been sufficiently well tested that they are commonly included with Linux distributions.

TIP To get help for a match extension, simply specify the extension name after the **-m** parameter and then give the **-h** parameter. For example, to get help for the ICMP module, use

```
[root@hostA ~]# iptables -m icmp -h
```

icmp This module provides an extra match parameter for the ICMP protocol:

```
icmp-type [!] typename
```

where **typename** is the name or number of the ICMP message type. For example, to block a ping packet, use the following:

```
[root@hostA ~]# iptables -t filter -A INPUT -m icmp --icmp-type echo-request
```

For a complete list of supported ICMP packet types, see the module help page with the **-h** option.

limit   This module provides a method of limiting the packet rate. It will match so long as the rate of packets is under the limit. A secondary "burst" option matches against a momentary spike in traffic but will stop matching if the spike sustains. The two parameters are

▼   `limit rate`

▲   `limit-burst number`

The **rate** is the sustained packet-per-second count. The **number** in the second parameter specifies how many back-to-back packets to accept in a spike. The default value for **number** is 5. You can use this feature as a simple approach to slowing down a SYN flood:

```
[root@hostA ~]# iptables -t filter -N syn-flood
[root@hostA ~]# iptables -t filter -A INPUT -p tcp --syn -j syn-flood
[root@hostA ~]# iptables -t filter -A syn-flood -m limit --limit 1/s -j RETURN
[root@hostA ~]# iptables -t filter -A syn-flood -j DROP
```

This will limit the connection rate to an average of 1 per second with a burst up to 5 connections. This isn't perfect and a SYN flood can still deny legitimate users with this method; however, it will keep your server from spiraling out of control.

state   This module allows you to determine the state of a TCP connection through the eyes of the conntrack module. It provides one additional option,

```
state state
```

where **state** is either INVALID, ESTABLISHED, NEW, or RELATED. A state is INVALID if the packet in question cannot be associated to an existing flow. If the packet is part of an existing connection, the state is ESTABLISHED. If the packet is starting a new flow, it is considered NEW. Finally, if a packet is associated to an existing connection (e.g., an FTP data transfer), then it is RELATED.

Using this feature to make sure that new connections have only the TCP SYN bit set, we do the following:

```
[root@hostA ~]# iptables -t filter -A INPUT -p tcp ! --syn -m state --state NEW -j
DROP
```

Reading this example, we see that for a packet on the INPUT chain that is TCP and does not have the SYN flag set, and the state of a connection is NEW, we drop the packet. (Recall that TCP connections must start with a packet that has the SYN bit set.)

tcp   This module allows us to examine multiple aspects of TCP packets. We have seen some of these options (like `--syn`) already. Here is a complete list of options:

▼   `source-port [!] port:[port]`   This option examines the source port of a TCP packet. If a colon followed by a second port number is specified, a range of ports is checked. For example, "6000:6010" means "all ports between 6000 and 6010, inclusive." The exclamation mark negates this setting. For example,

--source-port ! 25 means "all source ports that are not 25." An alias for this option is --sport.

- destination-port [!] port:[port] Like the --source-port option, this examines the destination port of a TCP packet. Port ranges and negation are supported. For example, -destination-port ! 9000:9010 means "all ports that are not between 9000 and 9010, inclusive." An alias for this option is --dport.

- tcp-flags [!] mask comp This checks the TCP flags that are set in a packet. The mask tells the option what flags to check, and the comp parameter tells the option what flags must be set. Both mask and comp can be a comma-separated list of flags. Valid flags are: SYN, ACK, FIN, RST, URG, PSH, ALL, NONE, where ALL means all flags and NONE means none of the flags. The exclamation mark negates the setting. For example, to use --tcp-flags ALL SYN,ACK means that the option should check all flags and only the SYN and ACK flags must be set.

- ▲ [!] --syn This checks if the SYN flag is enabled. It is logically equivalent to --tcp-flags SYN,RST,ACK SYN. The exclamation point negates the setting.

An example using this module checks if a connection to DNS port 53 originates from port 53, does not have the SYN bit set, and has the URG bit set, in which case it should be dropped. Note that DNS will automatically switch to TCP when a request is greater than 512 bytes.

```
[root@hostA ~]# iptables -t filter -A INPUT -p tcp --sport 53 --dport 53 ! --syn
--tcp-flags URG URG -j DROP
```

tcpmss This matches a TCP packet with a specific Maximum Segment Size (MSS). The lowest legal limit for IP is 576, and the highest value is 1500. The goal in setting an MSS value for a connection is to avoid packet segmentation between two endpoints. Dial-up connections tend to use 576-byte MSS settings, whereas users coming from high-speed links tend to use 1500-byte values. The command-line option for this setting is

```
mss value:[value]
```

where **value** is the MSS value to compare against. If a colon followed by a second value is provided, an entire range is checked. For example,

```
[root@hostA ~]# iptables -t filter -I INPUT -p tcp -m tcpmss --mss 576 -j ACCEPT
[root@hostA ~]# iptables -t filter -I INPUT -p tcp -m tcpmss ! -mss 576 -j ACCEPT
```

This will provide a simple way of counting how many packets (and how many bytes) are coming from connections that have a 576-byte MSS and how many are not. To see the status of the counters, use iptables -L -v.

udp   Like the TCP module, the UDP module provides extra parameters to check for a packet. Two additional parameters are provided:

▼ `source-port` `[!]` `port:[port]`   This option checks the source port of a UDP packet. If the port number is followed by a colon and another number, the range between the two numbers is checked. If the exclamation point is used, the logic is inverted.

▲ `destination-port` `[!]` `port:[port]`   Like the **source-port** option, this option checks the UDP destination port.

For example,

```
[root@hostA ~]# iptables -t filter -I INPUT -p udp --destination-port 53 -j ACCEPT
```

This example will accept all UDP packets destined to port 53. This rule is typically set to allow traffic to DNS servers.

COOKBOOK SOLUTIONS

So you just finished reading this whole chapter and your head is spinning a bit. So many options, so many things to do. Not to worry, that's what this section is for— some cookbook solutions to common uses of the Linux Netfilter system that you can put to immediate use as well as learn from. Of course, if you just skipped the entire chapter and just came to here, well, you'll find some cookbook solutions. However, taking the time to understand what the commands are doing, how they are related, and how you can change them is worthwhile. It will also turn a few examples into endless possibilities.

With respect to saving the examples for use on a production system, you will want to add the modprobe commands to your startup scripts. In Fedora and Red Hat, add the module name to the IPTABLES_MODULES variable in **/etc/sysconfig/iptables-config**. For other distributions, add the complete modprobe line to the **/etc/rc.d/rc.local** file. Any changes to /proc should also be added to **/etc/rc.d/rc.local**. Finally, Fedora and Red Hat users can save their **iptables** settings using the following command:

```
[root@hostA ~]# /etc/rc.d/init.d/iptables save
```

For other distributions, edit the appropriate startup script.

Rusty's Three-Line NAT

Rusty Russell, one of the key developers of the Netfilter system, recognized that the most common use for Linux firewalls is to make a network of systems available to the Internet via a single IP address. This is a common configuration in home and small office networks where DSL or PPP providers give only one IP address to use. In this section, we honor Rusty's solution and step through it here.

Assuming that you want to use your ppp0 interface as your connection to the world that and your other interfaces (e.g., eth0) connect to the inside network, do the following:

```
[root@hostA ~]# modprobe iptable_nat
[root@hostA ~]# iptables -t nat -A POSTROUTING -o ppp0 -j MASQUERADE
[root@hostA ~]# echo 1 > /proc/sys/net/ipv4/ip_forward
```

This set of commands will enable a basic NAT to the Internet. To add support for active FTP through this gateway, run the following:

```
[root@hostA ~]# modprobe ip_nat_ftp
```

If you are using Fedora Core or Red Hat or RHEL and want to make the **iptables** configuration part of your startup script, run the following:

```
[root@hostA ~]# /etc/rc.d/init.d/iptables save
```

NOTE For administrators of other Linux distributions, you can also use the **iptables-save** command (which is part of the **iptables** distribution and thus applies to all Linux distributions). This command in conjunction with **iptables-restore** will allow you to save and restore your **iptables** settings.

You will also need to make the system automatically do the "echo . . ." line at boot; add it to your **/etc/rc.d/rc.local** script.

Configuring a Simple Firewall

In this section we start with a deny-all firewall for two cases: a simple network where no servers are configured and the same network, but with some servers configured. In the first case, we assume a simple network with two sides: inside on the 10.1.1.0/24 network (eth1) and the Internet (eth0). Note that by "server," we mean anything that needs a connection made *to* it. This could mean a Linux system running ssh or a Windows system running BitTorrent.

Let's start with the case where there are no servers to support.

First we need to make sure that the NAT module is loaded and that FTP support for NAT is loaded. We do that with the **modprobe** commands.

```
[root@hostA ~]# modprobe iptable_nat
[root@hostA ~]# modprobe ip_nat_ftp
```

With the necessary modules loaded, we define the default policies for all the chains. For the INPUT, FORWARD, and OUTPUT chains in the filter table, we set the destination to be DROP, DROP, and ACCEPT, respectively. For the POSTROUTING and PREROUTING chains, we set their default policies to ACCEPT. This is necessary for NAT to work.

```
[root@hostA ~]# iptables -P INPUT DROP
[root@hostA ~]# iptables -P FORWARD DROP
[root@hostA ~]# iptables -P OUTPUT ACCEPT
```

```
[root@hostA ~]# iptables -t nat -P POSTROUTING ACCEPT
[root@hostA ~]# iptables -t nat -P PREROUTING ACCEPT
```

With the default policies in place, we need to define the baseline firewall rule. What we want to accomplish is simple: let users on the inside network (eth1) make connections to the Internet, but don't let the Internet make connections back. To accomplish this, we define a new chain called "block" that we use for grouping our state tracking rules together. The first rule in that chain simply states that any packet that is part of an established connection or is related to an established connection is allowed through. The second rule states that in order for a packet to create a new connection, it cannot originate from the eth0 (Internet-facing) interface. If a packet does not match against either of these two rules, the third rule forces the packet to be dropped.

```
[root@hostA ~]# iptables -N block
[root@hostA ~]# iptables -A block -m state --state ESTABLISHED,RELATED -j ACCEPT
[root@hostA ~]# iptables -A block -m state --state NEW -i ! eth0 -j ACCEPT
[root@hostA ~]# iptables -A block -j DROP
```

With the blocking chain in place, we need to call on it from the INPUT and FORWARD chains. We aren't worried about the OUTPUT chain, since only packets originating from the firewall itself come from there. The INPUT and FORWARD chains, on the other hand, need to be checked. Recall that when doing NAT, the INPUT chain will not be hit, so we need to have FORWARD do the check. If a packet is destined to the firewall itself, we need the checks done from the INPUT chain.

```
[root@hostA ~]# iptables -A INPUT -j block
[root@hostA ~]# iptables -A FORWARD -j block
```

Finally, as the packet leaves the system, we perform the MASQUERADE function from the POSTROUTING chain in the NAT table. All packets that leave from the eth0 interface go through this chain.

```
[root@hostA ~]# iptables -t nat -A POSTROUTING -o eth0 -j MASQUERADE
```

With all the packet checks and manipulation behind us, we enable IP forwarding (a must for NAT to work) and SYN cookie protection, plus we enable the switch that keeps the firewall from processing ICMP broadcast packets (Smurf attacks).

```
[root@hostA ~]# echo 1 > /proc/sys/net/ipv4/ip_forward
[root@hostA ~]# echo 1 > /proc/sys/net/ipv4/tcp_syncookies
[root@hostA ~]# echo 1 > /proc/sys/net/ipv4/icmp_echo_ignore_broadcasts
```

At this point, you have a working firewall for a simple environment. If you don't run any servers, you can save this configuration and consider yourself done. On the other hand, let's assume you have two applications that you want to make work through this firewall: a Linux system on the inside network that you need ssh access to from remote locations and a Windows system from which you want to run BitTorrent. Let's start with the ssh case first.

To make a port available through the firewall, we need to define a rule that says "if any packet on the eth0 (Internet-facing) interface is TCP and has a destination port of 22, change its destination IP address to be 172.16.1.3." This is accomplished by using the DNAT action on the PREROUTING chain, since we want to change the IP address of the packet before any of the other chains see it.

The second problem we need to solve is how to insert a rule on the FORWARD chain that allows any packet whose destination IP address is 172.16.1.3 and destination port is 22 to be allowed. The key word is insert (`-I`). If we append the rule (`-A`) to the FORWARD chain, the packet will instead be directed through the block chain.

```
[root@hostA ~]# iptables -t nat -A PREROUTING -i eth0 -p tcp --dport 22 -j DNAT
--to-destination 172.16.1.3
[root@hostA ~]# iptables -I FORWARD -p tcp -d 172.16.1.3 --dport 22 -j ACCEPT
```

We can apply a similar idea behind making BitTorrent work. Let's assume that the Windows machine that is going to use BitTorrent is 172.16.1.2. The BitTorrent protocol uses ports 6881-6889 for connections that come back to the client. Thus, we use a port range setting in the **iptables** command.

```
[root@hostA ~]# iptables -t nat -A PREROUTING -i eth0 -p tcp --dport 6881:6889 -j
DNAT --to-destination 172.16.1.2
[root@hostA ~]# iptables -I FORWARD -p tcp -d 172.16.1.2 --dport 6881:6889 -j
ACCEPT
```

Ta da! You now have a working firewall *and* support for an ssh server and a BitTorrent user on the inside of your network. You should feel so happy that you do the dance of joy.

SUMMARY

In this chapter we discussed the ins and outs of the Linux firewall, Netfilter. With this information, you should be able to build, maintain, and manage your own Linux firewall.

If it hasn't already become evident, Netfilter is an impressively complex and rich system. Authors have written complete books on Netfilter alone and other complete texts on firewalls. In other words, you've got a good toolkit under your belt with this chapter, but if you really want to take advantage of the awesome power of Netfilter, start reading now—you've got a lot of pages to go. In addition to this chapter, you may want to take some time to read up on more details of Netfilter. These can be found at http://www.netfilter.org. The book *Firewalls and Internet Security: Repelling the Wily Hacker, Second Edition* by Cheswick, Bellovin, and Rubin (Addison-Wesley, 2003) is also a good text.

Don't forget that security can be fun too. Take some time for a fun read with *The Cuckoo's Egg* by Clifford Stoll (Pocket, 2000). The book is a true story of an astronomer turned hacker-catcher in the late 1980s. It makes for a great read and gives you a sense of what the Internet was like before commercialization, let alone firewalls.

CHAPTER 14

Local Security

When you hear about a new attack against any operating system, one of your first questions should be whether it is accessible via the network or not. This makes the distinction between local security and network security, which, although related, have two different approaches to solving the problem. In this chapter, we focus on local security.

Local security addresses the problem of attacks that require the attacker to be able to do something on the system itself for the purpose of gaining root access. For example, there is a whole class of attacks that take advantage of applications that create temporary files in the **/tmp** directory but do not check the temporary file's ownership, its file permissions, or if it is a link to another file before opening and writing to it. An attacker can create a symbolic link of the expected temporary filename to a file that he wants to corrupt (e.g., **/etc/passwd**) and run the application; if the application is SetUID to root (covered later in this chapter), it will destroy the **/etc/passwd** file when writing to its temporary file. The attacker can use the lack of **/etc/passwd** to bypass possibly other security mechanisms so that he can gain root access.

For a system that has untrustworthy users on it, this can be a real problem. University environments are often ripe for these types of attacks, since students need access to servers for homework assignments but at the same time pose a great threat to the system because they can (a) get bored and (b) don't always think about the consequences of their actions.

Local security issues can also be triggered by network security issues. If a network security issue results in an attacker being able to invoke any program or application on the server, he can use a local security–based exploit not only to give himself full access to the server but to escalate his own privileges to the root user. "Script kiddies," that is, attackers that use other people's attack programs because they are incapable of creating their own, will use these kinds of methods to gain full access to your system. In their parlance, you'll be "owned."

In this chapter, we address the fundamentals of keeping your system secure against local security attacks. Keep in mind, however, that a single chapter on this topic will not make you an expert. Security is a field that is constantly evolving and requires constant updating. The Hacking Exposed series of books is an excellent place to jump-start your knowledge, and the BugTraq mailing list (http://www.securityfocus.com/) is often where the big security news is picked up in the first place.

In the rest of this chapter, you will notice two recurrent goals: mitigating risk and simpler is better. The former is another way of adjusting your investment (both in time and money, the former usually being worth the latter) given the risk you're willing to take on and the risk that a server poses if compromised. (A Web server dishing up your vacation pictures on a low-bandwidth link is a lower risk than a server handling large financial transactions for Wall Street.) The "simpler is better" comment is engineering 101—simple systems are less prone to problems, easier to fix, easier to understand, and inevitably are more reliable. Keeping your servers simple is a desired goal.

COMMON SOURCES OF RISK

Security is the mitigation of risk. With every effort of mitigating risk, there is an associated cost. Costs are not necessarily financial; they can take the form of restricted access, loss of functionality, or time. Your job as an administrator is to balance the costs of mitigating risk with the potential damage that an exploited risk can cause.

An example of balancing risk is running a Web server. The risk of opening a service that can be probed, poked at, and possibly exploited is inherent in exposing any network accessibility. However, you may find that the risk of exposure is low so long as the Web server is maintained and immediately patched when security issues arise. If the benefit of running a Web server is great enough to justify your cost of maintaining it, then it is a worthwhile endeavor.

In this section, we look at common sources of risk and examine what things you can do to mitigate those risks.

SetUID Programs

SetUID programs are those that run with the permissions of the program itself instead of the permissions given by the user that starts it. This enables administrators to make selected applications available with higher privileges to normal users without having to give those users any administrative rights. An example of such a program is **ping**. Because the creation of raw network packets is restricted to the root user (creation of raw packets allows the application to put any contents within the packet, including attacks), the ping application must run with the SetUID bit enabled and the owner set to root. Thus, even though user "sshah" may start the program, the ping program can elevate itself to the root user for the purpose of placing an ICMP packet onto the network. Administrative shorthand for this setup is "SetUID root."

The problem with programs that are running with root privileges is that they have an obligation to be very conscious of their security as well. It should not be possible for a normal user to do something dangerous on the system by using that program. This means many checks need to be written into the program and potential bugs have to be carefully removed. Ideally, these programs should be small and do one thing. This makes it easier to evaluate the code for potential bugs that can either harm the system or allow for the user to gain privileges that he should not have.

From a day-to-day perspective, it is in the administrator's best interest to keep as few SetUID root programs on the system as possible. The risk balance here is the availability of features/functions to users versus the potential for bad things to happen. For some common programs like **ping**, **mount**, **traceroute**, and **su**, the risk is very low for the value they bring to the system. Some well-known SetUID programs like the X Window System pose a low-to-moderate risk; however, given the exposure X Window has had, it is unlikely to be the root of any problems. If you are running a pure server environment where you do not need X Window, it never hurts to remove it.

SetUID programs executed by Web servers are almost always a bad thing. Take great caution with these types of applications and look for alternatives. The exposure is much greater, since it is possible for network input (which can come from anywhere) to trigger this application and affect its execution.

If you find that you must run an application SetUID with root privileges, find out if it is possible to run the application in a chroot environment (discussed later in this chapter).

Finding and Creating SetUID Programs

A SetUID program has a special file attribute that the kernel uses to determine if it should override the default permissions given to an application. When doing a directory listing, the permissions shown on a file in its `ls -l` output will reveal this little fact. For example,

```
[root@hostA ~]# ls -l /bin/ping
-rwsr-xr-x  1 root root 35108 Jun 15  2004 /bin/ping
```

If the fourth letter in the permissions field is an *s*, the application is SetUID. If the file's owner is root, then the application is SetUID root. In the case of ping, we can see that it will execute with root permissions available to it. Another example is the Xorg (X Window) program:

```
[root@hostA ~]# ls -l /usr/X11R6/bin/Xorg
-rws--x--x  1 root root 1995032 Oct 20 14:45 /usr/X11R6/bin/Xorg
```

As with ping, we see that the fourth character of the permissions is an *s* and the owner is root. The Xorg program is SetUID root.

To determine if a running process is SetUID, you can use the **ps** command to see both the actual user of a process and its effective user, like so:

```
[root@hostA ~]# ps ax -o pid,euser,ruser,comm
```

This will output all of the running programs with their process ID (PID), effective user (euser), real user (ruser), and command name (comm). If the effective user is different than the real user, it is likely a SetUID program.

> **NOTE**   Some applications that are started by the root user *give up* their permissions to run as a lesser user in order to help security. The Apache Web server, for example, must be started by the root user in order to listen to TCP port 80 (only root users can bind to ports lower than 1024), but it then gives up its root permissions and starts all of its threads as a lesser user (typically the user "nobody," "apache," or "www").

To make a program run as SetUID, use the **chmod** command. Prefix the desired permissions with a 4 to turn the SetUID bit on. (Using a prefix of 2 will enable the SetGID bit, which is like SetUID, but with group permissions instead of user permissions.) For example, if I have a program called "myprogram" and I want to make it SetUID root, I do the following:

```
[root@hostA ~]# chown root myprogram
[root@hostA ~]# chmod 4755 myprogram
```

```
[root@hostA ~]# ls -l myprogram
-rws--x--x  1 root sshah 9812 Mar 12 14:29 myprogram
```

Finding where those SetUID programs are can be pesky that first time around. A complete Fedora Core 3 installation can easily have hundreds of thousands of files on the system. (My system has 365,685 files.) Going from directory to directory to find SetUID programs can be tiresome and error prone. So instead of doing that manually, use the **find** command like so:

```
[root@hostA ~]# find / -perm +4000 -ls
```

Unnecessary Processes

When stepping through startup and shutdown scripts, you may have noticed that a standard-issue Linux system starts with a lot of processes running. The question that needs to be asked is *do I really need everything I start?* You might be surprised at your answer.

A Real-Life Example: Thinning Down the Author's Server

Let's take a look at a real life deployment of a FreeBSD server handling Web and e-mail outside of a firewall, and a Linux server sitting as a desktop workstation inside of a firewall with a trusted user. The two configurations represent extremes: tight configuration in a hostile environment and a loose configuration in a well-protected and trusted environment. (Before anyone looks too deeply into the Linux vs. FreeBSD debate, please note that the decision to use FreeBSD on the outside was done through the flip of a coin.)

The FreeBSD system runs release 4.9. With unnecessary processes thinned down, the FreeBSD system has 10 programs running with 18 processes when no one is logged in. Of the 10 programs, only SSH, Apache, and Sendmail are externally visible on the network. The rest handle basic management functions such as logging (syslog) and scheduling (cron). Removing nonessential services used for experimentation only (for example, Squid proxy server) and only available by logging into the server, the program count drops to 7 (init, syslog, cron, SSH, Sendmail, Getty, and Apache), with 13 processes running, 5 of which are Getty to support logins on serial ports and the keyboard. By comparison, a Fedora Core 3 system configured for desktop usage by a trusted user that has not been thinned down has 40 processes that handle everything from the X Window System to printing to basic system management services.

For desktop systems where the risk is mitigated (for example, where the desktop sits behind a firewall and the users are trusted), the benefits of having a lot of these applications running is well worth it. Trusted users appreciate having the ability to easily print and enjoy having access to a nice user interface. For a server such as the FreeBSD 4.9 system, the risk would be too great to have unnecessary programs running, and thus it has everything not needed removed.

The underlying security issue goes back to risk: Is the risk of running an application worth the value it brings you? If the value a particular process brings you is zero because you're not using it, then no amount of risk is worth it. Looking beyond security, there is the practical matter of stability and resource consumption. If a process brings zero value, even a benign process that does nothing but sit in an idle loop takes memory, processor time, and kernel resources. If a bug were to be found in that process, it could threaten the stability of your server. Bottom line: If you don't need it, don't run it.

If your system is running as a server, minimize what gets run. If there is no reason for the server to connect to a printer, disable the print services. If there is no reason the server should accept or send e-mail, turn off the mail server. Fully thinned down, the server should be running the bare minimum it needs in order to provide the services required of it. For example, if no services are run from **xinetd**, turn it off. No printer? Turn off CUPS. Not a file server? Turn off NFS and Samba. A Web server that is responsible for serving static images needs only Apache, SSH, cron, and syslog.

TIP You can quickly disable services in most Linux distributions by simply renaming the startup script in the appropriate **rc.d** directory. For example, if you don't need the Apache server and it starts at runlevel 3, you can simply do the following:

```
[root@hostA /root]# cd /etc/rc.d/rc3.d
[root@hostA rc3.d]# mv S15httpd K15httpd
```

After you change the first character of the startup script from *S* to *K*, the script will not start at boot time.

Picking the Right Runlevel to Boot With

Most default Linux installations will boot straight to the X Window System. This gives a nice startup screen, a login menu, and an overall positive desktop experience. For a server, however, all of that is typically unnecessary for the reasons stated.

The runlevel that Linux uses for booting with X Window is 5. Changing the runlevel to 3 will turn X Window off, and making the system boot to runlevel 3 will keep X Window from starting. To do this, edit the **/etc/inittab** file so that the line

```
id:5:initdefault:
```

is changed to

```
id:3:initdefault:
```

Notice that the 5 changed to a 3.

TIP You can see what runlevel you're in by simply typing **runlevel** at the prompt. For example,

```
[root@hostA /root]# runlevel
N 3
```

To force the change in runlevel when the system is running, invoke the **init** command with desired runlevel as the parameter. For example, to switch to runlevel 1 (single-user mode), run

```
[root@hostA ~]# init 1
```

Programs That Run as Root

Once you have only the bare essentials running to make your server fly, it's time to take a look at whether each program is running with only the necessary permissions.

Looking at the risk aspect, we want to gain the most benefit from having an application while exposing ourselves to the least amount of risk. Thus, if an application is able to deliver all of its functionality while running as a nonroot user, run the application as a nonroot user. We've already seen that some applications, like Apache, make an effort to do this. Other well-known server applications that drop root privileges include BIND (DNS) and SSH.

Of course, not everything can run (or run effectively) without root permissions. In these cases it is necessary to try to mitigate the risk. There are three things you can do to help that:

▼   Make sure you are running with a detailed configuration file that behaves exactly as you expect it to.

■   Keep the application up to date at all times. If the application has an "announce" mailing list, subscribe to it.

▲   If possible, run the application in a chroot environment (see later in this chapter).

Monitoring an application's Web page, mailing lists, and other sources of information like BugTraq can be tedious, but the time and risk averted in the end is worth it. As your systems grow, you may want to consider patch management systems to help in this effort.

Access Granted to Users

Users on a server need not always correspond to humans. Recall that every process running on a Linux system must have an owner. Running the **ps auxww** command on your system will show all of the process owners on the left-most column of its output. On your desktop system, for example, you could be the only human user, but a look at the **/etc/passwd** files shows that there are 57 accounts on the system.

For an application to drop its root privileges, it must have another user that it can run as. Here is where those extra users come into play; each application that gives up root can be assigned another dedicated user on the system. This user is used to own all of the application's files (including executable, libraries, configuration, and data), and the user is used to own the application processes while running. By having each application that drops privileges use its own user, the risk of a compromised application having access to other application configuration files is mitigated. In essence, an attacker is limited by what files the application has access to, which, depending on the application, may be quite uninteresting.

Limited Resources

To better control the resources available to a user, you can use the settings available in **ulimit** and globally configurable through the **/etc/security/limits.conf** file. This can restrict the number of files that may open, how much memory they may use, CPU time they may use, and how many processes they may open. The settings are read by the PAM (Pluggable Authentication Module) libraries when a user starts up.

The key to these settings is to consider the purpose of the server and (if applied to) the workstation. In the case of a server, if an application is going to require a lot of processes to run, be sure to have enough processes available to it. For other users (such as the BIND DNS server), there should never be more than a small handful of processes needed.

Before you get too excited, there is a caveat here: PAM has to have a chance to run to set the settings before the user does something. If the application starts as root and then drops permissions, PAM is not likely to run. From a practical point of view, this means that having individual per-user settings is not likely to do you a lot of good in most server environments. What will work are global settings that apply to both root and normal users. This detail turns out to be a good thing in the end; having root under control helps keep the system from spiraling away both from attacks and from broken applications.

The Fork Bomb

A common trick that students still play on other students is to log in to their workstations and run a "fork bomb." This is a program that simply creates so many processes that it overwhelms the system and brings it to a grinding halt. For a student, this is annoying. For a production server, this is fatal. A simple shell-based fork bomb using BASH is

```
[sshah@hostA ~]$ while true; do sh -c sh & done
```

If you don't have protections in place, *this script will crash your server.*

The interesting thing about fork bombs is that not all of them are intentional. Broken applications, systems under denial of service attacks, and sometimes just simple typographical errors entering commands can lead to bad things happening. By using the limits described in this chapter, you can mitigate the risk of a fork bomb by restricting the maximum number of processes that a single user can invoke. While the fork bomb may still cause your system to become highly loaded, it will still likely remain responsive enough to allow you to log in and deal with the situation, all the while hopefully maintaining the services offered. It's not perfect, but it is a reasonable balance between dealing with the malicious and not getting to do anything.

The format of each line in the **/etc/security/limits.conf** file is as follows:

```
<domain>    <type>    <item>    <value>
```

Any line that begins with a pound sign (#) is a comment. The *domain* value holds the login of a user or the name of a group. The *type* refers to the type of limit as "soft" or "hard." The *item* refers to what the limit applies to. The following items useful for an administrator are available:

Item	Description	Default
fsize	Maximum file size	Unlimited
nofile	Maximum number of open files	1024
cpu	Maximum amount of time (in minutes) a CPU can be used	Unlimited
nproc	Maximum number of processes that a user can have	Unlimited
maxlogins	Maximum number of logins for a user	Unlimited

A reasonable setting for most users is to simply restrict the number of processes unless there is a specific reason to limit the other settings. If you need to control total disk usage for a user, you should use disk quotas instead.

An example for limiting the number of processes to 128 for each user would be

```
* hard nproc 128
```

If you log out and log in again, you can see the limit take effect by running the **ulimit** command to see what the limits are

```
[root@hostA ~]# ulimit -a
core file size          (blocks, -c) 0
data seg size           (kbytes, -d) unlimited
file size               (blocks, -f) unlimited
pending signals                 (-i) 1024
max locked memory       (kbytes, -l) 32
max memory size         (kbytes, -m) unlimited
open files                      (-n) 1024
pipe size            (512 bytes, -p) 8
POSIX message queues     (bytes, -q) 819200
stack size              (kbytes, -s) 10240
cpu time               (seconds, -t) unlimited
max user processes              (-u) 128
virtual memory          (kbytes, -v) unlimited
file locks                      (-x) unlimited
```

The **-a** parameter tells **ulimit** to list all the settings.

MITIGATING RISK

Once you know what the risks are, mitigating them becomes easier. You may find that the risks you see are sufficiently low that no additional securing needs to be done. For example, a Windows XP desktop system used by a trusted, well-experienced user is a low risk for running with administrator privileges. The risk that the user downloads and executes something that can cause damage to the system is low. Furthermore, steps taken to mitigate the risk such as sticking to well-trusted web sites and disabling the automatic downloading of files further alleviate the risk. This well-experienced user may find that being able to run some additional tools and having raw access to the system are well worth the risk of running with administrator privileges. Like any nontrivial risk, the list of caveats is long. It simply boils down to a sufficient reward given to a user that has taken the time to learn how to work safely.

Using Chroot

The `chroot()` system call (pronounced "see-H-root" or "cha-root") allows a process and all of its child processes to redefine what they perceive the root directory to be. For example, if you were to `chroot("/www")` and start a shell, you could find that using the `cd` command would leave you at /www. To the program it would believe it is a root directory, but in reality it would not be. This restriction applies to all aspects of the process' behavior: where it loads configuration files, shared libraries, and data files.

> ▼ *NOTE* Once executed, the change in root directory by chroot is irrevocable through the lifetime of the process.

By changing the perceived root directory of the system, a process has a restricted view of what is on the system. Access to other directories, libraries, and configuration files is not available. Because of this restriction, it is necessary for an application to have all of the files necessary for it to work completely contained within the chroot environment. This includes any passwd files, libraries, binaries, and data files.

> ▼ *CAUTION* A chroot environment will protect against accessing files outside of the directory, but it does not protect against system utilization, memory access, kernel access, and interprocess communication. This means that if there is a security vulnerability that can be taken advantage of by sending signals to another process, it will be possible to exploit it from within a chroot environment. In other words, chroot is not a perfect cure, but rather an excellent deterrent.

Every application needs its own set of files and executables, and thus the directions for making an application work in a chroot environment vary. However, the principle remains the same: make it all self-contained under a single directory with a faux root directory structure.

An Example Chroot Environment

As an example, let's create a chroot environment for the BASH shell. We begin by creating the directory we want to put everything into. Since this is just an example, we'll create a directory in **/tmp** called **myroot**.

```
[root@hostA ~]# mkdir /tmp/myroot
[root@hostA ~]# cd /tmp/myroot
```

Let's assume we need only two programs: **bash** and **ls**. Let's create the **bin** directory under **myroot** and copy the binaries over there.

```
[root@hostA myroot]# mkdir bin
[root@hostA myroot]# cp /bin/bash bin
[root@hostA myroot]# cp /bin/ls bin
```

With the binaries there, we now need to check on whether these binaries need any libraries. We use the **ldd** command to determine what (if any) libraries are used by these two programs.

```
[root@hostA myroot]# ldd /bin/bash
        libtermcap.so.2 => /lib/libtermcap.so.2 (0x00b9d000)
        libdl.so.2 => /lib/libdl.so.2 (0x0098e000)
        libc.so.6 => /lib/tls/libc.so.6 (0x00840000)
        /lib/ld-linux.so.2 (0x00823000)
[root@hostA myroot]# ldd /bin/ls
        librt.so.1 => /lib/tls/librt.so.1 (0x006a8000)
        libacl.so.1 => /lib/libacl.so.1 (0x00abd000)
        libselinux.so.1 => /lib/libselinux.so.1 (0x0062b000)
        libc.so.6 => /lib/tls/libc.so.6 (0x00840000)
        libpthread.so.0 => /lib/tls/libpthread.so.0 (0x00a7f000)
        /lib/ld-linux.so.2 (0x00823000)
        libattr.so.1 => /lib/libattr.so.1 (0x00ab7000)
```

Now that we know what libraries need to be in place, we create **lib** and **lib/tls** directories and copy the libraries over.

```
[root@hostA myroot]# mkdir lib
[root@hostA myroot]# mkdir lib/tls
[root@hostA myroot]# cp /bin/bash bin
[root@hostA myroot]# cp /lib/libtermcap.so.2 lib
[root@hostA myroot]# cp /lib/libdl.so.2 lib
[root@hostA myroot]# cp /lib/libc.so.6 lib
[root@hostA myroot]# cp /lib/ld-linux.so.2 lib
[root@hostA myroot]# cp /lib/tls/librt.so.1 lib/tls
```

```
[root@hostA myroot]# cp /lib/libacl.so.1 lib
[root@hostA myroot]# cp /lib/libselinux.so.1 lib
[root@hostA myroot]# cp /lib/tls/libc.so.6 lib/tls
[root@hostA myroot]# cp /lib/tls/libpthread.so.0 lib/tls
[root@hostA myroot]# cp /lib/libattr.so.1 lib
```

Fedora Core includes a little program called **chroot** that invokes the system call for us, so we don't need to write our own C program to do it. It takes two parameters: the directory that you want to make the root directory and the command that you want to run in the chroot environment. We want to use **/tmp/myroot** as the directory and start **/bin/bash**, thus:

```
[root@hostA myroot]# chroot /tmp/myroot /bin/bash
```

Because there is no **/etc/profile** or **/etc/bashrc** to change our prompt, the prompt will change to bash-3.00#. Now try an **ls**:

```
bash-3.00# ls
bin   lib
```

Then try a **pwd** to see the current working directory:

```
bash-3.00# pwd
/
```

Since we don't have an **/etc/passwd** or **/etc/group** file, an **ls -l** command will show the raw UID values for each file. For example,

```
bash-3.00# cd lib
bash-3.00# ls -l
-rwxr-xr-x  1 0 0  108332 Mar 20 23:52 ld-linux.so.2
-rwxr-xr-x  1 0 0   23572 Mar 20 23:57 libacl.so.1
-rwxr-xr-x  1 0 0   26319 Mar 20 23:58 libattr.so.1
-rwxr-xr-x  1 0 0 1504728 Mar 20 23:51 libc.so.6
-rwxr-xr-x  1 0 0   16908 Mar 20 23:51 libdl.so.2
-rwxr-xr-x  1 0 0   56288 Mar 20 23:57 libselinux.so.1
-rwxr-xr-x  1 0 0   12592 Mar 20 23:51 libtermcap.so.2
drwxr-xr-x  2 0 0    4096 Mar 20 23:57 tls
```

With nothing else to use, the environment isn't terribly useful for practical work, which is what makes it great from a security perspective; we give only the minimum files necessary for an application to work, thus minimizing our exposure in the event the application gets compromised. Keep in mind that not all chroot environments need to have a shell and an **ls** command installed—if the BIND DNS server needs only its own executable, libraries, and zone files installed, then that's all you need.

SELinux

The United States government's National Security Agency (NSA) has taken an increasingly public role in information security, especially due to the growing concern over information security attacks that could pose a serious threat to the world's ability to function. Can any of us imagine the chaos if the world's financial markets were successfully attacked?

With Linux becoming an increasingly key component of enterprise computing, the NSA set out to create a set of patches to increase the security of Linux. The patches have all been released under the GPL license with full source code and thus subject to the scrutiny of the world, an important aspect given Linux's worldwide presence and developer community. The patches are collectively known as "SELinux," short for "Security-Enhanced Linux."

Many distributions of Linux, including Fedora Core and Red Hat, have accepted these patches as part of their normal kernel distribution. This has made the patches and improvements far reaching and an overall benefit to the Linux community.

The underlying concept behind the patches is that all objects within the system, both kernel and user space, have a Security Identifier (SID) associated with them. These SIDs are then associated with policies that dictate what actions may and may not be taken on the object by a given user. Given the extreme granularity of these objects, it is possible to express very rich and complex rules that dictate the security model and behavior of a Linux system.

The full scope of the patches is well beyond the scope of a single section in this book. If you are interested in these patches, visit the SELinux Web site at http://www .nsa.gov/selinux.

MONITORING YOUR SYSTEM

As you become familiar with Linux, your servers, and their day-to-day operation, you'll find that you start getting a "feel" for what is normal. This may sound peculiar, but in much the same way you learn to "feel" when your car isn't quite right, you'll know when your server is not quite the same.

Part of getting a feel for the system requires basic system monitoring. For local system behavior, this requires that you trust your underlying system as not having been compromised in any way. If your server does get compromised and a "root kit" that bypasses monitoring systems is installed, it may be very difficult to see what is happening. For this reason, a mix of on-host and remote host–based monitoring is a good idea.

Logging

By default, most of your log files will be stored in the **/var/log** directory with logrotate automatically rotating the log entries on a regular basis. While it is handy to be able to log to your local disk, it is often a better idea to have your system send its log entries to a dedicated log server that handles only syslog data and possibly an SSH server. With remote logging enabled, you can be certain that any log entries sent to the log server before an attack are 100% guaranteed not to be tampered with.

Because of the volume of log data that can be generated, you may find it prudent to learn some basic script skills so that you can easily parse through the log data and automatically highlight/e-mail anything that is peculiar or should warrant suspicion. For example, a filter that e-mails error logs is useful only to an administrator. This allows the administrator to track both normal and erroneous activity without having to read through a significant number of log messages every day.

Using ps and netstat

Once you have your server up and running, take a moment to study the output of the **ps auxww** command. Deviations from this output should catch your attention in the future. As part of monitoring, you may find it useful to periodically list what processes are running and make sure that any processes you don't expect are there for a reason. Be especially suspicious of any data capture programs like **tcpdump** that you did not start yourself.

The same can be said about the output of the **netstat -an** command. Once you have a sense of what represents normal traffic and normally open ports, any deviations from that output should trigger interest into why the deviation is there. Did someone change the configuration of the server? Did the application do something that was unexpected? Is there threatening activity on the server?

Between **ps** and **netstat**, you should have a fair handle on the goings-on with your network and process list.

Using df

The **df** command shows the available space on each of the disk partitions that are mounted. Running **df** on a regular basis to see the rate at which disk space gets used is a good way to see if there is any questionable activity. A sudden change in disk utilization should spark curiosity into where the change came from. In the past, we have found that some users had started using their home directories to store vast quantities of MP3 files. Legal issues aside, we weren't too happy about the repercussions that had on our backups, and if the backups failed because the tape ran out of space storing someone's music files instead of the key files necessary for the business, we would certainly have a disaster on our hands. In a security sense, if the sizes of the Web or FTP directories grow significantly without reason, there may be trouble looming with unauthorized use of your server.

Mailing Lists

As part of managing your system's security, you should be subscribed to key security mailing lists like BugTraq (http://www.securityfocus.com/archive/1). BugTraq is a moderated mailing list that generates only a small handful of e-mails a day, most of

Getting a Feel for My Server

Administrators have countless stories of how they knew something was not quite right. One such story comes from an admin managing a Sun IPX system many years ago. When walking into the server room, the administrator knew something was not right because the disk activity was frantic enough to be *heard* when it should have been quiet. Going immediately to its console, the response time between entering the system login and getting a shell prompt was also off—the server was clearly under some kind of significant load. With the disk working that hard, the administrator ran the **df** program to see how much free space there was. Sure enough, the mail spool was close to out of space, which was significantly off from where it was the day before. Less than a minute later, the culprit was found: someone had sent a massive e-mail distribution that caused a 40MB file to be copied hundreds of times. The sender had soaked up 1GB of space (which was huge at the time) before the e-mail was purged and the system brought back to normal. With the system behaving again, everything that made up the *feel* of the system—from the sounds it made to the response time of the prompts—had returned to normal.

which will not pertain to software you are running. However, this is where critical issues are likely to show up first. The last several significant worms that attacked Internet hosts were dealt with in real time on these mailing lists.

In addition to BugTraq, any security lists for software that you are responsible for are musts. Also look for announcement lists for the software you use. All of the major Linux distributions also maintain announcement lists for security issues that pertain to their specific distributions. Major software vendors also maintain their own lists. Oracle, for example, keeps their information online via their MetaLink Web portal and corresponding e-mail lists.

While this may seem like a lot of e-mail, consider that most of the lists that are announcement-based are extremely low-volume. In general, you should not find yourself needing to deal with significantly more e-mail than you already do.

SUMMARY

In this chapter you learned about securing your Linux system, mitigating risk, and learning what to look for when making decisions about how to balance features/functions with the need to secure. Specifically, we covered causes of risk such as SetUID programs, programs that run as root, and unnecessary programs. We also covered approaches to mitigating risk through the use of chroot environments and controlling access to users. Finally, we discussed some of the things that should be monitored as part of daily housekeeping.

In the end, you will find that maintaining a reasonably secure environment is largely a case of good hygiene. Keep your server clean of unnecessary applications, make sure the environment for each application is minimized so as to limit exposure, and patch your software as security issues are brought to light. With these basic tasks, you'll find that your servers will be quite reliable and secure.

On a final note, keep in mind that this section alone does not make you a security expert, much as the chapter on Linux firewalls didn't make you a firewalls expert. Linux is always evolving and always improving. You will need to continue to make an effort to learn about the latest and expand your general security knowledge.

CHAPTER 15

Network Security

In Chapter 14, we made the statement: "When you hear about a new attack against any operating system, one of your first questions should be whether it is accessible via the network or not." The answer to the question had a bearing on how the attack is approached. In other words, does the attack require local access to the system, or does the attack only need network connectivity that can send packets to the system? The former case was covered in Chapter 14. The latter case is covered in this chapter.

Network security addresses the problem of attackers sending malicious network traffic to your system with the intent to either make your system unavailable (denial of service attack) or exploit weaknesses in your system to gain access ("rooting" your system). However, network security is not a replacement for the local security approaches discussed in the previous chapter. Both local and network security approaches are necessary to keep things working the way that you expect them to.

In this chapter, we cover four issues in network security: tracking services, monitoring network services, handling attacks, and tools for testing. These sections should be used in conjunction with the previous chapter on local security, as well as Chapter 13.

TCP/IP AND NETWORK SECURITY

This chapter assumes you have experience configuring a system for use on a TCP/IP network. Because the focus here is on network security and not an introduction to networking, this section discusses only those parts of TCP/IP affecting your system's security. If you're curious about TCP/IP's internal workings, read Chapter 11.

The Importance of Port Numbers

Every host on an IP-based network has at least one IP address. In addition, every Linux-based host has many individual processes running. Each process has the potential to be a network client, a network server, or both. With potentially more than one process being able to act as a server on a single system, using an IP address alone to identify a network connection is not enough.

To solve this problem, TCP/IP adds a component identifying a TCP (or UDP) *port*. Every connection from one host to another has a *source port* and a *destination port*. Each port is labeled with an integer between 0 and 65535.

In order to identify every unique connection possible between two hosts, the operating system keeps track of four pieces of information: the source IP address, the destination IP address, the source port number, and the destination port number. The combination of these four values is guaranteed to be unique for all host-to-host connections. (Actually, the operating system tracks a myriad of connection information, but only these four elements are needed to uniquely identify a connection.)

The host initiating a connection specifies the destination IP address and port number. Obviously, the source IP address is already known. But the source port number, the value that will make the connection unique, is assigned by the source operating system. It searches through its list of already open connections and assigns the next available port number.

By convention, this number is always greater than 1024 (port numbers from 0 to 1023 are reserved for system uses). Technically, the source host can also select its source port number. In order to do this, however, another process cannot have already taken that port. Generally, most applications let the operating system pick the source port number for them.

Knowing this arrangement, we can see how source host A can open multiple connections to a single service on destination host B. Host B's IP address and port number will always be constant, but host A's port number will be different for every connection. The combination of source and destination IPs and port numbers (a 4-tuple) is therefore unique, and both systems can have multiple independent data streams (connections) between each other.

For a server to offer services, it must run programs that listen to specific port numbers. Many of these port numbers are called *well-known services* because the port number associated with a service is an approved standard. For example, port 80 is the well-known service port for the HTTP protocol.

In "Using the netstat Command," we'll look at the **netstat** command as an important tool for network security. When you have a firm understanding of what port numbers represent, you'll be able to easily identify and interpret the network security statistics provided by the **netstat** command.

TRACKING SERVICES

The services provided by a server are what make it a server. These services are accomplished by processes that bind to network ports and listen to the requests coming in. For example, a Web server might start a process that binds to port 80 and listens for requests to download the pages of a site. Unless a process exists to listen to a specific port, Linux will simply ignore packets sent to that port.

This section discusses the usage of the **netstat** command, a tool for tracking network connections (among other things) in your system. It is, without a doubt, one of the most useful debugging tools in your arsenal for troubleshooting security and day-to-day network problems.

Using the netstat Command

To track what ports are open and what ports have processes listening to them, we use the **netstat** command. For example,

```
[root@hostA ~]# netstat -natu

Active Internet connections (servers and established)
Proto Recv-Q Send-Q Local Address          Foreign Address        State
tcp        0      0 0.0.0.0:32768          0.0.0.0:*              LISTEN
tcp        0      0 0.0.0.0:111            0.0.0.0:*              LISTEN
tcp        0      0 0.0.0.0:113            0.0.0.0:*              LISTEN
tcp        0      0 127.0.0.1:631          0.0.0.0:*              LISTEN
```

```
tcp         0       0 127.0.0.1:5335       0.0.0.0:*               LISTEN
tcp         0       0 127.0.0.1:25         0.0.0.0:*               LISTEN
tcp         0       0 :::22                :::*                    LISTEN
tcp         0     132 192.168.1.4:22       192.168.1.33:2129    ESTABLISHED
udp         0       0 0.0.0.0:32768        0.0.0.0:*
udp         0       0 0.0.0.0:813          0.0.0.0:*
udp         0       0 0.0.0.0:5353         0.0.0.0:*
udp         0       0 0.0.0.0:5353         0.0.0.0:*
udp         0       0 0.0.0.0:111          0.0.0.0:*
udp         0       0 0.0.0.0:631          0.0.0.0:*
```

By default (with no parameters), **netstat** will provide all established connections for both network and domain sockets. That means we'll see not only the connections that are actually working over the network, but also the interprocess communications (which, from a security monitoring standpoint, are not useful). So in the command just illustrated, we have asked **netstat** to show us all ports (**-a**)—whether they are listening or actually connected—for TCP (**-t**) and UDP (**-u**). We have told **netstat** not to spend any time resolving IP addresses to hostnames (**-n**).

In the **netstat** output, each line represents either a TCP or UDP network port, as indicated by the first column of the output. The Recv-Q (receive queue) column lists the number of bytes received by the kernel but not read by the process. Next, the Send-Q column tells us the number of bytes sent to the other side of the connection but not acknowledged.

The fourth, fifth, and sixth columns are the most interesting in terms of system security. The Local Address column tells you your own server's IP address and port number. Remember that your server recognizes itself as 127.0.0.1 and 0.0.0.0 as well as its normal IP address. In the case of multiple interfaces, each port being listened to will show up on both interfaces and thus as two separate IP addresses. The port number is separated from the IP address by a colon. In the output from the **netstat** example just shown, the Ethernet device has the IP address 192.168.1.4.

The fifth column, Foreign Address, identifies the other side of the connection. In the case of a port that is being listened to for new connections, the default value will be 0.0.0.0:*. This IP address means nothing, since we're still waiting for a remote host to connect to us!

The sixth column tells us the State of the connection. The man page for **netstat** lists all of the states, but the two you'll see most often are LISTEN and ESTABLISHED. The LISTEN state means there is a process on your server listening to the port and ready to accept new connections. The ESTABLISHED state means just that—a connection is established between a client and server.

Security Implications of netstat's Output

By listing all of the available connections, you can get a snapshot of what the system is doing. You should be able to explain and justify *all* ports listed. If your system is listening to a port that you cannot explain, this should raise suspicions.

If you've been using your memory cells for other purposes and haven't memorized the services and their associated port numbers, you can look up the matching info you need in the **/etc/services** file. However, some services (most notably those that use the portmapper) don't have set port numbers but are valid services. To see which process is associated with a port, use the **-p** option with **netstat**. Be on the lookout for odd or unusual processes using the network. For example, if the BASH shell is listening to a network port, you can be fairly certain that something odd is going on.

Finally, remember that you are only interested in the destination port of a connection; this tells you which service is being connected to and whether it is legitimate. Unfortunately, **netstat** doesn't explicitly tell us who originated a connection, but we can usually figure it out if we give it a little thought. Of course, becoming familiar with the applications that you do run and their use of network ports is the best way to determine who originated a connection to where. In general, you'll find that the rule of thumb is that the side whose port number is greater than 1024 is the side that originated the connection. Obviously, this general rule doesn't apply to services typically running on ports higher than 1024, such as X Window (port 6000).

Binding to an Interface

A common approach to improving the security of a service running on your server is to make it such that it only binds to a specific network interface. By default, applications will bind to all interfaces (seen as 0.0.0.0 in the **netstat** output). This will allow a connection to that service from any interface so long as the connection makes it past any Netfilter firewalls you may have configured. However, if you only need a service to be available on a particular network, you should configure that service to bind to a specific interface.

For example, let us assume that there are three interfaces on your server: eth0, which is 192.168.1.4, eth1, which is 172.16.1.1, and lo, which is 127.0.0.1. Let us also assume that your server does not have IP forwarding (**/proc/sys/net/ipv4/ip_forward**) enabled. In other words, machines on the 192.168.1.0/24 side cannot communicate with machines on the 172.16/16 side. The 172.16/16 (eth1) network represents the "safe" network, and of course, 127.0.0.1 represents the host itself.

If the application binds itself to 172.16.1.1, then only those applications on the 172.16/16 side will be able to reach the application and connect to it. If you do not trust the hosts on the 192.168.1/24 side (e.g., it is a DMZ), then this is a safe way to provide services to one segment without exposing yourself to another. For even less exposure, you can bind an application to 127.0.0.1. By doing so, you arrange that connections will have to originate from the server itself in order to communicate with the service. For example, if you need to run the MySQL database for a Web-based application and the application runs on the server, then configuring MySQL to accept only connections from 127.0.0.1 means that any risk associated with remotely connecting to and exploiting the MySQL service is significantly mitigated. The attacker would have to compromise your Web-based application and somehow make it query the database on their behalf (SQL injection attack).

TIP If you need to provide a service to a group of technically proficient users across the Internet, binding a service to localhost and then forcing the group to use SSH tunnels is a great way to require authenticated and encrypted access to the service. My wife, for example, likes to download her e-mail via POP. Because she wants to access her e-mail from remote, we ended up binding the POP server to localhost, and then she used SSH with port forwarding to log in from her Macintosh to access the service (**ssh -1** *username* **-L 1110:127.0.0.1:110** *servername*). She then set her POP mail reader to pull mail from 127.0.0.1:1110 on her own machine. Anyone running a port scanner against my server will not see the POP mail server.

Shutting Down Services

One purpose for the **netstat** command is to determine what services are enabled on your servers. Making Linux easier to install and manage right out of the box has led to more and more default settings that are unsafe, so keeping track of services is especially important.

When you're evaluating which services should stay and which should go, answer the following questions:

1. *Do we need the service?* The answer to this question is very important. In most situations, you should be able to disable a great number of services that start up by default. A standalone Web server, for example, should not need to run NFS.

2. *If we do need the service, is the default setting secure?* This question can also help you eliminate some services—if they aren't secure and they can't be made secure, then chances are they should be removed. For example, if remote login is a requirement and Telnet is the service enabled to provide that function, then an alternative like SSH should be used instead due to Telnet's inability to encrypt login information over a network. (By default, most Linux distributions ship with Telnet disabled and SSH enabled.)

3. *Does the service software need updates?* All software needs updates from time to time, such as that on Web and FTP servers. This is because as features get added, new security problems creep in. So be sure to remember to track the server software's development and get upgrades installed as soon as security bulletins are posted.

Shutting Down xinetd and inetd Services

To shut down a service that is started via the **xinetd** program, simply edit the service's configuration file in **/etc/xinetd** and set disable equal to Yes. If you are using a stock **inetd**, edit the **/etc/inetd.conf** file and comment out the service you no longer want. To designate the service as a comment, start the line with a pound sign (#). See Chapter 8 for more information on **xinetd** and **inetd**.

Remember to send the HUP signal to **inetd** once you've made any changes to the **/etc/inetd.conf** file and a SIGUSR2 signal to **xinetd**. If you are using Red Hat Linux or Fedora Core, you can also type the following command:

```
[root@hostA /root]# /etc/rc.d/init.d/xinetd reload
```

Shutting Down Non-inetd Services

If a service is not run by **inetd**, then a process that is probably started at boot time is running it. If the service in question was installed by your distribution and your distribution offers a nice tool for disabling a service, you may find that to be the easiest approach.

Shutting Down Services in Red Hat and Fedora Core   For example, under Fedora Core, RHEL, and SuSE, the **chkconfig** program provides a very easy way to enable and disable individual services. For example, to disable the **portmap** service, simply run

```
[root@hostA ~]# chkconfig --level 35 portmap off
```

The parameter **--level** refers to what runlevels should be impacted by the change. Since runlevels 3 and 5 represent the two multiuser modes, we select those. The **portmap** parameter is the name of the service as referred to in the **/etc/rc.d/init.d** directory. Finally, the last parameter can either be "on", "off", or "reset". The "on" and "off" options are self-explanatory. The "reset" option refers to resetting the service to its native state at install time.

If you wanted to turn the **portmap** service on again, simply run

```
[root@hostA ~]# chkconfig --level 35 portmap on
```

Note that using **chkconfig** doesn't actually turn the service on or off but rather defines what will happen at startup time. To actually stop the process, use the **rc** script in the **/etc/rc.d/init.d** directory. In the case of **portmap**, we would stop it with

```
[root@hostA ~]# /etc/rc.d/init.d/portmap stop
```

Shutting Down Services in a Distribution Independent Way   To prevent a service from starting up at boot time, change the symlink in the corresponding runlevel's **rc.d** directory. This is done by going to the **/etc/rc.d/** directory and in one of the **rc*.d** directories finding the symlinks that point to the startup script. (See Chapter 6 for information on startup scripts.) Rename the symlink to start with an *X* instead of an *S*. Should you decide to restart a service, it's easy to rename it again starting with an *S*. If you have renamed the startup script but want to stop the currently running process, use the **ps** command to find the process ID number and then the **kill** command to actually terminate the process. For example, here are the commands to kill a **portmap** process, and the resulting output:

```
[root@hostA /root]# ps auxw | grep portmap
bin       255   0.0   0.1   1084   364 ?       S    Jul08    0:00 portmap
root      6634  0.0   0.1   1152   440 pts/0    S    01:55    0:00 grep portmap
[root@hostA /root]# kill 255
```

> **NOTE**   As always, be sure of what you're killing before you kill it, especially on a production server.

MONITORING YOUR SYSTEM

The process of tying down your server's security isn't just for the sake of securing your server; it gives you the opportunity to see clearly what normal server behavior should look like. After all, once you know what normal behavior is, unusual behavior will stick out like a sore thumb (e.g., if you turned off your Telnet service when setting up the server, seeing a log entry for Telnet means something is very wrong!).

Commercial packages that perform monitoring do exist and may be worth checking out for your site as a whole, but we'll leave the discussions of their capabilities to *Network World* or *PC Week*. Here, we'll take a look at a variety of other excellent tools that help you monitor your system. Some of these tools come with all Linux distributions; some don't. All are free and easily acquired.

Making the Best Use of syslog

In Chapter 8, we explored syslog, the system logger that saves messages from various programs into a set of text files for record-keeping purposes. By now, you've probably seen the type of log messages you get with syslog. These include security-related messages such as who has logged in to the system, when they logged in, and so forth.

As you can imagine, it's possible to analyze these logs to build a time-lapse image of the utilization of your system services. This data can also point out questionable activity. For example, why was the host crackerboy.nothing-better-to-do.net sending so many Web requests in such a short period of time? What was he looking for? Has he found a hole in the system?

Log Parsing

Doing periodic checks on the system's log files is an important part of maintaining security. Unfortunately, scrolling through an entire day's worth of logs is a time-consuming and unerringly boring task that reveals few meaningful events. To ease the drudgery, pick up a text on a scripting language (such as Perl) and write small scripts to parse out the logs. A well-designed script works by throwing away what it recognizes as normal behavior and showing everything else. This can reduce thousands of log entries for a day's worth of activities down to a manageable few dozen. This is an effective way to detect attempted break-ins and possible security gaps. Hopefully, it'll become entertaining to watch the script kiddies trying and failing to break down your walls.

Storing Log Entries

Unfortunately, log parsing may not be enough. If someone breaks into your system, it's likely that your log files will be promptly erased—which means all those wonderful scripts won't be able to tell you a thing. To get around this, consider dedicating a single host on your network to storing log entries. Configure your **/etc/syslog.conf** file to send all of its messages to this single host, and configure the host so that it's listening only to the syslog port (514). In most instances, this should be enough to gather, in a centralized place, the evidence of any bad things happening.

If you're *really* feeling paranoid, consider attaching a DOS-based PC to the serial port of the loghost and, using a terminal emulation package such as Telix, record all of the messages sent to the loghost. (You can also use another Linux box running **minicom** in log mode—just be sure *not* to network this second Linux box!) Have **/etc/syslog.conf** configured to send all messages to **/dev/ttyS0** if you're using COM1 or **/dev/ttyS1** if you're using COM2. And, of course, do *not* connect the DOS system to the network. This way, in the event the loghost also gets attacked, the log files won't be destroyed. The log files will be safe residing on the DOS system, which is impossible to log in to without physical access.

For the highest degree of monitoring capability, connect a parallel-port printer to the DOS system and have the terminal emulation package echo everything it receives on the serial port to the printer. Thus, if the DOS system fails or is damaged in some way by an attack, you'll have a hard copy of the logs. (Note that a serious drawback to using the printer for logging is that you cannot easily search through the logs. If you choose to set up this arrangement, consider also keeping an electronic copy for easier searching.)

TIP Consider using a package like **swatch** to page you when it sees a log entry that indicates trouble. You can find out more about it at http://swatch.sourceforge.net.

Monitoring Bandwidth with MRTG

Monitoring the amount of bandwidth being used on your servers produces some very useful information. The most practical use for it is justifying the need for upgrades. By showing system utilization levels to your managers, you'll be providing hard numbers to back up your claims. Your data can be easily turned into a graph, too—and managers like graphs! Another useful aspect of monitoring bandwidth is to identify bottlenecks in the system, thus helping you to better balance the system load. But the most useful aspect of graphing your bandwidth is to identify when things go wrong.

Once you've installed a package such as MRTG (Multi-Router Traffic Grapher, available at http://www.mrtg.org) to monitor bandwidth, you will quickly get a criterion for what "normal" looks like on your site. A substantial drop or increase in utilization is something to investigate, as it indicates a failure or a type of attack. Check your logs, and look for configuration files with odd or unusual entries.

HANDLING ATTACKS

Part of securing a network includes planning for the worst case: what happens if someone succeeds? It doesn't necessarily matter how, it just has. Servers are doing things they shouldn't, information is leaking that should not leak, or other mayhem is discovered either by you, your team, or by someone else asking why you're trying to spread mayhem to them.

What do you do?

Just as a facilities director plans for fires and your backup administrator plans for recovering data if none of your systems are available, a security officer needs to plan for how to handle an attack. In this section, we cover key points to consider with respect to Linux. For an excellent overview on handling attacks, visit the CERT Web site at http://www.cert.org.

Trust Nothing

If an attacker has successfully gotten into your systems, there is nothing that your servers can tell you about the situation that is completely trustworthy. "Root kits," or tool kits that attackers use to invade systems and then cover their tracks, can make detection difficult. With binaries replaced, you may find that there is nothing you can do to the server itself that helps. In other words, every server that has been successfully hacked needs to be completely rebuilt with a fresh installation. Before doing the reinstall, make an effort to look back at how far the attacker went so as to determine the point in the backup cycle when the data is certain to be trustworthy. Any data backed up after that should be closely examined to ensure that invalid data does not make it back into the system.

Change Your Passwords

If the attacker has gotten your root password or may have taken a copy of the password file, it is crucial that all of your passwords get changed. This is an incredible hassle; however, it is necessary to make sure that the attacker doesn't waltz back into your rebuilt server using the password without any resistance.

Note that it is a good idea to also change your root password if there are any staff changes. It may seem like everyone is leaving on good terms; however, finding out that someone on your team had issues with the company afterward could mean that you're already in trouble.

Stopping Network Traffic

Once you're ready to start cleaning up and need to stop any remote access to the system, you may find it necessary to stop all network traffic to the server until it is completely rebuilt with the latest patches before reconnecting it to the network. Putting a server back onto the network when it is still getting patches is an almost certain way to find yourself dealing with an attack again.

NETWORK SECURITY TOOLS

There are countless tools to help monitor your systems, including MRTG (http://www.mrtg.org) for graphing statistics (typically SNMP values from switches and routers), Big Brother (http://www.bb4.org), and of course the various tools we've already mentioned in this chapter. But what do you use to poke at your system for basic sanity checks?

In this section, we review a few tools that you can use for testing your system. Note that no one tool is enough and no combination of tools is perfect—there is no secret "Hackers Testing Toolkit" that security professionals have that we don't. The key to any tool is how you use it, how you interpret that data, and both what actions you take up front to protect your system and what actions you take after getting data from these tools.

A common thread that you'll see in a few tools listed here is that by their designer's intent, they were not meant to be security tools. Several of these tools were meant to aid in basic diagnostics and system management. What makes those tools work well for Linux from a security perspective is that they offer a deeper insight into what your system is doing. It is that deeper information that often proves to be more helpful than what you may have originally thought of it.

nmap

The **nmap** program scans a host looking for open TCP and UDP ports. When it can find one, it makes a connection attempt so that it can identify what application is active on that port. This is a powerful and simple way for an administrator to take a look at what their system exposes to the network and is frequently used by both attackers and administrators to get a sense of what is possible against a host.

What makes **nmap** powerful is its ability to apply multiple scanning methods. This is done because each method has its pros and cons with respect to how well it traverses firewalls and allows for anonymous scanning of hosts.

Snort

An intrusion-detection system (IDS) is a way of promiscuously monitoring a point in the network and reporting on questionable activity seen based on packet traces. The Snort program (http://www.snort.org) is an open-source implementation of an IDS that provides extensive rule sets that are frequently updated with new attack vectors. Any questionable activity is logged to syslog, and several open-source log processing tools are available (also on http://www.snort.org) to help make heads and tails of the information that is there.

Running Snort on a Linux system that is hanging off a key entry/exit point in your network is a great way to track the activity without having to set up a proxy for each protocol that you wish to support.

A commercial version of Snort called SourceFire is also available. You can find out more about SourceFire at http://www.sourcefire.com.

Nessus

The Nessus system (http://www.nessus.org) takes the idea behind **nmap** and extends it with deep application-level probes and a rich reporting infrastructure. Running Nessus against a server is a quick way to sanity-check your exposure.

The key to understanding Nessus is understanding its output. The report will log numerous comments from an informational level all the way up to a high level. Depending on how your application is written and what other services you offer on your Linux system, Nessus may log false positives or seemingly scary informational notes. Take the time to read through each one of them and understand what the output is, as not all of the messages necessarily reflect your situation. For example, if Nessus detects that your system is at risk due to a hole in Oracle 8 but your Linux system does not run Oracle, more than likely you have hit upon a false positive.

Although Nessus is open source and free, it is owned and managed by a commercial company, Tenable Network Security. You can learn more about Tenable at http://www.tenablesecurity.com.

Ethereal / tcpdump

We learned extensively about Ethereal and **tcpdump** in Chapter 11, where we used them to study the ins and outs of TCP/IP. While we have seen these tools used only for troubleshooting, they are just as valuable for doing network security functions.

Raw network traces are the food that all of the tools listed in the preceding sections feed off of in order to gain insight into what your server is doing. However, these tools don't have quite the insight into what your server is *supposed* to do that you do. Thus, it is useful to be able to take network traces yourself and read through them to see if there is any questionable activity going on. You may be surprised at what your server is doing!

For example, if you are looking at a possible break-in, you may want to start a raw network trace from another Linux system that can see all of the network traffic of your questioned host. By capturing all the traffic over a 24-hour period, you can go back and start applying filters to see if there is anything that shouldn't be there. Extending the example, if the server is supposed to only handle Web operations and SSH with reverse DNS resolution turned off on both, take the trace and apply the filter "not port 80 and not port 22 and not icmp and not arp." Any packets that show up in the output are suspect.

SUMMARY

In this chapter we covered the basics of network security as it pertains to Linux. With the information here, you should have the information that you need in order to make an informed decision about the state of health of your server and decide what, if any, action is necessary to better secure it.

As has been indicated in other chapters, please do not consider this chapter a complete source of network security information. Security as a field is constantly evolving and requires a careful eye toward what is new. Be sure to subscribe to the relevant mailing lists, read the Web sites, and if necessary, pick up a book like *Network Security, A Beginners Guide* by Eric Maiwald (McGraw-Hill/Osborne, 2003).

Internet Services

CHAPTER 16

DNS

The need to map unfriendly numerical IP addresses into people-friendly format has been an issue with TCP/IP since its creation in the 1970s. Although this translation isn't mandatory, it does make the network much more useful and easy to work with for humans.

Initially, IP address–to–name mapping was done through the maintenance of a **hosts .txt** file that was distributed via FTP to all the machines on the Internet. As the number of hosts grew (starting back in the early 1980s), it was soon clear that a single person maintaining a single file of all of those hosts was not a scalable way of managing the association of IP addresses to host names. To solve this problem, a distributed system was devised in which each site would maintain information about its own hosts. One host at each site would be considered "authoritative," and that single host address would be kept in a master table that could be queried by all other sites. This is the essence of the *Domain Name Service (DNS)*.

If the information in DNS wasn't decentralized as it is, one other choice would be to have a central site maintaining a master list of all hosts (numbering in the tens of millions) and having to update those host names tens of thousands of times a day—this alternative can quickly become overwhelming! Even more important to consider are the needs of each site. One site may need to maintain a private DNS server because its firewall requires that LAN IP addresses not be visible to outside networks, yet the hosts on the LAN must be able to find hosts on the Internet. If you're stunned by the prospect of having to manage this for every host on the Internet, then you're getting the picture.

NOTE In this chapter, you will see the terms "DNS server" and "name server" used interchangeably. Technically, "name server" is a little ambiguous because it can apply to any number of naming schemes that resolve a name to a number and vice versa. In the context of this chapter, however, "name server" will always mean a DNS server unless otherwise stated.

We will discuss DNS in depth, so you'll have what you need to configure and deploy your own DNS servers for whatever your needs may be.

THE HOSTS FILE

Not all sites run their own DNS servers. Not all sites need their own DNS servers. In sufficiently small sites with no Internet connectivity, it's reasonable for each host to keep its own copy of a table matching all of the host names in the local network with their corresponding IP addresses. In most Linux and UNIX systems, this table is stored in the **/etc/hosts** file.

NOTE Even in hosts that have access to a DNS server, there may still be valid reasons why you may want to keep a hosts file locally. This is useful so that a host can look up an IP address locally before going out to query the DNS server. Typically, this is done so that the system can keep track of hosts it needs for booting so that even if the DNS server may become unavailable, the system can still boot successfully. Less obvious might be the simple reason that you want to give a host a name but you don't want to (or can't) add an entry to your DNS server.

The **/etc/hosts** file keeps its information in a simple tabular format, and is a basic naming service. The IP address is in the first column, and all the related host names are in the second column. The third column is typically used to store the short version of the host name. Only white space separates the fields. Pound symbols (#) at the beginning of a line represent comments. Here's an example:

```
# Host table for Internal network
#
127.0.0.1    localhost.localdomain  localhost
192.168.1.1  serverA.example.org  serverA        # Linux server
192.168.1.2  serverB.example.org serverB         # Other Linux server
192.168.1.7  dikkog                               # Win2003 server
192.168.1.8  trillian                             # Cluster master node
192.168.1.9  sassy                                # FreeBSD box
10.0.88.20   laserjet5                            # Lunchroom Printer
```

In general, your **/etc/hosts** file should contain at the very least the necessary host-to-IP mappings for the loop-back interface (127.0.0.1) and the local host name with its corresponding IP address. A more robust naming service is the DNS system. The rest of this chapter will cover the use of the DNS name service.

UNDERSTANDING HOW DNS WORKS

In this section, we'll explore some background material necessary to your understanding of the installation and configuration of a DNS server and client.

Domains and Hosts Naming Conventions

Until now, you've most likely referenced sites by their *fully qualified domain name (FQDN)*, like this one: www.kernel.org. Each string between the periods in this FQDN is significant. Starting from the right end and moving to the left, you have first the top-level domain component, the second-level domain component, and the third-level domain component. This is illustrated further in Figure 16-1 in the FQDN for a system (serverA.example.org) and is a classic example of an FQDN. Its breakdown is discussed in detail in the following section.

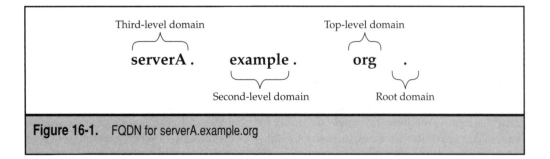

Figure 16-1. FQDN for serverA.example.org

The Root Domain

The DNS structure is like that of an inverted tree (upside-down tree); this therefore means that the root of the tree is at the top and its leaves and branches are at the bottom! Funny sort of tree, you'd say, eh?

At the very top of the inverted domain tree is the highest level of the DNS structure, aptly called the root domain and represented by the simple dot (.).

This is the dot that's supposed to occur after every FQDN, but it is silently assumed to be present even though it is not explicitly written. Thus for example, the proper FQDN for www.kernel.org is really www.kernel.org. (with the root period/dot at the end). And the FQDN for the popular Web portal for Yahoo! is actually www.yahoo.com. (likewise).

Coincidentally (or not) this portion of the domain name space is managed by a bunch of special servers known as the *root name servers*. At the time of this writing, there were a total of 13 root name servers managed by 13 providers (and each provider may have multiple servers that are spread all over the world. The servers are distributed for various reasons, such as security and load balancing). The root name servers are named alphabetically. They have names like a.root-server.net, b.root-server.net, . . . m.root-server.net. The role of the root name servers will be discussed further on.

The Top-Level Domain Names

The top-level domains (TLDs) can be regarded as the first branches that we would meet on the way down from the top of our inverted tree structure.

One can make bold and say that the top-level domains provide the categorical organization of the DNS namespace. What this means in plain English is that the various branches of domain namespace have been divided into clear categories to fit different uses (examples of such uses could be geographical, functional, etc.). At the time of this writing, there were roughly 258 top-level domains.

The TLDs can be broken down further into the generic top-level domain (e.g., .org, .com, .net, .mil, .gov, .edu, .int, .biz), country-code top-level domains (e.g., .us, .uk, .ng , and .ca, corresponding to the country codes for the United States, the United Kingdom, Nigeria, and Canada), and other special top-level domains (e.g., the .arpa domain).

The top-level domain in our sample FQDN (serverA.example.org.) is ".org."

The Second-Level Domain Names

The names at this level of the DNS make up the actual organizational boundary of the namespace. Companies, ISPs, educational communities, nonprofit groups, and individuals typically acquire unique names within this level. Here are a few examples: redhat.com, caldera.com, planetoid.org, labmanual.org, kernel.org.

The second-level domain in our sample FQDN (serverA.example.org.) is "example."

The Third-Level Domain Names

At this level of the domain namespace, individuals and organizations that have been assigned second-level domain names can pretty much decide what to do with the third-level names. The convention, though, is to use the third-level names to reflect host names or other functional uses. It is also common for organizations to begin the subdomain definitions from here. An example of functional assignment of a third-level domain name will be the "www" in the FQDN www.yahoo.com. The "www" here can be the actual host name of machine under the umbrella of the yahoo.com domain, or it can be an alias to a real host name.

The third-level domain name in our sample FQDN (serverA.example.org.) is "serverA." Here it simply reflects the actual host name of our system.

By keeping DNS distributed in this manner, the task of keeping track of all the hosts connected to the Internet is delegated to each site taking care of its own information. The central repository listing of all the primary name servers, called the *root server*, is the only list of existing domains. Obviously, a list of such a critical nature is itself mirrored across multiple servers and multiple geographic regions. For example, an earthquake in Japan may destroy the root server for Asia, but all the other root servers around the world can take up the slack until it comes back online. The only difference noticeable to users is likely to be a slightly higher latency in resolving domain names. Pretty amazing, isn't it? The inverted tree structure of DNS is shown in Figure 16-2.

Subdomains

"But I just saw the site www.support.example.org!" you say. "What's the host name component, and what's the domain name component?"

Welcome to the wild and mysterious world of *subdomains.* A subdomain exhibits all the properties of a domain, except that it has delegated a subsection of the domain instead of all the hosts at a site. Using the example.org site as an example, the subdomain for the support and help desk department of Example, Inc., is support.example.org. When the primary name server for the example.org domain receives a request for a host name whose FQDN ends in support.example.org, the primary forwards the request down to the primary name server for support.example.org. Only the primary name server for support.example.org knows all the hosts existing beneath it—hosts such as a system named "www" with the FQDN of "www.support.example.org."

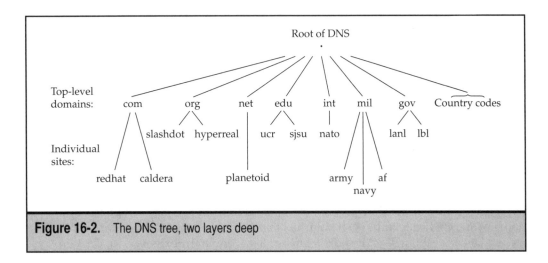

Figure 16-2.   The DNS tree, two layers deep

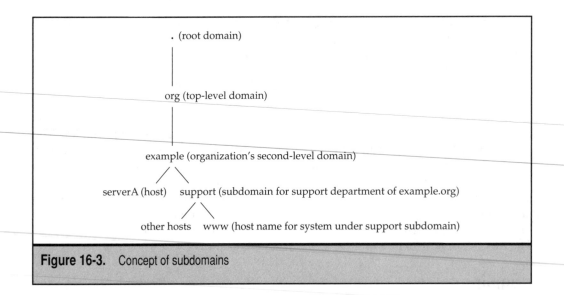

Figure 16-3. Concept of subdomains

Figure 16-3 shows you the relationship from the root servers down to example.org and then to support.example.org. The "www" is, of course, the host name.

To make this clearer, let's follow the path of a DNS request:

1. A client wants to visit a Web site called "www.support.example.org".

2. The query starts with the top-level domain "org.". Within "org." is "example.org".

3. Lets say one of the authoritative DNS servers for the "example.org" domain is named "ns1.example.org".

4. Since the host ns1 is authoritative for the example.org domain, we have to query it for all hosts (and subdomains) under it.

5. So we query it for info about the host we are interested in: "www.support .example.org".

6. Now ns1.example.org's DNS configuration is such that for anything ending with a support.example.org the server must contact another authoritative server called "dns2.example.org".

7. The request for "www.support.example.org" is then passed on to dns2.example.org, which returns the IP address for www.support.example.org—say, 192.168.1.10.

Note that when a site name appears to reflect the presence of subdomains, it doesn't mean subdomains in fact exist. Although the host name specification rules do not allow periods, the BIND name server has always allowed them. Thus, from time to time, you will see periods used in host names. Whether or not a subdomain exists is handled by the configuration of the DNS server for the site. For example, www.bogus.example.org does not automatically imply that bogus.example.org is a subdomain. Rather, it may also mean that "www.bogus" is the host name for a system in the example.org domain.

The in-addr.arpa Domain

DNS allows resolution to work in both directions. *Forward resolution* converts names into IP addresses, and *reverse resolution* converts IP addresses back into host names. The process of reverse resolution relies on the *in-addr.arpa* domain, where "arpa" is an acronym for "Address Routing and Parameters Area."

As explained in the preceding section, domain names are resolved by looking at each component from right to left, with the suffixing period indicating the root of the DNS tree. Following this logic, IP addresses must have a top-level domain as well. This domain is called the in-addr.arpa.

Unlike FQDNs, IP addresses are resolved from left to right once they're under the in-addr.arpa domain. Each octet further narrows down the possible host names. Figure 16-4 gives you a visual example of reverse resolution of the IP address 138.23.169.15.

Types of Servers

DNS servers come in three flavors: primary, secondary, and caching. Another special class of name servers consists of the so-called "root name servers." Other DNS servers require the service provided by the root name servers every once in a while.

The three main flavors of DNS servers are discussed next:

Primary servers are the ones considered authoritative for a particular domain. An *authoritative server* is the one on which the domain's configuration files reside. When updates to the domain's DNS tables occur, they are done on this server. A primary name server for a domain is simply a DNS server that knows about all hosts and subdomains existing under its domain.

Secondary servers work as backups and as load distributors for the primary name servers. Primary servers know of the existence of secondaries and send them periodic updates to the name tables. When a site queries a secondary name server, the secondary responds with authority. However, because it's possible for a secondary to be queried before its primary can alert it to the latest changes, some people refer to secondaries as "not quite authoritative." Realistically speaking, you can generally trust secondaries to have correct information. (Besides, unless you know which is which, you cannot tell the difference between a query response from a primary and one received from a secondary.)

Root Name Servers

The root name servers serve as the very first port of call for the topmost parts of the domain namespace. These servers publish a file called the "root zone file" to other DNS servers and clients on the Internet. The root zone file describes where the authoritative servers for the DNS top-level domains (com, org, ca, ng, hk, uk, etc.) are located.

A root name server is just an instance of a primary name server—it just delegates every request it gets to another name server. You can build your own root server out of BIND—nothing terribly special about it!

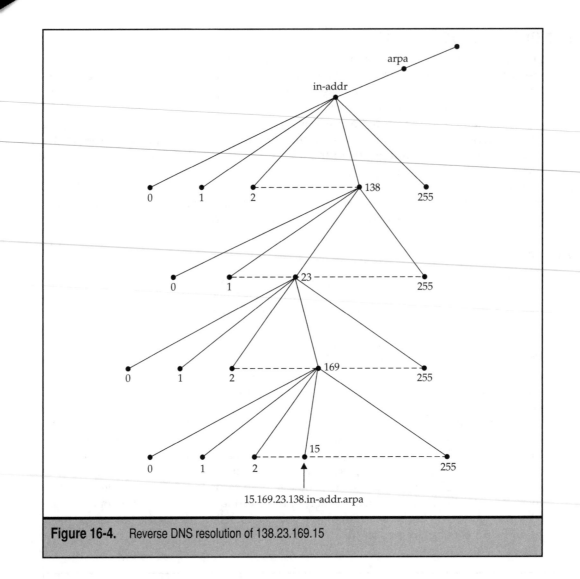

Figure 16-4.   Reverse DNS resolution of 138.23.169.15

Caching servers are just that: caching servers. They contain no configuration files for any particular domain. Rather, when a client host requests a caching server to resolve a name, that server will check its own local cache first. If it cannot find a match, it will find the primary server and ask it. This response is then cached. Practically speaking, caching servers work quite well because of the temporal nature of DNS requests. That is, if you've asked for the IP address to hyperreal.org, you are likely to do so again in the near future. (The Web has made this even more likely.) Clients can tell the difference between a caching server and a primary or secondary server, because when a caching server answers a request, it answers it "nonauthoritatively."

NOTE A DNS server can be configured to act with a specific level of authority for a particular domain. For example, a server can be primary for example.org but be secondary for domain.com. All DNS servers act as caching servers, even if they are also primary or secondary for any other domains.

INSTALLING A DNS SERVER

There isn't much variety of DNS server software available, but two particular flavors of DNS software abound in the Linux/UNIX world: djbdns and the venerable Berkeley Internet Name Domain (BIND) server. djbdns is a lightweight DNS solution that claims to be a more secure replacement for BIND. BIND is an older and much more popular program. It is used on a vast majority of name-serving machines worldwide. BIND is currently maintained and developed by the Internet Systems Consortium (ISC). More can be found out about the ISC at http://www.isc.org/. The ISC is in charge of development of the ISC DHCP server/client as well as other software.

Because of the timing between writing this book and the inevitable release of newer software, it is possible that the version of BIND discussed here will not be the same as the version that you will have access to; but you shouldn't worry at all, because most of the configuration directives, keywords, and command syntax have remained very much the same between recent versions of the software.

Our sample system runs the Fedora Core version of Linux, and as such we will be using the precompiled binary that ships with this OS. Software that ships with Fedora is supposed to be fairly recent software, so you can be sure that the version of BIND referred to here is pretty close to the latest version that can be obtained directly from the www.isc.org site (the site even has precompiled RPMs for the BIND program).

The great news is that once BIND is configured, you'll rarely need to concern yourself with its operation. Nevertheless, keep an eye out for new releases. New bugs and security issues are discovered from time to time and should be corrected. Of course, new features are released as well, but unless you have a need for them, those releases are less critical.

The BIND program can be found under the **/Fedora/RPMS/** directory at the root of the Fedora DVD media. You can also download it to your local file system from any of the Fedora mirrors, e.g., http://download.fedora.redhat.com/pub/fedora/linux/core/4/i386/os/Fedora/RPMS/bind-9*.rpm.

Assuming you downloaded or copied the BIND binary into your current working directory, you can install it using the **rpm** command. Type

```
[root@serverA root]# rpm -Uvh bind-9*
```

If you have a working connection to the Internet, installing BIND can be as simple as running this command:

```
[root@serverA  root]# up2date -i  bind
```

Once this command finishes, you are ready to begin configuring the server and running the DNS server.

Downloading, Compiling, and Installing the ISC BIND Software from Source

If the ISC BIND software is not available in a prepackaged form for your particular Linux distribution, you can always build the software from source code available from the ISC site at http://www.isc.org. It is also possible that you simply want to take advantage of the most recent bug fixes available for the software, which your distribution has not yet implemented. As of this writing, the most current stable version of the software was version 9.3.1, which can be downloaded directly from ftp://ftp.isc.org/isc/bind9/9.3.1/bind-9.3.1.tar.gz.

Once the package is downloaded, unpack the software as shown. For this example, we assume the source was downloaded into the **/usr/local/src/** directory. Unpack the tarball thus:

```
[root@serverA src]# tar  xvzf  bind-9.3.1.tar.gz
```

Change to the **bind*** subdirectory created by the preceding command. And then take a minute to study any README file(s) that might be present.

Next configure the package with the **configure** command. Assuming we want BIND to be installed under the **/usr/local/named/** directory, we'll run

```
[root@serverA bind-9.3.1]# ./configure --prefix=/usr/local/named
```

Create the directory specified by the "prefix" option, using **mkdir**:

```
[root@serverA bind-9.3.1]# mkdir   /usr/local/named
```

To compile and install, issue the **make; make install** commands:

```
[root@serverA bind-9.3.1]# make ; make install
```

The version of ISC BIND software that we built from source installs the Name server daemon (**named**) and some other useful utilities under the **/usr/local/named/ sbin/** directory. The client-side programs (**dig, host, nsupdate,** etc.) are installed under the **/usr/local/named/bin/** directory.

What Was Installed

Many programs come with the main **bind** package and **bind-utils** package that were installed earlier. The four tools that we are interested in are as follows:

Tool	Description
/usr/sbin/named	The DNS server program itself
/usr/sbin/rndc	The **bind** name server control utility
/usr/bin/host	Performs a simple query on a name server
/usr/bin/dig	Performs complex queries on a name server

The remainder of the chapter will discuss some of the programs/utilities listed here, as well as their configuration and usage.

Understanding the BIND Configuration File

The **named.conf** file is the main configuration file for BIND. Based on this file's specifications, BIND determines how it should behave and what additional configuration files, if any, must be read.

This section of the chapter covers what you need to know to set up a general-purpose DNS server. You'll find a complete guide to the new configuration file format in the **html** directory of BIND's documentation.

The general format of the **named.conf** file is as follows:

```
statement {
     options;     // comments
};
```

The **statement** keyword tells BIND we're about to describe a particular facet of its operation, and **options** are the specific commands applying to that statement. The curly braces are required so that BIND knows which options are related to which statements; there's a semicolon after every option and after the closing curly brace.

An example of this follows:

```
options {
    directory "/var/named";    // put config files in /var/named
};
```

The preceding **bind** statement means that this is an option statement. And the particular option here is the directive that specifies **bind**'s working directory, i.e., the directory on the local file system that will hold the name server's configuration data.

The Specifics

This section documents the most common statements you will see in a **named.conf** file. The best way to tackle this is to give it a skim but then treat it as a reference guide for later sections. If some of the directives seem bizarre or don't quite make sense to you during the first pass, don't worry. Once you see them in use in later sections, the hows and whys will quickly fall into place.

Comments

Comments may be in one of the following formats:

Format	Indicates
//	C++-style comments
/*...*/	C-style comments
#	Perl and UNIX shell script-style comments

In the case of the first and last styles (C++ and Perl/UNIX shell), once a comment begins, it continues until the end of the line. In regular C-style comments, the closing */ is required to indicate the end of a comment. This makes C-style comments easier for multiline comments. In general, however, you can pick the comment format that you like best and stick with it. No one style is better than another.

Statement Keywords

You can use the following statement keywords:

Keyword	Description
acl	Access Control List—determines what kind of access others have to your DNS server.
include	Allows you to include another file and have that file treated like part of the normal named.conf file.
logging	Specifies what information gets logged and what gets ignored. For logged information, you can also specify where the information is logged.
options	Addresses global server configuration issues.
controls	Allows you to declare control channels for use by the rndc utility.
server	Sets server-specific configuration options.
zone	Defines a DNS zone.

The include Statement

If you find that your configuration file is starting to grow unwieldy, you may want to consider breaking up the file into smaller components. Each file can then be included into the main named.conf file. Note that you cannot use the include statement inside another statement.

Here's an example of an include statement:

```
include "/path/to/filename_to_be_included";
```

NOTE To all you C and C++ programmers out there: Be sure not to begin `include` lines with the pound symbol (#), despite what your instincts tell you! That symbol is used to start comments in the **named.conf** file.

The logging Statement

The **logging** statement is used to specify what information you want logged, and where. When this statement is used in conjunction with the **syslog** facility, you get an extremely powerful and configurable logging system. The items logged are a number of statistics about the status of **named**. By default, they are logged to the **/var/log/messages** file. In its simplest form, the various types of logs have been grouped into predefined categories; for example there are categories for *security*-related logs, a *general* category, a *default* category, a *resolver* category, a *queries* category, etc.

Unfortunately, the configurability of this logging statement comes at the price of some additional complexity, but the default logging set up by **named** is good enough for most uses. Here is a simple logging directive example:

```
1    logging {
2    category default { default_syslog; };
3    category queries { default_syslog; };
4
5    };
```

NOTE Line numbers have been added to the preceding listing to aid readability.

The preceding logging specification means that all logs that fall under the default category will be sent to the system's syslog (the default category defines the logging options for categories where no specific configuration has been defined).

Line 3 in the listing specifies where all queries will be logged to; in this case all queries will be logged to the system syslog.

The server Statement

The **server** statement tells BIND specific information about other name servers it might be dealing with. The format of the **server** statement is as follows:

```
1    server ip-address {
2        bogus yes/no;
3    keys { string ; [ string ; [...]] } ; ]
4        transfer-format one-answer/many-answers;
5        ...<other options>...
6    };
```

where **ip-address** in line 1 is the IP address of the remote name server in question.

The **bogus** option in line 2 tells the server whether or not the remote server is sending bad information. This is useful in the event you are dealing with another site that may be sending you bad information due to a misconfiguration. The **keys** clause in line 3 specifies a **key_id** defined by the key statement, which can be used to secure transactions when talking to the remote server. This key is used in generating a request signature that is appended to messages exchanged with the remote name server. The item in line 4, **transfer-format**, tells BIND whether the remote name server can accept multiple answers in a single query response.

A sample **server** entry might look like this:

```
server 192.168.1.12 {
    bogus no;
    transfer-format many-answers;
};
```

Zones

The **zone** statement allows you to define a DNS zone—the definition of which is often confusing. Here is the fine print: *a DNS zone is not the same thing as a DNS domain.* The difference is subtle, but important.

Let's review: Domains are designated along organizational boundaries. A single organization can be separated into smaller administrative subdomains. Each subdomain gets its own zone. All of the zones collectively form the entire domain.

For example, .example.org is a domain. Within it are the subdomains .engr.example .org, .marketing.example.org, .sales.example.org, and .admin.example.org. Each of the four subdomains has its own zone. And .example.org has some hosts within it that do not fall under any of the subdomains; thus it has a zone of its own. As a result the "example.org" domain is actually composed of five zones in total.

In the simplest model, where a single domain has no subdomains, the definition of zone and domain are the same in terms of information regarding hosts, configurations, and so on.

The process of setting up zones in the **named.conf** file is discussed in the following section.

CONFIGURING A DNS SERVER

Earlier, you learned about the differences between primary, secondary, and caching name servers. To recap: Primary name servers contain the databases with the latest DNS information for a zone. When a zone administrator wants to update these databases, the primary name server gets the update first, and the rest of the world asks it for updates. Secondaries explicitly keep track of primaries, and primaries notify the secondaries when changes occur. Primaries and secondaries are considered equally authoritative in their answers. Caching name servers have no authoritative records, only cached entries.

Defining a Primary Zone in the named.conf File

The most basic syntax for a zone entry is as follows:

```
zone domain-name  {
      type master;
      file path-name;
};
```

The **path-name** refers to the file containing the database information for the zone in question. For example, to create a zone for the domain example.org, where the database file is located in **/var/named/example.org.db**, you would create the following zone definition in the **named.conf** file:

```
zone "example.org" {
      type master;
      file "example.org.db";
};
```

Note that the **directory** option for the **named.conf** file will automatically prefix the **example.org.db** filename. So if you designated **directory /var/named**, the server software will automatically look for example.org's information in **/var/named/example.org.db**.

The zone definition created here is just a *forward reference*—i.e., the mechanism by which others can look up a name and get the IP address for a system under the example .org domain that your name server manages. It's proper Net behavior to also supply an IP-to-host name mapping (also necessary if you want to send e-mail to some sites). To do this, you provide an entry in the in-addr.arpa domain.

The format of an in-addr.arpa entry is the first three octets of your IP address, reversed, followed by in-addr.arpa. Assuming that the network address for example .org is 192.168.1, the in-addr.arpa domain would be 1.168.192.in-addr.arpa. Thus, the corresponding **zone** statement in the **named.conf** file would be as follows:

```
zone "1.168.192.in-addr.arpa" {
      type master;
      file "example.org.rev";
};
```

Note that the filenames (example.org.db and example.org.rev) used in the zone sections here are completely arbitrary. You are free to choose your own naming convention as long as it makes sense to you.

The exact placement of our sample example.org zone section in the overall **named .conf** file will be shown later on.

Additional Options

Primary domains may also use some of the configuration choices from the **options** statement. These options are

- ▼ `check-names`
- ■ `allow-update`
- ■ `allow-query`
- ■ `allow-transfer`
- ■ `notify`
- ▲ `also-notify`

Using any of these options in a zone configuration will affect only that zone.

Defining a Secondary Zone in the named.conf File

The zone entry format for secondary servers is very similar to that of master servers. For forward resolution, here is the format:

```
zone domain-name {
    type slave;
    masters  IP-address-list; ;
    file path-name;
};
```

where **domain-name** is the exact same zone name as specified on the primary name server, **IP-address-list** is the list of IP addresses where the primary name server for that zone exists, and **path-name** is the full path location of where the server will keep copies of the primary's zone files.

Additional Options

A secondary zone configuration may also use some of the configuration choices from the **options** statement. Some of these options are

- ▼ `check-names`
- ■ `allow-update`
- ■ `allow-query`
- ■ `allow-transfer`
- ▲ `max-transfer-time-in`

Defining a Caching Zone in the named.conf File

A caching configuration is the easiest of all configurations. It's also required for every DNS server configuration, even if you are running a primary or secondary server. This is necessary in order for the server to recursively search the DNS tree to find other hosts on the Internet.

For a caching name server we define three zone sections. Here's the first entry:

```
zone "." {
    type hint;
    file "root.hints";
};
```

The first zone entry here is the definition of the root name servers. The line **type hint**; specifies that this is a caching zone entry, and the line **file "root.hints"**; specifies the file that will prime the cache with entries pointing to the root servers. You can always obtain the latest root hints file from http://www.internic.net/zones/named.root.

The second zone entry defines the name resolution for the local host. The second zone entry is as follows:

```
zone "localhost" in {
    type master;
    file "localhost.db";
};
```

The third zone entry defines the reverse lookup for the local host. This is the reverse entry for resolving the local host address (127.0.0.1) back to the local host name.

```
zone "0.0.127.in-addr.arpa" {
    type master;
    file "127.0.0.rev";
};
```

Putting these zone entries into **/etc/named.conf** is sufficient to create a caching DNS server. But of course the contents of the actual database files (**localhost.db**, **127.0.0.rev**, **example.org.db**, etc.) referenced by the **file** directive are also very important. The following sections will examine the makeup of the database file more closely.

DNS Records Types

This section discusses the makeup of the name server database files, i.e., the files that store specific information that pertains to each zone that the server hosts. The database files consist mostly of record types—therefore, you need to understand the meaning and use of the common record types for DNS: SOA, NS, A, PTR, CNAME, MX, TXT, and RP.

SOA: Start of Authority

The SOA record starts the description of a site's DNS entries. The format of this entry is as follows:

```
1      domain.name. IN SOA ns.domain.name. hostmaster.domain.name. (
2            1999080801              ; serial number
3            10800                   ; refresh rate in seconds (3 hours)
4            1800                    ; retry in seconds (30 minutes)
5            1209600                 ; expire in seconds (2 weeks)
6            604800                  ; minimum in seconds (1 week)
7             )
```

> **NOTE**   Line numbers have been added to the preceding listing to aid readability.

The first line contains some details you need to pay attention to: **domain.name.** is of course to be replaced with your domain name. This is usually the same name that was specified in the **zone** directive in the **/etc/named.conf** file. Notice that last period at the end of **domain.name.** It's supposed to be there—indeed, the DNS configuration files are extremely picky about it. The ending period is necessary for the server to differentiate relative host names from fully qualified domain names (FQDNs); for example, the difference between serverA and serverA.example.org.

IN tells the name server that this is an Internet record. There are other types of records, but it's been years since anyone has had a need for them. You can safely ignore them.

SOA tells the name server this is the Start of Authority record.

The **ns.domain.name.** is the FQDN for the name server for this domain (that would be the server where this file will finally reside). Again, watch out and don't miss that trailing period.

The **hostmaster.domain.name.** is the e-mail address for the domain administrator. Notice the lack of an @ in this address. The @ symbol is replaced with a period. Thus, the e-mail address referred to in this example is hostmaster@domain.name. The trailing period is used here, too.

The remainder of the record starts after the opening parenthesis on line 1. Line 2 is the serial number. It is used to tell the name server when the file has been updated. Watch out—forgetting to increment this number when you make a change is a mistake frequently made in the process of managing DNS records. (Forgetting to put a period in the right place is another common error.)

> **NOTE**   To maintain serial numbers in a sensible way, use the date formatted in the following order: YYYYMMDD*xx*. The tail-end *xx* is an additional two-digit number starting with 00, so if you make multiple updates in a day, you can still tell which is which.

Line 3 in the list of values is the refresh rate in seconds. This value tells the secondary DNS servers how often they should query the primary server to see if the records have been updated.

Line 4 is the retry rate in seconds. If the secondary server tries but cannot contact the primary DNS server to check for updates, the secondary server tries again after the specified number of seconds.

Line 5 specifies the expire directive. It is intended for secondary servers that have cached the zone data. It tells these servers that if they cannot contact the primary server for an update, they should discard the value after the specified number of seconds. One to two weeks is a good value for this interval.

The final value (line 6, the minimum) tells caching servers how long they should wait before expiring an entry if they cannot contact the primary DNS server. Five to seven days is a good guideline for this entry.

TIP   Don't forget to place the closing parenthesis (line 7) after the final value.

NS: Name Server

The NS record is used for specifying which name servers maintain records for this zone. If any secondary name servers exist that you intend to transfer zones to, they need to be specified here. The format of this record is as follows:

```
IN NS          ns1.domain.name.
IN NS          ns2.domain.name.
```

You can have as many backup name servers as you'd like for a domain—at least two is a good idea. Most ISPs are willing to act as secondary DNS servers if they provide connectivity for you.

A: Address Record

This is probably the most common type of record found in the wild. The A record is used for providing a mapping from host name to IP address. The format of an A address is simple:

```
Host_name        IN A        IP-Address
```

For example, an A record for the host serverB.example.org, whose IP address is 192.168.1.2, would look like this:

```
serverB            IN A          192.168.1.2
```

Note that any host name is automatically suffixed with the domain name listed in the SOA record, unless this host name ends with a period. In the foregoing example for serverB, if the SOA record above it is for example.org, then serverB is understood to be serverB.example.org. If you were to change this to serverB.example.org (without a trailing period), the name server would understand it to be serverB.example.org.example. org.—which is probably not what you intended! So if you want to use the FQDN, be sure to suffix it with a period.

PTR: Pointer Record

The PTR record is for performing reverse name resolution, thereby allowing someone to specify an IP address and determine the corresponding host name. The format for this record is very similar to the A record, except with the values reversed:

```
IP-Address       IN PTR     Host_name
```

The **IP-address** can take one of two forms: just the last octet of the IP address (leaving the name server to automatically suffix it with the information it has from the in-addr.arpa domain name); or the full IP address, which is suffixed with a period. The **Host_name** must have the complete FQDN. For example, the PTR record for the host serverB would be as follows:

```
192.168.1.2.     IN PTR     serverB.example.org.
```

MX: Mail Exchanger

The MX record is in charge of telling other sites about your zone's mail server. If a host on your network generates an outgoing mail message with its host name on it, someone returning a message would not send it back directly to that host. Instead, the replying mail server would look up the MX record for that site and send the message there instead.

When Internet sites were primarily composed of UNIX-based systems, with Sendmail configured as a NULL host forwarding to a mail hub, lack of an MX record was okay. But as more non-UNIX systems joined the Net, MX records became crucial. If pc.domain. name sends a message using its PC-based mail reader (which cannot accept SMTP mail), it's important that the replying party have a reliable way of knowing the identity of pc.domain.name's mail server.

The format of the MX record is as follows:

```
domainname.  IN MX weight Host_name
```

where **domainname.** is the domain name of the site (with a period at the end, of course); the **weight** is the importance of the mail server (if multiple mail servers exist, the one with the smallest number has precedence over those with larger numbers); and the **Host_name** is, of course, the name of the mail server. It is important that the **Host_name** have an A record, as well.

Here's an example entry:

```
example.org.     IN    MX    10    smtp1
                 IN    MX    20    smtp2
```

Typically, MX records occur close to the top of DNS configuration files. If a domain name is not specified, the default name is pulled from the SOA record.

CNAME: Canonical Name

CNAME records allow you to create aliases for host names. A CNAME record can be regarded as an alias. This is useful when you want to provide a highly available service with an easy-to-remember name, but still give the host a real name.

Another popular use for CNAMEs is to "create" a new server with an easy-to-remember name without having to invest in a new server at all. An example: Suppose a site has a Web server with a host name of zabtsuj-content.example.org. It can be argued that zabtsuj-content.example.org is not a very memorable nor user-friendly name. So since the system is a Web server, a CNAME record or alias of "www" can be created for the host. This will simply map the user-unfriendly name of zabtsuj-content.example.org to a more user-friendly name of www.example.org. This will allow all requests that go to www.example.org to be passed on transparently to the actual system that hosts the Web content, i.e., zabtsuj-content.example.org.

Here's the format for the CNAME record:

```
New_host_name   IN CNAME   old_host_name
```

For example, for our sample scenario described earlier, the CNAME entry will be

```
zabtsuj-content        IN    A        192.168.1.111
www                    IN    CNAME        zabtsuj-content
```

RP and TXT: The Documentation Entries

Sometimes it's useful to provide contact information as part of your database—not just as comments, but as actual records that others can query. This can be accomplished using the RP and TXT records.

A TXT record is a free-form text entry into which you can place whatever information you deem fit. Most often, you'll only want to put contact information in these records. Each TXT record must be tied to a particular host name. For example,

```
serverA.example.org.   IN TXT "Contact: Admin Guy"
                       IN TXT "SysAdmin/Android"
                       IN TXT "Voice: 999-999-9999"
```

The RP record was created as an explicit container for a host's contact information. This record states who is the responsible person for the specific host; here's an example:

```
serverB.example.org.   IN RP admin-address.example.org. example.org.
```

As useful as these records may be, they are a rarity these days, because it is perceived that they give away too much information about the site that could lead to social engineering–based attacks. You may find such records helpful in your internal DNS servers, but you should probably leave them out of anything that someone could query from the Internet.

SETTING UP BIND DATABASE FILES

So now you know enough about all the DNS record types to get you started. It's time to create the actual database that will feed the server.

The database file format is not too strict, but some conventions have jelled over time. Sticking to these conventions will make your life easier and will smooth the way for the administrator who takes over your creation.

> **NOTE**   Comment liberally. In this file, comment lines begin with a semicolon. Although there isn't a lot of mystery about what's going on in a DNS database file, a history of the changes is a useful reference about what was being accomplished and why.

The database files are your most important configuration files. It is easy to create the forward lookup databases; what usually gets left out are the reverse lookups. Some tools like Sendmail and TCP-Wrappers will perform reverse lookups on IP addresses to see where people are coming from. So it is a common courtesy to have this information.

Every database file should start with a $TTL entry. This entry tells BIND what the time-to-live value is for each individual record, whenever it isn't explicitly specified. (The TTL in the SOA record is for the SOA record only.) After the $TTL entry is the SOA record and at least one NS record. Everything else is optional. (Of course, "everything else" is what makes the file useful!) You may find the following general format helpful to follow:

```
$TTL
SOA record
NS records
MX records
A and CNAME records
```

Let's walk through the process of building a complete DNS server from start to finish to better show how the information shown so far comes together. For this example, we will build the DNS server for example.org that will accomplish the following goals:

▼ Establish two name servers: ns1.example.org and ns2.example.org.

■ Act as a slave server for the sales.example.org zone, where serverB.example.org will be the master server.

■ Define A records for serverA, serverB, smtp, ns1, and ns2.

■ Define smtp.example.org as the mail exchanger (MX) for the example.org domain.

■ Define www.example.org as an alternative name (CNAME) for serverA.example .org, and ftp.example.org as an alternative name for serverB.example.org.

▲ Finally, we will define contact information for serverA.example.org.

Okay, Mr. Bond, you have your instructions. Go forth and complete the mission. Good luck!

Breaking Out the Individual Steps

In order to accomplish our goal of setting up a DNS server for example.org, we will need to do a series of steps. Let's walk through them one at a time:

1. Make sure that you have installed the BIND DNS server software as described earlier in the chapter. Use the **rpm** command to confirm this. Type

```
[root@serverA ~]# rpm -q bind
bind-9.*
```

NOTE If you built and installed BIND from source, then the preceding **rpm** command will not reveal anything because the RPM database will not know anything about it. But you would know . . . what you installed and where.

2. Use any text editor you are comfortable with to create the main DNS server configuration file, i.e., the **/etc/named.conf** file. Enter the text that follows into the file:

```
options {
        directory         "/var/named";
        dump-file         "/var/named/data/cache_dump.db";
        statistics-file   "/var/named/data/named_stats.txt";
        notify            yes;
};

# The following zone definitions don't need any modification.  The first one
# is the definition of the root name servers and sets up our server as a caching
#  capable DNS server.
# The second one defines localhost.
# The third zone definition defines the reverse lookup for localhost.
zone "." in {
        type hint;
        file "root.hints";
};
zone "localhost" in {
        type      master;
        file      "localhost.db";
};
zone "0.0.127.in-addr.arpa" in {
        type      master;
        file      "127.0.0.rev";
};
# The zone definition below is for the domain that our name server is
# authoritative for i.e. the example.org domain name.
zone "example.org" {
        type      master;
        file      "example.org.db";
};

# Below is the zone for the in-addr.arpa domain, for the example.org site.
```

```
zone "1.168.192.in-addr.arpa" {
        type      master;
        file      "example.org.rev";
};
# Below is the entry for the sub-domain for which this server is a
# slave server IP address of sales.example.orgs master server is
# 192.168.1.2

zone  "sales.example.org"  {
          type  slave;
          file  "sales.example.org.bk";
          masters {192.168.1.2};

};
```

3. Save the preceding file as **/etc/named.conf** and exit the text editor.

4. Next we'll need to create the actual database files referenced in the file sections of the **/etc/named.conf** file. In particular, the files we want to create are **root .hints**, **localhost.db**, **127.0.0.rev**, **example.org.db**, and **example.org.rev**. All the files will be stored in BIND's working directory, **/var/named/**. We'll create them as they occur from the top of the **named.conf** file to the bottom.

5. Thankfully, we won't have to manually create the root hints file. Download the latest copy of the root hints file from the Internet. Use the **wget** command to download and copy it in the proper directory. Type

```
[root@serverA ~]# wget -O /var/named/root.hints  \
http://www.internic.net/zones/named.root
```

6. Use any text editor you are comfortable with to create the zone file for the local host. This is the **localhost.db** file. Enter the text that follows into the file:

```
$TTL 1W
@               IN SOA   localhost    root (
                              2006123100         ; serial
                              3H                 ; refresh (3 hours)
                              30M                ; retry (30 minutes)
                              2W                 ; expiry (2 weeks)
                              1W )               ; minimum (1 week)
              IN NS         @
              IN A          127.0.0.1
```

7. Save the preceding file as **/var/named/localhost.db** and exit the text editor.

8. Use any text editor to create the zone file for the reverse lookup zone for local host. This is the **127.0.0.rev** file. Enter the text that follows into the file:

```
$TTL 1W
@                IN SOA         localhost.   root.localhost. (
                                2006123100       ; serial
                                3H               ; refresh
                                30M              ; retry
```

```
                                  2W                      ; expiry
                                  1W )                    ; minimum


                   IN NS         localhost.
    1              IN PTR        localhost.
```

TIP It is possible to use abbreviated time values in BIND. For example, 3H means 3 hours, 2W means 2 weeks, 30M implies 30 minutes, etc.

9. Save the preceding file as **/var/named/127.0.0.rev** and exit the text editor.

10. Next create the database file for the main zone we are concerned with, i.e., the example.org domain. Use a text editor to create the **example.org.db** file and input the text that follows into the file:

```
$TTL 1W
@               IN SOA  ns1.example.org.   root (
                                2006123100       ; serial
                                3H               ; refresh (3 hours)
                                30M              ; retry (30 minutes)
                                2W               ; expiry (2 weeks)
                                1W )             ; minimum (1 week)
                IN      NS         ns1.example.org.
                IN      NS         ns2.example.org.
                IN      MX 10      smtp.example.org.
    ns1         IN      A          192.168.1.1   ;primary name server
    ns2         IN      A          192.168.1.2   ;secondary name server
    serverA     IN      A          192.168.1.1
    serverB     IN      A          192.168.1.2
    smtp        IN      A          192.168.1.25  ;mail server
    www         IN      CNAME      serverA       ;web server
    ftp         IN      CNAME      serverB       ;ftp server
    serverA     IN      TXT        "Fax: 999-999-9999"
```

11. Save the preceding file as **/var/named/example.org.db** and exit the text editor.

12. Finally, create the reverse lookup zone file for the example.org zone. Use a text editor to create the **example.org.rev** file and input the text that follows into the file:

```
$TTL 1W
@               IN SOA  ns1.example.org.   root (
                                2006123100      ; serial
                                3H              ; refresh (3 hours)
                                30M             ; retry (30 minutes)
                                2W              ; expiry (2 weeks)
                                1W )            ; minimum (1 week)
                IN      NS         ns1.example.org.
                IN      NS         ns2.example.org.
    1           IN      PTR        serverA.example.org. ; Reverse info for serverA
    2           IN      PTR        serverB.example.org. ; Reverse info for serverB
    25          IN      PTR        smtp.example.org.    ; Reverse for mailserver
```

13. We don't have to create any files to be secondary for sales.example.com. We only need to add the entries we already have in the **named.conf** file. (Although the log files will complain about not being able to contact the master, this is okay, since we have only shown how to set up the primary master for the zone for which our server is authoritative.)

    The next step will show how to start the **named** service. But because the BIND software is so finicky about its dots and semicolons, and because you may have had to manually type in all the configuration files, chances are great that you invariably made some typos (or we made some typos ourselves ☺). So your best bet will be to carefully monitor the system log files to view error messages as they are being generated in real time.

14. Use the **tail** command in another terminal window to view the logs and then issue the command in the next step in a separate window so that you can view both simultaneously. In your new terminal window, type

    ```
    [root@serverA named]# tail -f /var/log/messages
    ```

15. We are ready to start the **named** service at this point. Use the **service** command to launch the service. Type

    ```
    [root@serverA named]# service named start
    Starting named:                                    [  OK  ]
    ```

TIP   On a SuSE Linux system, the equivalent command will be

```
[root@serverA] # rcnamed start
```

16. If you get a bunch of errors in the system logs, you will find that the logs will usually tell you the line number and/or the type of error. So fixing the errors shouldn't be too hard. Just go back and put the dots and semicolons where they ought to be. Another common error is misspelling the configuration file's directives, e.g., writing master instead of masters; though both are valid directives, each is used in a different context.

TIP   If you have changed BIND's configuration files (either the main **named.conf** or the database files), you will need to tell it to reread them by sending the **named** process a HUP signal. Begin by finding the process ID for the **named** process. This can be done by looking for it in **/var/run/named/named.pid**. If you do not see it in the usual location, you can run the following command to get it:

```
[root@serverA ~]# ps -C named
 PID TTY   TIME CMD
 7706 ? 00:00:00 named
```

The value under the PID column is the process ID of the **named** process. This is the PID you want to send a HUP signal to. You can then send it a HUP signal by typing

```
[root@serverA ~]# kill -HUP 7706
```

Of course, replace **7706** with the correct process ID from your output.

17. Finally you may want to make sure that your DNS server service starts up during the next system reboot. Use the **chkconfig** command. Type

```
[root@serverA named]# chkconfig named on
```

The next section will walk you through the use of tools that can be used to test/query a DNS server.

THE DNS TOOLBOX

This section describes a few tools that you'll want to get acquainted with as you work with DNS. They'll help you to troubleshoot problems more quickly.

host

The **host** tool is really a very simple utility to use. Its functionality can of course be extended by using it with its various options.

Its options and syntax are shown here:

```
host [-aCdlrTwv] [-c class] [-n] [-N ndots] [-t type] [-W time]
                 [-R number] hostname [server]
    -a is equivalent to -v -t *
    -c specifies query class for non-IN data
    -C compares SOA records on authoritative nameservers
    -d is equivalent to -v
    -l lists all hosts in a domain, using AXFR
    -i Use the old IN6.INT form of IPv6 reverse lookup
    -N changes the number of dots allowed before root lookup is done
    -r disables recursive processing
    -R specifies number of retries for UDP packets
    -t specifies the query type
    -T enables TCP/IP mode
    -v enables verbose output
    -w specifies to wait forever for a reply
    -W specifies how long to wait for a reply
```

In its simplest use, **host** allows you to resolve host names into IP addresses from the command line. For example,

```
[root@serverA named]# host internic.net
internic.net has address 198.41.0.6
```

We can also use **host** to perform reverse lookups. For example,

```
[root@serverA named]# host 198.41.0.6
6.0.41.198.in-addr.arpa domain name pointer rs.internic.net.
```

dig

The domain information gopher, **dig**, is a great tool for gathering information about DNS servers. It is the official tool that has the BIND group's blessing and official stamp.

Its syntax and some of its options are shown here:

```
dig [@global-server] [domain] [q-type] [q-class] {q-opt}
        {global-d-opt} host [@local-server] {local-d-opt}
        [ host [@local-server] {local-d-opt} [...]]


Where:  domain are in the Domain Name System

        q-class  is one of (in,hs,ch,...) [default: in]
        q-type   is one of (a,any,mx,ns,soa,hinfo,axfr,txt,...) [default:a]
                    q-opt    is one of:
                 -x dot-notation     (shortcut for in-addr lookups)
                 -i                  (IP6.INT reverse IPv6 lookups)
                 -f filename         (batch mode)
                 -b address          (bind to source address)
                 -p port             (specify port number)
                 -t type             (specify query type)
                 -c class            (specify query class)
                 -k keyfile          (specify tsig key file)
                 -y name:key         (specify named base64 tsig key)

        d-opt    is of the form +keyword[=value], where keyword is:
                 +[no]vc             (TCP mode)
                 +[no]tcp            (TCP mode, alternate syntax)
                 +time=###           (Set query timeout) [5]
                 +tries=###          (Set number of UDP attempts) [3]
                 +domain=###         (Set default domainname)
                 +[no]recurse        (Recursive mode)
                 +[no]ignore         (Don't revert to TCP for TC responses.)
                 +[no]fail           (Don't try next server on SERVFAIL)
                 +[no]besteffort     (Try to parse even illegal messages)
                 +[no]aaonly         (Set AA flag in query)
                 +[no]cmd            (Control display of command line)
                 +[no]comments       (Control display of comment lines)
                 +[no]question       (Control display of question)
                 +[no]answer         (Control display of answer)
                 +[no]authority      (Control display of authority)
                 +[no]additional     (Control display of additional)
```

```
                  +[no]stats          (Control display of statistics)
                  +[no]short          (Disable everything except short
                                       form of answer)
                  +[no]all            (Set or clear all display flags)
                  +[no]qr             (Print question before sending)
                  +[no]nssearch       (Search all authoritative nameservers)
                  +[no]identify       (ID responders in short answers)
                  +[no]trace          (Trace delegation down from root)
                  +[no]dnssec         (Request DNSSEC records)
                  +[no]multiline      (Print records in an expanded format)

            global d-opts and servers (before host name) affect all queries.
            local d-opts and servers (after host name) affect only that lookup.
```

Dig's usage summary is

dig @*server* *domain* *query-type*

where **@*server*** is the name of the DNS server you want to query, ***domain*** is the domain name you are interested in querying, and ***query-type*** is the name of the record you are trying to get (A, MX, NS, SOA, HINFO, TXT, ANY, etc.).

For example, to get the MX record for the example.org domain we established in the earlier project from the DNS server we set up, you would issue the **dig** command like this:

```
[root@serverA ~]# dig @localhost example.org MX
...<OUTPUT TRUNCATED>...
;; QUESTION SECTION:
;example.org.                   IN      MX
;; ANSWER SECTION:
example.org.            604800  IN      MX      10 smtp.example.org.
;; AUTHORITY SECTION:
example.org.            604800  IN      NS      ns1.example.org.
example.org.            604800  IN      NS      ns2.example.org.
;; ADDITIONAL SECTION:
smtp.example.org.       604800  IN      A       192.168.1.25
...<OUTPUT TRUNCATED>...
```

To query our local DNS server for the A records for the yahoo.com domain, simply type

```
[root@serverA ~]# dig @localhost yahoo.com
...<OUTPUT TRUNCATED>...
;; QUESTION SECTION:
;yahoo.com.                     IN      A
;; ANSWER SECTION:
yahoo.com.              300     IN      A       216.109.112.135
yahoo.com.              300     IN      A       66.94.234.13
...<OUTPUT TRUNCATED>...
```

> **NOTE** You will notice that, for the preceding command, we didn't specify the query type, i.e., we didn't explicitly specify an "A"-type record. The default behavior for **dig** is to assume you want an A-type record when nothing is specified explicitly. You may also notice that we are querying our DNS server for the yahoo.com domain. Our server is obviously not authoritative for the yahoo.com domain, but because we also configured it as a caching-capable DNS server, it is able to obtain the proper answer for us from the appropriate DNS servers.

To reissue the previous command but this time suppress all verbosity, using one of **dig**'s options (**+short**), type

```
[root@serverA ~]# dig +short @localhost yahoo.com
66.94.234.13
216.109.112.135
```

To query the local name server for the reverse lookup info (PTR RR) for 192.168.1.1, type

```
[root@serverA ~]# dig -x 192.168.1.1  @localhost
...<OUTPUT TRUNCATED>...
;; QUESTION SECTION:
;1.1.168.192.in-addr.arpa.        IN        PTR
;; ANSWER SECTION:
1.1.168.192.in-addr.arpa. 604800 IN        PTR        serverA.example.org.
;; AUTHORITY SECTION:
1.168.192.in-addr.arpa. 604800   IN        NS         ns1.example.org.
1.168.192.in-addr.arpa. 604800   IN        NS         ns2.example.org.
...<OUTPUT TRUNCATED>...
```

The **dig** program is incredibly powerful. Its options are too numerous to properly cover here. You should read the man page that was installed with **dig** to learn how to use some of its more advanced features.

nslookup

The **nslookup** utility is one of the tools that you will find exists across various operating system platforms. And so it is probably one of the tools that most people are familiar with. Its usage is quite simple too. It can be used both interactively and noninteractively (i.e., directly from the command line).

Interactive mode is entered when no arguments are given to the command. Typing **nslookup** all by itself at the command line will drop you to the **nslookup** shell. To get out of the interactive mode, just type **exit** at the **nslookup** prompt.

TIP When **nslookup** is used in interactive mode, the command to quit the utility is `exit`. But most people will often instinctively issue the `quit` command to try to exit the interactive mode. **nslookup** will think it is being asked to do a DNS lookup for the host name "quit". It will eventually time out after a while. You can create a DNS record that will immediately remind the user of the proper command to use. An entry like this in the zone file for your domain will suffice:

```
use-exit-to-quit-nslookup        IN A        127.0.0.1
quit                             IN CNAME    use-exit-to-quit-nslookup
```

With the preceding entry in the zone file, whenever anybody queries your DNS server using **nslookup** interactively and then mistakenly issues the `quit` command, the user will get a gentle reminder that says *"use-exit-to-quit-nslookup."*

In the noninteractive mode, its usage is summarized here:

```
nslookup [ -option ]  [ name | - ]  [ server ]
```

For example, to use **nslookup** noninteractively, to query our local name server for information about the host www.example.org, type

```
[root@serverA ~]# nslookup www.example.org localhost
Server:         localhost
Address:        127.0.0.1#53

www.example.org canonical name = serverA.example.org.
Name:   serverA.example.org
Address: 192.168.1.1
```

NOTE The BIND developer group frowns on use of the **nslookup** utility. It is officially deprecated.

whois

The **whois** command is used for determining ownership of a domain. Information about a domain's owner isn't a mandatory part of its records, nor is it customarily placed in the TXT or RP records. So you'll need to gather this information using the **whois** technique, which reports the actual owner of the domain, their snail-mail address, e-mail address, and technical contact phone numbers.

Let's walk through an example of getting information about the yahoo.com domain. Type

```
[root@serverA ~]# whois yahoo.com
[Querying whois.internic.net]
[Redirected to whois.alldomains.com]
```

```
[Querying whois.alldomains.com]
[whois.alldomains.com]
...<OUTPUT TRUNCATED>...
Registrant:
        Yahoo! Inc.
        (DOM-272993)
   Technical Contact, Zone Contact:
        Domain Administrator
        (NIC-1372925)
...<OUTPUT TRUNCATED>...
   Created on.............: 1995-Jan-18.
   Expires on.............: 2012-Jan-19.
   Record last updated on..: 2005-Apr-05 16:34:22.
   Domain servers in listed order:
   NS4.YAHOO.COM                63.250.206.138
      ...<OUTPUT TRUNCATED>...
```

nsupdate

An often forgotten powerful DNS utility is the **nsupdate** utility. It is used to submit Dynamic DNS (DDNS) Update requests to a DNS server. It allows the resource records (RR) to be added or removed from a zone without manually editing the zone database files.

This is especially useful because DDNS-type zones should not be edited or updated by hand—since the manual changes are bound to conflict with the dynamic updates that are automatically maintained in journal files—which may result in zone data being corrupt.

The **nsupdate** program reads input from a specially formatted file or from standard input. The syntax for the command is

```
nsupdate [ -d ] [[ -y keyname:secret ] [ -k keyfile ] ] [-v] [filename ]
```

The rndc Tool

This is the "remote name daemon control" utility. It is very handy for controlling the name server and also debugging problems with the name server.

The **rndc** program can be used to securely manage the name server. To do this, a separate configuration file is required for **rndc**, since all communication with the server is authenticated with digital signatures that rely on a shared secret and this shared secret is typically stored in a configuration file, which is usually named **/etc/rndc.conf**. You will need to generate the secret that is shared between the utility and the name server by using tools such as **rndc-confgen** (we don't discuss this feature here).

The usage summary for **rndc** is listed here:

```
rndc [-c config] [-s server] [-p port]
        [-k key-file ] [-y key] [-V] command
command is one of the following:
```

```
reload          Reload configuration file and zones.
reload zone [class [view]]
                Reload a single zone.
refresh zone [class [view]]
                Schedule immediate maintenance for a zone.
reconfig        Reload configuration file and new zones only.
stats           Write server statistics to the statistics file.
querylog        Toggle query logging.
dumpdb          Dump cache(s) to the dump file (named_dump.db).
stop            Save pending updates to master files and stop the server.
halt            Stop the server without saving pending updates.
trace           Increment debugging level by one.
trace level     Change the debugging level.
notrace         Set debugging level to 0.
flush           Flushes all of the server's caches.
flush [view]    Flushes the server's cache for a view.
status          Display status of the server.
```

For example, you can use **rndc** to view the status of the DNS server. Type

```
[root@serverA ~]# rndc status
number of zones: 7
debug level: 0
xfers running: 0
xfers deferred: 0
soa queries in progress: 1
query logging is OFF
server is up and running
```

If, for example, you make changes to the zone database file (**/var/named/example .org.db**) for one of the zones under your control (e.g., example.org) and you want to reload just that zone without restarting the entire DNS server, you can issue the **rndc** command with the option shown here:

```
[root@serverA ~]# rndc reload example.org
```

> **NOTE**   You must remember to increment the serial number of the zone after making any changes to it!

CONFIGURING DNS CLIENTS

In this section, we'll delve into the wild and exciting process of configuring DNS clients! Okay, maybe they're not that exciting—but there's no denying their significance to the infrastructure of any networked site.

The Resolver

So far, we've been studying servers and the DNS tree as a whole. The other part of this equation is, of course, the client—the host that's contacting the DNS server to resolve a host name into an IP address.

> **NOTE**   You may have noticed earlier in the section "The DNS ToolBox" that most of the queries we were issuing were being made against the DNS server called "localhost." Localhost is, of course, the local system whose shell you are executing the query commands from. In our case, hopefully this system is serverA.example.org! The reason we specifically specified the DNS server to use was that by default the system will query whatever the host's default DNS server is. And if it so happens that your host's DNS server is some random DNS server that your ISP has assigned you, some of the queries will fail because your ISP's DNS server will not know about the zone you manage and control locally. So if we configure our local system to use our local DNS server to process all DNS-type queries, then we won't have to manually specify "localhost" any longer. This is called configuring the resolver.

Under Linux, the *resolver* handles the client side of DNS. This is actually part of a library of C programming functions that get *linked* to a program when the program is started. Because all of this happens automatically and transparently, the user doesn't have to know anything about it. It's simply a little bit of magic that lets them start browsing the Internet.

From the system administrator's perspective, configuring the DNS client isn't magic, but it's very straightforward. There are only two files involved: **/etc/resolv.conf** and **/etc/nsswitch.conf**.

The /etc/resolv.conf File

The **/etc/resolv.conf** file contains the information necessary for the client to know what its local DNS server is. (Every site should have, at the very least, its own caching DNS server.) This file has two lines. The first indicates the default search domain, and the second line indicates the IP address of the host's name server.

The *default search domain* applies mostly to sites that have their own local servers. When the default search domain is specified, the client side will automatically append this domain name to the requested site and check that first. For example, if you specify your default domain to be yahoo.com and then try to connect to the host name my, the client software will automatically try contacting my.yahoo.com. Using the same default, if you try to contact the host www.stat.net, the software will try www.stat.net.yahoo.com (a perfectly legal host name), find that it doesn't exist, and then try www.stat.net alone (which does exist).

Of course, you may supply multiple default domains. However, doing so will slow the query process a bit, because each domain will need to be checked. For instance, if both example.org and stanford.edu are specified, and you perform a query on www.stat .net, you'll get three queries: www.stat.net.yahoo.com, www.stat.net.stanford.edu, and www.stat.net.

The format of the **/etc/resolv.conf** file is as follows:

```
search domainname
nameserver IP-address
```

where **domainname** is the default domain name to search, and **IP-address** is the IP address of your DNS server. For example, here's a sample **/etc/resolv.conf** file:

```
search example.org
nameserver 127.0.0.1
```

Thus, when a name lookup query is needed for serverB.example.org, only the host part is needed, i.e., serverB. The example.org suffix will be automatically appended to the query. This is of course valid only at your local site, where you have control over how clients are configured!

The /etc/nsswitch.conf File

The **/etc/nsswitch.conf** file tells the system where it should look up certain kinds of configuration information (*services*). When multiple locations are identified, the **/etc/nsswitch.conf** file also specifies the order in which the information can best be found. Typical configuration files that are set up to use **/etc/nsswitch.conf** include the password file, group file, and hosts file. (To see a complete list, open the file in your favorite text editor.)

The format of the **/etc/nsswitch.conf** file is simple. The service name comes first on a line (note that **/etc/nsswitch.conf** applies to more than just host name lookups), followed by a colon. Next come the locations that contain the information. If multiple locations are identified, the entries are listed in the order in which the system needs to perform the search. Valid entries for locations are **files**, **nis**, **dns**, **[NOTFOUND]**, and **NISPLUS**. Comments begin with a pound symbol (#).

For example, if you open the file with your favorite editor, you'll see a line similar to this:

```
hosts:      files nisplus nis dns
```

This line tells the system that all host name lookups should first start with the **/etc/hosts** file. If the entry cannot be found there, NISPLUS is checked. If the host cannot be found via NISPLUS, regular NIS is checked, and so on. It's possible that NISPLUS isn't running at your site and you want the system to check DNS records before it checks NIS records. In this case, you'd change the line to

```
hosts:      files dns nis
```

And that's it. Save your file, and the system automatically detects the change.

The only recommendation for this line is that the hosts file (**files**) should always come first in the lookup order.

What's the preferred order for NIS and DNS? This is very much dependent on the site. Whether you want to resolve host names with DNS before trying NIS will depend on whether the DNS server is closer than the NIS server in terms of network connectivity, if one server is faster than another, firewall issues, site policy issues, and other such factors.

Using [NOTFOUND=action]

In the **/etc/nsswitch.conf** file, you'll see entries that end in **[NOTFOUND=action]**. This is a special directive that allows you to stop the process of searching for information after the system has failed all prior entries. The action can be either return or continue. The default action is to continue.

For example, if your file contains the line **hosts: files [NOTFOUND=return] dns nis**, the system will try to look up host information in the **/etc/hosts** file only. If the requested information isn't there, NIS and DNS won't be searched.

Configuring the Client

Let's step through the process of configuring a Linux client to use a DNS server. We'll assume that we are using the DNS server on serverA and we are configuring serverA itself to be the client. This may sound a bit odd at first, but it is important to recall that just because a system runs the server does not mean it cannot run the client. Think of it in terms of running a Web server—just because a system runs Apache doesn't mean you can't run Firefox on the same machine and access 127.0.0.1!

Breaking out the steps to configuring the client, we see the following:

1. Edit **/etc/resolv.conf** and set the **nameserver** entry to point to your DNS server. Per our example:

   ```
   search example.org
   nameserver 127.0.0.1
   ```

2. Look through the **/etc/nsswitch.conf** file to make sure that DNS is consulted for host name resolutions. Edit **/etc/nsswitch.conf** to make it perform name lookups.

   ```
   [root@serverA ~]# grep "^hosts"  /etc/nsswitch.conf
   hosts:       files dns
   ```

   If you don't have **dns** listed as in this output, use any text editor to include **dns** on the hosts line.

3. Test the configuration with the **dig** utility. Type

   ```
   [root@serverA ~]# dig +short serverA.example.org
   192.168.1.1
   ```

   Notice that you didn't have to explicitly specify the name server to use (like @localhost) for the preceding query.

SUMMARY

In this chapter, we covered all of the information you'll need to get various types of DNS servers up and running. We discussed

▼ Name resolution over the Internet

■ Obtaining and installing the BIND name server

■ The **/etc/hosts** file

■ The process of configuring a Linux client to use DNS

■ Configuring DNS servers to act as primary, secondary, and caching servers

■ Various DNS record types

■ Configuration options in the **named.conf** file

■ Tools for use in conjunction with the DNS server to do troubleshooting

▲ Additional sources of information

With the information available in the BIND documentation on how the server should be configured, along with the actual configuration files for a complete server presented in this chapter, you should be able to go out and perform a complete installation from start to finish.

Like any software, nothing is perfect, and problems can occur with BIND and the related files and programs discussed here. Don't forget to check out the main BIND Web site (http://www.isc.org) as well as the various mailing lists dedicated to DNS and BIND software for additional information.

CHAPTER 17

FTP

T he File Transfer Protocol (FTP) has existed for the Internet since around 1971. Remarkably, the protocol has undergone very little change since then. Clients and servers, on the other hand, have been almost constantly improved and refined. This chapter covers the Very Secure FTP Daemon (vsftpd) software package.

The vsftpd program is a fairly popular FTP server and is being used by major FTP sites such as kernel.org, redhat.com, isc.org, and openbsd.org. The fact that these sites run the software attests to its robustness and security. As the name implies, the vsftpd software was designed from the ground up to be fast, stable, and very secure.

> **NOTE**   Like most other services, vsftpd is only as secure as you make it. The authors of the program have provided all of the necessary tools to make the software as secure as possible out of the box, but a bad configuration can cause your site to become vulnerable. Remember to double-check your configuration and test it out before going live. Also remember to check the vsftpd Web site frequently for any software updates.

In this chapter, we will discuss how to obtain, install, and configure the latest version of vsftpd. We will show how to configure it for private access as well as anonymous access. And finally, we will show how to use the **ftp** client and test out your new FTP server.

THE MECHANICS OF FTP

The act of transferring a file from one computer to another may seem trivial, but in reality it is not—at least, not if you're doing it right. In this section, we step through the details of the FTP client/server interaction. While this information isn't crucial to being able to get an FTP server up and running, it is important when you need to consider security issues as well as troubleshooting issues—especially troubleshooting issues that don't clearly manifest themselves as FTP-related. ("Is the problem with the network, or is it the FTP server, or is it the FTP client?")

Client/Server Interactions

The original design of FTP, which was conceived in the early 1970s, assumed something that was reasonable for a long period of time on the Internet: Internet users are a friendly bunch.

After the commercialization of the Internet around 1990–1991, the Internet became much more popular. With the coming of the World Wide Web, the Internet's user population and popularity increased even more. Along with this came hitherto relatively unknown security problems. These security problems have made the use of firewalls a standard on most networks.

The original design of FTP does not play very well with the hostile Internet environment that we have today, which necessitates the use of firewalls. Inasmuch as FTP facilitates the exchange of files between an FTP client and an FTP server, its design has some built-in nuances that are worthy of further mention.

One of FTP's nuances stems from the fact that it utilizes two ports: a *control* port (port 21) and a *data* port (port 20). The control port serves as a communication channel between the client and the server for the exchange of commands and replies, whereas the data port is used purely for the exchange of data, which may be a file, part of a file, or a directory listing. FTP can operate in two modes: *active FTP* mode and *passive FTP* mode.

Active FTP

Active-mode FTP was traditionally used in the original FTP specifications. In this mode, the client connects from an ephemeral port (number greater than 1024) to the FTP server's command port (port 21). When the client is ready to transfer data, the server opens a connection from its data port (port 20) to the IP address and ephemeral port combination provided by the client. The key here is that the client does not make the actual data connection to the server but instead informs the server of its own port (by issuing the PORT command); the server then connects back to the specified port. The server can be regarded as the active party (or the agitator) in this FTP mode.

From the perspective of an FTP client that is behind a firewall, the active-mode FTP poses a slight problem. The problem is simply that the firewall on the client side might frown upon (or disallow) connections originating or initiated from the Internet from a privileged service port (e.g., data port 20) to nonprivileged service ports on the clients it is supposed to protect.

Passive FTP

The FTP client issues the PASV command to indicate that it wants to access data in the passive mode, and the server then responds with an IP address and an ephemeral port number on itself to which the client can connect, in order to do the data transfer. The PASV command issued by the client tells the server to "listen" on a data port that is not its normal data port (i.e., port 20) and to wait for a connection rather than initiate one. The key difference here is that it is the client that initiates the connection to the port and IP address provided by the server. And in this regard, the server may be regarded as the passive party in the data communication.

From the perspective of an FTP server that is behind a firewall, passive-mode FTP is a little problematic because a firewall's natural instinct would be to disallow connections that originate from the Internet that are destined for ephemeral ports of the systems that it is supposed to protect. A typical symptom of this behavior is when a client appears to be able to connect to the server without a problem, but the connection seems to hang whenever an attempt to transfer data occurs.

To address some of the issues pertaining to FTP and firewalls, many firewalls implement application-level proxies for FTP, which keep track of FTP requests and open up those high ports when needed, to receive data from a remote site.

Obtaining and Installing vsftpd

The vsftpd package is the FTP server software that ships with most modern Linux distributions. In particular, it is the FTP server package that comes with Fedora Core, RHEL, SuSE, and so on. The latest version of the software can be obtained from its official Web site, http://vsftpd.beasts.org. The Web site also hosts great documentation and the latest news about the software. But because it is the FTP server solution that ships with Fedora Core, you can very easily install it from the installation media or directly from any Fedora Core software package repository.

In this section and the next we will concentrate on showing how to install/configure the software from the prepackaged binary via RPM, but we will also briefly discuss the process of compiling and installing the software from source.

Building vsftpd from Source

The latest version of vsftpd that was available as at the time of this writing was vsftpd-2.0.3.tar.gz. This can be obtained directly from ftp://vsftpd.beasts.org/users/cevans/vsftpd-2.0.3.tar.gz. Follow these steps to download and build the program:

1. Use the **wget** command to quickly download the program into the **/usr/local/src** directory. Type

    ```
    [root@serverA src]# wget ftp://vsftpd.beasts.org/users/cevans/vsftpd-2.0.3.tar.gz
    ```

2. Use the **tar** command to untar and decompress the **vsftpd-2.0.3.tar.gz** file and then change into the **vsftpd** directory thus created. Type

    ```
    [root@serverA src]# tar xvzf vsftpd-2.0.3.tar.gz ; cd vsftpd-2.0.3
    ```

3. Take a moment to study the **README** and **INSTALL** files in the directory.

4. Run the **make** command to compile the software. This will also result in building the vsftpd executable in the root of the build directory. Type

    ```
    [root@serverA vsftpd-2.0.3]# make
    ```

5. Next you may run the **make install** command to automatically install the vsftpd executable and man pages to vsftpd's default locations on your local file system (e.g., the vsftpd binary will be installed under **/usr/local/sbin/**). Type

    ```
    [root@serverA vsftpd-2.0.3]# make install
    ```

If you want to use the sample **vsftpd.conf** configuration file, you'll have to manually copy that to somewhere like the **/etc** directory—if not, you can generate one from scratch.

First we discuss the process of installing the software from an RPM binary:

1. While logged in to the system as the superuser, use the **up2date** command to simultaneously download and install vsftpd. Type (enter **y** for "yes" when prompted)

```
[root@serverA ~]# up2date -i vsftpd
...<OUTPUT TRUNCATED>...
Installing...
   2:vsftpd                    ##################### [100%]
...<OUTPUT TRUNCATED>...
```

NOTE You can also manually download the software from a Fedora Core repository on the Internet, e.g., from http://download.fedora.redhat.com/pub/fedora/linux/core/4/i386/os/Fedora/ RPMS/vsftpd-2.0.3-1.i386.rpm. And alternatively, you can install directly from the mounted install media (CD or DVD). The software will be under the **/your_media_mount_point/Fedora/RPMS/** directory.

2. Confirm that the software has indeed been installed. Type

```
[root@serverA ~]# rpm -q vsftpd
vsftpd-*
```

Configuring vsftpd

Now that we have installed the software, the next step will be to configure it for use. The vsftpd software that was installed in the preceding section also installed other files and directories on the local file system. Some of the more important files and directories that come installed with the vsftpd RPM are discussed in Table 17-1.

The vsftpd.conf Configuration File

As stated earlier, the main configuration file for the vsftpd FTP server is **vsftpd.conf**. Performing an installation of the software via RPM will usually place this file in the **/etc/vsftpd/** directory. The file is quite easy to manage and understand, containing pairs of options (directives) and values that are in the simple format

```
option=value
```

TIP It is an error to put any space between the option, the equal sign (=), and the value.

As with most other Linux/UNIX configuration files, comments in the file are denoted by lines that begin with the pound sign (#). To see the meaning of each of the directives, you should consult the **vsftpd.conf** man page, using the **man** command like so:

```
[root@serverA ~]# man vsftpd.conf
```

File	Description
/usr/sbin/vsftpd	This is the main **vsftpd** executable. It is the daemon itself.
/etc/vsftpd/vsftpd.conf	This is the main configuration file for the **vsftpd** daemon. It contains the many directives that control the behavior of the FTP server.
/etc/vsftpd.ftpusers	Text file that stores the list of users *not* allowed to log in to the FTP server. This file is referenced by the Pluggable Authentication Module (PAM) system.
/etc/vsftpd.user_list	Text file used to either allow or deny access to users listed. Access is denied or allowed according to the value of the **userlist_deny** directive in the **vsftpd .conf** file.
/var/ftp	This is the FTP server's working directory.
/var/ftp/pub	This directory serves as the directory that holds files meant for anonymous access to the FTP server.

Table 17-1. The vsftpd configuration files and directories

The options (or directives) in the **/etc/vsftpd/vsftpd.conf** file can be categorized according to the role they play. Some of these categories are discussed in Table 17-2.

NOTE The possible values of the options in the configuration file can also be divided into three categories: the **Boolean** options (e.g., YES, NO), the **Numeric** options (e.g., 007, 700), and the **String** options (e.g., root, /etc/vsftpd.chroot_list)

Starting and Testing the FTP Server

The **vsftpd** daemon is pretty much ready to run out of the box. It comes with some default settings that allow it to hit the ground running.

We'll of course need to start the service. After that, the rest of this section will walk through testing the FTP server by connecting to it using an FTP client.

Type of Option	Description	Examples
Daemon options	These options control the general behavior of the **vsftpd** daemon.	**listen** When enabled, **vsftpd** will run in standalone mode instead of being run under a super-daemon like **xinetd** or **inetd**. **vsftpd** itself will then take care of listening for and handling incoming connections. Default value is NO.
Socket options	These are the networking and port-related options.	**listen_address** Specifies the IP address on which **vsftpd** listens for network connections. This option has no default value.
		anon_max_rate The maximum data transfer rate permitted, in bytes per second, for anonymous clients. The default value is 0 (unlimited).
		listen_port This is the port that **vsftpd** will listen on for incoming FTP connections. The default value is 21.
		pasv_enable Enables or disables the PASV method of obtaining a data connection. The default value is YES.
		port_enable Enables or disables the PORT method of obtaining a data connection. The default value is YES.
Security options	These options directly control the granting or denial of access to the server; i.e., the options offer a built-in access control mechanism to the FTP server.	**anonymous_enable** Controls whether anonymous logins are permitted or not. If enabled, both the usernames ftp and anonymous are recognized as anonymous logins. The default value is YES.

Table 17-2.   Configuration Options for vsftpd

Type of Option	Description	Examples
		tcp_wrappers Assuming **vsftpd** was compiled with tcp_wrappers support, incoming connections will be fed through tcp_wrappers access control. The default value is NO.
		local_enable Controls whether local logins are permitted or not. If enabled, normal user accounts in **/etc/passwd** may be used to log in. Default: NO.
		userlist_enable **vsftpd** will load a list of usernames from the filename specified by the userlist_file directive when this option is enabled. And if a user tries to log in using a name in this file, that user will be denied access before even being prompted for a password. The default value is NO.
		userlist_deny This option is examined if the userlist_enable option is active. When its value is set to NO, then users will be denied login unless they are explicitly listed in the file specified by userlist_file. When login is denied, the denial is issued before the user is asked for a password; this helps prevent users from sending clear-text across the network. The default value is YES.
		userlist_file This option specifies the name of the file to be loaded when the userlist_enable option is active. Default value: vsftpd.user_list.

Table 17-2.   Configuration Options for vsftpd (*cont.*)

Type of Option	Description	Examples
		cmds_allowed Specifies a list of allowed FTP commands. However, the post-login commands are always allowed, i.e., USER, PASS, QUIT; other commands are rejected, e.g., cmds_allowed=PASV, RETR, QUIT. This option has no default value.
File-transfer options	These options relate to file transfers to and from the FTP server.	**download_enable** If set to NO, all download requests will give permission denied. Default: YES.
		write_enable This option controls whether any FTP commands that change the file system are allowed or not. These commands are: STOR, DELE, RNFR, RNTO, MKD, RMD, APPE, and SITE. Default: NO.
		chown_uploads This option has the effect of changing the ownership of all anonymously uploaded files to that of the user specified in the setting chown_username. Default value: NO.
		chown_username Specifies the name of the user who is given ownership of anonymously uploaded files. Default value: root.
Directory options	These options control the behavior of the directories served by the FTP server.	**use_localtime** When enabled, **vsftpd** will display directory listings with the time in the local system time zone. The default behavior is to display the time in GMT; i.e., the default value is NO.

Table 17-2. Configuration Options for vsftpd (*cont.*)

Type of Option	Description	Examples
		hide_ids All directory listings will show ftp as the user and group for all files when this option is enabled. Default value: NO.
		dirlist_enable Enables or disables the ability to perform directory listings. If set to NO, a permission denied error will be given when a directory listing is attempted. Default value: YES.
Logging options	These options control how and where **vsftpd** logs information.	**vsftpd_log_file** This option specifies the main **vsftpd** log file. The default value is **/var/log/vsftpd.log**.
		xferlog_enable This option tells the software to keep a log of all file transfers as they occur.
		syslogd_enable If enabled, then any log output that would have gone to **/var/log/vsftpd.log** goes to the system log instead. Logging is done under the FTPD facility.

Table 17-2. Configuration Options for vsftpd (*cont.*)

So let's start a sample anonymous FTP session. But first we'll start the FTP service.

1. Start the FTP service. Type

```
[root@serverA ~]# service vsftpd  start
Starting vsftpd for vsftpd:                                    [  OK  ]
```

TIP If the **service** command is not available on your Linux distribution, you may be able to control the service by directly executing its run control script. For example, you may be able to restart **vsftpd** by issuing the command

```
[root@serverA ~]# /etc/init.d/vsftpd start
```

2. Launch the command-line FTP client program and connect to the local FTP server as an anonymous user. Type

```
[root@serverA ~]# ftp  localhost
Connected to localhost.localdomain.
220 (vsFTPd 2.0.1)
530 Please login with USER and PASS.
530 Please login with USER and PASS.
...<OUTPUT TRUNCATED>...
```

3. Enter the name of the anonymous FTP user when prompted; i.e., type **ftp**.

```
Name (localhost:root): ftp
331 Please specify the password.
```

4. Enter anything at all when prompted for the password.

```
Password:
230 Login successful.
Remote system type is UNIX.
Using binary mode to transfer files.
```

5. Use the **ls** (or **dir**) FTP command to perform a listing of the files in the current directory on the FTP server.

```
ftp> ls
227 Entering Passive Mode (127,0,0,1,41,244)
150 Here comes the directory listing.
drwxr-xr-x    2 0         0               4096 Oct 04  2004 pub
226 Directory send OK.
```

6. Use the **pwd** command to display your present working directory on the FTP server.

```
ftp> pwd
257 "/"
```

7. Using the **cd** command try to change to a directory outside of the allowed anonymous FTP directory; e.g., try to change your directory to the **/boot** directory of the local file system.

```
ftp> cd /boot
550 Failed to change directory.
```

8. Log out of the FTP server using the **bye** FTP command.

```
ftp> bye
221 Goodbye.
```

Next we'll try to connect to the FTP server using a local system account. In particular, we'll use the username "yyang," which was created in a previous chapter. So let's start a sample authenticated FTP session:

1. Launch the command-line **ftp** client program again. Type

```
[root@serverA ~]# ftp localhost
Connected to localhost.localdomain.
220 (vsFTPd 2.0.1)
530 Please login with USER and PASS.
530 Please login with USER and PASS.
KERBEROS_V4 rejected as an authentication type
```

2. Enter **yyang** as the FTP user when prompted.

```
Name (localhost:root): yyang
```

3. You must enter the password for the user yyang when prompted.

```
331 Please specify the password.
Password:
230 Login successful.
Remote system type is UNIX.
Using binary mode to transfer files.
```

4. Use the **pwd** command to display your present working directory on the FTP server. You will notice that the directory shown is the home directory for the user yyang.

```
ftp> pwd
257 "/home/yyang"
```

5. Using the **cd** command try to change to a directory outside of yyang's FTP home directory; e.g., try to change your directory to the **/boot** directory of the local file system.

```
ftp> cd /boot
250 Directory successfully changed.
```

6. Log out of the FTP server using the **bye** FTP command.

```
ftp> bye
221 Goodbye.
```

As demonstrated by these sample FTP sessions, the default **vsftpd** configuration on our sample Fedora Core system allows these things:

▼ **Anonymous FTP access** This means that any user from anywhere can log in to the server using the username ftp (or anonymous) with anything at all for a password.

▲ **Local user logins** This means that all valid users on the local system, with entries in the user database (the **/etc/passwd** file) are allowed to log in to the FTP server, using their normal usernames and normal passwords.

Customizing the FTP Server

The default out-of-the-box behavior of **vsftpd** is probably not what you want for your production FTP server. So in this section we will walk through the process of customizing some of the FTP server's options to suit certain scenarios.

Setting Up an Anonymous-Only FTP Server

First we'll set up our FTP server so that it does *not* allow access to users that have regular user accounts on the system. This type of FTP server is useful for large sites that have files that they want to make available to the general public via FTP. In such a scenario, it is of course impractical to create an account for every single user, when users can potentially number into the thousands.

Fortunately for us, **vsftpd** is ready to serve as an anonymous FTP server out of the box. But we'll examine the configuration options in the **vsftpd.conf** file that ensure this and also disable the options that are not required.

With any text editor of your choice, open up the **/etc/vsftpd/vsftpd.conf** file for editing. Look through the file and make sure that at a minimum the directives listed next are present (if the directives are present but commented out, then you might need to remove the comment symbol [#] or change the value of the option):

```
listen=YES
xferlog_enable=YES
anonymous_enable=YES
local_enable=NO
write_enable=NO
```

You will find that the options in the preceding listing are sufficient to enable your anonymous-only FTP server, and so you may choose to overwrite the existing **/etc/vsftpd/vsftpd.conf** file and enter just the options shown. This will help keep the configuration file simple and uncluttered.

TIP Virtually all Linux systems come preconfigured with a user called "ftp." This account is supposed to be a non-privileged system account and is especially used for anonymous FTP type access. You will need this account to exist on your system in order for anonymous FTP to work. To confirm the account exists use the `getent` utility. Type

```
[root@serverA ~]# getent passwd ftp
ftp:x:14:50:FTP User:/var/ftp:/sbin/nologin
```

If you don't get output similar to this, you can quickly create the FTP system account with the `useradd` command. To create a suitable "ftp" user, type

```
[root@serverA ~]# useradd -c "FTP User" -d /var/ftp -r -s /sbin/nologin ftp
```

If you had to make any modifications to the **/etc/vsftpd/vsftpd.conf** file, you need to restart the **vsftpd** service. Type

```
[root@serverA ~]# service vsftpd  restart
```

If the **service** command is not available on your Linux distribution, you may be able to control the service by directly executing its run control script. For example, you may be able to restart **vsftpd** by issuing the command

```
[root@serverA ~]# /etc/init.d/vsftpd  restart
```

Setting Up an FTP Server with Virtual Users

Virtual users are users that do not actually exist; i.e., these users do not have any privileges or functions on the system besides those for which they were created. This type of FTP setup serves as a midway point between enabling users with local system accounts access to the FTP server and enabling only anonymous users. If there is no way to guarantee the security of the network connection from the user end (FTP client) to the server end (FTP server), it will be foolhardy to allow users with local system accounts to log in to the FTP server. This is because the FTP transaction between both ends usually occurs in plain text. This is of course only relevant if the server contains any data of value to its owners!

The use of virtual users will allow a site to serve content that should be accessible to untrusted users but still make the FTP service accessible to the general public. In the event that the credentials of the virtual user(s) ever become compromised, one can at least rest assured that only very minimal damage can occur.

TIP It is also possible to set up **vsftpd** to encrypt all the communication between itself and any FTP clients by using SSL. This is quite easy to set up, but the caveat is that the clients' FTP application must also support this sort of communication—and unfortunately, not very many FTP client programs have this support. If security is a serious concern, you may want to consider using OpenSSH's **sftp** program instead—for simple file transfers.

In this section we are going to create two sample virtual users named "ftp-user1" and "ftp-user2." These users will not exist in any form in the system's user database (the **/etc/passwd** file). These steps detail the process:

1. First we'll create a plain text file that will contain the username and password combinations of the virtual users. Each username with its associated password will be on alternating lines in the file. For example, for the user ftp-user1 the password will be "user1," and for the user ftp-user2 the password will be "user2." We'll name the file **plain_vsftpd.txt**. Use any text editor of your choice to create the file. Here we use **vi**:

   ```
   [root@serverA ~]# vi plain_vsftpd.txt
   ```

2. Enter this text into the file:

   ```
   ftp-user1
   user1
   ftp-user2
   user2
   ```

3. Save the changes to the file and exit the text editor.

4. Convert the plain text file that was created in Step 2 into a Berkeley DB format (db) that can used with the pam_userdb.so library. The output will be saved in a file called **hash_vsftpd.db** stored under the **/etc** directory. Type

```
[root@serverA ~]# db_load  -T  -t  hash  -f plain_vsftpd.txt
/etc/hash_vsftpd.db
```

NOTE   You need to have the **db4-utils** package installed in order to have the **db_load** program. You can quickly install it using Yum with the command `yum install db4-utils`. Or look for it on the installation media.

5. Restrict access to the virtual users database file by giving it more restrictive permissions. This will ensure that it can not be read by any casual user on the system. Type

```
[root@serverA ~]# chmod    600    /etc/hash_vsftpd.db
```

6. Next we need to create a PAM file that the FTP service will use as the new virtual users database file. We'll name the file **virtual-ftp** and save it under the **/etc/pam.d/** directory. Use any text editor to create the file:

```
[root@serverA ~]# vi /etc/pam.d/virtual-ftp
```

7. Enter this text into the file:

```
auth required /lib/security/pam_userdb.so db=/etc/hash_vsftpd
account required /lib/security/pam_userdb.so db=/etc/hash_vsftpd
```

These entries tell the PAM system to authenticate users using the new database stored in the **hash_vsftpd.db** file.

8. Save the changes to the file into a file named **virtual-ftp** under the **/etc/pam.d/** directory.

9. Let's create a home environment for our virtual FTP users. We'll cheat and use the existing directory structure of the FTP server to create a subfolder that will store the files that we want the virtual users to be able to access. Type

```
[root@serverA ~]# mkdir   -p   /var/ftp/private
```

TIP   We cheated in Step 9 so that we won't have to go through the process of creating a guest FTP user that the virtual users will eventually map to, and also to avoid having to worry about permission issues, since the system already has an FTP system account that we can safely leverage off. Look for the **guest_username** directive under the **vsftpd.conf** man page for further information (`man vsftpd.conf`).

10. Now we'll create our custom **vsftpd.conf** file that will enable the entire setup. With any text editor of your choice, open the **/etc/vsftpd/vsftpd.conf** file for editing. Look through the file and make sure that at a minimum the directives listed next are present (if the directives are present but commented out, then you may

need to remove the comment sign or change the value of the option). Comments have been added to explain the less-obvious directives.

```
listen=YES
#We do NOT want to allow users to login anonymously
anonymous_enable=NO
xferlog_enable=YES
#This is for the PAM service that we created that was named virtual-ftp
pam_service_name=virtual-ftp
#Enable the use of the /etc/vsftpd.user_list file
userlist_enable=YES
#Do NOT deny access to users specified in the /etc/vsftpd.user_list file
userlist_deny=NO
userlist_file=/etc/vsftpd.user_list
tcp_wrappers=YES
local_enable=YES
#This activates virtual users.
guest_enable=YES
#Map all the virtual users to the real user called "ftp"
guest_username=ftp
#Make all virtual users root ftp directory on the server to be /var/ftp/private/
local_root=/var/ftp/private/
```

TIP If you choose not to edit the existing configuration file and create one from scratch, you will find that the options that follow will serve our purpose with nothing additional needed. The vsftpd software will simply assume its built-in defaults for any option that we didn't explicitly specify in the configuration file! You can, of course, leave out all the commented lines to save yourself the typing.

11. We'll need to create (or edit) the **/etc/vsftpd.user_list** file that was referenced in the configuration in Step 10. To create the entry for the first virtual user, type

    ```
    [root@serverA ~]# echo ftp-user1 > /etc/vsftpd.user_list
    ```

12. To create the entry for the second virtual user, type

    ```
    [root@serverA ~]# echo ftp-user2 >> /etc/vsftpd.user_list
    ```

13. We are ready to fire up or restart the FTP server now. Type

    ```
    [root@serverA ~]# service vsftpd restart
    ```

14. We will next verify that the FTP server is behaving the way we want it to behave by connecting to it as one of the virtual FTP users. Connect to the server as ftp-user1 (remember that the FTP password for that user is "user1").

    ```
    [root@serverA ~]# ftp localhost
    Connected to localhost.localdomain.
    220 (vsFTPd 2.0.1)
    ...<OUTPUT TRUNCATED>...
    Name (localhost:root): ftp-user1
    331 Please specify the password.
    ```

```
Password:
230 Login successful.
Remote system type is UNIX.
Using binary mode to transfer files.
ftp> ls -l
227 Entering Passive Mode (127,0,0,1,51,81)
150 Here comes the directory listing.
226 Directory send OK.
ftp> pwd
257 "/"
ftp> cd /boot
550 Failed to change directory.
ftp> bye
221 Goodbye.
```

15. We'll also test to make sure that anonymous users cannot log in to the server.

```
[root@serverA ~]# ftp localhost
Connected to localhost.localdomain.
...<OUTPUT TRUNCATED>...
Name (localhost:root): ftp
530 Permission denied.
Login failed.
ftp> bye
221 Goodbye.
```

16. We'll finally verify that local users (e.g., the user Ying Yang) cannot log in to the server.

```
[root@serverA ~]# ftp localhost
Connected to localhost.localdomain.
...<OUTPUT TRUNCATED>...
Name (localhost:root): yyang
530 Permission denied.
Login failed.
ftp> bye
221 Goodbye.
```

SUMMARY

The Very Secure FTP daemon is a powerful FTP server offering all of the features one would need for running a commercial FTP server in a secure manner. In this chapter, we discussed the process of compiling, installing, and configuring the vsftpd server from source and from binary RPM. Specifically, we covered

▼ Some important and often-used configuration options for vsftpd

■ Details about the FTP protocol and its effects on firewalls

■ Setting up anonymous FTP servers

▲ Setting up an FTP server that allows the use of virtual users

This information is enough to keep your FTP server humming for quite a while. Of course, like any printed media about software, this text will age, and the information will slowly but surely become obsolete. Please be sure to visit the vsftpd Web site from time to time to learn about not only the latest developments but also the latest documentation.

CHAPTER 18

Setting Up Your Web Server Using Apache

I n this chapter, we discuss the process of installing and configuring the *Apache HTTP server* (http://www.apache.org) on your Linux server. Apache is free software released under the Apache License. According to one of the most respected statistics on the Net (published by Netcraft Ltd., http://www.netcraft.co.uk), Apache has a market share of more than 50%. This level of respect from the Internet community comes from the following benefits and advantages provided by the Apache server software:

▼   It is stable.

■   Several major Web sites, including Amazon.com and IBM, are using it.

■   The entire program and related components are open source.

■   It works on a large number of platforms (all popular variants of UNIX, some of the not-so-popular variants of UNIX, and even Windows 2000/NT/2003).

■   It is extremely flexible.

▲   It has proved to be secure.

Before we get into the steps necessary to configure Apache, we will review some of the fundamentals of the HTTP protocol as well as some of the internals of Apache, such as its process ownership model. This information will help you understand why Apache is set up to work the way it does.

UNDERSTANDING THE HTTP PROTOCOL

HTTP (the Hypertext Transfer Protocol) is, of course, a significant portion of the foundation for the World Wide Web, and Apache is the server implementation of the HTTP protocol. Browsers such as Mozilla, Firefox, and Microsoft Internet Explorer are client implementations of HTTP.

As of this writing, the HTTP protocol is at version 1.1 and is documented in RFC 2616 (for details, go to http://www.ietf.org/rfc/rfc2616.txt).

Headers

When a Web client connects to a Web server, the client's default method of making this connection is to contact the server's TCP port 80. Once connected, the Web server says nothing; it's up to the client to issue HTTP-compliant commands for its requests to the server. Along with each command comes a *request header* including information about the client. For example, when using Mozilla under Linux as a client, a Web server might receive the following information from a client:

```
GET / HTTP/1.0
Connection: Keep-Alive
User-Agent: Mozilla/60.06 [en] (X11; U; Linux 2.6.12 i686)
Host: localhost:80
```

```
Accept: image/gif, image/x-xbitmap, image/jpeg, image/pjpeg,
image/png, /
Accept-Encoding: gzip
Accept-Language: en
Accept-Charset: iso-8859-1,*,utf-8
```

The first line contains the HTTP **GET** command, which asks the server to fetch a file. The remainder of the information makes up the header, which tells the server about the client, the kind of file formats the client will accept, and so forth. Many servers use this information to determine what can and cannot be sent to the client, as well as for logging purposes.

Along with the request header, additional headers may be sent. For example, when a client uses a hyperlink to get to the server site, a header entry showing the client's originating site will also appear in the header.

When it receives a blank line, the server knows a request header is complete. Once the request header is received, it responds with the actual requested content, prefixed by a server header. The server header tells the client information about the server, the amount of data the client is about to receive, and the type of data coming in. For example, the request header just shown, when sent to an HTTP server, results in the following server response header:

```
HTTP/1.1 200 OK
Date: Thu, 02 Jun 2005 14:03:31 GMT
Server: Apache/2.0.52 (Fedora)
Last-Modified: Thu, 02 Jun 2007 11:41:32 GMT
ETag: "3f04-1f-b80bf300"
Accept-Ranges: bytes
Content-Length: 31
Connection: close
Content-Type: text/html; charset=UTF-8
```

A blank line and then the actual content of the transmission follow the response header.

Ports

The default port for HTTP requests is port 80, but you can also configure a Web server to use a different (arbitrarily chosen) port that is not in use by another service. This allows sites to run multiple Web servers on the same host, each server on a different port. Some sites use this arrangement for multiple configurations of their Web servers, to support various types of client requests.

When a site runs a Web server on a nonstandard port, you can see that port number in the site's URL. For example, the address http://www.redhat.com with an added port number would read http://www.redhat.com:80.

TIP Don't make the mistake of going for "security through obscurity." If your server is on a nonstandard port, that doesn't guarantee that Internet troublemakers won't find your site. Because of the automated nature of tools used to attack a site, it takes fewer than 100 lines of C code to scan a server and find which ports are running Web servers. Using a nonstandard port does not keep your site secure.

Process Ownership and Security

As discussed in previous chapters, running a Web server under UNIX forces you to deal with the Linux (and UNIX in general) model. In terms of permissions, that means each process has an owner, and that owner has limited rights on the system.

Whenever a program (process) is started, it inherits the permissions of its parent process. For example, if you're logged in as root, the shell in which you're doing all your work has all the same rights as the root user. In addition, any process you start from this shell will inherit all the permissions of that root. Processes may give up rights, but they cannot gain rights.

NOTE There is an exception to the Linux inheritance principle. Programs configured with the SetUID bit do not inherit rights from their parent process but rather start with the rights specified by the owner of the file itself. For example, the file containing the program **su** (**/bin/su**) is owned by root and has the SetUID bit set. If the user yyang runs the program **su**, that program doesn't inherit the rights of yyang but instead will start with the rights of the superuser (root).

How Apache Processes Ownership

To do network setups, the Apache HTTP server must start with root permissions. Specifically, it needs to bind itself to port 80 so that it can listen for requests and accept connections. Once it does this, Apache can give up its rights and run as a nonroot user, as specified in its configuration files. By default, this is the user *nobody*.

As user nobody, Apache can read only the files that user nobody has permission to read. Thus, if a file's permissions are set so that they are readable only by the file's owner, the owner must be nobody. For any file that you want available to user nobody, set that file's permission to world readable:

```
chmod a+r filename
```

where **filename** is the name of the file.

TIP Most popular Linux distributions create a specific user for Apache to run as, and this user will automatically get added or created in the system user database if it does not already exist. In SuSE Linux, the default user is "www," and in Fedora Core and RHEL this user is named "apache."

Security is especially important for sites that use CGI scripts. By limiting the permissions of the Web server, you decrease the likelihood that someone can send a malicious request to the server. The server processes and corresponding CGI scripts can break only what they can access. As user nobody, the scripts and processes don't have access to the same key files that root can access. (Remember that root can access everything, no matter what the permissions.)

NOTE In the event that you decide to allow CGI scripts on your server, pay strict attention to how they are written. Be sure it isn't possible for input coming in over the network to make the CGI script do something it shouldn't. Although there are no statistics on this, most successful attacks on sites are possible because of improperly configured Web servers and/or poorly written CGI scripts.

INSTALLING THE APACHE HTTP SERVER

Most modern Linux distributions come with the binary package for the Apache HTTP server software in RPM format, so installing the software is usually as simple as using the **rpm** command. This section walks you through the process of obtaining and installing the program via RPM. Mention is also made of installing the software from source code if you choose to go that route. The actual configuration of the server covered in later sections applies to both classes of installation (from source or from RPM).

There are several ways to obtain the Apache RPM. Here are some of them:

▼ Download the Apache RPM for your operating system from your distribution's software repository. For Fedora Core, you can obtain a copy of the program from http://download.fedora.redhat.com/pub/fedora/linux/core/4/i386/os/Fedora/RPMS/httpd-2*.rpm.

■ You can install from the install media, from the **/Fedora/RPMS/** directory on the media.

▲ You can pull down and install the program directly from a repository using the Yum program. This is perhaps the quickest method if you have a working connection to the Internet. And this is what we'll do here.

To use Yum to install the program, type

```
[root@serverA ~]# yum install httpd
```

Type **y** when prompted to confirm that you want to install the program and any of its dependencies.

To confirm that the software is indeed installed, type

```
[root@serverA ~]# rpm -q httpd
httpd-2.0.*
```

And that's it! You now have Apache installed.

Installing Apache from Source

Just in case you are not happy with the built-in defaults that an RPM package forces you to live with and you want to build your Web server software from scratch, you can always obtain the latest stable version of the program directly from the apache.org Web site. The procedure for building from source is discussed here.

We'll download the latest program source into the **/usr/local/src/** directory from the apache.org Web site. You can use the **wget** program to do this. Type

```
[root@serverA src]# wget  http://www.apache.org/dist/httpd/httpd-2.0.54.tar.gz
```

Extract the tar archive. And then change to the directory that is created during the extraction.

```
[root@serverA src]# tar -xvzf httpd-2.0.54.tar.gz
[root@serverA src]# cd  httpd-2.0.54/
```

Assuming we want the Web server program to be installed under the **/usr/local/httpd/** directory, we'll run the **configure** script with the proper **prefix** option.

```
[root@serverA httpd-2.0.54]# ./configure  --prefix=/usr/local/httpd
```

Run **make**.

```
[root@serverA httpd-2.0.54]# make
```

Create the program's working directory (i.e., **/usr/local/httpd/**) and then run **make install**.

```
[root@serverA httpd-2.0.54]# make install
```

Once the **install** command completes successfully, a directory structure will be created under **/usr/local/httpd/** that will contain the binaries, the configuration files, the log files, etc., for the Web server.

Apache Modules

Part of what makes Apache so powerful and flexible is that its design allows extensions through modules. Apache comes with many modules by default and automatically includes them in the default installation.

If you can imagine "it," you can be almost certain that somebody has probably already written a module for "it" for the Apache Web server. The Apache module API is well documented, so if you are so inclined (and know how to), you can probably write your own module for Apache to provide a functionality that you want.

To give you some idea of what kinds of things people are doing with modules, visit http://modules.apache.org. There you will find information on how to extend Apache's capabilities using modules. Some common Apache modules are

▼ **mod_cgi**   Allows the execution of CGI scripts on the Web server

■ **mod_perl**   Used to incorporate a Perl interpreter into the Apache Web server

■ **mod_aspdotnet**   Provides an ASP.NET host interface to Microsoft's ASP.NET engine

■ **mod_authz_ldap**   Provides support for authenticating users of the Apache HTTP server against an LDAP database

■ **mod_ssl**   Provides strong cryptography for the Apache Web server via the Secure Sockets Layer (SSL) and Transport Layer Security (TLS) protocols

■ **mod_ftpd**   Allows Apache to accept FTP connections

▲ **mod_userdir**   Allows user content to be served from user-specific directories on the Web server via HTTP

If you know the name of a particular module that you want (and if the module is popular enough), you might find that the module has already been packaged in an RPM format and so you can install it using the usual RPM methods. For example, if you want to include the SSL module (**mod_ssl**) in your Web server setup, on a Fedora Core system you can issue this Yum command to automatically download and install the module for you:

```
[root@serverA ~]# yum install mod_ssl
```

Alternatively, you can go to the Apache modules project Web site and search for, download, compile, and install the module that you want.

TIP   Make sure nobody is there! If you build Apache from source, the sample configuration file (**httpd.conf**) expects that the Web server will run as the user nobody. Although that user exists on almost all Linux distributions, if something is broken along the way, you may want to check the user database (**/etc/passwd**) to make sure that the user nobody does indeed exist.

STARTING UP AND SHUTTING DOWN APACHE

One of the nicest features of Linux is the ability to start up and shut down system services without needing to reboot. This is easy to do in the Apache server.

To start Apache on a Fedora Core system or any other Red Hat-like system, use this command:

```
[root@serverA ~]# service httpd start
```

To shut down Apache, enter this command:

```
[root@serverA ~]# service httpd stop
```

After making a configuration change to the Web server that requires you to restart Apache, type

```
[root@serverA ~]# service httpd restart
```

TIP   On a system running SuSE Linux, the commands to start and stop the Web server, respectively, are

```
[serverA ~]# rcapache2 start
```

and

```
[serverA ~]# rcapache2 stop
```

Starting Apache at Boot Time

After installing the Web server, if you find that the Web service is a service that you want the system to provide at all times, you will need to configure the system to automatically start the service for you between system reboots. It is very easy to forget to do this on a system that has been running for a long time without requiring any reboots, because if you ever had to shut down the system due to an unrelated issue, you might be baffled as to why the Web server that has been running perfectly without incident failed to start up after starting the box. So it is good practice to take care of this during the early stages of configuring the service.

Most Linux flavors have the **chkconfig** utility available, which can be used for controlling which system services start up at what runlevels.

To view the runlevels the Web server is configured to start up in, type

```
[root@serverA ~]# chkconfig  --list httpd
httpd              0:off   1:off   2:off   3:off   4:off   5:off   6:off
```

This output shows that the Web server is not configured to start up in any runlevel in its out-of-the-box state. To change this and make Apache start up automatically in runlevels 2, 3, 4, and 5, type

```
[root@serverA ~]# chkconfig  httpd  on
```

NOTE   Just in case you are working with an Apache version that you installed from source, you should be aware that the **chkconfig** utility will not know about the startup and shutdown scripts for your Web server unless you explicitly tell the utility about it. And as such, you'll have to resort to some other tricks to configure the host system to automatically bring up the Web server during system reboots. You may easily grab an existing startup script from another working system (usually from the **/etc/init.d/** directory) and modify it to reflect correct paths (e.g., **/usr/local/httpd/**) for your custom setup. Existing scripts are likely to be called **httpd** or **apache**.

TESTING YOUR INSTALLATION

You can perform a quick test of your Apache installation using its default home page. To do this, first confirm that the Web server is up and running using the following command:

```
[root@serverA ~]# service httpd status
httpd (pid 26084 26080 26079 26078 26077 26074) is running....
```

On our sample Fedora Core system, Apache comes with a default page that gets served to visitors in the absence of a default home page (e.g., **index.html** or **index.htm**). The file that gets displayed to visitors when there is no default home page is **/var/www/ error/noindex.html**.

> **TIP**   If you are working with a version of Apache that you built from source, the working directory from which Web pages are served is **<PREFIX>/htdocs**. For example, if your installation prefix is **/usr/local/httpd/**, then Web pages will by default be under **/usr/local/httpd/htdocs/**.

To find out if your Apache installation went smoothly, start a Web browser and tell it to visit the Web site on your machine. To do this, simply type **http://localhost** in the address bar of your Web browser. You should see a page stating something to the effect that "your Apache HTTP server is working properly at your site." If you don't, retrace your Apache installation steps and make sure you didn't encounter any errors in the process.

CONFIGURING APACHE

Apache supports a rich set of configuration options that are sensible and easy to follow. This makes it a simple task to set up the Web server in various configurations.

This section walks through a basic configuration. The default configuration is actually quite good and (believe it or not) works right out of the box, so if the default is acceptable to you, simply start creating your HTML documents! Apache allows several common customizations. After we step through creating a simple Web page, we'll show how you can make those common customizations in the Apache configuration files.

Creating a Simple Root-Level Page

If you like, you can start adding files to Apache right away in the **/var/www/html** directory for top-level pages (for a source install, the directory would be **/usr/local/httpd/htdocs**). Any files placed in that directory must be world readable.

As mentioned earlier, Apache's default Web page is **index.html**. Let's take a closer look at creating and changing the default home page so that it reads "Welcome to serverA.example.org." Here are the commands:

```
[root@serverA ~]# cd /var/www/html/
[root@serverA html]# echo "Welcome to serverA.example.org" >>  index.html
[root@serverA html]# chmod 644 index.html
```

You could also use an editor such as **vi** or **pico** to edit the **index.html** file and make it more interesting.

Apache Configuration Files

The configuration files for Apache are located in the **/etc/httpd/conf/** directory on a Fedora Core or RHEL system, and for our sample source install, the path will be **/usr/local/httpd/conf/**. The main configuration file is named **httpd.conf**.

The best way to learn more about the configuration files is to read the **httpd.conf** file. The default configuration file is heavily commented, explaining each entry, its role, and the parameters you can set.

Common Configuration Options

The default configuration settings work just fine right out of the box and for basic needs may require no further modification. Nevertheless, site administrators may have need to customize their Web server/site further.

This section discusses some of the common directives or options that are used in Apache's configuration file.

ServerRoot

This is used for specifying the base directory for the Web server. On a Fedora and RHEL Linux systems, this value by default is the **/etc/httpd/** directory.

Syntax: `ServerRoot directory-path`

Listen

This is the port(s) on which the server listens for connection requests. It can also be used to specify the particular IP addresses over which the Web server accepts connections. The default value for this directive is 80 for nonsecure Web communications.

Syntax: `Listen [IP-address:]portnumber`

ServerName

This directive defines the host name and port that the server uses to identify itself. At many sites, servers fulfill multiple purposes. An intranet Web server that isn't getting heavy usage, for example, should probably share its usage allowance with another service. In such a situation, a computer name such as "www" (FQDN=www .example.org) wouldn't be a good choice, because it suggests that the machine has only one purpose.

It's better to give a server a neutral name and then establish DNS CNAME entries or multiple host name entries in the **/etc/hosts** file. In other words, you can give the system several names for accessing the server, but it needs to know only about its real name. Consider a server whose host name is dioxin.eng.example.org that is to be a Web server as well. You might be thinking of giving it the host name alias www .sales.example.org. However, since dioxin will know itself only as dioxin, users who visit www.sales.example.org might be confused by seeing in their browsers that the server's real name is dioxin.

Apache provides a way to get around this through the use of the **ServerName** directive. This works by allowing you to specify what you want Apache to return as the host name of the Web server to Web clients or visitors.

Syntax: `ServerName` *`fully-qualified-domain-name`*`[`*`:port`*`]`

ServerAdmin

This is the e-mail address that the server includes in error messages sent to the client.

It's often a good idea, for a couple of reasons, to use an e-mail alias for a Web site's administrator. First, there may be more than one administrator. By using an alias, it's possible for the alias to expand out to a list of e-mail addresses. Second, if the current administrator leaves, you don't want to have to make the rounds of all those Web pages and change the name of the site administrator.

Syntax: `ServerAdmin` *`e-mail_address`*

DocumentRoot

This defines the primary directory on the Web server from which HTML files will be served to requesting clients. On most Linux systems the default value of this directive is **/var/www/html/**.

TIP   On a Web server that is expected to host plenty of Web content, the file system on which the directory specified by this directive resides should have a lot of space.

MaxClients

This sets a limit on the number of simultaneous requests that the Web server will service.

LoadModule

This is used for loading or adding other modules into Apache's running configuration. It adds the specified module to the list of active modules.

Syntax: `LoadModule` *`module filename`*

User

This specifies the user ID as which the Web server will answer requests. The server process will initially start off as the root user but will later downgrade its privileges to those of the user specified here. The user should only have just enough privileges to access files and directories that are intended to be visible to the outside world via the Web server. Also, the user should not be able to execute code that is not HTTP- or Web-related.

On a Fedora system, the value for this directive is automatically set to the user named "apache." In SuSE Linux, the value is set to the user called "www."

Syntax: `User unix_userid`

Group

This specifies the group name of the Apache HTTP server process. It is the group with which the server will respond to requests. The default value under the Fedora and RHEL flavors of Linux is "apache." In SuSE Linux, the value is set to the group "www."

Syntax: `Group unix_group`

Include

This directive allows Apache to specify and include other configuration files at runtime. It is mostly useful for organization purposes; you can, for example, elect to store all the configuration directives for different virtual domains in appropriately named files and Apache will automatically know to include them at runtime.

Syntax: `Include file_name_to_include_OR_path_to_directory_to_include_`

UserDir

This directive defines the subdirectory within each user's home directory, where users can place personal content that they want to make accessible via the Web server. This directory is usually named **public_html** and is usually stored under each user's home directory. This option is of course dependent on the availability of the **mod_userdir** module in the Web server setup.

A sample usage of this option in the **httpd.conf** file is

`UserDir    public_html`

ErrorLog

This defines the location where errors from the Web server will be logged to.

Syntax: `ErrorLog file_path|syslog[:facility]`

Example: `ErrorLog /var/log/httpd/error_log`

Quick How-To: Serving HTTP Content from User Directories

After enabling the **UserDir** option and assuming the user yyang wants to make some Web content available from within her home directory via the Web server, following these steps will make this happen:

1. While logged in to the system as the user yyang, create the **public_html** folder.

   ```
   [yyang@serverA ~]# mkdir ~/public_html
   ```

2. Set the proper permissions for the parent folder.

   ```
   [yyang@serverA ~]# chmod a+x .
   ```

3. Set the proper permissions for the **public_html** folder.

   ```
   [yyang@serverA ~]# chmod a+x public_html
   ```

4. Create a sample page named **index.html** under the **public_html** folder.

   ```
   [yyang@serverA ~]# echo "Ying Yang's Home Page" >> ~/public_html/index.html
   ```

As a result of these commands, files placed in the **public_html** directory for a particular user and set to world readable will be on the Web via the Web server.

To access the contents of that folder via HTTP, you would need to point a Web browser to this URL:

   http://<YOUR_HOST_NAME>/~<USERNAME>

where *YOUR_HOST_NAME* is the Web server's fully qualified domain name or IP address. And if you are sitting directly on the Web server itself, you can simply replace that variable with **localhost**.

For the example shown here for the user yyang, the exact URL will be http://localhost/~yyang.

> **TIP** On a Fedora Core system with the SELinux subsystem enabled, you may have to do a little more to get the **UserDir** directive working. This is because of the default security contexts of the files stored under each user's home directory. The context by default is **user_home_t**. For this functionality to work properly, you will have to change the context of all files under ~/**username**/**public_html**/ to **httpd_sys_content_t**. This allows Apache to read the files under the **public_html** directory. The command to this is
>
> ```
> [yyang@serverA ~]$ chcon -Rt httpd_sys_content_t public_html/
> ```

LogLevel

This option sets the level of verbosity for the messages sent to the error logs. Acceptable log levels are emerg, alert, crit, error, warn, notice, info, and debug. The default log level is "warn."

Syntax: `LogLevel level`

Alias

The **Alias** directive allows documents (Web content) to be stored in any other location on the file system that is different from the location specified by the **DocumentRoot** directive. It also allows you to create abbreviations (or aliases) for path names that might otherwise be very long.

Syntax: `Alias URL_path actual_file_or_directory_path`

ScriptAlias

The **ScriptAlias** option specifies a target directory or file as containing CGI scripts that are meant to be processed by the CGI module (**mod_cgi**).

Syntax: `ScriptAlias URL-path actual_file-path_OR_directory-path`

Example: `ScriptAlias /cgi-bin/ "/var/www/cgi-bin/"`

VirtualHost

One of the most used features of Apache is its ability to support virtual hosts. It makes it possible for a single Web server to host multiple Web sites as if each site had its own dedicated hardware. It works by allowing the Web server to provide different, autonomous content, according to which host name, port number, or IP address is being requested by the client. This is accomplished by the HTTP 1.1 protocol, which specifies the desired site in the HTTP header rather than relying on the server to learn what site to fetch from its IP address.

This directive is actually made up of two tags: an opening <VirtualHost> tag and a closing </VirtualHost> tag. It is used to specify the options that pertain to a particular virtual host. Most of the directives that we discussed previously are valid here too.

```
Syntax: <VirtualHost ip_address_OR_hostname[:port] >
        Options
        </VirtualHost>
```

Suppose, for example, that we want to set up a virtual host configuration for a host named www.another-example.org. To do this, we can create a **VirtualHost** entry in the **httpd.conf** file (or use the **Include** directive to specify a separate file) like this one:

```
<VirtualHost www.another-example.org>
  ServerAdmin webmaster@another-example.org
  DocumentRoot /www/docs/another-example.org
```

```
      ServerName www.another-example.org
      ErrorLog logs/another-example.org-error_log
 </VirtualHost>
```

Don't forget that it is not enough to configure a virtual host using Apache's **VirtualHost** directive—the value of the **ServerName** option in the **VirtualHost** container must be a name that is resolvable via DNS (or any other means) to the Web server machine.

> **NOTE**   Apache's options/directives are too numerous to be covered in this section. But the software comes with its own extensive online manual, which is written in HTML, so that you can access it in a browser. If you installed the software via RPM, you might find that documentation for Apache has been packaged into a separate RPM binary and as a result you will need to install the proper package (e.g., httpd-manual) to have access to it. If you downloaded and built the software from source code, you will find the documentation in the **manual** directory of your installation prefix (e.g., **/usr/local/httpd/manual**). Apache's documentation is also available online at the project's Web site, http://httpd.apache.org/docs-2.0.

TROUBLESHOOTING APACHE

The process of changing configurations (or even the initial installation) can sometimes not work as smoothly as you'd like. Thankfully, Apache does an excellent job at reporting in its error log file why it failed or what is failing.

The error log file is located in your **logs** directory. If you are running a stock Fedora Core or RHEL-type installation, this is in the **/var/log/httpd/** directory. If you installed Apache yourself using the installation method discussed earlier in this chapter, the logs are in the **/usr/local/httpd/logs/** directory. In these directories, you will find two files: **access_log** and **error_log**.

The **access_log** file is simply that—a log of which files have been accessed by people visiting your Web site(s). It contains information about whether the transfer completed successfully, where the request originated (IP address), how much data was transferred, and what time the transfer occurred. This is a very powerful way of determining the usage of your site.

The **error_log** file contains all of the errors that occur in Apache. Note that not all errors that occur are fatal—some are simply problems with a client connection from which Apache can automatically recover and continue operation. However, if you started Apache but still cannot visit your Web site, then take a look at this log file to see why Apache may not be responding. The easiest way to see the most recent error messages is by using the **tail** command, like so:

```
[root@serverA html]# tail -n 10 /var/log/httpd/error_log
```

If you need to see more log information than that, simply change the number 10 to the number of lines that you need to see. And if you would like to view the errors or logs in real time as they are being generated, you should use the **-f** option for the **tail** command.

This provides a very valuable debugging tool, because you can try things out with the server (such as requesting Web pages or restarting Apache) and view the results of your experiments in a separate virtual terminal window. The tail command with the -f switch is shown here:

```
[root@serverA html]# tail -f /var/log/httpd/error_log
```

This command will constantly tail the logs until you terminate the program (using CTRL-C).

SUMMARY

In this chapter, we covered the process of setting up your own Web server using Apache from the ground up. This chapter by itself is enough to get you going with a top-level page and a basic configuration.

It is highly recommended that you take some time to page through the Apache manual. It is well written, concise, and flexible enough that you can set up just about any configuration imaginable.

In addition to the manual documentation, several good books about Apache have been written. Ben Laurie's and Peter Laurie's *Apache: The Definitive Guide, Third Edition* (O'Reilly, 2002) covers the details of Apache very well. The text focuses on Apache and Apache only, so you don't have to wade through hundreds of pages to find what you need.

CHAPTER 19

SMTP

The Simple Mail Transfer Protocol (SMTP) is the de facto standard for mail transport across the Internet. Anyone who wants to have a mail server capable of sending and receiving mail across the Internet must be able to support it. Many internal networks have also taken to using SMTP for their private mail services because of its platform independence and availability across all popular operating systems. In this chapter, we'll first discuss the mechanics of SMTP as a protocol and its relationship to other mail-related protocols, such as POP and IMAP. Then we will go over the Postfix SMTP server, one of the easier and more secure SMTP servers out there.

UNDERSTANDING SMTP

The SMTP protocol defines the method by which mail is sent from one host to another. That's it. It does not define how the mail should be stored. It does not define how the mail should be displayed to the recipient.

SMTP's strength is its simplicity, and that is due to the dynamic nature of networks during the early 1980s. (The SMTP protocol was originally defined in 1982.) People were linking networks together with everything short of bubble gum and glue. SMTP was the first mail standard that was independent of the transport mechanism. This meant people using TCP/IP networks could use the same format to send a message as someone using two cans and a string.

SMTP is also independent of operating systems, which means each system can use its own style of storing mail without worrying about how the sender of a message stores his mail. You can draw parallels to how the phone system works: each phone service provider has its own independent accounting system. However, they all have agreed upon a standard way to link their networks together so that calls can go from one network to another transparently.

Rudimentary SMTP Details

Ever had a "friend" who sent you an e-mail on behalf of some government agency informing you that you owe taxes from the previous year, plus additional penalties? Somehow a message like this ends up in a lot of people's mailboxes around April Fool's Day. We're going to show you how they did it, and what's even more fun, how you can do it yourself. (Not that we would advocate such behavior, of course.)

The purpose of this example is to show how the SMTP protocol sends a message from one host to another. After all, more important than learning how to forge an e-mail is learning how to troubleshoot mail-related problems. So in this example, you are acting as the sending host, and whichever machine you connect to is the receiving host.

The SMTP protocol requires only that a host be able to send straight ASCII text to another host. Typically, this is done by contacting the SMTP port (port 25) on a mail server. You can do this using the Telnet program. For example,

```
[root@hostA /root]# telnet mailserver 25
```

where the host **mailserver** is the recipient's mail server. The 25 that follows
mailserver tells Telnet that you want to communicate with the server's port 25
rather than the normal port 23. (Port 23 is used for remote logins, and port 25 is for the
SMTP server.)

The mail server will respond with a greeting message such as this:

```
220 mail ESMTP Postfix
```

You are now communicating directly with the SMTP server.

Although there are many SMTP commands, the four worth noting are

▼   **HELO**

■   **MAIL FROM:**

■   **RCPT TO:**

▲   **DATA**

The **HELO** command is used when a client introduces itself to the server. The parameter to **HELO** is the host name that is originating the connection. Of course, most mail
servers take this information with a grain of salt and double-check it themselves. For
example,

```
HELO super-duper-strong-coffee.com
```

If you aren't coming from the super-duper-strong-coffee.com domain, many mail
servers will respond by telling you that they know your real IP address, but they will not
stop the connection from continuing. (Some mail servers include a comment asking why
you didn't use a truthful **HELO** statement.)

The **MAIL FROM:** command requires the parameter of the sender's e-mail address.
This tells the mail server the e-mail's origin. For example,

```
MAIL FROM: dilbert@domain.com
```

means the message is from dilbert@domain.com.

The **RCPT TO:** command also requires the parameter of an e-mail address. This
e-mail address is of the recipient of the e-mail. For example,

```
RCPT TO: pointy-hair-manager@domain.com
```

means the message is destined to pointy-hair-manager@domain.com.

Now that the server knows who the sender and recipient are, it needs to know what
message to send. This is done by using the **DATA** command. Once issued, the server will
expect the entire message with relevant header information followed by one empty line,

a period, and then another empty line. Continuing the example, dilbert@domain.com might want to send the following message to pointy-hair-manager@domain.com:

```
DATA
354 Enter mail, end with "." on a line by itself
From: Dilbert <dilbert@domain.com>
To: Pointy Hair Manager <pointy-hair-manager@domain.com>
Subject: On time and within budget.
Date: Sat, 1 Apr 2000 04:01:00 -0700 (PDT)

Just an fyi, boss. The project is not only on time, but it is within
budget too!

.
250 NAA28719 Message accepted for delivery
```

And that's all there is to it. To close the connection, enter the **QUIT** command.

This is the basic technique used by applications that send mail—except, of course, they usually use C code rather than Telnet, but the actual content sent between the client and the server remains the same.

Security Implications

Sendmail, the mail server a majority of Internet sites use, is the same package most Linux distributions use. Like any other server software, its internal structure and design are complex and require a considerable amount of care during development. In recent years, however, the developers of Sendmail have taken a very paranoid approach to their design to help alleviate these issues. The Postfix developers took it one step further and wrote the server from scratch with security in mind. Basically, they ship the package in a very tight security mode and leave it to us to loosen it up as much as we need to for our site. This means the responsibility falls to us of making sure we keep the software properly configured (and thus not vulnerable to attacks).

These are some issues to keep in mind when deploying any mail server:

▼ When an e-mail is sent to the server, what programs will it trigger?

■ Are those programs securely designed?

■ If they cannot be made secure, how can you limit their damage?

▲ Under what permissions do those programs run?

In Postfix's case, we need to back up and examine its architecture.

Mail service has three distinct components. The *mail user agent (MUA)* is what the user sees, such as the Eudora, Outlook, and Pine programs. An MUA is responsible only for reading mail and allowing users to compose mail. The *mail transfer agent (MTA)* handles the process of getting the mail from one site to another; Sendmail and Postfix are MTAs. Finally, the *mail delivery agent (MDA)* is what takes the message, once received at a site, and gets it to the appropriate user mailbox.

Many mail systems integrate these components. For example, Microsoft Exchange Server integrates the MTA and MDA functionalities into a single system. (If you consider the Outlook Web Access interface to Exchange Server, it is also an MUA.) Lotus Domino also works in a similar fashion. Postfix, on the other hand, works as an MTA only, passing the task of performing local mail delivery to another external program. This allows each operating system or site configuration to use its own custom tool if necessary (that is, to be able to use a special mailbox store mechanism).

In most straightforward configurations, sites prefer using the Procmail program to perform the actual mail delivery (MDA). This is because of its advanced filtering mechanism as well as its secure design from the ground up. Many older configurations have stayed with their default **/bin/mail** program to perform mail delivery. The security issues in using that particular program vary from operating system to operating system.

INSTALLING THE POSTFIX SERVER

In this section we will cover the installation of the Postfix mail server. We chose it for its ease of use, and because it was written from the ground up to be simpler than Sendmail. (The author of Postfix also argues that the simplicity has led to improved security.) Postfix can perform most of the things that the Sendmail program can do—in fact, the typical installation procedure for Postfix is to replace the Sendmail binaries completely.

In this section we install Postfix in one of two ways: either using the RPM method (recommended) or via source code.

Installing Postfix via RPM

To install Postfix via RPM, simply use the Yum tool as follows:

```
[root@hostA /root]# yum install postfix
```

This may take a few minutes as Yum checks for updates and downloads any software it needs in order to install Postfix.

Since Sendmail is the default mailer that gets installed for most distributions, you will need to disable it using the **chkconfig** command and then enable Postfix.

```
[root@hostA /root]# chkconfig --level 35 sendmail off
[root@hostA /root]# chkconfig --level 35 postfix on
```

Finally, we can flip the switch and actually start the Postfix process. With a default configuration, it won't do much, but it will confirm whether the installation worked as expected.

```
[root@hostA /root]# /etc/rc.d/init.d/sendmail stop
[root@hostA /root]# /etc/rc.d/init.d/postfix start
```

Installing Postfix from Source Code

Begin by downloading the Postfix source code from http://www.postfix.org. As of this writing, the latest version is postfix-2.2.4.tar.gz. Once you have the file downloaded, use the **tar** command to unpack the contents.

```
[root@hostA src]# tar -xvzf postfix-2.2.4.tar.gz
```

Once it is unpacked, change into the **postfix-2.2.4** directory and run the **make** command like so:

```
[root@hostA src]# cd postfix-2.2.4
[root@hostA postfix-2.2.4]# make
```

The complete compilation process will take a few minutes, but it should work without event.

TIP If the compile step fails with an error about being unable to find "db.h" or any other kind of "db" reference, there is a good chance your system does not have the Berkeley DB developer tools installed. While it is possible to compile the Berkeley DB tools yourself, it is not recommended, as Postfix will fail if the version of DB being used in Postfix is different than what other system libraries are using. To fix this, install the db4-devel package. This can be done using Yum as follows:

```
[root@hostA postfix-2.2.4]# yum install db4-devel
```

Since Postfix will replace your current Sendmail program, you'll want to make a backup of the Sendmail binaries. This can be done as follows:

```
[root@hostA postfix-2.2.4]# mv /usr/sbin/sendmail /usr/sbin/sendmail.OFF
[root@hostA postfix-2.2.4]# mv /usr/bin/newaliases /usr/bin/newaliases.OFF
[root@hostA postfix-2.2.4]# mv /usr/bin/mailq /usr/bin/mailq.OFF
[root@hostA postfix-2.2.4]# chmod 755 /usr/sbin/sendmail.OFF
[root@hostA postfix-2.2.4]# chmod 755 /usr/bin/newaliases.OFF
[root@hostA postfix-2.2.4]# chmod 755 /usr/bin/mailq.OFF
```

Now we need to create a user and a group under which Postfix will run. You may find that some distributions already have these accounts defined. If so, the process of adding a user will cause an error to happen. Simply ignore the error message.

```
[root@hostA postfix-2.2.4]# useradd -M -d /no/where -s /no/shell postfix
[root@hostA postfix-2.2.4]# groupadd -r postfix
[root@hostA postfix-2.2.4]# groupadd -r postdrop
```

We're now ready to do the make install step to install the actual software. Postfix includes an interactive script that prompts for values of where things should go. Stick to the defaults by simply pressing the ENTER key at each prompt.

```
[root@hostA postfix-2.2.4]# make install
```

With the binaries installed, it's time to disable Sendmail from the startup scripts. We can do that via the **chkconfig** command like so:

```
[root@hostA postfix-2.2.4]# chkconfig --level 35 sendmail off
```

The source version of Postfix includes a nice shell script that handles the startup and shutdown process for us. For the sake of consistency, let's wrap it into a standard startup script that can be managed via **chkconfig**. Using the techniques learned from Chapter 6, we create a shell script called **/etc/rc.d/init.d/postfix**. We can use the following code listing for the **postfix** script:

```
#!/bin/sh
# Postfix      Start/Stop the Postfix mail system
#
#chkconfig:    35 99 01
#
. /etc/rc.d/init.d/functions

[ -f /usr/sbin/postfix ] || exit 0

# See how we were called.
case "$1" in
  start)
        echo "Starting postfix: "
        /usr/sbin/postfix start
        echo "done"
        touch /var/lock/subsys/postfix
        ;;
  stop)
        echo -n "Stopping postfix: "
        /usr/sbin/postfix stop
        echo "done"
        rm -f /var/lock/subsys/postfix
        ;;
  *)
        echo "Usage: postfix start|stop"
        exit 1
esac
exit 0
```

With the script in place, double-check that its permissions are correct with a quick **chmod**.

```
[root@hostA postfix-2.2.4]# chmod 755 /etc/rc.d/init.d/postfix
```

Then we use **chkconfig** to add it to the appropriate runlevels for startup.

```
[root@hostA postfix-2.2.4]# chkconfig --add postfix
[root@hostA postfix-2.2.4]# chkconfig --level 35 postfix on
```

CONFIGURING THE POSTFIX SERVER

By following the previous steps, you have now compiled and installed the Postfix mail system. The **make install** script will exit and prompt you for any changes that are wrong, such as forgetting to add the **postfix** user. Now that you have installed the Postfix server, you can change directories to **/etc/postfix** and configure the Postfix server.

Now that you have the Postfix server ready for use, you need to configure the server through the **/etc/postfix/main.cf** configuration file. It's obvious from its name that this configuration file is the main configuration file for Postfix. The other configuration file of note is the **master.cf** file. This is the process configuration file for Postfix, which allows you to change how Postfix processes are run. This can be useful for setting up Postfix on clients so that it doesn't accept e-mail and forwards to a central mail hub. For more information on doing this, see the documentation at http://www.postfix.org. Now let's move on to the **main.cf** configuration file.

The main.cf File

The **main.cf** file is too large to list all of its options in this chapter, but we will cover the most important options that will get your mail server up and running. Thankfully, the configuration file is well documented and explains clearly what each option is used for. The first option you will look at is the **myhostname** parameter.

myhostname

This parameter is used to set the name that Postfix will be receiving e-mail for. Typical examples of mail server host names are mail.wugaa.com or mail.yahoo.com.

```
myhostname = serverA.example.org
```

mydomain

This parameter is the mail domain that you will be servicing, such as homenet.com or yahoo.com.

```
mydomain = example.org
```

myorigin

All e-mail sent from this e-mail server will look as though it came from this parameter. You can set this to either **$myhostname** or **$mydomain**, like so:

```
myorigin = $mydomain
```

Notice that you can use the value of other parameters in the configuration file by placing a **$** sign in front of the variable name.

mydestination

This parameter lists the domains that the Postfix server will take as its final destination for incoming e-mail. Typically, this value is set to the host name of the box and the domain name, but it can contain other names, as shown here:

```
mydestination = $myhostname, localhost.$mydomain, $mydomain,
mail.$mydomain, www.$mydomain, ftp.$mydomain
```

If your server has more than one name, for example, serverA.example.org and serverA.another-example.org, you will want to make sure you list both names here.

mail_spool_directory

You can run the Postfix server in two modes of delivery, directly to a user's mailbox or to a central spool directory. The typical way is to store the mail in **/var/spool/mail**. The variable will look like this in the configuration file:

```
mail_spool_directory = /var/spool/mail
```

The result is that mail will be stored for each user under the **/var/spool/mail** directory with each user's mailbox represented as a file. For example, e-mail sent to yyang@example .org will be stored in **/var/spool/mail/yyang**.

mynetworks

The **mynetworks** variable is an important configuration option. This lets you configure what servers can relay through your Postfix server. You will usually want to allow relaying from local client machines and nothing else. Otherwise, spammers can use your mail server to relay messages. An example value of this variable would be

```
mynetworks = 192.168.1.0/24, 127.0.0.0/8
```

If you define this parameter, it will override the **mynetworks_style** parameter. The **mynetworks_style** parameter allows you to specify any of the keywords **class**, **subnet**, or **host**. These settings tell the server to trust these networks that the server belongs to.

CAUTION   If you do not set the **$mynetworks** variable correctly and spammers begin using your mail server as a relay, you will quickly find a surge of angry mail administrators e-mailing you about it. Furthermore, it is a fast way to get your mail server blacklisted by one of the spam control services like ORBS or RBL. Once your server is blacklisted, very few people will be able to receive mail from you and you will need to jump through a lot of hoops to get unlisted. Even worse, no one will tell you that you have been blacklisted.

smtpd_banner

This variable allows you to return a custom response when a client connects to your mail server. It is a good idea to change the banner to something that doesn't give away what server you are using. This just adds one more step for hackers to try to find faults in your software.

```
smtpd_banner = $myhostname ESMTP
```

There are many other parameters in the configuration file. You will see them when you set the preceding options. These other options will allow you to set security levels and debugging levels if you need them. Now we will move on to running the Postfix mail system and maintaining your mail server.

Checking Your Configuration

Postfix includes a nice tool for checking a current configuration and helping you troubleshoot it. Simply run

```
[root@hostA /root]# postfix check
```

This will list any errors that the Postfix system finds in the configuration files or with permissions of any directories that it needs. A quick run on our sample system shows this:

```
[root@hostA /root]# postfix check
postfix: fatal: /etc/postfix/main.cf, line 91: missing '=' after attribute
name: "mydomain example.org"
```

Looks like we made a typo in the configuration file. When going back to fix any errors in the configuration file, be sure to read the error message carefully and use the line number as guidance, not as absolute. This is because a typo in the file could mean that Postfix detected the error well *after* the actual error took place. In this example, a typo we made on line 76 didn't get caught until line 91 because of how the parsing engine works. However, by carefully reading the error message, we knew the problem was with "mydomain," so it was only a quick search before we found the real line.

Let's run the check again.

```
[root@hostA /root]# postfix check
[root@hostA /root]#
```

Perfect. We're ready to start using Postfix.

RUNNING THE SERVER

Starting the Postfix mail server is easy and straightforward. Just pass the **start** option to the **postfix** command:

```
[root@hostA /usr/sbin]# postfix start
```

> **NOTE**   Recall that if you are using Fedora Core and wish to use the preinstalled version, you can simply specify **/etc/rc.d/init.d/postfix start** to start Postfix.

When you make any changes to the configuration files, you need to tell Postfix to reload itself to make the changes take effect. Do this by sending the **reload** command to **postfix**:

```
[root@hostA /usr/sbin]# postfix reload
```

Checking the Mail Queue

Occasionally, the mail queues on your system will fill up. This can be caused by network failures or various other failures such as other mail servers. To check the mail queue on your mail server, simply type the following command:

```
[root@hostA /root]# mailq
```

This command will display all of the messages that are in the Postfix mail queue. This is the first step in testing and verifying if the mail server is working correctly.

Flushing the Mail Queue

Sometimes after an outage, mail will be queued up and it can take several hours for the messages to be sent. Use the **postfix flush** command to flush out any messages that are shown in the queue by the **mailq** command.

The newaliases Command

The file **/etc/aliases** contains a list of e-mail aliases. This is used to create site-wide e-mail lists and aliases for users. Whenever you make changes to the **/etc/aliases** file, you need to tell Postfix about it by running the **newaliases** command. This command will rebuild the Postfix databases and inform you of how many names have been added.

Making Sure Everything Works

Now that you have installed the Postfix mail server, you should test and test again to make sure that everything is working correctly. The first step in doing this is to use a local mail user agent like **pine** or **mutt** to send e-mail to yourself. If this works, great, you can move on to sending e-mail to a remote site, using the **mailq** command to see when the message gets sent. The final step is to make sure that you can send e-mail to the server from the outside network (that is, from the Internet). If you can receive e-mail from the outside world, your work is done.

Mail Logs

On a Fedora Core or Red Hat system, by default mail logs go to **/var/log/maillog** as defined by the syslog configuration file. If you need to change this, you can modify the syslog configuration file **/etc/syslog.conf** by editing the following line:

```
mail.*                    /var/log/maillog
```

Most sites run their mail logs this way, so if you are having problems you can search through the **/var/log/maillog** file for any messages.

If Mail Still Won't Work

If mail still won't work, don't worry. SMTP isn't always easy to set up. If you still have problems, step logically through all of the steps and look for errors. The first step is to look at your log messages, which might show that other mail servers are not responding. If everything seems fine there, check your DNS settings. Can the mail server perform name lookups? Can it perform MX lookups? Can other people perform name lookups for your mail server? Ninety percent of system administration is proper troubleshooting. Another source of troubleshooting is to look at what others have done. Check the Postfix Web site at http://www.postfix.org, or check the newsgroups at http://www.google .com for the problems you might be seeing.

SUMMARY

In this chapter we have learned about the basics of how SMTP works and configured/ installed the Postfix mail server. With this information, you have enough knowledge to set up and run a production mail server.

If you're looking for additional information on Postfix, start with the online documentation at http://www.postfix.org. The documentation is well written and easy to follow. There is a wealth of information on how Postfix can be extended to perform a number of additional functions that are outside of the scope of this chapter.

Another excellent reference on the Postfix system is *The Book of Postfix: State-of-the-Art Message Transport* by Ralf Hildebrandt and Patrick Koetter (No Starch Press, 2005). This book covers the Postfix system in excellent detail and is the most recent published text on the topic as of this writing.

As with any other service, don't forget to keep up on the latest news on Postfix. Security updates do come out from time to time, and it is important that you update your mail server to reflect these changes.

CHAPTER 20

POP and IMAP

In Chapter 19 we covered the differences between mail transport agents (MTAs), mail delivery agents (MDAs), and mail user agents (MUAs). When it came to the delivery of mail to specific user mailboxes, we assumed the use of Procmail, which delivers copies of e-mail to users in the mbox format. The mbox format is a simple text format that can be read by a number of console mail user agents like Pine, Elm, and Mutt, as well as some GUI-based readers.

The key to the mbox format, however, is that the client have direct access to the mbox file itself. This works well enough in tightly administered environments where the administrator of the mail server is also the administrator of the client hosts; however, this system of mail folder administration falls apart quickly in modern circumstances. Four specific circumstances most prominently show unworkable situations:

▼   Users cannot reasonably stay connected to a fast/secure network for file system access to their mbox file (e.g., roaming laptops).

■   Users demand local copies of e-mail for offline viewing.

■   Security requirements dictate that users do not have direct access to the mail store (e.g., NFS-shared mail spool directories are considered unacceptable).

▲   Mail user agents do not support the mbox file format (typical of Windows-based clients).

To deal with these user cases, the Post Office Protocol (POP) was created to allow for network-based access to mail stores. Many early Windows-based mail clients used the POP protocol for access to Internet e-mail, since it allowed users to access UNIX-based mail servers (the dominant type of mail server on the Internet until the rise of Microsoft Exchange in the late 1990s).

The idea behind POP is simple: a central mail server is managed such that it remains online at all times and can receive mail for all of its users. Mail that is received is queued on the server until a user connects via POP and downloads the queued mail, thus emptying his mailbox. The mail on the server itself can be stored in any format (e.g., mbox) so long as the POP protocol is adhered to. When a user wants to send an e-mail, it relays it through the central mail server via SMTP. This allows the client to disconnect from the network and gives the well-connected mail server the task of dealing with forwarding the message to the correct destination server, taking care of retransmits, delays, etc. Figure 20-1 shows this relationship.

Early users of POP found certain limitations of the protocol to be too limiting. Such features as being able to keep a master copy of a user's e-mail on the server with only a cached copy on the client were missing. This led to the development of the IMAP protocol (Interactive Mail Access Protocol), the earliest RFC version being IMAP2 in 1988 (RFC 1064). The IMAP protocol extended to version 4 (IMAPv4) in 1994. Most clients are compatible with IMAPv4. Recent extensions have taken it to IMAPv4rev1 (RFC 3501).

The essence of how IMAP has evolved can be best understood by thinking of mail access as working in one of three distinct modes: online, offline, and disconnected.

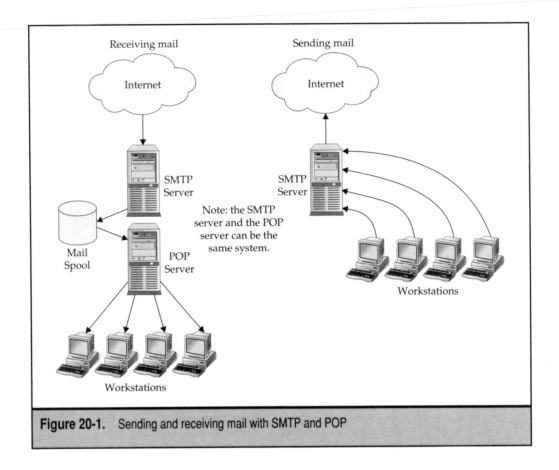

Figure 20-1.   Sending and receiving mail with SMTP and POP

The *online* mode is akin to having direct file system access to the mail store (e.g., having read access to **/var/mail**). The *offline* mode is how POP works, where the client is assumed to be disconnected from the network except when explicitly pulling down its e-mail. In offline mode, the server normally does not retain a copy of the mail.

Disconnected mode works by allowing users to retain cached copies of their mail stores. When connected, any incoming/outgoing e-mail is immediately recognized and synchronized; however, when the client is disconnected, changes made on the client are kept until reconnection, when synchronization occurs. Because the client only retains a cached copy, a user can move to a completely different client and resynchronize his or her e-mail.

By using the IMAP protocol, you will have a mail server that will support all three modes of access.

After all is said and done, supporting both POP and IMAP is usually a good idea. It allows users the freedom to choose whatever mail client and protocol best suits them. In this chapter, we cover the installation and configuration of the UW IMAP server, which includes a POP server hook. This particular mail server has been available for many years and comes with an easy-to-use installation process. For a small to medium-sized user base (up to a few hundred users), it should work well.

If you're interested in a higher-volume mail server for IMAP, consider the Cyrus or Courier IMAP server. Both offer impressive scaling options; however, they come at the expense of needing more complex installation processes.

THE MECHANICS OF POP AND IMAP

Like the other services we have discussed so far, POP and IMAP each need a server process to handle requests. The server processes listen on ports 110 and 143, respectively.

Each request to and response from the server is in cleartext ASCII, which means it's very easy for us to test the functionality of the server using Telnet. (This is especially useful when you have users who claim that the "mail server is broken," although the real problem is that they're unfamiliar with the system.) Like an SMTP server, a POP or IMAP server can be controlled with a very short list of commands.

To get a look at the most common commands, let's walk through the process of connecting and logging in to a POP server and an IMAP server. This simple test allows you to verify that the server does in fact work and is providing valid authentication.

Checking POP

We begin by using Telnet to connect to the POP3 server. From a command prompt, type

```
[root@hostA /root]# telnet pop3server.domain.com 110
```

The POP3 server responds as follows:

```
+OK ready.
```

The server is now waiting for you to give it a command. (Don't worry that you don't see a prompt.) Start by submitting your login name as follows:

```
USER yourlogin
```

where **yourlogin** is, of course, your login ID. The server responds with

```
+OK Password required for yourlogin
```

Now tell the server your password using the **PASS** command.

```
PASS yourpassword
```

where **yourpassword** is your password. The server responds with

```
+OK yourlogin has X messages (Y octets)
```

where *X* and *Y* will be actual numbers. *X* represents the number of messages in your mailbox, and *Y* represents the number of bytes in your mailbox. You're now logged in and can issue commands to read your mail. Since we are simply validating that the server is working, we can log out now. Simply enter **QUIT**, and the server will close the connection.

Checking IMAP

We begin by using Telnet to connect to the IMAP server. From the command prompt, type

```
[root@hostA /root]# telnet imap.domain.com 143
```

The IMAP server will respond with something similar to

```
* OK hostA Cyrus IMAP4 v2.2.6-Invoca-RPM-2.2.6-2.FC3.6 server ready
```

The server is now ready for you to enter commands. Note that like the POP server, the IMAP server will not issue a prompt.

The format of commands with IMAP is

```
<tag> <command> <parameters>
```

where *tag* represents a unique value used to identify (tag) the command. Commands can be executed asynchronously, meaning that it is possible for you to enter one command and while waiting for the response, enter another command. Because each command is tagged, the output will clearly reflect what output corresponds to what request.

To log in to the IMAP server, simply enter the **login** command like so:

```
A001 login username password
```

where **username** is the username you wish to test and **password** the user's password. If the authentication is a success, the server will return with

```
A001 OK User logged in
```

That is enough to tell you two things:

▼ The user's name and password are valid.

▲ The mail server was able to locate and access the user's mailbox.

With the server validated, you can log out by simply entering the **logout** command like so:

```
A002 logout
```

The server will reply with something similar to

```
* BYE LOGOUT received
```

Knowing When You Need Help

Author Steve *needs* to read his mail regularly. Nothing demonstrated this more clearly than something he experienced a few years ago. The server on which his home directory resided was down, and he was prevented from logging in. This was a system on which he didn't have administrative permissions, so he had to wait for the sysadmin to fix the server. Frustrated, he downloaded the RFC specifications for POP3 (RFC 1939, ftp://ftp.isi.edu/in-notes/rfc1939.txt), from which he figured out how to read his mail via POP3 commands and Telnet. He patiently read through all of his mail using this method (several dozen messages) and even responded to a few of them by using Telnet to issue SMTP commands directly to the SMTP server. By the time the sysadmin arrived, he had already read and replied to all of his e-mail for the morning. Sad, but true.

INSTALLING THE UW-IMAP AND POP3 SERVER

The University of Washington produces a well-regarded IMAP server that is used in many production sites around the world. It is a well-tested implementation; thus it is the version of IMAP that we will install.

Begin by downloading the UW-IMAP server to **/usr/local/src**. The latest version of the server can be found at ftp://ftp.cac.washington.edu/imap/imap.tar.Z. Once it is downloaded, unpack it as follows:

```
[root@hostA src]# tar -xvzf imap.tar.Z
```

This will create a new directory under which all of the source code will be present. For the version we are using, we will see a new directory called **imap-2004c1** created. Change into the directory as follows:

```
[root@hostA src]# cd imap-2004c1
```

The defaults that ship with the UW-IMAP server work well for most installations. If you are interested in tuning the build process, open the Makefile (found in the current directory) with an editor and read through it. The file is very well documented and shows what options can be turned on or off. For the installation we are doing now, we will want to stick with a simple configuration change that we can issue on the command line.

In addition to build options, the **make** command for UW-IMAP requires that you specify the type of system that the package is being built on. This is in contrast to many other open-source programs that use the **./configure** program (also known as Autoconf) to automatically determine the running environment. The options for Linux are as follows:

Parameter	Environment
ldb	Debian Linux
lnx	Linux with traditional passwords
lnp	Linux with Pluggable Authentication Modules (PAM)
lmd	Mandrake Linux (also known as Mandriva Linux)
lrh	Red Hat Linux 7.2 and later (covers Red Hat Enterprise and Fedora Core)
lsu	SuSE Linux
sl4	Linux with Shadow passwords (requiring an additional library)
sl5	Linux with Shadow passwords (not requiring an additional library)
snx	Linux needing an extra library for password support

A little overwhelmed with the choices? Don't be. Many of the choices are for very old versions of Linux that are not used any more. If you have a version of Linux that is recent (installed after 2002 or so), the only ones that you need to pay attention to are **lsu** (SuSE), **lrh** (Red Hat), **lmd** (Mandrake), **lnp** (PAM), and **ldb** (Debian).

If you are using SuSE, Red Hat/Fedora, Debian, or Mandrake/Mandiva, go ahead and select the appropriate option. If you aren't sure, the **lnp** option should work on almost all Linux-based systems. The only caveat with the **lnp** option is that you may need to edit the Makefile and help it find where some common toolkits such as OpenSSL are. (You can also simply disable those features as we do in this installation.)

To keep things simple, we will follow the generic case and disable OpenSSL. To proceed with the build, simply run

```
[root@hostA imap-2004c1]# make lnp SSLTYPE=none
```

The entire build process should take only a few minutes, even on a slow machine. Once complete, you will have four executables in the directory: **mtest**, **ipop2d**, **ipop3d**, and **imapd**. Copy these to the **/usr/local/bin** directory like so:

```
[root@hostA imap-2004c1]# cp mtest/mtest /usr/local/bin
[root@hostA imap-2004c1]# cp ipopd/ipop2d /usr/local/bin
[root@hostA imap-2004c1]# cp ipopd/ipop3d /usr/local/bin
[root@hostA imap-2004c1]# cp imapd/imapd /usr/local/bin
```

Be sure their permissions are set correctly. Since they only need to be run by root, it is appropriate to limit their access accordingly. Simply set their permissions as follows:

```
[root@hostA imap-2004c1]# cd /usr/local/bin
[root@hostA bin]# chmod 700 mtest ipop2d ipop3d imapd
[root@hostA bin]# chown root mtest ipop2d ipop3d imapd
```

With the necessary files in place, it is time to set up **xinetd** to accept connections for us. (For more information on **xinetd**, see Chapter 8.) Add the following lines to the **/etc/xinetd .conf** file:

```
service imap
{
 flags = REUSE
 socket_type = stream
 wait = no
 user = root
 server  = /usr/local/bin/imapd
 log_on_failure += USERID
}

service pop3
{
 flags = REUSE
 socket_type = stream
 wait = no
 user = root
 server  = /usr/local/bin/ipop3d
 log_on_failure += USERID
}
```

Before telling **xinetd** to reload its configuration, you will want to check that your **/etc/ services** file has both pop3 and imap listed. If **/etc/services** does not have the protocols listed, simply add the following two lines:

```
pop3 110/tcp
imap 143/tcp
```

Finally, tell **xinetd** to reload its configuration. If you are using Fedora Core or Red Hat, this can be done with the following command:

```
[root@hostA bin]# service xinetd reload
```

If you are using another distribution, find the **xinetd** process ID using the **ps** command like so:

```
[root@hostA bin]# ps -C xinetd
 PID TTY  TIME CMD
 2013 ? 00:00:00 xinetd
```

Then send the **xinetd** process ID a SIGHUP signal using the **kill** command as follows:

```
[root@hostA bin]# kill -HUP 2013
```

If everything worked, you should have a functional IMAP server. Using the commands and methods shown in the earlier section "The Mechanics of POP and IMAP," connect to the mail server and test if a valid user can log in to the server. If you get an error message along the way, check the **/var/log/messages** file for additional information.

OTHER ISSUES IN MAIL SERVICES

While there is enough infrastructure to get you started with a working mail server, there is still a lot of room for improvements. In this section, we step through some of the issues you may encounter and the methods by which you may want to address them.

SSL Security

The biggest security issue with the POP3 and IMAP servers is that in their simplest configuration, they do not offer any encryption. Advanced IMAP configurations offer richer password hashing schemes; however, common IMAP clients like Outlook and Outlook Express do not support them. Thus, your best bet is to encrypt the entire stream using SSL.

The way that we have configured this instance of the UW-IMAP server, we have not used SSL to keep the first install simple. (It's always nice to know that you can get something working first before tinkering too much with it!) If you do want to use SSL, you will need to take the following steps:

1. Recompile UW-IMAP, this time with SSL enabled.

   Change the **xinetd.conf** file to use the "imaps" and "pop3s" services instead of "imap" and "pop3," respectively. (The "imaps" service runs on TCP port 993, and "pop3s" runs on TCP port 995.)

2. Install an SSL certificate.

   Make sure that your clients use SSL. In Outlook, this choice is a simple check box in the "Add Mailbox" configuration.

Recompiling with SSL enabled may require more tinkering, depending on your installation. For the Linux types that are defined (Red Hat/Fedora, SuSE, etc.), the SSL libraries are already defined in the Makefile. If you are running another distribution, you may need to explicitly set the SSL variables in the Makefile first.

For example, to compile with SSL capability on Fedora Core 3, simply run

```
[root@hostA imap-2004c1]# make clean; make lrh
```

TIP You may want to recommend to all of your users that they use SSL encryption for checking their e-mail.

Don't forget to copy the newly compiled binaries to the **/usr/local/bin** directory and set their permissions accordingly.

With respect to creating an SSL certificate, you can create a self-signed certificate quite easily using OpenSSL. Simply run

```
[root@hostA imap-2004c1]# openssl req -new -x509 -nodes -out imapd.pem -keyout
imapd.pem -days 3650
```

This will create a certificate that will last ten years. Place it in your OpenSSL certificates directory. On Red Hat/Fedora, this is the **/usr/share/ssl/certs** directory.

> **NOTE**   Users will receive a warning that the certificate is not properly signed if you use this method of creating a certificate. If you do not want this warning, you will need to purchase a certificate from a certificate authority like VeriSign. Note that these certificates can cost hundreds of U.S. dollars. Depending on your users, this may be a requirement. However, if all you need is an encrypted tunnel for passwords to be sent through, a self-signed certificate works fine.

Testing IMAP Connectivity with SSL

Once you move to an SSL-based mail server, you may find that your tricks in checking on the mail server using Telnet don't work anymore. This is because Telnet assumes no encryption on the line.

Getting past this little hurdle is quite easy: simply use OpenSSL as a client instead of Telnet, like so:

```
[root@hostA ~]# openssl s_client -connect 127.0.0.1:993
```

In this example, we are able to connect to the IMAP server running on 127.0.0.1, even though it is encrypted. Once we have the connection established, we can use the commands that we went over in the first section of this chapter.

Availability

In managing a mail server, you will quickly find that e-mail qualifies as *the most* visible resource on your network. When the mail server goes down, everyone will know—and they will know quickly. Thus, it is important that you consider how you will be able to provide 24/7 availability for e-mail services.

The number one issue that threatens mail servers is "fat fingering" a configuration. In other words, making an error when doing basic administration. There is no solution to this problem other than *Be Careful!* When dealing with any kind of production server, it is prudent to take each step carefully and make sure that you meant to do what you're typing. When at all possible, work as a normal user rather than root and use **sudo** for specific commands that need root permissions.

The second big issue with managing mail servers is hardware availability. Unfortunately, this is best addressed with money—making an investment up front in a good case, adequate cooling, and as much redundancy as you can afford is a good way to make sure that the server doesn't take a fall over something silly like a CPU fan going out. Dual-power supplies are another way to help keep mechanical things from failing on you. Finally, disks configured in a RAID system help mitigate the risk of failure.

Finally, consider expansion early in your design. It is inevitable that your users will consume all of your available disk space. The last thing you will want is to start bouncing mail because the mail server has run out of disk! To address this issue, consider using disk volumes that can be expanded on the fly and RAID systems that allow new disks to be added quickly. This will allow you to add disks to the volume with minimal downtime and without having to move to a completely new server.

Log Files

Although we've mentioned this earlier in the chapter, watching the **/var/log/messages** and **/var/log/maillog** files is a prudent way to manage and track the activity in your mail server. The UW-IMAP server provides a rich array of messages to help you understand what is happening with your server and troubleshoot any peculiar behavior.

A perfect example of using log files came in writing this chapter, specifically the SSL section. After compiling the new version of the server, we forgot to copy the **imapd** file to **/usr/local/bin**. This led to puzzling behavior when we tried to connect to the server using Outlook. We tried using the **openssl s_client** command to connect and it gave an undescriptive error. What was going on?!

A quick look at the log files using the **tail** command revealed the problem:

```
Apr 27 21:27:37 hostA imapd[3808]: This server does not support SSL
Apr 27 21:28:03 hostA imapd[3812]: imaps SSL service init from 127.0.0.1
```

Well, that more or less spells it out for us. Retracing our steps, we realized that we forgot to copy the new **imapd** binary to **/usr/local/bin**. A quick run of the **cp** command, a restart of **xinetd**, and we were greeted with success.

In short, when in doubt, take a moment to look through the log files. You'll probably find a solution to your problem there.

SUMMARY

In this chapter we covered the logic behind IMAP vs. POP3, examples on how to manually test connectivity to each mail server, and the complete installation process required for the UW-IMAP server. With this chapter, you have enough information to run a simple mail server capable of handling a few hundred users without a problem.

As with any server software that is visible to the outside world, you will want to keep up-to-date with the latest releases. Thankfully, the package has shown sufficient stability and security so as to minimize the need for frequent updates, but a careful eye is still warranted.

Finally, we covered enabling SSL on your server and basic concerns in making sure your mail server is available 24/7. This method of security is an easy way to keep clear-text passwords embedded in IMAP traffic from making their way to hands that should not have them.

If you find yourself interested in building out a larger mail server, take the time to read up on the Cyrus and Courier mail servers. Both provide significant expansion capabilities at the expense of additional complexity in configuration. However, if you need a mail server that handles a lot of users, you may find the extra complexity a necessity.

Finally, consider taking a read through the latest IMAP and POP RFCs to understand more about the protocol. The more familiar you are with the protocols, the easier you'll find troubleshooting to be.

CHAPTER 21

The Secure Shell (SSH)

O ne unfortunate side effect of bringing your computer onto a public network (such as the Internet) is that, at one point or another, some folks out there will try to break into your system. This is obviously not a good thing.

In Chapter 15, we discussed techniques for securing your Linux system, all of which are designed to limit remote access to your system to the bare essentials. But what if you need to perform system administrative duties from a remote site? Telnet is woefully insecure, because it transmits the entire session (logins, passwords, and all) in cleartext. How can you reap the benefits of a truly multiuser system if you can't securely log in to it?

> **NOTE**   Cleartext means that the data is unencrypted. In any system, when passwords get sent over the line in cleartext, a packet sniffer could determine what a user's password is. This is especially bad if that user is root!

To tackle the issue of remote login versus password security, a solution called Secure Shell (SSH) was developed. SSH is a suite of network communication tools that are collectively based on an open protocol/standard that is guided by the Internet Engineering Task Force (IETF). It allows users to connect to a remote server just as they would using Telnet, **rlogin**, FTP, etc.—except that the session is 100% encrypted. Someone using a packet sniffer merely sees encrypted traffic going by. Should they capture the encrypted traffic, decrypting it could take decades.

In this chapter, we'll take a brief and general look at the cryptography concept. Then we'll examine the versions of SSH, where to get it, and how to install and configure it.

UNDERSTANDING PUBLIC KEY CRYPTOGRAPHY

A quick disclaimer is probably in place before proceeding: "This chapter is by no means an authority on the subject of cryptography and as such is not the definitive source for cryptography matters." What you will find here is a general discussion along with some references to good books that approach the topic more thoroughly.

Secure Shell relies on a technology called *public-key cryptography.* It works similarly to a safe deposit box at the bank: you need two keys to open the box, or at least multiple layers of security/checks have to be crossed. In the case of public-key cryptography, you need two mathematical keys, a public one and a private one. Your public key can be published on a public Web page, printed on a T-shirt, or posted on a billboard in the busiest part of town. Anyone who asks for it can have a copy. On the other hand, your private key must be protected to the best of your ability. It is this piece of information that makes the data you want to encrypt truly secure. Every public key/private key combination is unique.

The actual process of encrypting data and sending it from one person to the next requires several steps. We'll use the popular Alice and Bob analogy and go through the process one step at a time as they both try to communicate in a secure manner with one another. Figures 21-1 through 21-5 illustrate an oversimplified version of the actual process.

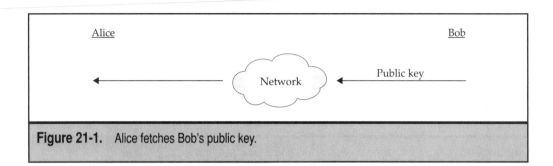

Figure 21-1. Alice fetches Bob's public key.

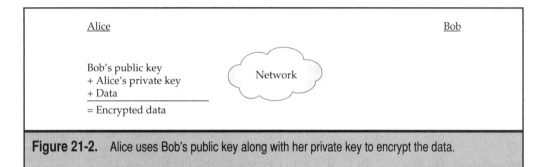

Figure 21-2. Alice uses Bob's public key along with her private key to encrypt the data.

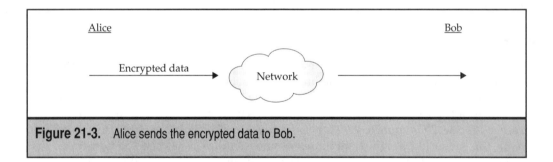

Figure 21-3. Alice sends the encrypted data to Bob.

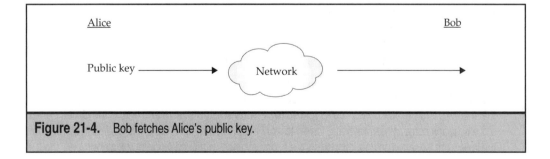

Figure 21-4. Bob fetches Alice's public key.

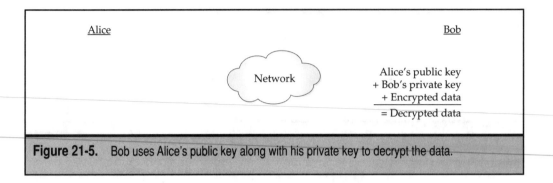

Figure 21-5. Bob uses Alice's public key along with his private key to decrypt the data.

Looking at these steps, notice that at no point was the secret key sent over the network. Also note that once the data was encrypted with Bob's public key and signed with Alice's private key, the only pair of keys that could decrypt it were Bob's private key and Alice's public key. Thus, if someone intercepted the data in the middle of the transmission, they wouldn't be able to decrypt the data without the proper private keys.

To make things even more interesting, SSH regularly changes its session key. (This is a randomly generated, symmetric key for encrypting the communication between the SSH client and server. It is shared by the two parties in a secure manner during SSH connection setup.) In this way, the data stream gets encrypted differently every few minutes. Thus, even if someone happened to figure out the key for a transmission, that miracle would be valid for only a few minutes until the keys changed again.

Key Characteristics

So what exactly *is* a key? Essentially, a key is a very large number that has special mathematical properties. Whether someone can break an encryption scheme depends on their ability to find out what the key is. Thus, the larger the key is, the harder it will be to discover it.

Low-grade encryption has 56 bits. This means there are 2^{56} possible keys. To give you a sense of scale, 2^{32} is equal to 4 billion, 2^{48} is equal to 256 trillion, and 2^{56} is 65,536 trillion. While this seems like a significant number of possibilities, it has been demonstrated that a loose network of PCs dedicated to iterating through every possibility could conceivably break a low-grade encryption code in less than a month. In 1998, the Electronic Frontier Foundation (EFF) published designs for a (then) $250,000 computer capable of cracking 56-bit keys in a few seconds to demonstrate the need for higher-grade encryption. If $250,000 seems like a lot of money to you, think of the potential for credit card fraud if someone successfully used that computer for that purpose!

NOTE The EFF published the aforementioned designs in an effort to convince the U.S. government that the laws that limited the export of crypto software were sorely outdated and hurting the United States, since so many companies were being forced to work in other countries. This finally paid off in 2000, when the laws were loosened up enough to allow the export of higher-grade cryptography. Unfortunately, most of the companies doing cryptography work had already exported their engineering to other countries.

For a key to be sufficiently difficult to break, experts suggest no fewer than 128 bits. Because every extra bit effectively doubles the number of possibilities, 128 bits offers a genuine challenge. And if you want to really make the encryption solid, a key size of 512 bits or higher is recommended. SSH can use up to 1024 bits to encrypt your data.

The tradeoff to using higher-bit encryption is that it requires more math processing power for the computer to churn through and validate a key. This takes time and therefore makes the authentication process a touch slower—but most people feel this tradeoff is worthwhile.

NOTE Though unproven, it is believed that even the infamous National Security Agency (NSA) can't break codes encrypted with keys higher than 1024 bits.

Cryptography References

SSH supports a variety of encryption algorithms. Public-key encryption happens to be the most interesting method of performing encryption from site to site and is arguably the most secure. If you want to learn more about cryptography, here are some good books and other resources to look into:

▼ *PGP* by Simson Garfinkel et al. (O'Reilly and Associates, 1994)

■ *Applied Cryptography: Protocols, Algorithms, and Source Code in C, Second Edition,* by Bruce Schneier (John Wiley & Sons, 1995)

■ *Cryptography and Network Security: Principles and Practice, Third Edition,* by William Stallings (Prentice Hall, 2002)

■ http://www.ietf.org/internet-drafts/draft-ietf-secsh-connect-25.txt

▲ http://www.apps.ietf.org/rfc/rfc3766.html

The *PGP* book is specific to the PGP program, but it also contains a hefty amount of history and an excellent collection of general cryptography tutorials. The *Applied Cryptography* book might be a bit overwhelming to many, especially nonprogrammers, but it very successfully explains how actual cryptographic algorithms work. (This text is considered a bible among cypherheads.) Finally, *Cryptography and Network Security* is heavier on principles than on practice, but it's useful if you're interested in the theoretical aspects of cryptography rather than the code itself.

UNDERSTANDING SSH VERSIONS AND DISTRIBUTIONS

The first version of SSH that was made available by DataFellows (now F-Secure) restricted free use of SSH to noncommercial activities; commercial activities required that licenses be purchased. But more significant than the cost of the package is the fact that the source code to the package is completely open. This is important to cryptographic software, for it allows peers to examine the source code and make sure there are no holes that may allow hackers to break the security. (In other words, serious cryptographers do not rely on security through obscurity.) Since the U.S. government has relaxed some of its encryption laws, work on the OpenSSH project has increased, and it is a viable alternative to some of the commercial versions of the SSH protocol.

Because the SSH protocol has become an IETF standard, there are also other developers actively working on SSH clients for other operating systems. There are many MS Windows clients, Macintosh clients, and even a Palm client, in addition to the standard UNIX clients. You can find the version of OpenSSH that we will be discussing at http://www.openssh.org/.

OpenSSH and OpenBSD

The OpenSSH project is being spearheaded by the OpenBSD project. OpenBSD is a version of the BSD operating system (another UNIX variant) that strives for the best security of any operating system available. A quick trip to their Web site (http://www.openbsd .org/) shows that they have gone *eight years* with only one remote exploit in their default installation. Unfortunately, this level of fanaticism on security comes at the expense of not having the most whiz-bang-feature-rich tools available, since they require that anything added to their distribution gets audited for security first. This has made OpenBSD a very popular foundation for firewalls.

The core of the OpenSSH package is considered part of the OpenBSD project and thus is very simple and specific to the OpenBSD operating system. To make OpenSSH available to other operating systems, a separate group exists to make OpenSSH portable whenever new releases come out. Typically, this happens very quickly after the original release. (For instance, OpenSSH 4.1 was released on May 26, 2005. And OpenSSH 4.1p1, the portable version, was released on the same day.)

> **NOTE** Since we are targeting Linux, we will use the versions suffixed with a *p*, indicating that they have been ported.

Alternative Vendors for SSH Clients

The SSH client is the client component of the SSH protocol suite. It is what allows users to interact with the service(s) provided by an SSH server daemon.

Every day, many people work with heterogeneous environments, and it's impossible to ignore all the Windows 98/NT/2000/XP/2003 and MacOS systems out there. In order to allow these folks to work with a *real* operating system (Linux of course!), there must be a mechanism for logging in to such systems remotely. Because Telnet is not secure, SSH provides an alternative. Virtually all Linux/UNIX systems come with their own built-in SSH clients, and as such, there isn't much of a need to worry about them; but the non-UNIX operating systems are a different story. Here is a quick rundown of several SSH clients:

▼ **PuTTY, for Win32 (http://www.chiark.greenend.org.uk/~sgtatham/putty)**
This is probably one of the oldest and most popular SSH implementations for the Win32 platforms. It is extremely lightweight—one binary with no DLLs, just one executable. Also on this site are tools like **pscp**, which is a Windows command-line version of SCP.

- **OpenSSH, for MacOS X**   That's right, OpenSSH is part of the MacOS X system. When you open the **terminal** application, you can simply issue the **ssh** command. (It also ships with an OpenSSH SSH server.)

- **MindTerm (Multiplatform) (http://www.appgate.com/products/80_MindTerm)** This program supports versions 1 and 2 of the SSH protocol. Written in 100% Java, it works on many UNIX platforms (including Linux) as well as Windows and MacOS. See the Web page for a complete list of tested operating systems.

- **FreeSSH, for Windows (http://www.freessh.org)**   The FreeSSH Web site tries to keep track of programs that implement the SSH protocol. The site lists both free and commercial SSH client and server implementations.

▲ **SecureCRT, for Windows (http://www.vandyke.com/products/securecrt)** This is a commercial implementation of SSH.

The Weakest Link

You've probably heard the saying, "Security is only as strong as your weakest link." This particular saying has a significance in terms of OpenSSH and securing your network: OpenSSH is only as secure as the weakest connection between the user and the server. This means that if a user uses Telnet from host A to host B and then uses **ssh** to host C, the entire connection can be monitored from the link between host A and host B. The fact that the link between host B and C is encrypted becomes irrelevant.

Be sure to explain this to your users when you enable logins via SSH, especially if you're disabling Telnet access altogether. Unfortunately, taking the time to tighten down your security in this manner will be soundly defeated if your users Telnet to a host across the Internet so that they can **ssh** into your server. And more often than not, they won't have the slightest idea of why doing that is a bad idea.

> **NOTE**   When you Telnet across the Internet, you are crossing several network boundaries. Each of those providers has full rights to sniff traffic and gather any information they want. Someone can easily see you reading your e-mail. With SSH, you can rest assured that your connection is secure.

DOWNLOADING, COMPILING, AND INSTALLING SSH FROM SOURCE

As previously mentioned, virtually all Linux versions ship with OpenSSH; however, you may have a need to roll your own version from source for whatever reason (e.g., you are running a version of Linux that was developed on the planet Pluto!). This section will cover downloading the OpenSSH software and the two components it needs, OpenSSL and zlib. Then you will compile and install the software. If you want to stick with the precompiled version of OpenSSH that ships with your distribution, you can skip this section and move straight to the configuring section.

As of this writing, the latest version of OpenSSH was 4.1p1. You can download this from http://www.openssh.com/portable.html. Select the site that is closest to you and download **openssh-4.1p1.tar.gz** to a directory with enough free space (**/usr/local/src** is a good choice, and we'll use it in this example).

Once you have downloaded OpenSSH to **/usr/local/src**, unpack it with the **tar** command, like so:

```
[root@serverA src]# tar xvzf openssh-4.1p1.tar.gz
```

This will create a directory called **openssh-4.1p1** inside of **/usr/local/src**.

Along with OpenSSH, you will need OpenSSL version 0.9.6 or later. As of this writing, the latest version of OpenSSL was openssl-0.9.8*.tar.gz. You can download that from http://www.openssl.org/. Once you have downloaded OpenSSL to **/usr/local/src**, unpack it with the **tar** command, like so:

```
[root@serverA src]# tar xvzf openssl-0.9.8*.tar.gz
```

Finally, the last package you need is the zlib library, which is used to provide compression and decompression facilities. Most modern Linux distributions have this already, but if you want the latest version, you need to download it from http://www .gzip.org/zlib/. The latest version as of this writing is version 1.2.2. To unpack the package in **/usr/local/src** after downloading, use **tar**, like so:

```
[root@serverA src]# tar xvzf zlib-1.2.2.tar.gz
```

The following steps will walk through the process of compiling and installing the various components of OpenSSH and its dependencies.

1. Begin by going into the **zlib** directory, like so:

   ```
   [root@serverA src]# cd zlib-1.2.2
   ```

2. Then run **configure** and **make**, like so:

   ```
   [root@serverA zlib-1.2.2]# ./configure
   [root@serverA zlib-1.2.2]# make
   ```

   This will result in the zlib library being built.

3. Install the zlib library by running

   ```
   [root@serverA zlib-1.2.2]# make install
   ```

   The resulting library will be placed in the **/usr/local/lib** directory.

4. Now you need to compile OpenSSL. Begin by changing to the directory that the downloaded OpenSSL was unpacked to; like so:

   ```
   [root@serverA ~]# cd /usr/local/src/openssl-0.9.8*
   ```

5. Once you are in the OpenSSL directory, all you need to do is run **configure** and **make**. OpenSSL will take care of figuring out the type of system it is on and configure itself to work in an optimal fashion. The exact commands are

```
[root@serverA openssl-0.9.8*]# ./config
[root@serverA openssl-0.9.8*]# make
```

Note that this step may take a few minutes to complete.

6. Once OpenSSL is done compiling, you can test it by running

```
[root@serverA openssl-0.9.8*]# make test
```

7. If all went well, the test should run without event. If there are any problems, OpenSSL will report them to you. If you do get an error, you should remove this copy of OpenSSL and try the download/unpack/compile procedure again.

8. Once you have finished the test, you can install OpenSSL by running

```
[root@serverA openssl-0.9.8*]# make install
```

This step will install OpenSSL into the **/usr/local/ssl** directory.

9. You are now ready to begin the actual compile and install of the OpenSSH package. Change into the OpenSSH package directory, like so:

```
[root@serverA ~]# cd /usr/local/src/openssh-4.1p1
```

10. As with the other two packages, you need to begin by running the **configure** program. For this package, however, you need to specify some additional parameters. Namely, you need to tell it where the other two packages got installed. You can always run **./configure** with the **--help** option to see all of the parameters, but you'll find that the following **./configure** statement will probably work fine:

```
[root@serverA openssh-4.1p1]# ./configure --with-ssl-dir=/usr/local/ssl/
```

11. Once OpenSSH is configured, simply run **make** and **make install** to put all of the files into the appropriate **/usr/local** directories.

```
[root@serverA openssh-4.1p1]# make
[root@serverA openssh-4.1p1]# make install
```

That's it, you are done. This set of commands will install the various OpenSSH binaries and libraries under the **/usr/local** directory. The SSH server, for example, will be placed under the **/usr/local/sbin** directory, and the various client components will be placed under the **/usr/local/bin/** directory.

INSTALLING OPENSSH VIA RPM

This is perhaps the easiest and quickest way to get SSH up and running on any Linux system. It is almost guaranteed that you will already have the package installed and running on most modern Linux distributions. Even if you choose a bare-bones installation (i.e., the most minimal option during operating system installation), OpenSSH is bound to be part of that minimum. This is more the norm than the exception. But again, just in case you are running a Linux distribution that was developed on the planet Neptune but at least has RPM installed, you can always download and install the precompiled RPM package for OpenSSH. On our sample Fedora Core system, you can query the RPM database to make sure that OpenSSH is indeed installed, by typing

```
[root@serverA ~]# rpm -q openssh
openssh-4.0p1-3
```

And if by some freak occurrence you don't have it already installed (or you accidently uninstalled it), you can quickly install it by using Yum, by issuing this command:

```
[root@serverA ~]# yum install openssh
```

The rest of this chapter will assume that we are dealing with OpenSSH as it is installed via RPM.

Server Startup and Shutdown

If you want users to be able to log in to your system via SSH, you will need to make sure that the service is running and start it if it is not. You should also make sure that the service gets started automatically between system reboots.

First let's check the status of the **sshd** daemon. Type

```
[root@serverA ~]# service sshd status

sshd (pid 7605 30397 2370) is running...
```

The sample output shows the service is up and running. But if, on the other hand, the service is stopped, issue this command to start it:

```
[root@serverA ~]# service sshd start
```

TIP On a SuSE Linux system the command to check the status of **sshd** is

```
serverA:~ # rcsshd status
```

And to start it, the command is

```
serverA:~ # rcsshd start
```

If for some reason you *do* need to stop the SSH server, type

```
[root@serverA ~]# service sshd stop
```

If you make configuration changes that you want to go into effect, you can restart the daemon at any time by simply running

```
[root@serverA ~]# service sshd restart
```

SSHD Configuration File

Most Linux systems out of the box already have the OpenSSH server configured and running with some defaults. On most RPM-based Linux distributions (such as Fedora, RHEL, or SuSE) the configuration file for **sshd** usually resides under the **/etc/ssh/** directory and is called **sshd_config**. For the OpenSSH that we installed from source earlier, the configuration file is located under the **/usr/local/etc/** directory.

Next we'll discuss some of the configuration options found in the **sshd_config** file.

▼ **AuthorizedKeysFile** Specifies the file that contains the public keys that can be used for user authentication. The default is **/<User_Home_Directory>/.ssh/ authorized_keys**.

■ **Ciphers** This is a comma-separated list of ciphers allowed for protocol version 2. Examples of supported ciphers are 3des-cbc, aes256-cbc, aes256-ctr, arcfour, and blowfish-cbc.

■ **HostKey** Defines the file containing a private host key used by SSH. The default is **/etc/ssh/ssh_host_rsa_key** or **/etc/ssh/ssh_host_dsa_key** for protocol version 2.

■ **Port** Specifies the port number that **sshd** listens on. The default value is 22.

■ **Protocol** This specifies the protocol versions **sshd** supports. The possible values are 1 and 2. Note that protocol version 1 is generally considered insecure now.

■ **AllowTcpForwarding** Specifies whether TCP forwarding is permitted. The default is yes.

▲ **X11Forwarding** Specifies whether X11 forwarding is permitted. The argument must be yes or no. The default is no.

NOTE **sshd_config** is a rather odd configuration file. You will notice that unlike in other Linux config files, comments (#) in the **sshd_config** file denote the default values of the options; i.e., comments represent already compiled-in defaults.

USING OpenSSH

OpenSSH comes with several useful programs that we will cover in this section. First, there is the **ssh** client program. Second, there is the Secure Copy (**scp**) program. And finally, there is the Secure FTP program. The most common application you will probably use is the **ssh** client program.

The ssh Client

With the **ssh** daemon started, you can simply use the **ssh** client to log in to a machine from a remote location in the same manner that you would with Telnet. The key difference between **ssh** and Telnet is that **ssh** will not prompt you for your login but instead will assume that you have the same login across both machines, which is typically the case.

However, if you need to use a different login (for instance, if you are logged in as root on one host and want to **ssh** to another and log in as yourself), all you need to do is provide the **-l** option along with the desired login. For example, if you want to log in to the host serverB as the user yyang from serverA, you would type

```
[root@serverA ~]# ssh  -l yyang  serverB
```

Or you could use the ***username@host*** command format, like so:

```
[root@serverA ~]# ssh  yyang@serverB
```

You would then be prompted with a password prompt from serverB for the user yyang's password.

But if you just want to log in to the remote host without having to change your login at the remote end, simply run **ssh**, like so:

```
[root@serverA ~]# ssh  serverB
```

With this command, you'll be logged in as the root user at serverB.

CREATING A SECURE TUNNEL

This section covers what is typically called the poor man's VPN. Essentially, you can use SSH to create a tunnel from your local system to a remote system. This is a very handy feature when you need to access an intranet or another system that is not exposed to the outside world on your intranet. For example, you can **ssh** to a file server machine that will set up the port forwarding to the remote Web server.

Let's imagine a scenario like this:

We have a system with two network interfaces. The system's host name is serverA. One of the interfaces is connected directly to the Internet. The other interface is connected to the local area network (LAN) of a company. Assume the first interface (the WAN interface) has a public/routable-type IP address of 1.1.1.1 and the second interface has a private-type IP address of 192.168.1.1. The second interface is connected to the LAN (network address

192.168.1.0), which is completely cut off from the Internet. The only service that is allowed on the WAN interface is the **sshd** daemon. The LAN has various servers and workstations that are *only* accessible by the hosts on the inside (including serverA).

Assume one of the internal servers hosts a Web-based accounting application that user yyang needs to access from home. The internal Web server's host name is "accounts," with an IP address of 192.168.1.100. And the user yyang's home workstation host name is homeA. We already said the internal network is cut off from the Internet and home systems are part of the public Internet, so—what gives? The setup is illustrated in Figure 21-6.

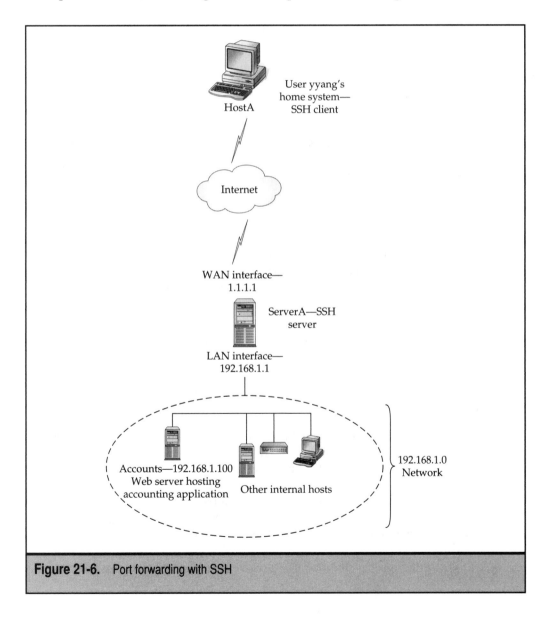

User yyang's
home system—
SSH client
HostA

Internet

WAN interface—
1.1.1.1

ServerA—SSH
server

LAN interface—
192.168.1.1

Accounts—192.168.1.100
Web server hosting
accounting application

Other internal hosts

192.168.1.0
Network

Figure 21-6.   Port forwarding with SSH

Enter the poor man's VPN, aka SSH tunneling. The user yyang will set up an SSH tunnel to the Web server running on "accounts" by following these steps:

1. While sitting in front of her home system—hostA—the user yyang will log in as herself onto the home system.

2. Once logged in locally, she will create a tunnel from port 9000 on the local system to port 80 on the system running the Web-based accounting software (named accounts).

3. In order to do this, yyang will connect via SSH to serverA's WAN interface (1.1.1.1) by issuing this command from her system at home (hostA):

```
[yyang@hostA ~] ssh -L 9000:192.168.1.100:80 1.1.1.1
```

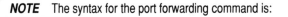

NOTE   The syntax for the port forwarding command is:

```
ssh -L local_port:destination_host:destination_port ssh-server
```

where ***local_port*** is the local port you will connect to after the tunnel is set up, ***destination_host:destination_port*** is the host:port pair where the tunnel will be directed, and ***ssh_server*** is the host that will perform the forwarding to the end host.

4. After yyang successfully authenticates herself to serverA and has logged on to her account on serverA, she can then launch any Web browser installed on her workstation (hostA).

5. User yyang will need to use the Web browser to access the forwarded port (9000) on the local system and see if the tunnel is working correctly. For this example, she needs to plug the URL http://localhost:9000 into the address field of the browser.

6. If all goes well, the Web content being hosted on the accounting server should show up on yyang's Web browser—just as if she were accessing the site from within the local office LAN (i.e., the 192.168.1.0 network).

7. To close down the tunnel, simply close all windows that are accessing the tunnel and then end the SSH connection to serverA by typing **exit** at the prompt you used to create the tunnel.

The secure tunnel affords you secure access to other systems within an intranet or a remote location. It is a great and inexpensive way to create a virtual private network between your host and another host. It is not a full-featured VPN solution, since you can't easily access every host on the remote network, but it gets the job done. In this project, you port-forwarded HTTP traffic. You can tunnel almost any protocol, such as VNC or Telnet. You should note that this is a way for people inside a firewall or proxy to bypass the firewall mechanisms and get to computers in the outside world.

OpenSSH Shell Tricks

It is also possible to create a secure tunnel after you have already logged in to the remote SSH server. That is, you don't have to set up the tunnel when you are setting up the initial SSH connection. This is especially useful for the times that you have a shell on a remote host and you need to hop around onto other systems that would otherwise be inaccessible.

SSH has its own very nifty little shell that can be used to accomplish this and other neat tricks.

To gain access to the built-in SSH shell, press SHIFT-~C on the keyboard after logging in to an SSH server. You will be dropped to a prompt similar to this one:

```
ssh>
```

To set up a tunnel similar to the one that we set up earlier, type this command at the **ssh** prompt/shell:

```
ssh> -L 9000:192.168.1.100:80
```

To leave or quit the ssh shell, just press ENTER on your keyboard and you'll be dropped back to your normal login shell on the system.

Simultaneously typing the tilde character (~) and the question mark (?) will display a listing of all the other things you can do at the **ssh** prompt.

```
[root@serverA ~]# ~?
```

These are the supported escape sequences:

~.	Terminate connection
~C	Open a command line
~R	Request rekey (SSH protocol 2 only)
~^Z	Suspend ssh
~#	List forwarded connections
~&	Background ssh (when waiting for connections to terminate)
~?	This message
~~	Send the escape character by typing it twice

Note that escapes are recognized only immediately after newlines.

Secure Copy (scp)

Secure Copy (**scp**) is meant as a replacement for the **rcp** command, which allows you to do remote copies from one host to another. The most significant problem with the **rcp** command is that users tend to arrange their remote-access settings to allow far too much access into your system. To help mitigate this, instruct users to use the **scp** command instead and then completely disable access to the insecure **rlogin** programs. The format of **scp** is identical to **rcp**, so users shouldn't have problems with this transition.

For example, say user yyang is logged in to her home workstation and wants to copy a file named **.bashrc** located in the local home directory over to her home directory on serverA. The command to do this is

```
[yyang@hostA ~]$ scp .bashrc      serverA:/home/yyang
```

If she wants to copy the other way—i.e., from the remote system, serverA, to her local system, hostA—the arguments only need to be reversed, like so:

```
[yyang@hostA ~]$ scp    serverA:/home/yyang/.bashrc    .
```

Secure FTP (sftp)

Secure FTP is a subsystem to the **ssh** daemon. You access the Secure FTP server by using the **sftp** command-line tool. To **sftp** from a system named hostA to an SFTP server running on serverA as the user yyang, type

```
[root@hostA ~]# sftp    yyang@serverA
```

You will then be asked for your password just as you are when you use the **ssh** client. Once you have been authenticated, you will be given a prompt like the following:

```
sftp>
```

You can issue various SFTP commands while at the SFTP shell. For example, to list all the files and directories under the **/tmp** folder on the SFTP server, you can use the **ls** command:

```
sftp> ls -l
drwxr-xr-x    2 yyang      yyang            4096 Jan 30 21:56 Desktop
-rw-r--r--    1 yyang      yyang            1344 Jan 22 21:13 anaconda-huu
.....<OUTPUT TRUNCATED>......
```

For a listing of all the commands, just type a question mark (**?**):

```
sftp> ?
Available commands:
cd path                        Change remote directory to 'path'
lcd path                       Change local directory to 'path'
```

```
chgrp grp path                  Change group of file 'path' to 'grp'
chmod mode path                 Change permissions of file 'path' to 'mode'
chown own path                  Change owner of file 'path' to 'own'
help                            Display this help text
get remote-path [local-path]    Download file
lls [ls-options [path]]         Display local directory listing
ln oldpath newpath              Symlink remote file
lmkdir path                     Create local directory
lpwd                            Print local working directory
ls [path]                       Display remote directory listing
lumask umask                    Set local umask to 'umask'
mkdir path                      Create remote directory
put local-path [remote-path]    Upload file
pwd                             Display remote working directory
exit                            Quit sftp
quit                            Quit sftp
rename oldpath newpath          Rename remote file
rmdir path                      Remove remote directory
rm path                         Delete remote file
symlink oldpath newpath         Symlink remote file
version                         Show SFTP version
!command                        Execute 'command' in local shell
!                               Escape to local shell
?                               Synonym for help
```

You will notice that the commands look strikingly familiar to the FTP commands in Chapter 17. This client is very handy if you forget the full name of a file you are looking for.

Files Used by SSH

The configuration files for the SSH client and SSH server typically reside in the directory **/etc/ssh/** on a distribution. (If you have installed SSH from source into **/usr/local**, the full path will be **/usr/local/etc/ssh/**.) If you want to make any system-wide changes to defaults for the SSH client, you need to modify the **ssh_config** file.

> **TIP** Remember that the **sshd_config** file is for the server daemon while the **ssh_config** file is for the ssh client!

Within a user's home directory, SSH information is stored in the directory **~username/ .ssh/**. The file **known_hosts** is used to hold host key information. This is also used to stop man-in-the-middle attacks. SSH will alert you when the host keys change. If the keys have changed for a valid reason—for instance, if the server was reinstalled—you will need to edit the **known_hosts** file and delete the line with the changed server.

SUMMARY

The Secure Shell tool is a superior replacement to Telnet for remote logins. Adopting the OpenSSH package will put you in the company of many other sites that are disabling Telnet access altogether and allowing only SSH access through their firewalls. Given the wide-open nature of the Internet, this change isn't an unreasonable thing to ask of your users.

Here are the key issues to keep in mind when you consider Secure Shell:

▼   SSH is very easy to compile and install.

■   Replacing Telnet with SSH requires no significant retraining.

■   SSH exists on many platforms, not just UNIX.

▲   Without SSH, you are exposing your system to potential network attacks in which crackers can "sniff" passwords right off your Internet connections.

In closing, you should understand that using OpenSSH doesn't make your system secure immediately. There is no replacement for a set of good security practices. Following the lessons from Chapter 15, you should disable all unnecessary services on any system that is exposed to untrusted networks (such as the Internet); allow only those services that are absolutely necessary. And that means if you're running SSH, you should disable Telnet, **rlogin**, and **rsh**.

Intranet Services

CHAPTER 22

Network File System (NFS)

Network File System (NFS) is the UNIX way of sharing files and applications across the network. The NFS concept is somewhat similar to that of Windows NT's disk sharing in that it allows you to attach to a disk and work with it as if it were a local drive—a very handy tool for sharing files and large storage space among users.

Aside from their similar roles, there are some important differences between NFS and MS Windows shares that require different approaches to their management. The tools that you use to control network drives are (of course) different, as well. In this chapter, we discuss those differences; however, the primary focus of the chapter is to show you how to deploy NFS under the Linux environment.

THE MECHANICS OF NFS

As with most network-based services, NFS follows the usual client and server paradigms; i.e., it has its client-side components as well as its server-side components.

Chapter 7 covered the process of mounting and unmounting file systems. The same idea applies to NFS, except each mount request is qualified with the name of the server from which the disk share is coming. Of course, the server must be configured to allow the requested partition to be shared with a client.

Let's look at an example. Assume there exists an NFS server named serverA that needs to share its local /home partition or directory over the network. In NFS parlance, it is said that the NFS server is exporting its /home partition. Assume there also exists a client system on the network named clientA that needs access to the contents of the /home partition being exported by the NFS server. Finally, assume all other requirements are met (permissions, security, compatibility, etc.).

In order for clientA to access the /home share being exported by serverA, clientA needs to make an NFS mount request for /home to be exported so that it can mount it locally, such that the share appears locally as the **/home** directory. The command to issue this mount request can be as simple as

```
[root@clientA ~]# mount   serverA:/home /home
```

Assuming that the command was run from the host named clientA, all of the users on clientA would be able to view the contents of **/home** as if it were just another directory. Linux would take care of making all of the network requests to the server.

Remote procedure calls (RPCs) are responsible for handling the requests between the client and the server. RPC technology provides a standard mechanism for any RPC client to contact the server and find out to which service the calls should be directed. Thus, whenever a service wants to make itself available on a server, it needs to register itself with the RPC service manager, *portmap*. Portmap takes care of telling the client where the actual service is located on the server.

Versions of NFS

NFS is not a static protocol. Standards committees have helped NFS evolve to take advantage of new technologies as well as changes in usage patterns. As at the time of this writing there are three well-known versions of the protocol: NFS version 2 (NFSv2), NFS version 3 (NFSv3), and NFS version 4 (NFSv4). There also existed an NFS version 1, but it was very much internal to Sun and as such never saw the light of day!

NFSv2 is the oldest of the three. NFSv3 is the standard with perhaps the widest use. NFSv4 has been in development for a while and is the newest standard. NFSv2 should probably be avoided if possible and should be considered only for legacy reasons. NFSv3 should be considered if stability and widest range of client support are desired. NFSv4 should be considered if its bleeding-edge features are needed and probably for very new deployments where backward compatibility is not an issue.

Perhaps the most important factor in deciding which version of NFS to consider would be to consider the version that your NFS clients will support.

Here are some of the features of each NFS version:

▼   **NFSv2**   Mount requests are granted on a per-host basis and not on a per-user basis. It uses TCP or UDP as its transport protocol. Version 2 clients have a file size limitation of less than 2GB that they can access.

■   **NFSv3**   This version includes a lot of fixes for the bugs in NFSv2. It has more features than version 2 of the protocol. It also has performance gains over version 2 and can use either TCP or UDP as its transport protocol. Depending on the local file system limits of the NFS server itself, clients can access files over 2GB in size. Mount requests are also granted on a per-host basis and not on a per-user basis.

▲   **NFSv4**   This version of the protocol uses a stateful protocol such as TCP or SCTP as its transport. It has improved security features thanks to its support for Kerberos; e.g., client authentication can be conducted on a per-user basis or a principal basis. It was designed with the Internet in mind, and as a result this version of the protocol is firewall friendly, and it listens on the well-known port 2049. The services of the RPC binding protocols (e.g., **rpc.mountd**, **rpc.lockd**, **rpc .statd**) are no longer required in this version of NFS because their functionality has been built into the server; in other words, NFSv4 combines these previously disparate NFS protocols in a single protocol specification. (The **portmap** service is no longer used.) It includes support for file access control list (ACL) attributes and can support both version 2 and version 3 clients. NFSv4 introduces the concept of the pseudo file system.

The version of NFS used can be specified at mount time by the client via the use of mount options. For a Linux client to use NFSv2, the mount option of **nfsvers=2** is used. For NFSv3, the mount option is specified by **nfsvers=3**. And for NFSv4, the **nfsvers** option is not supported, but this version can be used by specifying **nfs4** as the file system type.

The rest of this chapter will concentrate mostly on NFSv3 because it is considered very stable in Linux, it is very well known, and it also has the widest cross-platform support.

Security Considerations for NFS

Unfortunately, NFS is not a very secure method for sharing disks. The steps necessary to make NFS more secure are no different from those for securing any other system. The only catch is that you must be able to trust the users on the client system, especially the root user. If you're the root user on both the client and the server, there is a little less to worry about. The important thing in this case is to make sure nonroot users don't become root—which is something you should be doing anyway!

If you are in a situation where you cannot fully trust the person with whom you need to share a disk, it will be worth your time and effort to seek alternative methods of sharing resources (such as read-only sharing of the disk).

As always, stay up-to-date on the latest security bulletins coming from the Computer Emergency Response Team (http://www.cert.org/), and keep up with all the patches from your distribution vendor.

Mount and Access a Partition

Several steps are involved in a client's making a request to mount a server's partition (these steps mostly pertain to NFSv2 and NFSv3):

1. The client contacts the server's portmapper to find out which network port is assigned as the NFS mount service.

2. The client contacts the mount service and requests to mount a partition. The mount service checks to see if the client has permission to mount the requested partition. (Permission for a client to mount a partition is based on the **/etc/exports** file.) If the client does have permission, the mount service returns an affirmative.

3. The client contacts the portmapper again, this time to find out on which port the NFS server is located. (Typically, this is port 2049.)

4. Whenever the client wants to make a request to the NFS server (for example, to read a directory), an RPC is sent to the NFS server.

5. When the client is done, it updates its own mount tables but doesn't inform the server.

Notification to the server is unnecessary, because the server doesn't keep track of all clients that have mounted its file systems. Because the server doesn't maintain state information about clients and the clients don't maintain state information about the server, clients and servers can't tell the difference between a crashed system and a really slow system. Thus, if an NFS server is rebooted, all clients will automatically resume their operations with the server as soon as the server is back online.

Enabling NFS

Almost all the major Linux distributions ship with support for NFS in one form or another. The only task left for the administrator is to configure it and enable it. On our sample Fedora system, enabling NFS is very easy.

Because NFS and its ancillary programs are RPC based, you need to first make sure that the system **portmap** service is running. To check the status of the portmapper on Fedora, type

```
[root@serverA ~]# service portmap status
portmap is stopped
```

If the **portmap** service is stopped as in this example, start it like so:

```
[root@serverA ~]# service portmap start
Starting portmap:                                          [  OK  ]
```

Before going any further, use the **rpcinfo** command to view the status of any RPC-based services that might have registered with **portmap**. Type

```
[root@serverA ~]# rpcinfo -p
   program vers proto   port
    100000    2   tcp    111  portmapper
    100000    2   udp    111  portmapper
```

Because we don't yet have NFS running on the sample system, this output does not show too many RPC services.

To start the NFS service, enter this command:

```
[root@serverA ~]# service nfs start
Starting NFS services:                                     [  OK  ]
Starting NFS quotas:                                       [  OK  ]
Starting NFS daemon:                                       [  OK  ]
Starting NFS mountd:                                       [  OK  ]
```

Running the **rpcinfo** command again to view the status of RPC programs registered with the portmapper shows this output:

```
[root@serverA ~]# rpcinfo -p
program vers proto   port
100000    2   tcp    111  portmapper
100000    2   udp    111  portmapper
100011    1   udp    952  rquotad
100003    2   udp   2049  nfs
....<OUTPUT TRUNCATED>.....
100003    3   udp   2049  nfs
```

```
100021    1   udp   32791   nlockmgr
100005    1   udp     970   mountd
```

This output shows that various RPC programs (**mountd**, **nfs**, **rquotad**, etc.) are now running.

To stop NFS without having to shut down, enter this command:

```
[root@serverA ~]# service nfs stop
Shutting down NFS mountd:                          [  OK  ]
Shutting down NFS daemon:                          [  OK  ]
Shutting down NFS quotas:                          [  OK  ]
Shutting down NFS services:                        [  OK  ]
```

In order to have the NFS service automatically start up with the system with the next reboot, use the **chkconfig** command. First check the runlevels for which it is currently configured to start by typing

```
[root@serverA ~]# chkconfig --list  nfs
nfs            0:off   1:off   2:off   3:off   4:off   5:off   6:off
```

The service is disabled by default on a Fedora Core system; enable it to start up automatically by typing

```
[root@serverA ~]# chkconfig  nfs on
```

The Components of NFS

Versions 2 and 3 of the NFS protocol rely heavily on remote procedure calls (RPCs) to handle communications between clients and servers. RPC services in Linux are managed by the **portmap** service. As mentioned before, this ancillary service is no longer needed in NFSv4.

The following list shows the various RPC processes that facilitate the NFS service under Linux. The RPC processes are mostly relevant only in NFS versions 2 and 3, but mention is made wherever NFSv4 applies.

▼ **rpc.statd** This process is responsible for sending notifications to NFS clients whenever the NFS server is restarted with being gracefully shut down. It provides status information about the server to **rpc.lockd** when queried. This is done via the Network Status Monitor (NSM) RPC protocol. It is an optional service that is started automatically by the **nfslock** service on a Fedora system. It is not used in NFSv4.

■ **rpc.rquotad** As its name suggests, **rpc.rquotad** supplies the interface between NFS and the quota manager. NFS users/clients will be held to the same quota restrictions that would apply to them if they were working on the local file system instead of via NFS.

- **rpc.mountd**   When a request to mount a partition is made, the **rpc.mountd** daemon takes care of verifying that the client has enough permission to make the request. This permission is stored in the **/etc/exports** file. (The upcoming section "The /etc/exports Configuration File" tells you more about the **/etc/exports** file.) It is automatically started by the NFS server **init** scripts. It is not used in NFSv4.

- **rpc.nfsd**   The main component to the NFS system, this is the NFS server/ daemon. It works in conjunction with the Linux kernel to either load or unload the kernel module as necessary. It is of course still relevant in NFSv4.

NOTE   You should understand that NFS itself is an RPC-based service regardless of the version of the protocol. Therefore, even NFSv4 is inherently RPC-based. The fine print lies in the fact that most of the previously used ancillary RPC-based services (e.g., **mountd**, **statd**) are no longer necessary because their individual functions have now been folded into the NFS daemon.

- **rpc.lockd**   The **rpc.statd** daemon uses this daemon to handle lock recovery on crashed systems. It also allows NFS clients to lock files on the server. It is the **nfslock** service, no longer used in NFSv4.

- **rpc.idmapd**   This is the NFSv4 ID name mapping daemon. It provides this functionality to the NFSv4 kernel client and server, by translating user and group IDs to names, and vice versa.

- **rpc.svcgssd**   This is the server-side **rpcsec_gss** daemon. The **rpcsec_gss** protocol allows the use of the gss-api generic security API to provide advanced security in NFSv4.

- **rpc.gssd**   This provides the client-side transport mechanism for the authentication mechanism in NFSv4.

Kernel Support for NFS

NFS is implemented in two forms among the various Linux distributions. Most distributions ship with NFS support enabled in the kernel. And a few Linux distributions also ship with support for NFS in the form of a standalone daemon that can be installed via a package.

As far back as Linux 2.2, there has been kernel-based support for NFS, which runs significantly faster than earlier implementations. As of the time of writing, kernel-based NFS server support is considered production ready. It is not mandatory—if you don't compile support for it into the kernel, you will not use it. If you have the opportunity to try kernel support for NFS, it is highly recommended that you do so. If you choose not to use it, don't worry: the **nfsd** program that handles NFS server services is completely self-contained and provides everything necessary to serve NFS.

NOTE   On the other hand, clients must have support for NFS in the kernel. This support in the kernel has been around for a very long time and is known to be very stable. Almost all present-day Linux distributions ship with kernel support for NFS enabled.

CONFIGURING AN NFS SERVER

Setting up an NFS server is a two-step process. The first step is to create the **/etc/exports** file. This file defines which parts of your server's disk get shared with the rest of your network and the rules by which they get shared. (For example, is a client allowed only read access to the file system? Are they allowed to write to the file system?) The second step is to start the NFS server processes that read the **/etc/exports** file.

The /etc/exports Configuration File

This is the primary configuration file for the NFS server. This file lists the partitions that are sharable, the hosts they can be shared with, and with what permissions. The file specifies remote mount points for the NFS mount protocol.

The format for the file is very simple. Each line in the file specifies the mount point(s) and export flags within one local server file system for one or more hosts.

Here is the format of each entry in the **/etc/exports** file:

```
/directory/to/export client|ip_network(permissions) client|ip_network(permissions)
```

▼   **/directory/to/export** is the directory you want to share with other users, for example, **/home**.

■   **client** refers to the host name(s) of the NFS client(s).

■   **ip_network** allows the matching of hosts by IP addresses (e.g., 172.16.1.1) or network addresses with a netmask combination (e.g., 172.16.0.0/16).

▲   **permissions** are the corresponding permissions for each client. Table 22-1 describes the valid permissions for each client.

Following is an example of a complete NFS **/etc/exports** file. Please note that line numbers (1–4) have been added to the listing to aid readability.

```
1) # /etc/exports file for serverA
2) #
3) /home        hostA(rw) hostB(rw) clientA(ro,no_root_squash)
4) /usr/local   172.16.0.0/16(ro)
```

The first and second lines (lines 1 and 2) are comments and are ignored when the file is read. Line 3 exports the /home file system to the machines named hostA and hostB

Permission Option	Meaning
secure	The port number from which the client requests a mount must be lower than 1024. This permission is on by default. To turn it off, specify **insecure** instead.
ro	Allows read-only access to the partition. This is the default permission whenever nothing is specified explicitly.
rw	Allows normal read/write access.
noaccess	The client will be denied access to all directories below **/dir/to/mount**. This allows you to export the directory **/dir** to the client and then to specify **/dir/to** as inaccessible without taking away access to something like **/dir/from**.
root_squash	This permission prevents remote root users from having superuser (root's) privileges on remote NFS-mounted volumes. The "squash" here literarily means to squash the power of the remote root user.
no_root_squash	This allows the root user on the NFS client host to access the NFS-mounted directory with the same rights and privileges that the superuser would normally have.
all_squash	Maps all UIDs and GIDs to the anonymous user. The opposite option is **no_all_squash**, which is the default setting.

Table 22-1. NFS Permissions

and gives them read/write permissions, as well as to the machine named clientA, giving it read-only access but allowing the remote root user to have root privileges on the exported file system (/home).

Line 4 exports the **/usr/local/** directory to all hosts on the 172.16.0.0/16 network. Hosts in the network range are allowed read-only access.

Telling the NFS Server Process about /etc/exports

Once you have an **/etc/exports** file written up, use the **exportfs** command to tell the NFS server processes to reread the configuration information. The parameters for **exportfs** are as follows:

exportfs Command Option	Description
-a	Exports all entries in the **/etc/exports** file. It can also be used to unexport the exported file systems when used along with the **u** option, e.g., **exportfs -ua**.
-r	Reexports all entries in the **/etc/exports** file. This synchronizes **/var/lib/nfs/xtab** with the contents of the **/etc/exports** file. For example, it deletes entries from **/var/lib/nfs/xtab** that are no longer in **/etc/exports** and removes stale entries from the kernel export table.
-u clientA:/dir/to/mount	Unexports the directory **/dir/to/mount** to the host clientA.
-o options	Options specified here are the same as described in Table 22-1 for client permissions. These options will apply only to the file system specified on the **exportfs** command line, not to those in **/etc/exports**.
-v	Be verbose.

Following are examples of **exportfs** command lines.

To export all file systems,

```
[root@serverA ~]# exportfs -a
```

To export the directory **/usr/local** to the host clientA with the **read/write** and **no_root_squash** permissions,

```
[root@serverA ~]# exportfs -o rw,no_root_squash clientA:/usr/local
```

In most instances, you will simply want to use **exportfs -r**.

Note that Fedora Core and RHEL systems have a very capable GUI tool (Figure 22-1) that can be used for creating, modifying, and deleting NFS shares. The tool is called **system-config-nfs**. It can be launched from the command line by executing the following:

```
[root@serverA ~]# system-config-nfs
```

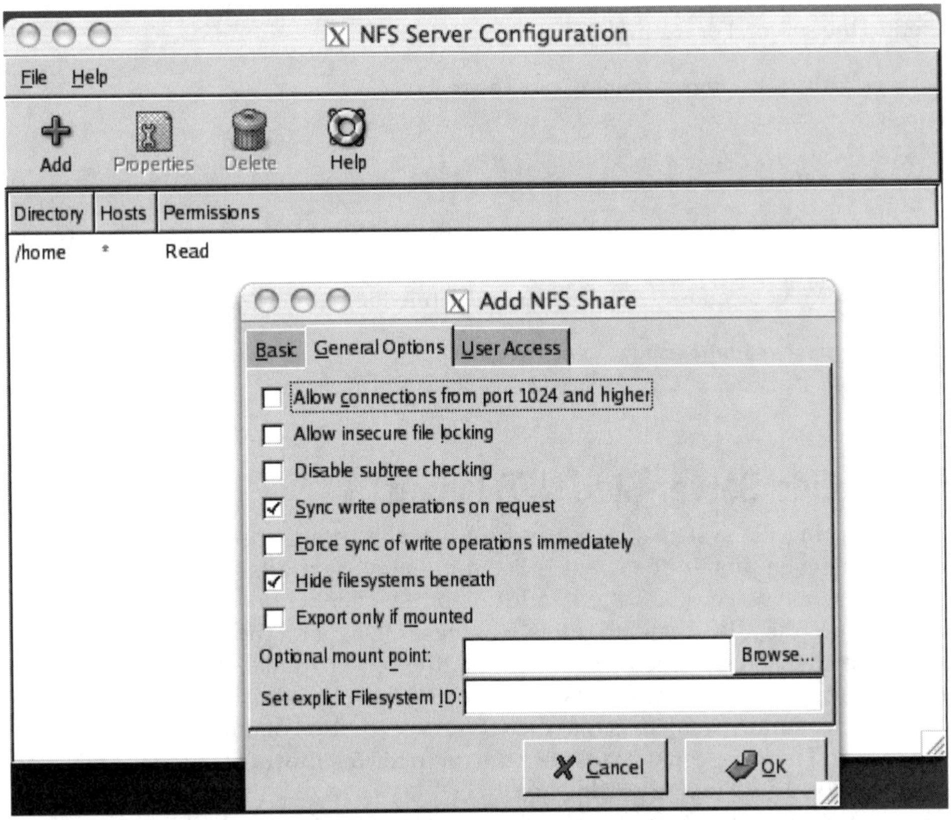

Figure 22-1.   NFS server configuration utility

The showmount Command

When configuring NFS, it is helpful to use the **showmount** command to see if everything is working correctly. The command is used for showing mount information for an NFS server.

By using the **showmount** command, you can quickly determine if you have configured **nfsd** correctly.

After you have configured your **/etc/exports** file and exported all of your file systems using **exportfs**, you can run **showmount -e** to see a listing of exported file systems on the local NFS server. The **-e** option tells **showmount** to show the NFS server's export list. For example,

```
[root@serverA ~]# showmount -e localhost
Export list for localhost:
/home *
```

If you simply run the **showmount** command with no options, it will list clients connected to the server. For example,

```
[root@serverA ~]# showmount  localhost
Hosts on localhost:
*
192.168.1.100
```

You can also run this command on clients by passing the server host name as the last argument. To show the exported file systems on the NFS server (serverA) from an NFS client (clientA), you can issue this command while logged in to clientA:

```
[root@clientA ~]# showmount -e  serverA
Export list for serverA:
/home *
```

Troubleshooting Server-Side NFS Issues

When exporting file systems, you may find that the server appears to be refusing the client access, even though the client is listed in the **/etc/exports** file. Typically, this happens because the server takes the IP address of the client connecting to it and resolves that address to the fully qualified domain name (FQDN), and the host name listed in the **/etc/exports** file isn't qualified. (For example, the server thinks the client host name is clientA.example.com, but the **/etc/exports** file lists just clientA.)

Another common problem is that the server's perception of the host name/IP pairing is not correct. This can occur because of an error in the **/etc/hosts** file or in the DNS tables. You'll need to verify that the pairing is correct.

For NFSv2 and NFSv3, the NFS service may fail to start correctly if the other required services such as the **portmap** service are not already running.

Even when everything seems to be set up correctly on the client side and the server side, you may find that the firewall on the server side is preventing the mount process from completing. In such situations, you will notice that the **mount** command seems to hang without any obvious errors.

CONFIGURING NFS CLIENTS

NFS clients are remarkably easy to configure under Linux, because they don't require any new or additional software to be loaded. The only requirement is that the kernel be compiled to support the NFS file system. Virtually all Linux distributions come with this feature enabled by default. Aside from the kernel support, the only other important factor is the options used with the **mount** command.

The mount Command

The **mount** command was originally discussed in Chapter 7. The important parameters to use with the **mount** command are: the specification of the NFS server name, the local mount point, and the options specified after the **-o** on the **mount** command line.

Following is an example of a **mount** command line:

```
[root@clientA ~]# mount -o rw,bg,soft serverA:/home /mnt/home
```

These **mount** options can also be used in the **/etc/fstab** file. This same entry in the **/etc/fstab** file would look like this:

```
serverA:/home      /mnt/home      nfs      rw,bg,soft 0 0
```

Here, **serverA** is the NFS server name. The **-o** options are listed in Table 22-2.

Soft vs. Hard Mounts

By default, NFS operations are *hard,* which means they continue their attempts to contact the server indefinitely. This arrangement is not always beneficial, however. It causes a problem if an emergency shutdown of all systems is performed. If the servers happen to get shut down before the clients, the clients' shutdowns will stall while they wait for the servers to come back up. Enabling a *soft* mount allows the client to time out the connection after a number of retries (specified with the **retrans=r** option).

There is one exception to the preferred arrangement of having a soft mount with a **retrans=r** value specified: don't use this arrangement when you have data that must be committed to disk no matter what, and you don't want to return control to the application until the data has been committed. (NFS-mounted mail directories are typically mounted this way.)

Cross-Mounting Disks

Cross-mounting is the process of having server A NFS-mounting server B's disks, and server B NFS-mounting server A's disks. While this may appear innocuous at first, there is a subtle danger in doing this. If both servers crash, and if both servers require mounting the other's disk in order to boot correctly, you've got a chicken and egg problem. Server A won't boot until server B is done booting, but server B won't boot because server A isn't done booting.

To get around this problem, make sure you don't get yourself into a situation where this happens. All of your servers should be able to completely boot without needing to mount anyone else's disks for anything. However, this doesn't mean you can't cross-mount at all. There are legitimate reasons for needing to cross-mount, such as needing to make home directories available across all servers.

`mount -o` Command Option	Description
`bg`	Background mount. Should the mount initially fail (for instance, if the server is down), the mount process will send itself to background processing and continue trying to execute until it is successful. This is useful for file systems mounted at boot time, because it keeps the system from hanging at the **mount** command if the server is down.
`intr`	Specifies an interruptible mount. If a process has pending I/O on a mounted partition, this option allows the process to be interrupted and the I/O call to be dropped. For more information, see "The Importance of the `intr` Option," later in this section.
`hard`	This is an implicit default option. If an NFS file operation has a major timeout, then a "server not responding" message is reported on the console and the client continues retrying indefinitely.
`soft`	Enables a soft mount for this partition, allowing the client to time out the connection after a number of retries (specified with the **retrans=r** option). For more information, see "Soft vs. Hard Mounts," earlier in this section.
`retrans=n`	The n value specifies the maximum number of connection retries for a soft-mounted system.
`rsize=n`	The value n is the number of bytes NFS uses when reading files from an NFS server. The default value is dependent on the kernel but is currently 4096 bytes for NFSv4. Throughput can be improved greatly by requesting a higher value (e.g., rsize=32768).

Table 22-2.   Mount Options for NFS

`mount -o` Command Option	Description
`wsize=n`	The value *n* specifies the number of bytes NFS uses when writing files to an NFS server. The default value is dependent on the kernel but is currently something like 4096 bytes for NFSv4. Throughput can be greatly improved by asking for a higher value (e.g., wsize=32768.) This value is negotiated with the server.
`proto=n`	The value *n* specifies the network protocol to use to mount the NFS file system. The default value in NFSv2 and NFSv3 is UDP. NFS version 4 servers generally support only TCP. Therefore, the valid protocol types are udp and tcp.
`nfsvers=n`	Allows the use of an alternate RPC version number to contact the NFS daemon on the remote host. The default value depends on the kernel, but the possible values are 2 or 3. This option is not recognized in NFSv4, where instead you'd simply state **nfs4** as the file system type.
`sec=value`	Sets the security mode for the mount operation to ***value***. ▼ **sec=sys** Uses local UNIX UIDs and GIDs to authenticate NFS operations (AUTH_SYS). This is the default setting. ■ **sec=krb5** Uses Kerberos V5 instead of local UIDs and GIDs to authenticate users. ■ **sec=krb5i** Uses Kerberos V5 for user authentication and performs integrity checking of NFS operations using secure checksums to prevent data tampering. ▲ **sec=krb5p** Uses Kerberos V5 for user authentication and integrity checking, and encrypts NFS traffic to prevent traffic sniffing.

Table 22-2.   Mount Options for NFS (*cont.*)

In these situations, make sure you set your **/etc/fstab** entries to use the **bg** mount option. By doing so, you will allow each server to background the **mount** process for any failed mounts, thus giving all of the servers a chance to completely boot and then properly make their NFS mountable partitions available.

The Importance of the intr Option

When a process makes a system call, the kernel takes over the action. During the time that the kernel is handling the system call, the process has no control over itself. In the event of a kernel access error, the process must continue to wait until the kernel request returns; the process can't give up and quit. In normal cases, the kernel's control isn't a problem, because typically, kernel requests get resolved very quickly. When there's an error, however, it can be quite a nuisance. Because of this, NFS has an option to mount partitions with the interruptible flag (the **intr** option), which allows a process that is waiting on an NFS request to give up and move on.

In general, unless you have reason not to use the **intr** option, it is usually a good idea to do so.

TIP   Keep those UIDs in sync! Every NFS client request to an NFS server includes the UID of the user making the request. This UID is used by the server to verify that the user has permissions to access the requested file. However, in order for NFS permission-checking to work correctly, the UIDs of the users must be synchronized between the client and server. (There is the **all_squash /etc/ exports** option that can circumvent this.) Having the same username on both systems is not enough. An NIS database or an LDAP database may help in this situation.

Performance Tuning

The default block size that gets transmitted with NFS versions 2 and 3 is 1KB (for NFSv4 it is 4KB). This is handy, since it fits nicely into one packet, and should any packets get dropped, NFS has to retransmit very few packets. The downside to this is that it doesn't take advantage of the fact that most networking stacks are fast enough to keep up with segmenting larger blocks of data for transport, and that most networks are reliable enough that it is extremely rare to lose a block of data.

Given these factors, it is often better to optimize for the case of a fast networking stack and a reliable network, since that's what you're going to have 99% of the time. The easiest way to do this with NFS is to use the **wsize** (write size) and **rsize** (read size) options. A good size to use is 8KB for NFS versions 2 and 3. This is especially good if you have network cards that support jumbo frames.

An example entry with **wsize** and **rsize** is as follows:

```
serverA:/home  /mnt/home  nfs      nfsvers=3,rw,bg,wsize=8192,rsize=8192 0 0
```

TROUBLESHOOTING CLIENT-SIDE NFS ISSUES

Like any major service, NFS has mechanisms to help it cope with error conditions. In this section, we discuss some common error cases and how NFS handles them.

Stale File Handles

If a file or directory is in use by one process when another process removes the file or directory, the first process gets an error message from the server. Typically, this error is "Stale NFS file handle."

Most often, stale file handles occur when you're using a system in the X Window System environment and you have two terminal windows open. For instance, the first terminal window is in a particular directory (say, **/mnt/usr/local/mydir/**), and that directory gets deleted from the second terminal window. The next time you press ENTER in the first terminal window, you'll see the error message.

To fix this problem, simply change your directory to one that you know exists, without using relative directories (for example, **cd /tmp**).

Permission Denied

You're likely to see the "Permission denied" message if you're logged in as root and are trying to access a file that is NFS mounted. Typically, this means that the server on which the file system is mounted is not acknowledging root's permissions.

This is usually the result of forgetting that the **/etc/exports** file will by default enable the **root_squash** option. And so if you are experimenting from a permitted NFS client as the root user, you might wonder why you are getting access denied errors even though the remote NFS share seems to be mounted properly.

The quick way around this problem is to become the user who owns the file you're trying to control. For example, if you're root and you're trying to access a file owned by the user mmellow, use the **su** command to become mmellow:

```
[root@clientA ~]# su - mmellow
```

When you're done working with the file, you can exit out of mmellow's shell and return to root. Note that this work-around assumes that mmellow exists as a user on the system and has the same UID on both the client and the server.

A similar problem is when users obviously have the same usernames on the client and the server but still get permission denied errors. This may be because the actual UIDs associated with the usernames on both systems are different. For example, the user mmellow may have a UID of 501 on the host clientA but a user with the same name, mmellow, on serverA may have a UID of 600. The simple work-around to this might be to create users with the same UIDs and GIDs across all systems. The scalable work-around to this might be to implement a central user database infrastructure such as LDAP or NIS so that all users have the same UIDs and GIDs independent of their local client systems.

CLIENT AND SERVER NFS CONFIGURATION

In this section we'll put everything we've learned thus far together by walking through the actual setup of an NFS environment. We will set up and configure the NFS server. Once that is accomplished, we will set up an NFS client and make sure that the directories get mounted when the system boots.

In particular we want to export the /usr/local file system on the host serverA to a particular host on the network named clientA. We want clientA to have read/write access to the shared volume and the rest of the world to have read-only access to the share. Our clientA will mount the NFS share at its /mnt/usr/local mount point. The procedure involves these steps:

1. On the server—serverA—edit the **/etc/exports** configuration file. You will share **/usr/local**. Input this text into the **/etc/exports** file.

   ```
   #
   /usr/local       clientA(rw,root_squash) *(ro)
   ```

2. Save your changes to the file when you are done editing and exit the text editor.

3. First you need to check if the portmapper is running. If it is not running, start it.

   ```
   [root@serverA ~]# service portmap status
   portmap is stopped
   [root@serverA ~]# service portmap start
   Starting portmap:                                        [  OK  ]
   ```

TIP On a SuSE system the equivalent of the preceding commands are `rcportmap status` and `rcportmap start`. And on a system that does not have the `service` command, you can try looking under the /**etc/init.d**/ directory for a file possibly named **portmap**. You can then manually execute the file with the `status` or `start` option to control the **portmap** service, e.g., by entering

```
[root@serverA ~]# /etc/init.d/portmap status
```

4. Next start the **nfs** service, which will start all the other attendant services it needs.

   ```
   [root@serverA ~]# service nfs start
   Starting NFS services:                                   [  OK  ]
   Starting NFS quotas:                                     [  OK  ]
   Starting NFS daemon:                                     [  OK  ]
   Starting NFS mountd:                                     [  OK  ]
   ```

   Typically the **nfs** startup script will let you know if it started or failed to start up. This sample output shows that all went well.

5. To check if your exports are configured correctly, run the **showmount** command:

   ```
   [root@serverA ~]# showmount -e localhost
   ```

6. If you don't see the file systems that you put into **/etc/exports**, check **/var/log/ messages** for any output that **nfsd** or **mountd** might have made. If you need to make changes to **/etc/exports**, run **service nfs reload** or **exportfs -r** when you are done and finally run a **showmount -e** to make sure that the changes took effect.

7. Now that you have the server configured, it is time to set up the client. First, see if the **rpc** mechanism is working between the client and the server. You will again use the **showmount** command to verify that the client can see the shares. If the client cannot, you might have a network problem or a permissions problem to the server. From clientA issue the command

```
[root@clientA ~]# showmount -e serverA
Export list for serverA:
/usr/local (everyone)
```

8. Once you have verified that you can view shares from the client, it is time to see if you can successfully mount a file system. First create the /mnt/usr/local/ mount point and then use the **mount** command as follows:

```
[root@clientA ~]# mkdir /mnt/usr/local
[root@clientA ~]#mount -o rw,bg,intr,soft serverA:/usr/local /mnt/usr/local
```

9. You can use the **mount** command to view only the NFS-type file systems that are mounted on clientA. Type

```
[root@clientA ~]# mount -t nfs
```

10. If these commands succeed, you can add the **mount** command with its options into the **/etc/fstab** file so that they will get the remote file system mounted upon reboot.

```
serverA:/usr/local    /mnt/usr/local    nfs    rw,bg,intr,soft 0   0
```

COMMON USES FOR NFS

The following ideas are, of course, just ideas. You are likely to have your own reasons for sharing disks via NFS.

▼ **To hold popular programs.** If you are accustomed to Windows, you've probably worked with applications that refuse to be installed on network shares. For one reason or another, these programs want every system to have its own copy of the software—a nuisance, especially if you have a lot of machines that need the software. Linux (and UNIX in general) rarely has such conditions prohibiting the installation of software on network disks. (The most common exceptions are high-performance databases.) Thus, many sites install heavily used software on a special partition that is exported to all hosts in a network.

■ **To hold home directories.** Another common use for NFS partitions is to hold home directories. By placing home directories on NFS-mountable partitions, it's possible to configure the Automounter and NIS or LDAP so that users can log in to any machine in the network and have their home directory available to them. Heterogeneous sites typically use this configuration so that users can seamlessly move from one variant of UNIX to another without worrying about having to carry their data around with them.

▲ **For shared mail spools.** A directory residing on the mail server can be used to store all of the user mailboxes, and the directory can then be exported via NFS to all hosts on the network. In this setup, traditional UNIX mail readers can read a user's e-mail straight from the spool file stored on the NFS share. In the case of large sites with heavy e-mail traffic, multiple servers might be used for providing POP3 mailboxes, and all the mailboxes can easily reside on a common NFS share that is accessible to all the servers.

SUMMARY

In this chapter, we discussed the process of setting up an NFS server and client. This requires very little configuration on the server side. The client side requires a wee bit more configuration. But in general the process of getting NFS up and running is relatively painless. Here are some key points to remember:

▼ NFS has been around for a long time now, and as such it has gone through several revisions of the protocol specifications. The revisions are mostly backward compatible, and each succeeding revision can support clients using the older versions.

■ NFS version 4 is the newest revision and is loaded with a lot of improvements and features that were not previously available. As at the time of this writing, the industry has been a little slow to adopt this version, probably because everybody is waiting for somebody else to adopt it and discover and fix any bugs or issues it might have. But it is gradually becoming popular.

■ The older NFS protocols (versions 2 and 3) are implemented as a stateless protocol. Clients can't tell the difference between a crashed server and a slow server; thus, recovery is automatic when the server comes back up. (In the reverse situation, when the client crashes and the server stays up, recovery is also automatic.)

▲ The key server processes in NFSv2 and NFSv3 are **rpc.statd**, **rpc.quotad**, **rpc.mountd**, and **rpc.nfsd**. Most of these functions have been rolled into one in NFSv4.

NFS is a powerful tool for sharing storage volumes across network clients. Be sure to spend some time experimenting with it before using it to try to meet your environment's resource-sharing needs.

Network Information Service (NIS)

The Network Information Service (NIS) facilitates the sharing of critical data stored in flat files among systems on a network. Typically, files such as **/etc/passwd** and **/etc/group**, which ideally would remain uniform across all hosts, are shared via NIS. Making such files available via NIS would allow any properly configured NIS client networked machine to access the data contained in these shared files and use the network versions of these files as extensions to the local versions. However, NIS is not limited to sharing just those two files. Any tabular file in which at least one column has a unique value throughout the file can be shared via NIS. Such files are very common on Linux/UNIX systems, e.g., the Sendmail aliases file, the Automounter files, or the **/etc/services** file.

The main benefit achieved from using NIS is that you can maintain a central copy of the data, and whenever that data is updated, it automatically propagates to all of the network users. To your users, features of NIS help to give the appearance of a more uniform system—no matter what host they may be working on.

If you're coming from a Windows background, you might think of NIS as the Linux/UNIX solution for some of the services offered by Active Directory. NIS of course is a much older technology and as such does not attempt to solve (or create ☺) the plethora of issues that Active Directory tackles.

In this chapter, we'll explore NIS, how it works, and how it can benefit you. We will then explain how to set up the client and server portions of the NIS configuration. Finally, we'll discuss some of the tools related to NIS.

INSIDE NIS

The Network Information Service is really just a simple database that clients can query. It contains a series of independent tables. Each table is created from straight text files, such as **/etc/passwd**, which is tabular in nature and has at least one column that is unique for every row (a database of key/value pairs). NIS keeps track of these tables by name and allows querying to happen in one of two ways:

▼ Listing the entire table

▲ Pulling a specific entry to match a search for a given key

Once the databases are established on the server, clients can query the server for database entries. Typically this happens when a client is configured to look to the NIS *map* when an entry cannot be found in the client's local database. A host may have a simple file containing only those entries needed for the system to work in single-user mode (when there is no network connectivity)—for example, the **/etc/passwd** file. When a program makes a request to look up user password information, the client checks its local **passwd** file and sees that the user doesn't exist there; the client then makes a request to the NIS server to look for a corresponding entry in the passwd table. If the NIS does have an entry, it is returned to the client and then to the program that requested the information in the first place. The program itself is unaware that NIS was used. The same is true if the NIS map returns an answer that the user password entry does not exist. The program would be passed the information without its knowing how much activity had happened in between.

This of course applies to all the files that we tell NIS to share. Other popular shared files include **/etc/group** and **/etc/hosts**.

> **NOTE** Although it is technically correct to refer to NIS's tables as a database, they are more typically called maps. (In this context, we are mapping keys to values.) Using the **/etc/passwd** file as an example, we map a user's login name (which we know is always unique) to the rest of the password entry.

Here is a listing of some daemons and processes that are associated with NIS:

▼ **ypserv** This daemon runs on the NIS server. It listens for queries from clients and responds with answers to those queries.

■ **ypxfrd** This daemon is used for propagating and transferring the NIS databases to slave servers.

▲ **ypbind** This is the client-side component of NIS. It is responsible for finding an NIS server to be queried for information. The **ypbind** daemon binds NIS clients to an NIS domain. It must be running on any machines running NIS client programs.

The NIS Servers

NIS can have only one authoritative server where the original data files are kept (this is somewhat similar to DNS). This authoritative server is called the *master* NIS server. If your organization is large enough, you may need to distribute the load across more than one machine. This can be done by setting up one or more *secondary (slave)* NIS servers. In addition to helping distribute the load, secondary servers also provide a mechanism to better handle server failures. The secondary NIS server can continue answering queries even while the master or other secondary servers are down.

> **NOTE** A server can be both a server and a client at the same time.

Secondary NIS servers receive updates whenever the primary NIS server is updated, so that the masters and slaves remain in sync. The process of keeping the secondary servers in sync with the primary is called a *server push*. As part of its update routine, the NIS master also pushes a copy of the map files to the secondary server. Upon receiving these files, the secondary servers update their databases, as well. The NIS master does not consider itself completely up-to-date until the secondary servers are up-to-date, as well.

NOTE   A server pull mechanism also exists for NIS. However, this solution is typically reserved for more complex configurations, such as when you have hundreds of slave servers. In a smaller network, this should not be an issue.

Domains

Primary NIS servers establish *domains* that are similar to the domains of a domain controller (DC) in Windows. A significant difference is that the NIS domain does not require the NIS server administrator to explicitly allow a client to join. (Bear in mind that the NIS model assumes that all clients are members of the same administrative domain and are thus managed by the same system administrators.) Furthermore, the NIS server only centralizes information/data; it does not by itself perform authentication—it defers to other system routines for this. The process of authenticating users is left to each individual host; NIS merely provides a centralized list of users.

TIP   Since NIS domains must be given names, it's a good practice (though not mandatory) to use names that are different from your DNS domain names. You'll have a much easier time discussing your network domains with fellow administrators when everyone knows which is which.

CONFIGURING THE MASTER NIS SERVER

Linux distributions typically have the client-side software for NIS already installed as a part of the initial operating system installation. This arrangement helps to make it easy to set up any system as an NIS client from the get go—some distributions will even give you the choice of configuring a machine to use NIS during the OS install.

Because not every system needs to act as an NIS server, you may have to manually install the NIS server component. This is usually very painless to do. The software required can be easily downloaded from your distribution's software repository (e.g., Web site or install media).

After installing the NIS server software, all that is usually left for you to do is to enable the service (if it isn't enabled already) and configure it. To make sure that the NIS server (ypserv) is started automatically between system boots, the **chkconfig** tool can be used.

First we'll install the server-side software for the NIS server. On a Fedora Core system and most other RPM-based Linux systems, the software package that provides the NIS server is aptly named **ypserv*.rpm** (where * represents the available version number).

Here we'll use the Yum program to quickly download and install the package from the Internet. Issue the Yum command:

```
[root@serverA ~]# yum install ypserv
...<OUTPUT TRUNCATED>...
Installing: ypserv                        ######################## [1/1]
Installed: ypserv.i386 0:*
Complete!
```

TIP   On a Fedora system, you can also install directly from the install media—the package can be found under the /media_mount_point/Fedora/RPMS directory). On a SuSE system, you can quickly install the ypserv package if it isn't already installed by using the Yast utility, as by entering `yast -i ypserv`.

Once NIS is installed and enabled, you'll need to configure it. There are four steps to doing this:

1. Establish the domain name.
2. Start the **ypserv** daemon to start NIS.
3. Edit the **Makefile**.
4. Run **ypinit** to create the databases.

The steps are examined in detail in the following section.

Establishing the Domain Name

Setting the NIS domain name is done with the **domainname** command. Let's say we're setting up a NIS domain called nis.example.org.

First use the **domainname** command to view the system's current NIS domain. Type

```
[root@serverA ~]# domainname
(none)
```

Now we'll go ahead and set the NIS domain like this:

```
[root@serverA ~]# domainname nis.example.org
```

Run the **domainname** command again to view your changes. Type

```
[root@serverA ~]# domainname
nis.example.org
```

To make your NIS domain name stick between each system reboot on a Fedora Core system and most other Red Hat–type systems, you can create a variable called NISDO-MAIN in the **/etc/sysconfig/network** file. Open up the file for editing and append an entry similar to this one at the end of the file:

```
NISDOMAIN=nis.example.org
```

We'll use the **echo** command to make the change to the **/etc/system/network** file. Type

```
[root@serverA ~]# echo "NISDOMAIN=nis.example.org" >> /etc/sysconfig/network
```

TIP In other Linux distributions you can achieve the same effect by adding the `domainname` command with the proper value to one of the **rc** scripts that gets executed while the system is booting; e.g., you can edit the **/etc/init.d/ypserv** script. Do a search for the line containing **domainname,** and if you can't find one, add one anywhere after the first line. The line should read like so:

```
domainname nis.example.org
```

Don't forget to replace `nis.example.org` with your own NIS domain name. The domain name should be set before the NIS server (**ypserv**) starts.

Starting NIS

The **ypserv** daemon is responsible for handling NIS requests. Starting the **ypserv** daemon is very easy on a Fedora Core or RHEL system. We'll use the **service** command to start it here. For other Linux distributions, you can directly execute the **ypserv** startup script (**/etc/ini.d/ypserv**) if you like, and for a SuSE system you can use the **rcypserv** command with the proper parameter.

NIS is an RPC-based service, and so you need to also make sure that the portmapper program is up and running before attempting to start NIS itself. To start the **portmap** service on a Fedora system, type

```
[root@serverA ~]# service portmap start
```

On our sample system, we'll start the NIS service like so:

```
[root@serverA ~]# service ypserv start
```

To confirm that the **ypserv** service has registered itself properly with the portmapper, use the **rpcinfo** command as shown here:

```
[root@serverA ~]# rpcinfo  -p
   program vers proto    port
    100000    2   tcp     111  portmapper
    100000    2   udp     111  portmapper
    100024    1   udp   32768  status
...<OUTPUT TRUNCATE>...
    100004    2   tcp     884  ypserv
    100004    1   tcp     884  ypserv
```

If you need to stop the NIS server at any time, you can do so with the command

```
[root@serverA ~]# service ypserv stop
```

Editing the Makefile

You've seen the use of the **make** command to compile programs in many other chapters. The **make** tool doesn't do the compilation, however—it simply keeps track of what files need to be compiled and then invokes the necessary program to perform the compilation. The file that actually contains the instructions for **make** is called a *makefile*.

The **make** tool is efficient because the programs it invokes are arbitrary. For example, you can substitute your preferred compiler in place of the one that comes with a particular Linux distribution. When **make** sees that a file's date and time have been modified, **make** takes that to mean that the file's contents have been modified. If the file has been modified, that tells **make** that the file needs to be recompiled.

Putting this concept to work on NIS is very straightforward. In this case, there's a series of straight text files that need to be converted into database format. We want a tool that will reconvert any files that have been changed—you can see how **make** fits the bill!

Changing over to the **/var/yp** directory, we see a file called **Makefile** (yes, all one word). This file lists the files that get shared via NIS, as well as some additional parameters for how they get shared and how much of each one gets shared. Open up the **Makefile** file with your favorite editor, and you can see all the configurable options. Let's step through the options in the **Makefile** file that apply to Linux.

But before proceeding, you should make a backup of the original untainted **Makefile**. You can use the copy (**cp**) command to do this:

```
[root@serverA ~]# cp /var/yp/Makefile   /var/yp/Makefile.original
```

The following section discusses some directives in the **Makefile** file that are of particular interest to us in this chapter. Sections of a sample **Makefile** are also quoted here along with their comments for clarity.

Designating Slave Servers: NOPUSH

If you plan to have NIS slave servers, you'll need to tell the master NIS server to push the resulting maps to the slave servers. Change the NOPUSH variable to false if you want slave servers.

> **NOTE**   If you don't need slave servers now but think you will need them later, you can change this option when you do add the servers.

```
# If we have only one server, we don't have to push the maps to the
# slave servers (NOPUSH=true). If you have slave servers, change this
# to "NOPUSH=false" and put all hostnames of your slave servers in the file
# /var/yp/ypservers.
NOPUSH=true
```

Remember to list the host names of your slave servers in the **/var/yp/ypservers** file. And for each host name you list there, be sure to list a corresponding entry in the **/etc/hosts** file.

Minimum UIDs and GIDs: MINUID and MINGID

When accounts are added, the minimum UID and GID created in the **/etc/passwd** and **/etc/group** files will be different depending on your Linux distribution. Be sure to set the minimum UID and GID values that you are willing to share via NIS. Obviously, you don't want to share the root entry via NIS, so the minimum should never be zero.

```
# We do not put password entries with lower UIDs (the root and system
# entries) in the NIS password database, for security. MINUID is the
# lowest uid that will be included in the password maps. If you
# create shadow maps, the UserID for a shadow entry is taken from
# the passwd file. If no entry is found, this shadow entry is
# ignored.
# MINGID is the lowest gid that will be included in the group maps.
MINUID=500
MINGID=500
```

Merging Shadow Passwords with Real Passwords: MERGE_PASSWD

So that NIS can be used for other systems to authenticate users, you will need to allow the encrypted password entries to be shared through NIS. If you are using shadow passwords, NIS will automatically handle this for you by taking the encrypted field from the **/etc/shadow** file and merging it into the NIS shared copy of **/etc/passwd**. Unless there is a specific reason why you do not want to enable sharing of the encrypted passwords, leave the MERGE_PASSWD setting alone.

```
# Should we merge the passwd file with the shadow file ?
# MERGE_PASSWD=true|false
MERGE_PASSWD=true
```

Merging Group Shadow Passwords with Real Groups: MERGE_GROUP

The **/etc/group** file allows passwords to be applied to group settings. Since the **/etc/group** file needs to be publicly readable, some systems have taken to supporting shadow group files—these are similar in nature to shadow password files. Unless you have a shadow group file, you need to set the MERGE_GROUP setting to false.

```
# Should we merge the group file with the gshadow file ?
# MERGE_GROUP=true|false
MERGE_GROUP=false
```

Designating Filenames

The following **Makefile** segment shows the files that are preconfigured to be shared via NIS. Just because they are listed here, however, does not mean they are automatically shared. This listing simply establishes variables for later use in the **Makefile**.

```
YPPWDDIR = /etc
```

This variable (**YPPWDDIR**) specifies the location of the passwd, group, and shadow files.

```
YPSRCDIR = /etc
```

The **YPSRCDIR** variable is generally used to specify the directory location of the other source files for NIS. It is used mostly for the network-related files such as the hosts file, protocols, file, and services file. The variable is used extensively in the rest of the file to specify the location of other files that might be of interest.

The listing that follows shows the actual usage of the YPPWDDIR and YPSRCDIR variables in the **Makefile**:

```
# These are the files from which the NIS databases are built. You may edit
# these to taste in the event that you wish to keep your NIS source files
# separate from your NIS server's actual configuration files.
#
GROUP        = $(YPPWDDIR)/group
PASSWD       = $(YPPWDDIR)/passwd
SHADOW       = $(YPPWDDIR)/shadow
GSHADOW      = $(YPPWDDIR)/gshadow
ADJUNCT      = $(YPPWDDIR)/passwd.adjunct
#ALIASES      = $(YPSRCDIR)/aliases  # aliases could be in /etc or /etc/mail
ALIASES      = /etc/aliases
ETHERS       = $(YPSRCDIR)/ethers      # ethernet addresses (for rarpd)
BOOTPARAMS   = $(YPSRCDIR)/bootparams # for booting Sun boxes (bootparamd)
HOSTS        = $(YPSRCDIR)/hosts
NETWORKS     = $(YPSRCDIR)/networks
PRINTCAP     = $(YPSRCDIR)/printcap
PROTOCOLS    = $(YPSRCDIR)/protocols
PUBLICKEYS   = $(YPSRCDIR)/publickey
RPC          = $(YPSRCDIR)/rpc
SERVICES     = $(YPSRCDIR)/services
NETGROUP     = $(YPSRCDIR)/netgroup
NETID        = $(YPSRCDIR)/netid
AMD_HOME     = $(YPSRCDIR)/amd.home
AUTO_MASTER  = $(YPSRCDIR)/auto.master
AUTO_HOME    = $(YPSRCDIR)/auto.home
AUTO_LOCAL   = $(YPSRCDIR)/auto.local
TIMEZONE     = $(YPSRCDIR)/timezone
LOCALE       = $(YPSRCDIR)/locale
NETMASKS     = $(YPSRCDIR)/netmasks
```

What Gets Shared: The all Entry

In the following **Makefile** entry, all of the maps listed after the **all:** are the maps that get shared:

```
all:  passwd group hosts rpc services netid protocols mail \
        # netgrp shadow publickey networks ethers bootparams printcap \
        # amd.home auto.master auto.home auto.local passwd.adjunct \
        # timezone locale netmasks
```

Notice that the line continuation character, the backslash (\ ), is used to ensure that the **make** program knows to treat the entire entry as one line, even though it is really three lines. In addition, note that the second, third, and fourth lines begins with a pound sign (#), which means the rest of the line is commented out.

Given this format, you can see that the maps configured to be shared are **passwd**, **group**, **hosts**, **rpc**, **services**, **netid**, **protocols**, and **mail**. These entries correspond to the filenames listed in the preceding section of the **Makefile**. Of course, not all sites want these entries shared, or they want some additional maps shared (such as the Automounter files, **auto.master** and **auto.home**). To change any of the maps you want shared, alter the line so that the maps you *don't* want shared are listed after a # symbol.

For example, let's say you want only the **passwd** and **group** maps shared over NIS. You'd change the **all:** line to read as follows:

```
all: passwd group \
     # hosts rpc services protocols netgrp mail \
     # shadow publickey networks ethers bootparams amd.home \
     # passwd.adjunct
```

Note that the order of the maps in the **all:** line doesn't matter. The placement of the foregoing entries simply makes them easily read.

Using ypinit

Once you have the **Makefile** ready, you need to initialize the YP (NIS) server using the **ypinit** command.

> **NOTE** Remember that you must already have the NIS domain name set before you run the **ypinit** command. This is done with the **domainname** utility as shown in "Establishing the Domain Name" earlier in this chapter.

```
[root@serverA ~]# /usr/lib/yp/ypinit  -m
```

Here, the **-m** option tells **ypinit** to set the system up as a master NIS server. Assuming we are running this command on our sample system named serverA, we would see the system respond as follows:

```
At this point, we have to construct a list of the hosts which will run
NIS servers.  serverA.example.org is in the list of NIS server hosts.
Please continue to add the names for the other hosts, one per line.
When you are done with the list, type a <control D>.
        next host to add:  serverA.example.org
        next host to add:
```

Continue entering the names of any secondary NIS servers if you plan on having them. Press CTRL-D when you have added all necessary servers. These entries will be placed in the **/var/yp/ypservers** file for you; if needed, you can change them by editing the file later.

You will next be prompted to confirm if the information you entered is correct. The current list of NIS servers looks like this:

```
serverA.example.org
Is this correct?  [y/n: y]  y
We need a few minutes to build the databases...
Building /var/yp/nis.example.org/ypservers...
gethostbyname(): Success
Running /var/yp/Makefile...
gmake[1]: Entering directory `/var/yp/nis.example.org'
Updating passwd.byname...
failed to send 'clear' to local ypserv: RPC: Program not registeredUpdating
passwd.byuid...
failed to send 'clear' to local ypserv: RPC: Program not registeredUpdating
group.byname...
...<OUTPUT TRUNCATED>...
serverA.example.org has been set up as a NIS master server.
Now you can run ypinit -s serverA.example.org on all slave servers.
```

(Ignore any error messages that may have resulted from this command for now. The possible errors are discussed in better detail in the following section.)

Once you are done, **ypinit** will run the **make** program automatically for you, to build the maps and push them to any secondary servers you have indicated.

This might be a good time to make sure that the **portmap** and NIS server services are running. Start them with the commands that follow if they are not running:

```
[root@serverA ~]# service portmap start
Starting portmap:                                      [  OK  ]
[root@serverA ~]# service ypserv start
Starting YP server services:                           [  OK  ]
```

Makefile Errors

Examine any errors that may have occurred from running the **ypinit** command in the previous section. The errors are most likely not fatal errors.

If you made a mistake in the **Makefile**, you may get an error when **ypinit** runs the **make** program. If you see this error,

```
gmake[1]: *** No rule to make target '/etc/shadow', needed by 'passwd.byname'.
Stop.
```

don't worry about it. This means you have specified a file to share that doesn't exist (in this error message, the file is **/etc/shadow**). You can either create the file or go back and edit the **Makefile** so that the file is not shared. (See the previous section "What Gets Shared: The all Entry.")

Another common error message is

```
failed to send 'clear' to local ypserv: RPC: Program not registered
Updating passwd.byuid...
failed to send 'clear' to local ypserv: RPC: Program not registered
gmake[1]: *** No rule to make target '/etc/gshadow', needed by 'group.byname'.
Stop.
gmake[1]: Leaving directory '/var/yp/serverA.example.org'
```

There are actually two error messages here. You can ignore the first one, which indicates that the NIS server hasn't been started yet. The second error message is the same one described in the preceding paragraph. Once you've fixed it, type in the following command to rebuild the maps, as described in the next section:

```
[root@serverA ~]# cd /var/yp ; make
```

Updating NIS Maps

If you have updated the files configured to be shared by NIS with the rest of your network, you need to rebuild the map files. (For example, you may have added a user to the central **/etc/passwd** file.) To rebuild the maps, use the following **make** command:

```
[root@serverA ~]# cd /var/yp ; make
```

CONFIGURING AN NIS CLIENT

Thankfully, NIS clients are much easier to configure than NIS servers! To set up an NIS client, you need to do the following:

1. Edit the **/etc/yp.conf** file.
2. Set up the startup script.
3. Edit the **/etc/nsswitch.conf** file.

Editing the /etc/yp.conf File

The **/etc/yp.conf** file contains the information necessary for the client-side daemon, **ypbind**, to start up and find the NIS server. You need to make a decision regarding how the client is going to find the server, either by using a broadcast or by specifying the host name of the server.

The broadcast technique is appropriate when you need to move a client around to various subnets, and you don't want to have to reconfigure the client so long as an NIS server exists in the same subnet. The downside to this technique, of course, is that you must make sure that there is an NIS server in every subnet.

NOTE   When you use the broadcast method, you must have an NIS server in every subnet because routers will not normally forward broadcast traffic; i.e., broadcasts do not span multiple subnets. If you are uncertain whether a particular NIS server is in the same subnet, you can find out by pinging the broadcast address. (Some systems have enabled protection against smurf attacks and so may not respond to broadcast pings—you may have to temporarily disable that protection to test properly.) If the NIS server is one of the hosts that responds, then you know for sure that the broadcast method will work.

The other technique for client-to-server contact is specifying the host name of the server. This method works well when you need to subnet your network, but you don't need an NIS server in every subnet. This allows a client to move anywhere inside your network and still be able to find the NIS server—however, if you need to change a client so that it points to another NIS server (to balance the network load, for example), you'll need to change that yourself.

▼   **Broadcast method**   If you choose the broadcast technique, edit the **/etc/yp.conf** file on the client so that it reads as follows:

```
domain nis.example.org broadcast
```

where **nis.example.org** is the name of our sample NIS domain. Remember that if you need failover support, you will need to have two NIS servers in every subnet in order for broadcast to find the second server.

▲   **Server host name method**   If you want to specify the name of the NIS server directly, edit the **/etc/yp.conf** file so that it reads as follows:

```
domain nis.example.org server serverA
```

where **nis.example.org** is the name of our sample NIS domain, and **serverA** is the name of the NIS server to which we want this client to refer.

NOTE   Remember that you also have to have an entry for **serverA** in the **/etc/hosts** file. At the time NIS is started, you may not yet have access to DNS, and you most certainly don't have access to the NIS hosts table yet! For this reason, the client must be able to do the host name-to-IP resolution without the aid of any other services.

Enabling and starting ypbind

The NIS client runs a daemon called **ypbind** in order to communicate with the server. Typically, this is started in the **/etc/init.d/ypbind** startup script. Check your startup scripts with the **chkconfig** program and verify that **ypbind** will start automatically at the desired runlevels.

▼ To start the daemon without having to reboot, use this command:

```
[root@serverA ~]# service ypbind start
```

■ If you need to stop the daemon, type

```
[root@serverA ~]# service ypbind stop
```

▲ Use the **chkconfig** utility to enable **ypbind**'s automatic startup in runlevels 3 and 5. Type

```
[root@serverA ~]# chkconfig  --level 35 ypbind on
```

If your system does not have the **service** utility available, you can manually execute the startup scripts with the appropriate parameter. For example, to start the **ypbind** service, you would type

```
[root@serverA ~]# /etc/init.d/ypbind start
```

Editing the /etc/nsswitch.conf File

The **/etc/nsswitch.conf** file is responsible for telling the system the order in which to search for information. The format of the file is as follows:

```
filename:    servicename
```

where **filename** is the name of the file that needs to be referenced, and **servicename** is the name of the service to use to find the file. Multiple services can be listed, separated by spaces. Here are examples of some valid services:

files	Use the actual file on the host itself.
yp	Use NIS to perform the lookup.
nis	Use NIS to perform the lookup (**nis** is an alias for **yp**).
dns	Use DNS for the lookup (applies only to hosts).
[NOTFOUND=return]	Stop searching.
nis+	Use NIS+. (Due to the experimental status of the NIS+ implementation under Linux at this writing, avoid using this option.)
ldap	Use the Lightweight Directory Access Protocol (LDAP).

Here is an example entry in the **/etc/nsswitch.conf** file:

```
passwd:    files nis
```

This entry means that search requests for password entries will first be done in the **/etc/passwd** file. If the requested entry isn't found there, NIS will then be checked.

The **/etc/passwd** file should already exist and contain most of the information needed. You may need to adjust the order in which certain **servicenames** are listed in the file.

GUI Tools for NIS

Fedora Core and RHEL have some GUI tools that can make configuring a host as an NIS client very easy. The first one is the ncurses-based command-line tool named **authconfig**. This is shown here:

To launch this tool, just type

```
[root@serverA ~]# authconfig
```

The second tool is the **system-config-authentication** tool, shown here:

This tool requires your X Window System to be running. To launch it, type

```
[root@serverA ~]# system-config-authentication
```

SuSE Linux has some very nice GUI tools that can aid in configuring both the NIS server and the NIS client. The server configuration tool is shown here:

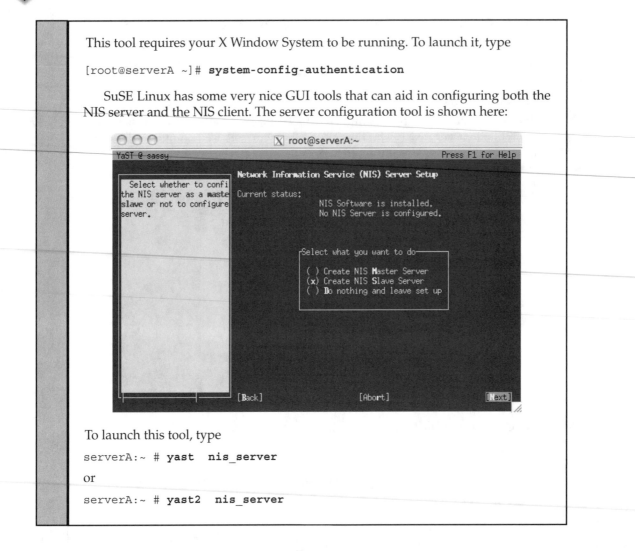

To launch this tool, type

```
serverA:~ # yast  nis_server
```

or

```
serverA:~ # yast2  nis_server
```

NIS at Work

The illustration in Figure 23-1 shows a sample usage of NIS. The illustration shows a user's login attempt before NIS was deployed. The second part of the illustration shows the same user's login attempt after NIS has been deployed for use.

The user testuser will attempt to log in to his local system as a user that does *not* exist in the hosts (serverB) local **/etc/passwd** file. The attempt will fail.

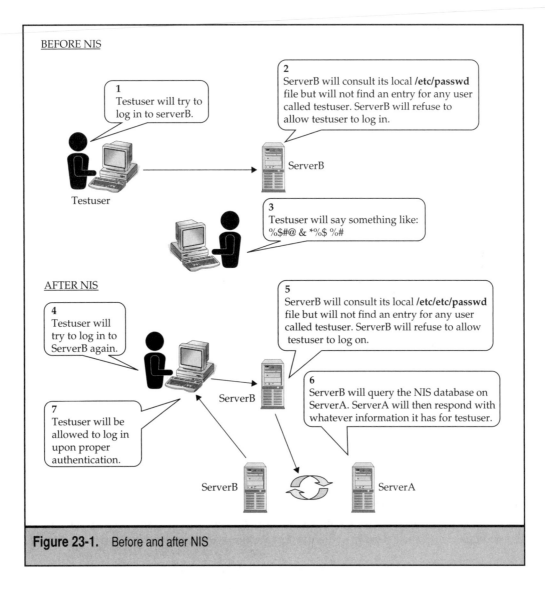

Figure 23-1.   Before and after NIS

After configuring NIS, a similar login attempt by the user is successful. It is successful because at this point serverB has been configured as an NIS client to serverA. The client—serverB—will again still check its local **/etc/passwd** file for an entry for testuser, but upon not finding it, it will next consult the NIS server at serverA. The NIS server has knowledge of the user and will pass on the same info to serverB, which will then perform the actual authentication.

Testing Your NIS Client Configuration

After the **/etc/yp.conf** and **/etc/nsswitch.conf** files have been properly configured and the **ypbind** client daemon is all set up, you should be able to use the **ypcat** command to dump a map from the NIS server to your screen. To do this, type the following command:

```
[root@serverA yp]# ypcat passwd
yyang:$1$Yn7AHj/:500:500:Ying Yang:/home/yyang:/bin/bash
mmellow:$1$jKv9B:501:501:Mel Mellow:/home/mmellow:/bin/bash
```

which dumps the **passwd** map to your screen—that is, of course, *if* you are sharing your **passwd** map via NIS. If you aren't, pick a map that you *are* sharing and use the **ypcat** command with that filename.

If you don't see the map dumped out, you need to double-check your client and server configurations and try again.

CONFIGURING A SECONDARY NIS SERVER

As your site grows, you'll undoubtedly find that there is a need to distribute the NIS service load to multiple hosts. NIS supports this through the use of secondary NIS servers. These servers require no additional maintenance once they are configured, because the master NIS server sends them updates whenever you rebuild the maps (with the **make** command, as described in "Editing the Makefile" earlier in this chapter).

There are three steps to setting up a secondary NIS server:

1. Set the NIS domain name.
2. Set up the NIS master to push to the slave.
3. Run **ypinit** to initialize the slave server.

Setting the Domain Name

As when configuring a master NIS server, you should establish the NIS domain name before starting up the actual initialization process for a secondary server (serverB):

```
[root@serverB ~]# domainname my_domain_name
```

where **my_domain_name** is the NIS domain name for your site.

Of course, the secondary server's domain name must be set up so that it automatically becomes established at boot time. If you are using the Fedora Core version of Linux, as in our sample system, you can do this by setting the NISDOMAIN variable in the **/etc/sysconfig/network** file. Otherwise, you can edit your **/etc/init.d/ypserv** file so that the first thing it does after the initial comments is set the domain name there.

NOTE   Be sure to set the domain name by hand before you continue with the `ypinit` step of the installation.

Setting Up the NIS Master to Push to Slaves

If you haven't already configured the master NIS server that will push to the slave NIS servers, you should do so now. This requires two tasks: First, edit the **/var/yp/ypservers** file so that it includes all the secondary NIS servers to which the master server will push maps. For example, if you want the master server to push maps to the hosts serverB and serverC, you'll edit **/var/yp/ypservers** so that it looks like this:

```
serverA
serverB
serverC
```

where serverA is the host name of the master NIS server.

Second, you'll need to make sure the **Makefile** has the line **NOPUSH=false**. See the section on configuring NIS master servers for details.

Running ypinit

With these setup steps accomplished, you're ready to run the **ypinit** command to initialize the secondary server. Type the following command on the secondary NIS server:

```
[root@serverB ~]# /usr/lib/yp/ypinit -s serverA
```

where the **-s** option tells **ypinit** to configure the system as a slave server, and **serverA** is the name of the NIS master server.

The output of this command will complain about **ypxfrd** not running—you can ignore this. What the secondary server is trying to do is pull the maps from the master NIS server, using the **ypxfrd** daemon. This won't work, because you didn't configure the master NIS server to accept requests to pull maps down via **ypxfrd**. Rather, you configured the master server to push maps to the secondaries whenever the master has an update. The server process at this point must be started by hand. It's the same process as for the primary server: **ypserv**. To get it started, run this command:

```
[root@serverB ~]# service ypserv start
```

NOTE   Be sure to have the server process start as part of the boot process. You can use the `chkconfig` program to do this. The `ypserv` program should start in runlevels 3 and 5.

To test the secondary server, go back to the master server and try to do a server-side push. Do this by running the **make** program again on the master NIS server, as follows:

```
[root@serverA ~]# cd /var/yp ; make
Updating passwd.byname...
Updating passwd.byuid...
```

```
Updating group.byname...
...<OUTPUT TRUNCATED>...
Updating mail.aliases...
```

This should force all of the maps to be rebuilt and pushed to the secondary servers.

NIS TOOLS

To help you work with NIS, a handful of tools have been written to let you extract information from the database via the command line:

▼ **ypcat**

■ **ypwhich**

■ **ypmatch**

▲ **yppasswd**

The first tool, **ypcat**, dumps the contents of an NIS map. This is useful for scripts that need to pull information out of NIS: **ypcat** can pull the entire map down, and then **grep** can be used to find a specific entry. The **ypcat** command is also useful for simple testing of the NIS service. For example, to use **ypcat** (and **grep**) to dump and search for the entry for user yyang in the passwd database, type

```
[root@serverA ~]# ypcat  passwd | grep  yyang
yyang:$1$ cXSafue2DYg0zskw.Hj/:500:500:Ying Yang:/home/yyang:/bin/bash
```

The **ypwhich** command returns the name of the NIS server that is answering your requests. This is also a good diagnostic tool if NIS doesn't appear to be working as expected. For example, let's say you've made a change in the master NIS tables, but your change can't be seen by a specific client. You can use **ypwhich** to see to which server the client is bound. If it's bound to a secondary server, it might be that the secondary server is not listed in the primary server's **/var/yp/ypservers** file.

Here is an example of **ypwhich** usage:

```
[root@serverA ~]# ypwhich
```

The **ypmatch** command is a close relative of **ypcat**. Rather than pulling an entire map down, however, you supply a key value to **ypmatch** and only the entry corresponding to that key is pulled down. Using the **passwd** map as an example, we can pull down the entry to the user yyang with this simple command:

```
[root@serverA ~]# ypmatch yyang passwd
```

The **yppasswd** command is the NIS version of the standard Linux **passwd** command. The difference between the two is that the **yppasswd** command allows the user to set his or her password on the NIS server. The behavior is otherwise identical to **passwd**. In fact, many sites rename the standard **passwd** command to something like **passwd .local** and then create a symlink from **passwd** to **yppasswd**.

USING NIS IN CONFIGURATION FILES

One of the most popular uses of NIS is the sharing of the **/etc/passwd** file so that everyone can log in to all hosts on the network by making a single modification to the master **/etc/passwd** map. Some distributions of Linux automatically support this feature once they see NIS running. Others still require explicit settings in **/etc/passwd** so that the login program knows to check NIS as well as the base password file.

Let's assume that you need to add the special tokens to your **/etc/passwd** file to allow logins from users listed in the NIS **passwd** file.

Here is the basic setting you might need to add to your client's **/etc/passwd** file to allow host login for all users listed in the NIS **passwd** list:

```
+:*:::::
```

> **NOTE**   Any glibc-based (e.g., Fedora, RHEL, Red Hat) systems do not need this addition to the /**etc/passwd** file, but having it there will not confuse glibc or otherwise make it behave badly.

And here is the setting if you want to prevent anyone from logging in to that host except for those listed explicitly in the **/etc/passwd** file:

```
+:::::::/bin/false
```

This overrides all the user's shell settings so that when a login to the client is attempted, the login program tries to run **/bin/false** as the user's login program. Since **/bin/false** doesn't work as a shell, the user is immediately booted out of the system.

To allow a few explicitly listed users into the system while still denying everyone else, use the sample entries that follow in the **/etc/passwd** file:

```
+username
+username2
+username3
+:::::::/bin/false
```

This allows only **username**, **username2**, and **username3**, specifically, to log in to the system.

IMPLEMENTING NIS IN A REAL NETWORK

In this section, we'll discuss deployment of NIS in real networked environments. This isn't so much a cookbook as it is a collection of samples. After all, we've already described the details of configuring and setting up NIS servers and clients. No need to repeat that!

Obviously, there will be exceptions to each scenario described here. Some small networks might generate an unusually high amount of NIS traffic, for some reason. On the other hand, some large networks might have such light NIS traffic that only a single master is needed. In any case, apply a liberal dose of common sense to the following, and you should be fine.

A Small Network

We define a small network to be one with fewer than 30–40 UNIX/Linux systems, all of which exist on the same subnet.

In this case, a single NIS master server is more than enough. Unless any of the systems in your network are generating an unreasonable amount of NIS requests, all of the other systems can be configured as clients to query the master server via either broadcast or direct connection. If you don't expect to segment your network, you'll probably want to stick with using broadcast, because it simplifies the process of adding hosts to the network.

The NIS server itself shouldn't have to be too beefy. If you do have a powerful machine handling the task, don't be afraid to have it share the load with another lightweight service or two. (DHCP is often a good candidate for load sharing.)

A Segmented Network

Segmented networks introduce complexity to the process of handling broadcast-style services (such as ARP or DHCP). For a growing network, however, segmenting is likely to be a necessity. By segmenting your traffic into two or more discrete networks, you can better keep traffic on each segment down to a controllable level. Furthermore, this arrangement helps you impose tighter security for inside systems. For instance, you can put Accounting and Human Resources onto another subnet, to make it harder for Engineering to put sniffers on the network and get to confidential information.

For NIS, segmenting means two possible solutions. The first solution assumes that even though you have a larger network, it doesn't require a lot of NIS traffic. This is typically the case in heterogeneous networks where Microsoft Windows has made its way to many desktop workstations. In this case, keeping a single NIS master server is probably enough. *In any event*, this network's clients should be configured to contact the server directly instead of using broadcasts. This is because only those clients on the same subnet as the NIS server will be able to contact it via broadcasts, and it's much easier to keep all your client workstations configured consistently.

On the other hand, if you do think there is enough NIS traffic, splitting the load across multiple servers—one for each subnet—is a good idea. In this case, the master NIS server is configured to send updates to the secondaries whenever the maps are updated, and clients can be consistently configured to use broadcasts to find the correct

NIS server. When you use broadcasts, clients can be moved from one subnet to another without your having to reassign their NIS server.

Networks Bigger Than Buildings

It isn't uncommon for networks to grow bigger than the buildings they're located in. Remote offices connected through a variety of methods mean a variety of administrative decisions—and not just concerning NIS!

For NIS, however, it is crucial that a server be located at each side of every WAN link. For example, if you have three campuses, connected to each other in a mesh by T1 links, you should have at least three NIS servers, one for each campus. This arrangement is needed because NIS relies on low-latency links in order to perform well, especially given that it is an RPC-based protocol. (Doing a simple `ls -l` command can result in hundreds of lookups, literally.) Furthermore, in the event one of the WAN links fails, it is important that each site be able to operate on its own until the link is reestablished.

Depending on the organization of your company and its administration, you may or may not want to split NIS so that multiple NIS domains exist. Once you get past this administrative decision, you can treat each campus as a single site and decide how many NIS servers need to be deployed. If you intend to keep a uniform NIS space, there should be only one NIS master server; the rest of the NIS servers at other campuses should be slaves.

SUMMARY

In this chapter, we discussed the process of installing master NIS servers, slave NIS servers, and NIS clients, as well as how to use some of the tools available on these servers. Here are the key points to remember about NIS:

▼ Although similar in nature to Windows domain controllers, NIS servers are not the same. Namely, NIS servers do not perform authentication.

■ Because anyone in your network can join an NIS domain, it is assumed that your network is already secure. Most sites find that the benefits of this arrangement outweigh the risks.

■ Once the **Makefile** file is set up and `ypinit` has been run, master NIS servers do not need additional setups. Changes to the files that you need to share via NIS (such as **/etc/passwd**) are updated and propagated by running `cd /var/yp;make`.

■ NIS slave servers are listed in the master server's file, **/var/yp/ypservers**.

■ NIS slave servers receive their information from the server via a server push.

■ Setup of an NIS slave server is little more than running the `ypinit -s` command.

■ NIS clients need their **/etc/yp.conf** and **/etc/nsswitch.conf** files to be configured properly.

▲ Be sure to establish the NIS-isms in the client-side password file whenever your particular Linux distribution requires it. Most Red Hat–based systems do not require these NIS-isms.

CHAPTER 24

Samba

Samba is a powerful tool for allowing UNIX-based systems (such as Linux) to interoperate with Windows-based systems and other operating system. It is an open-source implementation of the Server Message Block and Common Internet File System (SMB/CIFS) protocol suite.

Samba transparently provides file and print sharing services to Windows clients. Samba is able to do this through the use of the native Microsoft networking protocols SMB/CIFS. From a system administrator's point of view, this means being able to deploy a UNIX-based server without having to install NFS, LP, and some kind of UNIX-compatible authentication support on all the Windows clients in the network. Instead, the clients can use their native tongue to talk to the server—which means fewer hassles for you and seamless integration for your users.

This chapter covers the procedure for downloading, compiling, and installing Samba. Thankfully, Samba's default configuration requires little modification, so we'll concentrate on how to perform customary tasks with Samba and how to avoid some common pitfalls. In terms of administration, you'll get a short course on using Samba's Web Administration Tool (SWAT), and on the **smbclient** command-line utility.

No matter what task you've chosen for Samba to handle, be sure to take the time to read the program's documentation. It is well written, complete, and thorough. For the short afternoon it takes to get through most of it, you'll gain a substantial amount of knowledge.

> **NOTE**   Samba has actually been ported to a significant number of platforms—almost any variant of UNIX you can imagine, and even several non-UNIX environments. In this discussion, we are of course most interested in Samba/Linux, but keep in mind that Samba can be deployed on your other UNIX systems, as well.

THE MECHANICS OF SMB

To fully understand the Linux/Samba/Windows relationship, you need to understand the relationships of both operating systems to their files, printers, users, and networks. To better see how these relationships compare, let's examine some of the fundamental issues of working with both Linux and Windows in the same environment.

Usernames and Passwords

The Linux/UNIX login/password mechanism is radically different from the Windows PDC (Primary Domain Controller) model and the Windows 2000 Active Directory model. Thus it's important for the system administrator to maintain consistency in the logins and passwords across both systems. Users need to access both systems without having to worry about reauthentication or cached passwords that don't match a particular server.

You have several management options for handling username and password issues:

▼ **The Linux Pluggable Authentication Modules (PAM)**   Allows you to authenticate users against a PDC. This means you still have two user lists—one local and one on the PDC—but your users need only keep track of their passwords on the Windows system.

■ **Samba as a PDC**   Allows you to keep all your logins and passwords on the Linux system, while all your Windows boxes authenticate with Samba. When Samba is used with an LDAP backend for this, you will have a very scalable and extensible solution.

▲ **Rolling your own solution using Perl**   Allows you to use your own custom script. For sites with a well-established system for maintaining logins and passwords, it isn't unreasonable to come up with a custom script. This can be done using WinPerl and Perl modules that allow changes to the Security Access Manager (SAM), to update the PDC's password list. A Perl script on the Linux side can communicate with the WinPerl script to keep accounts synchronized.

In the worst-case situation, you can always maintain the two systems by hand (which some early sysadmins did indeed have to do!), but this method is error prone and not much fun to manage.

Encrypted Passwords

Starting with Windows NT 4/Service Pack 3, Windows 98, and Windows 95 OSR2, Windows uses encrypted passwords when communicating with the PDC and any server requiring authentication (including Linux and Samba). The encryption algorithm used by Windows is different from UNIX's, however, and therefore is not compatible.

Here are your choices for handling this conflict:

▼ Edit the Registry on Windows clients to disable use of encrypted passwords. The Registry entries that need to be changed are listed in the **docs** directory in the Samba package. As of version 3 of Samba, this option is no longer necessary.

▲ Configure Samba to use Windows-style encrypted passwords.

The first solution has the benefit of not pushing you over to a more-complex password scheme. On the other hand, you have to apply the Registry fix on all your clients. The second option, of course, has the opposite effect: For a little more complexity on the server side, you don't have to modify any of your clients.

Samba Daemons

The code of the Samba server is actually composed of three daemons: **smbd**, **nmbd**, and **winbindd**.

The **smbd** daemon handles the actual sharing of file systems and printer services for clients. It is also responsible for user authentication and resource locking issues.

It starts by binding to port 139 or port 445 and then listens for requests. Every time a client authenticates itself, **smbd** makes a copy of itself; the original goes back to listening to its primary port for new requests, and the copy handles the connection for the client. This new copy also changes its effective user ID from root to the authenticated user. (For example, if the user yyang authenticated against **smbd**, the new copy would run with the permissions of yyang, not the permissions of root.) The copy stays in memory as long as there is a connection from the client.

The **nmbd** daemon is responsible for handling NetBIOS name service requests. **nmbd** can also be used as a drop-in replacement for a Windows Internet Name Server (WINS). It begins by binding itself to port 137; unlike **smbd**, however, **nmbd** does not create a new instance of itself to handle every query. In addition to name service requests, **nmbd** also handles requests from master browsers, domain browsers, and WINS servers—and as such it participates in the browsing protocols that make up the popular Windows Network Neighborhood of systems. The services provided by the **smbd** and **nmbd** daemons complement each other.

Finally, the service provided by **winbindd** can be used to query native Windows servers for user and group information, which can then be used on purely Linux/UNIX platforms. It does this by using Microsoft RPC calls, PAM, and the name service switch (NSS) capabilities found in modern C libraries. Its use can be extended through the use of a PAM module (**pam_winbind**) to provide authentication services. This service is controlled separately from the main **smb** service and can run independently.

> **NOTE** With the release of Windows 2000, Microsoft moved to a pure DNS naming convention as part of its support for Active Directory in an attempt to make name services more consistent between the Network Neighborhood and the host names that are published in DNS. In theory, you shouldn't need **nmbd** anymore, but the reality is that you will, especially if you intend to allow non–Windows 2000 hosts on your network to access your Samba shares.

Installing Samba

Precompiled binaries for Samba exist for most Linux distributions. This section will show how to install Samba via RPM on a Fedora Core system. To provide the server-side services of Samba, two packages are needed on Fedora Core and RHEL-type systems. They are

▼ **samba*.rpm**   This package provides an SMB server that can be used to provide network services to SMB/CIFS clients.

▲ **samba-common*.rpm**   This package provides files necessary for both the server and client packages of Samba—files such as configuration files, log files, man pages, PAM modules, and other libraries.

To provide the client-side services of Samba, one package is needed on Fedora Core and RHEL-type systems. The package is

▼ **samba-client*.rpm**   It provides the SMB client utilities that allow access to SMB shares and printing services on Linux and non-Linux-type systems.

Assuming you have a working connection to the Internet, installing Samba can be as simple as issuing this command:

```
[root@serverA ~]# yum install samba
```

You can similarly install the **samba-client** package like so:

```
[root@serverA ~]# yum install samba-client
```

You may also choose to download and install the RPM package from the distribution's software repository (http://fedora.redhat.com/download/) or from the root of the install media's **/Fedora/RPMS/** directory using the usual RPM commands, e.g.,

```
[root@serverA ~]# rpm -ivh /media/cdrom/Fedora/RPMS/samba-*.rpm
```

Compiling and Installing Samba from Source

Samba comes installed on most Linux distributions. Nevertheless, as with all the other services we've discussed in this book, you should be able to compile the software yourself in the event you want to upgrade the package to a new release. Since its inception, Samba has had users across many different UNIX/Linux platforms and so has been designed to be compatible with the many variants. There is rarely a problem during the compilation process.

As of this writing, the latest version of Samba is 3.0.14a.

Begin by downloading the Samba source code from http://www.samba.org into the directory where you want to compile it. For this example, we'll assume this directory is **/usr/local/src**. You can download the latest version directly from http://us4.samba .org/samba/ftp/samba-latest.tar.gz.

1. Unpack Samba using the **tar** command.

   ```
   [root@serverA src]# tar xvzf samba-latest.tar.gz
   ```

2. Step 1 creates a subdirectory called **samba-3.0.14a** for the source code. Change into that directory. Type

   ```
   [root@serverA src]# cd samba-3.0.14a/
   ```

TIP Using your favorite text editor, start by reading the file titled **Manifest**. This explains all the files that came with Samba and gives you the location of the Samba documentation. While this isn't immediately crucial, it will help you in the long run.

3. Within the **samba-3.0.14** directory, there will be another subdirectory called **source**. Change into that directory like so:

   ```
   [root@serverA samba-3.0.14a]# cd source/
   ```

TIP   The Samba **source** directory may or may not contain the configure script. You may confirm this by doing a listing (**ls**) of the files in the folder. If the configure script is not present, you'll have to create it using the **autogen.sh** script under the source directory of the Samba source tree.

4. We'll run Samba's configure script and enable support for **smbmount**. The other options that you might want to consider are listed in Table 24-1. Here we'll enable only the **smbmount** option and accept the other defaults. Type

    ```
    [root@serverA source]# ./configure    --with-smbmount
    ```

5. Begin compiling Samba by running the **make** command.

    ```
    [root@serverA source]# make
    ```

6. Next run **make install**.

    ```
    [root@serverA source]# make  install
    ```

7. We are done. You will find all the Samba binaries and configuration files installed under the **/usr/local/samba/** directory. You can now carry on using them as you would if you had installed Samba via RPM. Of course, you should watch out for the paths!

Samba Configuration (`./configure`) Options	Description
`--prefix=PREFIX`	Install architecture-independent files in PREFIX.
`--with-smbmount`	Include support for the **smbmount** command. The **smbmount** command allows you to attach shares off of NT servers (or other Samba servers) much as you mount NFS partitions.
`--with-pam`	Include PAM support (default=no).
`--with-ldapsam`	Include LDAP SAM 2.2-compatible configuration (default=no).
`--with-ads`	Active Directory support (default auto.)
`--with-ldap`	LDAP support (default yes).
`--with-pam_smbpass`	Build PAM module for authenticating against passdb backends.
`--with-krb5=base-dir`	Locate Kerberos 5 support (default=/usr).
`--enable-cups`	Turn on CUPS support (default=auto).

Table 24-1.   Some Samba Configuration (./configure) Options

NOTE   The **/usr/local/samba/bin** directory is typically not found in the search path for most shells. You can either add it to your path or simply copy the binaries from **/usr/local/samba/bin** to a location where they will be searched (e.g., **/usr/sbin/** or **/usr/bin/**).

SAMBA ADMINISTRATION

This section describes some of the issues of administering Samba. We'll see how to start and stop Samba, how to do common administrative tasks with SWAT, and how to use **smbclient**. Finally, we'll examine the process of using encrypted passwords.

Starting and Stopping Samba

Most distributions of Linux have scripts and programs that will start and stop Samba without your needing to do anything special. They take care of startup at boot time and stopping at shutdown. On our sample system running Fedora with Samba installed via RPM, the **service** command and the **chkconfig** utility can be used to manage Samba's startup and shutdown.

For example, to start the **smbd** daemon, you can execute this command:

```
[root@serverA ~]# service smbd start
```

And to stop the service, type

```
[root@serverA ~]# service smbd stop
```

After making any configuration changes to Samba, you can restart it with this command to make the changes go into effect:

```
[root@serverA ~]# service smbd restart
```

The **smb** service on Fedora Core will not automatically start up with the next system reboot. You can configure it to start up automatically using the **chkconfig** utility like so:

```
[root@serverA ~]# chkconfig   smb   on
```

TIP   Starting the Samba that we installed from source earlier can be done from the command line with this command:

```
[root@serverA ~]# /usr/local/samba/sbin/smbd -D
```

The only command-line parameter used here (**-D**) tells **smbd** to run as a daemon. The **nmbd** daemon can be started in the same manner with

```
[root@serverA ~]# /usr/local/samba/sbin/nmbd -D
```

Stopping Samba without the use of proper scripts is a little trickier. But in general you may have to use the **ps** command to list all of the Samba processes. From this list, find the instance of **smbd** that is owned by root, and kill this process. This will also kill all of the other Samba connections.

USING SWAT

SWAT is the Samba Web Administration Tool, with which you can manage Samba through a browser interface. It's an excellent alternative to editing the Samba configuration files (**smb.conf** and the like) by hand.

Prior to version 2.0 of Samba, the official way to configure it was by editing the **smb .conf** file. Though verbose in nature and easy to understand, this file was rather cumbersome to deal with because of its numerous options and directives. It also meant that setting up shares under MS Windows was still easier than setting up shares with Samba. Many individuals developed graphical front ends to the editing process. Many of these tools are still being maintained and enhanced—you can read more about them by visiting Samba's Web site at http://www.samba.org. As of version 2.0, however, the source for Samba ships with SWAT, the Samba Web Administration Tool.

The SWAT software is packaged as a separate package on Fedora Core and RHEL systems. The binary RPM that provides SWAT is named **samba-swat**. In this section we'll install the RPM for SWAT using the Yum program.

Setting Up SWAT

What makes SWAT a little different from other browser-based administration tools is that SWAT does not rely on a separate Web server (like Apache). Instead, SWAT performs all the needed Web server functions without implementing a full Web server.

Setting up SWAT is pretty straightforward. Here are the steps:

1. Use Yum to download and install SWAT. Type

   ```
   [root@serverA ~]# yum install samba-swat
   ```

   Type **yes** to confirm the installation of **samba-swat** and any of its dependencies when prompted.

TIP SWAT is packaged with the main Samba source tree, and so it gets built when you build Samba itself from source. For our previous compile and build of Samba, SWAT was installed under the **/usr/ local/samba/swat/directory.**

2. Confirm that you have the **samba-swat** package installed. Type

   ```
   [root@serverA ~]# rpm -q samba-swat
   samba-swat-3.0.14a-2
   ```

3. SWAT runs under the control of the super-daemon, **xinetd**. It is disabled by default. Check its status by typing

   ```
   [root@serverA ~]# chkconfig --list swat
   swat            off
   ```

4. Enable it by typing

   ```
   [root@serverA ~]# chkconfig swat on
   ```

5. Restart **xinetd** to make your changes take effect. Type

```
[root@serverA ~]# service xinetd restart
Stopping xinetd:                                          [FAILED]
Starting xinetd:                                          [  OK  ]
```

6. Finally, you can connect to SWAT's Web interface using a Web browser on the system where it is installed. Point the Web browser to SWAT's URL,

```
http://localhost:901/
```

Upon entering this URL, you will be prompted for a username and password with which to log in to SWAT. Type in **root** as the username and type in root's password. Upon successfully logging in, you will be presented with a Web page similar to the one in Figure 24-1.

And that is pretty much all there is to installing and enabling SWAT on a Fedora system.

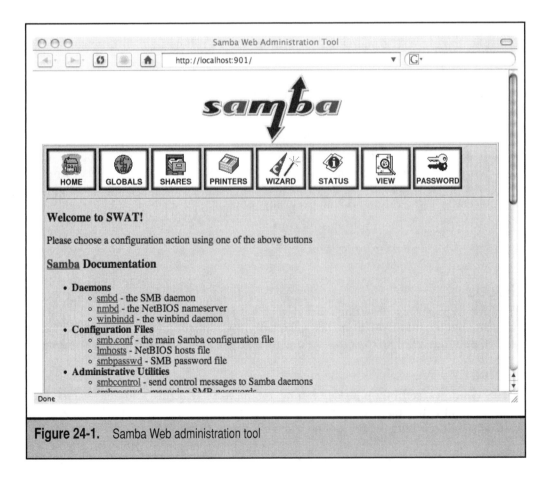

Figure 24-1. Samba Web administration tool

> **NOTE**   SWAT's default **xinetd** configuration allows you to connect to SWAT only from the same machine on which you are running Samba (i.e., the local host). This was done for the purpose of security, since you don't want to allow random people to be able to connect remotely to your server and "help" you to configure your Samba server.

> **CAUTION**   Logging in as root through SWAT causes the root password to be sent from the Web browser to the Samba server. Therefore, avoid doing administration tasks across an untrusted network. Preferably, connect only from the server itself, or set up an SSH tunnel between the client host and the Samba server host.

The SWAT Menus

When you connect to SWAT and log in as root, you'll see the main menu shown in Figure 24-1. From here, you can find almost all the documentation you'll need for Samba's configuration files, daemons, and related programs. None of the links point to external Web sites, so you can read them at your leisure without connecting to the Net.

At the top of SWAT's main page are buttons for the following menu choices:

Home	The main menu page
Globals	Configuration options that affect all operational aspects of Samba
Shares	For setting up disk shares and their respective options
Printers	For setting up printers
Status	The status of the **smbd** and **nmbd** processes, including a list of all clients connected to these processes and what they are doing (the same information that's listed in the **smbstatus** command-line program)
View	The resulting **smb.conf** file
Password	Password settings

Globals

The Globals page lists all settings that affect all aspects of Samba's operation. These settings are divided into five groups: base, security, logging, browse, and WINS. To the left of each option is a link to the relevant documentation for the setting and its values.

Shares

In MS Windows, setting up a *share* can be as simple as selecting a folder (or creating a new one), right-clicking it, and allowing it to be shared. Additional controls can be established by right-clicking the folder and selecting Properties.

Using SWAT, these same actions are accomplished by creating a new share. You can then select the share and click Choose Share. This brings up all the configurable parameters for the share.

Printers

The Printers page for SWAT lets you configure Samba-related setting for printers that are currently available on the system. Through a series of menus, you can add printer shares, delete them, modify them, etc. The one thing you cannot do here is add printers to the main system—you must do that by some other means (see Chapter 26).

Status

The Status page shows the current status of the **smbd** and **nmbd** daemons. This information includes what clients are connected and their actions. The page automatically updates every 30 seconds by default, but you can change this rate if you like (it's an option on the page itself). Along with status information, you can turn Samba on and off or ask it to reload its configuration file. This is necessary if you make any changes to the configuration.

View

As you change your Samba configuration, SWAT keeps track of the changes and figures out what information it needs to put into the **smb.conf** file. Open the View page, and you can see the file SWAT is putting together for you.

Password

Use the Password page if you intend to support encrypted passwords. You'll want to give your users a way to modify their own passwords without having to log in to the Linux server. This page allows users to do just that.

NOTE It's almost always a good idea to disallow access to your servers for everyone except support personnel. This reduces the chances of mistakes being made that could affect the performance or stability of your server.

Creating a Share

We will walk through the process of creating a share under the **/tmp** directory to be shared on the Samba server. We'll first create the directory to be shared and then edit Samba's configuration file (**/etc/samba/smb.conf**) to create an entry for the share.

This can of course be very easily done using SWAT's Web interface, which was installed earlier, but we will not use SWAT here. SWAT is very easy and intuitive to use. But it is probably useful to understand how to configure Samba in its rawest form, and this will also make it easier to understand what SWAT does in its backend so that you can tweak things to your liking. Besides, one never knows when one might be stranded in the Amazon jungle without any nice GUI configuration tools available. So let's get on with it:

1. Create a directory under the **/tmp/** folder called **testshare**. Type

   ```
   [root@serverA ~]# mkdir /tmp/testshare
   ```

2. Create some empty files (**foo1, foo2, moo3**) under the directory you created in Step 1. Type

   ```
   [root@serverA ~]# touch  /tmp/testshare/{foo1,foo2,moo3}
   ```

3. Set up the permissions on the **testshare** folder so that its contents can be browsed by other users on the system. Type

   ```
   [root@serverA ~]# chmod -R  755  /tmp/testshare/*
   ```

4. Open up Samba's configuration file for editing in any text editor of your choice and append the entry listed next to the end of the file. Please omit the line numbers 1–5. The lines are added *only* to aid readability.

   ```
   1)[samba-share]
   2)      comment=This folder contains shared documents
   3)      path=/tmp/testshare
   4)      public=yes
   5)      writable=no
   ```

   Line 1 is the name of the share (or service in Samba parlance). This is the name that SMB clients will see when they try to browse the shares stored on the Samba server.

   Line 2 is just a descriptive/comment text that users will see next to a share when browsing.

   Line 3 is very important. It specifies the location on the file system that stores the actual content to be shared.

   Line 4 specifies that no password is required to access the share (this is called connecting to the service in Samba-speak). The privileges on the share will be translated to the permissions of the guest account. If the value were set to "no" instead, then the share would not be accessible by the general public, but only to authenticated and permitted users.

   Line 5, with the value of the directive set to "no," means that users of this service may not create or modify the files stored therein.

   TIP   Samba's configuration file has options and directives that are too numerous to cover here. But you can learn more about the other possible options by reading the man page for **smb.conf** (`man smb.conf`).

5. Save your changes to the **/etc/samba/smb.conf** file and exit the editor.

   You should note that we have accepted all the other default values in the file. You may want to go back and personalize some of the settings to suit your environment.

One setting you may want to change very quickly is the directive ("workgroup") that defines the workgroup. This controls what workgroup your server will appear to be in when queried by clients or when viewed in the Windows Network Neighborhood.

Also note that the default configuration may also contain some other share definitions. You should comment (or delete) those entries if it is not your intention to have them.

6. Use the **testparm** utility to check the **smb.conf** file for internal correctness (i.e., absence of syntax errors). Type

```
[root@serverA ~]# testparm -s  | less
...<OUTPUT TRUNCATED>...
[samba-share]
        comment = This folder contains shared documents
        path = /tmp/testshare
        guest ok = Yes
```

Study the output for any serious errors and try to fix them by going back to correct them in the **smb.conf** file.

Note that because you piped the output of **testparm** to the **less** command, you may have to press Q on your keyboard to quit the command.

7. Now restart (or start) Samba to make the software acknowledge your changes. Type

```
[root@serverA ~]# service smb restart
Shutting down SMB services:                        [  OK  ]
Shutting down NMB services:                        [  OK  ]
Starting SMB services:                             [  OK  ]
Starting NMB services:                             [  OK  ]
```

We are done creating our test share. In the next section we will attempt to access the share.

USING SMBCLIENT

The **smbclient** program is a command-line tool that allows your Linux system to act as a Windows client. You can use this utility to connect to other Samba servers or even to real Windows NT/200x servers. **smbclient** is a very flexible program and can be used to browse other servers, send and retrieve files from them, or even print to them. As you can imagine, this is also a great debugging tool, since you can quickly and easily check whether a new Samba installation works correctly without having to find a Windows client to test it.

In this section, we'll show you how to do basic browsing, remote file access, and remote printer access with **smbclient**. However, remember that **smbclient** is a very flexible program, limited only by your imagination.

Browsing a Server

With so many graphical interfaces around, we've come to equate browsing with "point and click." But when your intention is to simply find out what a server has to offer, it's not enough of a reason in itself to support an entire GUI.

Using **smbclient** with the **-L** option allows you to view the offerings of a Windows file server or Samba server without having to use a GUI. Here's the format of the command:

```
[root@serverA ~]# smbclient  -L hostname
```

where **hostname** is the name of the server. For example, if we want to see what the local host (i.e., serverA) has to offer, we type

```
[root@serverA ~]# smbclient  -L localhost
```

You will be prompted for a password. You can just press ENTER to complete the command.

To list the shares on the Samba server again without being prompted for a password, you can use the **-U%** option. This implies that you want to be authenticated as the guest user, which has no password. Type

```
[root@serverA ~]# smbclient  -U% -L  localhost

Domain=[MYGROUP] OS=[Unix] Server=[Samba 3.0.14a-2]

        Sharename       Type        Comment
        ---------       ----        -------
        samba-share     Disk        This folder contains shared documents
        IPC$            IPC         IPC Service (Samba Server)
        ADMIN$          IPC         IPC Service (Samba Server)

Domain=[MYGROUP] OS=[Unix] Server=[Samba 3.0.14a-2]

        Server              Comment
        ---------           -------
        SERVERA             Samba Server
        Workgroup           Master
        ---------           -------
        MYGROUP             SERVERA
```

Notice the presence of the share we created earlier, in line 4 of the preceding output.

Remote File Access

The **smbclient** utility allows you to access files on a Windows server or a Samba server with a command-line hybrid DOS/FTP client interface. For its most straightforward usage, you'll simply run the following:

```
[root@serverB ~]# smbclient    //server/share_name
```

where *server* is the server name (or IP address) and *share_name* is the share name to which you want to connect. By default, Samba automatically sets up all users' home directories as shares. (For instance, the user yyang can access her home directory on the server serverA by going to **//serverA/yyang**.)

Following are some command-line parameters you may need to use with **smbclient** to connect to a server:

Parameter for smbclient	Description
-I *destIP*	The destination IP address to which you want to connect.
-U *username*	The user you want to connect as. This will be used instead of the user you are logged in as.
-W *name*	Sets the workgroup name to *name*.
-D *directory*	Starts from *directory*.

Once connected, you'll be able to browse directories using the **cd**, **dir**, and **ls** commands. You can also use **get**, **put**, **mget**, and **mput** to transfer files back and forth. The online help explains all of the commands in detail. Simply type **help** at the prompt to see what is available.

Let us attempt an actual connection to the share we created earlier (samba-share). To better demonstrate the process, the connection will be made from a different host named clientB.

We'll use the **smbclient** utility to connect to the server, connecting as a guest by specifying the **-U%** option. After connecting, we will be dropped down to an smb shell with the prompt **smb: \>**. While connected, we'll do a listing of the files available on the share using the **ls** command. Then we'll try to download one of the files that resides on the share using the FTP-like command **get**. Finally end the connection using **quit**. A sample session on clientB connecting to serverA is shown here:

```
[root@clientB ~]# smbclient -U%  //serverA/samba-share
Domain=[MYGROUP] OS=[Unix] Server=[Samba 3.0.14a-2]
smb: \> ls
  ..                                  D        0  Wed Jun 15 01:16:18 2005
  .                                   D        0  Wed Jun 15 00:12:20 2005
  moo3                                A        0  Wed Jun 15 00:12:20 2005
  foo2                                A        0  Wed Jun 15 00:12:20 2005
  foo1                                A        0  Wed Jun 15 00:12:20 2005
                37816 blocks of size 262144. 31717 blocks available
smb: \> get foo1
getting file \foo1 of size 0 as foo1 (0.0 kb/s) (average 0.0 kb/s)
smb: \> quit
```

The file (**foo1**) that was downloaded from serverA should be in the current working directory on the local file system of clientB.

MOUNTING REMOTE SAMBA SHARES

If your kernel is configured to support the SMB file system (as are most kernels that come with Linux distributions), you can actually mount a Windows share or Samba share onto your local system in much the same way you would mount an NFS export or a local volume. This is very handy for accessing a large disk on a remote server without having to shuffle individual files across the network.

While logged in to clientB, you can use the **mount** command with the proper options to mount a Samba share that resides on serverA.

First create the mount point if it does not exist. Type

```
[root@clientB ~]# mkdir -p /mnt/smb
```

Then run the command to do the actual mounting:

```
[root@clientB ~]# mount -t smbfs //serverA/samba-share /mnt/smb
```

where **//serverA/samba-share** is the remote share being mounted, and **/mnt/smb** is the mount point.

To unmount this directory, run **umount:**

```
[root@clientB ~]# umount /mnt/smb
```

CREATING SAMBA USERS

When configured to do so, Samba will honor requests from users that are stored in user databases that are in turn stored in various backends—e.g., LDAP (**ldapsam**), flat files (**smbpasswd**), or MySQL (**mysqlsam**).

Here, we will add a sample user that already exists in the local **/etc/passwd** file to Samba's user database. We will use Samba's native/default user database format (**smbpasswd** file) for demonstration purposes, as the other possibilities are beyond the scope of this chapter.

Let's create a Samba entry for the user yyang. We will also set the user's Samba password.

Use the **smbpasswd** command to create a Samba entry for the user yyang. Choose a good password when prompted to do so. Type

```
[root@serverA ~]# smbpasswd  -a yyang
New SMB password:
Retype new SMB password:
Added user yyang.
```

You can view the entry created for user yyang in the **/etc/samba/smbpasswd** file. Type

```
[root@serverA ~]# cat  /etc/samba/smbpasswd
yyang:500:93E28745F5C46E5169E95691975D12BC:[U          ]:LCT-42B0250C:
```

With a Samba user now created, you can now make the shares available to only authenticated users such as the one we just created for the user yyang.

If the user yyang now wants to access a resource on the Samba server that has been configured strictly for her use (a protected share or nonpublic share), the user can use the **smbclient** command shown here, for example:

```
[root@clientB ~]# smbclient  -Uyyang  -L   //serverA
```

It is of course also possible to access a protected Samba share from an MS Windows box. But the Samba username along with the corresponding Samba password will have to be entered in the Windows dialog box to connect to the share when prompted.

Allowing NULL Passwords

If you have a need to allow users to have no passwords (which is a bad idea, by the way), you can do so by using the **smbpasswd** program with the **-n** option, like so:

```
[root@serverA ~]# smbpasswd -n username
```

where **username** is the name of the user whose password you want to set to empty.

For example, to allow the user yyang to access a share on the Samba server with a null password, type

```
[root@serverA ~]# smbpasswd  -n yyang
User yyang password set to none.
```

You can also do this via the SWAT program using its Web interface.

Changing Passwords with smbpasswd

Users who prefer the command line over the Web interface can use the **smbpasswd** command to change their Samba passwords. This program works just like the regular **passwd** program, except this program does *not* update the **/etc/passwd** file by default. Because **smbpasswd** uses the standard protocol for communicating with the server regarding password changes, you can also use this to change your password on a remote Windows machine.

For example, to change the user yyang's Samba password, issue this command:

```
[root@serverA ~]# smbpasswd    yyang
New SMB password:
Retype new SMB password:
```

Samba can be configured to allow regular users to run the **smbpasswd** command themselves to manage their own passwords; the only caveat is that they must know their previous/old password.

USING SAMBA TO AUTHENTICATE AGAINST A WINDOWS SERVER

Thus far we've been talking about using Samba in the Samba/Linux world. Or to put it literally, we've been using Samba in its native environment, where it is lord and master of its *domain*. What this means is that our Samba server in combination with the Linux server has been responsible for managing all user authentication and authorization issues.

The simple Samba setup that we created earlier in the chapter had its own user database, which mapped the Samba users to real Linux/UNIX users. This allowed any files and directories created by Samba users to have the proper ownership contexts. But what if we wanted to deploy a Samba server in an environment with existing Windows servers that are being used to manage all users in the domain? And we don't want to have to manage a separate user database in Samba? Enter . . . the **winbindd** daemon.

The **winbindd** daemon is used for resolving user accounts (users and groups) information from native Windows servers. It can also be used to resolve other kinds of system information. It is able to this through its use of **pam_winbind** (a PAM module that interacts with the **winbindd** daemon to help authenticate users using Windows NT/LM authentication), the **ntlm_auth** tool (a tool to allow external access to **winbind**'s NT/LM authentication function), and **libnss_winbind** (**winbind**'s Name Service Switch library) facility.

The steps to set up a Linux box to consult a Windows server for its user authentication issues are very straightforward. They can be summarized in this way:

1. Configure Samba's configuration file (**smb.conf**) with the proper directives.
2. Add **winbind** to the Linux system's name service switch facility (**/etc/nsswitch .conf**).
3. Join the Linux/Samba server to the Windows domain.
4. Test things out.

Here we present a sample scenario where a Linux server named serverA wishes to use a Windows server for its user authentication issues. The Samba server is going to act as a Windows domain member server. The Windows server we assume here is running the Windows NT/200x Server operating system, and it is a domain controller (as well as the WINS server). Its IP address is 192.168.1.100. The domain controller is operating in mixed mode. (Mixed mode operation provides backward compatibility with Windows NT–type domains as well as Windows 200x–type domains.) The Windows domain name is "WINDOWS-DOMAIN." We have commented out any share definitions in our Samba configuration, so you'll have to create or specify your own (see the earlier parts of the chapter for how to do this). Let's break down the process in better detail:

1. First create an **smb.conf** file similar to this one:

```
#Sample smb.conf file
[global]
workgroup = WINDOWS-DOMAIN
security = DOMAIN
```

```
username map = /etc/samba/smbusers
log file = /var/log/samba/%m
smb ports = 139 445
name resolve order = wins bcast hosts
wins server = 192.168.1.100
idmap uid = 10000-20000
idmap gid = 10000-20000
template primary group = "Domain Users"
template shell = /bin/bash
winbind separator = +


# Share definitions
#[homes]
#    comment = Home Directories
#    browseable = no
#    writable = yes
```

2. Edit the **/etc/nsswitch.conf** file on the Linux server so that it will have entries
    similar to this one:

    ```
    passwd: files winbind
    shadow: files winbind
    group:  files winbind
    ```

3. On a Fedora Core or RHEL system, start the **winbindd** daemon using the `service`
    command. Type

    ```
    [root@serverA ~]# service winbind start
    Starting Winbind services:                              [  OK  ]
    ```

4. Join the Samba server to the Windows domain using the **net** command. Assum-
    ing the Windows Administrator account password, type

    ```
    [root@serverA ~]# net rpc join -U root%windows_administrator_password
    Joined domain WINDOWS-DOMAIN
    ```

    where the password for the account in the MS Windows domain with permis-
    sion to join systems to the domain is windows_administrator_password.

5. Use the **wbinfo** utility to list all users available in the Windows domain to make
    sure that things are working properly. Type

    ```
    [root@serverA ~]# wbinfo -u
    ```

TROUBLESHOOTING SAMBA

There are four typical solutions to connectivity problems with Samba.

▼ **Restart Samba** This may be necessary because either Samba has entered an
   undefined state or (more likely) you've made changes to the configuration but
   forgot to restart Samba so that the changes take effect.

- ■ **Make sure the configuration options are correct**   Errors in the **smb.conf** file are typically in directory names, usernames, network numbers, and host names. A common mistake is when a new client is added to a group that has special access to the server, but Samba isn't told the name of the new client being added. Don't forget that for syntax-type errors, the **testparm** utility is your ally.

- ▲ **Monitor encrypted passwords**   These may be mismatched—the server is configured to use them and the clients aren't, or (more likely) the clients are using encrypted passwords and Samba hasn't been configured to use them. If you're under the gun to get a client working, you may just want to disable client-side encryption using the **regedit** scripts that come with Samba's source code (see the **docs** subdirectory).

SUMMARY

In this chapter, we discussed the process of compiling, installing, and configuring Samba so that your Linux server can integrate into a Windows-based network. Samba is a powerful tool with the potential to replace MS Windows servers dedicated to disk and printer sharing.

Reading through tons of documentation probably isn't your favorite way to pass the day, but you'll find the Samba documentation to be complete, helpful, and easy reading. At least skim through the files to see what's there, so you know where you can go to get additional information when you need it. With all the Samba texts available (both free and non-free) today, you should have everything you need for configuring even the most complex setup. Two excellent texts dedicated to everything Samba immediately come to mind: *Samba-3 by Example*, by John Terpstra, and *The Official Samba-3 HOWTO and Reference Guide*, by John Terpstra and Jelmer Vernooij, both published by Prentice Hall (March, 2004). These are available in print and in electronic formats. The online versions of the book can be found at http://www.samba.org.

CHAPTER 25

LDAP

The Lightweight Directory Access Protocol (LDAP) has been referred to as many things, including the best thing since sliced bread. But it is actually a set of open protocols used to access and modify centrally stored information over a network. LDAP is based on the X.500 standard (X.500 is an ISO standard that defines an overall model for distributed directory services) but is a more lightweight version of the original standard. RFC 2251 explains the relationship thus: "LDAP is designed to provide access to directories supporting the X.500 models, while not incurring the resource requirements of the X.500 directory access protocol. Like traditional databases, an LDAP database can be queried for the information it stores."

LDAP was developed by the University of Michigan in 1992 as a lightweight alternative to the Directory Access Protocol (DAP). LDAP itself does not define the directory service. It instead defines the transport and format of messages used by a client to access data in a directory (such as the X.500 directory).

LDAP is extensible, relatively easy to implement, and based on an open standard (i.e., it is nonproprietary). This chapter will provide an introduction to the world of directory services, as implemented by OpenLDAP. Essential concepts governing the architecture and use of LDAP will be touched upon.

LDAP BASICS

LDAP is a global directory service. This directory can be used to store all sorts of information. The directory can be regarded as a database of sorts. But unlike traditional databases, an LDAP database is especially suited for read, search, and browse operations instead of write operations. It is with reads that LDAP shines the most.

Here are some popular LDAP implementations:

- ▼ OpenLDAP, an open LDAP suite
- ■ Novell's NetWare Directory Service (eDirectory)
- ■ Microsoft's Active Directory
- ■ iPlanet Directory Server (which was split between Sun and Netscape a while back. Netscape Directory Server has since been acquired by Red Hat, which has in turn released it to the Open Source community).
- ▲ IBM's SecureWay Directory

LDAP Directory

Just as in the popular Domain Name System (DNS), the directory entries in LDAP are arranged in a hierarchical tree structure. As in most hierarchical structures, the further you go down the tree, the more precise the content stored therein. The hierarchical tree structure of LDAP is known formally as the *directory information tree (DIT)*. The very top

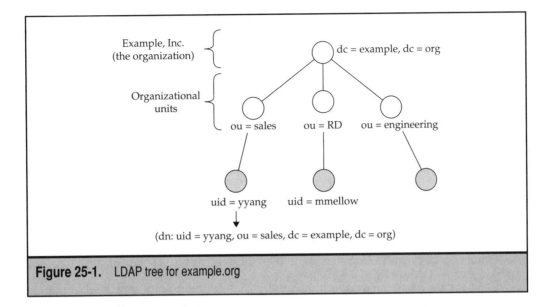

Figure 25-1.   LDAP tree for example.org

of the directory hierarchy has a *root* element. The complete path to any node in the tree structure, which uniquely identifies it, is known as the *distinguished name (DN)* of the node or object.

Again just as in DNS, the structure of an LDAP directory usually reflects geographic and/or organization boundaries. Geographic boundaries can be along country lines, state lines, city lines, or the like. Organizational boundaries can, for example, be along functional lines, departmental lines, or organization units.

For example, a company named Example, Inc., may decide to structure its directory tree using a domain-based naming structure. This company may have different subdivisions (organizational units, or OUs) within the company such as the Engineering department, the Sales department, and the R&D department. The LDAP directory tree of such a company is illustrated in Figure 25-1.

The DN of a sample object in the directory tree shown in the figure is "dn: uid=yyang, ou=sales,dc=example,dc=org".

Client/Server Model

As with most network services, LDAP adheres to the usual client/server paradigm. A typical interaction between the client and the server goes like this:

▼   An LDAP client application connects to an LDAP server. This is sometimes called binding to a server.

■   Based on the access restrictions configured on the server, the LDAP server either accepts or refuses the bind/connection request. Assuming it accepts . . .

- The client has the choices of querying the directory server, browsing the information stored on the server, or attempting to modify/update the information on the LDAP server.

▲ Again based on access restrictions, the server can allow or deny any of the operations attempted by the client. In the event that the server cannot answer a request, it may forward or refer the client to another upstream LDAP server that may have a more authoritative response to the request.

Uses of LDAP

LDAP is a distributed directory service and can be used as storage for various types of information. Just about any kind of information can be stored in an LDAP directory—information as varied in nature as plain textual information, images, binary data, or public key certificates.

Over the years various LDAP schemas have been created to allow the storage of different data sources in an LDAP directory. Here are some examples of uses of LDAP:

▼ LDAP can serve as a complete Identity Management Solution for an organization. It can provide authentication and authorization services for users. In fact, the services provided by the Network Information Service can be completely replaced by LDAP.

- The information stored in DNS records can be stored in LDAP.

- LDAP can be used to provide "yellow pages" services for an organization (for instance, users' or employees' contact info—phone numbers, addresses, departments, etc.).

- Mail routing information can be stored in LDAP.

▲ A Samba schema exists that allows a Samba server to store extensive object attributes in LDAP. This allows Samba to function as a robust drop-in replacement for MS Windows NT domain controllers in environments where redundancy and replication are needed.

LDAP Terminologies

If you are going to master LDAP-speak, you might as well know the essential LDAP technical jargon. In this section we attempt to define some terms you will often come across when dealing with LDAP.

▼ **Entry (or object)** This is one unit in an LDAP directory. Each entry is qualified by its distinguished name (DN), e.g., "dn: uid=yyang,ou=sales,dc=example,dc=com."

- **Attributes** These are pieces of information associated with an entry, e.g., an organization's address or people's phone numbers.

■ **objectClass**   This is a special type of attribute. All objects in LDAP must have an objectClass attribute. The objectclass definition specifies which attributes are required for each LDAP object. It specifies the object classes of an entry. The values of this attribute may be modified by clients, but the objectClass attribute itself cannot be removed.

The objectclass definitions are themselves stored in schema files.

■ **Schema**   A schema is a collection of rules that determine the structure and contents of the directory. The schema contains the attribute type definitions, object-class definitions, etc.

The schema lists the attributes of each object type and whether these attributes are required or optional. Schemas are usually stored in plaintext files.

Examples of schemas are

▼ **core.schema**   This schema defines the basic LDAPv3 attributes and objects. It is a required core schema in the OpenLDAP implementation.

▲ **inetorgperson.schema**   Defines the inetOrgPerson object class and its associated attributes. This object is often used to store people's contact information

▲ **LDIF**   This stands for the LDAP Data Interchange Format. It is a plaintext file for LDAP entries. Files that import or export data to and from an LDAP server must be in this format. The data used for replication among LDAP servers are also in this format.

OPENLDAP

OpenLDAP is the open-source implementation of LDAP that runs on Linux/UNIX systems. OpenLDAP is a suite of programs made up of the following components: **slapd**, **slurpd**, and **libraries**, which implement the LDAP protocol, along with various client- and server-side utilities.

Server-Side Daemons

The server side consists of two main daemons:

▼ **Slapd**   This is a standalone LDAP daemon. It listens for LDAP connections from clients and responds to the LDAP operations it receives over those connections.

▲ **Slurpd**   This is a standalone LDAP replication daemon. It is used to propagate changes from one **slapd** database to another. It is the daemon used for synchronizing changes from one LDAP server to another. It is only needed when more than one LDAP server is in use.

OpenLDAP Utilities

The OpenLDAP utilities are a set of command-line tools used for querying, viewing, updating, and modifying the data stored in the OpenLDAP directory. On a Fedora Core system and RHEL, this suite of programs is provided by the **openldap-clients*.rpm** package, and some of them are provided by the **openldap-server*.rpm** package. The programs are listed in Table 25-1.

Installing OpenLDAP

In order to get the OpenLDAP server and client components up and running, these packages are required on Fedora and Red Hat Enterprise Linux systems:

▼ **openldap-2*.rpm**   Provides the configuration files and libraries for Open-LDAP.

■ **openldap-clients*.rpm**   Provides the client programs needed for accessing and modifying OpenLDAP directories.

▲ **openldap-servers*.rpm**   Provides the servers (**slapd**, **slurpd**) and other utilities necessary to configure and run LDAP.

TIP   If you are configuring only the client side, you won't need the **openldap-servers*.rpm** package.

We will use the **up2date** program to automatically download and install the **open-ldap-servers** package on our sample system. The steps are listed here:

1. While logged in as root, first confirm which of the packages you already have installed by querying the RPM database.

   ```
   [root@serverA ~]# rpm -qa| grep -i openldap
   openldap-2*
   ...<OUTPUT TRUNCATED>...
   ```

NOTE   The installation process of most Linux distributions will automatically include the base OpenLDAP software as a part of the minimum software installed. This is done so that the system can be configured as an LDAP client from the get-go without any addition hassle.

2. Our sample system already has the basic **openldap** libraries in place, so we will next go ahead and install the OpenLDAP client and server packages using **up2date**. Type

   ```
   [root@serverA ~]# up2date -i openldap-servers  openldap-clients
   ```

3. Once the installation completes successfully, you can go on to the configuration section.

Utility	Description
ldapmodify	Used for modifying entries in LDAP. It accepts input either directly from the command line or via a file.
ldapadd	The **ldapadd** command is actually a hard link to the **ldapmodify -a** command. It is used to add new entries to an LDAP database. (The functionality provided by the **ldapadd** command can be obtained by adding the **-a** option to the **ldapmodify** command.)
ldapdelete	Used for deleting entries from an OpenLDAP directory.
ldappasswd	Sets the password for an LDAP user.
ldapsearch	Used for querying/searching an LDAP directory.
slapadd	Accepts input from an LDIF file to populate an LDAP directory. Located under the **/usr/sbin/** directory
slapcat	Dumps the entire content of the LDAP directory into an LDIF-type file. Located under the **/usr/sbin/** directory.
slapindex	Used for reindexing the LDAP database according to the actual current database content. Located under the **/usr/sbin/** directory.
slappasswd	Used for generating properly hashed/encrypted passwords that can be used with various privileged directory operations. Located under the **/usr/sbin/** directory.

Table 25-1.   OpenLDAP Utilities

Configuring OpenLDAP

Depending on what you want to do with your directory, configuring your directory server can be a real pain or it can be a very simple process. Setting up your directory is usually very easy if you are working on a brand-new deployment where you don't have to worry about any legacy issues, existing users or data, etc. For environments with existing infrastructure, extra precautionary measures have to be taken.

CAUTION   If you are deploying LDAP in an environment where you have to worry about backward compatibility issues, legacy architectures, existing users, or existing data, then you are advised to approach your OpenLDAP rollout with great caution. This may take months of planning in some situations. The planning should include extensive testing and actual staging of the current environment on test systems.

The pam_ldap and nss_ldap Modules

The **pam_ldap** module provides a means for Linux/UNIX hosts to authenticate against LDAP directories. The module was developed by the PADL software company (http://www.padl.com). It allows PAM-aware applications to authenticate users using information stored in an LDAP directory. Examples of PAM-aware applications are the login program, some mail servers, some FTP servers, OpenSSH, and Samba.

The **nss_ldap** module is a set of C library extensions that allow applications to look up users, groups, hosts, and other information by querying an LDAP directory. The module allows applications to look up information using LDAP as well as using the traditional methods such as flat files or NIS. The module was also developed by the PADL software company (http://www.padl.com).

On Fedora systems as well as RHEL systems, these modules are provided by the **nss_ldap*.rpm** package. These modules are required on systems where LDAP is to be used as a replacement for the traditional authentication mechanisms.

Let's check if the package is already installed by typing

```
[root@serverA openldap]# rpm -q nss_ldap
nss_ldap-*
```

If you find that the package is not installed, you can quickly install it by using the **up2date** command thus:

```
[root@serverA openldap]# up2date  -i  nss_ldap
```

Another very important factor to give adequate thought to when configuring your LDAP directory service is the structure of the directory. For example, you should have answers to these questions before proceeding: "What are the organizational divisions in your establishment?" "Along what boundaries will the structure be built?" Other questions that you should also keep in mind are: "How sensitive is the information you want to store in the directory?" "Will more than one LDAP server be required?"

Configuring slapd

The **/etc/openldap/slapd.conf** file is the configuration file for the **slapd** daemon. In this section, we will dissect the default configuration file that comes with our Fedora system and discuss some of its interesting portions.

Here is a truncated version of the **/etc/openldap/slapd.conf** file. Most of the comment entries in the original file have been removed as well as some other configuration directives that we don't want to address here. We display only the stripped-down version of the file that is relevant to our current discussion. And line numbers have also been added to the beginning of each line to aid readability.

```
1 # See slapd.conf(5) for details on configuration options.
2 # This file should NOT be world readable.
3 #
4 include          /etc/openldap/schema/core.schema
5 include          /etc/openldap/schema/cosine.schema
6 include          /etc/openldap/schema/inetorgperson.schema
7 include          /etc/openldap/schema/nis.schema
8 #
9 pidfile          /var/run/slapd.pid
10 argsfile         /var/run/slapd.args
11 database         bdb
12 suffix           "dc=my-domain,dc=com"
13 rootdn           "cn=Manager,dc=my-domain,dc=com"
14 # Cleartext passwords, especially for the rootdn, should
15 # be avoided.  See slappasswd(8) and slapd.conf(5) for details.
16 #
17 rootpw           {crypt}ijFYNcSNctBYg
18 #
19 # The database directory MUST exist prior to running slapd AND
20 # should only be accessible by the slapd and slap tools.
21 # Mode 700 recommended.
22 directory        /var/lib/ldap
```

From the preceding listing:

▼   Lines 1–3 are comment entries. Any text after the pound (#) symbol is a comment.

■   Lines 4–7 are **include** statements. The **include** statement is used to instruct **slapd** to read in additional configuration information from the file(s) specified. In this case, the additional files being pulled in are the specified OpenLDAP schema files stored under the **/etc/openldap/schema/** directory. The **core.schema** file must be present at a minimum.

■   In line 9, the **pidfile** directive points to the path of the file that will hold **slapd**'s process ID.

■   In line 10, the **argsfile** directive is used for specifying the path to a file that can be used to store command-line options used for starting **slapd**.

■   In line 11, the **database** option marks the beginning of a new database instance definition. The value of this option depends on the backend that will be used to hold the database. In our sample **slapd.conf** file, **bdb** (Berkeley DB) is used as the database type. Other supported database backend types are ldbm, sql, tcl, and meta. Some database backends are described in Table 25-2.

■   In line 12, the **suffix** directive specifies the DN suffix of queries that will be passed to this particular database backend. It defines the domain for which the LDAP server provides information or for which the LDAP server is authoritative. This entry should be changed to reflect your organization's naming structure.

Database Backend Type	Description
bdb	Berkeley database instance definition. This is the recommended database backend type. It uses the Sleepycat Berkeley DB to store data.
ldbm	Lightweight directory access protocol DBM (LDAP DBM) type. Very easy to configure but not as durable as the bdb database backend type. It also uses Berkeley DB, GNU DBM, and MDBM to store data.
sql	Uses a SQL database backend to store data.
ldap	Used as a proxy to forward incoming requests to another LDAP server.
meta	Metadirectory database backend. It is an improvement on the ldap type backend. It performs LDAP proxying with respect to a set of remote LDAP servers.
monitor	Stores information about the status of the **slapd** daemon.
null	Operations to this database type succeed but do nothing. This is the equivalent of sending stuff to **/dev/null** in Linux/UNIX.
passwd	Uses the system's plaintext **/etc/passwd** file to serve user account information.
tcl	An experimental backend that uses a Tcl interpreter that is directly embedded into **slapd**.
perl	Uses a Perl interpreter that is embedded directly into **slapd**.

Table 25-2.   OpenLDAP Database Backends

- In line 13, the **rootdn** directive specifies the DN of the superuser for the LDAP directory. This user is to the LDAP directory what the UNIX/Linux root user is to a Linux system. The user specified here is not subject to any access controls or administrative restrictions for operations on the database in question. The DN specified here need not exist in the directory.

- In line 17, the **rootpw** directive specifies the password for the DN specified by the **rootdn** directive. Needless to say, a *very* strong/good password should be used here. The password can be specified in plaintext (very, very bad idea), or the hash of the password can be specified. The **slappasswd** program can be used to generate password hashes.

▲ Finally, in line 22, the **directory** directive specifies the path to the BDB files containing the database and associated indices.

Having gone through a few important directives in the **slapd.conf** file, we will now make a few changes to the file to customize it for our environment.

▼ While logged in to the system as root, change to OpenLDAP's working directory. Type

```
[root@serverA ~]# cd /etc/openldap/
```

■ Make a backup of the original **slapd.conf** file by renaming it. This is so that you can always revert to it in case of mistakes. Type

```
[root@serverA openldap]# mv  slapd.conf   slapd.conf.original
```

■ Use any text editor to create a new **/etc/openldap/slapd.conf** file using the following text:

```
include        /etc/openldap/schema/core.schema
include        /etc/openldap/schema/cosine.schema
include        /etc/openldap/schema/inetorgperson.schema
include        /etc/openldap/schema/nis.schema
pidfile        /var/run/slapd.pid
argsfile       /var/run/slapd.args
database       bdb
suffix         "dc=example,dc=org"
rootdn         "cn=Manager,dc=example,dc=org"
#
# The hashed password below was generated using the command:
# "slappasswd  -s  test". Run the command and paste the output here.
rootpw  {SSHA}gJeD9BJdcx5L+bfgMpmvsFJVqdG5CjdP
directory      /var/lib/ldap
```

▲ Save your changes to the file and exit the editor.

Starting and Stopping slapd

After setting up **slapd**'s configuration file, the next step will be to start the daemon. Starting it on a Fedora system is very easy. But first we'll use the **service** command to check the status of the daemon.

```
[root@serverA ~]# service ldap status
slapd is stopped
```

The sample output shows that the daemon is not currently running. Start it with this command:

```
[root@serverA openldap]# service ldap start
Checking configuration files for slapd:  config file testing succeeded
                                                              [  OK  ]
Starting slapd:                                               [  OK  ]
```

And if you find that the **ldap** service is already running, you can instead issue the **service** command with the **restart** option, like so:

```
[root@serverA ~]# service ldap restart
Stopping slapd:                                          [  OK  ]
Checking configuration files slapd:  config file testing succeeded [ OK ]
Starting slapd:                                          [  OK  ]
```

TIP Watch out for the permissions of the OpenLDAP configuration files. For example, the **slapd** daemon will refuse to start on a Fedora or RHEL system if the "ldap" user cannot read the **slapd.conf** file. Also the contents of the database directory (/**var/lib/ldap**) must be owned by the user called "ldap" in order to avoid funny errors.

If you want the **slapd** service to start up automatically with the next system reboot, type

```
[root@serverA openldap]# chkconfig ldap on
```

CONFIGURING OPENLDAP CLIENTS

The notion of clients takes some getting used to in the LDAP world. Almost any system resource or process can be an LDAP client. And fortunately or unfortunately, each group of clients has their own specific configuration files. The configuration files for Open-LDAP clients are generally named **ldap.conf**. But they are stored in different directories depending on the particular client in question.

Two common locations for the OpenLDAP client configuration files are the /**etc/ openldap/** directory and the /**etc/** directory. The client applications that use the Open-LDAP libraries (provided by the **openldap*.rpm** package)—programs like **ldapadd**, **ldapsearch**, Sendmail, and Evolution—consult the /**etc/openldap/ldap.conf** file if it exists. The nss_ldap libraries instead use the /**etc/ldap.conf** file as the configuration file.

In this section, we will set up the configuration file for the OpenLDAP client tools. This configuration file is very straightforward; we will only be changing one of the directives in the file.

Open the /**etc/openldap/ldap.conf** file in any text editor and change this line in the listing:

```
BASE dc=example,dc=com
```

to look like this:

```
BASE dc=example,dc=org
```

> **TIP** One other particular variable/directive that you might also want to change in the **/etc/openldap/ldap.conf** file, if you are using the client tools from a host other than the server itself, is the HOST directive. This should be set to the IP address of the remote LDAP server. But because we are using the LDAP clients directly on the LDAP server itself, we have left the HOST directive at its default, **HOST 127.0.0.1**.

Creating Directory Entries

The LDAP Data Interchange Format (LDIF) is used to represent entries in an LDAP directory in textual form. As stated earlier, data in LDAP is presented and exchanged in this format. The data in an LDIF file can be used to manipulate, add, remove, and change the information stored in the LDAP directory. The format for an LDIF entry is

```
dn: <distinguished name>
<attribute_description>: <attribute_value>
<attribute_description>: <attribute_value>

dn: <yet another distinguished name>
<attribute_description>: <attribute_value>
<attribute_description>: <attribute_value>
...
```

The LDIF file is slightly strict in its format. You should keep these points in mind:

▼ Multiple entries within the same LDIF file are separated by blank lines.

■ Entries that begin with the pound sign (#) are regarded as comments and are ignored.

■ An entry that spans more than one line can be continued on the next line by starting the next line with a single space or tab character.

▲ The space following the colon (:) is important for each entry.

In this section we will use a sample LDIF file to populate our new directory with basic information to set up our directory information tree (DIT) and also information describing two users named bogus and testuser, respectively.

1. The sample LDIF file is presented next. Use any text editor to input the text in the listing into the file. Be very careful with the white spaces and tabs in the file and make sure that you maintain a newline after each DN entry, as shown in our sample file.

```
dn: dc=example,dc=org
objectclass: dcObject
```

```
objectclass: organization
o: Example inc.
dc: example

dn: cn=bogus,dc=example,dc=org
objectclass: organizationalRole
cn: bogus

dn: cn=testuser,dc=example,dc=org
objectclass: organizationalRole
cn: testuser
```

2. Next save the file as **sample.ldif** and exit your text editor.

3. Use the **ldapadd** utility to import the **sample.ldif** file into the OpenLDAP directory. Type

```
[root@serverA ~]# ldapadd  -x -D "cn=manager,dc=example,dc=org" -W -f sample.ldif
Enter LDAP Password:
adding new entry "dc=example,dc=org"
adding new entry "cn=bogus,dc=example,dc=org"
adding new entry "cn=testuser,dc=example,dc=org"
```

These are the parameters used in this **ldapadd** command:

▼ **x**   Means to use simple authentication instead of SASL.

■ **D**   Specifies the distinguished name with which to bind to the LDAP directory (i.e., the **binddn** parameter specified in the **slapd.conf** file).

■ **W**   Allows the user to be prompted for the simple authentication password, instead of specifying the password in plaintext on the command line.

▲ **f**   Specifies the file from which to read the LDIF file.

4. Enter the password that you created using the **slappasswd** utility earlier, i.e., the password that was specified in the **/etc/openldap/slapd.conf** file for the **rootpw** directive. We used "test" as the password in our example.

We are done populating the directory.

Searching, Querying, and Modifying the Directory

Here we will use a couple of OpenLDAP client utilities to retrieve information from our directory.

1. First we'll use the **ldapsearch** utility to search for and retrieve every entry in the database directory, by typing

```
[root@serverA ~]# ldapsearch  -x -b 'dc=example,dc=org' '(objectclass=*)'
# extended LDIF

...<OUTPUT TRUNCATED>...
```

```
# example.org
dn: dc=example,dc=org
objectClass: dcObject
objectClass: organization
o: Example inc.
dc: example

# bogus, example.org
dn: cn=bogus,dc=example,dc=org
objectClass: organizationalRole
cn: bogus

...<OUTPUT TRUNCATED>...

# numResponses: 4
# numEntries: 3
```

2. Let's repeat the search again, but without specifying the **-b** option and also making the output less verbose. Type

```
[root@serverA ~]# ldapsearch  -x -LLL    '(objectclass=*)'
dn: dc=example,dc=org
objectClass: dcObject
objectClass: organization
o: Example inc.
dc: example

dn: cn=bogus,dc=example,dc=org
objectClass: organizationalRole
cn: bogus

dn: cn=testuser,dc=example,dc=org
objectClass: organizationalRole
cn: testuser
```

Here, we didn't need to explicitly specify the **basedn** to search because that information is already defined in our **/etc/openldap/ldap.conf** file.

3. We'll next narrow down our query by searching only for the entry for the object whose common name (cn) is equal to bogus. Issue this command to do this:

```
[root@serverA ~]# ldapsearch -x -LLL  -b  'dc=example,dc=org' '(cn=bogus)'
dn: cn=bogus,dc=example,dc=org
objectClass: organizationalRole
cn: bogus
```

4. Now we'll attempt to perform a privileged operation on a directory entry using the **ldapdelete** utility. Let's delete the entry for the object with the DN of "cn=bogus,dc=example,dc=org". Issue this command:

```
[root@serverA ~]# ldapdelete -x -W -D 'cn=Manager,dc=example,dc=org' \
'cn=bogus,dc=example,dc=org'
Enter LDAP Password:
```

Enter the password for the cn=Manager,dc=example,dc=org DN to complete the operation.

5. Let's use the **ldapsearch** utility again to make sure that that entry has indeed been removed. Type

```
[root@serverA ~]# ldapsearch -x -LLL -b 'dc=example,dc=org' '(cn=bogus)'
```

This command should return nothing.

Using OpenLDAP for User Authentication

We will describe setting up the OpenLDAP server (and client) that we configured earlier in the chapter to also manage Linux user accounts. We will be using some of the migration scripts that come with the software to pull/migrate the users that already exist in the system's **/etc/passwd** file into LDAP.

Configuring the Server

Setting up a Linux system to use LDAP as the storage backend for user account information is very easy once you have all the other basic OpenLDAP configuration issues taken care of.

The software comes with various useful scripts to ease the migration of various databases into an OpenLDAP directory. These scripts are stored under the **/usr/share/openldap/migration/** directory on Fedora Core and RHEL systems.

We will begin by customizing the **/usr/share/openldap/migration/migrate_common .ph** file to suit our particular setup.

1. Open the file for editing and look for the lines/entries similar to these:

```
$DEFAULT_MAIL_DOMAIN = "padl.com";
$DEFAULT_BASE = "dc=padl,dc=com";
```

For example, we will change these variables to read

```
$DEFAULT_MAIL_DOMAIN = "example.org";
$DEFAULT_BASE = "dc=example,dc=org";
```

2. We will use one of the migration scripts (**migrate_base.pl**) to create the base structure for our directory. Type

```
[root@serverA ~]# cd /usr/share/openldap/migration/
```

3. And then execute the script thus:

```
[root@serverA migration]# ./migrate_base.pl >   ~/base.ldif
```

This command will create a file named **base.ldif** under your home directory.

4. Make sure **slapd** is running and then import the entries in the **base.ldif** file into the openLDAP directory. Type

```
[root@serverA ~]# ldapadd -c -x -D "cn=manager,dc=example,dc=org" \
-W -f base.ldif
```

5. Now we need to export the current users in the system's **/etc/passwd** file into an LDIF-type file. We will use the **/usr/share/openldap/migration/migrate_passwd.pl** script. Type

```
[root@serverA migration]# ./migrate_passwd.pl  /etc/passwd > \
~/ldap-users.ldif
```

6. Next we can begin importing all the user entries in the **ldap-users.ldif** file into our openLDAP database. We will use the **ldapadd** command. Type

```
[root@serverA ~]# ldapadd  -x -D "cn=manager,dc=example,dc=org" -W -f \
ldap-users.ldif
```

7. Enter the rootdn's password when prompted.

Configuring the Client

Configuring a client system to use an LDAP directory for user authentication is as easy as pie on a Fedora or RHEL system. Fedora Core has a GUI tool (**system-config-authentication**) that really dumbs down the procedure.

1. To launch the tool from the command line, type

```
[root@clientB ~]# system-config-authentication
```

A window similar to the one shown next will appear.

2. In the Authentication Configuration window, select the Enable LDAP Support option.

3. Next click the Configure LDAP button.

   A window similar to this one will open:

4. Enter in the appropriate information for your particular environment. Here we specify the Base DN as "dc=example,dc=org" and the LDAP server as serverA (you can also specify an IP address).

5. Click OK.

We just described a very simple way to enable a Fedora Core client system to use an OpenLDAP server for its user authentication. We did not bother with a lot of details because this is just a proof of concept. Here are some of the details you may have to deal with in a real production environment:

▼ **Home directories**   You may have to make sure that users' home directories are available to them when logging in from any system. A possible way to do this will be to share user home directories via NFS and export the share to all client systems.

■ **Security**   Our sample setup did not have any security measures built into the infrastructure. This should be of paramount importance in a production environment; so that user passwords do not go flying across the network in plaintext.

▲ **Other issues**   There are more issues that we didn't address here, but we'll leave those as a mental exercise for you to stumble over and ponder on.

SUMMARY

In this chapter we covered some LDAP basics. We concentrated mostly on the Open Source implementation of LDAP known as OpenLDAP. We discussed the components of OpenLDAP—the server-side daemons and the client-side utilities used for querying and modifying the information stored in an LDAP directory. We created a very simple directory and populated it with some sample entries.

We barely scratched the surface of the topic. LDAP is too large a topic to be done any justice in a single chapter. But hopefully, we whetted your appetite and got you started in the right direction with some essential concepts and ideas.

CHAPTER 26

Printing

Printing under Linux and UNIX typically has not been a straightforward process. With the advent of the Common UNIX Printing System (CUPS), Linux printing is much easier to configure and use. Previously, the printers most widely supported were PostScript printers from Hewlett-Packard and other manufacturers. As Linux has become a viable desktop workstation, a better printing solution was needed, and the solution is CUPS. This chapter will cover the installation of the CUPS system along with the administrative tasks involved in maintaining your printing environment.

PRINTING TERMINOLOGIES

There are several printing systems available in the Linux world today, all more or less based on the venerable BSD printing system. Here are some printing terms to be familiar with:

▼ **Printer** A peripheral device usually attached to a host computer or the network.

■ **Jobs** The file or set of files that is submitted for printing is called a job.

■ **Spooler** A spooler is the software that manages print jobs. It is responsible for receiving print jobs, storing jobs, queuing jobs, and finally, sending the jobs to the physical hardware that will do the actual printing. Spoolers run as daemon processes that are always sitting and waiting to service print requests, and for this reason they are often referred to as "print servers." These are examples of spoolers:

 ▼ **LPD** This is the original BSD Line Printer Daemon. It is the oldest printing system.

 ■ **LPRng** This is an enhanced, extended, and portable implementation of the Berkeley `lpr` spooler functionality It merges the best features of the System V printing system with that of the Berkeley system.

 ▲ **CUPS** This provides a portable printing layer for UNIX-based systems. It uses the Internet Printing Protocol (IPP) as the basis for managing print jobs and queues.

■ **PDL** This stands for *page description language*. Printers accept input in this form. PostScript and PCL are examples of PDLs.

■ **PostScript** PostScript files are programs. It is a stack-based programming language. Most UNIX/Linux programs generate output in PostScript format for printing. PostScript-based printers are printers that directly support this format.

■ **Ghostscript** A software-based PostScript interpreter for non-PostScript printers, it is used for software driven printing. It will generate the language of a printer from PostScript. Examples are Aladdin Ghostscript (commercial version), GNU Ghostscript (free version) and ESP Ghostscript (CUPS).

▲ **Filter** Filters are special programs or scripts that process data (jobs) before it is sent to the printer. Spoolers send the jobs to the filters and then the filter passes it on to the printer. File format translation and accounting usually take place at the filtering layer.

THE CUPS SYSTEM

CUPS is gaining widespread acceptance in Linux and the UNIX community as a whole. Even the new version of Apple's OS X supports CUPS. What this means is that you have a ubiquitous printing environment no matter what operating system you are using. Along with the standard UNIX printing protocol of LPR, CUPS supports Samba printing and the new Internet Printing Protocol. Using the concept of print *classes,* the CUPS system will print a document to a group of printers for use in high-volume printing environments. It can act as a central print spooler or just supply the printing method for your local printer.

Running CUPS

This section deals with the process of installing CUPS and controlling the service.

The CUPS software was developed by Easy Software Products and is available at http://www.easysw.com/. There are two methods of installation, through your Linux distribution or by compiling from source. The first method is highly recommended, as the distributions typically have all of the popular printer support built into CUPS. When compiling by hand, you have to get drivers for your printers yourself.

Installing CUPS

As with most of the software we've dealt with thus far, the CUPS software also comes in two forms: you have the CUPS source code itself, from which you can build the software, and you also have the prepackaged RPM binaries.

If you have to compile CUPS from source, follow the directions that come with the software package. The source code for CUPS can be found at http://www.cups.org/. Installation instructions are bundled with the software. You will also want to look at the Foomatic package located at http://www.linuxprinting.org; this site provides numerous printer drivers for various printing systems including CUPS.

If you have a Linux distribution such as Fedora Core, RHEL, SuSE, cAos, or Mandrake, CUPS should be available as an RPM package; in fact, CUPS is the default printing system used on those distributions.

Sticking with your distribution's package version of CUPS is the recommended method for installing CUPS. The distribution vendor has done the hard work to make sure that CUPS works well with their system. If you are unfortunate enough to have a Linux distribution that doesn't have CUPS, you can compile the package from source code (see the next section).

Because most systems have CUPS already installed during the initial operating system installation, you should first query the system's RPM database to see if the software is installed already. Type

```
[root@serverA ~]# rpm   -q cups
cups-1.1.23-15
```

If this query returns nothing, you can quickly install CUPS on a Fedora Core or RHEL system by typing

```
[root@serverA ~]# up2date -i cups
```

or

```
[root@serverA ~]# yum install cups
```

On a SuSE system, you should be able to type this command to get CUPS installed:

```
[root@serverA ~]# yast -i cups
```

Once you have installed the CUPS software, you need to turn on the CUPS daemon. On a Fedora system, you would do the following:

```
[root@serverA ~]# service cups restart
```

On a non-Fedora system, you might be able to start CUPS by executing the startup script directly, like this:

```
[root@serverA ~]# /etc/init.d/cups start
```

This will start the CUPS printing system and allow you to connect to the Web interface and add printers.

Configuring CUPS

The main configuration file for the CUPS print daemon is called **cupsd.conf**. It is usually located in the **/etc/cups/** directory. It is a plain text file with directives (syntax) similar to that of the Apache Web server. The directives determine how the server operates.

The file is very well commented, and all that usually needs to be done is to uncomment certain lines in the file to turn certain functions on or off.

Here are some interesting directives used in the **cupsd.conf** file:

▼ **Browsing**   This directive controls whether or not network printer browsing is enabled.

■ **BrowseProtocols**   This specifies the protocols to use when collecting and distributing shared printers on the local network.

■ **BrowseInterval**   This specifies the maximum amount of time between browsing updates.

■ **BrowseAddress**   This specifies an address to send browsing information to.

■ **Location**   This specifies access control and authentication options for the specified HTTP resource or path.

▲ **ServerName**   This directive specifies the hostname that is reported to clients.

A particularly interesting location is the root location represented by the slash symbol (/). This location in the default **cupsd.conf** file looks like this (please note that line numbers have been added to the listing to aid readability):

```
1) <Location />
2) Order Deny,Allow
3) Deny From All
4) Allow From 127.0.0.1
5) </Location>
```

▼ **Line 1** This is the start of the Location directive; here it defines the start of "/"—which is the path for ALL get operations, i.e., the topmost level of the Web server.

■ **Line 2** This is the Order directive. It defines the default access control for the location in question. These are the possible values for the Order directive:

    ▼ **Deny,Allow** *Only* allow requests from the hosts specified in the Allow directive.

    ▲ **Allow,Deny** Allow requests from all systems except those specified in Deny directive.

■ **Line 3** This Deny directive specifies the host(s) to deny access. In this case, the "All" keyword means all hosts.

■ **Line 4** The Allow directive specifies the host(s) to be allowed access. In this case, the only host allowed is the localhost, i.e., the loopback address (127.0.0.1).

▲ **Line 5** This is the closing tag for the Location directive.

TIP To change the default behavior of CUPS from allowing only access from the localhost, you could, for example, change the Allow directive from "Allow From 127.0.0.1" to "Allow From All" and then comment out the "Deny From All" directive.

ADDING PRINTERS

The first step after you have finished compiling and have turned on the CUPS system is to log in to the Web interface. The Web interface is available through port 631. In your Web browser, you just have to enter **http://localhost:631**. By default, you must be logged in to the same server that you are trying to administer. The interesting thing to note is that 631 is the same port that CUPS uses for accepting print jobs. When you connect to the Web page, you will see a page similar to Figure 26-1.

NOTE If you want to administer printers from other locations than the server that you are working on, you need to modify the **cupsd.conf** file to allow other hosts to connect. The **cupsd.conf** file typically resides in the directory **/etc/cups/**.

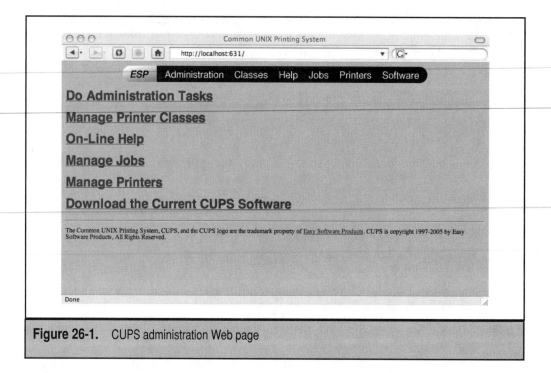

Figure 26-1. CUPS administration Web page

Local Printers and Remote Printers

Adding printers is very easy in CUPS. An important piece of information you will need is how the printer is attached to your system. Printers can be connected to hosts using two broad methods: locally attached printers and network printers. Several modes or possibilities exist under each method. The modes with which CUPS addresses the printer resources are specified by using what is known as the device *Uniform Resource Information (URI)* in CUPS. These are the possible device URIs that can be configured in CUPS:

▼ **Directly connected (local)** A standalone home system running Linux will most likely be connected to the printer directly through the use of a printer cable (commonly called a parallel cable) or perhaps connect using a USB cable to the printer's USB port. This is an example of a locally attached printer. In CUPS lingo, some possible device URIs for locally attached printer are specified as

    ▼ **parallel:/dev/lp*** For a printer attached to the parallel port

    ■ **serial:/dev/ttyS*** For a printer attached to the serial port

    ▲ **usb:/dev/usb/lp*** For a printer attached to the USB port

■ **IPP (network)** IPP is an acronym for the Internet Printing Protocol. It allows a printer to be accessed over the network using IPP. Most modern operating systems support this protocol, and so this is usually not a problem. And example of an IPP device URI in CUPS is ipp://*hostname*/ipp/.

- ■ **LPD (network)** LPD is the Line Printer Daemon. CUPS supports printers that are attached to systems running this daemon. Most UNIX/Linux systems (even some Windows servers) support this daemon. So if a printer is attached to a host that supports LPD, CUPS can be used to make that printer available on the network to other hosts that do not necessarily support LDP. Virtually all HP laser printers with network connectivity also natively support LPD.

  A sample device URI to address an LPD printer is lpd://*hostname*/queue, where *hostname* is the name of the machine where LPD is running.

- ■ **SMB (network)** SMB is the Service Message Block. This the foundation of file and printer sharing on Windows networks. Linux/UNIX hosts also support SMB through the use of the Samba software. If, for example, a Windows system (or a Samba server) has a printer shared on it, CUPS can be configured to access and make that printer available to its own clients. A sample device URI to address an SMB printer resource is smb://*servername*/*sharename*, where *sharename* is the name by which the printer has been shared on the Windows box or on the Samba server.

- ▲ **Networked Printer** (Duh!) This refers to a class of printers that have built-in networking capabilities. These printers don't need to be connected to any standalone system. They usually have some form of network interface of their own—either Ethernet, wireless, or some other method of connecting directly to a network. A very popular type of this printer group are the HP Jetdirect series. A sample URI to address such printers is socket://*ip_address:port*, where *ip_address* is the IP address of the printer and *port* is the port number on which the printer listens for print requests. This is usually port 9100 on the HP Jetdirect series.

Using the Web Interface

There are two ways in which printers can be added and configured in CUPS. One is through a Web interface using a browser of some sort, and the other is through the command line. The former method is probably easier because it uses a kind of wizard to walk you through the entire process.

This section will walk you through setting up a printer through the CUPS Web interface. We will set up an imaginary printer with the following properties:

```
Name:             Imagine-printer
Location:         Building  3
Description:      You only need to imagine to print here.
Connection Type:  Local. Connected to Parallel port
Make:             HP
Model:            LaserJet Series
```

Let's begin the process.

1. While logged in to the system running CUPS, launch a Web browser and connect to CUPS at this URL:

   `http://localhost:631`

   When prompted for a username and password, type **root** as the user and enter root's password.

2. After logging in, click the Do Administration Tasks link.

3. At the bottom of that page, click the Add Printer link.

4. On the Add Printer page, enter the information for the printer that was provided earlier, that is, the Name, Location, and so on.

5. Click the Continue button when done.

6. On the next page, use the drop-down box to select "parallel port #1" from the list and then click Continue.

7. At the Make/Model page, select the make for the printer (HP in this example) and click Continue.

TIP The printer makes shown in the list obviously do not cover all the printer makes that exist. If you need more variety/coverage, on a Fedora or RHEL-type system, you can install the gimp-print-cups rpm package. That package provides additional drivers for various printer manufacturers besides the ones that ship with the basic open-source version of the CUPS software. (Don't forget that CUPS is also available as a commercial product.)

8. Here you will select the Model/Driver for the printer. Select the HP Laserjet Series from the list of models shown and then click Continue.

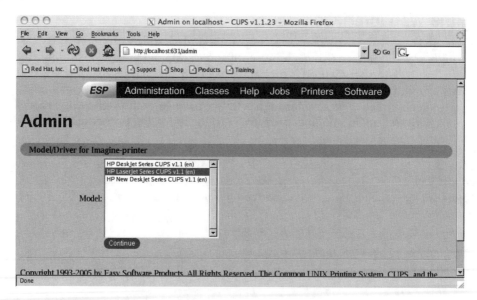

9. You will be presented with a page confirming that the printer has been successfully added. Click the printer name here (Imagine-printer).

10. You will see a page similar to the one shown next. The page shows the properties for the printer that was just added.

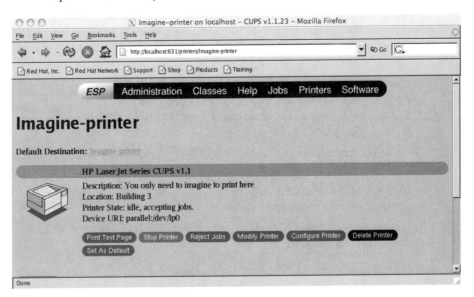

Observe that the software automatically created the proper device URI (parallel:/dev/lp0) to address the printer with.

Now put on your best imagination hat and imagine that you have clicked the "Print test page" link on the properties page for the printer that was just added. Next imagine the test page being printed successfully!

Using the Command-Line Tools to Add a Printer

Using the command line is the second method for adding a printer to the CUPS system. Once you are comfortable with how CUPS works, you may find managing the CUPS system through its command-line interface to be a little faster. To add a printer from the command line, you need some pertinent information, such as the printer name, the driver, and the URI.

This section will detail a simple example for setting up a printer through the use of the CUPS command-line tools. As in the preceding example, we will set up an imaginary printer. The new printer that we add will have mostly the same properties as the previous one, but we will change the name of the printer (also called the *printer queue*). We will name the second printer "Imagine-printer-number-2." We will also use a different device URI to address the printer, instead of the parallel port used previously. This time we will assume that the printer is a networked printer with the IP address of 192.168.1.200 listening on port 9100; that is, the device URI will be socket://192.168.1.200:9100.

1. While logged in to the system as the superuser, launch any virtual terminal and list the printer queues that you currently have configured for your system. Use the **lpstat** utility. Type

```
[root@serverA ~]# lpstat -a
Imagine-printer accepting requests since Jan 01 00:00
```

2. Now issue the **lpadmin** command to add the printer. The entire command is long because of all its options, and so it spans several lines in this sample listing. Type

```
[root@serverA ~]# lpadmin -p "Imagine-printer-number-2"  -E \
 -v socket://192.168.1.200  \
 -P /usr/share/cups/model/laserjet.ppd.gz  \
 -D "You only need to imagine to print here"  \
 -L "Building 3"
```

3. Use the **lpstat** command again to list all the printers that are present. Type

```
[root@serverA ~]# lpstat -a
Imagine-printer accepting requests since Jan 01 00:00
Imagine-printer-number-2 accepting requests since Jan 01 00:00
```

4. You can also view the printer you just added on CUPS Web interface. Point your Web browser to this URL:

```
http://localhost:631/printers
```

You should be greeted with a page similar to the one in Figure 26-2.

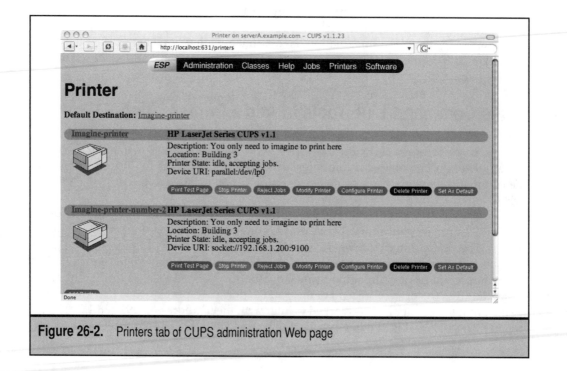

Figure 26-2. Printers tab of CUPS administration Web page

ROUTINE CUPS ADMINISTRATION

Setting up the printer(s) is one half of the battle in managing a printing environment. The preceding section hopefully gave you enough information to get you going in that regard. This section will discuss some routine printer administration tasks—tasks such as deleting printers, managing the printer queue, and viewing print job statuses. We will use both the command-line tools and the Web interface for some of these tasks.

Setting the Default Printer

On a system with multiple print queues set up, it may be desirable to set up a particular printer (queue) as the default printer for clients to use. The default printer is the printer that is used whenever a printer name is not specified explicitly for printing by clients.

For example, to set up the printer named "Imagine-printer-number-3" as the default printer on the system, type

```
[root@serverA ~]# lpadmin  -d  imagine-printer-number-3
```

Enabling and Disabling Printers

Disabling a printer is akin to taking the printer temporarily offline. In this state, the printer queue can still accept print jobs, but it will not actually print them. The print jobs are queued up until the printer is put in an enabled state or restarted. This is useful for situations when the physical print device is not working properly and the system administrator does not wish to interrupt users' printing.

To disable a printer named "imagine-printer-number-3," type

```
[root@serverA ~]# /usr/bin/disable  imagine-printer-number-3
```

To enable the printer named "imagine-printer-number-3," type

```
[root@serverA ~]# /usr/bin/enable  imagine-printer-number-3
```

Accepting and Rejecting Print Jobs

Any printer managed by CUPS can be made to accept or reject print jobs. This is a departure from disabled state of a printer in the sense that a printer that is made to reject print jobs will simply *not* accept any print requests. Making a printer reject print jobs is useful for situations where a printer needs to be put out of service for a long period but not deleted completely.

Whenever a printer is made to reject print jobs, it will first complete any print jobs in its queue and will immediately stop accepting any new requests.

As an example, to make a printer named "imagine-printer-number-3" reject print jobs, type

```
[root@serverA ~]# /usr/sbin/reject  imagine-printer-number-3
```

Use the `lpstat` command to view the state of this printer. Type

```
[root@serverA ~]# lpstat -a  imagine-printer-number-3
Imagine-printer-number-3 not accepting requests since Jan 01 00:00 -
        Rejecting Jobs
```

To make the printer named "imagine-printer-number-3" resume accepting print jobs, type

```
[root@serverA ~]# /usr/sbin/accept  imagine-printer-number-3
```

View the printer's status again. Type

```
[root@serverA ~]# lpstat -a  imagine-printer-number-3
Imagine-printer-number-3 accepting requests since Jan 01 00:00
```

Managing Printing Privileges

In its out-of-the-box state, all users can send print jobs to any printer managed by CUPS. In large multiuser environments it may be necessary to control which users or groups have access to which printer(s). This may be for security reasons or purely due to issues of office politics. CUPS offers a simple way to do this, through the use of the `lpadmin` utility.

For example, to allow *only* the users named yyang and mmellow to print to the printer named "imagine-printer," type

```
[root@serverA ~]# lpadmin  -p imagine-printer -u allow:yyang,mmellow
```

To perform the opposite of this command and deny the users yyang and mmellow access to the printer, type

```
[root@serverA ~]# lpadmin  -p imagine-printer -u deny:yyang,mmellow
```

To remove all the preceding restrictions and allow all users to print to the printer name "imagine-printer" type

```
[root@serverA ~]# lpadmin  -p imagine-printer -u allow:all
```

Deleting Printers

To delete a printer named "bad-printer," from the command line, type

```
[root@serverA ~]# lpadmin  -x  bad-printer
```

Managing printers via the Web Interface

Most of the preceding tasks can also be performed from the CUPS Web interface. Using buttons and links, you can easily delete printers, control print jobs, modify the properties of a printer, stop printers, reject print jobs, and so on.

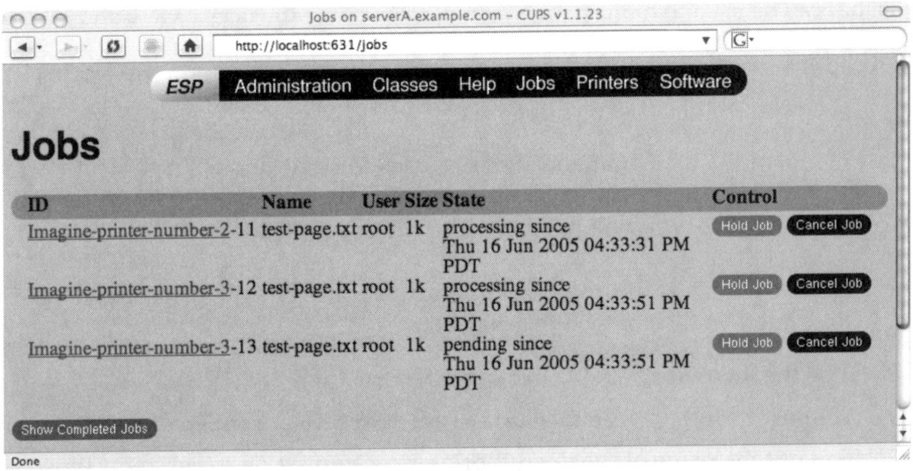

Figure 26-3. Jobs tab of CUPS administration Web page

For example, as an administrator, you may need to periodically check the print queues to make sure that everything is going smoothly. Clicking on the Jobs button (or going directly to http://localhost:631/jobs) on the Web interface will bring up a page similar to Figure 26-3. As you can see, you have three options to choose from if there are jobs in the queue. If not, you will only see a button called Show Completed Jobs. You have the option of either holding the job (pausing it) or canceling the job altogether.

You can also perform a host of other administrative tasks by pointing your browser to the Admin page for CUPS. On your local system, the URL for this page is http://localhost:631/printers/.

USING CLIENT-SIDE PRINTING TOOLS

Now that we've covered the aspects of installing CUPS and administering the system, it is time to cover how to do the actual printing with the Linux system.

When a client machine prints, the job gets sent to the print server and is spooled. Spooling is simply the act of putting a print job into the print queue. This is also known as a print job. The job typically has a couple of states that it can be in. One is *in progress*. The other is *paused*, where the administrator has paused printing. The printer being out of paper can also be a reason for a job being paused. When something goes awry with the printer, print jobs can queue up and create a problem when the printer comes back up.

In this section, we'll look at some commands that can be used to print, as well as commands that can be used to manage print queues. We cover the user's view and interaction with the printing system.

lpr

The **lpr** command is the command the user uses to print documents. Most PostScript and text documents can be printed by directly using the **lpr** command. If you are using AbiWord or StarOffice, you will have to set up those applications to print to the correct device.

Let's create a plain text file, that we'll attempt to print. The file will contain the simple text "Hello Printer" and be named **test-page.txt**.

1. Type the following:

   ```
   [root@serverA ~]# echo "Hello Printer" >>  test-page.txt
   ```

2. Find out the name of the default printer configured on the system. Type

   ```
   [root@serverA ~]# lpstat -d
   system default destination: Imagine-printer
   ```

3. Send the **test-page.txt** file to the default printer. Type

   ```
   [root@serverA ~]# lpr   test-page.txt
   ```

   This will print the document **test-page.txt** to the default printer, which is usually the first printer that was installed.

4. Now send the same document to the other imaginary printer that was installed earlier, the printer named "Imagine-printer-number-2." Type

   ```
   [root@serverA ~]# lpr -P Imagine-printer-number-2 test-page.txt
   ```

   Once you have entered this command, the printer should start printing fairly quickly unless you are printing a very large file.

5. To see the status of your print job, use the **lpq** command (discussed next).

lpq

After you have submitted the job, you can view what is on the print spooler by using the **lpq** command. If you've just printed a job and notice that it doesn't come out of the printer, use the **lpq** command to display the current list of jobs that are spooled on the printer. Typically, you'll see a bunch of jobs in the queue, and upon further investigation you may discover that the printer is out of paper. If you need to unspool the print job from the printer, you can use the **lprm** command discussed in the next section.

For example, to see the status of the print request that was sent to the default print, type

```
[root@serverA ~]# lpq -av
Rank     Owner    Job     File(s)                     Total Size
active   root     2       test-page.txt               1024 bytes
```

To view the status of the print job sent to the second printer, type

```
[root@serverA ~]# lpq -av  -P Imagine-printer-number-2
Imagine-printer-number-2 is ready and printing
Rank    Owner   Job    File(s)                     Total Size
active  root    2      test-page.txt               1024 bytes
```

As shown in both of the preceding outputs, both print jobs are stuck in the imaginary print queues because we didn't use our imagination well enough. We'll remove print jobs next.

lprm

When you've suddenly realized that you didn't mean to print the document you just printed, you might have a chance to delete it before it gets printed. To do this, use the **lprm** command. This will unspool the print job from the printer.

For example, to delete the print job with an ID of 2 from the default printer, type

```
[root@serverA ~]# lprm  2
```

To remove a job from a specific printer, simply add the **-P** option. For example, to remove the job with ID "2" from the printer named "Imagine-printer-number-2,", type

```
[root@serverA ~]# lprm  2  -P imagine-printer-number-2
```

If you are the root user, you can purge all print jobs from the printer named "Imagine-printer" by issuing the **lprm** command as follows:

```
[root@serverA ~]# lprm -P imagine-printer    -
```

The dash (-) at the end of this command means "all jobs."

TIP   Regular users can typically only manage their own print jobs; that is, user A cannot ordinarily go and delete a job submitted by user B from the print queue. The superuser can, of course, control everybody's print jobs. Also, you should understand that the window between sending a job to the printer being able to delete the job is very, very narrow. Therefore, you may find that the **lprm** requests fails because the command was issued too late. This will usually result in an error like "lprm: Unable to lprm job(s)!" As root, you may, of course, use the dash (-) option to clear the print queue of all jobs at any time.

SUMMARY

This chapter discussed the Common UNIX Printing System (CUPS). We touched on simple printer management tasks such as adding printers via the CUPS Web interface and from the command line, managing printers, and managing print jobs under Linux.

Usage of some common client tools to manage print jobs in Linux was discussed with examples. We also discussed some of the configuration directives that are used in CUPS' main configuration file, **cupsd.conf**.

However, we were only able to scratch the surface of the abilities and features of CUPS. Fortunately, the software comes with extensive online documentation, which is a highly recommended read if you are plan on using CUPS extensively to deploy and manage printers in your environment. The same documentation is also available online at the CUPS home page, http://www.cups.org.

Once you have printing set up on your Linux server, you'll find that it does its job very nicely and lets you focus on new and interesting challenges. Problems that arise with printing services afterward typically point to problems with the printer itself, such as paper jams, user abuse, or office politics.

CHAPTER 27

DHCP

Manually configuring IP addresses for a handful of systems is a fairly simple task. However, manually configuring IP addresses for an entire department, building, or enterprise of heterogeneous systems can be daunting.

The Linux DHCP (Dynamic Host Configuration Protocol) client and server can assist with these tasks. The client machine is configured to obtain its IP address from the network. When the DHCP client software is started, it broadcasts a request onto the network for an IP address. If all goes well, a DHCP server on the network will respond, issuing an address and other necessary information to complete the client's network configuration.

Such dynamic addressing is also useful for configuring mobile or temporary machines. Folks who travel from office to office can plug their machines into the local network and obtain an appropriate address for their location.

In this chapter, we'll cover the process of configuring a DHCP server and client. This includes obtaining and installing the necessary software and then walking through the process of writing a configuration file for it. At the end of the chapter, we'll step through a complete sample configuration.

NOTE   DHCP is a standard. Thus, any operating system that can communicate with other DHCP servers and clients can work with the Linux DHCP tools. One common solution includes using a Linux-based DHCP server in office environments where there are a large number of Windows-based clients. The Windows systems can be configured to use DHCP and contact the Linux server to get their IP addresses. The Windows clients will not necessarily know nor care that their IP configuration information is being provided by a Linux server, because DHCP is a standards-based protocol and most implementations try to adhere to the standard.

THE MECHANICS OF DHCP

When a client is configured to obtain its address from the network, it asks for an address in the form of a DHCP request. A DHCP server listens for client requests. Once a request is received, it checks its local database and issues an appropriate response. The response always includes the address and can include name servers, a network mask, and a default gateway. The client accepts the response from the server and configures its local settings accordingly.

The DHCP server maintains a list of addresses it can issue. Each address is issued with an associated *lease,* which dictates how long a client is allowed to use the address before it must contact the server to renew the lease. When the lease expires, the client is not expected to use the address any more. And as such, the DHCP server assumes that the address has become available and can be put back in the server's pool of addresses.

The implementation of the Linux DHCP server includes several key features common to many DHCP server implementations. The server can be configured to issue any free address from a pool of addresses or to issue a specific address to a specific machine. In addition to serving DHCP requests, the Linux DHCP server also serves BOOTP requests.

THE DHCP SERVER

DHCPD, the DHCP server, is responsible for serving IP addresses and other relevant information upon client request. Since the DHCP protocol is broadcast-based, a server will have to be present on each subnet for which DHCP service is to be provided.

Installing DHCP Software via RPM

The ISC DHCP server is the de facto implementation for Linux machines. This version is available in many Linux distributions in a prepackaged format, usually RPM.

In this section we run through the process of installing the ISC DHCP software using RPM. On Linux systems running Fedora Core or RHEL, the ISC DHCP software is separated into two different packages. These are

▼ **dhclient*.rpm** The dhclient package provides the ISC DHCP client daemon.

▲ **dhcp*.rpm** The dhcp package includes the ISC DHCP server service and relay agent.

On most Linux distributions you will most likely have the DHCP client-side software already installed. Let's check to see what we have already installed on our sample system. Type

```
[root@serverA ~]# rpm -qa | grep dhc
dhcpv6_client-0.10-13
dhclient-3.0.2-12
```

From the third line of this listing, we notice that the dhclient package is already installed.

To set up the DHCP server, we need to install the necessary package. We will use **up2date** to automatically download and install the software. Type

```
[root@serverA ~]# up2date -i  dhcp
```

Once this command completes successfully, you should have the necessary software installed.

Configuring the DHCP Server

The default primary configuration file of the ISC DHCP server is **/etc/dhcpd.conf**. The configuration file encapsulates two ideas:

▼ A set of declarations to describe the networks, hosts, or groups attached to the system and possibly the range of addresses that can be issued to each respective entity. Multiple declarations can be used to describe multiple groups of clients. Declarations can also be nested in one another when multiple concepts are needed to describe a set of clients or hosts.

▲ A set of parameters that describe the overall behavior of the server. Parameters can be global, or local to a set of declarations.

Downloading, Compiling, and Installing the ISC DHCP Software from Source

If the ISC DHCP software is not available in a prepackaged form for your particular Linux distribution, you can always build the software from source code available from the ISC site at http://www.isc.org. It is also possible that you simply want to take advantage of the most recent bug fixes available for the software, which your distribution has not yet implemented.

As of this writing, the most current stable version of the software was version 3.0.3b3, which can be downloaded directly from ftp://ftp.isc.org/isc/dhcp/dhcp-3.0.3b3.tar.gz.

Once the package is downloaded, unpack the software as shown. For this example, we assume the source was downloaded into the **/usr/local/src/** directory. Unpack the tarball thus:

```
[root@serverA src]# tar xvzf dhcp-3.0.3b3.tar.gz
```

Change to the **dhcp*** subdirectory created by this command. And then take a minute to study any Readme file(s) that might be present.

Next configure the package with the **configure** command.

```
[root@serverA dhcp-3.0.3b3]# ./configure
```

To compile and install, issue the **make; make install** commands.

```
[root@serverA dhcp-3.0.3b3]# make  ; make install
```

The version of ISC dhcp software built from source installs the DHCP server (**dhpcd**) daemon under the **/usr/sbin/** directory and the DHCP client (**dhcpclient**) under the **/sbin/** directory.

NOTE Since every site has a unique network with unique addresses, it is necessary that every site be set up with its own configuration file. If this is the first time you are dealing with DHCP, you might want to start with the sample configuration file presented toward the end of this chapter and modify it to match your network's characteristics.

Like most configuration files in UNIX, the file is ASCII text and can be modified using your favorite text editor. The general structure of the configuration file is as follows:

```
Global parameters;
Declaration1
    [parameters related to declaration1]
    [nested sub declaration]
```

```
Declaration2
    [parameters related to declaration2]
    [nested sub declaration]
```

As this outline indicates, a declaration block groups a set of clients. Different parameters can be applied to each block of the declaration.

Declarations

We may want to group different clients for several reasons, such as organizational requirements, network layout, and administrative domains. To assist with grouping these clients, we introduce the following declarations.

group   Individually listing parameters and declarations for each host again and again can make the configuration file difficult to manage. The **group** declaration allows you to apply a set of parameters and declarations to a list of clients, shared networks, or subnets. The syntax for the **group** declaration is as follows:

```
group label
    [parameters]
    [subd eclarations]
```

where **label** is a user-defined name for identifying the group. The **parameters** block contains a list of parameters that are applied to the group. The **subdeclarations** are used in the event that a further level of granularity is needed to describe any additional clients that may be a member of the current declaration.

Ignore the parameter field for now. We will go into further detail about it in the upcoming "Parameters" section.

host   A **host** declaration is used to apply a set of parameters and declarations to a particular host in addition to the parameters specified for the group. This is commonly used for fixed address booting, or for the BOOTP clients. The syntax for a **host** declaration is as follows:

```
host label
    [parameters]
    [subdeclarations]
```

The **label** is the user-defined name for the host group. The **parameters** and **subdeclarations** are as described in the **group** declaration.

shared-network   A **shared-network** declaration groups a set of addresses of members of the same physical network. This allows parameters and declarations to be grouped for administrative purposes. The syntax is

```
shared-network label
    [parameters]
    [subdeclarations]
```

The *label* is the user-defined name for the shared network. The **parameters** and **subdeclarations** are as described in the previous declaration.

subnet   The **subnet** declaration is used to apply a set of parameters and/or declarations to a set of addresses that match the description of this declaration. The syntax is as follows:

```
subnet subnet-number netmask netmask
    [parameters]
    [subdeclarations]
```

The **subnet-number** is the network that you want to declare as being the source of IP addresses for giving to individual hosts. The **netmask** is the netmask (see Chapter 12 for more details on netmasks) for the subnet. The **parameters** and **subdeclarations** are as described in the previous declaration.

range   For dynamic booting, the **range** declaration specifies the range of addresses that are valid to issue to clients. The syntax is as follows:

```
range [dynamic-bootp] starting-address [ending-address] ;
```

The **dynamic-bootp** keyword is used to alert the server that the following range of addresses is for the BOOTP protocol. The **starting-address** and optional **ending-address** fields are the actual addresses of the start and end blocks of IP addresses. The blocks are assumed to be consecutive and in the same subnet of addresses.

Parameters

We introduced this concept briefly earlier in the chapter. Turning on these parameters will alter the behavior of the server for the relevant group of clients. We'll discuss these parameters in this section.

always-reply-rfc1048   This parameter's syntax is as follows:

```
always-reply-rfc1048;
```

This is used primarily for BOOTP clients. There are BOOTP clients that require the response from the server to be fully BOOTP RFC 1048–compliant. Turning on this parameter ensures that this requirement is met.

authoritative   This parameter's syntax is as follows:

```
authoritative;
not authoritative;
```

The DHCP server will normally assume that the configuration information about a given network segment is not known to be correct and is not authoritative. This is so that if a user unknowingly installs a DHCP server without fully understanding how to configure it, it does not send spurious DHCPNAK messages to clients that have obtained addresses from a legitimate DHCP server on the network.

default-lease-time   This parameter's syntax is as follows:

```
default-lease-time seconds;
```

The value of **seconds** is the lease time allocated to the issued IP address if the client did not request any specific duration.

dynamic-bootp-lease-cutoff   This parameter's syntax is as follows:

```
dynamic-bootp-lease-cutoff date;
```

BOOTP clients are not aware of the *lease* concept. By default, the DHCP server assigns BOOTP clients an IP address that never expires. There are certain situations where it may be useful to have the server stop issuing addresses for a set of BOOTP clients. In those cases, this parameter is used.

The **date** is specified in the form *W YYYY/MM/DD HH:MM:SS*, where *W* is the day of the week in **cron** format (0=Sunday, 6=Saturday), *YYYY* is the year, *MM* is the month (01=January, 12=December), *DD* is the date in two-digit format, *HH* is the two-digit hour in 24-hour format (0=Midnight, 23=11 P.M.), MM is the two-digit representation of minutes; and *SS* is the two-digit representation of the seconds.

dynamic-bootp-lease-length   This parameter's syntax is as follows:

```
dynamic-bootp-lease-length seconds;
```

Although the BOOTP clients don't have a mechanism for expiring the addresses they receive, it's sometimes safe to have the server assume that they aren't using the address anymore, thus freeing it for further use. This is useful if the BOOTP application is known to be short in duration. If so, the server can set the number of **seconds** accordingly and expire it after that time has past.

CAUTION   Use caution with this option, as it may introduce problems if it issues an address before another host has stopped using it.

filename   This parameter's syntax is as follows:

```
filename filename;
```

In some applications, the DHCP client may need to know the name of a file to use to boot. This is often combined with **next-server** to retrieve a remote file for installation configuration or diskless booting.

fixed-address   This parameter's syntax is as follows:

```
fixed-address  address [, address ·];
```

This parameter appears only under the **host** declaration. It specifies the set of addresses assignable to the client.

get-lease-hostnames   This parameter's syntax is as follows:

```
get-lease-hostnames [true | false];
```

If this parameter is set to true, the server will resolve all addresses in the declaration scope and use that for the **hostname** option.

hardware   This parameter's syntax is as follows:

```
hardware hardware-type hardware-address;
```

In order for a BOOTP client to be recognized, its network hardware address must be declared using a hardware clause in the host statement. Here, **hardware-type** must be the name of a physical hardware interface type. Currently, only the ethernet and token-ring types are recognized.

The **hardware-address** (sometimes referred to as the MAC address) is the physical address of the interface, typically a set of hexadecimal octets delimited by colons. The hardware statement may also be used for DHCP clients.

max-lease-time   This parameter's syntax is as follows:

```
max-lease-time seconds;
```

A client has the option to request the duration of the lease. The request is granted as long as the lease time doesn't exceed the number of seconds specified by this option. Otherwise, it's granted a lease to the maximum of the number of seconds specified here.

next-server   This parameter's syntax is as follows:

```
next-server server-name;
```

The **next-server** statement is used to specify the host address of the server from which the initial boot file (specified in the **filename** statement) is to be loaded. Here, **server-name** is a numeric IP address or a domain name.

server-identifier   This parameter's syntax is as follows:

```
server-identifier hostname;
```

Part of the DHCP response is the address for the server. On multihomed systems, the DHCP server issues the address of the first interface. Unfortunately, this interface may not be reachable by all clients of a server or declaration scope. In those rare instances, this parameter can be used to send the IP of the proper interface that the client should communicate to the server. The value specified must be an IP address for the DHCP server, and it must be reachable by all clients served by a particular scope.

server-name   This parameter's syntax is as follows:

```
server-name Name;
```

The **server-name** statement can be used to inform the client of the name of the server from which it is booting. *Name* should be the name that will be provided to the client. This parameter is sometimes useful for remote clients or network install applications.

use-lease-addr-for-default-route   This parameter's syntax is as follows:

```
use-lease-addr-for-default-route [true|false];
```

Some network configurations use a technique known as *ProxyARP* so that a host can keep track of other hosts that are outside its subnet. If your network is configured to support ProxyARP, you'll want to configure your client to use itself as a default route. This will force it to use *ARP* (the Address Resolution Protocol) to find all remote (off the subnet) addresses.

CAUTION   The **use-lease-addr-for-default-route** command should be used with caution. Not every client can be configured to use its own interface as a default route.

Options

Currently, the DHCP server supports more than 60 options. The general syntax of an option is as follows:

```
option option-name [modifiers]
```

Table 27-1 summarizes the most commonly used DHCP options.

A Sample dhcpd.conf File

The following is an example of a simple DHCP configuration file:

```
subnet 192.168.1.0 netmask 255.255.255.0
        # Options
        option routers 192.168.1.1;
        option subnet-mask 255.255.255.0;

        option domain-name "example.org";
        option domain-name-servers ns1.example.org;

        # Parameters
        default-lease-time 21600;
        max-lease-time 43200;
        # Declarations
        range dynamic-bootp 192.168.1.25 192.168.1.49;

        # Nested declarations
        host clientA
            hardware ethernet 00:80:c6:f6:72:00;
            fixed-address 192.168.1.50;
```

Option	Description
broadcast-address	An address on the client's subnet specified as the broadcast address
domain-name	The domain name the client should use as the local domain name when performing host lookups
domain-name-servers	The list of DNS servers for the client to use to resolve host names
host-name	The string used to identify the name of the client
nis-domain	The name of the client's NIS (Sun Network Information Services) domain
nis-servers	A list of the available NIS servers available to the client
routers	A list of IP addresses for routers the client is to use in order of preference
subnet-mask	The netmask the client is to use

Table 27-1. Common dhcpd.conf Options

In this example, a single subnet is defined. The DHCP clients are instructed to use 192.168.1.1 as their default router (gateway address) and 255.255.255.0 as their subnet mask.

DNS information is passed to the clients; they will use example.org as their domain name and ns1.example.org as their DNS server.

A lease time of 21600 seconds is set, but if the clients request a longer lease, they may be granted a lease that can last as long as 43,200 seconds.

The range of IP addresses issued starts at 192.168.1.25 and can go as high as 192.168.1.49. The machine with a MAC address of 00:80:c6:f6:72:00 will always get assigned the IP address 192.168.1.50.

General Runtime Behavior

Once started, the daemon patiently waits for a client request to arrive prior to performing any processing. When a request is processed and an address is issued, it keeps track of the address in a file called **dhcpd.leases**. On Fedora systems and RHEL systems, this file is stored in the **/var/lib/dhcp/** directory.

THE DHCP CLIENT DAEMON

The ISC DHCP client daemon (named **dhclient**), included with many popular Linux distributions, is the software component used to talk to a DHCP server described in the previous sections. If invoked, it will attempt to obtain an address from an available DHCP server and then configure its networking configuration accordingly.

Configuring the DHCP Client

The client is typically run from the startup files, but it can also be run by hand. It's typically started prior to other network-based services; since other network services are of no use unless the system itself can get on the network.

On the other hand, the client can be invoked at the command line any time after startup. The client daemon can be started without additional options . . . but it will attempt to obtain a lease on all interfaces configured on the system.

Here is how to start the client from the command line in its most basic form:

```
[root@serverB ~]# dhclient
......<OUTPUT TRUNCATED>.....
Sending on    LPF/eth0/00:0c:29:f8:b8:88
Sending on    Socket/fallback
DHCPDISCOVER on lo to 255.255.255.255 port 67 interval 7
DHCPREQUEST on eth0 to 255.255.255.255 port 67
DHCPACK from 192.168.1.1
SIOCADDRT: File exists
bound to 192.168.1.36 -- renewal in 188238 seconds.
```

NOTE On a Fedora Core system or an RHEL system, network configuration scripts are available to automatically set up the system as a DHCP client between each system reboot, so that you will not need to manually run the **dhclient** daemon each time the system needs an IP address. To set this up, all that usually needs to be done is to edit the file **/etc/sysconfig/network-scripts/ifcfg-eth*** and make sure that at a minimum the **BOOTPROTO** variable is set to **dhcp** as in this sample listing:

```
DEVICE=eth0
BOOTPROTO=dhcp
ONBOOT=yes
```

Optionally, the client daemon can be started with additional flags that slightly modify the behavior of the software. For example, you can optionally specify the interface (such as eth0) for which an address lease should be requested.

The full syntax of the command is shown here:

```
Usage: dhclient [-1dqr] [-nw] [-p <port>] [-s server]
                [-cf config-file] [-lf lease-file][-pf pid-file] [-e VAR=val]
                [-sf script-file] [interface]
```

Some of the options are described in Table 27-2.

Option	Description
-p	Specifies a different UDP port for the DHCP client to use—instead of the standard port 68.
-d	Forces the DHCP client to run as a foreground process, instead of its normal behavior of running as a background process. This is useful for debugging.
-q	The -q flag prevents any messages other than errors from being printed to the standard error descriptor.
-r	This option tells the **dhclient** program to explicitly release the current lease, and once the lease has been released, the client exits.
-1	The -1 flag causes **dhclient** to try once to get a lease. If it fails, **dhclient** exits with exit code two.
-cf	Specifies the location of the configuration file for the **dhclient** program. The default location is **/etc/dhclient.conf**.
-lf	Specifies the location of the lease database. The default value is the **/var/lib/dhcp/dhclient.leases** file.
-pf	Defines the file that stores **dhclient**'s process ID.
interface	Specifies an interface to have **dhclient** configure.

Table 27-2.   dhclient Command-Line Options

SUMMARY

DHCP is a useful tool for dynamically configuring the addresses for large groups of machines or mobile workstations. Since DHCP is an open protocol, the architecture and platform of the server and the client are irrelevant.

A computer running Linux can serve DHCP requests. The software to do this is highly configurable and has mechanisms to persist after machine failures.

Software also exists to configure the networking of a Linux machine from a DHCP server on the network. This client daemon has a number of options that make it able to speak to a variety of DHCP servers.

CHAPTER 28

Backups

A server that is not backed up is a disaster waiting to happen. Performing backups is a critical part of any server's maintenance, no matter what operating system you use. In this chapter, we discuss the backup options that come with Linux. Many commercial packages exist as well, and you can purchase them for anywhere from a few hundred to many thousands of dollars. The best package for you depends on your site and its needs.

EVALUATING YOUR BACKUP NEEDS

Developing a backup solution is no trivial task. It requires that you consider the interactions among all the parts of your network, the servers, and the resources distributed among them. Even trickier is deciding the order in which backups are performed. For example, if you want to back up multiple partitions in parallel, you could end up losing the benefits of that parallelism if there is contention on the SCSI bus! And, of course, you must arrange for backups to occur regularly and to be verified regularly.

Unfortunately, no cookbook solution exists for setting up network backup. Every organization has different needs based on its site(s), its network, and its growth pattern. To make an educated decision, you need to consider the following questions:

▼ How much data do you need to back up?

■ What kind of hardware will you use for the backup process?

■ How much network throughput do you need to support?

■ How quickly must the data be recovered?

■ How often is data expected to be recovered?

▲ What kind of tape management do you need?

How Much Data?

Determining an accurate count of the data to be backed up is the most important issue for estimating your network backup needs. What makes this question tough to answer is that you must include anticipated growth in your determination. Given that most shops have tight purse strings, when planning for backup, it's always wise to try and plan as far ahead as financially possible.

It is also important to consider how often your data changes and with what frequency. Data that changes often (such as databases) need to be backed up frequently and quickly, whereas data that rarely changes (such as the **/etc** directory) doesn't need to be backed up often (if ever).

When examining your requirements, take careful stock of compressible vs. noncompressible data. With local disks becoming large, many individuals have taken to keeping private MP3 or image collections on their systems that have nothing to do with your organization. (In the case of personal backups, the exact opposite may be true.) It may be prudent to spell out your organization's policy on this so that expectations are set: If users think that all of the systems are being backed up, they may be taken aback when they find out that their MP3 collection wasn't covered in that. On the flip side, you may be taken aback by a sudden increase in capacity requirements when a user discovers P2P or brings their MP3 collection to work.

What Kind of Media?

The type of hardware you choose should reflect the amount of data you need to back up, the frequency of when you're backing it up, and whether it is necessary that backups get rotated to an offsite location.

Four common choices are available: tape, disk, recordable CDs, and recordable DVDs. Of the four, tape has been around the longest and offers the widest available choices in media density, form factor, and mechanisms.

Among your choices for tape, selecting the specific type can be tricky. Many of the high-density options are appealing for the obvious reason that you can cram more data onto a single tape. Of course, high-capacity tapes and tape drives typically cost more. Work toward finding an optimum solution that backs up the most system data at the best price, balanced with your requirements for media capacity.

NOTE Many advertisements for tape drives boast impressive capacities, but keep in mind that these numbers are for the compressed data on the tape, not the actual data. The amount of uncompressed data on the tape is usually about half the compressed capacity. This is important to note, because compression algorithms achieve various levels of compression depending on the type of data being compressed. For example, textual data compresses very well. Certain graphics or sound formats get little to no compression at all. When you estimate the amount of data you can store on a single unit, be sure to consider the mix of data on your servers.

Disk-based backups are a relatively new phenomenon. The concept is simple: if the primary goal of backups is to protect against simple accidents (file deletions, primary disk going bad, etc.), then this works well. Transfers are fast, media are cheap, and building a home-brew RAID system using a low-cost PC, a low-end RAID controller, and a few commodity disks can be done for less than $1000. (Commercial solutions such as those from NetApp offer more high-capacity options for larger installations.) Using this method, scheduled file copies can be automated with no tape swapping, and additional capacity can be added cheaply. The downside to this method is that offsite storage is not possible unless combined with removable storage. While getting hot-swappable hard disks is possible, they are not nearly as robust as a tape when it comes to being handled and moved. (A tape can be dropped several times with practically no risk. The same cannot be said of dropping a hard disk!)

With recordable CDs, and more recently recordable DVDs, low-cost backups have become a real possibility. These media are easy to use and come the cheapest. Unfortunately, they also hold a lot less than their tape and disk counterparts and have questionable lifetimes. If the amount of data that needs to be backed up is not too great or the data does not change once backed up (such as pictures taken from your digital camera), this type of media works well. The media lifetime varies by vendor and the research. For the purpose of backups, it is not unreasonable to assume a few years of life.

A combination between fixed and removable media is also increasing in popularity. In combination solutions, regular backups are done to disk, with periodic backups moved from the backup disk to tape.

In all of the preceding backup options, plan for media failure. That is, plan to move backed-up data to new media every few years. This is necessary to ensure that you're not just using new media, but that the drive itself is still correctly calibrated and modern equipment can still read and write it. In some cases, you may need to even consider the data format. After all, data that can be read but not understood doesn't do anyone any good. (Consider whether you could read a floppy disk given to you from your first computer today.)

Performance Considerations of Tape

When looking closely at tape-based backups, consider where the tape drive itself will be kept and what system it will be connected to. Will the tape be on a busy server that already has a lot of active disks? Will it be kept on a dedicated server with dedicated spooling disks? Is there any contention on the bus used to transfer data to it? (For example, if you're backing up to a SCSI tape drive, does that SCSI chain have other devices that are busy?)

Finally, are you able to feed data to the tape drive fast enough that it can stream? If the tape drive cannot stream, it will stop writing until it gets more data. This pause may be as long as several seconds on a slow mechanism, while the drive realigns itself with the tape and finds the next available position to write data. Even if the pause is brief, when it occurs thousands of times during a single backup, it can increase your backup runtimes by many hours.

How Much Network Throughput?

Unfortunately, network throughput is easily forgotten in the planning of backup operations. But what good do you get from a really fast backup server and tape drive if you feed in the data through a thin straw?

Take the necessary time to understand your network infrastructure. Look at where the data is coming from and where it's going. Use SNMP tools, such as MRTG (http://www.mrtg.org), to collect statistics about your switches and routers. If you need to back up machines that are connected via hubs, consider a backup sequence that won't back up two machines on the same collision domain at the same time.

Gathering all this information will help you estimate the bandwidth necessary to perform backups. With your analysis done, you'll be able to figure out which upgrades will net you the best return for your money.

What Speed of Recovery?

When requests to restore data from tape arrive, you're likely to be under the gun to get the data back to the user as quickly as possible. How long your users have to wait will depend on the tool used for backup. This means you need to incorporate the cost of response time into your backup evaluation. How much are you willing to spend to get the response time you need for a restore?

Disk-based restores are of course the fastest. They also offer the possibility of online backups where users can visit the backup server themselves and copy the file back. Recordable CDs and DVDs are also quick, since the file can be quickly pulled from disc and given to the user as well. Tape, by comparison, is much slower. The file on the tape needs to be found, the archive read, and an individual file extracted. Depending on the speed of the tape and the location of the file, this can take a little bit of time.

What Kind of Tape Management?

As the size of your backups grows, so will the need to manage the data you back up. This is where commercial tools often come into play. When evaluating your choices, be sure to consider their indexing and tape management. It does you no good to have 50 tapes worth of data if you can't find the right file. And unfortunately, this problem only gets worse as you start needing more tapes for each night's backups.

MANAGING THE TAPE DEVICE

The tape device interacts with Linux just as most other devices do: as a file. The filename will depend on the type of tape drive, your chosen mode of operation (auto-rewind or non-rewind), and how many drives are attached to the system.

SCSI tape drives, for example, use the following naming scheme:

Device Name	Purpose
/dev/st$X$	Auto-rewinding SCSI tape device; X is the number of the tape drive. Numbering of tape drives is in the order of the drives on the SCSI chain.
/dev/nst$X$	Non-rewinding SCSI tape device; X is the number of the tape drive. Numbering of tape drives is in the order of the drives on the SCSI chain.

NOTE   Under devfs, the naming scheme has changed to **/devfs/scsi/hostA/busB/targetT/lunL/mt** for the auto-rewinding tape and **/devfs/scsi/hostA/busB/targetT/lunL/mtan** for the non-rewinding tape. In both cases, A refers to the host card number, B refers to the channel number, T refers to the device ID, and L refers to the logical device on the physical device. (The logical device designation will vary by vendor. In the case of tape devices that have multiple mechanisms, it may refer to the mechanism number.)

Let's say you have a single SCSI tape drive. You can access it using either of these file-names: **/dev/st0** or **/dev/nst0**. If you use **/dev/st0**, the drive will automatically rewind the tape after each file is written to it. If you use **/dev/nst0**, on the other hand, you can write a single file to the tape, mark the end of file, but then stay at the tape's current position. This lets you write multiple files to a single tape.

> **NOTE** Non-SCSI devices will obviously use a different naming scheme. Unfortunately, there is no standard for naming backup devices if they are not SCSI devices. The QIC-02 tape controller, for example, uses the **/dev/tpqic*** series of filenames. If you use a non-SCSI tape device, you will need to find its corresponding driver documentation to see what device name it will use.

You may find it handy to create a symbolic link from **/dev/tape** to the appropriate device name for the rewinding mode and a link from **/dev/nrtape** for the non-rewinding mode (for example, **/dev/tape** → **/dev/st0** and **/dev/nrtape**→ **/dev/nst0**). This will make it easier to remember the name of the tape device when issuing commands. See Chapter 5 for information on using the **ln** command to create symbolic links.

What makes these backup device files different from disk files is that there is no file-system structure. Files are continuously written to the tape until it's full or until an end-of-file marker is written. If a tape device is in non-rewind mode, the write head is left in the position immediately after the last end-of-file marker, ready for the next file to be written.

Think of tape devices as similar to a book with chapters. The book's binding and the paper, like the tape itself, provide a place to put the words (the files). It's the markings of the publisher (the backup application) that separate the entire book into smaller subsections (files). If you (the reader) were an auto-rewinding tape drive, you would close the tape every time you were done with a single file and then have to search through the tape to find the next position (chapter) when you're ready to read it. If, however, you were a non-rewinding tape drive, you would leave the tape open to the last page you read.

Using mknod and scsidev to Create the Device Files

If you don't have the file **/dev/st0** or **/dev/nst0**, you can create one using the **mknod** command. (See Chapter 5 for an explanation of **mknod**.) The major number for SCSI tape drives is 9, and the minor number dictates which drive and whether it is auto-rewinding or not. The numbers 0 through 15 represent drive numbers 0 through 15, auto-rewinding. The numbers 128 through 143 represent drive numbers 0 through 15, non-rewinding. The tape drive is a character device.

So to create **/dev/st0**, we would type this **mknod** command:

```
[root@hostAhostA /root]# mknod /dev/st0 c 9 0
```

And to create **/dev/nst0**, we would use this command:

```
[root@hostAhostA /root]# mknod /dev/nst0 c 9 128
```

Another choice for creating the device names is to use the **scsidev** program. This will create device entries under the **/dev/scsi** directory that reflect the current state of your SCSI hardware with the appropriate device type (block or character) and corresponding major and minor numbers. This method, unfortunately, has yet another naming scheme.

The naming scheme for tape devices created using scsidev is as follows: /dev/scsi/ sth*A*-0c*BiTlL* where *A* is the host number, *B* is the channel number, *T* is the target ID, and *L* is the logical unit (lun) number.

All the different naming schemes may seem frustrating, which is understandable. The key to all of them, however, is that they are still using the same major and minor numbers. In other words, they all refer to the same driver! In the end, you could decide to call your rewinding and non-rewinding tape devices "Ted" and "Elaine" respectively, so long as they had the correct major and minor numbers.

Manipulating the Tape Device with mt

The **mt** program provides simple controls for the tape drive, such as rewinding the tape, ejecting the tape, or seeking a particular file on the tape. In the context of backups, **mt** is most useful as a mechanism for rewinding and seeking.

All of the **mt** actions are specified on the command line. Table 28-1 shows the parameters for the command.

mt Command Parameter	Description
-f *tape_device*	Specifies the tape device. The first non-rewinding SCSI tape device is **/dev/nst0**.
fsf *count*	Forward-spaces a number (*count*) of files. The tape is positioned on the first block of the next file; for example, **fsf 1** would leave the head ready to read the second file of the tape.
asf *count*	Positions the tape at the beginning of the file indicated by *count*. Positioning is done by first rewinding the tape and then forward-spacing over *count* file marks.
rewind	Rewinds the tape.
erase	Erases the tape.
status	Gives the status of the tape.
offline	Brings the tape offline and, if applicable, unloads the tape.
load	Loads the tape (applies to tape changers).
lock	Locks the drive door (only applies to certain tape drives).
unlock	Unlocks the drive door (only applies to certain tape drives).

Table 28-1.   Parameters for the **mt** Command

> *NOTE* If you do not use a non-rewinding tape device, the tape drive will automatically rewind after you perform your operation with **mt**. This can be rather frustrating if you are seeking to a specific file!

▼ To rewind the tape in **/dev/nst0**, use this command:

```
[root@hostAhostA /root]# mt -f /dev/nst0 rewind
```

▲ To move the head so that it is ready to read the third file on the tape, use this command:

```
[root@hostAhostA /root]# mt -f /dev/nst0 asf 2
```

COMMAND-LINE TOOLS

Linux comes with several tools that help you perform backups. Though they lack administrative front ends, they are simple to use—and they do the job. Many formal backup packages actually use these utilities as their underlying backup mechanism.

dump and restore

The **dump** tool works by making a copy of an entire file system. The **restore** tool can then take this copy and pull any and all files from it.

To support incremental backups, **dump** uses the concept of *dump levels*. A dump level of 0 means a full backup. Any dump level above zero is an incremental relative to the last time a **dump** with a lower dump level occurred. For example, a dump level of 1 covers all the changes to the file system since the last level 0 dump, a dump level of 2 covers all of the changes to the file system since the last level 1 dump, and so on—all the way through dump level 9.

Consider a case in which you have three dumps: the first is a level 0, the second is a level 1, and the third is also a level 1. The first dump is, of course, a full backup. The second dump (level 1) contains all the changes made since the first dump. The third dump (also a level 1) *also* has all the changes since the last level 0. If a fourth dump were made at level 2, it would have all the changes since the third level 1.

The **dump** utility stores all the information about its dumps in the **/etc/dumpdates** file. This file lists each backed-up file system, when it was backed up, and at what dump level. Given this information, you can determine which tape to use for a restore. For example, if you perform level 0 dumps on Mondays, level 1 incrementals on Tuesday and Wednesday, and then level 2 incrementals on Thursday and Friday, a file that was last modified on Tuesday but got accidentally erased on Friday can be restored from Tuesday night's incremental backup. A file that was last modified during the preceding week will be on Monday's level 0 tape.

> *NOTE* The **dump** tool comes with all distributions of Linux. This utility is file-system dependent, and the version for Linux only works on Linux's native file system (ext2 and ext3). If you use another file system such as ReiserFS, JFS, or XFS, be sure to use the appropriate **dump** tool.

Using dump

The **dump** tool is a command-line utility. It takes many parameters, but the most relevant are as shown in Table 28-2.

dump Command Parameter	Description
-n	The dump level, where *n* is a number between 0 and 9.
-a	Automatically size the tape. This is the default behavior of dump if neither -b, -B, -d, or -s (as documented later in this table) are specified.
-j	Use bzip2 compression. Note that bzip2, while being an excellent compression scheme, comes at the expense of needing more CPU. If you use this method of compression, be sure your system is fast enough to feed the tape drive without the tape drive pausing. Also note that this option may break compatibility with other UNIX systems.
-z	Use gzip compression. Note that this option make break compatibility with other UNIX systems.
-b *blocksize*	Sets the dump block size to *blocksize*, which is measured in kilobytes.
-B *count*	Specifies a number (*count*) of records per tape to be dumped. If there is more data to dump than there is tape space, **dump** will prompt you to insert a new tape.
-f *filename*	Specifies a location (*filename*) for the resulting dumpfile. You can make the dumpfile a normal file that resides on another file system, or you can write the dumpfile to the tape device. The SCSI tape device is **/dev/st0**.
-u	Updates the **/etc/dumpdates** file after a successful dump.
-d *density*	The *density* of the tape in bits per inch.
-s *size*	The *size* of the tape in feet.
-W	Displays what file systems need to be dumped without actually performing any dumps. This is based on the information in the **/etc/dumpdates** and **/etc/fstab** files.
-L *label*	Labels the dump with a name that can be read by the **restore** command.
-S	Performs a size estimate without performing the actual dump.

Table 28-2.   Parameters for the **dump** Tool

For example, here is the command to perform a level 0 dump to **/dev/st0** of the **/dev/hda1** file system:

```
[root@hostAhostA /root]# dump -0  -f /dev/st0 /dev/hda1
```

Suppressing the Tape Size Calculation   The **dump** tool must know the size of the tape it is working with. It uses this information to provide multivolume backups so that it can prompt the operator to insert the next tape when it is ready. But if you don't know the size of your tape and the **-a** option is unable to calculate it, you may still know the dump will fit on the tape. (For example, you may know that the partition you are dumping is 2GB and the tape capacity is 5GB uncompressed.) In this situation, you can do a little trick to keep **dump** from calculating the tape size. Instead of dumping straight to the device, send the output to the standard output, and then use the **cat** program to redirect the dump to the tape. Using the example in the previous section, you would enter this command:

```
[root@hostAhostA /root]# dump -0 -f - /dev/hda1 | cat >> /dev/st0
```

Since you're sending the output to standard out, you can also use this opportunity to apply your own compression filters to the stream instead of relying on hardware compression or the built-in compression command-line switches. For example, to use **gzip** to compress your dump, you'd type

```
[root@hostAhostA /root]# dump -0 -f - /dev/hda1 | gzip --fast -c >> /dev/st0
```

CAUTION   It's considered dangerous to dump file systems that are being actively used. The only way to be 100% sure that a file system is not in use is by unmounting it first. Unfortunately, very few people can afford the luxury of unmounting a system for the time necessary to do backup. The next best thing is to go through the unappealing task of verifying backups on a regular basis. Verification is best done by testing to see if the **restore** program (discussed in "Using Restore" later in this chapter) can completely read the tape and extract files from it. It's tedious, and it isn't fun. But many a system administrator has lost a job over bad backups—don't be one of them!

Using dump to Back Up an Entire System   The **dump** utility works by making an archive of one file system. If your entire system comprises multiple file systems, you need to run **dump** for every file system. Since **dump** creates its output as a single large file, you can store multiple dumps to a single tape by using a non-rewinding tape device.

Assuming we're backing up to a SCSI tape device, **/dev/nst0**, we must first decide which file systems we're backing up. This information is in the **/etc/fstab** file. Obviously, we don't want to back up files such as **/dev/cdrom**, so we skip those. Depending on our data, we may or may not want to back up certain partitions (such as **swap** and **/tmp**).

Let's assume this leaves us with **/dev/hda1**, **/dev/hda3**, **/dev/hda5**, and **/dev/hda6**. To back up these to **/dev/nst0**, compressing them along the way, we would issue the following series of commands:

```
[root@hostA /root]# mt -f /dev/nst0 rewind
[root@hostA /root]# dump -0uf - /dev/hda1 | gzip --fast -c >> /dev/nst0
[root@hostA /root]# dump -0uf - /dev/hda3 | gzip --fast -c >> /dev/nst0
[root@hostA /root]# dump -0uf - /dev/hda5 | gzip --fast -c >> /dev/nst0
[root@hostA /root]# dump -0uf - /dev/hda6 | gzip --fast -c >> /dev/nst0
[root@hostA /root]# mt -f /dev/nst0 rewind
[root@hostA /root]# mt -f /dev/nst0 eject
```

The first **mt** command is to make sure the tape is completely rewound and ready to accept data. Then come all the **dump** commands run on the partitions, with their outputs piped through **gzip** before going to the tape. To make the backups go a little faster, the **--fast** option is used with **gzip**. This results in compression that isn't as good as normal **gzip** compression, but it's much faster and takes less CPU time. The **-c** option on **gzip** tells it to send its output to the standard out. We then rewind the tape and eject it.

Using restore

The **restore** program reads the dumpfiles created by **dump** and extracts individual files and directories from them. Although restore is a command-line tool, it does offer a more intuitive interactive mode that lets you go through your directory structure from the tape.

Table 28-3 shows the command-line options for the **restore** utility.

A Typical Restore   A typical invocation of **restore** is as follows:

```
[root@hostA /root]# restore -ivf /dev/st0
```

This will pull the dump file from the device **/dev/st0** (the first SCSI tape device), print out each step **restore** takes, and then provide an interactive session for you to decide which files from the dump get restored.

A Complete Restore   Should a complete file system be lost, you can re-create the file system using the **mke2fs** command and then **restore** to populate the file system. For example, let's say our external SCSI drive (**/dev/sda**), which has a single partition on it (**/dev/sda1**), fails. After replacing it with a new drive, we would re-create the file system, like so:

```
[root@hostA /root]# mke2fs /dev/sda1
```

Next, we have to mount the partition in the appropriate location. We'll assume this is the **/home** partition, so we type the following:

```
[root@hostA /root]# mount /dev/sda1 /home
```

restore Utility Option	Description
-i	Enables interactive mode for **restore**. The utility will read the directory contents of the tape and then give you a shell-like interface in which you can move directories around and tag files you want to recover. When you've tagged all the files you want, **restore** will go through the dump and restore those files. This mode is handy for recovering individual files, especially if you aren't sure which directory they're in.
-r	Rebuilds a file system. In the event you lose everything in a file system (a disk failure, for instance), you can simply re-create an empty file system and restore all the files and directories of the dump.
-b blocksize	Sets the dump's block size to **blocksize** kilobytes. If you don't supply this information, **restore** will figure this out for you.
-f filename	Reads the dump from the file **filename**.
-T directory	Specify the temporary workspace (**directory**) for the restore. The default is **/tmp**.
-v	The verbose option; it shows you each step **restore** is taking.
-y	In the event of an error, automatically retries instead of asking the user if he or she wants to retry.

Table 28-3. Command-Line Options for the **restore** Utility

Finally, with the dump tape in the SCSI tape drive (**/dev/st0**), we perform the restoration using the following command:

```
[root@hostA /root]# cd /home; restore -rf /dev/st0
```

TIP If you used **gzip** to compress your dump, you'll need to decompress it before **restore** can do anything with it. Simply tell **gzip** to uncompress the tape device and send its output to the standard out. Standard out should then be piped to **restore**, with the - **f** parameter set to read from standard in. Here's the command:

```
[root@hostA /root]# gzip -d -c /dev/st0 | restore -ivf -
```

tar

In Chapter 5, we discussed the use of **tar** for creating archives of files. What we didn't discuss is the fact that **tar** was originally meant to create archives of files onto tape (**tar** = tape **ar**chive). Because of Linux's flexible approach of treating devices the same as files, we've been using **tar** as a means to archive and unarchive a group of files into a single disk file. Those same **tar** commands could be rewritten to send the files to tape instead.

The **tar** command can archive a subset of files much more easily than **dump** can. The **dump** utility works only with complete file systems, but **tar** can work on mere directories. Does this mean **tar** is better than **dump** for backups? Well, sometimes . . . .

Overall, **dump** turns out to be much more efficient than **tar** at backing up entire file systems. Furthermore, **dump** stores more information about the file, requiring a little more tape space but making recovery that much easier. On the other hand, **tar** is truly cross-platform—a **tar** file created under Linux can be read by the **tar** command under any other UNIX. And **gzip**ped **tar** files can even be read by the WinZip program!

Whether you are better off with **tar** or **dump** depends on your environment and needs.

> **NOTE** For more information on using **tar**, see Chapter 5.

SUMMARY

Backups are one of the most important aspects of system maintenance. Your systems may be superbly designed and maintained, but without solid backups, the whole package could be gone in a flash. Think of backups as your site's insurance policy.

This chapter covered the fundamentals of tape drives under Linux, along with some of the command-line tools for controlling tape drives and for backing up data to tape drives. With this information, you should be able to perform a complete backup of your system. Thankfully, **dump**, **restore**, and **tar** are not your only options for backup under Linux. Many commercial and noncommercial backup packages exist, as well. High-end packages such as Legato and Veritas have provided Linux backup support for quite some time now and offer some impressive solutions. Simpler programs such as bru and Lonetar are good for the handful of servers that are manageable by a single person. Open-source packages like Amanda and Dirvish are also viable choices. Dirvish is especially interesting because it is dedicated to the purpose of backing up to disk rather than tape.

However you decide to go about the task of backing up your data, just make sure that you do it.

INDEX

▼ E

▼ F

▼ G

▼ S